Thomas Bilson

The Effect of certaine sermons touching the full redemption of

mankind by the death and bloud of Christ Jesus

Thomas Bilson

The Effect of certaine sermons touching the full redemption of mankind by the death and bloud of Christ Jesus

ISBN/EAN: 9783337257538

Printed in Europe, USA, Canada, Australia, Japan

Cover: Foto ©Lupo / pixelio.de

More available books at **www.hansebooks.com**

TOVCHING

THE FVLL REDEMPT[ION]

of mankind by the death and blo[od]
CHRIST IESVS:

WHEREIN

Besides the merite of Christs suffering, the
of his offering, the power of his death, the co
of his Crosse, the glorie of his resurrection,

Are handled,

What paines Christ suffered in his soule on the C[rosse]

Together,

With the place and purpose of his descent to he[ll after]

Preached at Paules Crosse and else where in L[ondon]
by the right Reuerend Father Thomas B[ilson]
Bishop of Winchester.

With a conclusion to the Reader for the cleering
[of] the same doctrine.

---

1. Corinth. 3.

I [iudged] not to knowe any thing saue Christ Iesus, and him cruci[fied]

Athanasius de Incarnatione verbi dei.

Therefore the Sonne of God ought to haue a bodie that might die, [that]
[might] in such a one, [possible] soule, or might sustaine for a full [satisfaction]
Death for all.

[Im]printed at London by Peter Short for
[Walter Burre], and are to be sold in Paules Churchy[ard at]
the signe of the Flower deluce. 1599.

To the Chriſtian Reader.

IT is ſome time ſince (good Chri-
ſtian Reader)that lying in London,
and preaching at Paules Croſſe, as
the feaſt of Eaſter drawing neer did
admoniſh mee , I made choice to
ſpeake of the redemption of man-
kinde by the death and bloud of
Chriſt Ieſus. And becauſe that Citie then had, and yet
hah, as manie learned and religious preachers; ſo
ſome conceited and too much addicted to noueltíes,
whoſpared not in their Catechiſings and readings, to
vrge the ſuffering of the *verie paines of hell* in the ſoul
of Chriſt on the croſſe, as the chiefeſt part, and maine
ground of our Redemption by Chriſt: I, finding how
faſt that opinion had increaſed, ſince it was firſt deui-
ſed, and doubting where it would end, thought it my
dutie publikelie to warne them that were forward in
defending this fanſie, to take heed how farre they wa-
ded in that late ſprong ſpeculation. For as theſe words
of ⁱ *Dauid, The ſorrowes of hell beſieged me,* and theſe   ⁱ Pſa,18.&.116
of ᵇ *Ionas, Out of the belly of hel I cried, & thou heardeſt*   ᵇ Ionas,2.
myvoice, may be tolerablie applied to Chriſt, if they be
metaphorically interpreted of Chriſt, as the ſcriptures
meane them in *Dauid* and *Ionás*; ſo if wee grow from
the figuratiue vſe of the worde HELL, to the proper
ſignification thereof, and riſe from the degrees of ſor-

rowes and feares, which purſue the Saints in this life,
to the higheſt ſenſe and ſuffering of ALL, and THE VE-
RIE SAME paines and puniſhments which the dam-
ned do and ſhall endure for euer; freeing Chriſt from
nothing but from the place and continuance of hell:
vve make not a curious and ſuperfluous, but an erro-
neous and daungerous addition to the myſterie of
our Saluation.

The better to ſlacke their inconſiderate heate,
I laboured to prooue theſe foure pointes vnto
them. Firſt that, it was no where recorded in
the holie Scriptures, nor iuſtlie to bee con-
cluded by the Scriptures, that Chriſt ſuff-
red the true paines of hell; and ſo the Co-
ſciences of the faythfull coulde not iuſtlie bee for-
ced to the neceſſarie beleeuing of anie ſuch ſtrange
aſſertion. Secondlie, that as the Scriptures deſcribe
to vs the paines of the damned and of hell; th 'e are
manie terrors and torments, which, without euident
impietie, cannot be aſcribed to the Sonne of God, as
namely *extreame Darkeneſſe, Deſperation, Confu-
ſion, vtter ſeparation, reiection and excluſion* from
the grace, fauour, and kingdome of God; *remem-
brance* of ſinne *gnawing* the conſcience, *horrour* of
Diuels tormented and tormenting; and *flame* of *fire*
intolerablie burning both bodie and ſoule. Thirdlie,
that the death and bloud of Chriſt Ieſus were eui-
dentlie, frequentlie, conſtantlie ſet downe in the
writinges of the Apoſtles as the ſufficient price of
our Redemption, and true meane of our reconcili-
ation to God; and the verie ſame propoſed in the

figures

figures, refembled in the *facrifices* of the Lawe, and fealed with the *Sacraments* of the new Teftament as the verie grounde worke of our faluation by Chrift; and fo haue beene receaued and beleeued in the Church of God fourteene hundred yeares, before anie man euer made mention of hell paines to bee fuffered in the foule of Chrift. Laftlie, where the Scriptures are plaine and pregnant, that Chrift ᶜ DIED *for our finnes*, and by his ᵈ DEATH, *deftroi-ed him that had power of death, euen the Diuell, and reconciled vs, when we were ftrangers and enemies,* IN THE ᵉ BODIE OF HIS FLESH THROVGH DEATH, (for wee are *reconciled to God, by the* ᶠ DEATH *of his fonne, and fanctified by* THE OFFERING OF THE ᵍ BO-DIE *of Iefus Chrift once, who* ʰ *himfelfe bare our finnes in his* BODIE *on the Tree*: *where hee was put to death concerning the* FLESH;) Befides that the holie Ghoft in thefe places by expreffe wordes nameth the bodilie death of Chrift as the meane of our redemp-tion and reconciliation to God: no confiderate di-uine might affirme or imagine. Chrift *fuffered* the Death of the foule; for fo much as the Death of the foule muft exclude Chrift from the *grace, fpirit*, and *life* of God; and leaue in him neither *faith, hope*, nor *loue*, *fanctitie*, nor *innocencie*; which God forbid anie Chriftian man fhoulde fo much as dreame. Wee fhoulde therefore do well to reuerence the ma-nifeft wordes of Gods Spirit in fo high a pointe of Religion; and fuffer our felues as fchollers to bee taught by the leader into all trueth, what to beleeue and confeffe in the myftery of our redemp-tion; and not to controle or correct the doctrine fo

cleerely

4

ᶜ 1.Corin.15.
ᵈ Hebre.2
ᵉ Colof.1
ᶠ Rom 5.
ᵍ Hebr.10.
ʰ 1.Pet.2.

cleerelie deliuered in the Scriptures, ſo. conſonantlie retained of all learned and vnlearned in the Church of Chriſt, for ſo many hundred yeares: And if anie man to maintaine his deuiſe would inuent a newe hell and another death of the ſoule, then either ſcriptures or fathers euer heard or ſpake of, they ſhoulde keepe their inuentions to themſelues; it ſufficed me to beleeue what I read, and conſequently not to beleeue what I did not read in the word of God, which is and ought to be the foundation of our faith.

Thus farre I purpoſed, when I firſt entered, by Gods grace to proceede in this cauſe, according to ỹ ſimple vnderſtanding wherwith god hath endued me for the good of his Church. The article of the Creed, Chriſt DESCENDED INTO HELL I meant not to meddle with; chooſing rather to leaue ỹ vntouched, then to preſſe any ſenſe as a point of faith, for vvhich I had not ſo full and faire warrant, as for the redemption of man by the death and blood of Chriſt Ieſus; but the vehemencie of ſome contradicting that I taught, and the importunitie of others requeſting to knowe what they might ſafelie beleeue of that article, made mee to alter my minde. For whẽ ſome vrged, others doubted, that if Chriſt did not ſuffer the paines of hell whiles he hung on the Croſſe, that part of the Creed was added in vaine; and the wordes of *Dauid*, *Thou wilt not leaue my ſoule in hell*, applied by [k] *Peter* vnto Chriſt in the ſecond of the *Acts*, could hardly haue any good conſtruction: (becauſe it ſeemed farre fet, and altogither repugnant to the proper ſignification of the wordes, to take the *ſoule* for the *bodie*, and *hell* for the *graue*; and as for the locall deſcent of Chriſt

[l] Pſal. 16.
[k] Acts 2.

to hell after death ; they counted that but a fable.) I
was forced to promise that I would openlie deliuer,
which I thought was the likeliest and safest sense , as
well of that article in the Cre:de, as of those wordes
of *Dauid*, fulfilled in the person of our Sauiour. This
occasion drew mee to the next question of Christes
descent to hell. Wherin I resolued as by perusing the
later part of this treatise will better appeare , that
Chrifts descent to the verie place of hell after his ✕
death, did best concord both with the Creede , and
with the truth of Christian religion, so we tooke care
not to swarue frō the Scriptures, in setting downe the
cause why he went thither : which was to ouerthrow ＼
& deftroy the kingdom & might of Satan in the place
of his greatest ftrength, euen in hel, and as our head to ＼
free all his members from daunger and feare of com- ＼
ming thither: the sorrowes and terrors whereof hee
loosed vvith his presence , treading them vnder his
feete, and rose againe into a blessed and immortall
life, leading captiuitie captiue, and taking from hell
and Satan all povver to preuaile against his elect.

　　Both these resolutions that Christ suffered *not the*
true paines of hell in his soule on the crosse; and that hee ＼
personallie conquered and disarmed the *powers* and ＼
terrours *thereof before his resurrection* ; some (as in
such cases is common) misremembred, some miscon-
ftrued, and some misliked : vvhereupon I vvas both ＼
aduised and intreated by men of greater place then
I vvill name , to put the effect of that vvhich I had
deliuered in vvriting, that by mine ovvne vvords, and
not by other mens conceits or reports , the learned
might iudge of the doctrine. Which I did that verie
　　　　　　　　　　　　　　　　　　Summer

Summer, and had it readie for the preſſe before Bartle-
mewtide, but that the Parliament of States approch-
ing, wherein men ſhoulde be otherwiſe imploied;
and a great hurle raiſed againſt it by certaine popular
preachers in that citie, through whoſe mouthes the
contrarie had often paſſed to the people as currant, I
was deſired by the ſame perſons againe to ſtaie, till
that time of buſineſſe were ouer paſt, that heat of con-
tradiction ſomewhat alaied, and reſpite giuen that it
might be trãſlated into Latin; which alſo is now per-
formed, as wel as publiſhed in Engliſh. To whoſe coũ-
ſell I yeelded, referring the time wholy to their iudge-
ments, notwithſtanding I were by many traduced in
many places as a teacher of ſtrange and falſe doctrine.
But I haue beene and am the more willing to beare
the reproches of maligners, becauſe I ſeeke not my
ſelfe heerein, but that the church of Chriſt heere in
Englande ſhould hold faſt that ancient and ſure foun-
dation of faith which hitherto it hath kept; and pro-
feſſe that doctrine touching our Redemption by
Chriſt, which as wel the publike lawes of this realme,
as all the catholike fathers do vphold and allow.

In ſetting downe the ſumme of that which I prea-
ched, I neither do, nor can promiſe thee (gentle Rea-
der) the ſame words which I then ſpake; I wrote them
not; but I aſſure thee before him that knoweth all
things, that I haue not ſwarued nor altered anie ma-
teriall point from the methode, propoſitions, prooſes
and concluſions; which I then vſed, nor from the
wordes as farre as either my notes, or my memory
vpon the freſh foote coulde direct mee; which I haue
yet to ſhew. Manie prooſes and authorities I omitted

in

in the pulpit, which the time shut me from; and some obiections I haue answered here more largelie, then the course of Sermons would permit: but here is the selfe same in effect, which then I vttered and purposed, if the time woulde haue suffered. The manner of handling this question, I alwaies wished might bee temperate and sober, as best became christian professours and teachers; least by catching aduantages besides the cause, wee increased quarrels, and so much regarded our credits that wee neglected the truth. I haue therfore in the Treatise it selfe touched no mans name, oppugned no mans wordes, traduced no mans iudgement; but admitting and retaining as much as I thought might stande with the truth, I haue pared off certaine extremities, and reiected certaine additions, which the first inuentors did refraine; for that Christ suffered the death of the soule, or all the same tormentes, which the damned do and shall, are positions lately coined, and deriued from the proportion of Gods iustice as they call it, but as I thinke from presumption of mans reason intruding into Gods secrets. The doctrine which I defend, that we are sufficientlie redeemed by the death and bloud of Christ Iesus, (without adding of hell paines to bee suffered in the soule of Christ) hath the constant, full, and expresse warrant of the Scriptures, and the like approbation from al the fathers without exception. And therefore howsoeuer some men may despise all ancient writers, and frustrate the scriptures with their figures; al sober and wise christians will, I doubt not, beware how they admit this strange and late found nouelty into their Creede or consciences. The second point I presse not

vvith

with like vehemencie, becaufe it hath not like certain-
tie. So long as we confeffe (which the Scriptures do
confirme) that Chrifts humane nature after his ex-
treame humiliation on the Croffe, & before his refur-
rection, conquered & fpoyled not death only, but hell
& Satan alfo, of al their power & right ouer ŷ faithful,
& afcending on hie *lead captiuitie captiue*, & tooke the
keyes of death and of hell into his owne hands; with the
precife maner and hower I will not burden anie mans
confcience, that cannot be perfwaded by reading the
latter part of this treatife; though I my felfe, after long
& diligent fearch, find no fenfe fo agreeable to ŷ words
of the Creede, fo anfwerable to the rules of the facred
Scriptures, and fo fullie followed by all the Fathers,
as Chrifts defcent to the verie place of hell for the
purpofes aforefaid.

Hauing premonifhed thee (Chriftian reader) of thus
much, I am not willing to detayne thee anie longer
from vewing and examining the booke it felfe, but
onelie to tell thee that whiles I ftayed the printing
hereof, till others did like it, as wel as my felf, one more
haftie then either aduifed or learned, calling himfelfe
H. I. would needes traduce it and confute it before
he faw it, refting belike on fuch notes, as his angry
mind and brickle memorie tooke at the time
when I preached of thefe points. Wherein though
others condemne his follie, yet I commend his
pollicie, that leaft hee fhould trouble himfelfe
with more thē he could anfwere, he thought it ŷ beft
way to come into the field alone, and like a ftout
Champion fighting with his owne fhadow, to fay no
more thē he would be fure to deny or decline with one.

fhift

shift or other. To make the easier conquest of that
I preached, hee cleane changeth the state of the
first Question, hee offereth to prooue that which
I neuer denied; hee confuteth that which I ne-
uer affirmed, hee runneth at Random no man can
tell whither, hee peruerteth my wordes, hee may-
meth my reasons, hee skippeth all my authori-
ties; hee scornefullie reiecteth the iudgement of
the Fathers when I alleage them, the Scriptures
hee turneth and windeth at his pleasure, he wadeth
desperately through thicke and thinne in matters of
most importance, his best reason is euerie where his
own opinion, outfacing the world with his ignorance;
in summe, he sheweth vs by his example what it is for
a man in matters of faith to despise both 'authoritie
and antiquity, and trust onely to his own fancie. Such
an opponent the wiser sort will thinke I were better
neglect then encounter; which resolution I my selfe
do retayne; onely lest my silence should augment his
boldnes, I thought it not amisse in the conclusion se-
uered from the treatise, to giue thee a tast of the rash-
nes and weaknes of his enterprise, intreating thee in
the meane time to reade aduisedly and iudge indiffe-
rently, for that the cause is weighty and toucheth thee
as neere as mee. For if we suffer the mayne foundation
of our faith and hope in Christ to be wrenched neuer
so little awrie; the whole building is more endangered
then wee are ware of. In Gods causes, let Gods
booke teach vs what to beleeue, and what to professe.
If thou thinke it thy duetie in matters of faith to be-
ware of vnwritten verities, in the greatest point of
all, which is our redemption by Christ; take heede

To the Christian Reader.

thou eafilie admit not vnwritten abfurdities. This matter began in more generall and more tolerable tearmes, if they might bee rather foberly mitigated, then too vehemently preffed; but as when we runne downe an hill we can hardly ftaie; fo in matters of religion when we fal to inuenting beyond the fcriptures we quickly miffe and feldome recouer the truth. Farewell (gentle Reader) and pray that our thoughts and wits may be fubiected to the truth of Gods word, and that wee'loath not the fimplicitie which is in Chrift.

THE FVLL REDEMP-
tion of mankind, by the death
and bloud of Chrift.

GAL ATH. 6. - verſe. 14.

Be it far from me to reioice but in the Croſſe
of Chriſt.

AS the naturall man no where liketh nor alloweth the thinges of God, becauſe they ſeeme fooliſhnes vnto him: ſo of all the waies and workes of God there is none, that more diſpleaſeth and offendeth the vnbeleuer, then the Croſſe of Chriſt: a Wee preach Chriſt crucified (ſaith the Apoſtle) to the Iewes a ſtumbling blocke, to the Grecians fooluhneſſe. The Grecians ſauoring nothing but worldlie wiſedome, and fleſhlie reaſon, counted it a meere folly for the ſonne of God, to leaue his Throne of glorie in the heauens, and as a man amongſt men, to taſte of manie miſeries; and to ſuffer a cruell and ſhamefull death at the handes of his enemies. The price of our Redemption, for whoſe ſakes hee died, and the power of his reſurrection, by which hee raiſed vs to the imitation and expectation of a better life, they did neither conceiue, nor beleue; and therefore they reiected his birth, and ſpeciallie his death, as a dreame of ſimple and vnlearned men, ſuch as

a 1.Corinth 1.
The croſſe of Chriſt deſpiſed both of Iewes and Gentiles.

B 1.   they

they toke the Apostles to be. The Iewes hauing their eares full of those excellent promises, which God made by his prophets, concerning the kingdome of the Messias, and referring them to an earthlie king, that should sit on the throne of Dauid, bruising his enemies with a rod of Iron, and ruling the world with iustice and equitie: when they sawe the weake and base condition of our Sauiour, in outward shew promising nothing but reproch and penurie; they so disdained and detested him, that they could not bee quiet, till they had crucified him; being then, and euer since ashamed, and grieued that anie should saie, or thinke, he was the Messias, so much spoken of in the prophets. Thus the Iewes looking for wonders, and the Grecians for Wisedome, did both condemne the crosse of Christ: the one of weaknesse, the other of foolishnesse: and for that cause fell at the stone of offence: but such as were called both Iewes and Gentiles to bee heires of the promise, did plainelie perceaue, and fullie confesse Christ crucified to be the mightie power, and manifold wisedome of God for their euerlasting ioie and blisse; and were so far from being ashamed of Christs sufferings, that they were willing partakers and open reioicers in the crosse of Christ, as the Apostle here saieth of himselfe. [b] Be it farre from mee to reioice, but in the Crosse of Christ, by which the world is crucified to me, and I to the world. And indeede if we beholde Christ crucified with carnall eies, as did the Iewes, wee shall see nothing in him but earthlie weakenesse, and deadlie woundes, as they sawe: but if we bende the eies of our faith to the truth of his person, and to the force and fruite of his death, as must all his saints; we shall finde the power and wisedome, iustice and mercie of God so tempered in the crosse of Christ for our good; that by his paines we are eased, by his stripes we are healed, his weakenesse is our strength, his shame is our glorie, and his death our life: worthely therefore doth the Apostle professe, that he did, and we should not reioice but in the crosse of Christ.

And where hee saith, he did reioyce in nothing but in the crosse of Christ; he thereby teacheth vs to repose all our faith and

What it is to the beleeuers.

[b] Galath. 6

and hope, aſwell as our ioy, in the fauour of God, which Chriſt hath purchaſed for vs, by his death and bloud. Reioice in hope, ſaith the Apoſtle; that is in the expectation, not in the preſent fruition of heauenlie thinges, which God hath prepared for all that loue him. Now hope without faith there can bee none. Faith is the ground worke of that wee hope, for howe can we with patience looke for that, which we doe not belieue wee ſhall receiue? The doubting of Gods promiſes is the plaine diſtruſting of them; and breedeth rather a feare we ſhall miſſe them, then an hope to enioie them: and in feare there is PAINE, as ſaint Iohn ſaith, and no IOIE. Then as there is no perfect ioie, but in hope aſſured by faith; ſo if we muſt not reioice but in the croſſe of Chriſt, our faith and hope muſt wholie depende on that peace and attonement, which Chriſt hath made betwixt God and vs, by the ſheading of his precious bloud for our ſakes; that is by his croſſe. Since therefore Chriſt crucified is the wiſedome and power of God to ſaue all that belieue, and the croſſe of Chriſt is the ful ſupport of all our faith, hope and ioie; there is no one point in chriſtian religion, that more mainelie concerneth, and neerelie toucheth the ſaluation of our ſeules, then the right vnderſtanding and onely relying on the croſſe of Chriſt; leaſt we miſſtake the truth or diſtruſt the force thereof, to the diſhonour of Chriſt, and danger of our owne ſoules.

To preuent this perill, I thinke beſt to obſerue this order in that which ſhall be ſaide, to ſhewe firſt what the Croſſe of Chriſt CONTAINETH, next what the croſſe of Chriſt PERFORMETH: that knowing the contents and effectes of Chriſts croſſe, I meane the paines which he ſuffered; and the woorke which he accompliſhed by dying on the croſſe; we may be ſetled and aſſured, how far it extended, and what it effected for vs.

To begin with the CONTENTS of Chriſtes croſſe: The croſſe is ſometimes taken in the Scripture for all manner of afflictions, He that will come after me, let him denie himſelfe, and dailie take vp his croſſe and follow me. He that doth

Marginal notes:
- Rom.12
- Hebr.11
- 1.Iohn.4
- The methode of this treatiſe.
- Luke.9
- Matth.10.

not take vp his Crosse and follow me, is not worthy of me. In this sence, saieth Bernarde, h The whole life of Christ was a crosse and a martyrdom. The reason whie Christ so vsed the worde (for he first vsed it) was, for that he saw before hande, that going to his crosse he should taste all kindes of calamities: and so came it to passe. For betweene his last supper, and his death), hee was betraied of Iudas, abiured of Peter, forsaken of all his followers; hee was wrongfullie imprisoned, falselie accused, vniustlie condemned; he was buffeted, whipped, scorned, reuiled; he endured colde, nakednes, thirst, wounding, hanging, shame, reproch, and all sortes of deadlie paines; besides heauinesse of heart, and agonie of mind, which oppressed him in the garden. Rightlie then maie the crosse note all maner of miseries, forasmuch as our Sauiour going from the garden to the graue, suffered all sortes of afflictions: howbeit this is no different signification, but rather a participation of the crosse of Christ.

The Church of Rome hath wedded a great part of her deuotion to the crosse of Christ, but vnder that name she adoreth the matter and forme of the crosse: as for the force and effects of Christs death, which is remission of our sinnes, satisfaction of Gods wrath, and donation of eternall life, the prodigallie imparteth that to her pilgrimages, pardons, & purgatorie, yea to the workes and praiers of quicke and dead; and so magnifieng the signe and wood of the crosse, she dishonoreth the merite and fruit of Christ crucified. But of her painted and carued crosses, the scripture maketh no mention, and therefore I skipt it, rather as a manifest illusion, then anie signification of the crosse of Christ.

Most commonlie in the Scriptures by the crosse of Christ, the holie Ghost meaneth the person suffering, and the paine suffered on the crosse, that is, the punishments and torments which the sonne of God suffered for our sinnes; after he was fastened to the tree: the rest which went before not being excluded as superfluous, but continued and increased by that sharpe and extreame martyrdome which hee endured on the crosse.

b De passi.dom. cap.5. The crosse taken for all kind of affliction.

The church of Rome honoreth the crosse and dishonoreth the death of Christ.

What the scriptures meane by the crosse of Christ.

croſſe:And ſo Chriſt crucifico as the ſcriptures deſcribe him,
had from top to toe no part frée from paine and griefe; but
hong on the wood, hauing his fleſh tozne with whippes, his
chéekes ſwolne with buffets, his face defiled with ſpittle, his
head ſtucht full with thornes,his eies deiected for ſhame, his
eares burning with taunts,his mouth ſowzed with vineger;
his hands and féete wounded with Iron ſpikes, his bones
vniointed, his ſinewes pricked and ſtrained,his whole body
hanging by the ſozeneſſe of his hands and feet, and laſtlie
(though he were firſt dead) his heart pierced with a Speare,
whence iſſued bloud and water. His bodie thus wounded
and tortured vnto death;his bloud thus ſhed, and as it were
powzed on the earth,are ſaid in the ſcriptures to be the ran-
ſome of our ſinnes,and prjce of our redemption . [i] Hee bare
our ſinnes in his body vpon the Croſſe(ſaith Peter:)and again,
[k] You are redeemed with the precious bloud of Chriſt, as of a
lambe vnſpotted and vndefiled . I do not amplifie the bodilie
paines which Chriſt ſuffered, of purpoſe to make them ſéeme
greater then they were; I find my ſelfe rather vnable to ex-
preſſe them; but leaſt wee ſhould too much diminiſh them,
and aſke, What great matter it was for him to go ſecurely,
and as it were ſportinglie to his death, I thought good ſhortlie
to touch them, and leaue the fuller and further conſideration
of them to the godlie at their prjuate leyſure.

In the meane time I may not omit in his Stripes,Thornes,
Crucifying and Death,to obſerue that which the Reader will
happilie ouerſkippe in the hiſtozie of his paſſion,vnleſſe hee
be both aduiſed and learned. In his STRIPES I note,that
Pilate hauing a purpoſe to ſaue the life of Chriſt, and not
neglecting to ſatiſfie the people that were incenſed againſt
him,cauſed him extreamly to be whipped, and ſhewed to the
people in that plight with theſe wozds,[l] Ecce homo,Behold ã
man; to let them ſée that Chriſt had receiued very ſufficient
cozrection, nocrime being prooued againſt him, and ſo to
withozaw them from ſéeing his death. In CROWNING
him with thornes, the ſouldiers did not onelie wreath him

i 1 Peter.2,
k 1 Peter.1

The paines of
Chriſts croſſe.

l Iohn:)

Matth.27.
Marke.15.

a thicke crowne of thornes, to ſticke his head full of them:
but after the putting it on, to faſten it, they did ſtrike him on
the heade with their Canes; as [m] Matthew and Marke do
plainlie teſtifie. In NAILING him to the Croſſe, beſides
the greatneſſe and ſoreneſſe of his wounds, which were wor-
thie to be marked, they ſo ſtrained his bodie leaſt hee ſhould
ſtirre hand or fote, that all his bones might bee numbred.
The greatneſſe of his woundes Dauid foreſhewed by theſe
wordes : [n] *Foderunt manus meas, & pedes meos*; they digged
my handes and my feete ; noting howe wide woundes they
made in both, which were rather digged than pierced; and ſo
bigge were the nailes, as the Eccleſiaſticall hiſtorie repor-
teth, that Constantine made of them (when his mother had
found them in the mount where Chriſt was crucified) [o] A
bridle, and an helmet for his owne bſe. Howe tender and ſen-
ſible the hands & fæt are aboue other partes of the bodie, and
what paine and anguiſh the pricking, ſtraining and tearing
of the ſinewes, ligaments and ioynts in either (which are
berie thicke, and full of ſenſe in both thoſe places) did brede
and kindle in the whole bodie, nature can teach bs without
anie further proofe. Of RACKING his ioints, Bernard ma-
keth this collection out of Dauid: [P] *Tantum diſtentus ſum, ut
corpore nudo in modũ Tympanicæ pellis diſtento, faſ ſe poſſint om-
nia oſſa mea dinumerari.* I am ſo ſtrained (ſaith he in the per-
ſon of Chriſt) that my bodie naked beeing ſtretched like the
head of a timbrell (or drum) all my bones may be numbred. If
this proofe reach not home, Dauid hath plainer and expreſſer
wordes, in the 14. verſe of the ſame Pſalme , which can-
not be contradicted. HITHPAREDV.i. *Separauerunt ſe om-
nia oſſa mea*, All my bones are out of ioint, or pulled one from
the other. In this horrible torment of Stripes, Thornes,
Wounds, Sinewes and ioynts, our Sauiour hoong on the croſſe
aboue three houres, in moſt perfect ſenſe, with moſt extream
paine, till the berie inſtant that hee breathed out his ſoule.
A violenter death by fyre, or otherwiſe, our Sauiour might
happilie haue ſuffered; but a more painfull , with perfection

Pſa. 22.

Socrates lib.1.
cap.17

De paſſ.dom.
cap.7.

of patience, neuer martyr, much leſſe malefactor, did or could endure.

The torments of others when they are violent, do either haſten death, or ouerwhelme the ſenſe, and ſo the paine when it is moſt grieuous, is leaſt perceiued. In Chriſt there was no ſuch thing. He died not by degrées as we do ; his ſenſes did not decay, no pangs of death toóke hold of him, but in perfect ſenſe, and perfect patience both of bodie and ſoule, he did voluntarily and miraculouſly reſigne his ſpirit (as hee was praying) into his fathers handes. Longer tortures others haue endured, but neuer greater for the time, nor with like patience. For in all men (Chriſt excepted) though the ſpirit be neuer ſo willing, & the meaſure of faith neuer ſo ſtrong, yet vnles it pleaſe God to ſhorten or lighten the rage of their paine, the fleſh repineth at the preſent anguiſh, howſoeuer grace ſupport the ſoule, that it ſink not vnder the burthen. But [q] He which ſhortneth and lightneth the force of torments in his ſaints when they be grieuous, in his owne would doe neither. He ſpared not himſelfe, that knoweth how to ſpare his; but ſuffered and indured all to the vttermoſt, with ſo exact obedience and patience, that he did not ſhrinke at the paine, nor ſtriue with death, but yéelded ſo voluntarie a ſacrifice to god, that in the ſharpeſt torments he made no ſhew of ſenſe: nor ſuffered his fleſh ſo much as to tremble or ſtruggle with paine or death. The manner of rendring vp his ſoule the Scriptures and Fathers do carefullie obſerue. Saint Iohn thus deſcribeth it. [r] When Ieſus had taſted of the vinegar, hee ſaid (all) is finiſhed, & bowed his head, and gaue vp the Ghoſt. Whereupon Bernard ſaith: [ſ] It is a great infirmity to die, but ſo to die, doth plainlie proue an infinite power. S. Luke reporteth that Ieſus [t] cried with a loud voice (to ſhew himſelfe to be frée from any touch of death) and ſaide, Father into thy handes I commend my ſpirit. Whereupon Hierom obſerueth, that the Centurion hearing his prayer, and ſéeing him [u] Statim ſpiritum ſponte dimiſiſſe, preſently of his owne accord to ſende forth his ſpirite, Commotus ſigni magnitudine, mooued with the greatneſſe

Chriſt had no pangs of death but perfect ſenſe of paine vnto the end.

[q] Bernard de paſſ. dom. ca. 41.

He died voluntarily.
[r] Iohn. 19.

[ſ] Serm. 4. Hebdomadæ panoſæ.
[t] Luk. 23.

[u] queſt. 8. ad Hedibiam.

greatnesse of the wonder, saide ; Truly this man was the sonne of God. Augustine largely handling the maner of his death saith[x] ; Who can so sleepe when he wil, as Christ died when he would ? Who can so laie aside his garment at his pleasure, as Christ laid aside his flesh? Who can so leaue his place , as Christ left his life ? with how great power shall he come to iudge, that shewed so great power when he died ? Christ himselfe ratifieth these obseruations with his owne mouth in the Gospell of saint Iohn[y] : None taketh my soule from mee, but I laie it downe of my selfe. By this we may perceiue, the consunation of the Humane nature with the Diuine in the person of Christ was so fast and sure, that neither sinne, death, nor hell assaulting our Sauiour, could make anie separation, no not of his bodie; but he himselfe of his owne accord must put off his earthlie tabernacle, that dying for a season he might conquer death for euer; and so the laying downe of his life was no imposed punishment, nor forceable inuasion of death vpon him, but a voluntary sacrifice for sinne rendred vnto God for our sakes , to appease the wrath and satisfie the curse, which our manifold wickednes had most iustlie deserued.

Thus farre without feare we maie freelie extend the crosse of Christ by the warrant of the holie scriptures. Some men in our daies stretch it a great deale farther, to the death both of bodie and soule, and to the WHOLE PAINES OF THE DAMNED IN HELL; but vpon how iust grounds, when you heare, you may iudge as you see cause. This opinion hath growen by degrees; and euerie daie taketh newe encrease. At the first, men contented themselues to thinke Christ suffered the paines of hel, that is great and intolerable paines; which metaphoricall kind of speach the Scriptures will beare; if we conclude no worse meaning within those words; Out of the bellie of HEL, (saith Ionas) I cried and thou heardest my voice. The sorrowes of HEL compassed me about (saith Dauid) and the griefes of HEL tooke hold of me. Some others affirme; that Christ, in sustaining the wrath of God due to vs, wrastled with the verie powers of hell that sought

[x] Tract. 119. in Iohan.

[y] Iohn. 10.

How the opinion of Christs suffering hell paines hath growen by degrees.

Ionas. 2.
Psal. 18.
Psal. 116.

to faften on him, and howfoeuer beholding the terror of Gods vengeance prouoked by our finnes, he did fomtimes tremble, yet by firme faith alwaies fixed on God, he repelled and repreffed thofe affaults of Satan, and fo faued not him-felfe onely, but vs alfo. This might be induced if men could ftay here; & it were to be wifhed, that in matters of fo great weight and danger, we would rather try where we are, then haften to go onward. But as water breaking her bankes ftill runneth and neuer ftayeth; fo fome lighting on other mens inuentions neuer leaue adding till they marre all. In the cafe which we haue in hand, the name of Hell paines be-ing once admitted into the worke of our redemption, fome in our daies will no nay, but that Chrift on the croffe fuffe-red the felfe fame paines in foule, which the damned do in hell, and endured euen the death of the foule; yea others auouch that hee fuftained farre greater torments then anie are in hell, to wit, as much paine in 15. houres, as all the faithfull fhould haue fuffered euerlaftinglie, and that as well in body as in foule. To thefe dangerous deuifes are fome men flipt in our time. And becaufe I knowe not when or where they will make an ende, I thinke it needfull for difcharge of my dutie, and direction of your faith, as well to fet downe certaine limits beyond which you may not go, as alfo to re-iect fuch extremities as by no meanes may be clofed in the croffe of Chrift, without apparant impietie.

The paines of hell (if I be not deceiued) make a fourefold impreffion in the foules of men; a carefull feare, which decli-neth them; a doubtfull feare, which confifteth with them; a defperate feare which finketh vnder them, and a damned feare which fuffereth them. The firft is and muft be in all the god-lie; and chieflie in Chrift himfelfe: For the more we loue God, the more wee deteft and fhunne all feparation from God. Hell therefore which is an vtter exclufion from the kingdome of God, is moft iuftlie abhorred of all his faints, and fpeciallie of his owne Son: who not onelie by will, but by nature is one with his Father. A conflict with Hell

How many impreffions the paines of hell make in the foule of man.

if it come not from the inward motion of the mind, is but a
temptation to trie the heart, o; shew the strength of the god-
lie. So was Adam tempted in Paradise by Eue, and Eue by
the Serpent, to p;oue howe mindfull they were, and thank-
full they would be fo; the blessings of God bestowed vpon
them. So was Ch;ist tempted in the wildernesse by Sa-
tan, and all his life long by the wicked, which were to him
but occasions to declare the innocencie and integritie of his
humane nature. But the inwarde temptation of the
heart and conscience, though it bee in all the children of A-
dam, (the elect themselues not excepted,) by reason of their
flesh lusting agaynst the spirite, their conscience accu-
sing them fo; sinne, and their fayth sometimes fainting;
yet in Ch;ist wee must graunt no such thing, because
in him there was neither co;ruption of flesh, no; remo;se
of sinne, no; weakenesse of faith; that should anie
kinde of waie b;eede o; yeelde to the wo;me, that gnaw-
eth at our consciences. A desperate feare is when the
w;ath of God awaketh the wicked to knowe and ac-
knowledge, what vengeance is p;epared fo; them, in
the life to come, and so hauing lost both fayth and hope,
they fall to an ho;rible expectation of iudgement, and fla-
ming fy;e, which shall deuoure the aduersarie. But yet
euen these men, whose case is most despaired, are not
while they liue heere on earth, in the true paines of
Hell, but are as farre from that, as expecting is from
suffering. The last I knowe not howe to call, but by
the name of a damned, rather paine, then feare; which
the wicked departed this life doe p;esentlie feele. Fo;
paine that is p;esent, inflideth rather to;ment, then
feare; since feare is p;operlie the trembling at euill, be-
fo;e it come, and not the grieuing at it, when it is come.
Of these foure imp;essions, yee see which I attribute
vnto Ch;ist, and which not. Despairing, o; so much as
doubting of his saluation, we cannot ascribe to him with-
out euident impietie. And as fo; Ch;istes suffering the
                                                        same

ſame paines which the damned ſoules in Hell doe, to my
ſimple vnderſtanding, it is rather a dreame then a doc-
trine to bee taught in the Church of Chriſt. Did they de-
fende as great ſenſe and anguiſh of paine to haue beene
in Chriſtes bodie or ſoule, as hell fire doth inflict to the dam-
ned, though that were a verie preſumptuous and audacious
poſition, yet is it not ſo impious, as when they affirme he ſuf-
red the ſelfeſame which the damned do. For the damned haue
many ſorts of paines in hel, which by no means could faſten
on Chriſts perſon; and ſince there be degrées of paine in hell
euen for the damned; theſe curious teachers muſt ſhewe vs
which of theſe degrées Chriſt ſuffered, & by what warrant of
gods word, they adiunge the very paines of hell to the croſſe
of Chriſt.

　To perſwade them to hold faſt the forme of wholſom words, 2. Tim. 1.
which the holy gheſt obſerueth throughout the ſcriptures, I
feare is but loſt labor; hauing lighted on a ſtrange doctrine,
they are forced to vſe ſtrange ſpéeches, ſuch as no where are
found in the word of truth, expreſſing mans redemption by
the death and bloud of Chriſt; yet ſomwhat to rebate the heat
of ſuch as deſpiſe all other ſufferings of Chriſt in reſpect of
their hell-paines, I think it not amiſſe to examine the weight
of thoſe allegations and reaſons that are brought to ſupport
their aſſertion. The proofs that are pretended for this opinion The proofes
which are
brought that
Chriſt ſuffered
the paines
of hell.
a Pſal. 16.
b Pſal. 18.
may be recalled to thrée principal heds, which are theſe, P RE-
DICTIONS that Chriſt ſhould ſuffer the paines of hell in
ſoul; CAVSES, why he muſt ſuffer them; SIGNES that he did
ſuffer them. Predictions, that Chriſt ſhould ſuffer the paines
of hel are cited theſe, a Thou wilt not leaue my ſoule in hell: and
againe, b The ſorowes or ſtreights of hell haue found me out, &
beſet me round. The cauſes why he muſt ſuffer them are en-
larged by ſome into many branches, but may bee contracted
into theſe two; THE PART that chiefly ſinned in man; & the
WAGES due to man for ſin. The WORKE of ſin appeared
firſt & moſt in the ſoul of Adam, & therfore in ŷ ſatiſfaction for
ſin, the ſoul of Chriſt, as they ſay, muſt properly & principally
C 2　　　　　　　　　　　　　　　　　　　　　ſuffer

suffer. The vv a ges of sin is expressely death both of soule and bodie, and therfore Christ, as our suretie and for our sinnes, must taste of both, (as they affirm) before he can discharge vs from both. Signes that he did suffer, were his Agonie in the garden, when he sweat blood; which for a corporall death he would neuer haue don: his Complaint on the crosse, that he was forsaken of God, which (as they thinke) proueth he felt in soule a most fearefull iudgement of God, pronounced against our sinnes. To euerie of these I will speake in order, that finding the weaknesse of their foundation, we maie the sooner see the lamenesse of their conclusion.

Predictions that Christ should suffer y̆ paines of hel.
c Augu∫t. epi. 99

To the first I might answere with Saint Austen; these words of Dauid specifie not anie suffering of hell paines on the crosse, but rather a descent to the place of hell. c That the Lord after his bodie was dead came to hell is certaine enough; for neither can the prophecie be contradicted, which said, Thou wilt not leaue my soule in hell; (which least anie man shoulde dare otherwise to interpret, Peter in the Acts of the Apostles so expoundeth;) nor the wordes of Peter bee auoided, where hee saith that Christ brake the sorrowes of hell, the which could not possiblie take hold on him; who then but an infidell will denie that Christ was in hell? But with antiquitie I will not vrge them; if the text doe not refuse their exposition, I will release them this authoritie. That this saying of Dauid doth not import anie paines suffered while Christ liued, but some honour done to his soule after his death, maie three waies be proued; by the wordes next præcedent, by the words next adioyned, and by the application which Peter maketh, when he citeth this place. The wordes next before, (which are these, d My flesh shall rest in hope) note Christs buriall: and this is brought as a reason why Christes bodie should rest in hope, not on the crosse where it had no rest, but in the graue after he was dead; because thou wilt not leaue my soule in hell. If this respected any thing endured on the crosse, the holy ghost must haue saide in the person of Christ, because Thov Hast Not Left My Sovle In Hel: the paines, and

d Psal. 16.

time

time were both paſt; but he ſpeaketh in the future tenſe, & of future things, Thou wilt not leaue my ſoule in hell. And this was the hope in which Chriſt died. Now hope neuer tendeth to things paſt and known, but to that which is to come. This therefore toucheth ſomthing conſequent after Chriſts death, which he hoped for when he died, and not anie paines ſuffered on the croſſe, or in the garden, whiles he liued. The words annered inſer the ſame. d Thou wilt not leaue my ſoule in hell, **d** Pſal.16.
nor ſuffer thine holie one to ſee corruption. Both theſe being ſointlie ſpoken of Chriſt, muſt both bee ſointlie verified in Chriſt; wherefore Chriſtes ſoule muſt then not bee left in hell, when his fleſh lying in the earth ſawe no corruption. They may not bee ſeuered in performance, which the holie ghoſt knitteth together in coherence. Laſtlie Peter in plaine words ſaieth, c Dauid ſpake (this) of Chriſts reſurrection. If **e** Acts 2.
this concerned his reſurrection, then not his paſſion on the croſſe; but after death, and before he roſe, as his fleſh ſaw no corruption; So his ſoule was not left in hell. Yea, God f raiſed him vp (as Peter ſaith) breaking the ſorrowes of death (or hell **f** Ibidem.
before him) of which it was impoſſible he ſhould be held; g not that hee was euer in them, and ſo looſed them, as a man doth chaines, wherewith hee was once bound : but as the ſnares of hunters (ſaith Auſten) are broken, *Ne teneant, non quia tenue-* **g** Auguſt epiſt.
runt : before they take hold, not after they haue taken holde. 99.
For Chriſt was to riſe againe, not as others before him were reſtored to this preſent life; but as the full and firſt conquerour of death and hell, hee was to riſe both in bodie and ſoule to eternall & celeſtial glory; and therfore he brake, when he roſe, the paines and powers of death and hell ; that they ſhould not preuaile for euer againſt him or his.

The other places of the Pſalmes, haue as manie anſweres as they haue words; for euerie word is an anſwere. Firſt Dauid ſpeaketh of himſelfe, not of Chriſt; and Dauids words to Chriſts perſon we may not refer at our pleaſures, without farther and better warrant. Againe, Dauid doth not **h** Pſal.18. &
ſaie, the TORMENTS, but the h SNARES, or STREIGHTS 116.

C 3. of

of DEATH, as well as of HELL (for the worde Sheol is differentlie signifieth both, if there bee none other circumstance to limite it to either; and Dauid by the rules of diuinitie was neuer here on earth in the true paines of the damned,) haue FOVND me out, or BESET, and besieged mee, but not oppressed, nor ouerwhelmed me. And if we take the name of HELL neuer so properlie, it is no inconuenience, that the gates of hell, I meane the craft and power of Satan, should hunt after the godlie here on earth, and seeke to entrap, euen Christ himselfe; but the true paines of hell, the wicked and desperate do not suffer in this life, much lesse the elect, least of all Christ. It is a iudgement following death, and maie no more be defended to bee here on earth, then the ioies of heauen may be possessed in this life.

In the causes, why Christ should suffer the paines of hell, we may do well not to be too forwarde with the rules of reason: as well for that there is no proportion betwixt the person of Christ and vs, as also for that wee may not sit iudges with God, and prescribe when or howe his iustice should bee satisfied. It is requisite in our selues to confesse that as both parts of man sinned in Adam, so the wages of sinne, which is euerlasting death, is due to both: and as the soule shoulde haue principallie entoied God, which is her life, if shee had persisted in obedience; so in falling from God, her losse, and smart, must of the twaine bee farre the greater; though the bodie shall not wante both grieuaunce and vengeance intolerable: but if wee stretch these rules to Christ, and subiect his person, as our suretie, to the verie SAME WAGES of sinne, which we should haue suffered, I knowe not howe in fewer wordes a man maie couch more grosse and open impietie. For we should haue béene WHOLY SEVERED, IVSTLY HATED, and VTTERLY REIECTED from God, yea ETERNALLY CONDEMNED BODIE AND SOVLE to hell fire. May anie of these thinges be affirmed or imagined of Christ without hainous and horrible blasphemie? This was the wages of our sinne; must

be

The causes why Christ must suffer the paines of hel.

be endure THE SAME, before wee can bee redeemed, or Gods iuſtice be ſatiſfied? I hope no ſound diuine will ſo conclude.

They will releaſe eternall death to the dignitie of Chriſts perſon, but he was (as they ſaie) for the time to taſte the verie ſame death both in ſoule and bodie which wee ſhould haue done; and which in vs ſhould haue béene euerlaſting. Firſt by their leaues; hell in the ſcriptures is an euerlaſting torment, and therefore if the excellencie of Chriſtes perſon exempt him from euerlaſting miſerie, that cléerelie quiteth him in bodie and ſoule from ſuffering hell. Againe, as ſinne is the voluntarie defection of the ſoule from God, ſo hell is the TOTAL, if not FINAL EXCLVSION of the ſoule from all fellowſhip with God; leſſe then the death of ſoule it cannot be. It is the wages of ſinne, and therefore it muſt bee the death as well of the ſoule, as of the bodie; and chiefelie of the ſoule, becauſe the ſoule of man is the principall agent in ſinne. S. Iohn calleth hell the [i] ſecond death. If then the ſoule of Chriſt ſuffered either hell, or the wages of our ſinne, of neceſſitie for the time it muſt be dead. The[k] wages of ſinne is death. If for the time Chriſtes ſoule were dead, it had no communion with God, nor God with it, no more then death hath with life, or darkenes with light: It loſt for that time all faith and loue of God. For by faith the iuſt doe[l] liue: and he that [m] abideth in loue abideth in God. And ſince God is the life of the ſoule, Chriſt could not ſuffer the death of the ſoule, which is the wages of our ſinne, no not for a day, or an houre, but he muſt be ſeuered from God, & forſaken of God. [n] *Mors anima fit cum eam deſerit deus*, the death of the ſoule is when God forſaketh it. [o] *Mors eſt ſpiritus, à deo deſeri*, it is the death of the ſpirit to bee forſaken of God. [p] *Mors anima deus amiſſus* : the loſſe of God is the death of the ſoule. To loſe God, or to be forſaken of God, is to haue no communion, nor fellowſhip with God; the ſoule then that is dead, is excluded from the fauour, and grace; truth, and ſpirit of God; and if anie bee ſo irreligious or impious, as once to affirme theſe

things

Christ could not ſuffer the death of the ſoule, which was the chiefe wages of our ſinne.

[i] Apocal. 2.

[k] Rom. 6.

[l] Galat. 3
[m] 1. Iohn. 4.

[o] Auguſt. de ciuitate dei lib. 13. cap. 2.
[o] Idem de Trinitate. lib. 4. c. 14
[p] Idem de verbis domini ſuper Matthæum. ſerm. 6.

things of Chꝛist, he may auouch, that Chꝛists soule suffered
the true wages of our sin; but if we abhoꝛre these things as
sacrilegions and monstrous absurdities, as I doubt not
but we do; then certainelie the soule of Chꝛist could not bee
dead, no not foꝛ an instant, and consequentlie the true wa-
ges of our sinne the soule of Chꝛist could not receaue, noꝛ suf-
fer on the crosse, oꝛ in the garden: but wee must rather giue
eare to Peter, which saith, ⸿ Christ bare our sinnes in his bodie
on the tree; where he was quickened in spirite, though moꝛti-
fied in flesh, and strengthened in the inward man by the ioy
pꝛoposed, foꝛ which hee sustained the crosse, and despised the
shame thereof. Chꝛist then tooke the burden of our sinnes
from vs, and laied it on his owne shoulders, yea the Loꝛde
⸿ Laid vpon him the iniquity of vs all; but when it came to light
vpon him, the verie iustice of God found great difference
betwixt his person and ours; and so great, that what should
haue condemned vs bodie and soule foꝛ euer, that could take
no hold on him; but so far foꝛth, as he did voluntarilie yeelo
himselfe to bee obedient vnto the death of the crosse, and in
our flesh to quench the curse of the lawe pꝛonounced against
our sinnes; insomuch that neither sinne noꝛ death were able
to seaze on his bodie, till he did of his owne accoꝛd resigne it
into their handes. If we thinke it strange to see so much dif-
ference betwixt him and vs, we must remember, wee were
sinnefull, he was innocent; we were defiled, hee was holie;
we were hatefull, he was beloued; we were the seruants of
sinne, and enemies vnto God, he was the Loꝛd of life and of
gloꝛie; we were seuered and estranged from God both in bo-
die and soule, his verie flesh was personallie vnited and in-
separablie ioined vnto God; besides that himselfe was the
true and euerliuing sonne of God. What maruell then if
sinne, which should haue wrought in vs an eternall destruc-
tion both of body and soule, could not farther pꝛeuaile in him,
but to the wounding of his flesh, and shedding of his blood
foꝛ the iust and full satisfaction of all our sinnes, euen in the
righteous and sincere iudgement of God? Though therefore

THE

⸿ 1.Pet.2

⸿ Esay.53.

THE SAME PART might, and did fuffer in Chrift, which finned in man, I meane the foule; yet by no meanes could it receaue THE SAME WAGES which we fhould haue recei-ued. And fince hell is the greateft vengeance, that God in-flicteth for finne, if Chriftes foule were free from anie, it muft nedes be cleered and acquited from that, which is greateft, and moft repugnant to the fulneffe of grace, truth and fpirit, that dwelt in the humane foule of Chrift: but hereof I fhall haue occafion to fpeake afterward againe.

The fignes that Chrift fuffered the paines of hell are left: and thofe are his agonie in the garden, and his complaint on the croffe, that he was forfaken. Of Chrifts agonie, fince the fcriptures haue not reuealed the right caufe, it is curiofitie to examen, prefumption to determine, impoffibilitie to con-clude certainelie what was the true caufe thereof. Howbeit if we will nedes coniecture at caufes, wee muft take hede, that with our obfcure and priuate gueffes, we do not contra-dict fuch plaine and euident places, as teftifie the perfection and coniunction of Chrifts humane nature with his diuine, and fo wrong the perfon of our Sauiour. This rule remem-bred (though I bee moft willing to refraine the fearching of that, which is concealed from vs) yet fince they make this the moft aduantage of their caufe, that there cãnot be anie other reafon affigned of Chriftes forrow, befides his fuffering the paines of hell: I will let you vnderftand how manie there might be befides that which they bring; and that theirs of all others, is leaft probable, if not altogether intolerable. I will offer you fixe caufes, that might be, of Chrifts agonie; eue-rie one of them more likelie, and more godlie then this de-uife of hell paines; others at their leifures maie thinke on moe, which I fhall be content to heare. Thofe fixe are thefe. Chrifts SVBMISSION to the maieftie of God fitting in iudge-ment; The REIECTION of the Iewes; The DISPERSION of his Church; The LAMENTATION of mans finne; The DE-PRECATION of Gods wrath; The VOLVNTARY DEDI-CATION of his bloud to be fhed for the finnes of the world,

D 1　　　　　and

The fignes y̆ Chrift did fuf-fer the paines of hell, are his agonie in the garden, and his complaint on the croffe.

Sixe caufes that might be of Chrifts ago-ny in y̆ garden.

and ſanctificatiõ of his perſon to offer his true & eternal ſacrifice.

So great is the MAIESTY OF GOD, euerie where and at all times, but ſpeciallie ſitting in iudgment, and ſo farre excelling the capacitie of all his creatures, that no fleſh liuing is able to appeare before him without feare and trembling, ᶠThe day of the Lord (whenſoeuer hee riſeth to iudge) is great and fearefull, and who ſhall indure it? When God gaue his lawe, which was but the rule of his iudgement, ſo ᵗterrible was the ſight, that *Moſes* ſaid, I feare and tremble. ᵘMy fleſh (ſaith Dauid to God) trembleth for feare of thee, and I am afraide of thy iudgements. Since then it is a point not onelie confeſſed but vrged, by the defenders of this new deuiſe, that Chriſt appeared here before the tribunall of God, to ſubmit himſelfe to his fathers pleaſure; and the wordes of Chriſt in the twelfth of Iohn tend to that effect, where he ſaith, ˣNowe (euen at hand) is the iudgement of the world. Now (euen ſhortlie) ſhall the prince of this world be caſt out, and if I were lift vp from the earth, I will draw all vnto me: whie might not the humane nature of Chriſt tremble before the maieſtie of that iudge, whoſe glorie the Seraphins in heauen doe not behold, withoutvvealing their faces? whereby Chriſt teacheth vs not to preſſe into Gods preſence, whiles wee are loden with ſin, but in much feare and trembling; ſince he would not appeare before God to take our ſinnes on him, but in this agonie.

The REIECTION OF THE IEVVES might be another cauſe of his agonie. ᶻHe weptouer their cittie, when he beheld it, and remembred the ſubuerſion of it; how woulde he then be grieued when he foreſawe the finall reiection of þ whole nation? and his bloud to be laid on them and their children for euer? for their ſakes Moſes deſired ᵃTo bee wiped out of Gods booke, and Paule ᵇ could haue wiſhed himſelfe to be ſeparated from Chriſt for his brethren the Iſraelites. If the ſeruants of Chriſt had ſo great heauineſſe and ſorrow in their hearts for their kinſmen according to the fleſh; what agonie muſt it needes breede in their king, and Meſſias, in whome were the bowels of mercie and pittie, to ſee the wicked rage of

ᶠIoel.2

ᵗHebre.12
ᵘPſalm.119

ˣIohn.12

ᶻEſay.6

The reprobati
on of ÿ Iewes.
ᶻLuke.19

ᵃExod 32
ᵇRom.9.

of the people kindling Gods fearefull vengeance againſt
themſelues, and their offspring by putting him to a moſt cru-
ell and ſhamefull death, that came to redeeme them from ſin
and death ? This cauſe is obſerued by Ambroſe, Hierom,
Auguſtine and Bede. ᶜ *Nec illud diſtat à vero, ſi triſtis erat pro
perſecutoribus :* neither is that diſſonant from truth (ſaith Am-
broſe) if he were heauy (in ſoule) for his perſecutors, whom hee
knewe ſhould dearelie pay for their ſacrilegious putting him to
death. Hee was not then afraide to die, but hee was loath to
haue them though they were euill, to periſh ; leaſt his paſſion
ſhould bee their deſtruction, which hee meant for the ſaluation
of all. Chriſts ſoule was not heauie (ſaith Icrom and Bede)
ᵈfor any feare of his paſſio, but for that moſt vnhappy Iudas, for
the ſcandall of all his Apoſtles, for the reiection of the Iewes, and
ſubuerſion of wretched Ieruſalem. And Auſten, If wee ſaie the
Lorde was ſorrowfull (for the Iewes) when his paſſion drewe
neere, where they would commit ſo haynous a ſinne, ᶜ*non in-
congrnè nos dicere exiſtimo,* I think we ſpeake not without reaſo.

¶ If reſpect of his perſecutors could thus agonize him, what
could the regard of his own followers doe? how did the weak-
neſſe of his owne diſciples afflict him, when the wilfulneſſe
of his enemies did ſo prepaile with him? Hee warned his
diſciples of the danger, and they vaunted of their ſtrength;
he willed them to ᶠ praie, and they ſlept; and when he was ap-
prehended they did euerie one forſake him ; yea the ſtouteſt
of them did plainelie forſweare him. Hee might therefore
iuſtlie be grieued with their infirmitie, and earneſtlie prate
for their ſecuritie. His tender care of them, and earneſt prai-
er for them appeareth in the 17. of Iohn, euen as hee entred
into the garden; hee called vpon them to ᵍ watch and praie,
that they entred not into temptation. ʰ *Dormiunt* (ſaith Am-
broſe) *& neſciunt dolere pro quibus Chriſtus dolebat:* the Diſci-
ples ſlept, and cãnot tel how to ſorrow, for whom Chriſt ſorow-
ed: *Triſtis erat non pro ſua paſſione, ſed pro noſtra diſperſione.
Triſtis erat, quia nos paruulos relinquebat.* Hee was ſorrowfull

ᶜ *Ambroſ. in Lu-
cam. lib. 10. de
triſtitia & dolo-
re Chriſti.*

ᵈ *Hieron. in
Matth. cap. 26*
ᵈ *Beda in matth.
cap. 26.*

ᵉ *Auguſt. in
Pſal. 87.*

The diſperſion
of his church.

ᶠ *Luke. 22*

ᵍ *Ibidem.*
ʰ *Ambroſ. in Lu-
cam. lib 10. de
triſtitia & do-
lore Chriſti.*

not for his owne suffering, but for our dispersing. He was grieued because hee left vs yong and weake. Hilarie in his tenth booke *de Trinitate* largely pursueth this occasion of Christs agonie, & concludeth; *Non ergo sibi tristis erat, neq̉ sibi*

i *Hilarius de trinitate. lib* 10.

orat, sed illis, quos monet orare peruigiles; Christ is not sorrowfull for himself, nor praieth for himself; but for those who he warneth to watch and pray. And for their sakes he saith, the Angell was sent to comfort Christ, that hee should take no longer griefe and feare for his Disciples. k The Angell being sent to

k *Ibidem.*

protect the Apostles, and the Lord receiuing comfort thereby *Ne pro his tristis esset; iam sine tristitiæ metu ait, dormite & requiescite:* That he should no longer grieue for them, beginneth nowe to be without griefe and feare, and saith to them, sleepe now, and take your rest. k *Nam qui nobis tristis est, id est propter*

k *Ibidem.*

nos tristis est, necesse est vt propter nos sit comfortatus, & nobis; for he that was sorrowfull for our sakes, and in our behalfe, must of force be comforted for vs, and to our vse.

His sorrow for our sinne.

The desire and care Christ had to see his kept safe from the rage of Satan, leadeth me to the fourth cause of Christs agonie. For if Christ were so sad for our infirmitie, how sorrowfull then was he for our iniquitie, whereby we doe not onelie laie our selues open to danger, but euen wound our selues to death and destruction? Well saith Ambrose of this

l *Ambrose de fide lib. 2. cap. 3.*

matter, l *Mihi compatitur, mihi tristis est, mihi dolet. Ergo pro me, & in me doluit, qui pro se nihil habuit quod doleret. Dolet igitur domine Iesu, non tua, sed mea vulnera, non tuam mortem, sed nostram infirmitatem.* Christ is affected for mee, sadde for mee, and greeued for mee, Hee sorroweth for mee, and in mee, who had nothing in himselfe to bee sorowed for. Thou grieuest Lord Iesu, not at thine owne wounds, but at mine; not for thy death, but for my weakenesse. Inward sorrow for sin is præciselie requisite in all remission of sinnes. To sinne and not to be sorie for it, is first to displease, and then to despise God. Wherefore it is not possible to appease Gods wrath once prouoked, but with earnest and heartie sorrowe that euer we offended. Then as corruption is the mother, and

plea

pleaſure is the life of ſinne : ſo the inward affliction and con-
trition of the ſoule in all the godlie, is the death of ſinne. And
ſince we are neither willing, nor able to ſorrow ſufficientlie
for our ſinnes, why might not the ſon of God, when hee tooke
vpon him the purgation of our ſins in his own perſon, take
likewiſe vnto him that inward & earneſt ſorow for our ſins,
which neuer creature before him, or beſides him did, or could
expreſſe. [m] Godly ſorrow cauſeth (in vs) repentance vnto ſalua-
tion; and a [n] troubled ſpirit is a ſacrifice vnto God. Of this kind
of ſorrow to ſupplie the weakneſ and want of true repen-
tance in vs all, and to teach vs heartilie to lament our ſins,
the more wee attribute vnto the ſoule of our Sauiour, the
more ſufficient euerie way we make his ſatiſſaction for ſin,
that did not onelie render recompence by his life, and ſuffer
vengeance by his death for our ſins, but ſo deepelie ſorrowed
for them that in his agonie, aboue nature, he ſweate bloud
after a ſtrange and marueilous maner.

[m] 2. Cor. 7.
[n] Pſal. 51.

　The fift cauſe of Chriſts agonie, might be the cup of gods
wrath, tempered and made readie for the ſinnes of men. [o] In
the hand of the Lorde is a cuppe (ſaith Dauid) it is mixed full,
the wine thereof is redde ; all the wicked of the earth ſhall
wring and drinke the dregges thereof. In this cuppe are all
manner of plagues and puniſhmentes for ſinne, as well
ſpirituall, as corporall; eternall, as temporall. The mix-
ture of which cuppe Chriſt perfectlie knowing; and care-
fullie ſhunning the dregges thereof, earneſtlie prayed this
cuppe might paſſe from him. I knowe diuers men haue
diuerſlie expounded theſe wordes of Chriſt, ſome there-
by collecting two willes ſhewed in Chriſt, a diuine and
humane, the one ſubmitting it ſelfe to the other : ſome no-
ting a difference betwixt the vnwillingneſſe of our fleſh,
and readineſſe of the ſpirite, euen in the manhoode of
Chriſt: ſome alſo thinking that Chriſt corrected and reuo-
ked his petition, ſuddenly ſlipt from him, by the vehemencie of
griefe, which tooke from him the preſent remembrance of gods
heauenly decree. In this varietie of iudgements, to refuſe

The depreca-
tion of Gods
wrath.
[o] Pſal. 75

none that agræth any way with the rules of truth, Chrift might behold three things in the cuppe of Gods wrath, and by his praier accordinglie decline them; to wit, eternal male-diction, corporall caftigation aboue his ftrength, and the fepa-ration of his bodie by death from the fruition of God.

Chrift might pray againft the eternal malediction of our finnes.

‡ Heb.5.

¶ Theodoret in c.5.epift.ad Heb.

What was due to our finnes Chrift could not be ignorant; and as he became man to quicken our fouls that were dead, not to kill his owne; and to bring vs to God, not to feuer himfelfe from God: fo knowing what our finnes deferued, he might intentiuelie pray to haue That cup paffe from him, which was prepared for vs; & was heard in that he declined or feared, ‡ Chrift (faith Paule) in the dayes of his flefh did of-fer vp praiers and fupplications to him, that was able to faue him from death, and was heard ἀπὸ τῆς εὐλαβείας, for the reue-rence had of him; for fo Chryfoftome, Theodorete, Oecumenius and others not vnlearned (as I thinke) in the Græke tongue doe interprete the worde; or as others delight rather to fay: He was heard in that he feared; εὐλάβεια fignifying feare and care, as wel as reuerence. ¶ Paule meaneth that praier (faieth Theodorete) which CHRIST made before his paffion, when he faid, Father if it be poffible let this cup paffe from me: And in deed but in the garden, Chrift neuer praied with ftrong cries and teares to be faued from death, that we read in the fcrip-tures: and He was heard (faith the Apoftle) in that he feared or fhunned. From the death of the croffe hee was not faued, that therfore was not the effect of his praier; for he was heard in that hee afked . He defired therefore to be faued from ETERNALL death, and that the cup of Gods euerlafting malediction might paffe from him, and in that he was heard.

[At leaft then (wil they fay) Chrift feared euerlafting death, againft which he inftantlie praied with ftrong cries & tears.] The number of our finnes, and power of Gods wrath hee coulde not chofe but fee, being ordained the fauiour of the world, to beare the one, and appeafe the other; and therefore if we grant that the fight of both, did for the time fomewhat aftonifh the humane nature of Chrift, aduifedly confidering
the

the waight of both, I ſee no great inconuenience therein, ſo long as they impreſſed nothing in the ſoule of Chriſt, but a religious feare to Sorrow foꝛ the one, and to pray againſt the other. But diſtruſt of his owne ſaluation, oꝛ doubt of Gods diſpleaſure againſt himſelfe, we cannot ſo much as imagine in Chriſt, without euident want of grace, and loſſe of Faith; which we may not attribute to Chriſts perſon, no not foꝛ an inſtant. It is weakeneſſe of faith in vs to feare, oꝛ foꝛget the pꝛomiſes of God, when the conſcience of ſinne accuſeth vs. What then will it be foꝛ the ſoule of Chriſt, after ſo manie pꝛomiſes and oathes made by God, to annoint and ſend the Sauiour of the woꝛld, after ſo manie cleare and full aſſurances of Gods loue and fauour towards his perſon, to ſtagger at the certaintie of Gods counſell, at the light of his owne knowledge, and at the truth of his fathers voice ſo often denounced, and confirmed with thunder from heauen? I refraine to ſpeake what wꝛong it is, to put either doubtfulnes, oꝛ foꝛgetfulneſſe of theſe thinges in any part of Chriſtes humane nature.

[Why then did hee pꝛaie that the cup might paſſe from him?] he had no néed to pꝛay foꝛ himſelf, but onely foꝛ vs; who then ſuffered with him, and in him. On vs it might haue ſtaied being ſeuered from him, as the iuſt wages of our ſin: againſt him it could not pꝛeuaile, becauſe nothing could befall him either againſt his will, oꝛ vnfit foꝛ the ſonne of God. Wherefoꝛe the foꝛce and effect of his pꝛaier chieflie concerned vs, Being then compriſed in his bodie, in which wee were crucified, buried, and raiſed, togither with him, And touching himſelfe, albeit the innocencie of his cauſe, the holineſſe of his life, the merit of his obedience, the aboundance of his ſpirit, the loue of his father, and vnitie of his perſon, did moſt ſufficientlie gard him from all danger, and doubt of eternal death; yet to ſhew the perfection of his humilitie, he woulde not ſuffer his humane nature to require it of right, but pꝛoſtrate on the earth beſought his Father, That cuppe might paſſe.

Christ praied as the heade of his bodie, and ſo one perſon with his members.

Galath. 2.
Rom. 6.
Coloſ. 3.

paſſe from him, and was heard in that he ſhunned, oꝛ auoided. Foꝛ though God were long befoꝛe reſolued to accept the death and blood of his ſonne foꝛ the ſinnes of the woꝛld; yet by this meanes Chꝛiſt did ſée howe déerelie God loued him, that foꝛ his ſake, and at his requeſt releaſed the iuſt vengeance of mans ſinne, & tooke the cup of eternall malediction not from him onlie, but from vs all at his mediation: howbeit to ſhew the confidence he had in his father, and to bꝛing his obedience to the higheſt degrée that might be; hee did after his religious diſlike of that cup, which wee had deſerued, ſimplie and wholie ſubmit himſelfe to his fathers pleaſure, without anie condition oꝛ exception, in ſaying to his father; *r* Not as I will, but as thou wilt: Not thereby ſtriking any terroꝛ of hell into the ſence of his fleſh, as ſome would haue it; but fully reſting on his fathers will and goodneſſe towardes him, as in the ſureſt hauen of his hope, and our helpe, againſt all the power of death and hell.

r Matth. 26

A ſecond thing which Chꝛiſt might iuſtlie feare, and earneſtlie pꝛaie againſt, (though his ſoule were neuer ſo ſafe,) was the power of Gods wꝛath to be executed on his bodie, vnleſſe it pleaſed God to lighten the burden of mans ſinne. Foꝛ God was armed with infinite vengeance to afflict and puniſh the bodie, aboue that the humane fleſh of Chꝛiſt was able to endure. Since therefoꝛe Chꝛiſt was not or elie with méekeneſſe to beare, but with al willingnes to offer to abide the hand of God laid vpon him, by what meanes ſoeuer; hee might pꝛay that the cup of his paſſion might be pꝛopoꝛtioned to the ſtrength of his fleſh, which was but weake in reſpect of Gods power; and therein alſo he was heard. Foꝛ the cup which his father gaue him to dꝛinke by the hands of the twicked, did paſſe from him, without oppreſſing his patience, oꝛ ſhaking his obedience.

Thirdlie Chꝛiſt might feare his verie paſſion; not as weaker in courage then martyꝛs oꝛ malefactoꝛs, but as perfecter in nature then either of them. The moꝛe we enioie the
pꝛeſence

Chriſt might deſire the puniſhment of our ſinnes to be proportioned to the ſtrength of his humane fleſh.

Chriſt might pray againſt death, not as weaker but as perfecter then others.

presence of God in soule or in bodie; the greater griefe it will be, and must be to lacke the sence hereof, euen for a short time. The flesh of Christ then, which had not onlie a personall coniunction, but also a wonderfull fruition of God aboue all men liuing, might well be loath to leaue the same, and yeeld to death, not as timorous through infirmitie, but as desirous in pietie to kepe that sence and feeling of Gods presence, which not onlie the soules, but also the bodies of his Saintes shall hereafter enioie; and which Christ had here on earth in greater measure, then we can expresse, as being personallie vnited to the diuine nature, though as yet not glorified with immortalitie.

And where some auouch, it had beene in Christ a shamefull nicenesse to be so afflicted with the feare of his passion; albeit S. Augustine saie well : ^c *Non est vllo modo dubitandum , non enim animi infirmitate , sed potestate turbatum* ; We may by no meanes doubt that Christ was troubled not for any weakenesse of hart , but through (his own) power : yet Cyril granteth that Christ as a man abhorred and feared death, and addeth that except he had voluntarily shewed our feare in himselfe , and quenched it, we had neuer beene freed from it. ^c *Omnia Christus perpessus est , vt nos ab omnibus liberaret . Sicut igitur nisi mortuus esset, mors non extingueretur, sic nisi timuisset, non essemus nos à metu liberati: nisi doluisset non cessassent dolores nostri.* Christ suffered all, that he might free vs from al. As therefore except he had died, death had not beene conquered ; so vnlesse he had feared, we had not beene deliuered from feare; and if he had not sorrowed, our sorrowes could not haue ceased . And in like manner shalt thou finde all the passions of (our) flesh , to haue beene stirred in Christ, but without sinne, that beeing stirred they might be repressed , by the power of the godheade dwelling in him; and our nature by that meanes reduced to a better temper. Ambrose in other wordes saieth, as much: ^d *Sequestrata delectatione diuinitatis æternæ, tædio meæ infirmitatis afficitur. Suscepit enim tristitiam meam, vt mihi suam lætitiam largiretur, &*

C I.

Augusti. tra. 60. in Iohannem. Christ cured our infirmities in his owne person.

Cyril. thesauri. lib. 10.cap. 3.

Ambrosius in Lucam lib. 10. de tristitia dolore & tædia vestigiis Christi.

vestigijs nostris descendit vsque ad mortis ærumnam, vt nos suis vestigijs reuocaret ad vitam. Debuit ergo & dolorem suscipere, vt vinceret tristitiam, non excluderet; & nos disceremus in Chri-sto, quemadmodum futuræ mortis mæstitiam vinceremus. And so he concludeth. *Hic alio operatur effectu, vt quia in carne sua, peccata nostra perimebat, mærorem quoque animæ nostræ, suæ animæ mærore aboleret.* Laying aside the delight of his æternall deitie, (Christ) is affected with the tediousnesse of my infirmity, and deiected himselfe to feele the griefe of death as we doe, that by following his steps he might reduce vsto life: hee was there-fore to admit sorrowe that he might conquer sorrowe, and not keepe it off; and wee to learne in Christ howe we should ouer-come the feare of death approching. (In his agonie) hee wrought with a deepe effect, that because in his flesh hee killed our sinnes, he might also with the sorrow of his soule extinguish the sorrowe of our soules. So the sorrowe and feare of death, which it pleased our sauiour to feele in our nature came not for want of strength: but of purpose to quench and abolish those affections and passions in vs, that the faithfull for euer might bee freed from them, through his grace working in their hearts. And therefore we haue no cause to excuse, much lesse to reproch Christes weakenesse, but rather to admire his power, and praise his mercie, that woulde submit himselfe to these infirmities of our nature, thereby to cure them in vs, and to strengthen vs against them; and to make vs parta-kers of his wonderfull courage, and patience, the steps wher-of we may daille find, not in martyrs onelie, but in all his members, when they are tried with anie kinde of outwarde or inward afflidion.

We must pre-fer Christs suf-fering before all martyrs, not for his paines, but for his pa-tience.

Howbeit, I may not omit, how great an ouersight it is to conclude, that Christ, if he feared death in his agony, was far feebler then martyrs which ioyfullie die; yea, then malefactors which oftentimes go to their death verie resolutely. The desp-ratenesse of the wicked which haue neither feare nor care of God, till they feele the force of his wrath in hell fire, is no fit

comparison

compariſon fo2 the ſonne of God ; no mo2e then the ſinke of ſinne is to ſwæeten the fountaine of grace ; I will therefo2e ſkippe that ouer with ſilence. But if death bee not fearefull to the ſeruants of Ch2iſt, as indæede it is not, they are the mo2e bound to their Lo2d and maſter, who in his owne perſon to make the waie eaſie fo2 them, with the loſſe of his life diſarmed death fo2 euer, and b2ake the chaines in ſunder therewith death and hell were coupled together. Fo2 Ch2iſt was the firſt that by ſeuering death from the terro2 and power of hell, made the ſtroke of death contemptible to all the godlie; which otherwiſe was and would haue bæene the harbinger of hell. So that when death p2eſented it ſelfe to the ſight of our ſauiour purpoſing to redæeme the wo2ld, it came ſo faſt claſped with hell; that none but the ſonne of God could diſſolue the band, therewith they were linked. And therfo2e Ch2iſt had far greater cauſe then anie of his members, to feare; and with earneſt p2aier to decline the taſte of death, which did wound both bodie and ſoule with euerlaſting deſtruction, if he did not take awaie the ſting thereof; and by his ſund2ing the one from the other, (which was the hope of all his ſaints, befo2e he died, and faith of al the godlie ſince) death was and is to all belæeuers no cauſe of feare, but reſt from their labo2s, and paſſage to a better life. The feare then which Ch2iſt had and ſhewed of death, was either the curing of our infirmities in his fleſh; o2 the breaking the knot betwixt death and hell, which none but he was able to doe; o2 the mitigating of Gods anger, which might be executed on his bodie, o2 laſtlie the deſire hee had to continue the fæeling and enioying of Gods p2eſence, and coherence with bodie and ſoule in the vnitie of his perſon : and if in anie of theſe wee charge Ch2iſt with niceneſſe, wee knowe not what we ſaie, except we will bee guiltie in a wo2ſe iſſue, which I perſwade my ſelfe was no part of their meaning, that firſt b2ochet this matter.

The laſt cauſe of Ch2iſts agony might be the ſanctifying of himſelfe to p2aie fo2 trangreſſo2s, and the voluntarie dedi-

cating

Chriſt might by his agony voluntarilie dedicate his

bloud to mans
redemption.

cating of his bloud to bee shed for the redemption of mankind: for where some coniecture Christ did sweate bloud for feare, Hilarie plainelie denieth it, and saieth, ^x *Sudorem nemo audebit infirmitati deputare; quia & contra naturam est sudare sanguinem, nec infirmitas est, quod potestas, non secundum naturæ consuetudinem, gessit.* No man shoulde dare attribute (Chrifts bloudy) sweate to infirmitie, because it is against nature to sweat bloud, and can bee no weakenes, which power did aboue the courſe of nature. Austen maketh it a significati on of the martyrs bloud, that should willinglie bee shedde throughout the church for the testimonie of the truth. ^y *Ideo toto corpore sanguinē sudauit, quia in corpore suo, id est Ecclesia, Martyrum sanguinem ostendit.* Christ sweat bloud along all his bodie, to this ende, that he might shew the bloud of martyrs in his bodie, which is the church. Prosper agreeth with S. Augustine in iudgement and saith. ^z *Orans cum sudore sanguineo dominus Iesus, significabat de toto corpore, quod est Ecclesia, emanaturas martyrum passiones.* The Lorde Iesus praying with a bloudy sweat, signified the sufferings of the martyrs that should be in his whole body which is the church. Bede thereby noteth that Chriſtes prayer made for his Apoſtles was hearde; and that by his bloud he should not onelie redreſſe the frailtie of his diſciples, but quicken the whole earth being dead in their sinnes. ^a *Nemo sudorem hunc infirmitati deputet, sed intelligat per irrigatam sacratamque eius sanguine terram, non sibi, qui nouerat, sed nobis aperiē declarātum, quod effectum suæ precis iam obtineret, vt fidem discipulorum, quàm terrena adhuc fragilitas arguebat suo sanguine purgaret, & quicquid illa scandali de eius morte pertulisset, hoc totū ipse moriendo deleret; immo vniuersum latē terrarū orbem peccatis mortuum sua innoxia morte cælestem resuscitaret ad vitam.* Let no man attribute Chrifts bloudie sweat to infirmitie, but rather learne that by sprinkling and hallowing the earth with his bloud, it was declared, not to him who knewe it, but vnto vs, that he had obtained the effect of his praier, with his bloud to purge the faith of his Disciples, which earth

lie

^x*Hilar. lib. 10
de triniate.*

^y*August. in
Psalm. 93.*

^z*Prosper sentent. ex August.
sent. 68.*

^a*Bede in Luc.
cap. 22.*

lie frailtie did weaken, and whatſoeuer offence (the earth) had taken at his death, al that he dying ſhould aboliſh, yea with his innocent death he ſhould raiſe vnto an heauenlie life the whole world then dead in their ſinnes. Bernard taketh hold on S. Pauls wordes, where hee calleth Chriſtes ſweate by the name of teares: and ſaith, *Ventum eſt adorationem, & vſque tertiò factus in Agonia orabat; vbi quidem non ſolis oculis, ſed quaſi omnibus membris fleuiſſe videtur, vt totū corpus ēius, quodeſt eccleſia, totius corporis lachrymis purgaret in.* Chriſt came to praier, and being in an agony he praied thriſe: where he ſeemed to weepe, not onelie with his eies, but with all the parts of his body; that the whole body of his Church might bee purged with the teares of his whole body.

Bernard in ramis palmarum ſermon. 3.

S. Paul alleageth the cries and teares of Chriſt in the garden as a proofe of his prieſthood, & ſaith, that not onlie [b] He offered praiers & ſupplications, which was one part of the prieſts office, wherein hee was heard for the reuerence had of him: But alſo τελειωθεὶς, being ſanctified, to offer ſacrifice, (for ſo the word doth often ſignifie,) or elſe conſummated by the offering of himſelfe on the croſſe, (which was the other part of his prieſtlie function) was made authour of eternall ſaluation to all that obey him, being thus called and allowed of God to bee an high prieſt after the order of *Melchizedec.* Chriſt readie to enter the garden ſaith, [c] *Pro eis ſanctifico meipſum;* for their ſakes I ſanctifie my ſelfe: and ſanctification properlie belongeth to the prieſts perſon, before hee might appeare in Gods preſence to offer for the ſinnes of the people; and by the rite of Moſes lawe, the prieſtes, when they were ſanctified vnto God, had their bodies [d] ſprinkled with the bloud of their ſacrifice from top to toe. Chriſt then being the truth of all their figures as well in the ſanctification, as oblation of himſelfe, might miraculouſlie ſprinkle his whole bodie with his own bloud; (for it was aboue nature as Hilarie noteth) to conſecrate his perſon, as approued of God, to be the true prieſt after the order of Melchizedec, and voluntarilie deuotrate his bloud to

[b] Hebe. 5.

Or ſanctifie his perſon to offer the true ſacrifice for ſinne.

[c] Iohn. 17

[d] Exod. 29

be ſhed for the remiſſion of our ſinnes, which hee did of his owne accord yeeld, to be diſpoſed of at his fathers pleaſure, before the Iewes or Gentiles wounded his bodie, that his whole paſſion which followed, might bee a willing ſacrifice, and no forced violence by the handes or weapons of the wicked. Chriſtes agonie then being alleaged by the Apoſtle to demonſtrate Chriſts prieſthood, muſt not riſe from the terror of his owne death, but rather from the vehemencie of his prayer for vs, that it might bee aſwell an interceſſion for ſinners, as a ſanctification of himſelfe, to offer the ſacrifice auaileable for the ſinnes of the world. To which if anie will adde the ſignification of the martyrs bloud, which Auſten ſpeaketh of, as if Chriſt in the garden did not onelie preſent his owne bloud to be the true propitiation of our ſinnes, but alſo the bloud of his martyrs, to make their death acceptable to God, that willinglie laide downe their liues for the witnes of his truth; I can be well content to admit that expoſition, conſidering Chriſt muſt offer both the liues and deathes of all his ſaintes to God his father, before they can be holie or precious in his ſight.

The ſuffering of hell paines not ẙ cauſe of Chriſts agony.

But ſince Chriſtes feare (as they expound the Apoſtles words Hebre. 5.) is made the groundworke of this conceipt, let vs ſee whether their owne foundation will not ouerthrow their owne building. The paines of hell, did Chriſt when hee prayed in the garden, feare them or no? If hee did not feare them, hee did not feele them; for they are fearefull: yea the verie *expectation of them is verie dreadful, as the Apoſtle ſaith Hebre. 10; and if he feared them not, howe could they bee the cauſe of his agonie, which theſe men ſo ſtiflie maintaine? If he feared them, he was freed from them, as they themſelues interprete the worde εὐλάβεια, for hee was heard in that he feared. His prayer was to haue that cup paſſe from him, and God neuer denied whatſoeuer he aſked. ſ I know (ſaith Chriſt to his father) that thou heareſt me alwaies. Whence they conclude, he feared hell paines, thence I infer

*Hebre.10

ſIoh.11.

he

hee ſuffered them not . for being deliuered from the feare of hell
approching, he could not be left vnder the burden of hell abi-
ding. Againe, if the ſuffering of hell were the cauſe of Chriſts
agony, the cauſe continuing, the effect could not ceaſe . But
his agonie ended in the garden; how then could the paines
of hell endure on the croſſe, and be lengthened almoſt to the
end of his life? Ierome ſaith vpon theſe wordes of Chriſt to
his diſciples, [Ariſe let vs go :] g leaſt they finde vs, as though
we were fearefull, and drawing backe , let vs of our owne ac-
corde goe towardes them; *vt confidentiam , & gaudium paſſuri
videant*; that they may ſee the confidence and gladneſſe (of
Chriſt) going to his paſsion.

 The continuance of Chriſtes agonie they proue by his
complaint on the croſſe, where not long before he yælded vp
his ſpirit, he cried; h My God, my God, why haſt thou forſaken
me? and theſe wordes, they ſaie, do plainelie conuince , that
Chriſt felt himſelfe forſaken of God , and that this was the
true cauſe of his agonie, whatſoeuer pretences are inuented
by others to excuſe , or colour his feare . Indeede this place
moſt beare the burden of the whole frame; for the reſt are on-
lie ſignes of ſorrowe and zeale, the ſcriptures not expreſsing
the cauſe; but here are manifeſt wordes if wee miſtake not
their reference. i My father is greater then I am , were wordes
as cleare as daie light : but the referring that to the diuine
which hee ſpake of his humane nature , bero the Arrian he-
reſſe, My God, my God, why haſt thou forſaken mee; are not
ſo plaine. for the ſaints of God haue often complained vnto
God that they were forſaken of him, when he withdrew nei-
ther his fauour, grace, nor ſpirit from them; but onelie with-
helde his helpe or comfort for the time, to make them more
earneſt to ſeeke and flie to him. But were they neuer ſo preg-
nant, if we applie them to the wrong part, which God neuer
forſooke, we may incurre as groſſe an errour as euer did Ar-
rius. And yet if we ſtraine them to the vttermoſt, they will
neuer proue that Chriſt on the croſſe ſuffered the paines of
                    hell.

g *Hieron. in
Matth. ca.26*

h Matth. 27.

What is meant
by Chriſts cō-
plaint on the
croſſe that he
was forſaken.

i Iohn. 14.

hell. For if we should grant, which were diuelish impietie to thinke, that God forsooke Christes soule as verelie, as euer hee did anie of the wicked heere on earth, Cain, Saul, Iudas not excepted; yet that doth not conclude he suffered the true paines of hell. For those in this life did not suffer as much, as their soules doe now in hell, make their case neuer so desperate. And therefore I marueile howe wise men were bewitched with the sound of these wordes, which hence resolued that out of all question, Christ suffered the paines of the damned in hell, where as the wordes inferre no such thing, though we stretch them neuer so farre. For in spite of our hearts, before we can bring that conclusion to follow, this

The wicked are here forsaken, and yet not in hell.

must be the iointure of our reason. All men any way forsaken of God in this life are in the true paines of hell: Christ was forsaken of God, *ergo* he was in the true paines of hell. Now howe fond, false, and absurd the generall assertion is, that all anie way forsaken of God, are in the true paines of hell, to men of learning and religion needeth no long discourse. Cain was a [k]runnagate and accursed by Gods mouth; Esau was a [l]prophane person, and [m]hated of God; Saul was verie desperate when he sought to the witch, for God was [n]departed from him, and become his enemie; Iudas was the [o]sonne of perdition, and a [P]diuell: yea manie were starke mad, and possessed with diuels; and yet none of them in those verie tormentes, which are reserued for the damned in hell. The [q]Gentiles as Paul saith, were strangers from the life of God, and had [r]no hope, and were without God in the world, yet were they not in the paines of hell, here on earth. But I hope we be not so far drowned in the depth of hell, that wee will for our fansie range the sonne of God, and sauiour of the world, in this rable of wicked and desperate castawaies; and yet though men could be so dangerouslie deuoted to their dreames, this proueth not their purpose. Desperation they may stumble at, if they will presse the wordes without anie difference betweene the dereliction of Gods saintes and his enemies; but toleration

[k]Genes.4
[l]Hebre.12
[m]Rom.9.
[n]1 Samuel 28
[o]Iohn.17
[P]Iohn.6
[q]Ephes.4.18
[r]Ephes.2.12.

tion of hell paines theſe words will neuer conclude, vnleſſe we make hell to be no iudgement, nor puniſhment after this life, but onelie a terror and horror of conſcience, ſuch as pur＊ſeth the wicked here in reuenge of their ſinnes.

When the godlie complaine, as often they do in the ſcrip-tures, that they were forſaken of God, it is not onlie a plaine abſurditie, but a groſſe impietie to conclude of their words, that they then ſuffered the verie paines of the damned in hell. For example, Sion, which is the whole church of God, ſaith in the prophet Eſay, ᶠ the Lorde hath forſaken me : and God himſelfe aſſureth her words to bee true, ᵗ For a while I forſooke thee, for a moment in mine anger, I hid my face from thee: Was the whole church for that time in the true paines of hell? Dauid ſaith of himſelfe, ᵘ Thou haſt reiected and ab-horred, thou haſt beene angrie with thine annointed. Was Dauid then in the verie paines of the damned? of his whole realme he ſaith; ˣ O God thou haſt caſt vs off, and beene angry with vs. Did all the people then ſuffer the torments of hell? reiecting and abhorring are words of greater diſlike, and more deteſtation, then forſaking; and yet they infer not the paines of hell. Whie then doe wee ſo fondlie miſconſter the one, when we well inough vnderſtande the other? why ſtumble we at a ſtrawe, when we canne ſtep ouer a blocke? To be forſaken of God as the wicked are, is to bee depriued of his fauour, grace, and ſpirit: and yet they are not forth-with in hell. To be forſaken, as the godlie complaine they are, is to be voide of comfort, or deſtitute of helpe, when their enemies aſſault or afflict them, which is nothing neere the ſtate of the damned. For as God is ſaid to be preſent by his gifts and graces: ſo he hideth his face, or forſaketh vs, when he reſtraineth his eie from watching, his eare from hearing, or his hand from helping vs in the miſeries and aduerſities of this life.

If I be thought partiall, let vs heare what the ancient and learned fathers purpoſelie write of our ſauiours complaint

How the godly
are forſaken.

ᶠ Eſay 49.
ᵗ Eſay.54

ᵘ Pſalm.89

ˣ Pſalm.60

on the croſſe; in whome I finde ſundꝛie, and all godlie expoſi-
tions, accoꝛding with the truth of the ſcriptures, and no way
bending oꝛ inclining to this late deuiſe of hell paines.

1.

*Diuers expo-
fitions of the
fathers, how
Chriſt was for-
ſaken on the
croſſe.*

The firſt; that as Chriſt is our heade, and we his mem-
bers in ſuch ſoꝛt ioyned in one bodie with him, that hee ſuffe-
reth in vs, and we in him; ſo were we not onlie crucified and
buried, but alſo raiſed, and gloꝛified in him, and with him;
and therefoꝛe hee ſhewed and vttered manie thinges in his
paſſion, which ought to be referred directlie to vs, and not to
him, but as bearing our perſon, and ſpeaking in our names.

*¹ Auguſt. epiſto-
la. 120.*

My God, my God, why haſt thou forſaken mee? ¹ *Hanc inſe
vocem transfigurauit Ieſus, vocem corporis ſui, hoc eſt eccleſia.*
This ſpeech Chriſt transferred to himſelfe, (ſaith *Auſten*) being
the ſpeach of his body, which is the church. The church ſuffered
then in him, when he ſuffered for the church, euen as hee ſuffe-
red in the church, when the church ſuffered for him. And as we
heard the voice of the church ſuffering in Chriſt, when he ſaide;
my God, my God, why haſt thou forſaken me: ſo haue we heard
the voice of Chriſt ſuffering in his church, when bee ſaide; *Saul,*

*² Idem in Pſal-
mum. 21.*

Saul, why perſecuteſt thou mee? And againe; ² *quid voluit di-
cere dominus? non enim dereliquerat illū deus, cum ipſe eſſet deus,
atque filius dei. Quare dicitur, niſi quia nos ibi eramus, niſi quia
corpus Chriſti eccleſia?* Why would the Lord ſaie, my God, my
God, why haſt thou forſaken me? God had not forſaken him, for
ſo much as he was God, and the ſon of God. Why then was it
ſaid, but becauſe we were there in him, & the church which was

*ᵇ Leo de paſſio.
ſerm. 16.*

*ᶜ Athanaſius de
incarnat, Chriſti.*

his bodie? ᵇ *Sub redemptorum ſuorum voce clamabat, deus de-
us meus, quare me dereliquiſti,* In the name of his redeemed
Chriſt ſaid, my God, my God, why haſt thou forſaken me: ᶜ *Ex
noſtra perſona verba illa proloquitur, non enim ipſe à deo deſti-
tutus fuit, ſed nos.* In our perſon Chriſt ſpeaketh theſe wordes,
for he was not forſaken of God, but we.

2.

The ſecond expoſition of theſe woꝛds is, that Chꝛiſtes hu-
mane nature was not pꝛotected from the rage of the Iewes,
but left without helpe in the power of his enemies, to bee
vſed

vfed at their pleafures, which he calleth a kind of forfaking.
For God then feemeth to leaue vs, whē he doth not defend vs
from the furie of our foes, which feeke our ouerthrow. *Erat*
aliqua caufa, eaque non parua, quare Chriftum de manibus Iu-
deorum non liberaret deus, eumque in poteftate fauientium, vf-
que ad mortis exitum derelinqueret. There was a caufe, faieth
Auguſtine, and that no fmall caufe, why God did not deliuer
Chriſt out of the handes of the Iewes, but let him alone in the
power of his purfuers, vntill he died. ᵉ *Vt homo loquitur meos* ᵉ Ambroſ. de fuk
circumferens metus, quod in periculis pofiti a domino deferi nos lib. 2. cap 3.
putamus. Chriſt fpeaketh as a man (faith Ambrofe) bearing a-
bout him my feares, for y̌ we, when we are in danger, think our
felues forfaken of God. ᶠ *Ne mireris querimonias derelicti; cum* ᶠHieron in ca.27
fcandalum crucis videas. Maruaile not at Chriftes complaint Matthe.
that he was forfaken, when as thou feeſt how he was vfed on the
croffe. ᵍ *Derelictus eft Chriftus pro parte carnis.* Chriſt was ᵍ Idē in Pfal. 21
forfaken in his paſſion as touching his flefh.

A third is, that Chriſts godhead together with his humane 3.
foule were then departing from his bodie, and leauing it vn-
to death. Tertullian, (*Deus*) *Filium* ʰ *dereliquit, cum hominem* ʰ Tertul. aduer-
eius tradidit in mortē. Ita relinqui a patre, fuit mori filio. God fus Praxeam.
forfooke his fonne, in that he deliuered his humanity vnto death.
So for the fonne to die, was to be forfaken of his father. Hilarie,
ⁱ *Habes conquerentem fe effe relictum ad mortem, quia homo eſt:* ⁱ Hilar. lib. 10
vt intelligentia noſtra fit, & homo mortuus, & deus regnans. de Trinitate.
Thou heardeſt Chriſt complaine that hee was left vnto death,
that we fhould conceiue he died as a man, he raigned as a God.
And againe; ᵏ *Clamor ad deum, corporis vox eſt, recedentis a fe* ᵏ Idem in Matth.
verbi dei conteſtata diſſidium: relinquitur, quia erat homo etiam cap. 33.
morte peragendus. Chriftes complaint vnto God, that hee was
forfaken, is the voice of his body, teſtifying the feparation of the
diuine nature from it for a time. He is forfaken, becaufe he was a
man to be confummated by his death. Epiphanius faith, hee
fpake thefe words, ˡ When he faw his deitie with his foule readie ˡ Epiph. lib. 2. t.
to depart from the perfon of his humanity & to forfake his body. 2. contra. Ario-
A manitas.

4

A fourth is, that where God for sin had refused and forsaken man, euen from the fall of Adam, Christ nowe exalted on the tree, reconciled mankind vnto God, and slue hatred, making peace by his prayer betwixt God & man. *Cyril:* ᵐ whē Adam transgressed the diuine commaundement, mans nature was after a sort forsaken of God, and therby subiected to a curse and death. These words of Christ therfore, *Erant soluentis manifestè derelictionem quæ nobis acciderat, & quasi placantis in hoc patrē, &c.* Were the manifest remouing of that derelictiō, which fel on vs, and as it were an appeasing his father, and procuring his fauor towards vs, as towards himself. *Basil:* ⁿ *Dicit hæc dom. inus, primitiæ humanæ naturæ pro vniuersa.* The lord speaketh these words for all mankind, as being the first fruits of mãs nature. Otherwise of his own person it is true that Athanasius saith. ᵒ *Neq̃; enim à patre derelinqui potuit, quia semper est in patre. & antequam hancvocem ederet & postquam edidisset. Ecce enim dicente, cur me dereliquisti: ostendit pater se vt semper antea, ita tum quoq̃, in filio fuisse.* He could not be forsaken of his father, who was alwaies in his father, both before and after he spake these words. Behold as hee vttered these words (why hast thou forsaken me) the father shewed himselfe to be euen then in his sonne, as he was at all times before. For the earth feeling the weight of her Lord, straight wayes trembled, the vaile rent, the Sunne darkened, the stones claue, the dead rose.

5.

The fift, that Christ putteth vs in mind by these words to acknowledge the cause, why God doth often not heare our prayers, but in refusing our desires prouideth better for vs, then if we had our wils. ᵖ *Vox ista, quare me dereliquisti, doctrina est, nõ querela. Nam cum in Christo dei & hominis vna sit persona, nec ab eo potuerit relinqui, à quo non poterat separari, pro nobis trepidis & infirmis interrogat, cur caro pati metuens exaudita non fuerit.* This speach (saith Leo) My God, my God, why hast thou forsaken me, is an instruction, and no complaint: For where in Christ there is but one person of God and man, and he could not be forsaken of God, from whom he could not bee separated,

---

ᵐ *Cyril de recta fide ad reginas.*

ⁿ *Basil. in Psal. 21.*

ᵒ *Athan. contra Arrianos serm. 4.*

ᵖ *Leo de Pass. serm. 16.*

parated,he asketh the queſtion for vs that are fearefull & weak, why fleſh fearing to ſuffer is not heard. ¶ *Vnde ipſa vox non exauditi, magni eſt expoſitio ſacramenti: quòd nihil humano generi conferret redemptoris poteſtas, ſi quod petebat noſtra obtineret infirmitas.* The verie wordes of him,that was not heard, open to vs a great myſterie,to **witte**, that the power of the redeemer coulde doe mankinde no good, if our infirmitie might obtaine what it woulde aske : Origen **ſayth** : [r] In reſpect of that,in which conſiſted the inuiſible forme of God,Chriſt was forſaken of his father, where hee tooke the ſhape of a ſeruant, and came to the death of the Croſſe, which amongſt men was moſt ſhamefull. So that for Chriſt to become man, and to ſuffer on the Croſſe, was to bee forſaken of God, in compariſon of that glorie, **which hée had with his Father before all worldes.**

The laſt expoſition is, that when the Iewes reprochcd Chriſt on the Croſſe,as reiected of God,he with a loud voice, that all might hear, ſang or cited the beginning of the 21. Pſalme, wherein it was by the Prophet Dauid foreſhewed, that the true Meſſias and ſauiour of the worlde ſhould ſuffer all thoſe wronges,and ſhames, which they had heaped on him : and thereby taught them, that they had [ſ] gathered themſelues togither to do whatſoeuer the hand and counſaile of God had determined before to be done. [t] The Lord (ſaith Ierom)hanging on the Croſſe,vſeth this verſe , My God my God,why haſt thou forſaken me ; by which wee perceiue, that in the Croſſe he ſang the whole Pſalme, as directly pertaining to his paſſió. [u] Chriſt ſpake theſe words(ſaith Chryſoſtom) that the Iewes might know hee honoured his father to the laſt breath, and that God was not his enemie (**as they obiected:**) for which cauſe he vſed the Prophet *Dauids* words,to verifie or fulfill the ſcripture of the old teſtament.

All theſe interpretations are ſound,and ſtand well with the rules of chriſtian pietie, without diſhonouring the perſon,or diſturbing the faith of Chriſt;: therfore I cannot but maruel

that

Marginal notes:

[q] *Ibidem.*

[r] *Origen in Mat.cap.27.*

6

[ſ] *Act. 4.*

[t] *Hieron.in Pſa. 21.*

[u] *Chryſoſt.homo in Mat.89.*

what reason our late writers had to refuse them all, and deuise another exposition of their owne which imploieth not onlie desperation in Christs soule, if wee presse the wordes, and the dissolution of Christes person, but an euident contradiction to all that Christ did, or saide on the crosse, or in iudgement after the Iewes had once laide handes on him. For if these wordes be referred to the soule of Christ, and import a generall and true detestation, which must be supposed, before the paines of hell can thence be concluded; Christ feeling and confessing himselfe to bee forsaken of God, coulde haue neither faith, nor hope. For he that beleeueth, and hopeth in God, cannot trulie saie, that God hath forsaken his soule; he may complaine that God doth not deliuer him from dangers and troubles assaulting him; which the weakenesse of man thinketh a kinde of forsaking. *Mine enemies (saith Dauid) take counsell, saying, God hath forsaken him, pursue him, there is none to deliuer him. But this is no forsaking of the soule, so long as that part of man trusteth in God, which is created chiefelie to enioie God. Nowe by faith, hope, and loue, the soule of man enioieth God in this life; and hee that enioieth God is not forsaken of God. Yea whosoeuer hopeth in him, neither is nor euer shall be forsaken. *For hope doth not confound, *was there euer any confounded, that put his trust in the Lorde? or who hath continued in his feare, and hath beene forsaken? or whome did he euer despise that called vpon him? Then if out of these wordes we will infer, that Christes soule was truelie forsaken of God, it cannot bee auoided, but this inwarde perswasion in Christ (that his soule was forsaken) during from the time of his agonie in the garden, till his complaint on the crosse (which was aboue 18. houres) was manifest desperation: vnlesse wee saie Christ was deceiued in so thinking, which is as great an errour on the other side. For if his faith, hope, and loue were still fixed on God, and no waie decaied, he could with no truth saie, that his soule was vtterlie forsaken.

Againe

Againe, the soule that is forsaken of God must needes be
separated from God. a For he that cleaueth vnto the Lorde, is
one spirit with him, & so not forsaken of him. If then Christs
soule were seuered from God, it could haue no mutuall con-
gruence, much lesse naturall coherence with God. There
must bee a spirituall communion in grace, or else there
can be no personall vnion in nature. As the soule doth com-
municate her effects to the bodie, with which shee is coupled:
so must the deitie make the humane nature of Christ parta-
ker of those graces and giftes, which maie come from the
godhead, before we can truli saie, that the one is personal-
lie ioyned with the other. The participation and fruition of
God is not in words or thoughtes, but in deedes and effects.
In whom then the spirit of God dwelleth not, with his force
and fruites, let him neuer deceiue his hart, that he hath any
fellowship with God. Nowe that Christ was the fulnesse of
Gods spirit and grace. God b measured not his spirit to him,
but of his fulnesse we all haue receaued. So that if the fulnesse
of grace failed in the soule of Christ, the vnitie of his person
was vtterly dissolued. For without a communion, there can
be no coniunctiō of two natures in Christ. If there were an
effectuall and full communion, there could be no reall nor
generall derelictiō. Insomuch that the verie flesh of Christ,
though it were left vnto death; yet was it not vtterlie forsa-
ken of the deitie, but preserued euen in the graue from cor-
ruption, and raised againe with greater perfection then be
fore; besides the wonderfull conquest it had ouer death.
Which plainelie proue the Godheade was neuer separated
from the bodie of Christ, though the soule for a time de-
parted, that death and hell might bee destroied. If the deitie
did neuer forsake the bodie, no not in death; much lesse did it
euer forsake the soule, which alwaies had an vnseparable
coniunction, and vnseaseable communion with the godhead
of Christ.

Lastlie, no sence could bee deuised, more repugnant and
opposite

margin: a 1.Cor.6. If Christs soule were forsaken the vnion of his two natures was dissolued. b Iohn.1.

Chrifts words
& deeds proue
his foule was
not forfaken
of God.
ᶜMark.14.

ᵈLuke.23

ᵉLuke.23.

ᶠMatth.27.
ᵍIohn.18
ʰIohn.16

ⁱ. Acts.2.

oppofite to all that Chꝛiſt ſaide oꝛ did after his agonie, then this laſt found expoſition,oꝛ rather depꝛauation of his woꝛds. To the high pꝛieſt aſking him whether he were Chriſt the ſon of ỹ bleſſed (God,)he anſwered ᶜI am ; and ye ſhall ſee the ſon of man ſit at the righthande of the power of God, and come in the cloudes ofheauen. Chꝛiſt was and muſt be farre from diſtruſting oꝛ doubting that, which he reſolutelie affirmeth ſhal come to paſſe euen in the eies of his enemies. When they faſtened him to the croſſe hee ſaſt, ᵈ Father,forgiue them,they know not what they do. Could he intreate and obtaine pardon foꝛ others, that found himaſelfe to be foꝛſaken of God? To the thiefe that hung vp him, and deſired to be remembꝛed when he came to his kingdome,he anſwered, ᵉVerilie, I ſaie to thee,thou ſhalt this day bee with me in paradiſe. Could hee giue paradiſe to others,with ſo great confidence,that coulde not then aſſure himſelfe of Gods fauour, yea, as theſe men will haue it, that was abandoned and foꝛſaken of God?The Centurion that had the charge to ſee him put to death, and heard him ſpeake theſe woꝛds,neuer conceiued that he was reiected oꝛ eſtranged from God,but contrariwiſe confeſſed; ᶠTruelie this man was the ſonne of God. Chꝛiſt himſelfe ᵍKnowing all thinges that ſhould come vnto him, ſaide to his diſciples; ʰBehold the houre is come,that ye ſhall be ſcattered, and leaue me alone, but I am not alone,for the father is with me. Now if God were with him,when his diſciples left him, as he himſelfe witneſſeth, howe could his ſoule be foꝛſaken of God? of Chꝛiſt crucified Dauid ſaith (as Peter expoundeth his woꝛdes) ⁱ I alwaies beheld the Lord before me, euen at my right hand, that I ſhould not bee ſhaken. If Chꝛiſt had all the time of his paſſion the fauour of God ſo conſtant,and the power of God ſo pꝛeſent ,that hee coulde not be ſo much as mooued oꝛ ſwaied to and fro, foꝛ ſo the woꝛdes ἵνα μὴ σαλευθῶ doe ſigniſie , that I ſhould not waue vp and downe, but ſtand fixed and aſſured; how could that parte of Chꝛiſt,which enioied ſo manifeſtlie the ſight of Gods countenance, and ſtrength

ſtrength of Gods aſſiſtance, be forſaken or refuſed of God?
And out of this complaint, that he was forſaken, if we inferre
the paines of hell, wee conclude directlie againſt Chriſtes
woordes in the 16. pſalme, *Non derelinques animam meam in*
inferno, Thou wilt not forſake my ſoule in hell. Chriſts ſoule
was not forſaken in hell; if then it were forſaken on the
croſſe, it is euident that there it ſuffered not hell, for in hell
it was neuer forſaken. And therefore turne and winde the
woordes of Chriſt which way they will or can, this expoſition,
which they faſten vnto them, is a manifeſt contradiction to
all that Chriſt did or ſaide on the croſſe, and namelie to that
aſſertion of Dauid, in the perſon of Chriſt, Thou wilt not for-
ſake my ſoule in hell.

　　Then are there in the ſacred ſcriptures neither anie pre-
dictions that Chriſt ſhoulde ſuffer the paines of hell in his
ſoule here on earth; nor cauſes why he muſt ſuffer them; nor
Signes that he did ſuffer them; and conſequentlie, whatſoeuer
is pretended, no proofe that theſe ſufferings muſt be added
to the croſſe of Chriſt, before the worke of our ſaluation can
be perfect. And for my part, which moderation I wiſh in you
all, What I reade in the word of God that I beleeue, what I do
not reade that I doe not beleeue. In Gods cauſes wee maie
not eaſily leaue Gods woords, and with a new kind of ſpeach
make way for a new kinde of faith. We muſt learne from
God what to beleeue, and not by correcting or inuerting his
woords teach him how to ſpeake. Since therefore redempti-
on and remiſſion of ſinnes are euerie where in the ſcriptures
referred to the death and bloud of Chriſt, I dare not ſo much
as thinke the woords of the holie ghoſt in one of the greateſt
myſteries of our chriſtian faith to be improper, or imperfect.
And that you may the better perceaue how plainelie and ful-
lie this doctrine is deliuered in the propheticall & apoſtolical
ſcriptures; I thinke it good to go forwardes with the effects
of Chriſtes croſſe; by which it ſhall appeare howe ſufficient
the price of our redemption is, in the bloud of Chriſt, without

anie supplie of hell paines to be suffered in y⸍ soule of Christ.

The effectes of Christs crosse though I might reckon manie, yet to keep my selfe within some compasse, I restraine to fiue chiefe branches: the MERITE of his suffering, which was INFINITE; the MANER of his offering, which was BLOVDY; The POVVER of his DEATH, which was mighty; the COMFORT of his CROSSE which was NECESSARIE, ⸍ the GLORY of his RESVRRECTION which was heauenly. These fiue will direct vs not onely what to beléeue, but what to refuse in the person and passion of our Sauiour. I will therefore take them as they lie in order.

The merite of Christs suffering must be simply infinite, that it may worke two things for vs; to wit, redeeme vs from Sathan, and reconcile vs vnto God: cleere vs from hell, and bring vs to heauen; ⸍ in either respect it must be infinite. The wages of sinne is death, both of bodie and soule, here and for euer. With the Iudge of the world is no vnrighteousnesse. He therefore punisheth no man, without cause, or aboue desert. Since the reuenge of each mans sinne is eternall, ⸍ is infinite in time; the waight of each mans sinne must needs be infinite, as being rewarded with euerlasting death. It may séeme much to carnal men, that God should requite sin with euerduring reuenge; but if we seriouslie bethinke our selues, what it is for earth and ashes to waxe proud against God, ⸍ after so manifold ⸍ abundant blessings to cast off his yoake, ⸍ readily, yea gréedily to prefer euerie vanitie and fansie before his heauenlie truth, ⸍ glory; we shall presently perceiue how iust cause God hath infinitely to hate our vncleannes, ⸍ eternallie to pursue the pride, contempt, ⸍ rebellion of wicked and wilfull men against his diuine maiestie; howsoeuer we digest it, it is a thing determined with God, and no doubt balanced in his vpright and sincere iudgment. [k]The soule that sinneth, that soule shal die. Death ⸍ life are both eternall, ⸍ is, infinite in length, though not in weight; in durance, though not in degree and sence of ioy, or paine. Then in either respect

to

to countervaile our deliuerance from hell, & our inheritance in heauen, the merit of Chriſts ſuffering muſt be infinite. An infinite purchaſe cannot be made, but with an infinite price.

For this infinite price whither ſhall we ſeeke? to the paines of hell, or to the powers of heauen? ⸀ paines of hel are neither meritorious nor infinite. What thanks with God to be ſeparated from God? and the ſoule being alienated from God, that other part of man can merite his fauor? If any man fal away, my ſoule ſhall haue no pleaſure in him. Hel paines therefore are accurſed, not accepted of God; and hee that ſuffereth them is hated, and no way beloued, ᵐ Depart from me ye curſed into euerlaſting fire. As they are not meritorious, no more are they infinite; I meane in waight; but they muſt euerlaſtingly be ſuffered, before they can be infinite. For not only diuels, but men of all ſorts ſhal ſuffer them, who cannot endure any infinite ſence of paine. All creatures are finite both in force to do, & ſtrength to ſuffer. Infinit is as much as God himſelf hath, & therefore God alone is infinite. So that neither hel fire is of infinite force to puniſh, nor men nor angels of infinite ſtrength to ſuffer, but the vengeance of ſinne continueth for euer; by reaſon no creature is able to beare an infinite waight of puniſhment. Since then the paines of hel haue neither worth nor waight ſufficient in themſelues to ſatiſfie the anger, & procure the fauor of God, we muſt ſeeke to heauen, euen to God himſelfe, for the true ranſome for our ſinnes, and redemption of our ſoules, which we no where find, but in the perſon of Chriſt Jeſus, who being true God tooke our nature vnto him, and by the infinite price of his bloud bought vs from ⸀ power of hel, & brought vs vnto God. For neither ⸀ vertues of Chriſts humane ſoule, though they were many; nor the ſufferings of his fleſh, though they were painful, are ſimply infinite, til we looke to his perſon, & then ſhall we find that ⁿGod vouchſafed with his own bloud to purchaſe his Church, & that ° we were reconciled to God by the death of his ſonne when we were his enemies. Bernarde expreſſing the

infinite

Margin notes:

Hell is not infinite, but onlie in time.

ˡHebre. 10.

ᵐMatth. 25.

Nothing infinite but only God.

The merite of Chriſt is infinite in reſpect of his perſon.

ⁿActs. 20
°Roman. 5.

infinite merite of Christes death and passion saith. p *Incomprehensibilis (deus voluit) comprehendi, summus humiliari, potentissimus despici, pulcherrimus deformari. sapientissimus vt iumentũ fieri, immortalis mori, vt compendio absoluam, deus fieri (voluit) vermiculus: quid excelsius deo? quid inferius vermiculo?* The incomprehensible (God woulde) be comprehended, the highest humbled, the most mighty despised, the most beautifull deformed, the most wise bee like a beast, the immortall (would) suffer death; to speake all in fewe wordes, God would become a Worme: what is higher then God? what is baser then a Worme? If betweene the Creator and the best of his creatures there be an infinite distance; what thinke yee then was there betwixt the throne of God in heauen, and the crosse of Christ on earth? not an infinite distance? and so infinite that neither men nor Angels can comprehend it? The ground of our saluation then is the obedience, humility and charitie of the sonne of God, yeelding himselfe not onelie to serue in our steed, but to die for our sinnes. For when he was equall with God in nature, power, and glory, hee refused not to take the shape of a seruant vpon him, and to humble himselfe to the death of the crosse, not onelie obeying his fathers will, which we had despised; but abiding his hand for the chastisement of our peace. The Apostle noteth these three vertues in the person of Christ; q Let the SAME AFFECTION (of loue) bee in you, which was in Christ Iesus, vvho being in the forme of God, emptied and humbled himselfe and became obedient to the death, euen to the death of the crosse. By his humilitie, obedience, and charity, hee purged the pride, rebellion, and selfe-loue, which our first father shewed when he fell, and we all expresse in our sinnes; and therefore as wee all died in Adams transgression, so we are all iustified, that is absolued from our sinnes, and receaued into fauour, by the obedience of Christ.

p Bernard de passione cap. 17

q Philip. 2

Yea the obedience of Christ did in farre higher degree please God the Father, then the rebellion of Adam did displease.

pleafe him. For there the vaffall rebelled, here the equall o-
beied: there earth pzefumed to be like vnto God, here God
vouchfafed to bee the loweft amongft men: there the crea-
ture neglected his maker; here the creatoz fo loued his ene-
mies,euen his perfecutozs,that hee tooke the burthen from
their fhoulders,and laid it on his owne,contentedly giuing
his life foz them,(who cruellie tooke his life from him: to con-
clude,thofe were the finnes of men; thefe are the vertues of
God,which doe infinitelie countervaile the other,and foz that
caufe the iuftice of God is farre better fatiffied with the obe-
dience of Chzift, then with the vengeance it might iuftlie
haue executed on the finnes of men. For God hath no [r] plea-
fure in the death of the wicked, neither doth hee delight in
mans deftruction; but with the obedience of his fonne he is
well pleafed,and therein euen his foule delighteth. [ſ] This is
my beloued fonne in whom I am well pleafed. [t] Loe my cho-
fen,my foule taketh pleafure in him. In which wozds God doth
not onlie note the naturall loue betwixt his fonne and him-
felfe;but he giueth full appzobation of his obedience, as be-
ing thereby thzoughlie fatiffied foz the finne of man. By
Chzifts obedience I doe not meane the holineffe of his life,
oz perfozmance of the lawe, but the obedience of the perfon
vnto death,euen the death of the Croffe; which was volun-
tarilie offered by him,not neceffarily impofed on him,aboue
and befides the lawe,and no way required in the lawe. Foz
it could be no dutie to God oz man, but onelie mercie and
pitie towardes vs, that caufed the fonne of God to take
our moztall and weake flefh vnto him; and therein,and ther-
by to pay the ranfome of our finnes, and to purchafe eter-
nall life foz vs. He muft be a Sauiour, no debter;a redeemer,
no pzifoner;Lozd of all,euen when hee humbled himfelfe to
be the feruant of all; his diuine glozie, power and maieftie
make his fufferings to be of infinite fozce and value. And
from this dignitie, and vnitie of his perfon, which is the
maine pillar of our redemption, if we caft our eies on any

Marginal notes:

Chrifts obedi-
ence doth
more then
countervaile
Adams difo-
bedience.

[r] Ezech.33.

[ſ] Matt 3.
[t] Efay.42.

C 5.

other.

other cause, oz deuise any new help to ſtrengthen the merits of Chziſt, wee diſhonour and diſable his diuinitie, as if the ſonne of God were not a full and ſufficient pzice, to ranſome the bodies and ſoules of all mankind.

On this foundation doe the ſcriptures build the whole frame of mans redemption. God purchaſed his church (ſaith Paule) WITH HIS OVVNE BLOVD; GOD, noting the dignitie; HIS OVVNE, the vnitie of his perſon, and both impozting a pzice far wozthier then the thing purchaſed. God ſpared not his owne ſonne, but gaue him for vs all. In that he was the ſonne of God, al nations are counted vnto him (oz in ballance with him) leſſe the nothing, and vanitie; in that he was giuen foz vs, the ranſome excelleth the pziſoner, as much as God doth man. We are reconciled to God by the death of his ſonne. Maruell we to ſee Chziſts death of that power & pzice with God, that it appeaſed his wzath, when he was angrie with vs, as with his enemies; when as his owne ſon being equall with him in the fozme of God, humbled himſelfe to the death of the croſſe foz our ſakes? Fairer oz fuller cauſes of our redemption we neede not aſke, the holie Ghoſt doth not expzeſſe, God cannot haue. If the ſon of God be not able with his bloud to redeeme vs, wee muſt giue ouer all hope; and deſpaire. Foz heauen cannot yeeld vs a greater value, and the earth hath none like. Wherfoze if any man be diſpoſed to ſeale his own condemnation, with his own heart, let him diſtruſt the merits of Chziſts death: but all that will be ſaued muſt acknowledge the infinite pzice of his death, and bloud aboue our wozth, and we muſt learne being ſinfull and wzetched creatures, not to amend the wozdes of God, in the myſterie of our redemption, but ſuffer him that is trueth to be the guider of our faith, and not by figures to fruſtrate all that is wzitten in the wozd of God touching our ſaluation, purchaſed by the death and bloud of Chziſt Ieſus.

I am not the firſt that obſerued oz vzged this doctrine, it is auncient and Catholike. ᵃ Cum ſuper omnes eſſet Dei
verbum

Margin notes:

u Acts. 20
The ſcriptures ground our ſaluation on the dignitie of Chriſts perſon
x Rom. 8.
y Eſay. 40.

z Rom. 5.

And ſo do the fathers.

verbum, merito ſuum ipſius templum & corporale inſtrumen- a *Athanaſus de*
tum pro omniũ animis pretium offerens, id quod morti debebatur *incarnatione ci-*
perſoluit. Whereas the word (or ſonne) of God, (ſaith Athana- *tatus a Theodo-*
ſius) was aboue al, worthily then by offering his owne temple & *reto dialogo.3.*
bodily inſtrument, as a price for the ſoules of all men, did he pay
that was due vnto death. *Cyril.* b *Si non eſſet deus quomodo ipſe* b *Cyril de recta*
& ſolus ſufficeret ad hoc, vt ſit pretiũ? Sed ſuffici ſolus pro omni- *fide ad reginas in*
bus mortuus, quia ſuper omnes eſt; deus igitur eſt, morte ſuã car- 1. *Timothei.2.*
nis à mundo mortē depellens. If Chriſt were not God, how could *dedit ſemetipſit*
he alone ſuffice to be the ranſome (for al?) but he alone dead ſuf- *pretium pro*
ficeth for all, becauſe he is aboue all; he is therefore God, by the *nobis.*
death of his fleſh, driuing away death from the worlde. And
againe; c *Redempti ſamus Chriſto proprium corpus dante pro no-* c *Cyril ibidem*
bis. Sed ſi vt communis homo intelligerétur Chriſtus, quomodo *in 1.Petri. 1.*
corpus eius ad rependéndam ómnium vitam ſufficéret? *At ſi deus* *pretioſo ſanguine*
fuit in carne, qui digniſſimus, ſufficiens ad redemptiónem totius *Chriſti reden.2.*
mundi per ſuum ſanguinẽ mérito fuit. We are redeemed, Chriſt *s. eſta.*
giuing his own body for vs. But if Chriſt be taken to be no more
then a man, how ſhould his body be ſufficient to reſtore life to al
men: but if he were God in our fleſh, worthily thẽ did he ſuffice
to redeem the whole world with his blond. Auſten. d *Si propter* d *Auguſt. in pſa.*
hominẽ mortuus eſt deui. nõ eſt victurus homo cum deo? quomodo 148.
mortuus eſt deus? accipit ex te vnde moreretur pro te; nõ poſſet
mori niſi caro nõ poſſet mori niſi mortale corpus. If god died for mã
ſhall not mã liue with god? but how died god? he took of thine
wherin to die for thee. There could nothing die but fleſh, there
could die nothing but a mortal body. And elſewhere an anciẽt
writer vnder his name, if not himſelfe. *Indubitanter creda-*
mus quod totum mundum redemit, qui plus dedit quã totius mun-
dus valeret: inter redimentẽ & redemptum diſpenſatio, non com- e *Auguſt. de*
penſatio. fuit. Let vs vndoubtedly beleeue that hee redeemed *tempore.114.*
the whole worlde, which gaue more then the whole world was
worth. Betweene the redeemer and the redeemed there was a
diſpenſation (of humilitie) no compenſation (of equality.) And
to ſhewe the truth of his ſpéech he addeth; f Innocency was f *Ibidem.*
arraigned for the guiltie, mercie was buffeted for the cruell; pietie
was

was whipped for the vngodlie, wisdom was mocked for the foolish, righteousnes was condened for the vnrighteous, truth was slaine for the liar, life died for him that was dead. And doe wee yet, remembring who he was, and what we were, stagger to confesse with these Christian and Catholike Fathers, that his bloud was a most sufficient price for all the world: or wonder we to see death ouerthrowne by his death, who was the fountaine of life, and could no more bee swallowed vp of death, then God himselfe could be conquered by the power of darkenesse.

The mightier Christs person the fitter to conquer, but not to suffer hel.

[The mightier Christs person, the more able he was (some will say) to suffer death & hell.] he would be partaker of our mortall infirmitie, that by suffering death for the time hee might conquer the force thereof for euer; but the gates of hel could not preuaile against him, because the Prince of this world had nothing in him. The inward man may be strongest when the outward man is weakest; and when the flesh is nearest vnto death, the spirit may cleaue fastest vnto God. Christ therefore in dying for our sakes shewed a most euident, and eminent example of his obedience, loue, and patience; but in suffering hel there is no signe of grace, nor shew of vertue. Voluntarilie to forsake God, or willinglie to be forsaken of God, is the greatest impietie that can bee committed. And against his will Christ neuer did, nor might suffer anie thing: for that had beene violence, not obedience; vengeance, not patience; force, not loue. But all constraint was farre from Christ, that his sufferings might be a voluntary sacrifice to witnesse his loue, and declare his merits, which in compulsion could be none. Since then the sonne of God neither willinglie would, nor forciblie could be forsaken of his Father; it is a dangerous deuise to subiect his soule to hell, which is the totall and finall separation of the wicked from God, and his kingdome.

Eight things in hel paines, which by no means Christs

And that wee may a little the better bethinke our selues, before we growe too resolute in this assertion, that Christs soule suffered the verie paines of hell; I will obserue some things,

things, which the ſcriptures affirme of hell; it may not be ap-
plied to Chriſt without apparãt iniurie. Firſt hel is outward
and inward darkeneſſe; nowe Chriſt was light, and in him
was no darkeneſſe of the ſoule. g As long as I am in the worlde
I am (ſayth hée) the light of the worlde. Then as the h light
hath no fellowſhippe with darkeneſſe, no moꝛe had Chriſt
with hell; which is the i power of darkeneſſe, from whence
hee hath deliuered vs. Seconðlie, hell is deſtruction both
of bodie and ſoule. kFeare not them (ſaith Chꝛiſt) which kill
the bodie, but cannot kill the ſoule; ſeare him rather which is
able to deſtroie both ſoule and bodie in hell. In the Saui-
our of both, wee maie not admitte the deſtruction of both:
howe ſhall he ſaue vs, that could harðlie, and as ſome wꝛite,
MAXIMA CVM DIFFICVLTATE, with much a do ſaue
himſelfe? But l God ſent his ſonne to bee the Sauiour of the
worlde. Wee muſt not therefoꝛe wꝛappe him withïn the de-
ſtruction of bodie and ſoule; no not foꝛ an howter, oꝛ an in-
ſtant. Thirðlie, hell is the ſecond death. The firſt is of the bo-
die foꝛ a time, the ſecond is of the ſoule foꝛ euer. m The lake
burning with fire and brimſtone, this is the ſecond death(ſaith
Saint Iohn.). Of this death Auſten ſaith, n De prima cor-
poris morte dici poteſt quòd bonis bona ſit & malis mala; ſecunda
vero ſine dubio ſicut nullorum eſt bonorum, ita nulli bona. Ideo
vero ſecunda, quia poſt illam primam eſt. The fiſt death of the
bodie is good to the good, and euill to the euill; but the
ſeconde death without doubt, as no good man ſuffereth it,
ſo is it good to none: and therefore it is called the ſeconde
death, becauſe it followeth after the firſt. Befoꝛe the firſt
death, no man ſuffereth hell, which is the ſeconde death,
and befoꝛe wee maie auouch it of Chꝛiſt, wee muſt take
all goodneſſe from him; foꝛ doubtleſſe (ſayeth Auſten) no
good man dooth ſuffer it. And inðéede howe pernicious it
is to make the ſoule of Chꝛiſt lyable to the death of the
ſoule; I ſhall afterwarðe haue occaſion to ſpeake. In
the meane time S. Iohn affirmeth, that hell goeth not befoꝛe
death,

H

1
g Iohn.9.
h 2.Cor.6.
i Coloſ.1.

2
k Mat.10.

l 1 Iohn.4.

3
m Apoc.20.

n Auguſt.de ciui. dei.lib. 13 cap.2

death, but followeth after death. [p] I looked (saith he) and beheld
[p] Apoc. 6. a pale horse, and his name that sate on him, was death, and HEL
FOLLOVVED AFTER HIM: and therefore it cannot stand
with truth to subiect the soule of Christ yet liuing on earth, to
4. the very paines of the damned. Fourthly, their [p] WORME in
[p] Mark 9. hell neuer dieth, for so much as the remembrance of their
sinnes committed against God euerlastinglie biteth and af-
flicteth the conscience. Now in Christ as there was no taint
of sinne, so could there bee no touch of conscience accusing,
nor remorse of any transgression agaynst God. With com-
passion of our sinnes he might be moued and troubled; but
worme of conscience hee could haue none, who was priuie to
his owne heart, that he was [q] holie, harmlesse, vndefiled, and
[q] Hebr. 7. separated from sinners, and therefore needed no sacrifice for
his owne sinnes; but as [r] a faythfull and mercifull high Priest
[r] Hebr. 2. by the offering of him selfe once, made an attonement for
the sinnes of the people.

But what the paines of the damned are, the sentence of the
Iudge will best declare. [s] *Discedite à me maledicti in ignem*
[s] Mat. 25. *aeternum*; Depart from mee ye cursed into euerlasting fire, pre-
pared for the diuell and his Angels. In which wordes there are
foure things, which by no meanes can agree vnto Christ; RE-
IECTION, MALEDICTION, VENGEANCE OF FIRE,
& CONTINVANCE THEREIN FOR EVER. As sinne is a
voluntary separation of man from god, so hell is a totall and
finall exclusion of the sinfull from enioying the presence or pati-
ence of God anie longer. The time of this life is the respite
of Gods patience towards all the wicked; with the ende
thereof, beginneth his eternall vengeaunce, which who-
lie and for euer debarreth the workers of wickednesse from
5 the kingdome of God. This reiection the soule of Christ
could not suffer, beeing inseparablie ioyned to the Godhead
of Christ. We must not in stead of a naturall and mutuall
coniunction, beleeue or teach a reall & effectuall separation
betwixt God and man, in the person of Christ, no not a

perſwaſion thereof in the ſoule of our Sauiour, which is all
one with Deſperation, and ſheweth the condition rather
of the Reprobate, then of the childzen of God, much
leſſe of him that was God and man. As the Sonne of
God coulde not bee REIECTED; no moze could hee bee
ACCVRSED. He that is ioyned with God, muſt nœdes
bee partaker of Gods goodneſſe. God is the fountaine
of all bliſſe; hee therefoze filleth with his bleſſing all that
are vnited vnto him. And if we, when we cleaue vnto him
by faith and loue, muſt nœds deriue from him ioy and bliſſe;
coulde the ſoule of Chziſt bee perſonallie ioyned with
him, and not be perpetuallie bleſſed by him? Though then it
pleaſed our Sauiour to ſuffer a curſed kinde of death fo?
our ſinnes, and by receyuing that curſe in his fleſh to
quench the ſpirituall and eternall curſe that hung ouer our
heades; yet his ſoule was neuer accurſed, ſince he was al-
waies beloued; and the curſe of God compziſeth not onelie
the anger and hatred, but the inſolerable and vnceaſeable
vengeance of God, which purſueth the ſouls and bodies of the
wicked with flaming fire fo? euer. Fo? how could al nations ⸀Gen.22.
of the earth be bleſſed in him; if he himſelfe were accurſed? ᵃActs 3.
but God ᵃ ſent him to bleſſe vs: hee muſt therefoze be ſtozed
with ſtoꝛies of bleſſing, firſt fo? himſelfe, then fo? vs all.

And could we frame our tongues, which I hope all Chzi-
ſtians with heart deteſt, ſo much to diſhonour the perſon
of Chziſt as to auouch him to be trulie reiected and accurſed
of his Father, fo? the time bee it neuer ſo ſhozt; yet we muſt
not ſhew our ſelues ſo void of al ſenſe, as to ſay that Chziſts
ſoule ſuffered HEL FIRE; which is the perpetuall and eſſen-
tiall puniſhment of all the damned. Let vs not come within
that danger of ſo deſperate follie; not to knowe, o? not to
care, what we defend o? affirme. It ſhould haue ſome pzoofe,
it ſhould haue ſome truth, whatſoeuer is held fo? matter
of faith. That Chziſtes ſoule was tozmented with hell fire
I aſke not what pzoofe, o? truth, but what ſhe we can bee

6.

7.

pretended : The fire of hell, they will say is metaphoricall; they that go thither shall find it no metaphore. It is no good dallying with Gods eternall, and terrible iudgements. The Scriptures are so plaine, and so full of the parts and effects of fire in hell, that I dare not allegorize them. Christ maketh the rich mans soule in hell to saie, [x] I am tormented in this flame. Saint Iohn saith it is a [y] lake burning with fire and brimstone . Daniel saith, [z] a firie streame issued from before Christ sitting in iudgement. Paul saith, it is [a] a violent fire which shall deuoure the aduersaries. God himselfe saith, a [b] fire is kindled in my wrath, and shall burne to the bottome of hell, and shall enflame the foundations of the hilles. If therefore the paines of the damned come in question, it is not safe to measure them by our imaginations, but to giue eare to the holie ghost, who can best expresse them; and by him wee learne, that if anie man worshippe the beast and his image, he shall [c] drinke of the wine of the wrath of God, and shall bee tormented in fire and Brimstone before the holie Angels, and before the lambe. And the smoke of their torment shall ascende euermore; and they shall haue no rest night nor daie. Into this fire if wee cast Christes soule, wee must take heede our proofes bee sound and sure; least our presumption exclude vs from the place where Christ is; and leaue vs in the lake where hee neuer was : there to learne what it is rashlie to conclude the thinges that are not confirmed by the word of God. But I perswade my self, few men of learning or religion, will venter on this desperate resolution, that Christs soule here on earth suffered hell fire, and therefore to propose it, is inough to confute it.

The last thing in hell fire, is that it is eternal. For as there is no remission of paine, so thence is no redemption; but once adiudged thither is euerlastinglie fastened to that place of torment . And this is cause inough to staie all men, that bee soberlie minded, from defending that Christs soule suffered the paines of hell, which the holie Ghost

saith

Luke 16.
Reuel. 21.
Dan. 7.

Heb. 10.
Deut. 32.

Reuel. 14.

faith are endles. d They which knowe not God, and obey not
the gofpell fhall fuffer paines, euen euerlafting perdition, from
the prefence of the Lord, faith the Apoftle to the Theffalonians.
And fo Peter, c to whom the myft. of darkeneffe is referued for
euer. And Iude, f Sodome and Gomorrhe are fet for an exam-
ple, which fuffer the punifhment of euerlafting fire, Yea Chrift
himfelfe pronounced that fire to be g. vnquenchable. Where-
fore vnleffe we can fhew a later and better warrant then I
yet fee, we fhall do well not to enterprize to quench hell fire;
but to let it burne eternallie, and to confeffe with Peter that
God raifed Chrift breaking the paines of death and hell, of
which it was h impoffible he fhould be held. For fince he was
and is the i Sauiour of his body, the paines of hell, which are
eternall, could not take hold on him. He was mightier then
hell, that faued vs from hell; bee could not free vs from the
chaines of darkeneffe, but he muft firft breake them in fun-
der. His deliuering vs from the power of Satan, proueth
him to be ftronger then Satan; and the ftronger could ne-
uer be bound by the weaker; but contrariwife he entred into
Satans k houfe, where his chiefe ftrength was, and bound him
and fo fpoiled him. This comparifon Chrift maketh betwixt
Satan & himfelfe; by which he concludeth that he was ftron-
ger then Satan; and confequentlie could not himfelfe bee
bound by death or hell, but l ouercame fatan, and tooke all his
armour from him wherein he trufted, and deuided the fpoiles.

  And where fome men begin to doubt, whether eternall con-
tinuance be of the nature & fubftance of hell or no, they fhall
doe well to leaue thefe dangerous and fruitleffe fpeculati-
ons: For whether they looke to the perfons for whom; or the
crimes for which, or the Iudge by whom it was prepared; they
fhall euerie waie find it muft be eternall. It was m prepared
for the diuell and his Angels, and to them could be no punifh-
ment be allotted but euerlafting, except we will giue poffi-
bilitie of grace, and hope of repentance vnto diuels. It is
the wages of finne, which being an infinite contempt of the

d 2.Thef 1.

c 2.Peter.2.
f Iud. epift.

g Mark.9.

h Acts.2.
i Ephef 5.

k Matth 12.

l Luke. 11

The paines of
hel are eternal

m Matth.2 5.

diuine

diuine maiestie, must by the balance of iustice haue infinite vengeance in waight, or in length. And since no creature is able to beare an infinite burden and sence of paine, of force all sinnefull creatures must bee contemned to an infinite length of punishment; which is hell fire. Lastlie, as God is eternall and cannot change; no more can his iustice, or iudgement alter with time; but as his truth abideth for euer, so his iudgment being iust and good is irreuocable; & consequently the vengeance of sinne can neuer cease, as proceeding from the righteous iudge of the world, in whom is ⁿ no shadowing, nor varying. And therefore Paul calleth the iudgement ° æternal, wherby God shall rewarde euerie man according to his workes; & our sauior forwarneth vs not in vaine, that hel fier is PVNQVENCHABLE, & EVERLASTING. Since then neither the remorse, reiection, malediction, nor desperation of the damned; nor the darkenes, destruction, death, & fire of hel can without euident impietie be attributed to the soule of Christ; I am farre from admitting into anie part of the Creed this ambiguous, if not dangerous assertion, that Christ in his soule on the crosse felt the verie paines, and torments of the damned: but I preferre the simple and plaine doctrine of the holie Ghost, which teacheth vs that Christ ᵖ died for our sinnes according to the scriptures, and that he was buried, and that hee rose againe the thirde daie according to the scriptures, and by Christs so doing, death was ᵠswallowed vp into victory, and we may ioyfully saie, ᵠ O death where is thy sting? O hell where is thy victory? thanking God which hath giuen this victorie through our Lorde Iesus Christ, as it was foretold by the prophet Esay, The Lorde will ʳ destroy death for euer; and by Osee, ˢO death I will bee thy death, O hell I will bee thy destruction.

The manner of Christes offering is the second effect of Christs crosse, which must be bloudie; before it can be propitiatorie. In this part I will deliuer you three thinges worthie to be obserued; with what Sacrifice God was pleased for our sinnes,

* Iames, I.
° Heb. 6.

ᵖ Mark. 9.

ᵠ 1. Corinth. 15

ᵠ Ibidem.

ʳ Esay. 25.
ˢ Ose. 13.

The sacrifice for sinne must be bloudy, before it could be propitiatorie.

ſinnes, with what price the Diuell was concluded for our ranſome, with what Seale the newe couenant of grace and mercie was confirmed vnto vs for our ſafetie. Theſe three depend eache on other. God, as the Iudge offended, was to haue a ſacrifice for our ſinne, that might content him; the Diuell as the Iailour, was to haue a ranſome for vs, that were by Gods Iuſtice deliuered into his handes; Our ſelues as priſoners were to bee reſtored by GOD S pardon, and to be aſſured of his protection, that the like miſerie might not the ſecond time preuaile againſt vs; which is performed by the newe Teſtament of mercie forgiuing, and grace repreſſing ſinne, that wee relapſe not into the pit of perdition whence wee were deliuered.

What was the true propitiatorie ſacrifice which God accepted for the ſinnes of the world, if the new teſtament did not plainelie declare, the olde teſtament would ſufficientlie witneſſe vnto vs. For as well Patriarks as Prophets, yea all the goodlie from Abel to Chriſt did by their ſacrifices and ſeruice of God profeſſe and confirme their faith to be this, that they looked for the Seede of the woman, who by his death and bloud ſhould purge their ſinnes, and make peace betweene God and them. This was the promiſe of grace which God made in Paradiſe to our firſt parents, threatning the ſerpent with the ſeede of the woman in theſe words, He ſhall cruſh thine heade, and thou ſhalt bruiſe his heele. As the heele of man is the baſeſt part of his bodie, and neareſt the earth; ſo the Serpent ſhoulde bruiſe the weakeſt and earthlieſt part of Chriſt; but euen that bruized heele ſhould be of force enough to cruſh the Serpentes head. For by the fleſh of Chriſt wounded, and bloud ſhed, the power & pride of ſatan ſhould be conquered and confounded: This ſence of Gods promiſe made to his parents, Abell the firſt martyr by faith accepted, by ſacrifice adored; and in that reſpect his bodilie and bloudie offering was preferred before his brothers.

The true ſacrifice for ſinne was ſhadowed in the figures and ſacrifices of the former teſtament.

Geneſ.3:

brothers. This faith did all the Patriarkes testifie by their bloudie sacrifices, that they expected the bodie of the Messias to be bruized, and his bloud to be shed for the remission of their sinnes. And as they received it from their fathers, so they delivered it to their children for the shot anchor of all their hope. This God did ratifie by his lawe written, suffering his people to haue no sacrifices for sinne, but such as represented the bloudie offering of Christ on the crosse. So that all the sacrifices and sacraments of Moses lawe were nothing else but figures and [u] examples of better thinges, as the Apostle calleth them, namelie of Christes bodie once to bee offered, and his bloud once to bee shed for the abolishing of sinne. The FIGVRES of Christ before and vnder the lawe, what else doe they point, but to the death, bloud, and crosse of Christ to be the redemption and saluation of all mankinde? Abrahams readinesse to offer vp Isaac, for which the blessing was annexed to him with an othe, what doth it import but the loue of God [x] Not sparing his owne sonne, but giuing him for vs all? The bloud of the passeouer sprinkled on the postes of the Israelites to auert the destroier, doth it not represent the blond of that immaculate lambe, which saueth vs from the fiercenesse of Gods wrath? The lifting vp the brasen serpent to cure the people that were stung with fierie Serpents, doth it not foreshewe Christ hanging on the crosse to cure our soules from the poison of sinne, which is the sting of that deadlie serpent? The strength of Sampson pulling the house on his owne and his enemies heades, doth it not declare the voluntarie death of Christ, to be the destruction of death and hell, which insulted at him on the crosse?

When the truth came expressed by all these sacrifices, and resembled in all these figures, what offering made he on the altar of the crosse? Did he yeelde his soule to the paines of hell, or his bodie to be crucified of the Iewes? both they will saie; for so they must saie, except they will haue their supposall of hellpaines cleane excluded from the sacrifice for sin.

But

[r] Rom. 8

The Patriarks
and prophets
did not mistake
the true sacrifice for sinne.

But which of theſe two was beleeued of the Patriarks, wit-
neſſed by the ſacrifices, ſhadowed in the figures of the law,
expected of the faithfull from the foundation of the worlde?
The bloudie ſacrifice of Chriſtes bodie is ſo plainelie pro-
claimed by them all, that there can bee no queſtion of their
faith and expectation. And were they deceiued in the obiect
of their faith, and hope? Did they all miſtake the true ſa-
crifice for their ſinnes? and did God by his lawe confirme
them in that errour? And doeth the Apoſtle falſelie con-
clude from the ſacrifices of the lawe, that Chriſtes offe-
ring before it coulde take awaie ſinne, muſt of force bee
bloudie? Theſe were verie ſtrange poſitions in Chriſtian
religion, and yet I ſee not howe wee ſhall auoide them, if
we ſtillie maintaine the ſuffering of hell paines to bee the
chiefer and principaller part of our redemption, without
which the reſt is nothing. If their faith faſtened on the
death and bloud of Chriſt for the remiſſion of their ſinnes
did ſaue them, then was the death of Chriſt of force e-
nough, without the paines of Hell to releaſe them from
their ſinnes; and bring them vnto God. And if it wrought
that effect in them, it is ſtill of the ſame power and ſtrength
to worke the like in vs. If it were inſufficient to re-
leaſe them from the rigour of GODS wrath, then are
the Patriarkes periſhed in their ſinnes, by miſta-
king the true price of their redemption. For that they
knewe anie thing of Chriſts ſuffering Hell paynes, I
thinke will hardlie bee prooued. But out of queſtion
their faith was right which was ſettled on the bloud of
Chriſt to bee ſhedde for the redeeming of their ſinnes;
and themſelues are Saintes in Gods kingdome: Wee
muſt therefore take heede that wee doe not raſhlie varie
from the foundation of their faith and hope; which muſt like-
wiſe be ours, with this onelie difference, that they beleued
in him, which ſhould take away the ſins of the worlde by his
death and croſſe, and we in him that hath taken them away.

J i.   The

The time doth differ; but the meanes are still the same. The

’Reuel. 13

ʼlamb was slaine from the beginning of the world; not actually, but in the counsaile of God, which did purpose it; and in the truth of God, which did promise it ; as likewise in the faith of al his saints, which did rest & reioice in it; frō whose steps if we swarue, we may not looke to be Abrahās childzen, ỹ refuse A-brahās faith as erroneous, & chalēge our father for misbeliefe.

Three proper-ties of the true sacrifice for sinne, vrged by the Apostle.

If the offerings and faith of the Patriarks were not preg-nant enough to lead vs to the true sacrifice for sinne ; the A-postle to the Hebrewes doth so purposelie and positiuely han-dle it, that I much muse how any man of iudgement or lear-ning can mistake it. For if we marke but thrée conclusions, which the Apostle maketh; we cannot erre from the truth in this behalfe. The true sacrifice for sinne must be but O N E,

1.

and O N C E O F F E R E D, not often, nor iterated, by reason it is perfect and able to clense vs from all sinne. It must bee

2.
ᵃHebre. 9.
3.

B L O V D Y, for so were all the offeringes of the lawe, and ᵗʸwithout shedding of bloud is no remission. It must bee C O N-FIRMED B Y D E A T H, that redemption purchased might neuer bee reuoked, nor altered. These thrée positions are mainelie and mightilie vrged by the holie ghost, the 9. and 10. to the Hebrues; and for this faith, are all the fathers of the old Testament from Abel to Samuel praised in the 11. chap-

ᵃHebre.10

ter of that Epistle. This ᵃ man (saith Paul meaning Christ) after he had offered O N E S A C R I F I C E F O R S I N N E, sit-teth for euer at the right hand of God. For with O N E O F F E-RING had he made perfit for euer those which are sanctified. Now where remission (of sinne) is, there is no more offering for sinne. Christ then making but one offering for sinne, we must not make two; but rather learne what that one was, which we may do without any difficultie, since the Apostle so plain-lie teacheth vs, that we are sanctified by T H E O F F E R I N G

ᵇHebre.9

O F T H E B O D Y O F I E S V S O N C E ; that ᵇ BY HIS OWNE BLOVD CHRIST ENTERED in Once into the holy place, and FOVND ETERNALL REDEMPTION. Almost all things are by

the

the law purged with bloud, and without ſhedding of bloud is
no remiſſion. It was then neceſſary that the ſimilitudes of hea-
uenlie thinges (in the law) ſhould be purified with ſuch thinges
(as the bloud of bulles and goates) but heauenly things them-
ſelues with better ſacrifices then theſe; euen with the bloud of
Chriſt. For ᶜ if the bloud of bulles and goates ſanctifieth as tou-
ching the purifying of the fleſh; howe much more ſhall THE
BLOVD OF CHRIST, who through the eternall ſpirit of-
fered himſelfe without ſpot to God, PVRGE YOVR CONSCI-
ENCES FROM DEAD WORKS to ſerue the liuing God? And
ᵈ for this cauſe is he the Mediator of the newe Teſtament, that
THROVGH DEATH which was for THE REDEMPTION OF
THE TRANSGRESSIONS IN THE FORMER TESTAMENT,
they which were called might receiue the promiſe of eternal in-
heritance. For where a teſtament is, there muſt be THE DEATH
OF HIM THAT MADE THE TESTAMENT. For it is of no
force, ſo long as he that made it, is aliue; wherefore neither was
the firſt teſtament ordained without bloud. ᵉ Ieſus then ſuffe-
red without the gate, that hee might SANCTIFIE the people
WITH HIS OWNE BLOVD; and this is the bloud of the euer-
laſting Teſtament, through which God brought againe from the
dead our Lorde Ieſus. Chriſt confirmeth the ſame when hee
ſaith. This is ᶠ MY BLOVD of the new teſtament WHICH IS
SHED for many for THE REMISSION OF SINNES.

The words be plainer then that they neede anie commen-
tarie. There was but ONE ſacrifice that could aboliſh
ſinne; euen THE OBLATION OF THE BODIE OF IESVS
ONCE, whoſe BLOVD purged our conſciences from deade
works, and purchaſed eternal inheritance, by the TESTATORS
DEATH, FOR THE REDEMPTION of thoſe ſinnes, which
we committed againſt the former Teſtament. What ſhift
haue we to ſhun the force of theſe words, or to bring in the
paines of hell in Chriſtes ſoule, as a part of the propitiatory
ſacrifice for ſinne? Chriſt made but one oblation of him-
ſelfe for ſinne, and that was the ſuffering of death in his body,

ᶜ Hebre.9

ᵈ Ibidem.

ᵉ Hebre.13

ᶠ Matth.26.

The ſacrifice
for ſinne was
bodily, blou-
dy, and deadly.

R 2.   for

for the redemption of our tranfgreffions, and fhedding of his bloud for the remiffion of our finnes. More then one, hee neeðeð not make; for that one obtained eternall redemption: and other then this, he ðið not make, for his offering was both BODILY and BLOVDIE. § This is my body, which is giuen, (and) h broken for you; this is i my bloud, which is fhed for manie. THE OBLATION OF THE BODY of Iefus once & THE SHEDDING OF HIS BLOVD are of ftrength ₹ force enough to clenfe vs from our fins, ₹ to procure vs the promife of euerlafting inheritance, which beeing confirmeð by the death of the teftator ftandeth irreuocable. How canne wee then bring in another facrifice of Chriftes foule fuffering the paines of hell, which coulð be neither bodily nor bloudy, but wee muft increafe the number, and confounde the differences of Chrifts offerings; and weaken the force of his externall ₹ corporal facrifice, which was the truth that anfwereð ₹ accomplifheð al the fignes of the law? For the inuifible paines of hel are no where prefigureð in the facrifices of the law, that I finð; nor fo much as once mentioneð in the Apoftles difcourfe, of Chrifts facrifice for finne, that I reaðe; ₹ therfore if we adde them as a neceffary part of our reðemption, we ðerogate from the bloud of Chrift, as infufficient without thofe torments to clenfe vs from our fins, ₹ pacifie the wrath of God, that was kinðleð againft vs.

The force of Chrifts bloud expreffed in the fcriptures.

What ðanger it is to ðepart from ȳ manifeft worðs of the holy ghoft in fo high a point of faith, ₹ by things vnwritten to ðifcreðit things written, I neeðe not aðmonifh fuch as be learneð, let the fimple take heeð, that they fuffer not reafon to ouerrule religion, ₹ obfcure and ðoubtful places in the fcriptures to wreft from them the perfpicuous and perpetuall ðoctrine of the holy ghoft. Howeful and perfect the reðemption is, which wee haue by the bloud of Chrift, if you fearch the Scriptures you fhall eaftlie fee; if you ðoe but hearken you fhall prefentlie learne. The bloud of Chrift ðoth REDEEME, CLENSE, WASH, IVSTIFIE, ₹ SANCTIFY the elect

elect; It doth PACIFIE and PROPITIATE the Iudge; It
doth SEALE THE COVENANT of mercie. grace & glorie, be-
twixt God & man; It doth CONCLVDE and bind the diuell;
what more can be required I verily cannot coniecture. If the
blood of Chriſt performe al theſe things for vs, & more we can-
not aſk; or expect; why ſhrinke we from it as vnable to ſaue
vs, except it be ſupplied with the paines of hell? Whether I
affirme any thing of mine owne, or deliuer you that which is
plainly taught in ſ ſcriptures, iudge you, k Ye were REDEE-
MED(ſaith Peter) by the pretious bloud of Chriſt as of a Lambe
vnſpotted; and vndefiled. l Chriſt by his own bloud(ſaith Paul)
entered once into the holy place OBTAINING eternall RE-
DEMPTION. m The bloud of Ieſus Chriſt CLENSETH vs fró
all our ſinnes. n He WASHED vs from our ſinnes in his bloud.
o Beeing now IVSTIFIED by his bloud, we ſhall bee ſaued
from wrath through him. p Ieſus ſuffered ⬤t hee might
ſanctifie the people with his bloud. By Chriſt then q wee
haue redemption through his bloud, euen the remiſſion of
ſinnes. and r nowe in Chriſt Ieſus yee which once were farre
off, are made neere by the bloud of Chriſt. ſ For it
hath pleaſed (the Father) by him to reconcile all thinges
vnto himſelfe. And to pacifie through the bloud of his Croſſe
both thinges in earth, and things in heauen: t Whome God
hath purpoſed to bee a . Reconciliation through ſayth in his
bloud.

And therefore the new teſtament is ſealed with Chriſtes
bloud. This is (ſaith hee) my bloud of the u new Teſtament,
which is ſhed for manie for the remiſſion of ſinnes. x Yee are
come to Ieſus the mediatour of the newe Teſtament (ſaith
Paul) & to the blood of ſprinkling which ſpeaketh better things
then that of Abell. For Abels bloud cried for vengeance: but
Chriſts bloud ſpeaketh for mercie and grace. And for that
cauſe Paul calleth it, y The bloud of the euerlaſting Te-
ſtament; For z this is the Teſtament, that I will make with the
houſe of Iſrael; after thoſe dayes ſayth the Lorde, I will

I 3   pus

Marginal notes:
k I Pet. 2.
l Hebr. 9.
m I Iohn I.
n Reuel I
o Rom. 5.
r Heb. 13.
q Epheſ. I.
r Epheſ. 2.
ſ Coloſ. I.
t Rom. 3.
u Mat. 26.
x Heb. 12.
y Heb. 13.

put my lawes in their minde, and in their heart I will write
them, and I will bee their God, and they shall bee my people;
I will be mercifull to their vnrighteousnesse, z and I will remem-
ber their sinnes and iniquities no more. This testament of
mercie, grace and glorie is confirmed by the death of Christ,
and sealed with his blood, which if we weaken or frustrate
with our inuentions, or additions, wee must looke for that
fearefull iudgement which the Apostle threatneth. a He that
despiseth *Moses* lawe dieth without mercie vnder two or
three witnesses: Of how much sorer punishment suppose ye shal
he be worthie, which treadeth vnder foote the sonne of God,
and counteth vnholie the bloud of the Testament, wherewith
he was sanctified, and reprocheth the spirite of grace? The
wrong that is offered to the bloud of the newe Testament,
treadeth vnder foote the sonne of God, and reprocheth the
spirit of grace. Now howe can we more vnsanctifie the
bloud of the Testament, then to make it so vnprecious, that
it cannot redeeme vs without the paines of hell, or to set vp
another price, for which we haue no expresse record, against,
or aboue the bloud of Christ, by which we are cleansed from
our sinnes, and reconciled to God?

I knowe they will and must answere, the paines of hell
are contained in the bloud of Christ; for so much as he suffe-
red the one in their imagination, when hee shed the other.
Could they proue by expresse and infallible testimonies
(which they cannot do) that Christ suffered in soul the paines
of the damned, they had some reason to comprise the one
within the other; but no such thing being warranted, or wit-
nessed in the scriptures, they must take heed, that they do not
elude, rather then expound the words of the holie ghost with
a perpetuall Synecdoche, which shall frustrate the very force
of all those euident and vehement speeches. For it is strange
to mee, first, that without iust proofe any such thing should be
ioined to the bloud of Christ, to helpe the price thereof.
Next that the holie ghost should alwayes vrge the one, and
                                                          as

:Heb.8.

:Heb.10.

Whether the
paines of hell
be comprised
in the bloud
of Christ.

as it were continuallie forget the other. Thirdlie, the things which are named in the Scriptures, as they were the laſt, ſo are they the chiefeſt parts of Chriſts ſufferings, the reſt being vnderſtood as antecedent to them, and not eminent aboue them. Nowe the CROSSE, BLOVD, and DEATH of Chriſt are euerie where mentioned in the ſcriptures, as the verie groundworke and pillars of our redemption. Laſtlie the bodie of Chriſt wounded, and his bleud ſhed for the remiſſion of ſinnes, are the ſeales that confirme and ratifie the new teſtament; and therefore they giue chiefeſt power and ſtrength to the whole couenant; as appeareth by the Sacraments: which import vnto vs not the paines of hell, but the death and bloud of Chriſt, as the right and true meanes of our redemption. [b] Know ye not (ſaith Paule) that all we which haue beene baptiſed into Ieſus Chriſt, haue beene baptiſed into his death? Wee are buried then with him by baptiſme into his death. And ſpeaking of the Lords Supper he ſaith: [c] As often as ye ſhall eate this bread, and drinke this cuppe, ye ſhewe the Lords death vntill he come. [d] The cuppe of bleſſing which wee bleſſe, is it not the communion of Chriſtes blood? The bread which we breake, is it not the communion of Chriſts bodie? By theſe we are grafted into Chriſt, by theſe wee are quickned, & nouriſhed into life euerlaſting: And theſe propoſe vnto vs no inuiſible paines of hell, but the bodie of Chriſt wounded, and his bloud ſhed for the remitting of our ſinnes, and vniting vs vnto Chriſt, that we may be [e] members of his bodie, of his fleſh, and of his bones.

Yea that an vnthankefull part were it for the captiues that are inlarged, to chalenge the ranſome, which was paide for their freedome, as defectiue; when the aduerſarie from whom we were bought, receyued it by the rule of Gods iuſtice, as a price moſt ſufficient for vs all that were deliuered? [f] I will redeeme them from the power of hell, I will ranſome them from death (ſaith God by his Prophet:) [g] you were bought with a PRICE (ſaith Paul,) The price then which Chriſt paide.

Marginal notes:
[b] Rom. 6.
[c] 1. Cor. 11.
[d] 1. Cor. 10.
[e] Epheſ. 5.
Chriſts bloud the verie price of our redemption.

paid muſt be fully worth the thing redeemed. For ſince it pleaſed God, not by force to take vs from Satan, but with a price to buie vs ont of his hands, it were diſhonour to God, and a kinde of reproch to giue leſſe for vs , then might counteruaile vs. And therefore let vs reſt aſſured that the price which Chriſt payed for vs , was of farre greater value then we were , not onelie in the vpright iudgement of God, but euen in the malicious and furious deſire of Satan, who thirſted after the bloud of the ſonne of God, with greedier iawes, then after all the worlde beſydes , and tryumphed more in bringing him to a ſhamefull death, then in the deſtruction of all the faythfull . Wherefore the wiſedome and iuſtice of God , ſuffered him to ſhewe his rage on the fleſh of Chriſt , and as it were to trample in his bloud , which hee ſpilt like water on the earth ; and left him that, which hee ſo eagerly purſued, and in his malice againſt Gods glorie preferred before all the worlde, as a full payment for all thoſe that ſhoulde be deliuered by the death of Chriſt. And for this cauſe the bloud of Chriſt is called by ý holie ghoſt the PRICE of our REDEMPTION. [h] Ye were REDEEMED (ſaith Peter) WITH THE PRECIOVS BLOVD of Chriſt as of a lambe vnſpotted and vndefiled. Yea the ſong which the Saints in heauen do ſing vnto the lambe is this, Thou waſt killed, and [i] HAST REDEEMED VS TO GOD BY THY BLOOD.

[h] 1 Pet. 1.

[i] Reuel. 5.

How the price of our redemption was paid.   When I ſay the bloud of Chriſt was the price, wherewith God redeemed vs out of Satans power, I doe not meane that God made anie contract with Satan, or tooke his conſent to exchange ; much leſſe, that Chriſt did profer his bloud to the diuell , to ſet vs free : it were an iniurie to Chriſt for vs to thinke his bloud was ſhed to [k] ſatisfie the diuell as Gregory Nazianzene wel obſerueth in his oration de Paſchate ; but Chriſt offered his bloud as a ſacrifice to god his father to verifie the iudgement pronounced againſt vs, [l] Thou ſhalt die the death, and to ſatisfie the iuſtice of God prouoked
with

[k] Nazianzen. orat. 42. in Paſchat. 2.
[l] Gene. 2.

with our finnes; yet in comming to his death, fince his life
might not be ended, neither with his owne hand, nor by the
hand of his Father, the wifedome of God ᵐ deliuered him
into the handes of finners, by whofe blinde zeale and bloudie
rage the diuell, that worketh in the children of difobedience,
confpired and compaffed his death, and with all maner of
contumelie and crueltie abufed his body, and fpilt his blood,
infulting at him by the mouthes of the wicked, and reioy-
cing in the conqueft he gate ouer Chrift in bringing him to
a reprochfull death. But this extreame rage of Satan a-
gainft the perfon of Chrift, turned to the bitter ruine of his
owne kingdome. For God did not onely raife againe the
Lord Iefus from death, as dying an innocent without all
defert, but in recompence of the wrong, which he receiued at
Satans hands, to the which he willingly fubmitted himfelfe,
God gaue him power to fpoyle the kingdome of the diuell,
and to deliuer all that euer did or fhould beleeue in his death
and paffion. And in this fort Chrift bought vs with his pre-
cious blood from the daunger of finne and hell; not of-
fering, but fuffering Satan by the hands of the Iewes to
take his life from him; neither compounding with his
aduerfarie, but repreffing him in the mideft of his ma-
lice, who affaulting Chrift Iefus our head, as he had done all
the members was ouerthrowne by him, and vanquifhed
with an euerlafting victorie.

ⁿ *Mortuus eft volens, vt inuoluntarie mortuos exufci-*
t.ret. Deuorauit ipfum mors ignorans, vbi deuoraffet, cognouit
quem non deuorauit. Deuorauit vnum cum omnibus; perdidit
omnes propter vnum. Rapuit vt leo; confracti funt dentes ipfius.
Chrift died willinglie (faith Bafill) that hee might raife thofe
which died againft their wils. Death ignorantly deuoured him,
which when hee had done, hee knewe whom he had not de-
uoured. Hee fwallowed vp one as he did all; and for that one,
hee loft all. Hee feafed on him as a Lion, but his teeth were
therwith broken. The creed extant vnder the name of Ruffinus;

ᵐ Mark. 14.

ⁿ Bafil. oration.
in fine epifto-
larum.

B   ᵒ *Sacra-*

• *Symbolum Ruffini tomo Hieronymi. 4.*

° *Sacramentum carnis suscepta hanc habet causam, vt diuina filij dei virtus velut hamus quidam, habitu humana carnis obtectus principem mundi inuitare posset ad Agonem, cui ipse carnem suam velut escam tradens, hamo eum diuinitatis intrinsecus teneret insertus ex profusione immaculati sanguinis.* The mysterie of Christes taking flesh was to this end, that the diuine power of the Sonne of GOD couered-as a hooke vnder the shewe of mans flesh, might prouoke the Prince of this worlde to assault him; to WHOM(CHRIST) DELIVERING HIS FLESH AS A BAITE helde fast (the diuell) with the hooke of his diuinitie sticking in him, through the shedding of his immaculate bloud.

P *Gregor. Moralium.lib.3,ca.11*

P *Conditorem omnium Satana manui traditum, quis vel desipiens credat? sed tamen edoctus veritate quis nesciat; —— cum se pro nostra redemptione Dominus membrorum Satana manibus tradidit, (quod) eiusdem Satana manum in se sauire permittit, vt vnde ipse exterius occumberet, inde nos exterius interiusque liberaret?* That the maker of all was deliuered into the hande of Satan, who is so foolish as to beleeue? And yet who taught by the trueth is ignorant, that when the Lorde for our redemption yeelded himselfe into their handes that were the members of Satan; hee suffered the hande of Satan to rage agaynst him, that whence he outwardlie dyed (in body) thence he might both outwardlie and inwardlie deliuer vs? And therefore hee concludeth, q *Cum corpus eius ad passionem accipit; electos eius à iure sua potestatis amittit.*

q *Ibidem.*

When(Satan) receyued the bodie(of Christ) to crucifie it; hee lost the elect of Christ from subiection to his power.

Saint Austen shewing howe Christ conquered the Diuell first by iustice, and then by power, sayeth; r *Placuit Deo vt propter eruendum hominem de Diaboli potestate, non potentia Diabolus sed iustitia vinceretur.* It pleased God for the deliuering of man out of the Diuels power, that the diuell should be conquered by iustice, and not by might

r *August. de trinitate li.13 cap.13.*

might. *Quæ eſt igitur iuſtitia, qua victus eſt Diabolus? Quæ*　ᶜ*Ibidem.*
niſi iuſtitia Ieſu Chriſti? Et quomodo victus eſt? Quia
cum in eo nihil morte dignum inuenit, occidit eum tamen : &
vtique iuſtum eſt, vt debitores quos tenebat, liberi dimit-
tantur, in eum credentes, quem ſine vllo debito occidit, Hoc
eſt quod iuſtificari dicimur in ſanguine Chriſti. What then
is the iuſtice whereby the Diuell was conquered ? What
but the iuſtice of Ieſu Chriſt ? And howe ? Becauſe that
when the Diuell founde in Chriſt nothing woorthie of death,
hee killed him notwithſtanding : and ſurelie iuſtice requi-
reth that the debtours, which Satan helde ſhoulde bee ſette
free, beleeuing in him whome Satan ſlue without any debt.
This is it that wee are ſayde to bee iuſtifyed in the bloud of
Chriſt . ᵗ*Sanguis enim ille quoniam eius erat qui nullum*　ᵗ*Ibidem.cap.13*
habuit: omnino peccatum, ad remiſſionem noſtrorum fuſus
eſt peccatorum; vt quia eos Diabolus merito tenebat, quos
peccati reos conditione mortis obſtrinxit, hos per eum meritò
dimitteret, quem nullius peccati reum immerito pœna mortis
affecit: hac iuſtitia victus, & hoc vinculo vinctus eſt for-
tis, vt vaſa eius eriperentur. For that bloud becauſe it
was his, who was vtterlie voyde of ſinne, was ſhedde for
the remiſſion of our ſinnes; that whom the Diuell iuſtlie held
as guiltie of ſinne, and obnoxious to death, thoſe hee might
woorthilie looſe through him, whome hee wrongfullie ſlue
beeing guiltie of no ſinne : with this iuſtice the Diuell was
conquered, and with this band was hee bound, that his goods
might bee ſpoyled. And ſo Saint Auſten concludeth in ex-
preſſe woordes, that THE BLOVD OF CHRIST, which
the Diuell was permitted to ſhedde by the handes of the
wicked, VVAS GIVEN AS A PRICE IN OVR
REDEMPTION, Which when the Diuell had ſpilt, it was
reckoned to him as a ranſom for vs ſince Chriſt owed none
for himſelf, & ſo were we diſmiſſed out of his power. ᵘ*In hac*　ᵘ*Ibidem.cap.13*
redemptione tanquam pretiũ pro nobis datus eſt Chriſti ſanguis, quo
　　　　　　　　　　　　accepto

accepto diabolus non ditatus, sed ligatus est, vt nos ab eius nexibus solueremur. In this redemption the bloud of Christ was giuen as a ransome for vs, which being receiued the diuell was not inriched, but concluded that wee might bee loosed from his snares.

° *Ambros̄ lib.* 9
Epist. 77.

°S. Ambrose affirmeth as much. *Si redempti sumus non corruptibilibus argento, & auro, sed pretioso sanguine domini nostri Iesu Christi(quo vtiq; vendente* NISI Eo *qui nostrū iam peccatricis successionis are quæsitum seruitium possidebat.) Sine dubio* IPSE *flagitabat pretium vt seruitio exueret quos tenebat obstrictos. Pretiū autem nostræ liberationis erat sanguis domini Iesu, quod necessaria soluendum erat* EI, CVI *peccatis nostris venditier umus.* If we bee redeemed not with corruptible things as siluer and golde, but with the precious bloud of our Lorde Iesus Christ(who selling vs, BVT HE that possessed vs as his seruants by reason of our sinfull succession)doubtlesse euen HE required a ransome to dismisse vs from the seruitude which he had ouer vs. Now the price of our deliuerance was the bloud of the Lord Iesus, which (price) was necessarilie to bee payde to HIM, TO WHOM we were sold through our sinnes: They which traduce this doctrine, as inclining to Manicheisme, had more neede of Elleborus to purge their braines, then of authorities to perswade their hearts, For since Christ paid no ransome for himselfe, but for vs, and his innocent bloud could not be shed but by the hands of the wicked; what tauch of vntruth can it haue, that God accounted the bloud of Christ to bee of more value then all the sonnes of men; and consequentlie, that, which the diuell eagerlie thirsted, and wrongfullie shed, to be reputed as mans ransome; and a price most sufficient for all the world? Yea the scripture, which is the word of truth, doth not onely teach vs, who redeemed vs, and with what price, as, ˣGod bought his Church with his owne bloud : but in manifest words from whom we were redeemed; euen from the power of ʸDARKNES, ᶻDEATH and HEL; that being ᵃdeliuered out of the hands of our enemies, wee should serue God without feare in holines and righteousnes all the daies of our life.

ˣ Acts. 20.
ʸ Colos̄. 1.

ᶻ Ofee. 13.
ᵃ Luke 1.

Whether

Whether therefore wee resemble the bodie and bloud of Christ to a PRAY that brake the teeth of the deuourer; to a BAITE that held fast the swallower; to a PRICE that concluded the challenger; to a RANSOME that freed the prisoner; or to a CONQVEST that ouerthrew the inspirer; in effect it is all one. Satan by killing him, that was the authour of life, lost both him and all his members; the Lorde rising againe by his owne power, and raising them all, that could not bee seuered from him; by the might and merite of his death and suffering. And so the godlie, which now liue on the earth, are not their [h] OWNE, but his that bought them with a price; being before [c] solde vnder sinne, whose [d] seruants they were till Christ with his bloud [e] redeemed them vnto GOD, and made them kinges and priestes to God his father. [f] *Venit redemptor & dedit pretium, fudit sanguinem suum, emit orbem terrarium, Videte quid dederit, & inuenite quid emerit. Sanguis Christi pretium est: tanti quid valet? quid nisi totus orbis? quid nisi omnes gentes?* The redeemer came (saith Austen) and paied the price? hee shed his bloud; and purchased the worlde. Consider what he gaue, and marke what he bought. The bloud of Christ was ye price: what was valued ac so great a price? What but the whole world? what but all the nations of the earth? [g] *Hic sanguis effusus totum terrarum orbem abluit, hic sanguis antea semper praefigurabatur in sacrificijs, iniustorum cædibus, Hic orbis terrarum est pretium. Hoc Christus emit ecclesiam. Hoc eam omnem adornauit.* This bloud (saith Chrysostom) being shed washed the whole world. This bloud was euer before figured in the sacrifices, and martyrdomes of the righteous. This bloud is the price of the world; with this Christ bought his Church; with this he wholy adorned it. [h] *Christus non esset condignam pretium totius creaturae redimendae, neque sufficeret ad bene redimendam mundi ruinam, etiamsi suam deponeret animam vt pretium pro nobis, nec illo pretiosum sanguinem, nisi vere esset filius, & tanquam ex deo deus.* Christ had not beene a iust price (saith Cyril) to redeeme all creatures, nor sufficient to purchase the life of the

Margin notes:
b 1.Corinth.6.
c Rom 7.
d Rom.6
e Reuelat.5.
f August.in Psal.95.
g Chrysost.ad popul.Antioch homil.61.
h Cyril. dialog. de trinitat.lib.4.

world, though he would haue laid down his life and his precious
bloud as a ranfome for vs , if he had not beene the true fonne of
God, & as it were, God of God . Where as now [i] *Vnus digni-
tate vniuerfos fuperans, pro omnibus mortuus eft, & quacunq̃ fub
cœlo funt fanguine fuo redemit, deoq̃, & patri vniuerfe terr.e habi-
tatores acquifiuit.* He alone exceeding al other in worth & valew
died for al, & by his bloud redeemed all things vnder heauen, &
purchafed to God his father the inhabitants of the whole earth.

[But our fauioʒ faith the fon of man came [k] *dare animã fuã
redemptionem pro multis,* to giue his foule a ranfome for many.
And Efay foʒetold as much, that he fhould [l] make his foule an
offering for fin] It is no great mafterie to cite places of fcrip-
ture in fhew repugnant one to the other ; howbeit in trueth
thefe are not contrarieties, but cõfequents to the foʒmer au-
thoʒities ; Foʒ where the foule of man is the life of his bodie;
Chʒift could not die foʒ our finnes, but he muſt laie down his
foule to death, that it might be feperated from his bodie & fo
giue His sovle, that is, his life & a ranfome foʒ many, & an
offering foʒ fin. And fo the very trãflatoʒs, ỹ otherwife fanoʒ
this opinion of hel-paines, do interpʒete thofe woʒds: [m] The
fon of man came not to be ferued but to ferue, & to giue His life
a ranfome for many. And the like elfewhere : [n] *Bonus paftor dat
animã pro ouibus,* The good fhepheard giueth His life for his
fheep [n] *Animã meã pono pro ouibus meis;* I lay down my life foʒ
my fheep. [n] *Diligit me pater quia pono animã meã, vt iterũ fumã
eam.* My father loueth me becaufe I lay downe my life to take it
againe. And indeed that phʒafe ponere animam in the Scrip-
tures doth alwaies note a voluntary yeelding of the life, which
is a laying aside of the sovle, foʒ ỹ loue of otherʒ; as where
Peter faith, [o] *Ponam animam meã pro te;* he did not meane he
would go to hel foʒ his maſter, there was no-caufe noʒ neede
thereof; but I will lay down my life for thee. And when S. Iohn
telleth vs, [p] *Quoniam ille animã fuã pofuit pro nobis, & nos debe-
mus animas ponere pro fratribus;* hee doth not charge vs to ha-
zard our foules by fin oʒ hel foʒ otherʒ; but infomuch as Chʒift
gaue

gaue His life for vs; wee ought to give ovr lives. for our bre-
thren. So that for Chriſt to lay aside his sovle, or to po vre
it ovt vnto death; was not to ſuffer hell paines for our
ſakes, but to die for our ſins; al thoſe places are rather cohe-
rent, the diſſident to the reſt of ſcriptures, which I alleaged.

And yet becauſe the ancient fathers ſome times ſaie that
Chriſt gaue his ſoule for our ſoules, as hee did his fleſh for our
fleſh, & the ſcriptures often affirme hee gaue himſelfe; I will
come to the third effect of Chriſts croſſe, which is the MIGHTY
POVVER OF. HIS DEATH; and there examine what part of
Chriſt died for our ſinnes, and howe by his death the guilt of
ſinne, the curſe of the lawe, the ſting of death, and the ſtrength
of Satan are not onelie weakened, and waſted, but extingui-
ſhed and abolished, that they ſhal neuer preuaile againſt him
or his elect.

That the Sonne of God loued vs & gaue ⁹ himſelfe for vs, ma-
king the purgatió of our ſinnes in his ʳ own perſon, by the ſ ſacri-
fice of himſelf to put away ſinne; is a caſe ſo cleere, that it néed
not to be prooued, much leſſe may be doubted without appa-
rant ſubuerſion of the Chriſtian faith: but whether Chriſt ſuf-
fered the death of the whole man, his ſoule faſting for the
time an inwarde and ſpirituall death in ſatiſfaction of our
ſinnes; as his fleſh did an externall & corporall diſſolution of
nature, this by ſome men is queſtioned in our daies. That
for our ſakes he humbled himſelf, & was obedient vnto death
euen the death of ſ croſſe, is out of al donbt; the Euangeliſts
deſcribe the maner of his death, the apoſtles the cauſe; to wit
the REDEMPTION of our ſins, the CONFIRMATION of the new te-
ſtament, the RECONCILIATION of man to God, the DESTRVCTI-
ON of him that was ruler of death, & the IMITATION of his
obedience; who ſuffered for vs leauing an exáple ᵗ y we ſhould
follow his ſteps. Al this he performed with ſ death of his fleſh,
the Scriptures no where mentioning anie other kinde of
death, that I can read. Where a teſtament is, there muſt be
the death of him that made the teſtament. For the teſtamēt is

The power of
Chriſts death.

⁹ Galat. 2
ʳ Hebre. 1
ᵗ Hebre. 9
By Chriſtes
death the ſcrip
tures meane
the death of
his body.

ᵗ 1. Peter. 2.

confirmed

confirmed when men are dead. Christ is the mediator of the new
Testament; that through death which was for the redemption
of the trespasses in the former Testament; they which are
called might receiue the promise of eternall inheritance . This
plainelie expresseth the death of the bodie. For God forbid
their Testaments should be frustrate, till their soules haue
tasted the second death: but from the death of the bodie all te-
staments take their force. Wherefore the new testament is
confirmed by the bodilie death of Christ, and there neede no
paines of hell before it can be good. You ý in times past were
strangers and enemies in mind by euill works, hath he nowe re-
conciled in the body of his flesh through death to make you ho-
lie, vndefiled, and faultlesse before him. Paul thought it not e-
nough to saie, Wee were reconciled vnto God by the death of
his sonne; but that death, he addeth, was IN THE BODY OF
HIS FLESH, to exclude all supposals of the death of the soule;
since THE BLOVD OF CHRISTS CROSSE did PACIFY
thinges in earth and in heauen. For so much as the children
were partakers of flesh and bloud, hee also did therein partake
with them, that through death hee might destroy him that had
power of death euen the deuill. The death of the spirit maie
bee without flesh and bloud; as we see in the Deuils who are
dead in spirite. But Christ tooke flesh and bloud, that by the
death of his flesh hee might destroie the deuill, that insulted
and raigned ouer the weakenesse of mans flesh. Wee are
buried (with Christ) by baptisme into his death, and if we bee
grafted with him into the similitude of his death, we shalbe like-
wise into his resurrection: knowing this that our old man is cru-
cified with him that the body of sinne might bee destroied, that
henceforth wee should not serue sinne, for hee that is dead is
freed from sinne. So manie wordes, so manie reasons to
proove that Christ died not for vs the death of the soule, but
onelie of the bodie. Wee are buried with him by Baptisme;
his bodie not his soule was buried. Wee are grafted into
the similitude of his death; not the soule but sinne dieth in

vs

* Colos. 1

ʸ Hebre. 2

ᶻ Rom. 6

bs, when we are grafted into Chriſt, for hee quickneth our
ſpirits. Our olde man was crucified with him; his ſoule was
not crucified but his fleſh : that the body of ſinne might be de-
ſtroied, by the death of the ſoule the body of ſinne is ſtrength-
ned and encreaſed. That henceforth we ſhould not ſerue ſinne;
they muſt needes ſerue ſinne, whoſe ſoules are deade with
ſinne. He that is dead is freed from ſinne, but he that is deade
in ſpirit, is ſubiected to the force & furie of ſinne. The death
of Chriſt then is mentioned no where in the Scriptures, but
the verie words or circumſtances, doe cleerely confirme that
they ſpeake of the death which he ſuffered for vs on the croſſe,
IN THE BODY OF HIS FLESH.

　That Chriſt did or could ſuffer the death of the ſoule, is a
poſition far from the words, but farther from the groundes
of the ſacred ſcriptures. For in God there is no death, and
without God there is no life of the ſoule. So that it is nei-
ther poſſible for the ſoule ioyned with God to die, nor for the
ſoule ſeparated from God to liue. Then if Chriſts ſoule were
at anie time deade, it loſt all coniunction and communion
with God; and conſequentlie the perſonall vnion of God and
man in Chriſt was for that time diſſolued; and the grace and
preſence of Gods ſpirit were vtterlie taken from him; and ſo
during that ſpace, there coulde bee in Chriſt neither obedi-
ence, humility, patience, holines nor loue; which are the fruits of
Gods ſpirit; yea the ſoule of Chriſt, if it were but for an houre
depriued of Gods grace and ſpirit, muſt needes for that time
be ſubiected to all ſinne and wickedneſſe; which the diuel him-
ſelfe dare not auouch of the ſoule of Chriſt. Men maie doe
well therefore to beware how they venture vnaduiſedlie to
ſaie, that Chriſt ſuffered the death of the ſoule; for howſoeuer
they may frame vnto themſelues a new kind of death in the
ſoule of Chriſt, as they thinke far from theſe abſurdities and
blaſphemies; yet both ſcriptures & fathers mightillie contra-
dict that loſe, if not lewde aſſertion. With thee is the foun-
taine of life, ſaith Dauid to God. Then if the ſoule of Chriſt

Chriſt could
not die the
death of the
ſoule.

* Pſal. 36.

L i.　　　were.

were alwaies ioined with God, or so much as in Gods fauor,
it must needs haue life; for [b] in (Gods) fauour there is life. Yea
the presence of Gods spirit giueth life. [c] *Spiritus est qui viui-*
ficat; it is the spirit y̌ quickneth, saith our Sauiour; and Paul ci-
teth the same words. Where then THE SPIRIT OF GOD
is, there is LIFE, and consequently the soule y̌ is dead is depri-
ued of Gods spirit. Now from whom the spirit of God is de-
parted; in him must needs want al the fruits of Gods spirit;
and so the soule, that is dead, is excluded from all godlinesse
and vertue. For these are not onelie signes, but effectes of
Gods spirit working in the soule of man. And since be-
twœn righteousnes and vnrighteousnes there is no middle,
the soule of man wanting light, truth, and sanctitie, of force
must be filled with darkenes, error, & iniquity; which to surmise
in the soule of Christ, is the hight of all impietie. [d] As manie
as are led by the spirit of God, they are the sonnes of God. If
Christes soule wanted at anie time the spirit of God, he was
not the sonne of God. If he euer and alwaies had the spirit
of life dwelling in him, his soule coulde at no time be dead.
For the [e] spirite is life through righteousnesse. But whie
seeke we proofes that Christes soule could not die, since he
himselfe is the AVTHOR and GIVER OF LIFE? [f] I am
the waie, the truth, and THE LIFE saith our Sauiour, & He
that beleeueth in me hath euerlasting life. [h] I am the resurrec-
tion and the life: hee that beleeueth in mee, though bee were
dead, he shall liue: And hee that liueth, and beleeueth in me,
shal neuer die. If the soule of him that beleeueth in Christ shal
neuer die, how could Christ himself at anie time die in soule?
[i] Christ is our life; howe then shall we be sure neuer to die, if
the fountaine of our life in Christes person might for the
time bee dried vp with death? shall we haue fuller or perfi-
ter fruition of life then Christ Iesus our heade, who [k] giueth
life to all his sheepe? but he had so plentifull, perpetuall, and
personall possession of life, not onelie for himselfe, but for vs
all, that the Apostle saith, the first *Adam* was made a liuing
soule,

[a] Psal.30.
[a] Iohn.6
[a] 2.Corinth.3.

[d] Rom.8

[e] Rom.8.

[f] Iohn.14
[g] Iohn.6.
[h] Iohn.11

[i] Colos.3.

[k] Iohn.10

foule, the laſt *Adam* was made a quickening ſpirit; that is not
only to haue life in himſelf, but to giue life to others. Could
hee then at anie time be a deade ſoule, whome the holy ghoſt
affirmeth to be made a QVICKENING SPIRIT? could he
giue that to others, which himſelfe did lacke? or looſe that
which he once had? I know to giue life is proper to God, and
for that cauſe the ſoule of Chriſt could not haue that power
by creation, but by coniunction with his godhead; and in that
reſpect was the receptacle whereby the life and grace of his di‐
uine nature was deriued into his humane, with ſuch abun‐
dance, and aſſurance, that of his [m]fulnes we al haue receaued;
inſomuch that the [n]words which he ſpake, were ſpirit and life;
and the [n]fleſh which he tooke, was the bread of life; yea the bo‐
dy of Chriſt dying did not only reſiſt and repreſſe the force of
death; but riſing againe deſtroied death, & reſtored life to the
world. If the temple of his bodie were ſtronger then death,
that was the ſanctuarie of his ſoule?

I.Corinth.15

[m]Iohn.1
[n]Iohn.6

I wiſh therfore all men, that profeſſe themſelues chriſtiās,
to be ſoberlie minded; and with the learned and aunctient fa‐
thers to acknowledge, that there is not mentioned in the
ſcriptures anie death of the ſoule, beſides SINNE, & eternall
DAMN̄ATION̄, or of the which with anie moderation
or mitigation attributed to Chriſt without ſhamefull
blaſphemie, *peccans ipſa morietur*. The ſoule
that . . . . die. In theſe wordes are both
dea. . . . . ; the firſt voluntarie when for
the . . . . uſe the preceptes of God: the o‐
ther . . . . God by his iuſtice withdraweth his
preſence . . . . executeth his VENGEANCE on vs,
that neuer ſhall haue end. That ſinne is a death of the ſoule,
cannot be denied. Let the dead bury their dead, ſaith Chriſt
to one of his diſciples; follow thou me: which muſt needes be
meant of ſuch as are liuing in body, & dead in ſoule, as Paule
ſpeaketh of wanton widowes, ſhe which liueth in pleaſure, is
dead whiles ſhee liueth. Theſe the ſcripture calleth DEAD

The death of
the ſoule is ei‐
ther ſinne, or
damnation.

[o]Ezech.18

[p]Matth.8

II.Timoth.5

† Ephes.2
‡ Colos.2

IN SINNE. When we were ‖ dead by sinnes, God quickened vs together with Christ. And again, You, which ‖ were dead in sinnes, hath he quickened together with Christ, forgiuing you all your trespasses. From this death I make no doubt but all christian men with heart and voice will cheerelie discharge the ‖ VNSPOTTED and VNDEFILED Lambe of God, who did ᵘ no sinne, neither was there any guile found in his mouth.

? 1.Pet.1
a 1.Peter.2

The other kinde of the death of the soule, which is damnation, must be farther from Christ then euer was sinne. For not onelie Christes innocency should bee vniustlie condemned, which were altogether repugnant to Gods righteousnesse; but the sonne of God wronged, and mans saluation wholy subuerted. Nothing might befall the humane nature of Christ, which was vnfitting for his diuine, both being ioyned in one person. And if our Sauiour were condemned to hell; which way shall we thinke to scape the iust and fearefull iudgement of God for our manifold and grieuous sinnes? he was indeed condemned by man, that gaue wrongfull sentence of death against him; but hee was acquitted of God. And because hee humbled himselfe to the death of the crosse, God highly ˣ exalted him, and gaue ▓▓▓▓▓▓▓▓ aboue all names, as well in witnesse of his ▓▓▓▓▓▓▓▓ward of his humility. Yea the holie ghost ▓▓▓▓▓▓▓▓eth Christes assurance, confidenc ▓▓▓▓▓▓▓▓ hee hung on the crosse, cleane exclu▓▓▓▓▓▓on th▓▓ he suffered the death of the soule. For ▓▓▓▓▓▓▓▓aue no fuller, nor faster coherence ▓▓▓▓▓▓▓▓ill had. And since God is the true life of the ▓▓▓▓▓▓▓▓rable coniunction of Christes soule with God ▓▓▓▓▓▓ continuall perswasion, and fruition of eternal life; which by no meanes admitteth anie danger or doubt, much lesse anie sence or sufferance of the second death being the iust wages of sinne, whereby the wicked are euerlastinglie punished. ᶻ Certe a-nima Christi non solum immortalis secundum cæterarū naturam,

a Philip.2

y Psal.16.

a August.epi. 64.

sed

fed etiam nullo mortificata peccato, vel damnatione punita eft:
quibus duabus caufis mors animæ intelligi poteft. Surely the foule
of Chrift (faith Auften) was not only irmortall in nature as the
reft ; but was NEITHER DEAD WITH ANY
SIN, nor PVNISHED WITH DAMNATION:
which two wayes the death of the foule may be vnderftood. If
then neither tranfgreffion, nor damnation may be afcribed
to the foal of Chrift, it is euident he fuffered not the death of
the foule ; yea to fubiect the foule of Chrift to either of thefe
two deaths, which onelie are the deaths of the foule, were
more horrible blafphemie, then I hope anie Chriftian man
meaneth to incurre.

[But I miftake the death of the foule.] I muft con-
feffe I therein followe the facred Scriptures, and ancient
fathers; other kinde of death of the foule I know none, be-
caufe I reade none iuftlie proued. Thefe two are manifeft
in the fcriptures. That finne killeth the foule, befides ma-
nie other places before cited, Saint Paule fhortly fheweth
in thefe words. [a] SIN REVIVED, BVT I DIED: for finne
deceiued me, and flaue me. And likewife our Sauiour, except
you beleeue, you fhall [b] die in your finnes. That euerlafting
death is ▓▓▓▓▓ finne, I take it to be as cleare a cafe,
as the f▓▓▓▓▓▓▓ go into [c] euerlafting punifhmét, faith
Ch▓▓▓▓▓▓▓▓ they fhall be [d] punifhed with euerla-
fting▓▓▓▓▓▓▓ the ignorant and difobedient.
The ▓▓▓▓▓▓▓ al afcend euermore, faith Iohn
in h▓▓▓▓▓▓▓ burning with fire and brimftone,
this is ▓▓▓▓▓▓▓ the ancient fathers define the
death of ▓▓▓▓▓▓ feene by their writings. *Dicam au-*
dacter fra▓▓▓▓▓▓em verum. Duæ vitæ funt, vna corporis, al-
tera animæ, ficut vita corporis anima, fic vita animæ deus. Quo-
modo fi animæ deferat, moritur corpus; fic moritur anima fi deferat
Deus. [e] I wil fpeake boldlie (faith Auften) but trulie. There are
two fortes of life, one of the bodie, another of the foule. As the
foule is the life of the body, fo God is the life of the foule; & as if
L.3 the

The death of
the foule is a
feparation frô
God.

[a] Rom 7.
[b] Iohn.8.

[c] Mat 25.
[d] 2 Thef.1.

[e] Reuel.14.
[f] Reuel.20.

[g] Auguft. in
Pfal.70.

the soule depart, the body dieth; so dieth the soule, if God forsake it. [h] *Mors propriè non est ea, quæ animam à corpore, sed quæ animam à Deo separat. Deus vita est, quia Deo separatur, mortuus est.* That is not properly death (saith Cyrill) which seuereth the soule from the bodie, but that which seuereth the soule from God. God is life; and therefore hee that is separated from God, is dead. [i] *Anima quæ peccat moritur, non vtique aliqua sui dissolutione, sed merito moritur Deo, quia viuit peccato. Ergo quæ non peccat, non moritur.* The soule which sinneth dieth, (sayeth Ambrose) not by anie dissolution of her substaunce, but worthilie dieth shee vnto God, because shee liueth vnto sinne. The soule then which sinneth not, dieth not. [k] *Anima in corpore vita est carnis; Deus vero qui viuificat omnia, vita est animarum.* [l] *Sicut mors exterior ab anima diuidit carnem, ita mors interior à Deo separat animam.* The soule in the bodie (saith Gregorie) is the life of the flesh, but God that quickeneth all things is the life of the soule; as the outwarde death diuideth the bodye from the soule, so the inward death diuideth the soule from God. [m] *Sicut anima vita est corporis, ita Deus vita est animæ.* [n] *Mors animæ separatio à Deo; mors corporis separatio animæ à corpore.* As the soule is the life of the bodie, so God is the life of the soule, saith Bernard. The death of the soule is to be separated from God; the death of the bodie is the departure of the soule from the bodie. Neither doe I see howe this . . . . the soule can be suopped or amended . . . . . . from any other, but onelie from God . . . . . must come from the fountaine of all good . . . . is good but onelie God. Then the soule which is . . . . of God, is partaker of life; and to be seuered from God, is to be seuered from life which is the true description of death.

Rightly therefore do the auncient Fathers teach, that Christ dying for our sinnes, suffered ONLY THE DEATH OF THE BODIE, but not of the soule: and the scriptures wheresoeuer they mention the death of Christ, must haue the

Marginal notes

[h] *Cyril. homil. 10. de exitu animæ.*

[i] *Ambros. de bono mortis ca 9*

[k] *Gregor. in Ezech. homil. 17*

[l] *Idem moralis lib. 9. Cap. 38.*

[m] *Bernard. serm. part. 3. & alii ser. part. num. 7*

[a] *Luc. 18.*

The fathers mainely teach that christ died the death of ye flesh ONELY.

the like conſtruction. For the ſoule of Chriſt could not die, ſo
long as it had the preſence and aſſiſtance of Gods ſpirit; yea
we leaue him neither faith nor hope, loue nor ioy, obedience
nor patience, nor any other merites or vertues, if wee ſub-
iect him to the death of the ſoule; for theſe are the buds and
fruits of life. From which if we cannot excluse the ſoule
of Chriſt, no not for a moment, without ſacrilegious impie-
tie, it remaineth that Chriſt neither ſuffered nor taſted the
death of the ſoule, but onelie the death of the bodie. ° In his
bodie he bare our ſinnes on the tree; and ᴾ reconciled vs vnto
God, in the BODY OF HIS FLESH THROVGH DEATH,
when we were ſtraungers and enemyes in heart; by reaſon
of our euill workes. �q *Quid eſt enim quod viuificatus eſt
ſpiritu, niſi quod eadem caro* QVA SOLA FVERAT MOR-
TIFICATVS *viuificante ſpiritu reſurrexit? Nam* QVOD
ANIMA FVERAT MORTIFICATVS IESVS, *hoc eſt eo
ſpiritu qui hominis eſt,* QVIS AVDEAT DICERE, *cum
mors anima non ſit niſi peccatum, à quo ille omnino immu-
nis fuit? Mortificatus ergo carne dictus eſt, quia ſecun-
dum* SOLAM CARNEM *mortuus eſt.* What is meant by
this, that Chriſt was quickened in ſpirite, but that the ſame
fleſh, IN WHICH ONELIE HE DIED, roſe againe
quickened by the ſpirite? For that Ieſus was DEAD IN
SPIRIT, WHO DARE AVOVCH, I meane in his
humane ſpirit, ſince as the death of the ſoule is no-
thing but ſinne, from which hee was altogither free? And
leaſt wee ſhoulde thinke this ſlipte his penne, elſe-
where hee largelie and learnedlie handleth the ſame
matter. (*Diabolus*) ʳ *per impietatem* MORTVVS EST IN
SPIRITV, *carne vtique mortuus non eſt: nobis autem
& impietatem perſuaſit, & per hanc vt in mortem car-
nis venire mereremur effecit. Quò ergo nos Mediator mortis
tranſmiſit, & ipſe* NON VENIT, *hoc eſt ad* MORTEM CAR-
NIS: *ibi nobis Dominus Deus noſter medicinam emendatio-
nis inſeruit quam ille non meruit.* By ſinne the Diuell

DIED

Marginal notes:
- ° 1 Pet. 2.
- ᴾ Coloſ. 1.
- q *Auguſt. epiſt.* 99.
- ʳ *Idem de trini-
tate lib. 4 ca. 13*

Dïed In Spïrït; in flesh he died not : but to vs hee perswaded sinne, and thereby brought vs to deserue the death of the flesh. Whither then the mediator of death cast vs, and came not himselfe, that is to the death of the bodie ; euen there the Lord our God appointed a medicine to cure vs, which the Diuell neuer obtained. And noffing the remedie prouided for vs in the bodilie death of Chrift, he faith, ʿ Vitâ mediator oſtendens, quam non ſit mors timenda, qua per humanam conditionem iam euadi non poteſt, ſed potius impietas qua per fidem caueri poteſt occurrit nobis Ad Finem Qvo venimus, ſed Non Qva Venimvs. Nos enim ad mortem per peccatum venimus, ille per iuſtitiam ; & ideo cum ſit mors noſtra pœna peccati, mors illius facta eſt hoſtia pro peccato : The Mediatour of life (Chrift Jesus) to shewe vs that death is not to bee feared, which by humane condition can nowe not bee escaped, but rather impietie, which by fayth may be auoyded ; mette vs in the ende whither wee were come, but not in the way by which we came . For we came by sinne to death ; but hee by righteousnesse : and so where our death is the punishment of sinne ; his death is the sacrifice for sinne . And therefore the death which Chrift suffered in his bodie on the Croffe, did purge, abolish, and extinguish all our sinnes ; whereby the power of satan iuffly detained vs to abide the punishment of our transgreffions. Quia viuum ſpiritu mortuus ſpiritu non inuaſit, quoquo modo auidus mortis humanæ conuertit ſe ad faciendam mortem quam potuit ; & Permissvs Est In Illvd Qvod Ex Nobis Mortale vinus mediator acceperat ; Et vbi potuit aliquid facere, ibi omni ex parte deuictus eſt, & vnde accepit exterius poteſtatem dominica carnis occidenda, inde interior eius poteſtas, qua nos tenebat, occiſa eſt. Factum eſt enim, vt vincula peccatorum multorum In Mvltis Mortibvs Per Vnivs Vnam Mortem, quam peccatum nullum præceſſerat , ſoluerentur. Ita Diabolus hominem in ipſa morte Carnis amiſit. Because (the Diuell) deade in spirite coulde not inuade (Chrift) liuing in spirite ; as most desirous

Ibidem.

Ibidem. cap. 13

to kill man, hee faſtened on that death which hee coulde compaſſe and was ſuffered to kill that mortall (bodie) which the liuing Mediatour tooke from mankinde; and where he could doe anie thing, euen there was hee euerie waie conquered; and whence hee receyued outwardlie power to kill the Lords bodie, thence was his inwarde power, whereby hee helde vs, ouerthrowne. By which it came to paſſe, that the chaines of manie ſinnes deſeruing manie deathes were looſed by the one death of one, in whome was no ſinne. So the Diuell loſt man BY THE VERIE DEATH OF (Chriſts) FLESH. Yea the death of Chriſt ſhould leade vs patientlie to ſuffer the ſame death for him which hee ſuffered for vs. [n] *Hactenus morerentur ad Chriſti gratiam pertinentes, quatenus pro illis ipſe mortuus eſt Chriſtus*, CARNIS TANTVM MORTE NON SPIRITVS. So farre ſhoulde they, which belong to the grace of Chriſt, die as Chriſt died for them; that is, the DEATH OF THE BODIE ONELIE, AND NOT OF THE SPIRIT. And by that death of his bodie he freed vs from both. SOLIVS CORPORIS MORTEM *Dei filius pro nobis accepit, per quam à nobis & dominationem peccati, & pœnam æterna punitionis excluſit.* The death OF THE BODIE ONLIE THE SONNE OF GOD SVFFERED FOR Vs, by which he deliuered vs both from the dominion of ſin, and from eternall damnation.

Cyrillus teacheth the ſame doctrine. [y] *Si intelligatur Deus incarnatus, & propria carne paſſus, parua eſt erga ipſum omnis creatura, & ſufficit ad redemptionem mundi* VNIVS CARNIS MORS. If wee vnderſtand (Chriſt) to bee God incarnate, and to haue ſuffered in his owne fleſh; of ſmall valoe in reſpect of him are all creatures, and ſufficient to redeeme the worlde is the DEATH OF HIS ONELY FLESH. And likewiſe Gregorie. [z] *Nos, quia mente à Deo receſſimus, & carne ad puluerem redimus, pœna dupla mortis aſtringimur: Sed venit ad nos qui* SOLA CARNE PRO NOBIS MORERETVR, ET SIMPLAM SVAM DV-

[n] *Auguſt. de Trinitate lib. 11 cap. 15.*

[x] *Idem de tempore. Serm. 162.*

[y] *Cyril. de recta fide ad reginas lib. 2.*

[z] *Greg. moral. lib. 9. cap. 15.*

PLAE NOSTRAE *iungeret & nos* ABVTRAQVE MORTE *liberaret.* Becaufe in heart wee were departed from God, and in flefh returning to duft ; wee are tied to the punifh-ment OF A DOVBLE DEATH, But (Chrift) came vnto vs, which DIED IN THE FLESH ONLY FOR VS, and ioyning HIS ONE KINDE OF DEATH TO BOTH OVRS, DELIVERED VS FROM BOTH . And more at large, the fame father debating the fame matter ; [a] *Vmbra mortis mors carnis accipitur quia ficut vera mors eft; qua anima feparatur à Deo, ita vmbra mortis eft, qua caro feparatur ab anima . Quos enim conftat* NON SPIRITV SED SOLA CARNE MORI, *ne-*

[a] *Idem moralium lib.4.cap.17.*

quaquam fe vera morte,fed vmbra mortis dicunt operiri. Quid eft ergo quod beatus Iob poftulat vmbram mortis nifi quod ad de-lenda peccata ante Dei oculos , Dei & hominum Mediato-rem requirit,qui SOLAM PRO NOBIS MORTEM CAR-NIS *fufciperet,& veram mortem delinquentium, per vmbram fue mortis deleret ? Ad nos quippe venit qui* IN MORTE SPIRITVS CARNISQVE TENEBAMVR VNAM *ad nos fuã morte detulit , &* DVAS NOSTRAS, *quas reperit fol-uit,*SI ENIM IPSE VTRAMQVE SVSCIPERET NOS A NVLLA LIBERARET:*fed* VNAM *mifericorditer accepit,* & IVSTE V-TRAMQVE *damnauit* SIMPLAM SVAM DVPLAE NO-STRAE *cõtulit &* DVPLAM NOSTRAM MORIENS SVBE-GIT. *Qui ergo* SOLAM PRO NOBIS MORTEM CARNIS SVSCEPIT *vmbrã mortis pertulit,& à dei oculis culpam quam fecimus,abfcondit.* The fhadow of death is takē for the death of the bodie , for that as it is the true death, whereby the foule is feparated from God ; fo it is but the fhadow of death, whereby the bodie is feparated from the foule. For they which affuredly die NOT THE DEATH OF THE SPIRIT,BVT ONLY OF THE FLESH, they doe not fay they are couered with the true death ; but with the fhadow of death. To what end then doth bleffed Iob aske for the fhadow of death,but that to wipe away finne out of Gods fight, hee feeketh for the Mediator of God & man,who fhould vndertake FOR VS THE DEATH

OF

Of The Bodie Only, and by the ſhadow of his death might extinguiſh the true death of ſinners? . Hee came to vs that Were Svbiect Both To The Death Of The Spirit And Of The Flesh , and by His Single Death He Loosed Both Ovr Deaths. If he ſhould haue Svffered Both, He Covld Have Delivered Vs From Neither. But he mercifully Vndertooke One Of Them and iuſtlie Condemned Both. He ioyned His Single Death To Ovr Dovble Death, and dying Conqvered Both Ovr Deaths. He then which for vs Tooke Vpon Him Only The Death Of The Body ſuffered the ſhadow of death, and hid from Gods eies, the ſinne which we had committed. Bernard likwiſe. *Cum gemina* *Bernard.* *ad milit.tem-* *morte ſecundum vtramq̃, naturam homo damnatus fuiſſet, altera* *pli.cap.11.* *quidem ſpiritali & voluntaria, altera corporali & neceſſaria ; v-* *triq̃, deus homo,* Vna Sva Corporali *ac voluntaria benigne* *& potenter occurrit,* Illaqve Sva Vna Nostram Vtramqve Damnavit. Where man was condemned vnto a double death, to witte, in either part of his nature ; the one death ſpirituall and voluntarie ; the other corporall and neceſſarie ; God beeing made man did mightilie and mercifullie releaſe both our Deathes , with his One Corporall and voluntarie Death ; and with That One Death Of His Destroyed Both Ovrs. And ſo concludeth ; *Dum* *ſponte , & tantum in corpore moritur , & vitam nobis &* *iuſtitiam promeretur.* VVhiles Chriſt dyed willinglie and only in his body he merited for vs both righteouſnes and life.

I hope to all men learned, or well aduiſed it will ſeeme no *How Chriſt* Ieſuiticall phraſe, but rather chriſtian & catholike doctrine, *gaue himſelfe* that the ſon of God dying for our ſinnes, ſuffered Not The *wholy for vs.* death of the sovle, but onlie of the bodie by the hands of the Iewes: and by the bodily & bloudie ſacrifice of himſelf, did not only redeeme & clenſe both our ſouls & bodies, but deſtroied ſin & death , purging our tranſgreſſions by the merit of his obedience,& ſwalowing vp death by power of his life b 1.Tim.2

And howsoeuer the scriptures sometimes affirme that hee gaue b himselfe a ransome for all men, and the Fathers like-wise teach, that hee gaue his flesh for our flesh, and his soule for our soules: yet neither Scriptures nor Fathers haue a-nie meaning either to subiect Christ to the death of the soule, which assertion they abhorre as wicked; or to diminish the force or fruit of his bodily death, which they extoll as most sufficient; but to expresse that in the death of his flesh on the crosse his soule did suffer the sense of paine, and smart of death which parted the bodie and soule in sunder; and so ioyntlie with the bodie, and seuerallie by it selfe, the soule of Christ had not onely temptations, afflictions and passions, but euen endured the naturall sting and sharpenesse of death, to which he submitted his soule, that he might haue the feeling of our infirmities, and in all things bee tempted as wee are: but still without sinne. How Christ gaue himselfe wholy for vs, we maie learne out of Bernard. d Sicut Totvm Hominem

c Heb.4.

d Bernard in
ramis palma-
rium. Serm.3.

salutum fecit, sic De Toto Se Hostiam fecit salutarem, corpus exponens tantis supplicijs & iniurijs, animam vero gemi-ne cuiusdam humanissimae compassionis affectui; inde (super maerore inconsolabili sanctarum foeminarum, inde super de-speratione & dispersione discipulorum. In his quatuor crux domi-nica fuit. As Christ saued the WHOLE MAN, so of HIM-SELFE WHOLIE hee made a wholesome sacrifice, yeel-ding his bodie to so great torments and wrongs, and his soule to the feeling of a double most tender compassion; on the one side for the vncomfortable greefe of the holie women; on the other side for the desperation and dispersion of his dis-ciples. In these foure consisted the crosse of Christ. Since then the death of Christ did both affect and afflict his soule and his

e Irenaeus. lib.5
cap.1.

bodie; iustlie might Irenaeus say, e The Lord bought vs with his owne bloud, and gaue his soule for our soules, and his flesh for our flesh. For in dying hee layde downe his soule not onelie to sorrowe, greefe and paine, but euen to the bitter diuorce of death, that brake the communion of bodie

                                                                                     and

and ſoule : ᶠ *Sicut* TOTVS-SEMETIPSVM *tradidit* , & ᶠ *Fulgentius ad*
TOTVS HOMO SEMETIPSVM OBTVLIT,*ita totus homo* ANI- *Traſimundum*
MAM SVAM POSVIT,*cū anima, in cruce moriente carne, diſ-* *lib 3.*
ceſſit. As WHOLE Chriſt gaue HIM SELFE (ſaith Fulgen-
tius) and the WHOLE MAN OFFERED HIMSELFE , ſo the
whole man LAYD DOWNE HIS SOVLE, whē, the fleſh dying
on the croſſe, the ſoule departed. So that Chriſt yeelded his
ſoule fo; our ſoules to the ſuſception of ſo;row, prepaſsion of
paine, and diſſolution of nature ; but vnto the death of the
ſoule he did neither offer, no; yeelde himſelfe: ſince that is a
ſeparation from God, and excluſion from grace, from which it
was vtterlie impoſsible the ſoule of Chriſt could either will-
ingly, o; fo;ceablie fo; an houre be remoued: yea where you
find the ſuffering of his ſoule witneſſed, there ſhall you ſee
the DEATH OF HIS FLESH ONELIE to be auouched.
ᵍ *Quia* TOTVM HOMINEM *deus ille ſuſcepit, ideo* TOTIVS
HOMINIS *in ſe paſſiones in veritate monſtrauit, & animam qui-* ᵍ *Fulgentius ad*
dem rationalem habens , quicquid fuit infirmitatis anima ſine *Traſimundum*
peccato ſuſcepit & pertulit ; vt dum humanæ animæ paſſiones, in *lib: 3.*
anima quam accepit vinceret, noſtras quoque animas ab infirmi-
tatibus liberaret. Carnem quoque humanam accipiens, in eiuſdem
veritate carnis , veritatem voluntaria habuit paſſionis , vt IN
CARNE MORTVS TOTAM *in ſe* HOMINIS OCCI-
DERET MORTEM. Becauſe (the ſonne of God) tooke vnto
him the WHOLE NATVRE of man, therefore he ſhewed in
himſelfe the ſufferings OF THE VVHOLE MAN; and hauing
a reaſonable ſoule , he tooke vpon him and endured all the infir-
mities of the ſoule , but without ſinne; that whiles in the ſoule,
which he tooke, hee conquered the paſsions of mans ſoule, he
might free our ſoules alſo from infirmities. Taking likewiſe mans
fleſh, in the truth of the ſame fleſh he ſuffered a true and volun-
tarie paſsion, that DYING IN THE FLESH, hee might kill
in his perſon the WHOLE DEATH dew to man. Chriſt en-
dured the paſsions of the whole man ; hauing neither bodie
no; ſoule free from ſuffering; but yet he died ONLY in the
M 3.   FLESH,

FLESH, and thereby he killed the WHOLE DEATH inflicted on the body and soule of man. [h] *Quis ignorat Christum* IN SO-LO CORPORE MORTVVM *& sepultū?* Who is ignorāt that Christ in BODY ONLY DIED, and was buried? And againe, [i] *Sicut in* MORTE SOLIVS CARNIS *immortalis fuit, sic in passionibus totius hominis impassibilis ōmnino permansit.* The godheade of Christ was immortall when ONELY HIS BODY DIED, and impassible, when the whole man suffered. [k] *Moriente carne, non solùm deitas sed* NEC ANIMA CHRISTI POTEST OSTENDI COMMORTVA. When Chrifts bodie died, not onelie his deitie, but his SOVLE CANNOT BE SHEWED TO HAVE BEEN PARTAKER OF DEATH. Wherefore I cannot admitte the wordes of Nazianzene to be true, that euerie part in man is [l] sanctified by the like in Christ, our condemned flesh by his flesh, our soule by his soule, our vnderstanding by his vnderstanding; yea I dislike not the wordes of Cyrill; [m] *Carnem suam in redemptionis pretium pro omnium carne dependit; & animam suam similiter pro omnium anima redemptionis pretium constituit, quamuis iterum renixerit, vita secundum naturam existens.* Christ yeelded his flesh, as a ransome for the flesh of all men, and made his soule likewise a price to redeeme the soules of all, though he were restored againe to life, as beeing life by nature: so long as we abufe not his wordes to maintaine our fansies impugning his generall and setled doctrine; that [n] sufficient for the redemption of the world, is the DEATH OF HIS FLESH ONLY: not thereby take occasion to defend that his blood is not able to suffice, or sanctifie the beleeuers. [o] *Sanguine suo; hoc est* SVAE CARNIS SANGVINE *iustificat omnes in se credentes.* With his blood, that is with THE BLOVD OF HIS FLESH he iustifieth all that beleeue in him. P SI NON A-LIO MODO SALVANDVS ERAT *mundus nisi in* SANGVINE ET CORPORE *morti* VTILITER *derelicto, quo pacto non necessarius verbo incarnationis modus vt iustificet in sanguine suo credētes in se, & conciliet patri per mortē sui corporis?* If the world MIGHT
NONE

[b] *Ibidem.*

[i] *Ibidem.*

[k] *Ibidem.*

[l] *Nazianzen.in tract.49. ad Cledonium.*

[m] *Cyril. de recta fide ad Theodosium.*

[n] *Cyril de recta fide ad reginas lib.2.*

[o] *Idem de recta fide ad reginas lib.1*

[p] *Ibidem.*

NONE OTHER WAY BE SAVED but by Chriftes leauing his BODIE AND BLOVD VNTO DEATH for our good, howe was not the taking of flesh neceffarie for the fonne of God, that by his bloud hee might iustifie such as beleeued in him, and BY THE DEATH OF HIS BODIE reconcile them to God his father? ¶ *Quomodo fanguis communis hominis nos fanctos efficeret? fed fanctificauit fanguis Chrifti. Deus igitur & non fimpliciter homo; deus enim erat in carne*, SVO SANGVINE *nos purificans*. How could the bloud of a common man make vs holie? BVT THE BLOVD OF CHRIST DID SANCTIFIE VS. He was therefore God and not fimplie a man. For he was God in FLESH THAT CLENSED VS WITH HIS BLOVD.

When the ancient fathers affirme, that Chrift died for vs THE DEATH OF THE BODY ONLY, and that the BLOVD OF HIS FLESH doth faue and fanctifie the beleeuers; we muft not like children imagine they fpeake of infenfible flefh, or that in thefe wordes they exclude the vnion, operation or paffion of the foule, whiles Chriftes bodie fuffered and died: that were to make Chrift a ftocke, not a man, and to giue him carrion, and not humane flefh quickened and coupled with life and foule; but in the death of his bodie & fhedding of his bloud, they include all thofe afflictions and paffions of the foule, which naturally & neceffarily follow paine & accompany death. For thefe fufferings of Chrifts foule confirme his obedience, & witnes his patience; only their intent is by all meanes to free Chrift from THE DEATH OF THE SOVLE, and then to propofe the death which hee fuffered in the bodie of his flefh on the croffe, with all painefull, but no finnefull concomitants and confequents, as the propitiation for our finnes, redemption of our foules, and reconciliation vnto God; by which al þ aduerfaries of our faluation the law, finne, death and Satan are vtterlie conquered and abolifhed. And thus farre forth they haue the fcriptures expreffelie concurring

The death of Chrifts flefh redeemeth as well foule as bodie.

¶ Ibidem.

ᵇ 2.Iohn, 1

concurring with them. ᵇ The bloud of Iesus Christ his sonne clenseth vs from all sinne. It must clense then our soules, as wel as our bodies; for they are the chiefe agents in sin. ᶠMuch more shall the bloud of Christ purge your consciences from dead works. Conscience is a part of the soule; not of the bodie. ᵗ Thou hast redeemed vs to God by thy bloud, saie the saintes in heauen, whose bodies lie in the dust of the earth. Redemption, remission of sinnes, iustification, sanctification, and such like effectes of the bloud of Christ are PRINCIPALLY and PRIMARILY in the soule; and by consequent in the bodie. And therefore there can be no question, but the bodilie death of Christ is the redemption of our soules, as well as of our bodies, in as much as the whole man in Christ died the death of the crosse, to redeeme the whole man in vs; both partes in him ioyntlie feeling; but with admirable patience enduring, the bitter and sharpe paines antecedent, and annexed to the death of his bodie. ᵘ Cum caro in doloribus est, & in pœnis, profecto anima tunc habet maximum agonem patientiæ. When the flesh is in anguish and paine, (saith Austen) then the soule certainly hath the greatest triall of patience. For the soule is so created and ordained that shee feeleth the pleasure and paine of her bodie; and howsoeuer the flesh bee subiected to violence, the sence and grieuance thereof is in the soule; both in this life, and in the next.

ᶠHebre.9

ʳReuelat.5.

ᵘ August. epist. 120.

As the bodilie death of Christ paieth the price of our redemption: so it remoueth all the impediments of our saluation, which are manie and mightilie linked together. For by the CORRVPTION of nature descending from our parents, and dwelling within vs, wee are ˣ solde vnder sinne, ʸ fulfilling the will of the flesh, and louing ᶻ pleasures more then God; whereby we neglect and breake the LAVV of God, and so incurre the CVRSE pronounced against the transgressours of the law; and by that obligation are liable to ETERNAL DEATH. This is the chaine of originall infection, actuall transgression, legall malediction, and eternal damnation, which

The bodilie death of christ ouerthrew all the enemies of our saluation.
ˣRom. 7.
ʸEphes. 2.
ᶻ2.Timoth.3

which draweth vs from God, and bindeth vs as priſoners and captiues to death, and hell. If then the DEATH of Chriſt ſuffered [a] IN THE BODY OF HIS FLESH loſed euery linke of this chaine, and not onelie cleered vs from all theſe enemies and exactors, but reconciled vs to God, and made peace for vs [b] by the bloud of his croſſe; it is a wrong to the death & bloud of Chriſt either to diſable thē as not ſufficient to redéem vs; or to ſupplie them with anie better or other addition, which the holie ghoſt doth not mention. Examine theſe particularlie, and ſee whether the power of Chriſtes death doe not perfectlie diſſolue them all. [c] Our olde man is crucified with him, that the bodie of ſinne might bee deſtroied, that henceforth we ſhould not ſerue ſinne. Let not ſinne raigne therefore in your mortall bodie, (ſaieth the Apoſtle) that you ſhould obey it in the luſtes thereof. The force and ſtrength of originall ſinne and corruption in all the faithfull is crucified and dead with Chriſt, except they reuiue it by voluntarie obeying the luſtes thereof. [d] For they which are Chriſtes, haue crucified the fleſh with the affections and luſtes; by reaſon not onelie the guilt, but alſo the life and power of ſinne died in Chriſtes fleſh, when it was crucified. So that [e] ſinne nowe hath no dominion ouer them, becauſe they are not vnder the lawe, but vnder grace. And likewiſe for actuall ſinne, (by Chriſt) [f] we haue redemption, through his bloud, that is the forgiuenes of ſinnes. For God hath [g] propoſed him to be a reconciliation through faith in his bloud by the forgiueneſſe of the ſinnes that are paſſed, through the patience of God. [h] The bloud (therefore) of Chriſt Ieſus his ſonne clenſeth vs from all ſinne, ſince he is the [i] mediator of the new Teſtament, (whoſe) death was for the redemption of the tranſgreſſions, that were in the former teſtament.

If the death of Chriſt on the croſſe, and the ſhedding of his bloud were the iuſt and full redemption of all our ſinnes, then apparentlie it eaſed and ended the curſe which the lawe inflicted, for ſinne. For where he is [k] accurſed, that continueth not

Margin notes:
[a] Coloſ.1.
[b] Ibidem.
[c] Rom.6.
[d] Galat.5
[e] Rom.6.
[f] Epheſ.1.
Coloſ.1.
[g] Rom.3.
[h] 1.Iohn.1
[i] Hebre.9
The death of Chriſt on the croſſe quencheth y̆ curſe of the law.
[k] Galat 3.

not in al things written in the book OF THE LAVV, to do thē; the remitting of sinne, is the releasing of the curse that is consequent to sinne. The curse importeth vengeance due to sinne. Then where sinne is pardoned the curse is determined. But [1] wee haue redemption, euen remission of sinnes through his blood. *Ergo* the bloud of Christ doth quench the curse of the law. The maner, how the curse of the law lighted & seased on the person of Christ, is thus expressed by S. Paule. [m] Christ redeemed vs from the curse of the lawe, being made a curse for vs. For it is written, accursed is euery one that hangeth on the tree. As by his stripes we are healed: so by his curse we are blessed. In as much as he submitted himselfe to the curse of the law for our sinnes, not only our transgressions are pardoned, for which Christ suffered; but the law stinging him to death, lost his force for euer. For the vengeance of the law once executed on our suertie, can no more in Gods iustice be exacted of vs. But Christ receiued the sentence of the lawe in himselfe, when he bare our sinnes in his bodie on the tree; wee therefore are quited for euer from the power of the lawe. Since then by his receiuing and suffering the curse of the lawe in his owne person, wee are freed and blessed; it remaineth wee search howe farre the curse preuailed against him. Wherein we must take heede that wee step not an hayres breadth from the Apostles words. For if we stretch the curse farther on Christ, then in truth it did, or coulde take place, wee arrogantlie and impiouslie pronounce that cursed, which indeede was blessed; and falsifie the promise of God, made to Abraham, that in his seede, which was Christ, [n] All the nations of the earth should be blessed. For howe could the blessing of Abraham be deriued from Christ to vs, if euerie part of his humane nature were accursed? Wherefore Christ must receiue the curse of the lawe in one part of himselfe, which was his flesh, and in the other which was his soule, retaine the blessing of God, as well for his flesh to bee raised againe, as for his members to bee vnited vnto him.

Margin notes:
[1] Ephes.1
[m] Galat.3
[n] Genes.22

him. If this bee not the doctrine of the holie Ghoſt, I
vrge no man to beléeue it ; if it bee, let ſuch as will wante
G O D S curſe, beware howe they refuſe it . It is no
ſmall aduenture to extende the curſe of God vpon the ſoule
of Chriſt Ieſus, without cléere, ſound, and ſure teſtimonie of
the holie ſcriptures.

To ſhew that Chriſt ſuſtained the curſe of the lawe ; and ┃ How Chriſt
by his enduring it , acquited vs ; Saint Paul in effect vſeth ┃ was made a
this reaſon . ° C V R S E D ſaieth Moſes is euerie one that ┃ curſe for vs.
is hanged on the tree. But Chriſt was content for our ſinnes ┃ °Deuter.21
to be hanged on the trée of the croſſe. He therfore ſubmitted
himſelfe to the curſe of the law to redéeme vs from it . That
this is Saint Paules argument, the thirde to the Galathians,
to proue Chriſt vnder the curſe of the lawe, I hope the ſim-
pleſt amongſt you, will ſoone perceiue, the learnedeſt dare
not denie. By which it is euident, that part of Chriſt which
hung on the croſſe was ſubiected to the curſe : but the ſoule
of Chriſt was not crucified : Ergo the ſoule of Chriſt
was not made a curſe ; but onelie his bodie . And by
ſuffering this curſe, that is by hanging on the tree, hee re-
déemed vs from the curſe of the lawe, which wee had deſer-
ued both in bodie and ſoule . Which of theſe thinges canne
we contradict? Shall wee ſaie the Apoſtle miſt his marke,
in that hee cleareth vs from the ſpirituall and perpetuall
curſe of the lawe, by Chriſtes ſuffering a corporall and
temporall parte thereof ? or ſhall wee chalenge him to be ſo
ſimple that he knew not the difference betwixt the one & the
other? I am far from any ſuch thought; I loue to follow and
not to leade the holie ghoſt. In matters of ſo great depth
I dare not wade, without, or before my guide . That ┃ ᴾ Matth 27
Chriſt died hanging on a tree, the ᴾ Euangeliſtes are plaine. ┃ Marke.15
That hanging on a tree is a curſed kinde of death in the ┃ Luke 23.
q lawe of Moſes, is as manifeſt. That by hanging on the ┃ ᵠDeutero.21
trée hee was made a curſe for vs , and thereby redéemed ┃
vs from the curſe of the lawe, the ʳ Apoſtle is reſolute. ┃ ʳGalat.3.

N 2. If

If anie man will offer farther, I must leaue him. To fasten the internall or eternall curse of the lawe, on the soule of Christ, is to my vnderstanding verie desperate diuinitie. For men might naile his bodie to the trée, as did the Iewes; but none coulde inflict the curse on his soule, but onelie God. Since then the innocencie, obedience, patience, humilitie, and sanctitie of his soule were so perfect euen in the sight of God, that it could not suffice be but blessed, howe shoulde the righteousnesse of God immediatelie, and vniustlie laie the curse, which bringeth inwarde and enerlasting death, on the soule of Christ? Againe, God spirituallie curseth none, but whome hee first deseruedlie hateth; as all vncleane and wicked persons. If then the soule of Christ could not worthilie be hated of God, it coulde not truelie bee cursed of God; for the hatred and curse of God cannot bee seuered.

Christ was not accursed in soule.

This doctrine is ancient and catholicke. Saint Austen ripping this matter to the quicke, saieth. *Securus Apostolus ait de Christo, factus est pro nobis maledictum, sicut non timuit dicere, pro omnibus mortuus est; hoc est enim mortuus, quod maledictus; quoniam mors ipsa ex maledicto est: & maledictum est omne peccatum, siue ipsum quod fit, vt sequatur supplicium, siue ipsum supplicium, quod alio modo vocatur peccatum, quia fit ex peccato. Suscepit autem Christus sine reatu supplicium nostrum, vt inde solueret reatum nostrum, & finiret etiam supplicium nostrum.* Securely the Apostle saieth of Christ that he was made a curse for vs, euen as he feared not to say, Christ DIED FOR ALL. For, HEE DIED, IS ALL ONE VVITH HE VVAS ACCVRSED, BECAVSE DEATH CAME FROM THE CVRSE; and all sinne is accursed, as well that which is committed and deserueth punishment, as THE PVNISHMENT IT SELFE, which in a sort is called sinne, because it is consequent to sinne. Nowe Christ bare our punishment without any desert, that thereby hee might acquite our guiltinesse, and ende our punishment. And againe. *Male-dictus*

a August. contra Faustum Manicheū. lib. 14. ca. 4.

Christ was in that part accursed in which he died.

dictus omnis qui pendet in ligno, non hic aut ille, ſed omnis omnino.
Etiamne & filius dei ? etiam prorſus. DISPLICET VOBIS
MALEDICTVS PRO NOBIS, QVIA DISPLICET
MORTVVS PRO NOBIS. *Tunc extra maledictum illius*
Adam, ſi extra illius mortem. *Cum vero ex homine, & pro ho-*
mine mortem ſuſcepit, ex illo & pro illo etiam maledictum quod
mortem comitatur ſuſcipere non dedignatus eſt etiam ille, prorſus
etiam ille filius Dei, ſemper viuus in ſua iuſtitia, mortuus autem
propter delicta noſtra in carne ſuſcepta ex pœna noſtra. Sic & ſem- `¹Ibid, in cap.6`
per benedictus in ſua iuſtitia, maledictus autem propter delicta
noſtra, in morte ſuſcepta ex pœna noſtra ; ac per hoc additum eſt,
OMNIS: *ne Chriſtus ad veram mortem non pertinere diceretur,*
ſi à maledicto, quod morti coniunctum eſt, inſipienti honorificen-
tia ſepararetur. Curſed is euerie one that hangeth on the wood:
not this or that man, but euery man without exception. What
the ſonne of God himſelfe ? yea in anie caſe . . You (*Mani-*
chees) miſlike Chriſt ſhould be accurſed for vs; becauſe you be
leeue not hee died for vs. Then is Chriſt without the curſe of
Adam, when he is without the death of *Adam.* But for ſo
much as from man, and for man he did admit death ; euen from
man, and for man he vouchſafed to admit the curſe, which ac-
côpanieth death; I meane euen that verie ſon of God, alwayes
liuing in his owne righteouſneſſe, but dying for our ſinnes in the
fleſh which he tooke from our puniſhment. So alwayes bleſſed
in his owne righteouſneſſe, he was accurſed for our ſinnes in the
death which hee ſuffered by reaſon of our puniſhment ; and
therefore the Scripture ſayth, EVERIE ONE; leaſt Chriſt
ſhould be thought not truly to haue died, if by an intent of foo-
liſh honour he ſhould be excepted from the curſe, which is vni-
ted vnto death. And anſwering Fauſtus obiection ; if a king
command anie Chriſtian to worſhip the Sunne & Moone,
or to be hanged on a trée; hee muſt either way of neceſſitie
be accurſed: Auſten ſaieth, ᵘ *Chriſtianus videt vnum male-* `²Ibid.cap.13`
dictum pertinere ad corpus mortale, quod ligno ſuſpenditur ; al-
terum ad animum, quò ſol adoratur: ſicut mors eſt corporis in

ligno pendere, ita mors est animi solem adorare. Eligendum est igitur maledictum in corporis morte, quo maledicto & ipsum corpus in resurrectione liberabitur : deuitandum autem maledictum in animi morte, ne cum suo corpore in æterno igne damnetur. Nolite timere maledictum corporalis mortis, quod temporaliter soluitur ; sed timete maledictum mortis spiritualis, per quod anima in æternum cum suo corpore cruciatur. A Christian perceiueth the one curse to belong to the mortall bodie, that hangeth on the woodde ; the other whereby the Sonne is worshipped, to pertaine to the soule. Hee must therefore choose the curse of the corporall death, from which curse euen his verie bodie shall be deliuered in the resurrection ; and shunne the curse of the spirituall death, least togither with the bodie the soule bee damned in euerlasting fire. Feare not the curse of the corporall death, which is dissolued with time ; but feare the curse of the spirituall death, by which the soule is euerlastingly tormented with her bodie. This doctrine is so sounde, it cannot bee confuted ; and so cleare, it neede not bee explained. The temporall death of the bodie came first from sinne, as a part of the curse and punishment of sinne ; and so to this daie doth it continue. Christ therefore in that hee yeelded his bodie to die on the Crosse, subiected himselfe to the curse of our sinne, and by suffering a part of the curse, abolished the whole : but the curse of the soule, which is the spirituall death, Christ coulde not taste ; because that damneth bodie and soule for euer.

[x] Chrysost. in cap.3.epist.ad Galatas.
The kinde of Christs death was accursed, & so the force of the lawe dissolued.

The rest of the ancient fathers tredd the same path.[x] The people (saith Chrysostome) were subiect to the curse, which saith, accursed is euery one y̌ abideth not in those things which are written in the booke of the law. For none of them had continued therein, neither had any man fulfilled the whole lawe, but Christ exchanged the curse with another, which saith, accursed is euerie one that hangeth on the tree. Where then he that hangeth on the tree is accursed, and he that transgresseth the law is
likewise

likewiſe accurſed, he that ſhall diſſolue this curſe, muſt not bee
ſubiect to the ſame ; but muſt admit an other in ſteede of that;
which Chriſt did, and ſo by the one looſed the other. y The croſſe
therefore tooke away the curſe. Can we with plainer words,
then that Chriſt by ſuffering the CVRSE OF SVSPEN-
SION on the croſſe, tooke away THE CVRSE OF TRANS-
GRESSION, to which the people were ſubiect? *Theodorete:*
z When all were ſubiect to the curſe of the lawe, Chriſt ſuffered
that kinde of death, which is accurſed in the lawe, that hee
might deliuer all men from the curſe. *Cyril.* a *Factus eſt pro
nobis maledictum, crucem ferens & pendens in ligno vt ſol-
uat peccatum mundi.* Chriſt was made a curſe for vs; when
hee endured the Croſſe, and hung on the tree , that hee
might releaſe the ſinne of the worlde. *Ambroſe.* b *Quare
maledictum dicatur Apoſtolus te. docet dicens, quia ſcriptum
eſt: maledictus omnis qui pendet in ligno. Hoc eſt qui in carne
ſua noſtram carnem, in ſuo corpore noſtras infirmitates , & noſtra
maledicta ſuſcepit, vt crucifigeret.* Why Chriſt is called a curſe,
the Apoſtle teacheth thee, when hee ſayth, becauſe it is writ-
ten; accurſed is euerie one that hangeth on the tree, that is, which
in his fleſh bare our fleſh , AND IN HIS BODIE TOOKE
OVR INFIRMITIES, AND OVR CVRSES, that he might
faſten them to his Croſſe.   *Hierom.* c It ought to trouble no
man that Chriſt was made a curſe for vs; becauſe God, who is
ſaide to make him a curſe, did alſo make him ſinne for vs, though
he knew no ſinne ; yea, being life he died, and being the wiſe-
dome of God, he is called fooliſhnes: but he died, that we might
liue; he was made fooliſhnes that we ſhould be made wiſdome;
hee hung on the tree, that being faſtened to the tree, hee might
wipe out the ſin , which we had committed in y tree of the know-
ledge of good and euil. *Oecumenius.* d We were vnder the curſe,
becauſe wee had not kept the lawe ; Chriſt was free from that
becauſe he had fulfilled the law; and yet hee ſuffered a curſe not
due to him, when he was hanged on the tree, that he might diſ-
ſolue the curſe pronounced againſt vs.

y *Ibidem.*

z *Theodoret. in
cap. 3. epiſt. ad
Galat.*
a *Cyril. de recta
fide ad reginas
lib. 1.*

b *Ambroſ. epiſti.
lib. 5. oration.
in Auxenſium
de baſilicis
tradendis.*

c *Hierom. in cap.
3. epiſt. ad Gala.*

d *Oecumenius
in cap. 3. epiſt.
ad Galatas.*

Other

Other expositions if anie man séeke, hee shall find euen in the learned and ancient writers. [c] *Non maledictum, vel peccatum factum, est (verbum) sed cum iniquis reputatus est iustus existens, vt aboleat peccatum : & appellatus est maledictus, qui benedixit creaturam, vt soluat nostrum maledictum, & liberet à pœnâ credentes in ipsum. Igitur non est factus secundum veritatem maledictum & peccatum , appellatus autem illorum nominibus, vt aboleat maledictum & peccatum.* Christ was not made indeede a curse, or sinne (sayth *Cyrill*)but hee was reputed amongst the wicked, beeing iust, that hee might put awaie sinne ; and he who did blesse the creature, was called a curse, that he might dissolue our curse, and free from vengeance such as beleeued in him. Therefore he was not in truth made a curse and sin ; but he was called by those names, that he might abolish both the curse and sinne . Christ was no more a curse, then hee was sinne ; who indæde, and with God was neither ; but with men he was reputed both wicked and accursed, by reason God suffered him to endure that vilde and shamefull kinde of death, which hee did to saue vs from the curse of sinne. Epiphanius saith he was A CVRSE VNTO THE CVRSE, that is, a dissoluer and finisher of the curse. [f] *Ignorat omnino miser ille, quod neq; Christus maledictio factus fit ; absit : sed maledictionem, qua propter peccata nostra fuit, abstulit se ipsum cruci dedens ; & factus est mors morti propter peccata nostra, & MALEDICTIO MALEDICTIONI. Quapropter non est Christus maledictum, sed maledicti solutio ; benedictio autem omnibus verè in ipsum credentibus.* That wretch (*Marcion*) is vtterly ignorant, that Christ was not accursed ; God forbid : but he tooke away the curse that lay on our sinnes, in yeelding himselfe to the crosse, and was made death vnto death for our sinnes, and A CVRSE VNTO THE CVRSE. Wherefore Christ was NOT A CVRSE , but THE DISSOLVER OF THE CVRSE, and A BLESSING to all that trulie beleeue in him.

These, though they diuerslie applie the Apostles speach,

Factus

Factus pro nobis maledictum , Chriſt was made a curſe for vs, ſome to the toleration of death, ſome to the opinion of men, and ſome to the depulſion of the curſe from vs; yet in this they all agrée, that by giuing his bodie to die on the Croſſe, Chriſt receiued, ſuſtained, and aboliſhed the curſe due to vs for tranſgreſſing the law of God. And to iuſtifie their aſſertion they haue not onelie the plaine text of g Paule and g Moſes, Curſed is he that hangeth on the tree; but the manifeſt wordes of Peter, h He bare our ſinnes in his bodie on the tree. To proue the death which Chriſt ſuffered to be a curſed kinde of death, the place of Moſes is verie pregnant; to proue the perſon to bee accurſed in ſoule, it hath neither cauſe, nor truth. For innocents maie ſuffer that wrong to bee hanged on trées; and ſhall they then be accurſed in ſoule? And be they malefactors, they may repent as did ſhe theefe on the croſſe; and ſhall they notwithſtanding their repentance bee accurſed? Shall we cloſe both penitent and innocent within the true curſe of the ſoule, rather then we will ſuffer Pauls wordes to be referred to the death of the bodie? For he ſaith, Curſed is EVERIE ONE that hangeth on the tree; excuſing none; and if anie might bee excepted out of the generall rule, Chriſt Ieſus moſt of all . But euerie one that hangeth on the tree, hath a curſed kinde of death; though a bleſſed ſoule. Paule therefore expreſſelie teacheth , that Chriſt ſubiected himſelfe to a curſed kind of death; and in ſo dying, he deliuered vs from the curſe of the Lawe. i *Ex parte quippe mortali pependit in ligno , mortalitas autem vnde ſit , notum eſt credentibus. Ex pœna quippe eſt , & maledictio peccati primi hominis , quam Dominus ſuſcepit , & peccata noſtra pertulit in corpore ſuo ſuper lignum .* That part (ſayth Auſten) which was mortall (in Chriſt) hung on the Croſſe ; and whence mortalitie came the faythfull knowe. It came from the puniſhment of ſinne, and is the malediction of the ſinne of the firſt man ; which the Lorde tooke vnto him and bare our ſinnes in his bodie on the tree. Yea when

D　　　　　　　　　　　　　　　Chriſt

[margin notes:]

Theſe three wayes Chriſt is ſaid to be accurſed for vs.

g Galat. 3.
g Deut. 21.
h 1. Peter. 2.

i Auguſt. in expoſition. epiſt. ad Galat.

Chꝛiſt tooke the curſe , hee tooke the ſinne of the olde man into his fleſh , and faſtened it togither with his fleſh vnto the Croſſe. k *Quid pependit in ligno, niſi peccatum veteris hominis , quod Dominus pro nobis in ipſa carnis mortalitate ſuſcepit? Vnde nec erubuit nec timuit Apoſtolus dicere, peccatum eum feciſſe pro nobis ; addens vt de peccato condemnaret peccatum . Non enim & vetus homo noſter ſimul crucifigeretur , ſicut Apoſtolus alibi dicit , niſi in illa morte Domini , peccati noſtri figura penderet.* What hung on the tree but the ſinne of the olde man, which . (ſinne) the Lorde tooke vpon him for vs in the verie mortalitie of his fleſh ? Wherefore the Apoſtle was neither aſhamed , nor afraied to ſay, that (God) made him ſinne for vs, that by ſinne he might condemne ſin. For our olde man could not be crucified togither with Chriſt, as the Apoſtle elſe where writeth, except the figure of our ſinne did hang on the Croſſe in that death which the Lord died. And if Peters woꝛds be true, (which can not be falſe) Chriſt bare our ſinnes, that is , the malediction and puniſhment of our ſinnes, in his body on the tree, and thereby ſaued vs from the eternall malediction, which is, Go you curſed into euerlaſting fire.

My reſolution then is, which I hope will bee receyued, becauſe it is the Apoſtles; WE ARE DEAD TO THE LAVV BY THE BODIE OF CHRIST, that we ſhould be to another, euen to him that is raiſed from the dead. We are quit from the feare, from the yoke, from the curſe, from the vengeance of the law; in one woꝛd, WE ARE DEAD to the lawe; which hath no moꝛe chalenge to vs nowe , then a man hath to his wife that is long ſince dead . And if you aſke when, and how we became dead to the lawe, Saint Paul anſwereth; BY THE BODIE OF CHRIST , when hee ſuffered on the Croſſe foꝛ our ſinnes. And as m he that is dead is freed from ſinne; ſo we dying in , and with the bodie of Chꝛiſt, are n LOOSED FROM THE LAVVE OF SINNE, AND DEATH ; Sinne breing condemned, and death conquered

b Ibidem

l Rom. 7.
We are dead to the law in the bodie of Chriſt.

m Rom. 6.

n Rom. 8.

red in the flesh of Christ, WHICH IS OUR FLESH, not onelie because it was taken of vs, but also for that it is vnited vnto vs, as the heade to the members; and communicateth with vs both in life and death, as appeareth by that we died and rose againe in him; and to this daie he suffereth in vs, then which no coniunction can be surer, or neerer. Since then the corruption of our flesh, the guilt of our sinne, the curse of the lawe, the sting of death were all closed and crucified in the bodie of Christ on the Crosse, and his death hath discharged vs from their dominion; fullie doth the Apostle saie of Christ, that hee did [o] partake with flesh, and bloud, that through death hee might destroy him that had power of death, euen the diuell. For in that wee bee freed from the curse of the lawe, which brought and bound sinners by death to hell: the chaynes of darkenesse are broken, and Satans force wholie frustrate; and he himselfe nowe left to beholde the ruine of his kingdome, to grieue at the spoyle of his goodes, and to feare the vengeance prouided for him, howsoeuer for a season hee bee suffered to pursue the members of Christ here on earth, to his owne shame, and their greater comfort, in trying the mightie power and steadfast fauour of God for their perpetuall defence, and eternall recompence. So that in all thinges [p] wee are more then conquerours through him that loued vs, [q] and gaue himselfe for vs, [r] who will tread downe Satan vnder our feete, [s] that God may bee all in all. Verie mightie then is the power of Christes death, by whose BLOVD the Saintes [t] OVERCOME the greate Dragon, that olde Serpent called the Diuell; and his ouerthrow prooueth all the enemies of mans saluation to bee vanquished, and impediments remooued; since he was the first perswader and procurer, and is the Prince and ruler of them all.

[o] Hebr.2.
[p] Rom.8.
[q] Galat.2.
[r] Rom.16.
[s] 1.Cor.15.
[t] Reuel.12.

We haue seene the power of Christs death in subduing sin and Satan, as likewise in ending & abolishing the curse of

The bodilie death of christ doth more

expresse Gods
mercies and
Chriſts merits,
then if the
paines of hell
were ioyned
with it,

of the lawe, which obliged man for his vncleannesse and vn-
righteouſneſſe to euerlaſting condemnation; and find that
hee, which bare our ſinnes in his bodie on the tree, did in that
mortall part which hee tooke of vs , crucifie as well the
fleſh, and ſinne of man, as the curſe and death, that raig-
ned ouer man: and ſo much hee performed in the bodie, of
his fleſh through death , by which hee reconciled vs vnto
God, to make vs holie and blamvleſſe in his ſight: let vs
nowe ſee whether the death of the ſpirite, and the curſe
of the ſoule will anie thing helpe the woorke of our re-
demption , or whether the death of Chriſtes bodie , doe
not more fullie demonſtrate the mercies of God, and me-
rits of Chriſt, then if the paines of hell had beene ioyned
with it . And where ſome men thinke it woulde much com-
mende the TRVTH, POVVER, and IVSTICE of God,
and more amplie declare the OBEDIENCE, PATIENCE,
and LOVE of Chriſt , if hee refuſed not the verie tor-
ments of hell for our ſakes, ſhunning no part of the bur-
then that preſſed vs, I muſt confeſſe I am rather of a con-
trarie minde; that the bodilie death of Chriſt on the croſſe
doth more plainlie expreſſe the vertues of God, and Chriſt
his ſonne, then if the terror and horror of hell were there-
with coupled.

1

And firſt for the TRVTH of god, his threatning Adam in this
wiſe, " Thou ſhalt die the death, or thou ſhalt certainely die,
was truelie performed in the bodie of Chriſt; in the ſoule of
Chriſt it could not without ſinne or damnation ; neither of
which with anie truth can be aſcribed vnto Chriſt . That the
mouth of God lied, or the ſoule of Chriſt died, is a choiſe ſo
hard, that I wiſh all men that haue anie care of Chriſtian
religion to refraine either . Next, touching the POVVER of
God; the weaker the inſtrument which God vſeth to ouer-
throwe his enemies, the greater is both his glory and their
ſhame. Then, for fleſh which was the feebleſt part of Chriſt,
after it was deade, and voide of all hope in ſhew, to riſe a-
againe

* Gen. 2.

As namely the
truth of God

2

The power
God.

gaine into a bleſſed and heauenlie life, and to foile both
death and Satan by recouering it ſelfe into the full poſſeſſi-
on, and all his members into the ioyfull expectation of euer-
laſting glorie, was farre a mightier conqueſt, then for his
ſoule with much adoe at length to eſcape, and reſiſt the aſ-
ſaultes of hell. From the depth of hell here on earth manie
ſinnefull ſoules haue by grace ſtruggeled, and cleered them-
ſelues; from the graue neuer roſe none into an immortall, &
incorruptible life, before the fleſh of Chriſt. Deeper in de-
ſperation, and al other temptations of hel haue others been,
that yet were ſaued, then anie man dare affirme of Chriſt:
deeper in death without corruption, then the bodie of Chriſt,
neuer was, nor euer ſhall be anie of the ſonnes of men. It
was therefore an harder thing for the bodie of Chriſt, paſt
all ſenſe, to riſe from death, to immortalitie, then for his
ſoule voide of ſinne, and full of grace to repell the force of
Satan; and yet to repell it, ſheweth greater power then to
ſuffer it; to conquere it, ſheweth greateſt of all.

[But to beare the burden of Gods wrath due to our
ſinnes, and to free vs from it, needed greater ſtrength, (they
will ſaie) then Chriſtes fleſh could haue.] To ſupport and
auert Gods iuſt indignation from vs, the humane bodie or
ſoule of Chriſt of themſelues were not able; but the DIGNI-
TIE and VNITIE of his perſon muſt be placed in the gap to
quench the flame of Gods iuſt vengeãce againſt our ſinnes,
which was euerlaſting deſtruction both of bodie and ſoule;
yet for ſo much as the ſincerity and ſanctitie of Chriſtes ſoule,
perſonallie ioyned, quickened, and bleſſed with the perpetual
vnion, communion, and fruition of his deitie, could feele no
want of grace, no lacke of ſpirit, no loſſe of fauour with God
(in which thinges conſiſt the inwarde death, and curſe of the
ſoule:) the wrath of God was executed on the fleſh of his
ſonne, which hee tooke of purpoſe from Adam, that therein
he might beare the ſinne, and curſe of Adam; and ſo by his
death might ſatiſfie the ſentence, and pacifie the diſpleaſure of

To auert Gods wrath from vs, the dignity of Chriſts perſon was neceſſary.

God

God againſt our vnrighteouſneſſe.

And this is moꝛe agrǽable to Gods iuſtice, then if Chꝛiſts ſoule had ſuffered the death and curſe of the ſoule. Foꝛ to take life from the ſoule, muſt be Gods proper and peculiar action. No creature can giue the grace oꝛ ſpirit of God to the ſoule of man, which is the life of the ſoule, but onelie God. Therefoꝛe no creature can take it from the ſoule, but God alone that GIVETH it, muſt TAKE IT AVVAY. Since then Chꝛiſt might ſuffer nothing iuſtlie, but as the [x] iuſt for the vniuſt, that is willinglie, but vniuſtlie; his death muſt come by the handes of the wicked, who might wꝛongfullie take his life from him, but not touch his ſoule; and not by the immediate hande of GOD, who will doe no wꝛong, and can kill the ſoule. [y] I haue ſinned, ſaith Iudas, in betraying the INNOCENT bloud. [z] You denied the HOLIE AND IVST, and killed the Lorde of life, ſaith Peter to the Iewes, warning them howe great a ſinne they had committed in putting Chꝛiſt to death. If hee were an INNOCENT, and deſerued no puniſhment; if hee were HOLIE and IVST, and could not bee perſecuted oꝛ put to death without haynous impietie and iniurie, wee may doe well to remember that the death of his ſoule had beene a farre greater wrong, then the death of his bodie was. And therefoꝛe if the iuſtice of God would not farther interpoſe it ſelfe in killing his bodie, then by deliuering him into the handes of the wicked, permitting them to ſhed his blond, which hee woulde accept foꝛ the ſinnes of the woꝛlde; much leſſe woulde God with his owne mouth accurſe; oꝛ with his owne hande ſlea the ſoule of his ſonne, whome hee ſent to reſtore and quicken thoſe that were accurſed, and dead in their ſinnes. Againe, corporallie oꝛ temporallie God puniſheth one foꝛ anothers fault, bicauſe he can recompence them eternally, that thereby repent and turne from their ſinnes; but eternally oꝛ ſpiritually he puniſheth no man, but foꝛ his owne vncleannes, either naturally ſticking in him, oꝛ voluntarily committed by him.

3.
The iuſtice of God.

[x] 1.Pet.3

[y] Matth.27
[z] Actes.3.

The death of Chriſts ſoule could neither proceed from God, nor be acceptable vnto God.

him. Chriſt then beeing frée from all ſinne, might not ſuffer
the inwarde oz euerlaſting death of the ſoule, but corporall and
temporall reproch, and paine, which God might and did re-
compence with eternall ioye, and glorie. Thirdlie that ᵃEzechiel, 18
ſoule which ſinneth, that ſoule ſhall die. This is the ſetled rule
of Gods iuſtice; and therefoze Chriſts ſoule which ſinned not,
could by no iuſtice die the death of the ſoule. To laie down
his life foz vs was loue and thankes with God: but willing-
lie to ſeparate himſelfe from God foz vs, was no waie to
reconcile God to vs, oz to bzing vs to God. He muſt there-
foze cleaue faſt to God in ſoule, whoſe death ſhall bze pzeti-
ous in Gods ſight, as was Chriſts. If the ſoule bze ſeuered
from God, the death of the bodie is deteſtable in his eies, as
beeing the wages of ſinne; and therefoze no moze accepta-
ble to G O D then ſinne it ſelfe, but where the ſoule, ha-
ting the infection of ſinne, and loathing the infirmitie of
the fleſh, reſigneth it vnto death foz Gods glozie, and the good
of others. And in this reſpect the death of the bodie maie
bee a ſacrifice vnto God, but not except the ſoule doe liue,
and cleaue to God, without ſeparation. Then hatefull to
G O D was the death of Chriſt, if his ſoule were firſt ha-
ted oz accurſed; if that were beloued and bleſſed of God,
it coulde not chooſe but liue; foz God is not the ᵇ God of the ᵇMatth. 22.
deade, but of the liuing. So that the death of Chriſtes bo-
die on the Croſſe, was by no iuſtice an acceptable ſacri-
fice vnto God, if his ſoule were firſt deade. But his death
was ſo pzecious in Gods ſight, that in ᶜ the bodie of his fleſh ᶜColoſ. 1.
through death, he reconciled vs vnto God: his ſoule was there-
foze aliue and in fauour with God, yea ſo abundantly bleſſed,
and highly accepted, foz the holines, humilitie, and obedience
thereof, that God was pacified, and pleaſed, and we all ſanc-
tified with THE OBLATION OF THE BODY of Ieſus on
the altar of the croſſe.
  Laſtlie, the fleſh of Chriſt by Gods iuſtice muſt bze
as able to purge vs from ſinne, as Adams was to poyſon
                                                            vs

Christes flesh must be as able to quicken vs, as Adams flesh was to kill vs.

d 1.Corinth.15

e Rom.5.

f Philip.2 Rom.3. verse g 25, & h 24.

i Psal.51.

k Iob.14.

l Ephes.1.
m Ephes.4
n Rom.7.
o Rom.7

p Galat.5
q Rom.8

φρόνημα.

r Rom.1
ſ Rom.7
ſ Rom.6

vs with sinne. But the flesh of Adam infected all his posteritie with sinne, and death; ergo the flesh of Christ must haue as much force, to clense and quicken the faithfull both in this life, and the next. Of this iustice Paul speaketh, when he saith, since by man came death, by man must come the resurrection of the dead: For as in *Adam* all die, euen so in Christ shal al be made aliue. The first Adam WAS THE FIGVRE of the second Adam, that where e sinne abounded, there grace might abound much more. e As then by one mans disobedience manie were made sinners; so by the obedience of one shall many bee made righteous. The obedience of Christ which here Paule mentioneth, is his f obedience vnto death, euen to the death of the crosse; and the g righteousnesse of the faithfull is the forgiuenes of their sinnes, h through the redemption that is in Christ Iesus. I wil not here dispute whether the soule be created, and infunded; or else traduced from Adam, as well as the flesh: I meane not with curious or superfluous questions to busie mens heades; that which the scriptures deliuer touching the deriuation of sinne and death from our first parents, I may safelie teach, and you must necessarily belieue. That we were i fashioned in iniquitie, and conceaued in sinne, the words of Dauid doe exactlie witnesse, and no maruaile. For k who can make that to bee cleane, which commeth from the vncleane? yea sinne cleaueth so fast vnto our flesh, that when the l eies of our heart are lightened, and the m spirit of our minde is renued, so that the n inwarde man delighteth in the law of God; EVEN THEN haue we an o other law in our members rebelling against the lawe of our minde, and leading vs captiue vnto the lawe of sinne; the p one so contrarie to the other, that we cannot doe the things which we would; by reason the affection or q liking of the flesh cannot be subiect to the lawe of God. This fight betwixt the flesh and the spirit is so durable, that it cannot bee dissolued but onelie by death. Though r Christ bee in vs, and the spirit liue for righteousnesse sake; yet ſ sinne so dwelleth in vs, (that is) in our ſ mortall bo-

dies,

dies, that whiles we liue, ᵘ in minde we ſerue the law of God, but in our fleſh the lawe of ſinne. From Adams fleſh wee deriue this infection of ſinne, that ſticketh ſo faſt vnto vs after we are regenerate, and new boꝛne againe of water and the holie ghoſt, and this is the roote and nurſe of all ſinne, and the cauſe of death to al men. ˣ If Chriſt be in you, the bodie is dead becauſe of ſinne. From Chꝛiſtes fleſh then we muſt receiue the purgation of ſinne both inherent in vs, and committed by vs; oꝛ elſe Adams fleſh is ſtronger to wound vs, then Chriſts is to heale vs; which is repugnant to the iuſtice of God; by which the grace of God muſt bee farre mightier vnto ſaluation in the bodie of Chꝛiſt, then the foꝛce of ſinne was vnto condemnation in the bodie of Adam; vnleſſe wee make ſinne of moꝛe power to kill, then God is to quicken; which is to exalt the diuell aboue God, and his ſonne. For ʸ God was in Chriſt, reconciling the worlde to himſelfe; by whoſe bloud the ᶻ partition wal is broken down, and hatred abrogated ᶻ through his fleſh; that wee might bee reconciled vnto God in one bodie by his croſſe.

^u Rom. 7

^x Rom. 8.

^y 2. Corinth. 5

^z Epheſ. 2

[But the death of the bodie, they will ſaie, hath no pꝛopoꝛtion to the death of the ſoule; and therefoꝛe the one cannot in iuſtice excuſe the other.] There is farre greater diſtance betwixt the ſonne of God, and the ſonnes of men, then betwixt the bodies and ſoules of men. Theſe differ as creatures, and both inferiour vnto the angels; but there is the excellencie of the Creatoꝛ aboue the creature, which is ſimplie infinite. Whatſoeuer therefoꝛe it pleaſed the ſonne of God to ſuffer foꝛ our ſakes, it was moſt ſufficient foꝛ our redemption; howbeit to demonſtrate his loue, hee would be partaker of our infirmitie and mortality; leaſt we ſhould loath our condition, oꝛ grudge at the chaſtiſement of our ſinnes; but if we ſet aſide the dignitie and vnitie of his perſon, then is no waie the death of the ſoule oꝛ the paines of hell, which they imagine Chꝛiſt ſuffered, pꝛopoꝛtionable in exact iuſtice to the true wages of our ſinne. Foꝛ what equiualence hath one ſoule with

why the death of Chriſts body doth counteruaile all the bodies & ſoules of men.

all

all the foules of the Saints? or one daies anguish which Christ felt in foule, as they fuppofe, with that euerlafting fire which wee shoulde haue fuffered in bodie and foule for euer? fet afide I faie the refpect of the perfon, which fuffered for vs; and in the reft they shall neuer bee able to prooue anie proportion of iuftice diuine or humane. But as I haue fullie shewed before, the worthineffe of the perfon is the furelt ground of our faluation, and <u>chiefeft weight of our</u> redemption; and therefore his death is of infinite force, and his bloude of infinite price, euen as his perfon is. For fince all mens actions are and ought to bee efteemed according to the giftes which they haue, and place which they holde from G D D; whie shoulde not the death and bloud of Chrift bee valued in Gods iuftice according to the height and worth of his perfon? and if in all thinges wee receaue honour not due to our fieshe wherein wee partake with Beaftes, but fitte for the foule wherein wee communicate with Angels; howe feemeth it ftrange in our eyes, that the dooinges and fufferinges of Chrift Iefus, which hath the natures of God and man in a furer and nearer coniunction, then wee haue our foules and bodies, shoulde not bee reckned and accepted in G D D S iuftice, as the ACTIONS and PASSIONS OF HIS OVVNE SONNE; and haue their value from the diuiner and worthier parte of Chrift?

As the death of Chriftes flesh ONELIE doth more expreffe the TRVETH, POVVER, AND IVSTICE of God, then if the death of the foule had beene ioyned with it; fo the fame fetteth forth Chriftes merites, namelie his OBEDIENCE, PATIENCE, and LOVE in farre better forte, then if wee adde vnto it the death of the fpirite, which is the rewarde of all the reprobate and damned. For that a man vnwillinglie fuffereth, that sheweth neyther obedience, nor patience. Obedience hath readineffe; and patience, if it bee perfect, hath gladneffe; both haue willingneffe.

The bodilie death of chrift doth more cómend the merits of Chrift then if ý paines of hell were ioyned with it.

willingneſſe. If then wee bee forced againſt our willes to endure that which wee woulde gladlie auoide, it is violence; it is neither obedience nor patience; and conſequentlie it hath neither merite nor thankes with GOD. The death then of the ſoule, which is a ſeparation from the fauour and grace of God, did Chriſt ſuffer it willinglie, or vnwillinglie? if willinglie; there coulde bee no greater neglect of GOD, then to bee willing to bee ſeparated from God. It were diſobedience and inſolence in the higheſt degree, to be glad and forwarde to forſake God, or to bee forſaken of him. Chriſt therefore muſt not bee willing to ſuffer the death of the ſoule, leaſt wee wrap him within the compaſſe of contemning and reiecting the grace and fauour of GOD, which are ſinnefull enormities. Was hee vnwilling to ſuffer it? then coulde hee bee neither obedient, nor patient in ſuffering it. All vertue is voluntarie, compulſion hath no merite. [a] God loueth a cheerefull giuer, and ſufferer. Hee that murmureth, in heart rebelleth, though hee holde ſtill his tongue. So likewiſe I muſt aſke, if Chriſt ſuffered the death of the ſoule, did hee ſuffer it iuſtlie or vniuſtlie? if vniuſtlie: God could not be the ſole and immediate agent in impoſing it; and beſides God, no creature canne bereaue the ſoule of life. Did hee ſuffer it iuſtlie? then muſt hee be voide of all vertue; for nothing but ſinne deſerueth the death of the ſoule. Obedience and patience, merite thankes with God; and cannot wante the bleſſing of God: where the death of the ſoule is the greateſt curſe, that God inflicteth heere on earth.

And where they thinke it woulde greatelie increaſe the loue of Chriſt towardes vs if hee vouchſafed to taſte the death of the ſoule for our ſakes; I replie, that ſuppoſition woulde make Chriſt a ſinner, if not a lyar; which God forbid ſhoulde once enter our thoughtes. For firſt Chriſt ſaieth, [b] Greater loue then this hath no man,

P 2.   that

Margin notes:
In the death of the ſoule there could neither be obedience nor patience.

[a] 2. Corinth. 9.

It is no loue to renounce God for mans ſake.
[b] Iohn. 15

Rom.5

that one should laie downe his life for his friendes. But ᶜ God commendeth his loue towards vs; that whiles we were yet sinners Christ died for vs. If it be loue for a man to loose his soule for his friend, then is there found a greater loue, then Christ euer knew: for he saith, there is no greater loue the for a mã to laie downe his life. And the Apostle applying it to Christ saith, The height of Gods loue was this, that Christ died for sinners: that is, for his enemies, not for his friendes; sinne beeing enmitie to God, and sinners enemies to the holinesse of his will, and glory of his kingdome. This loue of Christ by which he died for vs, we reie as little worth, vnlesse hee endured the losse of Gods fauour for vs; which I take to bee sinne and not loue. For loue is due first and aboue all to God, then to men; this order of loue if we breake, it is no charitie, it is iniquitie. What doe all wicked ones, but preferre the loue of themselues, or of others, before the loue of God? to loue men so well, that wee ware willing to forsake the fauour and fellowship of God, is transgression against God, and not compassion towards men; and therefore wee maie not bring the sonne of God within the listes of this loue, no not for an houre; by reason the loue of God afore all others may not faile in the hart of Christ, not for a moment, bee it neuer so short.

Chrifts loue
towards vs in
dying for vs.

For our loue then he tooke flesh, when he was God; which was infinite humilitie; and gaue his life for his enemies, which was exceeding charitie; and in the course thereof referred himself wholie to the wil and pleasure of God, which was exact obedience; willinglie, but wrongfullie suffering, whatsoeuer the malice of Satan, and rage of the wicked contriued against him: the wise and gracious counsell of God so turning the mischiefe of the diuell and his members to the generall good of mankind, that Christes innocent and righteous bloud, being furiously and vniustly shed by the hands of his enemies, became the true sacrifice for sinne, and the full
price

price of mans redemption. Farther then this, if we will
force the ſonne of God with our fancies, as namelie to the
death or curſe of the ſoule, wee doe not onelie diminiſh the
ſtrength of his loue towardes God, but we debaſe the price
of his bloud; and make it rather deteſtable, then acceptable
in Gods ſight. For nothing can pleaſe God, but that which
is RIGHTEOVS, INNOCENT, HOLIE, ¶ VNDEFILED.
And in a dead or curſed ſoule what place leaue we for theſe
giftes and graces of the holie Ghoſt? Since then our high
Prieſt muſt be d holie, harmeleſſe, vndefiled, and ſeparate from
ſinners, before his ſacrifice coulde bee accepted; the ſoule of
Chriſt muſt neceſſarilie bee repleniſhed with all goodneſſe,
and embraced with all fauour, before the death of his bodie
could be an e offering of a ſweete ſauour vnto God: and ſo the
power of Chriſtes death is no whitte encreaſed, but alto-
gither weakened, if wee conioyne it with the death of the
ſoule.

  The death of the ſoule then doth not encreaſe the obe-
dience, patience, and loue of Chriſt towardes vs, but doth ra-
ther decreaſe and endanger all the vertues of our Sauiour.
For if Chriſt ſuffered the death of the ſoule, which is Gods
immediate action; ſince God will offer his owne ſonne
neither violence nor wrong; wee muſt confeſſe that Chriſt
deſerued the death of the ſoule, and admitted it as due vnto
him; to which abſurdities if wee come, wee leaue nothing
ſound in our ſaluation. Call we him iuſt that deſerueth, or
holie that deſireth to be forſaken of God? I thinke not. Then
all Chriſts ſufferings muſt be INIVRIOVS, before hee can
be IVST; and VOLVNTARIE, before they can be a SACRI-
FICE vnto God. Both which are witneſſed by the worde
of God, as likewiſe by the ancient fathers. THIS IS f THANK-
WORTHIE (ſaith Peter) if a man for conſcience towards God
endure grief, SVFFERING WRONGFVLLY. For what praiſe
is it, if when ye be BVFFETED for your FAVLTS, ye take it
PATIENTLIE? But if, when ye doe well, ye ſuffer patientlie,

d Heb. 7.

e Epheſ. 5.

All Chriſts
ſufferings were
INIVRIOVS in
reſpect of the
doers, and VO-
LVNTARIE in
reſpect of him
ſelfe.
f 1. Peter. 2.

this is acceptable vnto God. For hereunto are ye called : for s o
CHRIST SVFFERED FOR VS, leauing vs an example that
we should follow his steppes. Christ therfore suffered as well
VVRONGFVLLY AS PATIENTLY. Malefactors may be
patient, but that is no merit with God. He must be both in-
nocent and patient that will haue thanks from God. So was
Christ. g He did no sin, and so was innocent; g when he was re-
uiled, he reuiled not againe: when he suffered, he threatned not,
which proueth his patience. This verie testimonie, the theefe
on the crosse giueth him. h We receiue punishment worthie of
that we haue done; but this mā hath done nothing amisse. i *Quod
iuste debebat* Adam, *Christus iniuste mortem suscipiendo persol-
uit.* What *Adam* iustly owed (saith Austen) that Christ vniustlie
paied by suffering death. k *Pergit ad passionem, vt pro debitoribus
nobis quòd ipse nō debebat, exsolueret.* Christ goeth to his passion
to pay that for vs debtors , which bee did not owe. l *De huma-
nitate suscepta tantum beneficij collatum est hominibus, vt . à dei
sempiterno filio, eodemque hominis filio mors temporalis indebita
redderetur, qua eos a sempiternâ morte debitâ liberaret. Peccata
nostra Diabolus tenebat , & per illa nos merito figebat in mor-
te. Demisit ea ille, qui sua non habebat, & ab illo imme-
rito est perductus ad mortem : Tantum valuit sanguis ille,
vt neminem Christo indutum in eterna morte debita detinere
debuerit; qui Christum morte indebita vel ad tempus occi-
dit.* By Christ taking mans nature , this benefite men get,
that the eternall Sonne of God , and the same also the sonne
of man , suffered a temporall death not due, to deliuer
them from an euerlasting death due ; The Diuell laide sure
holde on our sinnes , and by them holde vs deseruedlie in
death. Those hee remitted, that had no sinnes of his owne;
and was without anie desert brought by the Diuell vnto death.
But such was the force of Christes bloud, that the Diuell had
no right to detaine anie man (that put on Christ) in eternall
death due, for so much as hee slue Christ with death for the
time, which was no way due. m *Mediator noster puniri pro se*
ipso

g 1. Pet. 2.

h Luke 23.

i *August. de tem-
pore, serm. 101.*

k *Idem de vini-
tate li. 13. ca. 14*

l *Ibid. cap. 16*

m *Greg. mora-
lium. li. 3. ca. 11.*

ipſo non debuit ∴ quia nullum culpæ contagium perpetrauit. Sed ſi ipſe indebitam mortem non ſuſciperet , nunquam nos à debita morte liberaret. Our Mediatour for himſelfe ought not to bee puniſhed, becauſe hee neuer ſinned . But if hee had not ſuffered a death not due , hee coulde neuer haue freed vs from the death that was due. If the tempozall death of the bodie were not due to our Sauiour , much leſſe was the death of the ſoule due vnto him . And if no death were due ; that which hee ſuffered was wrong-full. Then might God bee the permitter, directer, orderer, and accepter of Chꝛiſtes death on the Croſſe ; but hee coulde not bee the immediate inflicter of it, becauſe it was wrongfull and vndeſerued : much leſſe might GOD in iuſtice forſake his ſoule ; that with ſo great obedience, patience and innocencie humbled himſelfe to the will of his heauenlie father.

That likewiſe hee ſuffered nothing agaynſt his owne liking, his owne mouth teſtified when he ſaid. [n] *Nemo tollit animam meam à me, ſed pono eam à meipſo.* No man taketh my life from mee, but I lay it downe of my ſelfe . And elſe where. [o] The ſonne of God loued mee; and gaue himſelfe for mee. [p] Loue your wiues as Chriſt loued the Church , and gaue himſelfe for it. If it were loue , then was it no conſtraint, noꝛ violence , that foꝛced him thereto . If hee gaue himſelfe foꝛ vs; it muſt needes bee voluntarie whatſoeuer hee ſuffered . [q] *Demonſtrauit ſpiritus mediatoris quàm nulla pœna peccati vſque ad mortem carnis acceſſerit, quia non eam deſeruit inuitus, ſed* QVIA VOLVIT, QVANDO VOLVIT, QVOMODO VOLVIT . The ſpirite of the Mediator ſhewed that without anie puniſhment of ſinne it came euen to the death of the fleſh, which hee did not leaue agaynſt his will , but BECAVSE HE VVOVLDE, VVHEN HE VVOVLDE, AND HOVVE HE VVOVLDE. *Et* [r] *natus , & paſſus , & mortuus eſt, nulla ſua neceſſitate, ſed voluntate, & poteſtate .* Chriſt was borne , and ſuffered and

[a] Iohn. 10.

[o] Galat. 2.
[p] Epheſ. 5.

[q] Auguſt. de trinitat. li. 4. ca. 13.

[r] Auguſt. de fide contra Manicheos cap. 26.

and died, not for anie necessitie that vrged him, but of his owne will, and hauing it in his owne power. If Christ might suffer nothing but what hee woulde, and as hee would; the death of the soule hee did neuer suffer; for thereto hee coulde not be willing without sinne, by reason it is a separation from God, and a losse both of his heauenlie fauour, and holie spirite, from which Christ willinglie would neuer be excluded.

The summe is, since the TRVTH and IVSTICE of God might not release the sin of man, without fulfilling the sentence of the Iudge, THOV SHALT DIE THE DEATH, and that by man; for so much as man was the trespasser: God so loued the world, when none of the sonnes of Adam was able to restore his owne soule, much lesse to ransome others; that hee sent his owne sonne to become man ; and as by the dignitie and puritie of his person to counteruaile and ouerweigh the soules of all men ; so by his paines and death on the Crosse, to verifie and satisfie the iudgement of God pronounced against man, and to quit him from all danger following death. And to trie the obedience, shew the patience, and augment the merits of the Redeemer, the wisedome of God decreed, that his sonne in our substance should violentlie and wrongfullie bee put to death euen by their handes, for whose sakes he laid downe his life; that his loue might so much the more exceede in praying for his persecutours, and dying for his tormentors. The shame and sharpenesse of the crosse, so iniuriouslie imposed on the holinesse, and worthinesse of Christes person, and yet so obedientlie and patientlie endured by him, God so highlie esteemed, and recompenced, that hee made his death the ransome of all mankinde, and his bloud to bee the purgation and propitiation of our sinnes: his obedience wyping awaie our disobedience; his fauour quenching the displeasure ; his blessednesse altering the curse ; his death finishing the vengeance that was due to our iniquities. This is the manner and merit of Christs

suffering

The recapitulation of ỹ maner and merit of Christs death.
ſ Gen. 2.
‖ Iohn. 3.

ſuffering death on the croſſe, to ſaue vs from the wrath of God, that was kindled againſt our tranſgreſſions. And ſince the ſcriptures mention none other meanes of our redemption but the DEATH and BLOVD of the SONNE of God, I hold them wiſeſt, that leaue deuiſing any better or other help for our ſaluation then God himſelfe hath reuealed. And as for the death of the ſoule, I take that to be the greateſt hinderance that may be to the worke of our redemption, and to ſhake the verie foundation of our faith and hope in the croſſe of Chriſt. Which leaſt I ſhould ſeeme to ſay, & no way to proue: let vs view the COMFORT of Chriſtes croſſe, and thereby ſee howe his ſoule was affected towardes God, euen whiles his bodie ſuffered that grieuous, and opprobrious death of the croſſe.

I haue often muſed what made men of great learning and iudgement otherwiſe, to ſwarue ſo much from the plain tenor of the ſcriptures; and to imagine in the ſoule of our ſauiour, ſuch doubt and feare of Gods fauour, ſuch horrors and torments of hell, that they ſticke not to match them with the paines of the damned; conſidering there is no manifeſt ground, nor euident proofe of ſo dangerous doctrine in the word of God: but contrariwiſe, when the ſcriptures deſcribe Chriſt on the croſſe, they propoſe his bodie martyred with al kinde of crueltie, but his ſoule cleauing to God, with all perfection of conſtancie. Read the xvi. and xxii. Pſalme. who will, which purpoſelie treate of Chriſtes paſſion; and tell mee whether there bee ſo much as a worde importing anie diſtruſt of Gods fauour, or anie ſuſpicion of the paines of hell ſuffered in the ſoule of Chriſt? [The firſt entrance of the xxii. Pſalme, you will ſay is, "My God, my God, whie haſt thou forſaken me?] This is that Helen, that hath bewitched the world; I meane the miſconſtruing of theſe words. Of which though I haue ſpoken before, as much as may content any man that is not faſtned to his fancies, more then to the truth; yet let vs ſhortlie ſee whether the reſt of the

The comfort of Chriſts croſſe taken out of the 22. Pſalme.

"Pſalm. 22.

D   Pſalme

Psalme admit their new found exposition, o: no. It followeth in the same place. ˣ Thou didst bring me out of my mothers wombe; thou gauest mee confidence at my mothers breasts. ʸ On thee was I cast from my birth. THOV ART MY GOD FROM MY MOTHERS BELLIE. ᶻ Bee not farre from mee, for trouble is neere, and there is none to helpe. ᵃ Bee not farre, O Lord my strength: hasten to helpe me. ᵇ I will declare thy name vnto my brethren, in the midst of the congregation, I will praise thee, ᶜ for HE HATH NOT DESPISED, nor abhorred the weakenesse, or basenesse of the poore: neither HATH HE HID HIS FACE FROM HIM; but when he called vnto him HE HEARD HIM. Is this the praier of a man whose soule is forsaken of God? Did he doubt of Gods fauour, that with such confidence pronounced, Thou gauest me assurance at my mothers breasts, thou art my God from my mothers belly? Was he perswaded that god had refused and left him when as he saith, God hath not DESPISED ŷ weaknes of the poore: he hath not hid his face from him; when he called, God heard him? If these be flat contradictions to their imaginations, why wrest they the first verse to euert all the rest? Christ therfore in the beginning of the Psalm might well complain that god had for the time of his passion withheld his PROTECTION, or diminished his CONSOLATION; but in no wise that God had decreased his loue, or shut vp his fauor towards the humane soule of his sonne. Yea the next words are an explication of the former. Why hast thou forsaken me, ᵈ and art so farre from mine helpe? Not to helpe in trouble is to forsake, though God bee not angrie with the soules of such as suffer affliction. The very words agree, to GO FARRE OFF frō a man, is to FORSAKE HIM; so he that desireth God not to be far off, praieth not to be forsaken; but rather to receiue helpe in time of need. Merilie S. Ambroses iudgement and reason doth satisfie me, whatsoeuer it doth others. ᵉ *Ille nunquam derelictus est à patre, cum quo pater semper erat. Sed secundum corpus; in quo traditus est passioni vox ista processit; quoniam derelinqui nobis*

ᵍVerf 9.

ʸ 10
ᶻ 11

ᵃ 19
ᵇ 22
ᶜ 24

ᵈ Verf. 1.

ᵉ Ambrof. in Pfal. 118. fer. 1.

nobis videmur, quando ſumus in periculis conſtituti . Chriſt
was neuer forſaken of his Father , with whome the father
alwayes was ; but this complaint came from his bodie,
which was left to ſuffer death , for ſo much as wee thinke
our ſelues forſaken when wee are oppreſſed with anie trou-
bles.

If the xxii. Pſalme content vs not, let vs examine the
ſixteenth, and there marke that the holie Ghoſt doth attri-
bute to the ſoule of Chriſt in the middes of his ſufferings
on the Croſſe ; and then iudge which opinion draweth nea-
reſt to the truth of the ſacred Scriptures. f I haue alwayes
SET the Lord BEFORE ME ; for hee IS AT MY RIGHT
HAND THAT I SHOVLD NOT BE SHAKEN, therefore my heart is
glad, & my tongue reioiceth; my fleſh alſo ſhall REST IN HOPE.
Becauſe thou wilt not leaue my ſoule in hell, nor ſuffer thine ho-
lie one to ſee corruptiō. Thou wilt SHEVV ME THE VVAY OF LIFE;
THE FVLNES OF IOY IS IN THY PRESENCE, and delectation at thy
right hand for euer.   Three plentifull and wonderfull graces
of the holie Ghoſt are here deſcribed in our Sauiour, as he
hung on the croſſe, in the middeſt of his miſeries; abundance
of FAITH, aſſurance of HOPE, perſiſtance in IOY . The ground
of our faith is the truth of Gods word, ſealed in our hearts,
by the working of his ſpirite.   The faith of Chriſt had a
farre ſtronger foundation, and clearer reuelation , then ours
can poſſiblie haue. He was hoped for by the Patriarks, ſear-
ched after by the Prophets; he was the end of all the lawe,
and truth of all the former teſtament. He was ſerued by An-
gels, acknowledged by ſtarres, ſeas, windes, beaſts, fiſhes, and
trees ; hee was obeyed by diſeaſes, death and diuels, the holie
Ghoſt viſiblie deſcended on him when hee was baptiſed,
the father by thunder from heauen often proclaimed him to
be his welbeloued ſonne, and commaunded all men to heare
him; he knewe the thoughts of mens hearts, yea the ſecrets
of heauen; he was transfigured in the Mount, and taſted of
that heauenlie glorie prepared for him. The confeſſing him
to

The ſame out
of the 16.
Pſalme.
f Pſal. 16.

The ground of
Chriſts faith.

to bee the sonne of God, openeth heauen, preuaileth agaynst hell, supporteth his Church, and obtaineth blessednes. This he heard with his eares, sawe with his eyes, and wrought with his hands: yea, he spake with his mouth, & knew in his heart that God had sanctified him, and sent him to saue the world. I aske now a meane diuine; was it possible that Christ Iesus after all this intelligence, euidence and experience both of his owne person who he was, and of his fathers loue and purpose, how setled, determined, and euerlasting it was, should feare or doubt, least he should be forsaken, or want the fauor and help of god in those afflictions, which he willingly suffered for our safetie: For vs to distrust or doubt Gods promise côfirmed by his word, & perswaded to our spirits by his spirit, is diffidêce and incredulitie. What hainous and horrible sinne then were it for the soule of Christ, after so cleare perspicuitie, so full certaintie, so firme stabilitie of Gods COVNSEL AND PROMISE, OATH & PERFORMANCE, that in him all nations of the earth should be blessed: to haue so much as a feare, doubt, or thought, that God would faile him, or forsake him? Let me fatherlie aduise, and brotherly intreate you all in the bowels of Christ Iesus, that you take good heed how you venter on any such doctrine. Ioine rather with S. Peter, and stedfastlie beleeue, that Dauid spake concerning Christ, when he said: ^g I saw the Lord alwayes before me, for he is at my right hande, that I should not be mooued. If ALVVAIES, then was there no intermission: If BEFORE HIS FACE, then was there no obscuration: If AT HIS RIGHT HAND, then God was neuer absent: If hee COVLD NOT BE MOOVED, then could he not be forsaken.

[But Christ himselfe sayth, he was forsaken?] hee doth not say he was forsaken, either in soule, or else of Gods fauour and grace, as some in our dayes woulde faine make him speake: but he saith, My God, my God, why hast thou forsaken me? And his words stand true, if any kind of dereliction be confessed. ^h *Quasi quædam ibi dereliction fuit, vbi nulla fuit in tanta*

g Act. 2.

h *Bernard de verbis Esaiæ serm. 5.*

tanta neceſſitate virtutis exhibitio ; nulla maieſtatis oſtenſio.
There was on the croſſe a kind of forſaking ; in as much as there
was in ſo great neceſſitie, no declaring of his power; no ſhew-
ing of his maieſtie. Diuers other kindes of forſaking may
bee verie well allowed and beleeued in the ſufferings of our
Sauiour; but that he ſhould be deſtitute of FAITH, HOPE,
LOVE, or IOY, or forſaken of Gods FAVOVR, GRACE, or
SPIRIT, that is ſo dangerous to the office, and pernicious to
the perſon of Chriſt, that it may in no wiſe bee admitted.
[i] Whatſoeuer is not of faith is ſinne. Then howe much we de-
creaſe faith in Chriſt, ſo much wee increaſe ſinne in Chriſt.
WAVERING, STICKING, DOVBTING are all rebate-
ments of faith, and degrees of diffidence, and greater ſinnes
in Chriſt, then in any other man, becauſe of his infallible
REVELATION FROM GOD, vnſpeakeable FRVITI-
ON OF GOD, and inſeparable COMMVNION WITH
GOD. [k] *Modica fidei, quare dubitaſti?* O thou of LITTLE
faith, why diddeſt thou DOVBT? ſaith Chriſt to Peter. Then
doubting is the diminiſhing of faith. [l] Abraham (ſaieth the
Apoſtle) did not DOVBT of the promiſe of God THROVGH
VNBELIEFE; but was ſtrengthned in faith, and gaue the glo-
rie vnto God; being fullie aſſured, that hee which had promiſed,
was able to performe it. Then doubting, by the expreſſe rule
of the holie ghoſt is VNBELIEFE; and a DISHONOR VN-
TO GOD, as if he were not able to make good his promiſe.
So that wee muſt in ſpite of our heartes either CLEERE
CHRIST FROM DOVBTING, or CHARGE HIM WITH
VNBELEEVING, and DISHONOVRING GOD. [m] If any
man lacke wiſedome (ſaith Iames) let him aske of God, and it
ſhall be giuen him: but let him aske in faith, and not doubt, (or
diſpute with himſelfe,) for he that doubteth, is like a waue of the
Sea, toſt with the winde; neither let that man thinke he ſhall re-
ceaue any thing of the Lorde. Doubtfulneſſe differeth from
incredulitie in this, that the incredulous as yet beleeueth
not: the doubtful wauereth betwixt faith and infidelitie; as

Marginal notes:
[i] Rom. 14

Doubting of
Gods fauour is
ſinne in Chriſt

[k] Matth. 14.

[l] Rom. 4.

[m] Iacob. 1.

a waue of the sea doth, that is tost with the winde, enclining sometimes one way, sometimes another way. But this man for his inconstancie, shall obtaine nothing at Gods haiues, whose truth when we but DOVBT wee DENIE; and whose promise when wee DISPVTE wee DISBELEEVE. The soule of Christ then maie not bee touched VVITH ANIE DOVBT, much lesse distrust of Gods fauour and loue towards him, and to imagine or affirme so much of Christes person, is to drawe him within the compasse of inconstancie, infidelitie, and Apostasie from GOD; which I assure my selfe, no Christian Diuine will attempt or endure.

Feare is more intolerable in Christ then doubting.

If the humane soule of Christ must bee so setled and resolued in faith, that it might not doubt of Gods fauour; much lesse might it be perplexed or amazed with the feare, terror, or sense of Gods displeasure against himselfe, as our suretp. For to that ende did it please the sonne of God to take our nature into the unitie of his person, that it shoulde utterlie bee impossible for sinne, death, or hell to separate. us from him, or him from God. Whereof because hee was infalliblie assured, hee must needes be throughlie perswaded, and in that perfect perswasion, knowledge, and assurance of Gods euerlasting purpose, fauour, and loue towardes him, that he should be the Sauiour of the world, if doubting bee not tolerable, howe inexcuseable is feare and terror, as if hee were forsaken of God? which could not bee, except God would breake his promise; and othe. giuen to Abraham and Dauid, and falsifie his truth expressed with his own voice from heauen; yea, and reuerse his eternall counsell and decree, forespoken by the mouthes of so many Prophets, confirmed with so manie miracles, and executed and accomplished so euidentlie in the birth of our Sauiour. The soule of Christ must therefore bee farre from fearing or doubting, least God woulde change his minde, recall his worde, frustrate his promise, and violate his oath; for these are blasphemies against
God

God in the higest degrée; wee must rather receaue Saint Peters assertion out of Dauid, that Christ did.[n] ALWAIES see God on HIS RIGHT HANDE that hee shoulde NOT BEE MOOVED; And therefore his heart was gladde, and his tongue ioyfull: yea, wee must not onelie leaue him faith, but so perpetuall, constant, and strong, that nothing might shake it, or abate it. For if wee giue vnto men faith that shal withstand, and conquere al temptations, much more must we allow the Sauior of the world faith, as farre aboue ours, in validitie, stability, and certainty, as the rest of his virtues and graces exceede the measure of our gifts. As therefore in wisdome and holines, power and prudence, counsell and strength, righteousnesse and faithfulnesse, no creature might excéed the humane soule of Christ; so in patience and assurance, hope and loue, courage and confidence no earthlie wight might come néere him. For hee had the [o] fulnesse of Gods spirite, as much as the creature was capable of; we haue but a portion according to the [p] measure of the gifte of Christ. Since then [q] God did not giue him the spirit by measure, it is an euident absurditie, if not impietie, to diminish his faith with doubting, his loue with feare, his hope with horrour of reiection, alienation, or separation from GOD; but as constant faith STAGGERETH NOT, perfect loue FEARETH NOT, assured hope TREMBLETH NOT; so the faith, hope, and loue of Christ must not stumble at anie of these stones, much lesse make such a shipwracke of faith and hope, as if hee DID ALMOST PERSWADE HIMSELFE that hee was DROWNED, and PERISHED in the gulfe of perdition.

[n] Acts.2.
[o] Iohn. 1.
[p] Ephes.4
[q] Iohn 3.

[But the vehemencie of paine (some thinke) might for the time wrest frō Christ the remembrāce of Gods eternal decree & promise, & so shake ȳ perswasion otherwise settled in his hart ȳ God had sworne he would not faile Dauid.] I had rather confesse mine ignorāce in not vnderstanding, then shew any

Christ was not amazed on the Crosse.

skill

skill in refelling this answere. It is true that a mightie feare may so affect a man for the time, that it shall hinder the sences from recouering themselues, and stop the faculties from informing one the other. But this must bee some suddaine obiect astonishing the heart; and so terrible that it suffereth vs not presentlie to gather our wits together, and to consider of it. But what is this to our purpose? was Christ in a traunce on the crosse? and so continued eightteen houres, from his entering into the garden after supper, to the ending of his life the next daie at three of the clocke after noone? and all this while so affrighted and amazed that hee could not remember he was the sonne of God, and sent to redeeme the world? his words and deedes at his apprehension, at his examination before the chiefe Priestes and Elders, at his condemnation by Pilate, at his crucifixion and expiration doe they make anie proofe, or giue anie signe of a man in a maze? when hee boldelie professed himselfe before the high Priest [r] TO BE THE SONNE OF GOD; when he tolde Pilate as well the cause why [s] HE WAS BORNE, as the place whence he had [t] POWVER OVER HIM; when hee warned the women of Ierusalem TO [u] VVEEPE FOR THEMSELVES and their children; when hee praied for his persecutors, as [x] NOT KNOVVING VVHAT THEY DID, and promised PARADISE to the penitent thiefe that hung by him; when he bequeathed the care of his [y] MOTHER to the fidelitie of his DISCIPLE, and [z] COMMENDED HIS SPIRIT into the handes of his father; was his memorie or vnderstanding taken from him by feare in anie of these actions? or doe we not rather see his death answerable to his life, that is full of constancie, clemencie, fidelitie and pietie? If anie be otherwise minded, God graunt they be not in a deepe traunce of selfe-liking: that will rather challenge Christes memorie, then suspect their owne fanfie. Coulde he forget himselfe to be the sonne of God, that so often and openlie called God his FATHER? that in the heate of his agonie

[r] Mark.14.
[s] Iohn.18
[t] Iohn.19
[u] Luke.23

[x] Luke.23.

[y] Iohn.19
[z] Luke.23

agony praying vſed none other ſtile, but a O MY FATHER? that in the counſell of the Scribes and Elders woulde not conceale himſelfe to be b THE SONNE OF GOD, no not to ſaue his life, but ſaid b I AM the ſonne of the bleſſed? that dying committed his ſpirit to his c FATHERS HANDS? he remembred to call for drinke, that the d ſcripture might bee fulfilled; and d knew that all things touching him were performed; and had he forgotten who he was, or why he came into the world, euen e to ſaue that which was loſt?

　And in all good ſort to admoniſh them that are learned, to looke a little better, before they reſolue on ſo ſtrange a concluſion in diuinitie; if wee put Chriſt in ſuch a maze on the croſſe, that for feare he forgate his fathers counſell, purpoſe, promiſe, voice, and oath; yea his own function, vnion and perſon: what obedience or patience, what humility or charitie do we leaue him, in ſuffering the death of the croſſe? what vertue find we, where remembrance faileth? or what merite is it for a man to be amazed? how hangeth this with their owne poſition, that the ſenſe and ſuffering of Gods wrath in the ſoule of Chriſt is the chiefeſt and principalleſt part of our redemption? is it ſo materiall for mans ſaluation, as they affirme, and can it not be maintained but by taking from Chriſt both iudgement and memorie? is this that great myſterie of deuotion, which true religion may not endure, except wee ſuppoſe the ſonne of God to be for feare beſides himſelfe? haue they not ſpun a faire thread, to be ſo zealous for Chriſts ſuffering the verie paines of hell, here on earth, and when all is done, their aſſertion cannot bee ſaued from impietie, but by caſting Chriſt into a fit of a Lethargie? for that God was in deede angrie, and offended with his owne ſonne, is odious and enormous blaſphemie. That Chriſt ſo conceaued, and perſwaded himſelfe, or ſo diſſembled, when there was no ſuch cauſe; chargeth the ſonne of God not onelie with falſitie, but with infidelitie. To decline both theſe miſchiefes there is no meane left, but to ſaie, that the verie force of paine made

Marginal notes:
a Matth. 26
b Marke. 14
c Luke 23.
d Iohn. 19
e Matth. 18

The ſufferings of Chriſt are no way meritorious, if he were in a trace al the while he hung on the croſſe.

Chꝛiſt foꝛget both his owne perſon, and his Fathers eter-
nall counſell and loue towardes him; which is to tie one
abſurditie with an other . Foꝛ though by this maze they
excuſe Chꝛiſt from ſinne, as being neither aduiſed, noꝛ ſuffe-
red by feare to be maſter of himſelfe; yet by the ſame they ex-
clude him from all the graces and vertues of his paſſion, on
which our ſaluation is grounded; and leaue him as without
memoꝛie, ſo without merite; ſince the faculties of the mind,
ouerwhelmed and aſtoniſhed with feare oꝛ paine, haue no full
apprehenſion, much leſſe iuſt deliberation, and leaſt of all free
election of good and euil. In which caſe if we ſuppoſe our Sa-
uiour to haue bin during his ſuffering on the croſſe we ſhew
our ſelues to be void of all vnderſtanding, in that we cleaue
to our own fanſies againſt the wittnes both of nature & ſcrip-
ture. Read who liſt the maner of Chꝛiſts praying, anſwering &
ſuffering, before & at his death; & tel me wherin he ſhewed any
defect of iudgment, oꝛ want of remēbꝛing? Peter ſaith, Chriſt
ſuffered for vs, leauing vs an example, that we ſhould follow his
ſteps. If he were ſtroken with feare beſides himſelfe, it is a
bad example foꝛ vs to follow. But in deede he neither did, noꝛ
ſpake anie thing, no not in the mids of his paines, but verie
aduiſedlie, quietly, religiouſly, & obediently; ſuch as might wel
beſeeme the Sauiour of the woꝛld, humbled in our fleſh, and
chaſtiſed foꝛ our ſinnes, but no way partner of our impatient
and ſinnefull affections.

He wauered (ſome thinke) in his pꝛaiers; and corrected
himſelfe as ouerſhot, in that he aſked at his fathers hands:]
ſuch holdfaſt they take of his woꝛdes, that faine would haue
his wittes amazed with their imagined fears and horrour
of hell fire. But by their patience, their expoſitions muſt
not looke to bee canonicall in the church of God. If they
ſaie anie thing well, wee take it with their pꝛayſe; if o-
therwiſe as men, they miſſe their marke, wee refuſe it with
their leaues. God hath called vs vnto libertie, not to be
ſeruantes of men; and to ſerue erroneous conſtructions, is
woꝛſe

f 1.Peter.2

Chriſt wauered
not in his prai-
ers in ỹ garden

g Galat.5
h 2.Corinth.7

woꝛſe than to beare tyrannous exactions. Was Chꝛiſt vn-
aduiſed in his pꝛaiers in the garden? and did hee reuoke that
which ſuddainly ſlipt from him? All pꝛaier without faith is ſin
in Gods ſight. What then was Chꝛiſts pꝛaier, if it were diſ-
realie bent againſt the determined purpoſe, and reuealed
will of God, but euident ſinne? His thꝛiſe repeating [i] the ſelfe
ſame words with good diſtance of time betwéene, and aduiſed
and vehement zeale, what was it, if it ſtill needed to bee re-
uoked and amended, but a voluntary ſpurning at the ſtedfaſt
decrée and eternall counſell of God foꝛ mans redemption?
But god foꝛbid, we ſhould ſo côceiue of our ſauioꝛ, as if there
were in his deeds, woꝛds oꝛ thoughts the leaſt inclination to
contradict his fathers reſolution. He was not onely patient
without refuſing, but obedient without miſliking his fathers
will. Eſay ſaith of him. [k] He was oppreſſed and afflicted, yet did
hee not open his mouth. Hee was brought as a ſheepe to the
ſlaughter, and as a Lambe is dumbe before his ſhearer, ſo ope-
ned hee not his mouth. Doth the holie ghoſt giue him this
teſtimonie, that hee mildelie and ſilentlie bare all the
oppꝛeſſions and afflictions, that were laide on him, and
ſhall we dare auouch, that hee vehementlie and often ſtrug-
gled, and ſtriued in his pꝛaiers againſt the knowne will of
his Father; and ſought by all meanes to decline the
woꝛke foꝛ which hee came into the woꝛlde? [His fleſh
(they will ſaie,) feared death, though his ſpirit ſubmit-
ted it ſelfe to the will of his heauenlie Father.] As if
his fleſh did pꝛaie, and not his ſpirite? if then his pꝛaiers
were paſſionate and vnaduiſed, his ſpirit cannot bee ex-
cuſed from conſenting and yeelding thereto. And where do
we learne that Chꝛiſtes fleſh refuſed the lawe of his minde,
and ſo pꝛeuailed againſt the ſpirite, that it wꝛeſted from
him inconſiderate and diſobedient thoughtes, and woꝛdes?
oꝛ when wee thus ſaie, doe wee not plainelie bꝛing the
ſonne of GOD within the communion of our ſinnefull
coꝛruption?

R 2　　　　But

[l] Matth.26.
verſe 44.

[k] Eſay. 53

Christ praied often and earnestly but with full assurance to be heard,
'Hebre 5.

[But his spirit was amazed with feare, and so hee knewe not what he praied.] We take to much vpõ vs to put Christ besides himselfe, when it pleaseth vs. His praiers in the garden were zealous, but religious; vehement, but reuerent; mournesul, but faithful. He offered vp [1] strong cries and teares, but HE VVAS HEARD in that he asked; and so long as God performed, what Christ desired, it is more then presumption to chalenge his praiers as inconstant and wauering. For my part though I could not conceiue the sense of Christes praier in the garden, yet do I fully resolue he was most assured in faith, his praier should take effect. His oftē repeating the same words, noteth how great a thing hee requested at his fathers hands, which yet he obtained, though it were neuer so great. That which you call a reuocation, I take to bee a limitation, wherby Christ declared, he neuer ment to aske or haue any thing against his fathers liking; nor in any sort to prefer his owne choise or ease, before his fathers will. If this be a trance, then faith and obedience are no fruits of Gods spirit, but fits of a distempered humor, and in the end we shall conclude godlines to be madnes. For greater submissiõ or more deuotiõ, then Christ vttered in that agony, can no man shew. If therfore we condemne this as a maze in Christ, when that zealous and deuout persons be in their wits.

=Mark.14. verse.33. Christ might at the first be abashed with Gods maiesty, or mans misery; but he recouered himselfe before he entered into his praiers.

[But the scripture saith, he was ᵐ AFRIGHTED, & ASTONISHED.] The liuely beholding of Gods maiesty, or mãs misery might both afright & astonish his humane nature on the suddaine, but presently, recollecting himselfe, he fell to be content and intentiue praier, and therein continued almost an houre, not warbling in his wordes, nor wauering in his petitions or affections; but perseuering in the same minde, & in the same matter, till he obtained his desire. Nowe to be abashed at Gods presence, declared his pietie: and to bee stricken at the heart with the feeling of vengeance prouided for vs, commended his charitie. Lay these two, deuotion to God, and compassion towards men, as the grounds & causes

of his Agonie, and you shall easily cleare this soule heape of
absurdities and impieties, that now pursueth the contrarie
position . It is humilitie for mans infirmitie to shake and
tremble at the appearance of Gods glorie. It is mercie, to
stand defixed and euen astonished with the sense and griefe of
mans finall iudgement and eternall punishment. From this
fountaine, that is from the meditation of the diuine Maie-
stie, and commiseration of humane miserie; if we deriue the
HEAVINES of heart, FEARE and ASTONISHMENT,
which Christ suffered or shewed in his agony, we can do him
no wrong; because the more violent, the more eminent signes
they were of submission to God, and compassion on man: his
faith and loue not being oppressed with stupiditie, but infla-
med with such vehemencie, that the weakenesse of mans flesh
not able to followe the readinesse of his spirit, rauished with
a wonderfull feruencie to giue himselfe to saue the world,
might for the time faile in the exteriour actions, and offices
of the bodie. But we must beware that we continue not this
astonishment, when he came to his praiers. For in praier the
heart must be, not onelie prepared and aduised, but sincerelie
affected and wholie deuoted to aske nothing, but that which
tendeth to Gods glorie, and agreeth with Gods will. He that
otherwise asketh anie thing at Gods hands, prayeth not, but
presumptuouslie tempteth God, and seeketh to make the
wisedome and power of God seruiceable to his corrupt ap-
petites. You knowe not what you aske, said Christ to the
sonnes of Zebedee, when he refused their petition, and repro-
ued their follie. How shall we beleue, wee shall receiue, if
we aske we knowe not what? Faith must be rightlie direc-
ted, and throughlie perswaded, before it can obtaine. Christes
prayers then in the garden were neither abrupt without
sense, nor wauering without faith, that they needed bee excu-
sed or corrected; but his deuotion was instant, and perswa-
sion constant that he should preuaile; and therefore hee ceased
not to aske the selfe same thing thrise, till hee was heard, and

K 3 streng-

How and why
Christ might
be rauished.

Mat. 20.

ſtrengthened by an Angel from heauen.

[He aſked that, they will ſay, which was not granted.]
I am reſolutelie of another minde . My reaſons are,
firſt the Apoſtle ſayeth . ᵒ HE VVAS HEARD offering
vp ſtrong cries and teares . Secondlie , Chriſt himſelfe
ſayeth; ᵖ Father I thanke thee, becauſe thou haſt heard me.
I knowe THOV HEAREST ME ALVVAYES. And howe
coulde it be otherwiſe? For if he prayed according to the
will of God , he muſt needes bee heard; and agaynſt the
will of God bee neither did, nor woulde praie. For that
were ſinne in him, that was not ignorant of Gods will,
both determined and reuealed. And God forbid, we ſhould
bee ſo wicked, as to ſay or thinke, that Chriſt would thriſe in
moſt earneſt prayer , impugne his fathers will ſo well
knowne, and ſo often foretolde by his owne mouth. I be-
lieue rather his owne report of himſelfe; for hee coulde
not lie. ᑫ I doe nothing (ſayde hee) of my ſelfe, but as my
father hath taught mee , ſo ſpeake I theſe thinges. For hee
that ſent mee is with mee : the Father hath not left mee a-
lone, becauſe I DOE ALVVAYES the thinges , THAT
PLEASE HIM. Though I beare recorde of my ſelfe, my
recorde is true ; FOR I KNOVVE VVHENCE I CAME,
AND VVHITHER I GOE. As hee coulde not bee ig-
norant, ſo coulde hee not bee forgetfull of his Fathers
counſell and decree . The glorie of God might appall
him at the entrance into his prayers : but his conſtant
continuing one and the ſame requeſt to his Father
three ſeuerall turnes ; with intermiſſion of time , and ad-
monition to his Diſciples to watch and praie , prooueth
hee had not forgotten himſelfe, that ſtill perſiſted in his
purpoſe ; nor yet ſtriued agaynſt his Fathers will,
in that his prayer was accepted, and aſſured from hea-
uen.

[Did then the cup paſſe from him ; which was the ſumme
of his prayer?] No doubt it did in that ſenſe which he deſired.

The

The cup mingled by Gods iuſt iudgment for the ſin of man, did paſſe both from him, and vs, by force of his prayer; not that hee did not taſte of it, but in that yeelding himſelfe to the temporall and corporall chaſticement thereof, hee quenched the ſpirituall and eternall vengeance, that was conſequent after death: the aboliſhing whereof was a worke worthie of the ſonne of God; and a memorable effect of that earneſt and inſtant prayer, which our Sauiour made in the Garden, thereby ſhutting vp hell, and opening heauen to all his members. And for that cauſe the Prophet Eſay ioyneth his patient ſuffering and vehement praying, as needfull groundes of our redemption; hee bare the ſinne of manie, and ʳ PRAYED for the TRESPASSERS: and the Apoſtle reckoneth Chriſts ſ PRAYERS OFFERED VVITH TEARES, and his paines ſuffered through obedience as principall parts of his Prieſthood, and effectuall ſacrifices for the ſinnes of the people.

ʳ Eſay. 53.

ſ Hebr. 5.

As praying in the garden Chriſt muſt be free from forgetting either his fathers will or loue, ſo ſuffering on the croſſe he muſt haue not onely patience and obedience, but intelligence & aſſurance that the bloody ſacrifice, which he offered, ſhould be accepted as the propitiation for our ſinnes, and himſelfe exalted from the ſhame and paine of the croſſe to euerlaſting honour, ioy, and glorie. He did not offer himſelfe on the altar of the croſſe, ſuppoſing or preſuming it might pleaſe God thereby to be fauourable vnto man; but as hee came into the world, annointed and ſent of purpoſe to ſaue his people from their ſinnes, ſo did hee ᵗ humble himſelfe to the death of the Croſſe, beeing thereto appoynted by his heauenlie father; and therefore moſt aſſured that God was immutablie determined to accept his ſacrifice for the ſin of the world, and ˣ by the bloud of his croſſe to ſet at peace thinges both in heauen and in earth: and to reconcile vs that were ſtraungers and enemies in euill woorkes, through death in the bodie of his fleſh, to make vs holie and without fault in

Chriſt on the croſſe muſt be aſſured his ſacrifice ſhould be accepted.

ᵗ Matt. 1.
ˣ Phil. 2.

ˣ Coloſ. 1.

in the sight of God . This Saint Paule saith was Gods
ᵞ GOOD PLEASVRE, to which Christ was ᶻ OBEDIENT, &
therefore neither ignorant of it, nor doubtfull in it; but assured-
lie resolued with fulnesse of faith and hope, that he which had
decreed it, could not be changed; and that God which had
sent him, would not deceiue him. And for that cause the Apo-
stle maketh the death of Christ to be a ᵃ SACRIFICE OF
A SWEET SMELLING SAVOVR VNTO GOD; and
saith, that ᵇ Iesus the authour & finisher of our faith, FOR THE
IOY WHICH WAS SET BEFORE HIM, endured the
crosse, and despised the shame, (thereof) and is placed on the
right hand of the throne of God. So that howsoeuer late wri-
ters haue found out the terror of Gods wrath, and horror of
eternall death in the soule of Christ suffering; the Apostle tea-
cheth vs, that Christ hanging in the shame and paine of the
crosse, had not onelie peace and fauour with god, as offering a
sweet smelling sacrifice, but also ioy before his eies of euerla-
sting glory at the right hand of ẏ throne of God. And with him
agree both Peter & Dauid, when they bare witnes of Christ,
that his HEART WAS GLAD, HIS TONGVE IOIFVL,
and that euen ᶜ HIS FLESH should REST IN HOPE, not-
withstanding the anguish of death, force of the graue, and fury
of hell. For God would neither forsake his soule in hell, nor
suffer his flesh to see corruption.

Dare anie man doubt of this doctrine, which is so cleare-
lie and fullie deliuered vs in the Scriptures ? Or make
wee a pastime of it, in fauour of our fansies to ouer-
turne the verie principles of truth? ᵈ Christ suffered
for vs, leauing vs an example, that wee shoulde followe his
steppes. For if ᵉ wee suffer with him, wee shall bee glorified
with him. Must we suffer the paines of the damned, afore we
may hope to be partakers of his glorie? The gaine which
we haue in Christ, when we haue refused all thinges
as vile for his sake, is to knowe the fellowshippe of his
afflictions, and to bee conformed vnto his death; if by
anie

ᵞ Colos.1.
vers.19. & 20
ᶻ Phil.2. ver. 8.

ᵃ Ephe.5.

ᵇ Heb.12.

ᶜ Acts.2.
ᶠ Psal.16.

We must suffer
as Christ did;
which I hope
is not the
paines of hell.
ᵈ 1.Pet.2.
ᵉ Rom.8.

ᶠ Phil.3.

anie meanes wee may attaine to the refurrection of the deade. Shall the communion of Chriftes fufferings bring vs to the true torments of hell, and muft wee perfwade our felues that wee are forfaken of God, afore wee can bee conformed to his death? g Reioyce (fayth Peter,) when yee doe communicate with Chriftes fufferings. Muft wee then RE IOICE **g** 1 Peter. 4. in the horror of hell, and bee glad of Gods difpleafure towards vs? I thinke not. Howe farre fuller of comfort is the Apoftles doctrine, where he faith; h As the fufferinges of **h** 2. Cor. 1. Chrift abound in vs; fo our confolation aboundeth through Chrift. And our hope is ftedfaft concerning you, that as you Chrifts afflicti- are partakers of the fufferinges, fo fhall you bee of the com- on on ẏ croffe forts. What comfort thefe men can finde in the paines of confolation, the damned, I knowe not; they elfe where feeme to fay, that all feares and griefes, all terrors and torments are trifles vnto the fenfe and feeling of Gods difpleafure and iuft indignation; but the holie Ghoft I am fure propo- feth to vs the Croffe of Chrift as the waie to perfection, that neuer wanteth confolation. For therein though our **i** 2. Cor. 4. i outwarde man perifh, yet the inwarde man is daylie renued; and when our bodies die to fhine, as did Chriftes, our foules liue to God, as did his. Excellentlie doth the Apoftle defcribe the comfort of Chriftes Croffe in all the faythfull, when hee fayeth. k Wee are afflicted on euerie **k** Ibidem. fide, but not ouerpreffed; wanting, but not vtterlie defti- tute; perfecuted; but not forfaken; falling, but not pe- rifhing; alwayes bearing about in our bodie the dying of the Lorde Iefu, that the life of Iefu might bee manifeft in our bodyes. For wee, whiles wee liue, are ftill deliuered vnto death for Iefus fake, that the life of Iefu might bee manifeft in our mortall flefh. Chrift then in the mortifi- cation of his bodie on the Croffe, was neither OVER- PRESSED, FORSAKEN, nor PERISHING; but relieued & fupported inwardly by the power of gods fpirit, in which he reioiced, whiles his flefh indured bitter and fharpe torments.

S And

And this rule, [1] When I am weake, then am I strong, was true in Christ, and after his example shall be in all his members. For Gods [m] power is perfited in infirmitie. Very gladly therefore must all the godlie reioice and take pleasure in their infirmities, that the power of Christ may dwell in them. How can this be called Christs power, if he wanted it in his infirmities and afflictions? And if we haue it from him, why presume we to take it from him in the time of his sufferinges? Shall the scholler be aboue his maister? or the seruant more perfect then his Lord? Yea, then God manifested in the flesh? But I hope men learned will take good heede howe they diminish the comfort of Christs crosse; we must [n] looke to Iesus the authour and finisher of our faith. If he were amazed, perplexed, and forsaken in his afflictions, who shal raise and comfort vs in our extremities? Hee that himselfe was astonished and ouerwhelmed with his sufferings on the crosse? It may then be said vnto him, [o] Phisition heale thy selfe. Shall hee comfort vs, that could NOT COMFORT himselfe? Can wee REIOICE AND TAKE PLEASVRE in following his steppes, when hee sanke vnder the burthen, and suffered both his fayth and hope for the time to faile? But farre be from vs these vnsauorie thoughts, and vnseemlie speeches. [P] It was fit that hee from whom, and by whom are all things, should CONSVMMATE BY AFFLICTIONS THE PRINCE OF OVR SALVATION, that shoulde bring many sons vnto glorie; the selfe same way that he went before them. Which cannot be by doubting & distrusting the fauor and help of god, much lesse by suffering & induring the paines of the damned; but by desiring through loue, and reioicing vnder hope to take vp Christs crosse and follow him; [q] delighting in reproches, necessities, persecutions and anguish for Christs sake, that [r] when his glorie shal appeare, we may be glad and reioice with fulnesse of euerlasting ioy.

Do we then exempt the Lord Christ from all sense of his fathers wrath against our sins; while we defend in him peace and

[l] 2. Cor. 12.

[m] Ibidem.

[n] Heb. 12.

[o] Luke 4.

[p] Heb. 2.

[q] 2. Cor. 12.
[r] 1. Pet. 4.

and ioy of the holie ghoſt, as he hung on the croſſe? There is a feeling of gods wrath which may ſtand with the pacification. & conſolation of the inward man; and there is a ſenſe of Gods wrath which ouerthroweth both, and breedeth a fearful apprehenſion of Gods diſpleaſure towards vs; in which is neither peace nor comfort. All the miſeries of mans life, whatſoeuer they be, came firſt fro the force of gods wrath reuenging ſin; and therfore not only death & damnation, but al kinds of troubles, paines & griefs, in our ſtates, bodies and minds, which ſhorten or ſower this preſent life, are degrees of gods wrath, & chaſticements of our tranſgreſſion and corruption. When the plague was kindled amongſt the people for murmuring againſt Moſes & Aaró, Moſes ſaid to Aaron, take ẙ cenſer & put fire & incenſe therein, & go quickly vnto the congregation, and make an atonemét for theefor there is VVRATH GONE OVT FROM THE LORD; the plague is begun. When the prophet Iehu reproued Iehoſaphat for aiding Achab the king of Iſrael; he ſaid wouldſt thou help the wicked? and loue them that hate the lord? euen for this cauſe WAS THE VVRATH OF THE LORD VPON THEE. The prophet Eſay comforting the church, ſaith Awake, awake and ſtand vp ó Ieruſalem, which haſt drunke at the hand of the Lord, THE CVP OF HIS VVRATH. By the prophet Micheas the Church humbleth her ſelfe vnder the hande of God in theſe wordes, I will BEARE THE VVRATH of the Lord, becauſe I haue ſinned againſt him, vntill he plead my cauſe, and execute iudgement for me. Euerie where the like is vſed in the ſcriptures. I VVAS VVROTH with my people, and gaue them into thine hand, (ſaith God to Babylon) and thou didſt ſhewe them no mercie; but didſt lay a verie heauie yoke vpon the auncient. So Ieremie complaineth to God, Thou haſt vtterly reiected vs, thou art EXCEEDINGLY ANGRY VVITH VS. Theſe, and many ſuch places more, mention the wrath of God, which the ſaints & ſeruants of god taſted and felt for their ſinnes; but they do not import that Gods eternall fauour and loue towards his children in heauenlie things, was vaniſhed or changed. The a foundation of God ſtandeth ſure ; yea the b gifts and calling of

S 2 God

Marginal notes:
All miſeries are the effects of gods wrath.
f Num.16.
t 2.Chro.19
* Eſay.51
x Mich.7.
y Eſay.47.
z Lament.5,
a 2.Tim.2.
b Rom.11.

God are without repentance. And therefore it is vtterlie impossible, that Gods election should alter, or that hee should not [c] loue his owne vnto the end; but [d] iudgement beginning at the house of God, [e] wee are chastened of the Lord, that wee should not be condemned with the world. And albeit the bitternes of affliction some time bite so neere, that the conscience of our sinnes accusing vs as vnworthie to bee the sonnes of God, feare calleth Gods fauour in question for the time; yet that temptation riseth from the guiltines of our hearts, and weaknesse of our faith, which giueth way to the diuel: otherwise as we ought to belieue god will be [f] merciful to our iniquities, & remember our sinnes no more, for his couenant made with vs in the bloud of his sonne; so should we bee fullie perswaded, that when we endure chastening, bee it neuer so sharpe, Gods offereth himselfe vnto vs, as vnto sonnes; for what sonne is it, whome the father chasteneth not? So that if wee bee without correction, whereof all are partakers, wee are bastards and not sonnes, since God chasteneth vs for our profite, that wee might be partakers of his holines.

This correction and chastisement of God, because it [h] seemeth greeuous for the present, and not ioyous, is called in the scriptures the rodde and wrath of God; not that Gods loue ceaseth when he correcteth his children; (for [i] whom the Lord loueth he chasteneth, and he scourgeth euery sonne, that hee receiueth;) But as the blessings which he abundantly bestoweth on vs, do manifest his gracious and vndeserued mercy; so the plagues, with which he visiteth our sinnes, do witnes his righteous and prouoked iudgement. And in that sense must we reckon them to be the signes and effects of Gods wrath. For as he is iustly offended with our iniquities because they resist his will, [k] dishonour his name, and [l] grieue his holie spirit, by whom we are sealed vnto the day of redemption; so when hee chasteneth our transgressions, the scourge which we feele is trulie said to be the wrath of God; not that God is touched with anie perturbation or alteration in himselfe, but his iustice

leadeth

Margin notes:
[c] Iohn.13.
[d] 1 Peter.4.
[e] 1.Cor.11.

[f] Heb.8.

[g] Heb.12.

[h] Heb.12.

[i] Heb.13.

[k] Rom.2.
[l] Ephe.4.

leadeth him to inflict that punishment on vs, as well to bring vs to hate that we haue done, by godlie sorrow; as to make vs more warie how we attempt the like, which is religious feare restraining vs from often and easie offending the maiestp and sanctitie of God. But this vengeance of our sinnes because it is temporall, when it should iustlie be eternall; and afflicteth the bodie, where it might worthilie kill the soule; it is rather the chastisement of a father, then the rigour of a Iudge. And yet the scriptures call it wrath, because God neuer proceedeth to punish, but when he is prouoked and despised, in such sort, that were it not for smart of correction, wee would fall to the rage of open rebellion.

Wherefore the displeasure of God against our sinnes was verie great, that pursued our suertie, beeing innocent and obedient, and euen his owne and only sonne, with all maner of corporall and temporall scourges vnto death, before it could bee pacified; but that Gods fauour towards his sonne was altered or diminished, or that Christ in feare and terror apprehended anie such change in his father, or so much as doubted the constant and eternall counsell, and decree of God, to make him the Sauiour of the worlde, and by the bloud of his crosse to make peace in heauen and earth; these are so dangerous doctrines; that I thinke no learned diuine will vndertake them. [m] Though he were the sonne, yet learned he obedience, by that which he suffered, saith the Apostle; Now obedience could not breed diffidence but confidence; and was the vertue, that so highlie pleased God in Christ, that hee was [n] made the authour of eternall saluation vnto all that OBEY HIM. A double sense then of Gods wrath Christ Iesus had. The first that pursued his bodie vnto death on the tree, where [o] hee bare our sinnes; that is the [p] chastisement of our peace; the STRIPES of our iniquities, and WOVNDES of our transgressions. The next was the serious contemplation of that eternall and intolerable vengeance; which the iustice of God had in store for vs, by reason of our manifold sinnes; whose

Gods wrath towards his is mixed with mercy and iustice.

The wrath of God against our sinnes was very great in the crosse of Christ.

[m] Hebre. 5

[n] Ibidem.

[o] 1. Peter. 2.
[p] Esay. 53.

whofe danger and deſtruction touched him as nere, through the tenderneſſe of his loue and pietie, as if it had beene imminent ouer his owne heade. And therefore euen ſicke with ſorrowe foꝛ vs, & trembling at the terror of Gods wꝛath pꝛepared to reuẽge our vnrighteouſnes, he neuer left SVVEA-TING, VVEEPING and CRYING to God foꝛ vs, that his ſtripes might heale vs, his anguiſh excuſe vs, his death quicken vs, and his perſon ſuſtaine and ſuffer foꝛ vs, whatſoeuer the iuſtice of God would late on him, till he was heard, and allowed of God to offer the ſacrifice, that ſhould pꝛopitiate the ſinnes of the woꝛlde. In theſe paines and ſcares, whiles hee felt the arrowes of God ſticking in his fleſh, and ſawe the terror of eternall death readie to ſwallow vp all his members, we maie grant, that the CONSOLATION and IOIE, which the humane ſoule of Chꝛiſt befoꝛe had of his Fathers continuall pꝛeſence and aſſiſtance, was foꝛ the time ſomewhat diminiſhed; his heart being oppreſſed with ſoꝛrow, his bodie afflicted with ſharpe and bitter paine, his ſoule beſieged with feare and care foꝛ vs, that neither the dreadfull wrath of God ouerwhelmed vs, noꝛ the deceitfull fraude of Satan vndermined vs: but by no meanes we maie admit in Chꝛiſt either feare oꝛ doubt of his owne ſaluation; noꝛ forgetfulnes of his perſon oꝛ function; but the harder the woꝛk he vndertooke, the ſtronger his faith, that performed it; the more terrible our danger, the more ſtedfaſt his loue, that ſhꝛunke not from vs in ſo great extremitie.

[Might not yet the ſoule of Chꝛiſt in this conſtant and full aſſurance of Gods loue towardes him, and mercie towards vs, feele the toꝛments of hell foꝛ the time without anie diſtruſting oꝛ doubting of his ſaluation, oꝛ our redemption?] The eſſentiall toꝛments of hell, are the abſolute loſſe of Gods kingdome, without recouerie, and exquiſite ſenſe of hell fire euerlaſtinglie without releaſe. Neither of theſe without hoꝛrible blaſphemie can be imagined in the ſoule of Chꝛiſt: the reſt that are conſequents to theſe, as deſperation, murmura-
tion,

tion, darkeneſſe, horrour and ſuch other impreſſions are like
to theſe; and coulde no more haue place in Chriſtes perſon,
then the antecedentes might. And ſince it is no where wit-
neſſed in the Scriptures, nor anie waie prooued, that
Chriſt ſuffered the paines of hell; whie ſtriue we to eſtabliſh
a meere conceite of men, neuer written or ſpoken of, be-
fore our age? beare wee ſo ſmall regarde to the Church of
Chriſt, and to all the learned fathers and teachers in the
ſame, that for thirteene hundred yeeres no man euer knew
or heard the right waie, and true meane of our redemption
and reconciliation to God, till the paines of hell were late-
lie deuiſed? Abuſes and errours did by little and little creepe
into the church by the wilineſſe of Satan, and wilfulneſſe of
men; but that the gates of hell ſhoulde ſo much preuaile a-
gainſt it, as from the Apoſtles time to this preſent age, no
chriſtian ſhould euer trulie teach or rightlie beleeue how we
are ſaued by the croſſe of Chriſt, is to me ſo ſtrange; that I
will be ten times aduiſed, before I will once admit it. Let vs
giue thankes to God, for diſpelling the miſt of darkenes and
ignorance, that querſpred the world vnder Antichriſt: but let
vs neuer gloze that we firſt inuented a newe faith, neither
teſtified in the ſcriptures, nor mentioned in anie ancient wri-
ters, nor euer heard of amongſt chriſtians before our time.
It is no corne but cockle that ſpringeth ſo late in the Lordes
field; it is no faith, but fanſie that neuer before was in ye foun-
dation of Chriſts church. The ſimplicitie therfore of the ſcrip-
tures continually PRESSING the DEATH and BLOVD of Chriſt,
as the TRVE CAVSES of our ſaluation & redemption; and
the conſonancy of all antiquity according therewith, do ſo cha-
lenge my faith, and eſtabliſh my hart, that I will ſee this new
deuiſe of hel paines ſuffered in the ſoule of Chriſt, better
warranted, before I wiſh it to be beleeued.

And as for the doctrine of the church of England, which
ſome men would faine infect with this late fanſie, giue mee
leaue, men and brethren to admoniſh you ſhortlie but
trulie;

It ſhould ſom-
what moue vs,
ye hell paines
were neuer ad-
ded to Chriſts
croſſe for 1300
yeeres ſince the
Apoſtles time.

The doctrine
here deliuered
is authoriſed
by the lawes of
this realme.

⁹ _Num. 3._

ʳ _Num. 13._

trulie; that who ſo will reade the ſermon of the ⁹ ſaluation of al mankinde, in the firſt volume of Homilies; and likewiſe the two Homilies, concerning the death and ʳ paſſion of our Sauiour Jeſus Chriſt, contained in the ſecond tome of Homilies; ſhall finde that the doctrine which I haue deliuered you, hath the publike approbation of Prince and Parliament, the conſent and agreement of all the Biſhops, and the ſubſcription of all the clergie of this kingdome, to bee taught as truth in all the churches of this realme, and ſo hath had, as well in the daies of king Edwarde the ſixt, as all the time of her maieſties moſt happie raigne, whatſoeuer ſome forward nouices haue told you to the contrarie. And thus much let me ſpeake in the Honor of her maieſtie, and this realme; I ſee no cauſe; why the doctrine of the church of England ſo plainelie warranted by the Scriptures, ſo fullie confeſſed by all the Fathers, ſo long continued in Chriſts church without contradiction, ſo ſufficiently authorized, ſo generally acknowledged, ſhould bee controlled or corrected, either by the dangerous deuiſes of ſome late writers, or by the vnſetled humours of ſome late teachers. Hold therefore in Gods name cloſe to the rules of the holie ghoſt, cloſe to the words of the chriſtian & catholicke Fathers, cloſe to the lawes of this realme : they all concur and conſoine together, howſoeuer ſome giddie ſpirits haue lately buzzed in your eares that I impugned the doctrine of the church of England.

The fift effect of Chriſtes croſſe; which is the glory of his reſurrectiō.

I Haue deliuered you foure effectes of Chriſtes croſſe; the merite of his ſuffering which was infinite ; the maner of his offering, which was bloudie; the power of his death, which was mightie; the comfort of his croſſe, which was and is neceſſary for vs all; there remaineth the glorie of his reſurrection, which was heauenlie, of which I did not purpoſe to ſpeake, when I firſt entred this matter; but the ignorance of ſome, imagining I denied the Article of the Creede, HE DESCENDED INTO HELL (for deſcent but on the croſſe they admit none) and

and the zeale of others importuning me to knowe what they
might safelie beléeue touching that article, hath made me to
change my mind; and in this last part to shewe, that I nei-
ther frustrate the faith, nor alter the Créede by anie thing
that I affirme, or refuse. Whereto let you see the multipli-
citie of mens wits and conceites; there are foure seuerall
opinions that take holde euerie one of this Article of our
Créede, and chalenge the true meaning thereof as their pe-
culiar and vndoubted right. The FIRST applieth it to the
soule of Christ suffering on the crosse; the SECOND to the
bodie of Christ buried; the THIRD to the state of Christes
soule seuered by death from the bodie; the LAST to the con-
quest and triumph which the humane soule of Christ had ouer
hell by the glorie of his resurrection, as his bodie had ouer
death. Which of these hath the best right, and fittest sense to
be an article of our créede, will appeare by comparison in the
end and vpshot of all; in the meane while, I will shortlie sift
them, that you maie sée the substance of them, and so be able
the better to iudge of them.

    The first is the verie same, which I haue alreadie handled,
and refused as not consonant to the christian faith; but rather
repugnant to the dignitie, certaintie, sanctity of Christs per-
son, consanction, & communion with God. The scriptures a-
uouch, that Christs SOVLE was IN HELL, but not whiles
he liued here on earth: it was a consequent to his death, and
no part of his suffering on the crosse, as I shewed before. And
since the times do so much varie, there can be no truth in ta-
king the one for the other. In this life God sometimes suf-
fereth the sorowes and feares of hell to bestege his seruantes,
and bringeth them euen vnto hell; but his saints descend not
into hell: feare may humble them, that would otherwise pre-
sume of themselues, or make triall howe fast they stande on
that foundation against the which the gates of hell shall not
preuaile: but this conflict of conscience must resolue on the
assurance of Gods fauour, except they yélde themselues vn-

(margin notes)

Foure opinions touching the article of the Creede he de-scended into hell.

1.Samuel.&c.

The feare of hell may fall on vs, but not on Christ,

    T 3   to

to deſpaire . In Chriſt as there was no vſe, ſo was there no place for anie ſuch temptation . There was in him no danger of pride to exalt him; and therefore no neede of feare to depreſſe him: no ſlackneſſe or coldneſſe coulde take holde of him; and ſo no terror requiſite to awake him from ſleepe, or inflame his zeale: generallie there was in him no corruption of nature, no infection of ſinne, no wauering of faith, no want of grace, no doubt of Gods fauour; and ſo thoſe dreadfull thoughts and feares of hell, which amaze other, could not ariſe within his heart; but all the paines and griefes, which the ſonne of God felt in his pretious bodie, or righteous ſoule, as they were VOLVNTARY for our example, and SATISFACTORIE for our ſinne; and not MEDICINABLE for anie infirmitie of his, nor PROFITABLE to bring him to perfection of holineſſe, as they are in vs: ſo were they proportioned to his perſon, that was moſt aſſured of Gods euerlaſting loue; and to his gifts, that could endure no inward decreaſe; and therefore hee muſt in this point differ from all the ſaints of God, that euer were or euer ſhall be on earth. For they may be toſſed with the waues of temptation, riſing from the remembrance of ſinne, & remorſe of conſcience; but our Sauiour, as he was free from all touch of ſinne, ſo was he free from all feare of heart, that hee ſhould or might bee reiected from Gods fauour, or adiudged to euerlaſting death. Smart, paine and griefe of bodie or minde, be it neuer ſo great, will commende his obedience and patience; but the SENSE of damnation or ſeparation from God, or the FEARE or DOVBT thereof in Chriſt, as they quench faith, and aboliſh grace, ſo they diſſolue the vnion and communion of both his natures; or elſe breede a falſe perſwaſion, and ſinnefull temptation in the ſoule of Chriſt. In vs that haue infinitelie prouoked the iuſtice of God, it is the true beholding what wee haue deſerued, if God be not pleaſed for Chriſts ſake to pardon and forgiue vs; In Chriſt, that was perfectlie righteous, and perſonallie ioyned with God, there coulde

be

bre no apprehenſion of hell paines as due vnto him, or de-
termined for him, without renouncing his innocencie, and
leauing the vnitie of his perſon; and conſequentlie hee muſt
find or feare, that God would be inconſtant, and vniuſt; which
are more then hainous impieties. For Chriſt could not
FEARE OR DOVBT his owne ſaluation, but he muſt feare or
doubt, that either his humane nature ſhould bee ſeparated
from his diuine, or his diuine together with his humane bee
caſt into hell fier; from which the Lord bleſſe the tongues and
thoughts of al chriſtian men. As for Chriſts not remembring in
a maze, that he was the ſon of God, & ſaior of the world; is a
ſeely ſhift to ſhun theſe inconueniencies; I had rather ſimply
deny, then any way beleeue this kind of deſcending into hel.

Do I charge then anie man with vpholding theſe impie-
ties? God forbid. I ſee by their own words they purpoſe and
profeſſe by al means to decline them, & no doubt deteſt them;
but I confeſſe my dulnes, that ſee not how to auoide the one,
if I auouch the other. If we take hell paines METAPHORI-
CALLY for great and intolerable paines; in which ſenſe the
word male bee vſed; then it is no daunger to ſaie, Chriſt
ſuffered on the croſſe the paines of hell: becauſe there caune
bee no doubt, but HIS PAYNES were exceeding
GREATE, and more SHARPE, then inee canne
conceiue or vtter. But this is not the meaning of the
Creede. In that Article hee deſcended into Hell; by rea-
ſon there are words before inferring the paynes, which
bee SVFFERED, when hee was CRVCIFIED. If
wee attribute the ſenſe of Gods wrath, and feeling of hell
paynes vnto Chriſt by waie of COGNITION and COM-
PASSION towardes vs, forſomuch as the ſoule hath her
ſight, and pittie hath her inwarde feeling of other mens
miſeries, as if they were our owne; it is no wrong
to the perſon or fundion of our Sauiour for vs to
confeſſe, that hee conſidered and grieued to ſee the bur-
then of Gods euerlaſting wrath due to our ſinnes, none

How Chriſt in ſome ſenſe may be ſaid to haue ſuffered the paines of hel on ỹ croſſe

otherwise then if himselfe had béene subiect thereto: so long
as we leaue him certaintie and securitie of his owne saluati-
on & our redemption; that his bowels of mercie maie bee
moued and affected for our danger, and not for his owne. It
is farre more religious to presse the soule of Christ with vio-
lent panges of griefe and sorrowe for our inquities and mi-
series; then to touch him with anie feare or doubt of his own
innocencie or safetie. Charitie is a fitter Agonie for the sonne
of God in our flesh, then either timiditie or stupiditie; and
yet I do not thinke this to be the sense of the Créede, when it
saieth hee descended into hell; for that it were somewhat
strange to expresse the vertues of Christs suffering, by his de-
scending into hell.

Papists were
the first bro-
chers of this o-
pinion, that
Christ suffered
hell paines on
one crosse.

And least the insolent sect of Iesuites shoulde take such
pleasure as they doe, in misconstruing other mens words,
and blazing them vnto the worlde as erroneous and impi-
ous; let them remember, that some of their owne side, and
those not of the meanest both for learning and religion a-
mongst them, haue not onelie waded as farre as anie other
newe writers in this position; but for ought that I reade,
haue gone farther; howsoeuer they will defende it or excuse
it. Nicholaus Cusanus a Cardinall of their church, and a
great admirer of the councell of Basill, 50. yéeres before Lu-
ther appeared, first broched this assertion. ^t *Passio Christi,
(qua maior nulla potest esse) fuit vt damnatorum, qui magis
damnari nequeunt; scilicet* VSQVE AD POENAM INFER-
NALEM. The suffering of Christ, (then the which there can
be no greater,) was as of the damned, which cannot bee more
condemned, EVEN VNTO THE PAINES OF HELL.
And againe. ^u *Illam pœnã sensus* CONFORMEM DAMNA-
TIS IN INFERNO, *pati voluit in gloriam dñi patris sui.* That
paine of feeling agreeable to the damned in hell, Christ would
suffer for the glory of God his father. Augustinus Iustinianus,
that set out the Psalter in Hebrew with fiue translations
and obseruations, the same yéere, that Luther beganne to
write,

write; in his ſcholies vpon the 30 Pſalme, mentioneth this opinion of Cuſanus, and ſaith, ˣ *Se huius eruditiſſimi viri, & in omni ſcientia eminentiſſimi opinionem, nec amplecti, nec aſpernari;* He neither embraceth nor reiecteth the opinion of that moſt learned man and excelling in all kinde of knowledge. *Iohannes Ferus* a Franciſcane and preacher at *Mogunce*, about the ſame time that Caluine wrote, goeth further then anie other wri-ter, that I haue read. Commenting vpon theſe wordes of Chriſt, My God, my God, why haſt thou forſaken me, he ſaith, ʸ*Exuit Chriſtus hac horâ* DEVM, *non abijciendo, ſed non* SEN-TIENDO: *ſepoſuit patrem vt hominem ageret. Sic & Deus pa-ter, nunc non patrem, ſed* TYRANNVM AGIT, *quamuis in-terim amiciſſimo in Chriſtum ſit animo. Illa Chriſti derelictio pa-uor eſt conſcientia noſtra ob admiſſa peccata, qua iudicium dei & iram aeternam experitur : & ſic afficitur, quaſi in perpetuum derelicta & reiecta à facie Dei eſſe.* That verie hower Chriſt put off GOD, not caſting him away, but not FEELING him; he laid aſide his father, that he might ſhew himſelfe to be a man. So alſo God the father now taketh vnto him the PERSON not of a father, but OF A TYRANT; though in heart hee were moſt louing vnto Chriſt. That forſaking of Chriſt is the feare of our conſcience for ſinne committed, which feeleth the iudgment and eternall wrath of God;& is ſo affected, as if it were forſaken and reiected from the face of God for euer. And as if this were not inough to ſay, that Chriſt put off his diuine nature, as ha-uing no feeling of it, and God the father played the PART OF A TYRANT; he goeth on and addeth. ᶻ*Non ſolum ſup-plicium à nobis meritum, verum etiam* DESPERATIONEM NOSTRAM *in ſe tranſtulit. Itaque Chriſtus vt peccatores libe-raret conſtituit ſeipſum in locum omnium peccatorum, non qui-dem furans, adulterans, occidens, &c: ſed ſtipendium, pœnam & meritum peccatorum, qua ſunt frigus, calor, eſuries, ſitis, timor, tremor, horror mortis, horror inferni,* DESPERATIO, *mors,* INFERNVS IPSE) *in ſe transferens, vt famem fame, timorem timore, horrorem horrore,* DESPERATIONEM DESPERA-TIONE,

T.3

(marginal notes)
ˣ Auguſt. Iu Ti-niarui in ſcho-liis O.Tapli in Pſal.30.

ʸ Ferus. lib 4.in Mat.cap.27.in illa verba, Deus meus, deus meus

ᶻ Ibidem.

TIONE,*mortem morte*, INFERNVM INFERNO, *breuiter*
SATANAM SATANA, *vinceret*. Chriſt did transferre to him-
ſelfe not onelie the puniſhment which wee had deſerued, but
euen OVR DESPERATION And therefore Chriſt, that hee
might deliuer ſinners,ſet himſelfe in the place of all ſinners, not
by ſtealing, adultering, killing, but by transferring vnto him-
ſelfe, the wages, puniſhment, and deſert of ſinners, which are
heate and colde, hunger and thirſt,ſeare and trembling, horror
of death, HORROR OF HELL DESPERATION, death,
HELL IT SELFE.: that he might ouercome hunger with
hunger, ſeare with ſeare, horror with horror, DESPERA-
TION VVITH DESPERATION, death with death, HELL
VVITH HELL, and laſtlie, SATAN VVITH SATAN.
Trulie I knowe no man that ſo plainlie auoucheth, Chriſt
admitted and receyued vnto himſelfe DESPERATION, as
this Frier doth. For where other men warilie decline to ſay
that CHRIST DESPAIRED, this Franciſcane boldlie ſaith,
Chriſt transferred vnto himſelfe DESPERATION, HELL,
yea, THE DIVELL and all; and was ſo affected for the
time,as if he had FELT THE ETERNALL VVRATH OF
GOD,and were REIECTED FOR EVER. Could thoſe quar-
rellers haue gotten the like aduantage againſt anie of our
writers, they would haue filled the world with their tragi-
call exclamations of HERESIE, BLASPHEMIE, TVR-
CISME, PAGANISME, and I knowe not what; and there-
fore let them goe and waſhe their owne faces from theſe
ſpottes, before they declaime ſo violentlie agaynſt our de-
formities.

And albeit I like not theſe ſpeeches either in theirs or ours,
Charitie ſup-
poſeth the beſt yet I cleare them both from anie purpoſe of wilfull blaſ-
phemie. They might be deceiued in the ſequele of their
aſſertion, but ſure they were neuer ſo vnaduiſed, as to
faſten either DESPERATION OR DAMNATION on the
ſoule of Chriſt. Perhappes they thought hee was be-
ſieged and aſſaulted with theſe temptations, and that the
humane

humane nature of Chriſt, being left to it ſelfe, could not preſentlie & eaſilie ſtand cleare from the vengeance due to our ſinnes, but with ſome conflict and feare, wreſtled from vnder the weight of our iniquities, and in this fight did ſweat bloud, and ſpake as if he were forſaken: yea Ferus ſeemeth to meane that Chriſt did voluntarilie take the burthen of deſperation and damnation from vs, and laid it on himſelfe; againſt whom it could not preuaile; that by transferring thoſe dangers from our perſons to his, & ſuffering them for the time, he might breake them, and diſſolue them for euer.

Naturall infirmities, which are outragious in vs by reaſon of our corruption, Chriſt might ſuffer to ariſe within him, and there temper them, as Cyrill & other ancient fathers do teach; but ſinfull extremities, as deſperation, confuſion, reiection, damnation, Chriſt muſt conquere by repelling, not by ſuffering: leaſt the fellowſhip of our ſinnes be more hainous in him, then in vs. For as his faith, hope and loue muſt by manie degrees exceed ours in perfection; ſo the quenching or ſlaking of theſe graces in him, is greater ſinne then in vs. Doubt and diſtruſt is farre more impious in Angels, by reaſon of their excellent knowledge and ſtrength, then in men; and moſt impious in the ſoule of Chriſt, who by his perſonall vnion with God, deriued clearer intelligence in knowing Gods will, and greater aſſurance to perſiſt therein, then either man or Angell. For the verie Angels haue but the condition of their creation, from which ſome fell; and confirmation of grace, in which the reſt ſtand: but no creature euer had ſo faſt conjunction, and full communion with the godhead, as the ſoule of Chriſt. And therefore DVBITATION, DESPERATION, TREPIDATION in his ſoule are more hainous ſinnes, then in any other creature; for ſomuch as they beleeue not truth, truſt not the promiſe, reſt not ſecured in the VOICE and OATH of God, which all are immutable and impoſſible to bee falſe; and feare leaſt Gods goodneſſe and loue will faile; and in fine doe depriue him of his diuine nature, ſince without

Sinful infirmities are more hainous in Chriſt then in vs.

without veritie, bonitie, and conſtancie, there can be no God. If then Chriſts ſoule could not be infected with ſinne, nor haue anie ſocietie with euill, no not for an inſtant; theſe doubts and feares of Gods fauour, and his ſaluation muſt be farre from him; and in the full perſwaſion, and ſteadfaſt expectation of eternall ioy and bliſſe, howe deſperation ſhould lodge, I yet vnderſtand not.

God might reueale, and the ſoule of Chriſt in this life beholde, as all ours ſhall when we appeare before the face of God after this life, what cup was prepared for the wicked to drinke, and the ſight thereof as it is moſt fearefull, ſo might it make him tremble, though he were neuer ſo free from it; but more then the VISION of Gods wrath, and COMMISERATION of mans danger, if wee attribute to the ſoule of Chriſt; we muſt either grant he was tempted as well with our iniquities, through lacke of grace, as with our infirmities through want of ſtrength; or elſe caſt him into a traunce at the time of his paſſion, as ſome doe, to excuſe him from ſinne. For that in the fulneſſe of Gods fauour, grace and ſpirite, the ſoule of Chriſt ſhoulde feele the flames of hell fire; can neither bee prooued, nor defended by the worde of God. The proofe I leaue to them that like the poſition; which if anie man affirme, he were beſt bee ſure of his footing. It is no ſmall arrogancie, and blaſphemie to ſit Iudge in Gods place, and to condemne Chriſts ſoule to hell fire, without a ſounde and cleare commiſſion, to warrant that aſſertion. Beſides hell fire in the Scriptures being ETERNALL; by what authoritie will they quench it at their pleaſure, and make it temporarie? And if Chriſtes ſoule beeing perſonallie ioyned to the Deitie, notwithſtanding might feele the furie of hell fire, when ſhall the Saints of God, that can neuer bee ſo vnited vnto his glorie, nor aſſured of his ſocietie, nor ſo endued with his ſanctitie, bee free from the flames of hell? If that vnion and communion which Chriſt had with God, coulde not exclude

Chriſts ſoule freer from hel. then either ſaints or angels.

erclude hell fire; what ſhall hinder but that the Angels in heauen male for the time likewiſe feele the flames therof? Can they haue faſter coherence, or fuller preſence of God, then hee which was ioyned with God in vnitie of perſon? They come not neere the fauour and grace, knowledge and truth, power & ſtedfaſtnes of the manhoode of Chriſt, which here on earth they did ſerue and adore. But none of theſe things can be intended in the Creede; for there the articles are placed in ORDER AND TIME, as they were performed. And therfore when Chriſt was DEAD AND BVRIED, he then DESCENDED INTO HELL.

The ſecond opinion is, that Chriſts deſcent to hell is all one with his buriall, for that SHEOL in the olde teſtament doth moſt commonlie, if not continuallie ſignifie the graue. But this is nothing to the Creede, whoſe authoritie and antiquitie if wee reuerence, it is ſoone concluded, that hell there doth not ſignifie the graue. For firſt it is abſurde, that in a ſhort rehearſall of the faith made for the ſimpleſt to conceiue, one article ſhoulde bee twice repeated; and after a plaine and knowne worde, hee was buried which no man could doubt of; a darke and enigmaticall phraſe of ſpeech, HE DESCENDED INTO HELL, which fewe men did vnderſtande, ſhould bee added, rather to obſcure then to expound the former. Againe, HE DESCENDED, ſigniſieth a voluntarie motion, where as the bodie dead hath neither VVILL nor MOTION. Thirdlie, HELL in the new teſtament, is ſo vnuſuall for the graue, that I thinke no example can be ſhewed thereof. Though therefore this expoſition cannot be charged with falſitie, for Chriſt was trulie buried; yet may it not bee endured by reaſon of the idle repetition, and ſtrange circumloquution, which troubleth and confoundeth the hearer; beſides the improprietie and incoherence of the worde, that a deade corps ſhould deſcend, and ſpeciallie vnto hell.

The third opinion doth neither miſtake the TIME nor the PART which deſcended: for they referre the wordes of the

This opinion is not falſe, but impertinent and idle.

Creede to Chriſtes ſoule after DEATH, but they
change the name of hell into the ſtate of the deade; and
ſo confeſſe, that Chriſtes ſoule after ſeparation from the
bodie endured THE STATE OF THE DEAD. To this a
number of learned men incline, becauſe they woulde auoyde
Limbus patrum; diſliking by all meanes that the ſoules of
the righteous and faithfull before Chriſtes ſuffering ſhoulde
be kept in a region or part of hell; and thence deliuered by
his deſcent. I ſee well enough what they woulde faine
decline; but what if by their farre ſet expoſition they fall
into that errour which they ſeeke to flie? Doe they not
fairelie profer, and quite beſides the marke? Let vs looke
a little into their conceite. Chriſt deſcended into hell, that is,
ſaie they, his ſoule after death, conuerſed among the ſoules
of the iuſt, that were dead before him. But where were the
ſoules of the iuſt? In a place, or no? Without a place can
nothing be; but onelie God. All creatures be they ſoules or
angels are deſined with place, though they do not reple-
niſh their places as bodies do; yea whatſoeuer is not circum-
ſcribed within a place, is infinite, which no creature can bee.
The ſoules then of the righteous muſt of neceſſitie bee in a
place. And what call you that place by your opinion? For
ſothe euen HELL. For Chriſtes deſcending into hell, as you
expound it, was his conuerſing among the ſoules of the
dead. Thoſe ſoules then were in a place, and that place by your
conſtruction the Creed calleth Hell. Their ſtate you will ſay,
is called hell, but not their place. A wittie difference I aſ-
ſure you. The place for ſoules after this life, is anſwerable
to their ſtate. If their ſtate bee hell; their place can nei-
ther bee Heauen, nor Paradiſe. As is their receptacle; ſo
is their reſt; the place doth bring either ioy or paine,
which is their ſtate. So that if Chriſt deſcending into hell
conuerſed with the ſoules of the righteous; of force the
ſoules of the righteous were in hell, which is the ſelfe
ſame errour, that you woulde ſeeme by your newe founde
word   interpre-

interpretation to preuent.

[But the state of the deade, is in Hebrew noted by the worde Sheól ; and thither Christ descended.] And the state or place whither Christ descended, is in the Creede named hell, and so Sheól is that which the Creede calleth hell. In deede some say, that Sheól doth neuer in the olde testament signifie the place of the damned: but I must be one with, if I bee not of their minde. Manie men saie, that they neder proue; and some speake they know not what. As both partes of man sinned in the first transgression ; so was there a pit of perdition prouided for either part; the graue for the bodie, which there should rot ; and hell for the soule, which there should bee tormented with euerlasting fire. Both these pits, because they alwayes expect and exact as their due, the bodies and soules of mortall and sinfull men, and neuer are satisfied, are contained in the word Sheól; and are note distinguished by the nature of the worde, which is common to both; but by the circumstances added which are proper to either. For example, when the word Sheól is qualified with an OPPOSITION to heauen with a difference of SCITVATION, as the LOWER PIT, with an ADDITION of the soule there suffering, or of the pain there suffered; all these are proofe that the word Sheól, which is otherwise indifferent, must there be taken not for the buriall of the body, nor for the change from this life, but for the state of destruction, and place of damnation. a Whither shall I go from thy spirit? or whither shall I flie from thy presence? If I ascend into heauen, thou art there ; If I lodge BENEATH IN HEL, thou art there. Opposite to heauen is not the graue, where the bodies of all gods saints do lie, but hell, as being the farthest from it, and most repugnant to it; since from hel to heauen there is no passage for man; but from the graue to heauen is the assured hope of all the faithfull. This opposition our Sauiour expressing in the new testament, saith, b And thou Capernaum which art exalted to heauen, shalt bee thrust downe to hell.

U 2 Christ

Sheól as well hell as the graue.

a Psal. 139.

b Mat. 11, ve. 23

Chriſt doth not threaten the contemners of his doctrine, and myracles with the graue, which is common to all the godlie; but with perpetuall deſtruction and puniſhment proportionable to the height of their pride, which muſt needes be hell. And ſo much followeth in plaine wordes in the next verſe. ^e I ſay to you, it ſhall be eaſier for them of the land of Sodome in the day of iudgement, then for thee. In the daic of iudgement as death, ſo the graue are at an ende, for the bodies of the wicked ſhall then liue for euer; and then ſhall Capernaum be caſt downe to hell for the contempt of Chriſts preaching.

^e Ibid. ver. 24.

As hel is the fartheſt place from heauen, that can be named, ſo it is the loweſt, and therefore by the lower pit, is ment not the graue, but hell, which in ſcituation is far lower then the outſide of the earth where men are buried. ^d Canſt thou by ſearching find out God ? canſt thou find out the perfection of the almightie? to the height of heauen what canſt thou do? it is deeper then hell; how canſt thou know it? Gods perfection is higher then the higheſt place, which is heauen; & deeper then the deepeſt place, which is hel. To compare his power or iuſtice with the depth of the graue, which is not foure peards deepe at the moſt, were a very ſlender compariſon for the incomprehenſible greatnes of god; but ſince in height & depth it excedeth all things; there can be no doubt, but it is compared with the higheſt & deepeſt places that are; which are heauen and hel. In like ſort, ^e Thou haſt deliuered my ſoule from the loweſt pit, can not be ment of the graue. For mens ſouls are not incloſed in graues with their bodies, but as the pit prouided for the body is the higher of the twaine, and the pit prepared for the ſoule is the lower; ſo the loweſt pit out of queſtion is hell, where the ſoules of ſuch as are reiected from God are detained againſt the day of vengeance. And albeit ſome of theſe ſpeeches may perchance admit an allegoricall ſenſe, and ſo ſignifie the greateſt and extreameſt dangers that might be; yet the ground of the allegorie dependeth on the nature of hell, and not of the graue, becauſe of the two ſortes of pittes,

^d Iob. 11

The *loweſt* place and *fartheſt* from heauen is hell.

^e Pſal. 85.

hell

hell is the loweſt; and made to receaue the ſoules of men, which the graue doth not.ᶠ A fire,(ſaith God by Moſes) is kind- ᶠDeut.32
led in my wrath, and ſhall burne to the bottome of hell, and ſet
on fire the foundations of the mountaines. Fire in the graue
there is none, in hell there is; neither can the ſepulcher, where
mens bodies lie buried, be the bottome of hell. For ſo ſhall
we make the place of hell higher then the earth, which the
ſcripture euerie where croſſeth, when it calleth hell the deepe,
or loweſt pit. A fire then burning to the bottome of hell, and
inflaming the verie foundations of the hils, can haue no reſem-
blance to the graue, nor performance in the graue; but Sheol
in that ſcripture, as in manie others, muſt ſignifie the verie
place of the damned, which we call hell.

The wordes then of the Creede, hee deſcended into hell;
ſince the defenders of this thirde opinion doe not referre to
the bodie of Chriſt buried, but to the ſoule of Chriſt after
death; it is euident by their poſition, that not onelie Chriſts
ſoule after this life deſcended to hell, but all the ſoules of the
iuſt and righteous leauing this worlde before Chriſtes com-
ming, deſcended likewiſe into hell. And this euaſion of
theirs, that Sheol in Hebrew ſignifieth the ſtate of the deade
after this life, be it good or bad, ſtandeth them in little ſteed.
For firſt they doe not auoid that obſcure and idle repetition,
wherewith the ſecond opinion was charged; that, after a
plaine and eaſie article, hee was deade, the ſelfe ſame thing
ſhould bee iterated againe with a verie darke and doubtfull
kind of hebraiſme, he deſcended into Sheol. By this former,
he was dead, euerie man muſt needes conceaue, not onelie
the ſeparation of the ſoule from the bodie, but alſo the ſubiec-
tion of either part to the ſtate of the deade. What needed
then an vnknowne hebrew phraſe hee deſcended into Sheol,
to expreſſe the verie ſame point, which before was fullie and
fairelie deliuered? Againe, though Sheol be common to the
bodies of the faithfull and infidels, yet may it bee verie
well doubted, whether the ſoules of the righteous departed

this

this life be in Sheôl, or no. And vnder correction I take it to bee more, then the Scripture anie where doeth positiuelie affirme. My reason is, that Abrahams bosome is by our Sauiour placed ABOVE, FARRE OFF from the place, where the wicked after this life are tormented. Now to Sheôl the Scripture maketh a DESCENT, not an ascent; as when Iacob saieth, I WILL GOE DOVVNE to Sheôl vnto my sonne, mourning. And againe, you will bring my gray hayres with sorrow DOVVNE TO SHEOL. And least thee should dreame of a metaphoricall kinde of descent; in the rebellion of Corah, Dathan, and Abiram, the scripture saieth, THE GROVNDE claue asunder, that was vnder them; and the earth opened her mouth, and swallowed them vp, with their families. So they, and all that were with them, WENT DOWNE aliue into Sheôl; and the earth COVERED THEM. To Sheôl then the scripture maketh a locall descent; which is either of the bodie to the graue, (for so Iacobs words must be vnderstood, when he saith, I will descende to Sheôl vnto my sonne:) or of the soule after death, to the place of torment, which is the rewarde of all the wicked. The wicked (saith Dauid) shall be turned into Sheôl, and al nations that forget God. Where he doth not meane, they shall die, as wel as the godly, which is likewise the lot of all the iust & righteous; but that al shall haue the due wages of sinne; both body and soule descending to Sheôl; that is, the one to corruption in the earth, the other to damnation in hell. For Sheol conteineth both; and supposeth both to the forgetters and despisers of God, albeit it fasten no farther on the godly, then to bring their bodies to the graue, which is the gate of hell. Ezechiah mentioning in his praiers, how he was willed by the prophet to prepare himselfe to die, thus expresseth it, I said in the cutting off of my daies, I shal goe to the gates of Sheol, I am depriued of the residue of my yeeres; but the wicked go to THE DEPTH OF SHEOL, which is the place of euerlasting punishment. The way of life (saith Salomon) is ON HIGH, to
him

The scripture maketh a descent to Sheol.
c Luke.16
b Genes.37
l Genes.42
k Numb.16
l Psal.9.
The soules of ye wicked were in Sheol before Christs comming, but not of the godly.
a Esay.38
a Prouerb.15

him that vnderstandeth to decline from SHEOL BENEATH. So that after this life, the soules that liue, are aboue, so the way to life is on high, the soules that die go to the depth of Sheol, euen to the bottomles pit of perdition. Of him that hanteth harlots Salomon saith. ° He knoweth not ỹ her ghests are in the depth of Sheol, that is, so wrapped in their sinnes, that they cannot preuent euerlasting damnation. And againe, ᵖ Thou shalt smite the child with the rod, and shalt deliuer his soule from Sheol. Correction will not saue a childe that hee shall not see death, but it will bow him to obedience, and so saue his soule from destruction. Yea how should Dauid so often confesse to God that his soule was freed from Sheol, if by Sheol hee ment the state after death: for thence it was impossible his soule shuld be deliuered. ᑫWhat man liueth, & shal not see death? So precious is the redemption of the soule (frō death) that it must cease for euer. And yet comparing himself with the wicked, & his state with theirs, he saith. ʳ Like sheepe shall they lie in Sheol, death shal deuoure thē, and the righteous shall haue dominiō ouer thē, in the day spring: But God wil deliuer my soule from the power of Sheol, for he will receiue me. Doth Dauid meane he shal neuer die, or that his soule shalbe deliuered from Sheol, that is from the state of such as were departed this life: ỹ imagination were both false & absurd: but he meaneth, that death shal deuoure the wicked wholle, as well soule as bodie; whereas he did firmly beleeue, ỹ God would deliuer his soule from the power of Sheol, & would receaue him after death: though his body must of force by the condition of nature weare olde as a garment, and rot in the graue, til the day of resurrectiō. And if a rite man thinke good in some such places, as these are, to interp: of the S O V R C E for L I F E, because it is the spring and cause of life in the bodie; and S H E O L for the G R A V E, where life endeth, I will not vtterlie condemne his exposition, so long as he leaueth a different power of Sheol ouer ỹ iust & but iust, frō which Dauid saith, God will deliuer his soule, and do not make the soules of the righteous D E S C E N D T O SHEOL

° Prouerb.5

ᵖ Prouerb.23

ᑫPsal.89.
ʳPsal.49

ʳPsal.49.

Abrahams bosome is no part of Sheol, or hel.

SHEOL after death. For that directlie impugneth the doc-
trine, as well of the olde teſtament, which ſaith the [t] way
of life is on high; as of our Sauiour, who placeth Abrahams
boſome VPVVARD A FAR OFF from hell; when he ſaith
of the rich man; that "being in hell in torments, hee LIFT VP
his eies and ſaw *Abraham* A FAR OFF, and *Lazarus* in his
boſome. Vpon which place, S. Auguſten learnedlie and tru-
lie inferreth, [x] *Ne ipſos quidem* INFEROS VSPIAM *ſcriptu-*
rarum locis IN BONO APPELLATOS *potui reperire. Quòd*
ſi nuſquam in diuinis authoritatibus legitur, non vtique ſinus ille
Abrahæ, id eſt, ſecreta cuiuſdam quietis habitatio ALIQVA
PARS INFERORVM *eſſe credenda eſt : quanquam in ijs ipſis*
tanti magiſtri verbis, vbi ait dixiſſe Abraham, Inter nos & vos
chaos magnum firmatum eſt ; SATIS VT OPINOR APPA-
RET, NON ESSE QVANDAM PARTEM, ET QVASI
MEMBRVM INFERORVM, *tanta illius felicitatis ſinum:*
Chaos enim magnum, quid eſt niſi quidam hiatus multum ea ſe-
parans, inter qua non ſolum eſt, verum etiam firmatus eſt ? The
name of *Inferi* I could no where finde in anie place of ſcripture
vſed IN ANY GOOD SENSE : which if wee doe no where
reade in the authorities of the ſcripture, ſurelie *Abrahams* bo-
ſome, which is an habitation of ſecret reſt, may not be thought
to bee ANY PEECE OF THE LOVVER PARTS albeit in
the words of ſo ſufficient a maiſter (as our Sauiour) where he
maketh *Abraham* ſay, betwixt vs and you there is a GREATE
GVLFE ESTABLISHED, it is EVIDENT ENOVGH, as
I take it; that the boſome of ſo great felicitie, is NO PART
NOR MEMBER of hell. For what is a great gulſe, but a great
diſtance ſeparating thoſe places, betweene which it lieth? *Inferi*
are the lower parts where the dead remaine, which the He-
brew calleth Sheòl; and touching Inferi, which are the pla-
ces, or ſpirits beneath, we maie with S. Auſten conclude two
thinges out of the manifeſt wordes of our Sauiour. Firſt
that Abrahams boſome is VPVVARD towards heauen, and
therfore the ſoules of the righteous before the death of Chriſt

aſcended

[t] Prouerb. 13

[*] Luke 16.

[x] *Auguſt. epiſt.*
99.

ascended rather, then descended. Next, that neither paradise,
nor Abrahams bosome, (which was the receptacle for ꝑ soules
of all the sonnes of Abraham, that held the faith, and did the
workes of Abraham,) was anie part or member of hell. So
that CHRISTS DESCENDING INTO HELL cannot be
expounded of his conuersing with the spirites of the iust and
perfect men after his death; nor of his enduring the state of
the deade; since the place, where their soules doe rest after
death, is no where in the scriptures called HELL or SHEOL,
or, as S. Austen speaketh, INFERI. And this I take to be so
cleare, that neither Iewish Rabbines with their grammatt-
ickll obseruations, nor Greeke poets with their fantasticall
imaginations may be suffered to contradict it. Howe easie
it is to wrangle with the words, NEPHESH, SHEOL, and
HADES a meane scholar mate soon perceiue; but I hold it no
sound course to fetch the explication of the mysteries of chri-
stian religion, either from such impudent impugners of it,
as were the Rabbines, or from such ignorant deluders of it,
as were the prophane poets, who talke euerie where of hea-
uen and hell, according to the false and lewde perswasion of
their own hearts. And therfore they may spare their paines,
that promise vs so manie thousand deponentes both Iewish
and heathen, that Sheol and Hades do not signifie hell. It will
trouble them more then they thinke, to bring vs but one good
proofe out of the scripture, that the soules of the righteous be-
fore Christs comming. were in Sheol or Hades; and till they
doe, I rest on Saint Austens collection out of the wordes of
Christ; that Abrahams bosome is no péece nor part of Ha-
des, or Inferi, which the hebrew calleth Sheol, as being deui-
ded from it with a mightie distance; and that the soules of
the iust departing this life before Christs death, were ᵛ CA- ˒Luke.16.
RIED VP BY THE ANGELS, INTO ABRAHAMS BO-
SOME.

So that as yet wee haue not the true meaning of these
words of our creed, he was CRVCIFIED, DEAD, & BVRIED;

XI.   HE

HE DESCENDED INTO HEL; neither doeth anie of the precedent opinions come néere the plaine and true exposition thereof. For in my iudgement they must haue a sense both DIFFERENT in matter; and CONSEQVENT in order, euen as they lie, before we can rightlie vnderstand thē. First he must be DEAD; then BVRIED in body, which was laid in ye earth: lastlie the soule after it was seuered by death from the bodie, DESCENDED INTO HEL; & this third point, he descended into hell, must neither be ALLEGORIZED, which in matters of faith is verie dangerous, so long as the proper sense containeth a truth; nor CONFOVNDED VVITH THE FORMER: for so the Créed shal not shortly touch mysteries of religion, but darckly trouble vs with phrases of variation. And therefore for my part, I retaine in expounding this Article, 3. things; DISTINCTION of matter, CONSEQVENCE of order, & PROPRIETY of words; and those thrée considered, the sense of the Article maie & must be, that Christ, after his BODY was BVRIED, in SOVLE DESCENDED VNTO that place, which the scripture properly calleth HEL; & this sense I find to be so far from any falsity or absurdity, that it is more honorable to Christ, and more comfortable to christians, then any of the rest, that we haue yet examined. Which that you may the better perceiue, giue me leaue somewhat farther to repeat the fruit and force of his glorious resurrection.

Christ is called * the first fruits of them that slept; not that neuer none before Christ was restored from the deade, to liue héere on earth; but though many were so reuiued againe, yet from the foundation of the worlde not one was euer raised vnto a blessed and immortall-life before Christ. Elias raised the [a] widow of Sareptas sonne; Elizeus the [b] Sunamites; Christ himself restored to life the [c] daughter of Iairus, the [d] widowes onlie sonne of Naim, and [e] Lazarus; yet all these after their returne to life were still subiect to sinne and death, as they were before; but he whom the scripture nameth [f] the first begotten of the dead, was indéede the first, that euer rose from the

How ye words of the Creed are best expounded.

* 1.Corinth.15

[a] 1.Regum.17.
[b] 2.Regum.4
[c] Marci.5.
[d] Luke.7
[e] Iohn.11

[f] Reuelat.1.

the deade into an happy and heauenly life. For where man
here on earth is befet with three dangers, with SINNE du-
ring life, with DEATH fhortning life, with HEL tormenting
after life; (the iuft vengeance of finne deliuering the body to
death, the foule to hel:) the refurrection of Chrift, being the ful
conqueft of all his & our enemies, that impugne either his
glory or our fafety, muft ouerthrowe, finne, death & hel; not in
his own perfon onlie, to whom no fuch thing was due, but in
our ftead, & for our good; y we might bee likewife freed from
the power of thofe foes; and as members be ioyned vnto our
head, wholy without any hinderance, euerlaftingly without
anie difturbance, and ioyfully without any greeuance. Wher-
fore Chrift rifing into a SPIRITVAL, IMMORTAL, & CE-
LESTIAL life, freed vs from the dominion of finne, feare of
death, and fury of Satan; and by s quickening vs, raifing vs vp,
and fetting vs together with himfelfe, in heauenly places, hath
not only giuen vs the victorie againft finne, and death; but
euen trodden down Satan vnder our feet.

s Ephef.1

Of Chrifts conqueft againft finne & death, I fhall not need
to fay much; things not impugned require leffe paines to be
defended; his conqueft ouer hel, as in himfelf it fhewed moft
power, & purchafed moft honor; fo from vs it deferueth grea-
teft thanks; as bringing vs greateft comfort, that though finne
remaine, & death preuaile againft our bodies; there is yet no
caufe to feare or doubt the fulneffe and fureneffe of our re-
demption, fince the ftrength of hel is altogether conquered
& abolifhed from the faithfull; which before was the very fting
of finne and death. As therfore Chrift was h deliuered to death
for our finnes; and is rifen againe for our iuftification; fo by
MERCY REMITTING, and GRACE REPRESSING, he pareth the
branches, and drieth the roote of finne; till the bodie of finne
and death turning to duft, & withering in the graue, be refto-
red againe after Chrifts example to perpetuall & celeftial life
and bliffe. Infomuch that by lamenting finne paft; and refi-
fting finne to come, fin daily dieth in vs; and the inward man

h Rom.4.

Chrift the firft
that euer rofe,
conqueror of
finne, death
and hell.

The conqueft
of Chrift ouer
finne & death.

X 2. of

of the heart being lightened and renewed by grace doth daily moꝛe and moꝛe, by deſire and delight of heauenly thinges, aſpire to the imitation and participation of Chꝛiſtes reſurrection. The foꝛce of ſinne then being quenched by Chꝛiſtes dying vnto ſinne, and his riſing againe vnto righteouſneſſe, the power of death is aboliſhed by the pardoning and decreaſing of our ſinnes; that being nowe the paſſage to gloꝛie foꝛ all repenters, which befoꝛe was the gate to hell foꝛ all tranſgreſſoꝛs. In his owne perſon Chꝛiſt ſhewed his conqueſt ouer death, not by keeping his fleſh from death, which he could eaſilie haue done, but by ſauing it from rotting in the ſepulchꝛe, and by raiſing it againe into an immoꝛtall and gloꝛious ſtate: that death being ſwallowed vp by the power of his life, hee might take from vs the feare of death, whiles here wee liue: and change the curſe of death, making it nowe a reſt from all labours, which befoꝛe was an entrance into perpetuall paine. This enemie, becauſe he doth leaſt harme, ſhall bee laſt deſtroied: euen at the daie of the generall reſurrection, and not befoꝛe: and ſerueth now rather to repreſſe ſinne, then to reuenge ſinne; the godlie being by death deliuered from the committing, louing, oꝛ feeling ſinne; and the wiſedome of God pꝛouiding, that as ſinne brought death into the woꝛld, ſo death ſhould aboliſh ſinne out of the woꝛlde. This is byte the victoꝛie, that Chꝛiſt obtained againſt ſinne and death, by his dying and riſing from the dead. His conqueſt ouer hell, as it is moꝛe queſtioned, and moꝛe expected, ſo will I not refuſe to ſhew you, what I thinke maie be ſafelie beleeued, and muſt not raſhlie be reiſcted of any chꝛiſtian.

The conqueſt of Chꝛiſt ouer hell and Satan may bee no way doubted by any diuine, that rightly handleth the myſterie of our ſaluation. In vaine do we ſpeake of releaſing ſinne, oꝛ deſpiſing death, if the right of hell to vs, and power of hell ouer vs doe ſtill remaine. And therefoꝛe the verie ground of Chꝛiſts conquering ſinne and death, is his ſubduing of hell and Satan, that they ſhould lay no chalenge to, noꝛ haue no foꝛce

i Reuel. 14

In vaine is all that chriſt did for vs, if hel be not cōquered.

force againſt the faithful. It is then on all ſides accorded, that hell and Satan muſt be fullie conquered by Chriſt, before the worke of our redemption can be perfectlie ſetled or aſſured; but as well the time when, as the maner how, are ſomewhat queſtioned, and that maketh the whole matter the more needfull to be diſcuſſed. To refute euerie mans fanſie that ſpeaketh hereof, were an infinite labour; to ſearch out a truth in this caſe, that maie ſafelie be receiued, and comfortablie embraced, if not neceſſarilie vrged, is the ſumme of mine intention, and ſhould bee the ende of your expectation; with this prouiſo, that no man carpe before hee righlie conceiue; nor pronounce before hee well crammine that which ſhall be ſpoken; leaſt hee checke the Scriptures before he be ware, and condemne the whole Church of God without anie cauſe.

In expreſſing Chriſtes conqueſt ouer hell and Satan, I thinke beſt to obſerue theſe three things : VVHAT hee did vnto Satan and his kingdomie; VVHEN; and with VVHICH PART OF HIMSELFE hee did execute this triumph. VVHAT HE DID vnto Satan, wee ſhall learne, by ſeeing what he ſuffered at Satans hands. Proportionable to Chriſts humiliation was his exaltation; and for the violence which he endured, he receiued full ſatiſfaction. As then on the croſſe Chriſt ſuffered at Satans hands, and by Satans meanes REPROCHE, RAGE, & VVRONG; ſo in his reſurrection he reaped a triple recompence from Satan : SVBMISSION, whereby his pride was ſubiected vnder Chriſt; CAPTIVATION, whereby his rage was reſtrained, and himſelfe chained by Chriſt; RESTITVTION, whereby his ſpoiles were diuided, and deliuered vnto Chriſt. When I ſay that Satan was SVBDVED, TIED, and SPOILED by Chriſt riſing from the dead, let no vnſetled braine imagine, this is ſuperſtitious and popiſh; as I meane them, and as the ſcriptures deliuer them, they are propheticall and Apoſtolicall. And leaſt you ſhould thinke I delude

The methode of handling Chriſts deſcent.

Chriſts conqueſt ouer Satan had theſe three effects.

you with woordes, I will shewe you whence I take them;
first iointlie all in one sentence, then seuerallie from sun-
drie places of the holie scriptures. Our Sauiour in the Gos-
pell doth purposelie make this comparison, or rather this pa-
rable concerning himself and the kingdom of Satan. ᵏ How
can a man ENTER into a strong mans house, and spoile his
goods, except he first 'B I N D the strong man, and then S P O I L E
his house? Christ then ENTERED vpon Satans house as
A CONQVERER; TIED him as the STRONGER; SPOI-
LED him as the right OVVNER of that, which Satan vniust-
lie detained from him. And albeit it maie not bee denied,
but Christ whiles hee liued on earth, made some proofe,
of his right and power, to dissolue the workes, and displace
the force of Satan, from the bodies and soules of men; yet it
is euident that the full demonstration of his victorie, and
perfection of his glorie were reserued to the time of his re-
surrection, when he brake the chaines and sorrowes of death
and hell, and ascended to his father, not onelie clothed with
honour, and immortalitie, but armed with power and princi-
palitie; ˡ all knees bowing vnto him, in heauen, earth and hell,
and all tongues confessing that Iesus was the Lord, to the glorie
of God. These varie parts of Christs conquest ouer Satan,
the Apostle doth comprise in one sentence to the Colossians,
saying: Christ ᵐ S P O I L E D powers and principalities, and
made A SHEVV of them openlie, TRIVMPHING ouer
them in his owne person. That powers and principalities
in this place doe signifie wicked and sinfull spirites there
can bee no question; those names in the scriptures are
proper to Angels, bee they good or badde; as Roman. 8
vers. 38. Ephes. 3. vers. 10. & 6. vers. 12. Colos. 1. vers. 16
1. Peter. 3. vers. 20. And heere must needes import euill
Angels, because Christ had no cause to conquere or spoile
the elect Angels, which serued him, and ministred vn-
to him; but the badde, that impugned his trueth, and
enuied his glorie. Ouer those then Christ TRIVMPHED

as

The proofe of
these three by
the scriptures
ᵏ Mat. 12.
Mark. 3.

ˡ Phil. 2.

ᵐ Colos. 2.

as a conquerer; thoſe bee OPENLIE SHEVVED as cap-
tiues bounde with chains; thoſe be STRIPT OR SPOI-
LED of the goodes which they had vnlawfullie gotten. And
this the Apoſtle ſaith he did execute in his owne perſon, as a
triumph fit for the ſonne of God, [n] all things being ſubiected
vnder his feete, yea, [o] Angels, powers, and mights ſubdued vnto
him, when he aſcended into heauen.

    And though ſome late tranſlators, to decline the deſ-
cent of Chriſt to hell after death, doe imagine that the wic-
ked Angels were CONQVERED, SHEVVED and SPOI-
LED by Chriſt in his ſuffering the paines of hell on the
croſſe; and to that ende doe alter the ancient and conſtant
reading of the text; putting in ſteade of ἐν αὐτῷ, in his owne
perſon, ἐν αὐτῷ in the ſame croſſe; yet ſince both ſcriptures
and fathers with one conſent doe contradict that daun-
gerous ſpeculation, I maie not admitte it as conſonant,
either to the faith or truth of the Scriptures . For the
conqueſt which Chriſt had ouer Satan and his King-
dome, was not by RESISTING, much leſſe by SVFFE-
RING the aſſaults of hell. He is no conquerer that with
much adoe ſaueth himſelfe and his from the furie of his
enemies; but hee that ſubdueth and treadeth his aduerſa-
ries vnder his feete, and ſo maiſtreth them, that hee may diſ-
poſe of them at his will, he is truly called a conquerer. And
ſince the Apoſtle ſaith, Chriſt SPOILED the powers of dark-
nes, and made AN OPEN SHEVV of them, and TRIVM-
PHED ouer them, it is all euident wrong to Chriſt to thinke
that all the conqueſt hee had ouer them, was at length to
REPELL them, with mightie feares and cries TO SCAPE
their force. Yea the redemption of mankind is altogither
vncertaine and vnſufficient, if our head being God and man,
could doe no more but by long ſtruggling winde himſelfe out
of Satans clawes. Wee muſt confeſſe an other kind of con-
queſt, before the kingdome of Chriſt can ouerrule all as it
muſt; and his Church bee ſecure from the gates of hell;

                                                         to

[n] 1.Cor.15.
[o] 1.Peter.3.

*On the croſſe
Chriſt obtai-
ned his tri-
umph, but he
executed it at
his reſurrectió*

p Mat. 28.
q Philip. 2
r Reuel. 1.

f Psal 2.
t Heq. 2.

to wit, that p ALL POVVER in heauen and earth was giuen vnto him; that q EVERIE KNEE in heauen, and earth, and hell bowed vnto him; that he had and hath THE r KEFES of death and OF HELL; and could f RVLE his enemies with a rodde of yron, and breake them like a potters vessell; that by his death, hee t DESTROIED him, that was the ruler of death, euen the diuell. This conquest Christ purchased by his passion, but he did not execute it till his resurrection; otherwise he could not haue died, if death on the crosse had beene throughlie conquered. But hee was humbled and crinanited on the crosse, euen vnto death, that he might after hr his resurrection bee exalted, and replenished with all honour, power, and principalitie, in heauen, earth and hell. Howbeit of the time VVHEN hee triumphed, wee shall afterwarde speake; we nowe obserue VVHAT hee did in his triumph ouer hell and Satan; and by the Scriptures wee finde that Christ ENTERED Satans house, TIED him, and SPOILED his goodes; or as the Apostle expresseth it, hee SPOILED POVVERS & PRINCIPALITIES, MADE AN OPEN SHEVV of them, and TRIVMPHED OVER THEM IN HIS OVVNE PERSON.

And least I be thought to pretend an ancient and vniforme reading of Paules wordes in this place without iust proofe, let vs see what ancient fathers haue followed the same. The Siriacke translation of the newe Testament, which is of no small antiquitie, readeth IN SEMETIPSO, IN HIS OVVNE PERSON, as I doe. So do Origen, m Epistola ad Romanos, lib. 5. cap. .. Epiphanius in Anchorato, & contra Pneumatomacheos hæres. 74. Chrysostome homili. 6 or .. ca. ad Colos. and Theodorete likewise in 2 cap. ad Colos. Of the Latine Fathers, in whome it miste better bee distinguished, the booke de Trinitate vnder Tertullians name, Augustine contra Faustum: lib. 16. cap. 29 & Epistola 59. a Hilarius de Trinitate. lib. 1. & lib. 9. Fulgentius ad Thrasimundum. lib. 3. Hieronymus in cap. 2. ad Colos. Ambrose vpon the same place, Ruffinus

a Colos. 2. The fathers read in semetipso in his own person, and those y reade εν αυτῷ applie it to Christ, & not to the crosse, laue onelie Occumenius.

Ruffinus *in Symbolum Apoftolicum,* and fo throughout the Latine Church without anie diffenting. Onelie the Greeke collections vnder Oecumenius name, referre that triumph which faint Paul here fpeaketh of, to the Croffe, faying that Chrift fhamed and confounded the diuell on the croffe, in that he was openlie crucified in the eies of all the people . And although J condemne not the fenfe as falfe, that Chrift wreftled with Satan on the croffe, and euen there ouermaftred his power, yet that Chrift had no further or greater triumph ouer hell and Satan, then by dying on the croffe in the fight of men, doth vtterlie abolifh the glorie of his refurrection, and contradicteth the whole courfe of the fcriptures. By his fuffering and dying on the croffe; hee deferued and purchafed the exaltation, and triumph which he had afterwards, when he rofe from the dead; and euen before he died, he was fafflie affured, that neither his foule fhould be left in hell, nor his flefh fee corruption; but that God would raife him again, and giue him all power in heauen and earth ; and make all knees in heauen, earth, and hell to bow vnto him , and place him at his right hand in the brightneffe of eternall glorie. Jt may therefore be confeffed + beleeued, that Chrift ouerthrew Satan on the croffe; and fo triumphed in fpirit againft him, or had a fpirituall triumph ouer him, as Dauid foretolde, when he faid in the perfon of Chrift ; Mine heart was glad , and my tongue ioyfull; yea my flefh fhall reft in hope ; but that the glorie of his refurrection did not farre excell the fhame of his paffion , and that his rifing from the deade was no more victorious and triumphant, then his yeelding himfelfe vnto death, is directlie repugnant to the truth of the fcriptures. Though he were ᵡ C R V C I F I E D T H R O V G H I N: F I R M I T I E, yet liueth he (faith Paul) through T H E P O VV E R of God. So that to die , euen in Chrift, was infirmitie, though voluntarie ; to liue againe as hee liueth in the height of celeftiall glorie, was a cleare demonftration of the power of God in him. ʸ He was declared to be the fon of God,

Oecumenius in 2. cap. ad Colof.

Chrifts refurrectio was a far more glorious triumph ouer Satan, then his paffion was.

ᵡ 2. Cor. 13.

ʸ Rom. 1.

Y 1　　　　in

in power by the resurrection from the dead. Insomuch that if Christ had died, and not risen againe, his conquest had not beene worth the speaking of . ^z If Christ bee not raised, your faith is in vaine, saith Paule; and ye are yet in your sinnes . Christes death then without his resurrection had béene a full conquest of Satan ouer Christ, and all his members. That which Paule sayeth , is true, as well in Christ as in vs ; ^a It is sowen in dishonour , it is raised in glorie; it is sowen in VVEAKENESSE,it is raised in power. Since then in the death and crosse of Christ the holie ghost noteth ^b reproach, ^c shame and weakenesse ; wee do foulie erre, if wee ascribe no greater , nor other triumph to Christ ouer death and hell , then his crosse and passion. ^d These things Christ was to suffer, and (so) to enter into his glorie ; but we must make as great difference betwixt his dying , and his rising againe, as wee woulde betwixt his weakenesse and his power; his conflict, and his conquest;his depression, and his exaltation ; his suffering in reproch, and his raigning in glorie.

For the better euidence thereof, you shall see the holie scriptures at large expresse the verie same parts,and the verie same time,which I obserued vnto you . ^e Christ humbled himselfe,and became obedient vnto the death , euen the death of the crosse. WHEREFORE God also highly EXALTED him,and gaue him a name aboue euery name, that at the name of Iesus euery KNEE SHOVLD BOVV,of things IN HEAVEN IN EARTH,AND BENEATH THE EARTH, Under the earth are no reasonable creatures to knéele to Christs person and scepter, but the damned spirits and soules in hell, except we take holde of Purgatorie, or Limbus patrum; the elect in heauen doe willinglie serue him ; such as liue on earth, doe endure his iustice or loue his mercie; tho spirits beneath doe finde his truth , and feele his hand ; the most aduerse acknowledge his name,and feare his force. This exaltation of Christ to raigne ouer heauen , earth and hell;

carte

^z 1.Cor.15.

^a Ibidem.

^b Heb.13.
^c Heb.12.

^d Luke.24.

^e Phil.2.

The cause and time of chrifts triumph.

caure after his death, as being the rewarde and effect of his obedience vnto death. So faith the Apoſtle. He humbled himſelfe, and became obedient to the death, euen the death of the Croſſe. WHEREFORE (or for which cauſe) God highlie exalted him, that in the name of Ieſus all knees in heauen, earth and hell ſhould bowe. Then on the croſſe, or afore his death the time was not yet come, that Chriſt ſhould be thus exalted; but there rather was the time and place of his humiliation; and when he roſe againe, [f] all power in heauen and earth was giuen vnto him. [g] I was dead (ſaith hee himſelfe) and behold I am aliue for euermore; and I HAVE THE KEIES OF HELL AND OF DEATH; that is all power ouer death and hell, to [h] ſhut and no man may open; to open, and no man may ſhut. The Prophet Eſay pointeth to the verie ſame CAVSE and TIME of Chriſtes exaltation. [i] BECAVSE he hath powred out his ſoule vnto death: THEREFORE will I giue him his portion with the great, and hee ſhall diuide the ſpoiles with the mightie. If FOR THAT CAVSE; then AFTER THAT TIME, Chriſt diuided the ſpoyles of the mightie; or (as the Apoſtle ſpeaketh) hee ſpoyled powers and principalities. And noting exactlie the TIME of Chriſtes triumph, the Apoſtle ſaith ἀναβὰς εἰς ὕψος, ASCENDING ON HIGH, HE LED CAPTIVITIE CAPTIVE. This that hee aſcended, what meaneth it, but that hee firſt deſcended into the lower partes of the earth? Chriſt did not leade captiuitie captiue, when hee deſcended into the lower partes of the earth, but when hee aſcended from thence. The Diuels then which helde vs in captiuitie, were themſelues leade captiue, when Chriſt aſcended from the lower partes of the earth; and then were powers and principalities SPOILED, and openlie SHEVVED, Chriſt TRIVMPHING OVER THEM, not on the Croſſe at the time of his paſſion; but IN HIS OVVNE PERSON, at the time of his reſurrection and aſcenſion.

[f] Math. 28.
[g] Reuel. 1.

[h] Reuel. 3.

[i] Eſay. 53.

[k] Epheſ. 4.

An

¹Reuel.20.

An effect of this triumph is this, that an Angell was ſent (in the Reuelation of Saint Iohn) from heauen hauing the key of the bottomleſſe pit, and a great chaine in his hand. And hee tooke the Dragon that olde Serpent, which is the diuel & Satan, and bound him a thouſand yeares. And caſt him into the bottomles pit, and ſhut him vp, and ſealed vpõ him, that he ſhould deceiue the people no more. If a meſſenger from Chriſt had this power ouer Satan, to binde him, and ſhut him vp, what commaund then had Chriſt himſelfe ouer hell and Satan? And how wholeſome and gladſome a thing is it for vs to beleeue and confeſſe, that Chriſt Ieſus our Lord and ſauiour hath Satan, and all the powers of hell chained at his will, and by his conqueſt ouer them ſo ruleth and reſtraineth them that they can not ſtirre but by his leaue and appointment; and thus ſhall he hold them captiue, till hee deliuer the kingdome to God his father, and throughly tread both death and Satan vnder our feete. This doctrine I truſt maintaineth no ſuperſtition, but ſound and true religion, as well touching the partes, as the time of Chriſts conqueſt and triumph ouer death and hell.

It reſteth now to ſearch what part of Chriſt had this triumph ouer hell; for ſo much as Chriſt conſiſted of two natures, diuine, and humane; his manhood by death was then diuided into two places, the bodie being ſeparate from the ſoule, and lying in the duſt of the earth, but without corruption. And firſt, we muſt not referre this triumph to his diuine nature; by reaſon it was no maiſterie for god to conquer his vaſſall. The ᵐ ſeede of the woman muſt bruize the ſerpents heade, and not the maker of heauen and earth with his almightie power & maieſtie. Beſides the godhead of Chriſt coulde neither truly DESCEND, nor ASCEND; as being euery where preſent; nor be EXALTED as being equall with the higheſt, nor RECEIVE GIFT, as hauing all fulnes in it: but that nature which led captiuitie captiue, did firſt DESCEND into ẙ lower parts of the earth, & after ASCENDED, & was EXAL-
TED

Chriſts manhood muſt triumph and not his Godhead.

ᵐ Gen.3.

TED, AND RECEAVED this power and honour as a GIFT from God, in refpect of his obedience, patience, and humilitie. The places are before alleaged, there is no neede to repeat them. It was then Chriftes humane nature, which God fo highlie EXALTED for his former obedience vnto death, and to which all power was giuen in heauen and earth; his diuine was euer in euen degree with his father, full of maieftie, power and glorie. It is not to be neglected, that Ireneus faith. ⁿ Si homo non viciffet inimicum hominis, non iuftè victus effet inimicus. If a man had not ouercome the enemy of man, the enemie had not lawfully beene ouercome. Which pro-portion of iuftice the Apoftle vrgeth, when he faith; as ° by a man came death, fo by a man came the refurrection of the dead. Since then the humane nature of Chrift by condition might, and by defert muft bee exalted aboue all creatures; and by the rule of iuftice had the conqueft of fatan and his kingdome; it is no harde matter to difcerne, which part of Chrifts manhood muft ouerthrow death, and which muft tri-umph ouer hell. The bodie of man, whiles the firft death la-fteth, is not due to hell; it muft lie dead and fenfeleffe in the earth; and fo can neither liue, nor feele the paines of hell. Chriftes bodie then lying in the graue without SENSE, MO-TION, OR LIFE, could haue no conqueft ouer hell; ouer death it had, being preferued in the graue without all corrup-tion; and raifed from the deade to a bleffed and immortall ftate without all imperfection: Ouer hel it had none, becaufe that part of Chrift which did conquere hel, muft haue as well MOTION TO DESCEND thither, and POVVER TO RE-PRESSE there the rage of fatâ; as alfo LIFE AND SENSE TO SPOILE powers and principalities, and by leading them captiue to make an open fhewe of them; from al which, the firft death kept the bodie of Chrift; till the time that his foule afcending with triumph from hell, tooke his body from death, and fo made a perfect conqueft ouer hell and death, not onlie for his owne perfon, to whome all power was giuen

° Irenæus.lib.3. cap.20.

° 1.Corinth.15

And in his mã-hood the foule, not the bodie, which lay dead in earth.

P 3.   in

in heauen and earth, but foʒ his members alſo, foʒ whoſe ſaꝼ
fety he tooke from Satan the keyes of hell, and of death, that

ᵖRom.14

he himſelfe might be ᵖ Lord of the dead & the liuing. So that
now the power of hell is deſtroied, and Satan reſtrained,
and the faithfull freed from all feare, & aſſured that

ᑫMatth.16.

ᑫ the gates
of hel ſhal not preuaile againſt them. And this is that victoʒie,
which God thʒeatened to death and hell by his pʒophet, ſay-

ʳOſee.13

ing: ʳ I will redeeme them from THE POVVER OF HEL;
I will deliuer them from death. O death I will be thy death: O
HEL I VVIL BE THY DESTRVCTION; repentance is hid
from mine eyes.

Whether
Chriſts deſcēt
to hel be writ-
ten in the ſcrip-
tures, or no.

So agréeable is this doctrine to the chʒiſtian faith, & ſo com-
foʒtable to all the godly, that few would refuſe it, except ſuch
as are waſpiſhlie wedded to their owne fanſies; if it might
appeare where this is wʒitten in the ſcriptures. The which
deſire of religious mindes, whiles I laboʒ to ſatiſfie, I muſt
foʒwarne them, how eaſie it is foʒ cōtentions ſpirits to fruſ-
trate the ſtrength of all that God ſaith, if they may be ſuffe-
red with diuerſe ſignifications, & figuratiue interpʒetations,
to elude when they liſt, the woʒds of the holie ghoſt, & decline
the literall & pʒoper ſenſe of the diuine oʒacles at their plea-
ſures. This rule therefoʒe muſt be helde thʒoughout the ſcrip-
tures, ÿ in myſteries of religion, we diuert not from the na-
tiue & proper ſignifications of the woʒdes, but when the letter
impugneth the grounds of chʒiſtian faith & charity. Otherwiſe
we ſhal leaue nothing ſound & ſure in the woʒd of God; if we
may auoid al things by figures: that pleaſe not our humoʒs.

ſ *Auguſt. de
doctri. Chriſtia-
na. lib.3.cap.10.*

ſ To this leſſon, (ſaith Auſten) whereby wee take heede not
to interpret a figuratiue ſpeach, as if it were proper; we muſt
adde another, that wee take not a proper ſpeach, as if it were
figuratiue. Firſt then we muſt ſhewe the meane, how to finde
out whether the ſpeach bee figuratiue or proper. And this is

ᵗ *ibidem.*

the way to diſcerne them; ᵗ *vt quicquid in ſermone diuino, ne-
que ad morum honeſtatem, neque ad fidei veritatem proprie refer-
ri poteſt, figuratum eſſe cognoſcas;* that whatſoeuer in the diuine
ſcripture

ſcripture CANNOT PROPERLY be referred to the honeſtie of maners, or to the verity of faith, thou maiſt be ſure it is FIGV-RATIVE. So long then as the proper ſenſe of the ſcriptures may ſtand with the Analogy of faith, and direction of charity; we offer violence to the word of God, if wee wreſt it to a figuratiue vnderſtanding.

From this rule, (which muſt be obſerued throughout the body of the ſcripture,) if we do not raſhly ſlide; it is no harde matter to ſhew where Chriſtes deſcent to hell is expreſlie recorded in the ſcriptures. The words are well knowen, & often alleaged, if men were not diſpoſed to peruert, or elude them with their enigmaticall & allegoricall conſtructions. u Thou VVILT NOT FORSAKE MY SOVLE IN HELL, nor ſuffer thine holy one to ſee corruptió. If Chriſts ſoule in hel were aſſiſted with the glorious power and preſence of God; ergo Chriſtes ſoule vvas in hel. And THERE it could not be, without DESCEN-DING THITHER. The deſcent then of Chriſtes ſoule into hell, when it was ſeuered from the bodie, is apparantly witneſſed in the ſcriptures, howſoeuer the diuers conceits of men doe diuerſly expound it. To take the SOVLE for the CARCAS; & HEL for the GRAVE, (as ſome do) if it be not a wreſted expoſition, I am ſure it is not the proper interpretation of the words; and therefore in myſteries of faith by no meanes to be admitted. To let the ſoule retaine her true ſignification, and by hell to meane paradiſe (where others defend the ſoule of Chriſt was al the time, that his bodie lay in the graue;) if it be not a miſconſtruction, it is no literall expoſition of the place, and in my iudgement a verie ſtrange kind of figure it is, to expreſſe Chriſts aſcent into Paradiſe, by his deſcent into hell; & ſo to expound the words of the Crẽd, that we draw them to a cleane contrary ſenſe. If therefore we leaue forcing & wreſting the words of the holy ghoſt, & let their proper & true ſignification ſtand, as wel ʒ words, as the circumſtances wil exactly proue that ʒ ſoule of Chriſt after death DESCENDED INTO HEL. That this was performed after Chriſt was dead, and conſequently when

* Pſal. 16.
Acts. 2
The words are plaine enough if we wreſt the not from their proper ſenſe.

when his soule was seuered from his bodie, there can bee no question, as I haue shewed before; for that Christ saieth, his flesh [*]SHAL LIE DOVVN (or take rest in the tabernacle of his graue) IN HOPE that God VVIL NOT FORSAKE HIS SOVLE IN HEL; and in this hope Christ died: this assistance was therfore giuen him after death. That his soule must be taken properlie for that part, which after death sawe the power and presence of God not forsaking him, as well the separation of the bodie, as fruition of Gods assistance do plainelie proue. Whiles we liue, the bodie or soule may rightlie import the whole man; but after death it is more then absurd to take the soule for the bodie, or the bodie for the soule: yea in men here liuing, wee must take hæde that in matters of doctrine we mistake not the one for the other. In matters of fact, to note the person by either part, can be no danger; but in their attributes and properties, to confounde them, is to leaue nothing certaine in christian religion. Tertullian saith truly. [y] *Certe peruersissimū, vt carnem nominantes animā intelligamus; & animam significantes, carnē interpretemur. Omnia periclitabuntur aliter accipi, quam sunt; & amittere quod sunt, dum aliter accipiuntur: si aliter, quam sunt, cognominantur. Fides nominum salus est proprietatum.* It is most peruerse, that the flesh being named, wee should vnderstande the soule, or the soule being signified, wee should interpret it for the flesh. All thinges shall be in danger to bee otherwise taken then they are, and to loose that they are, while they are mistaken, if wee call them by other names then their owne. The distinction of their names is the preseruation of their properties. And yet in these words the case is clærer. For heere are both partes expressed and distinguished as well by their NATVRES, and PLACES, as by their NAMES. Christs soule was not forsaken in hell, but enioyed the glorious assistance of God, euen there, where God forsaketh all others: Christes flesh lying dead without sense in the graue, was there preserued from all corruption. For Dauid, saith Peter, [z] spake of Christs

[*]Psal.16.

The soule must not be taken for the bodie, though man may be signified by either.

[y]*Tertullian. de carne Christi. cap.13.*

[z]Actes.2.

Chrifts refurrection, that his s o v l e was not forſaken, (o₂ left) in hel, nor his f l e s h ſaw corruption . ᵃ *Quum diuidit ſpecies, carnem & animam, duo oſtendit* , faith Tertullian . When (the ſcriptnre) deuideth the kindes, as the ſoule and the fleſh, it noteth two diſtinct things . Since then Peter doth not onlie ſo repo₂te, but ſo interp₂et Dauids wo₂des , that hee ſpake of Ch₂iſts ſoule and Ch₂iſts fleſh; it is euident they muſt be two diſtinct and different thinges, both in Dauids p₂ediction, and in Peters application.

ᵃ *Tertullian. de carne Chriſti. cap. 13*

Againe in theſe wo₂ds is not comp₂iſed the generall ſtate of the dead common to Ch₂iſt with all other, but a ſpeciall p₂erogatiue verified in none, but in the true Meſſias and Sauiour of the wo₂lde . Fo₂ neither of theſe was euer accompliſhed in anie, but in Ch₂iſt . Then as no fleſh in the ſepulch₂e was euer free from corruption, but onlie Ch₂iſts; ſo no ſoule in hell was euer ſuppo₂ted and aſſiſted by God, and not forſaken, but onely Chriſtes. If by hell , wee vnder ſtand Paradiſe; it was no p₂iuiledge to be there not fo₂ſaken, but rather a childiſh abſurditie to thinke that any ſoule might there be fo₂ſaken; and ſo no cauſe fo₂ Ch₂iſt ſo ſtrongly to hope, and ſo greatly to reioice, that h i s s o v l e ſhould not bee fo₂ſaken; where it was impoſſible, that anie ſoule ſhould be fo₂ſaken : but this is rather a iuſt grounde of exceeding ioie, if where all ſoules were fo₂ſaken of God, as in hell they are; there Ch₂iſtes ſoule ſhould not be fo₂ſaken, but aſſiſted with the might and maieſtie of God, to b₂eake the fo₂ce, and tread the power of hell vnder his fæt. And this p₂ooueth Ch₂iſtes refurrection mo₂e ſtronglie, (fo₂ which cauſe Dauid ſpake it) then if wee applie the name of hell to the ſtate of Paradiſe . Fo₂ if Ch₂iſt did riſe againe without co₂ruption, becauſe his ſoule was not fo₂ſaken of God in Paradiſe; then all the ſoules that riſe not in like maner, are fo₂ſaken of God, though they ſtill remaine in the reſt and cō fo₂t of Paradiſe; which is a palpable falſity, if not impietie. But if neither the graue could corrupt his fleſh, no₂ hell detaine his ſoule; what better aſſurance could be b₂ought of his

The circumſtances proue the words muſt be properly taken.

resurrection, then that neither death could diſſolue his bodie into duſt, nor hell preuaile againſt his ſoule. And this I take to be S. Peters reaſon when hee ſaith to the Iewes: b Ieſus of Nazareth haue ye taken by the handes of the wicked,& crucified, and ſlaine : whom God raiſed againe , BREAKING THE SORROVVES OF DEATH, in as much as it was IMPOSSIBLE he ſhould BE HELD THEROF. God made way for Chriſt to riſe againe by BREAKING THE SORROVVES OF DEATH before him, that they ſhould not hinder him. Chriſtes bodie lying dead in the graue,& lacking ſenſe could haue no ſorrow. In Paradiſe a place of reſt & ioie, if his ſoule were there , much leſſe may we imagine any ſorrow. Since then the ſepulchre hath no SENSE where Chriſts fleſh lay; & Paradiſe hath NO SORROVV; the SORROVVES OF DEATH muſt nœdes be referred to the paines of hel,which were all loſed and diſſolued before Chriſt , becauſe IT VVAS IMPOSSIBLE THEY SHOVLD TAKE HOLD OF HIM.

[But Peter,they will ſay, nameth the SORROVVES OF DEATH , and not of hell:] as if the name of death did not extende, as well to the c SECOND DEATH, which is hell, as to the firſt, which is the diſſolution of nature: and THE SORROVVES OF THE FIRST DEATH Chriſt apperantly ſuffered, as much as any man; and they ended with death, they dured not after death. But in Peters words the ſorrows of death were broken at Chriſts reſurrection . God d raiſed him vp, looſing the ſorrowes (or paines) of death . Wherefore the SORROVVES OF THE SECOND DEATH muſt neceſſarilie be vnderſtode; & thoſe were all broken and diſſolued before Chriſt, by reaſon his ſoule was not forſaké in hell, but vnited vnto God, & aided by the mighty hand of God, to tread vpon al the power of ꝥ aduerſary,& in his own perſon to triumph ouer Satan, and al the ſtrength of the kingdom of darknes.

Laſtly howſoeuer ſome preſumers on their Hebrew may wrangle with the word Sheôl in Dauids ſpeach, thou wilt not forſake my ſoule in hel : yet the worde ᾅδης, by which S. Luke expreſſeth Dauids meaning,doth properly import in the new teſta-

b Actes. 2.

c Apoc. 2
20.
21.
Death is either the firſt or the ſecond
d Actes. 2

The word
ᾅδης by
which S. Luke
expreſſeth Da-
uids meaning

teſtament the place of the damned. I remit poets & Pagans v- d oth alwaies note hel in the new teſtament
ſing that word after their prophane imagination, to the allea
gers; in what ſenſe the Euangeliſts and Apoſtles take it, will
ſone appeare by their writings. c Vpõ this Rock (ſaith Chriſt) c Matth. 16
wil I build my church, & the gates ἅδ̈ε (of hel) ſhal not preuaile
againſt it. The church doth not aſſure the godly, that they ſhall
not die.; but, that the gates of the f ſecond death ſhal not hurt f Reuelat. 2.
thẽ. When the merciles rich man died & was buried, as wee
read in the goſpel of S. Luke, ŷ ſcripture ſaith ε ͫ ἐν τῷ ἅδη, g Luke. 16
& being in hel, in TORMENTS, he lift vp his eies, and ſaw Abrahã
a far off, & Lazarus in his boſome. I hope the ſoule of this rich
man, was neither in the graue, nor in paradiſe, but plainelie
IN HEL, euen in the h PLACE OF TORMENTS, where no mercy h Ibidem, ver. 23
can be ſhewed, nor releaſe hoped for; and that place & ſtate of
the damned S. Luke calleth ἅδης, and our Sauior expreſſing
it, maketh the rich man moſt truly to ſaie; i I AM TORMEN- i Ibidem, ver. 24
TED IN THIS FLAME; S. Iohn in his Reuelation noting the co-
herence of death and hell in the deſtruction of the wicked,
ſaith. k Behold, a pale horſe, and his name, that ſate thereon was k Reuel. 6.
death, & (ἅδης) HEL FOLLOVVED AFTER HIM, and power was
giuen THEM ouer the fourth part of ŷ earth. After death follow-
eth none other death, but HEL, which is the ſecond death, and ŷ
as it commeth AFTER the death of the body; ſo is it diſtingui-
ſhed from the death of the bodie, becauſe it killeth the ſoule for
euer; and that S. Iohn calleth ἅδης. He doth the like in the 20.
chap. of the ſame booke. The l ſea (ſaith he) gaue vp her dead, l Reuelat. 20
which were in her, & death & (ἅδης) HEL deliuered vp her dead,
that were in them, and death & (ἅδης) HEL were caſt into ŷ lake
of fire; this is the ſecond death. When our ſauiour then ſaith, I
haue ŷ keies of death, m (καὶ τῶ ἅδε) & of hel, he doth not onlie m Reuel. 1
mean the graues of dead bodies are ſubieded to his power,
but the place and paines of damned ſoules are likewiſe at
his diſpoſition. And when Paule ſaith; O death, where is thy n 1. Corinth. 15
ſting (ἅδη) ò hel where is thy victory? he teacheth vs that God
hath giuen vs the victory ouer DEATH AND HEL, through
our Lord Ieſus Chriſt. That victorie Chriſt could not make

vs partakers of, except hee had firſt triumphed ouer them
both in his owne perſon. And that victorie Chriſt did foreſee
and foreſhew, when he ſaid to God, thou wilt not forſake my
ſoule (εἰς ᾄδℵ) in hell; (or leaue it to the power of hell;) but
aſſiſt me there, and bring me thence with ſafetie and victory.

If my collections were not allowed by the ſcriptures; the
generall faith and confeſſion of all the fathers in all ages and
countries, ſince the firſt foundation of Chriſts church, ſhould
moue men that are modeſt, not haſtelie to leape from the v-
niuerſall conſent of al places, and perſons grounding them-
ſelues on the manifeſt words of the ſacred ſcriptures. To
quote them all, were to increaſe another volume; I will
therefore content my ſelfe with ſhewing you, how ſoone it
began, and howe long it continued in the church of Chriſt,
to be receaued and beleæued as a matter of faith. Thaddæus
one of the 70. diſciples, mentioned in the tenth of Luke,
taught the citizens of Edeſſa, within ten yeares after Chriſts
death, amongſt other points of faith, as Euſebius reporteth,

* Euſeb. eccleſi-
aſt. hiſtor. lib. 1
cap. 13.

° Quomodo (Chriſtus) crucifixus fuerit, & ad inferos deſcende-
rit, ſepemque illam antea nunquam diruptam ſciderit: reſurrexe-
rit etiam, ac mortuos qui à ſeculo dormierant, vnâ excitauerit;
& quomodo ſolus quidem deſcenderit, multâ vero turbâ comita-
tus ad patrem ipſius aſcenderit. Howe Chriſt was crucified, and
deſcended into hell, and ouerthrew the wall, which was neuer
before that time broken; and roſe againe, and raiſed vp with him
thoſe v̈ had bin dead long before; & how he deſcéded alone, but
aſcended vp to his father with a great multitude. This report by
ſome men is counted fabulous, for ÿ the letters ſent to Chriſt
and receaued from him by the ruler of that city, are no where
remembred in the Euangeliſts: but by their leaues that rea-
ſon is rather friuolous: for ſo much as S. Iohn ſaith; ᵖ There
are alſo many other thinges, which Ieſus did, the which if they
ſhould be writté euery one, I ſuppoſe the world could not con-
taine the bookes, that ſhould be written. Since then this is no
ſure ground to reiect a ſtorie, for that it is not contained in
the

ᵖ Iohn. 21

the fcriptures, I fee no caufe either to preiudice the publike and ancient records of the citie of Edeffa, remaining at that verie time when this report was made; or to miftruft the credite of Eufebius, as if he had impudentlie forged the olde monuments of that citie, where he might fo eafilie bee reproued. His words are. ¶ *Habes harum rerum teſtimoninm ſcriptis comprehenſum, & ex Grammatophylacio vrbis* Edeſſæ *tunc regiæ deſumptum. Nam in ipſis publicis chartis, quæ res priſcas continent, iſta ad hunc vſq̃ diem ex eo tempore ſeruata reperiuntur. Nihil autem impedit, quo minus literas ipſas, quæ nobis ex Archinis deſumptæ, & e Syrorum lingua his verbis tranſlatæ ſunt, audiamus.* Thou haft the teftimonie of thefe thinges comprifed in writing, and taken out of the chamber of *Edeſſa*, that then was a princely Citie. For in the publike recordes, of things aunciently paft, thus much is there extant T O T H I S V E R I E D A Y, preferued from the time wherein thefe things were done. And I thinke it beft to fet downe the letters, which I my felfe C O P I E D out of the Authentick records, and T R A N S L A-T E D from the Syrian tongue in thefe wordes. How the report of a writer, y̆ is not canonical, fhould haue more credite then this hath, I know not. The records were auncient and publique, and then extant to be viewed by euerie man, when Eufebius did exemplifie them . If wee difcredite all antiquitie and teftimonie which wee fee not with our owne eies ; wee muft looke to recefue the like rewarde from our pofteritie . Ignatius that liued with ; and after the Apoftles, in his Epiftle to the Church of Trallis, confeffeth the fame Article, almoft in the fame words. καὶ κατῆλ-θεν εἰς ἅδην μόνος . Chrift defcended into Hell alone, and returned (or rofe againe) with a greate number, and brake downe the rampiere that had ftoode from the beginning, and ouerthrewe the mid-wall thereof . Athanafius prefent at the great councell of Nice as a Cleargie man, though not then a Bifhop, in his fhort recapitulation of the Catholike faith, addeth this Article, as neceffarie to be be-

Z 3   leiued

leeued of all Christians. [r] *Passus est pro salute nostra, descendit ad inferos, tertia die resurrexit a mortuis: hæc est fides Catholica quam nisi quis firmiter fideliterq́, crediderit, saluus esse non poterit.* Christ suffered for our saluation, descended into hell, rose againe the third day from the dead. This is the Catholike faith, which except a man doe firmelie and fastlie beleeue he cannot bee saued. Saint Austen doth so presse it, that hee pronounceth it infidelitie to denie it. [s] *Secundum animam* (Christum) *apud inferos fuisse apertè scriptura declarat, & per Prophetam præmissa, & per Apostolicum intellectum satis exposita, qua dictum est, non derelinques animam meam in inferno.* That Christ according to his soule was in hell, the Scripture plainelie declareth, forespoken by the Prophet (*Dauid*) and sufficientlie expounded by the Apostles application, where it was saide, Thou wilt not leaue my soule in hell. [t] *Quis ergo nisi infidelis negauerit fuisse apud inferos Christum?* Who then but an infidell will denie, that Christ was in Hell? Hilarius maketh it a necessarie cause of our redemption. [u] *Crux, mors, inferi, salus nostra est.* Christes Crosse, death, and beeing in Hell, are the meanes of our saluation. For as hee died that wee might liue, so hee went to hell by Hilaries assertion, that wee might goe to heauen. [x] *Christus Dei filius moritur, sed omnis caro viuificatur in Christo. Dei filius in inferis est, sed homo refertur ad cœlum.* Christ the sonne of God dieth, but all flesh is quickened in Christ. The sonne of God is in Hell, but man is restored to Heauen. And least wee shoulde thinke that Hilarie dreamed of Christes suffering hell paines on the Crosse, as some haue alledged him; his wordes are plaine else where, that Christs soule after death descended into hell. [y] *Humanæ ista lex necessitatis est, vt sepultis corporibus ad inferos animæ descendant. Quam descensionem, Dominus ad consummationem veri hominis non recusauit.* This is the lawe of mans miserie, that their bodies goe to the graue, their soules to hell: WHICH DESCENT the Lorde did not refuse, to prooue

[r] *Athanas. in Symbolo.*

[s] *August. epist. 99.*

[t] *Ibidem.*

[u] *Hilarius de trinitat. lib. 2.*

[x] *Ibid. lib 3.*

[y] *Hilarius in Psal. 138.*

prooue himfelfe iu euerie point to bee a true man . This ne∙
ceffitie was the wages of mans finne ; the ftrength where∙
of coulde none abolifh but onelie Chrift. [z] *Hic vnus eft , ad-*
uerfantes nobis inimicaſque virtutes ligno paſſionis affigens, mor-
tem in inferno perimens, ſpei noſtræ fidem reſurrectione confir-
mans, corruptionem humanæ carnis gloria corporis ſui perimens.
Chrift alone was hee that faftened to the wood of his paffion
the powers which were aduerfaries and enemies to vs ; that
vanquifhed death euen in hell ; that confirmed the ftedfaft-
neffe of our hope with his refurrection , and abolifhed the
corruption of mans flefh with the glorie of his bodie . Leo
likewife . [a] *Reſurrectio ſaluatoris , nec animam in infer-*
no , nec carnem diu moxata eft in ſepulchro; quoniam deitas, quæ
ab vtraque ſuſcepti hominis ſubſtantia non receſſit , quod po-
teſtate diuifit, poteſtate coniunxit. The refurrection of our Sa∙
uiour neither ftayed his foule long in hell, nor his flefh in the
graue ; becaufe his Godhead which did not depart from either
part of his manhoode, mightilie conioyned, what it mightilie
feuered.

But no man hath moze pithilie ; oz moze foundlie
deliuered the full courfe , and caufe of Chziftes defcent
to Hell , then Fulgentius ; which I mufte repeate at
large , becaufe euerie wozde is woozth the marking.
[b] *Reſtabat ad plenum noſtræ redemptionis effectum , vt il-*
luc vſque homo ſine peccato à Deo ſuſceptus deſcenderet , quo-
uſque homo ſeparatus à Deo peccati merito cecidiſſet : id eſt
ad infernum ; vbi ſolebat peccatoris anima torqueri , & ad
ſepulchrum; vbi conſueuerat peccatoris caro corrumpi: ſic ta-
men, vt nec Chriſti caro in ſepulchro corrumperetur, nec in-
ferni doloribus anima torqueretur . Quoniam anima immunis
à peccato non erat ſubdenda ſupplicio , & carnem ſine peccato
non debuit vitiare corruptio . Nam quia peccans homo me-
ruit in ſeipſo per ſupplicium diuidi, quia maluit à Deo præuarica-
tionis reatu diſiungi, propterea factum eſt, vt peccatoris mort
carnem peccati ad ſepulchrum corrumpendam perduceret , ani-
mam

[z] *Idem de trinit. lib. 4.*

[a] *Leo de reſur. domini. ſerm. 1.*

[b] *Fulgentius de paſſione domini ad Traſim. lib. 3*

mam inferno torquendam protinus manciparet. Vt autem peccator fuiſſet gratuito munere liberatus, factum eſt, vt mortem corporis, quam à Deo iuſto peccator homo pertulerat iuſtè, Dei filius a peccatore pateretur iniuſtè : & ad ſepulchrum perueniret caro iuſti, quouſque fuerat caro deuoluta peccati : & vſq̃; ad infernum deſcenderet anima ſaluatoris, vbi peccati merito torquebatur anima peccatoris. Hoc autem ideo factum eſt, vt per morientem temporaliter carnem iuſti, donaretur vita æterna carni : & per deſcendentem ad infernum animam iuſti, dolores ſoluerentur inferni. It remained for the full effecting of our redemption, that man aſſumed of God without ſinne, ſhoulde thither deſcend, whither man ſeuered from God fell by deſert of ſinne : that is, vnto hell, where the ſoule of the ſinner was woont to bee tormented; and to the graue, where the fleſh of the ſinner was woont to bee corrupted; yet ſo, that neither Chriſtes fleſh ſhoulde bee corrupted in the graue, nor his ſoule bee tormented with the paines of hell; becauſe the ſoule free from ſinne was not to be ſubiected to that puniſhment; nor fleſh cleane from the contagion of ſinne ſhoulde ſuffer corruption. In ſo much, as man ſinning deſerued by puniſhment to bee ſeuered from himſelfe; who by his tranſgreſſion woulde needes bee ſeuered from God, therefore it was appointed that the death of the ſinner ſhould bring his ſinfull fleſh to the graue, there to rotte; and preſentlie ſhould ſend his ſoule to hell, there to bee tormented. But when the ſinner by the gift of (Gods) grace, was to bee deliuered; it was prouided, that the ſonne of God ſhould vniuſtlie ſuffer at the hands of ſinners the death of the bodie; which ſinfull man had iuſtlie beene wrapped in by the iuſtice of God, and the fleſh of the iuſt ſhould come to the graue; whither ſinfull fleſh was tumbled : and that the SOVLE OF OVR SAVIOVR SHOVLD DESCEND TO HELL, VVHERE THE SINFVL SOVLE VVAS TORMENTED FOR THE REVVARD OF SINNE. This was therefore done, that by the fleſh of the iuſt temporally dying, eternall life might be giuen to (our) fleſh, and by the ſoule

of

of the iuſt defcending to hell,the torments of hell might be abo-
liſhed.

Out of Fulgentius I obſerue two things; which if it pleaſe
men to marke, they ſhall cleare themſelues from all abſur-
dities touching Chriſts defcent to hell. The firſt is, THE
PLACE, VVHITHER he defcended;the next is, THE CAVSE,
VVHY he defcended. The place whither hee defcended was
hell ; whither the foule of man finning againſt God was
adiudged for the wages of his tranſgreſſion. The caufe of
his defcent, was to free all the faithfull from the begin-
ning of the world to the ende thereof from comming thi-
ther.And in both thefe, the Scriptures and fathers doe ful-
lie concurre ; though fome auncient wziters doe fwarue,
and ſtriue about Chriſtes deliuering fome from hell , that
were there at the time of his defcent,as they fuppofe. Which
varietie and vncertaintie of opinions concerning the ſtate
of the deade before Chriſtes comming hath verie much en-
tangled this queſtion, and induced manie men of learning
and iudgement otherwife,to reiect Chriſts defcent to hell as
a fable, oz to wzeſt it to an other fenſe , with newe foonde
expofitions. Howbeit I fee no caufe,but the doctrine of the
Scriptures confeſſed by all the fathers may ſtande verie
cleare, whatſoeuer we refolue of this other affertion , tou-
ching the ſtate of the righteous departed this life before
Chriſts death. I will therefore ſhortly difcuſſe both the place
and the caufe,and fo dzaw to an end.

As for the place whither Chriſt defcended, the Church of
Rome greedily hunteth after it, to heare of her Purgatozie;
hoping , whence the foules of the righteous were by Chriſt
deliuered, there to make a ſtand for foules,not perfectlie con-
feſſed and abfolued in this life ; that ſhe maie fet to fale her
pzaiers and pardons . But if ſhee follow Chriſt defcen-
ding , her deuotion muſt reach to the place and paines of
the damned, foz thither Chriſt defcended. And fo by their
leaues both Scriptures and fathers auouch.   Firſt the

Aa 1   wozdes

Chrift defcen-
ded to ẙ place
of the damned

c Act. 2.
d Symbol. Apoſt.

wordes are plaine, and muſt bee proper, as well in the c Canon as in the d Creed. Thou wilt not leaue my ſoule in hell: and d he deſcended into hell. Againe the kingdom of Satan conſiſteth of theſe three; SINNE, DEATH, and HELL: SINNE RAIGNING, whiles the bodie and ſoule are ioined togither; DEATH SEVERING them both, and TVRNING the bodie to earth; HELL RECEIVING and TORMENTING the ſoule, till the date of iudgement, when bodie and ſoule ſhall for euer bee caſt into hell fire. If theſe three bee not aboliſhed by Chriſt, Satans kingdome is not deſtroyed by Chriſt; and ſpeciallie if hell bee not vanquiſhed; no part of our ſaluation is performed. The womþke of ſinne is ſweete, if the wages were not ſower, which is hell fire. To raiſe our bodies from death, is no fauour, if Hell bee not ouerthrowen; it were more eaſie for them to lie in duſt, then to burne in hell. Howe hath Chriſt reſtored vs to Heauen, if hee haue not yet freed vs from Hell? Or brought vs to God, if he haue not yet taken vs from Satan? Wherefore either Hell muſt bee deſtroyed, or wee are no waie redeemed, And in all theſe, when I ſpeake of Hell, I ſpeake of the place of the damned. For if the feare of damnation continue, what hope of ſaluation can wee conceiue? But the Apoſtle ſaieth plainlie, that Chriſt through death

c Heb. 2.

c DESTROIED HIM, that had power of death, euen the DIVELL; and DELIVERED ALL them which for feare of death were all their life time ſubiect to ſeruitude. If the DIVELL bee DESTROIED, then

To deſtroy the diuell, and to deliuer man.

Hell is fullie conquered; for whiles that retaineth force againſt the faithfull, the Diuell is in the height of his kingdome. Neither is death to bee feared at all, but in reſpect of hell following after death. If then all the Saintes heere on earth be f DELIVERED FROM THE FEARE OF DEATH, and g from the handes of all that hate (them) to ſerue (God) without feare all the dayes of their

f Heb. 2.
g Luke 1.

life,

life, in holineffe and righteoufneffe before him ; it is eui=
dent that hell is fpoyled of all right and claime to the
members of Chzift , by reafon our heads breing there
in our names, and fo2 our finnes, b2ake the ftrength of
hell , abolifhed the power, and loofed the fo2rowes and
paines thereof ; that they fhoulde not take holde on him,
no2 enter after on anie of his . fo2 as hee fuffered and
died, not fo2 his owne fake, but fo2 ours ; fo hee defcen=
ded and loofed the fo2rowes of death and hell , not as p2o=
uided fo2 him, but fo2 bs . And fince to our finnes was
due damnation, and no leffer o2 eafier punifhment ; it was
requifite that Chzift fhoulde thither defcende, and by dif=
foluing the wages of our finne in his owne perfon, thence
deliuer bs ; though not there tormented , yet thither ad=
iudged, and fo releafe bs, not as breing there, but from
comming thither.

Touching the place , Thaddæus one of the feuentie
taught, as wee heard out of Eufebius , that Chzift def=
cended into hell ; and brake the wall that was neuer be= **Whither chrift**
fore broken.   from the deade manie rofe befo2e Chziftes **defcended af=**
death), and therefo2e the partition betwixt death and life **ter death.**
was often b2oken by others , befo2e Chziftes refurrec=
tion ; but from hell neuer returned anie , but onelye
Chzift ; by reafon that wall was neuer b2oken , but by
the Sonne of GOD . Athanafius in like fo2te . *In fua* **d** *Athanaf de*
ad noftri fimilitudinem forma , noftram inibi depingens mor- *falutari aduentu*
tem , vt in ea refurrectionem pro nobis concinnaret, ex fepulchro *chrifti.*
quidè corpus,animam vero ex ORCO *reducem faceret,vt in morte*
mortem diffolueret per exhibitionem anima , & per fepul-
chrum corporis in fepulchro , corruptionem aboleret ; ex orco
verò & fepulchro immortalitatem & incorruptionem often-
dit, in forma nobis confimili viam noftram emerfus, noftram-
que detentionem relaxans , & hoc ipfum eximij miraculi
fuit : In his likeneffe to our nature (Chzifte) accom-
plifhing our death, that in the fame hee might perfoime his
refurrection

reſurrection for vs, brought his BODIE OVT OF THE GRAVE, & his SOVLE OVT OF HEL; that in death he might diſſolue death by preſenting his ſoule there, and by the buriall of his bodie, he might aboliſh corruption in the graue. So that euen from hell, and from the graue, hee ſhewed immortalitie (of the ſoule) and incorruption (of the body) treading the verie way that we ſhould haue trod, in the likeneſſe of our nature, and releaſing of our detention. And this was a marueilous wonder. When Athanaſius ſaith, that Chriſt in his humane nature trodde the verie ſame way of death that wee ſhould haue done; his bodie and ſoule going to thoſe very places whither ours ſhould haue gone; he doth not mean the place of reſt, where ẏ ſoules of the righteous were before Chriſts comming; but the place whither the ſouls of men were condemned for the ſin of their firſt father; which is not Paradiſe, nor Abrahams boſome, but the place of the damned, where the true death of the ſoule and wages of ſin are by Gods iuſtice inflicted. Heare his owne words.

[1] Athanaſ. de incarnatione Chriſti.

[1] Vbi corruptum fuerat humanum corpus, eó ſuum corpus proiecit Ieſus: & vbi tenebatur anima humana in morte, ibi exhibuit humanam ſuam animam, vt ipſe inuictus à morte, tanquam hominem ſe præſentem oſtenderet, & ſolueret catenas mortis vt Deus; vt vbi ſeminata fuerat corruptio, inde exoriretur incorruptibilitas; & VBI REGNAVERAT MORS IN FORMA HVMANAE ANIMAE, ibi ipſe ille mortalis præſens, immortalitatem exhiberet, atq́, ita NOS PARTICIPES redderet ſuæ incorruptibilitatis, & immortalitatis per ſpem reſurrectionis ex mortuis. Where the bodie of man vſed to rot, thither Ieſus caſt his body: and VVHERE THE SOVLE OF MAN VVAS HELD IN DEATH, there did he exhibite his humane ſoule; that hee being in no wiſe to bee conquered by death, might both ſhewe himſelfe there preſent as man; and yet break the chaines of death as God; that where corruption was ſowed, thence incorruption might riſe (euen from the graue;) & where death raigned ouer mens ſoules (which muſt needes be in hell) there he being preſent as a mortall man, might demonſtrate his immortalitie, and

ſo

fo make vs partakers, of his incorruption (in fleſh,) and immortalitie (in foule) by the hope of refurrection from the dead.

And becauſe Hilarius and Fulgentius doe fo fullie concurre with Athanaſius, that if we trulie conceiue the one, we ſhall eaſilie vnderſtand the other; you ſhall ſee the ſame doctrine, which the other two follow, more fullie deliuered by Athanaſius. Athanaſius agreeth in this point with Hilary and Fulgentius. ᵏ *Qui de Adæ inobedientia quæſtionem habuit, iudicioque peracto duplicem pœnam in ſententia ſua complexus erat, dum rei terreſtri ita loquitur, Terra es, & in terram reuerteris,(atque ita pro decreto, domini corpus in terram abſcedit;) animæ dixit, morte morieris; atq; hinc eſt, quod homo in duas partes diſcerpitur; et vt ad duo loca diſcedat, condemnatur. Ac proinde opus fuit illo ipſo iudice, qui hoc decretū tulerat, vt ipſe per ſe ſententiā ſolueret ſub ſpecie condēnati, incondēnatū ſe ſincerūque a peccatis oſtēdens, vt hominem deo reconciliaret, hominemque totum in libertatem vindicaret. Iam ſi mihi alium locum condemnationis præter hos duos oſtendere poteſtis, merito hominem dixeritis tripliciter diuidi. Quod ſi tertium aliquem locum oſtendere non p:teſtis,* PRAETER SEPVLCHRVM ET INFERNVM, *ex quibus plané ereptus eſt homo Chriſto aſſertore, per ſuam ſpeciem cum noſtri ſimilitudine congruentem, cur igitur dicitis, deum nondum propitiatum eſſe?* Hee that examined *Adams* difobedience, and in the ende of his iudgement comprifed in his fentence (againſt Adam) a double punifhment; fpeaking thus to the terreſtriall part (of man,) *earth thou art, and to earth ſhalt thoureturne;* and according to this decree, the Lords body was laid in earth; euen he faid to the foule, thou fhalt *die the death*; and thereupon man (dying) is diſtracted in two partes, and condemned to two places. Infomuch that it was requifite, the verie fame iudge, which pronounced this decree, fhould by himfelfe diſſolue this fentence in the fhew of a man condemned, but yet prouing himfelfe to be vncondemned, and cleere from finne, that he might reconcile man to God, and reduce the whole man to libertie. Nowe if you can name me any other place, whereto man was condemned befides thefe two, rightly may you thinke man

ᵏ Athanaſ. ibidē.

(after

(after death) is to be deuided into three (places;,) but if you can ſhewe me no third place, beſides the graue, (for the bodie) and hell, (for the ſoule;) from both which man is fullie freed, Chriſt deliuering him with like parts of himſelfe anſwerable to our nature, how ſay you then, that God is not yet ſatisfied? The whole man in Adam was in ſuch ſort condemned for ſinne, that his bodie returned to corruption in the earth, and his ſoule departed to tormentes in hell, which is the death of the ſoule after this life. To the verie ſame places whither man was condemned, & in the ſame partes of our nature, the ſonne of GOD vouchſafed to deſcende, that by the lying of his bodie in the earth, our bodies might at the laſt date bee raiſed out of the earth; and by the preſence of his ſoule in hell, on which the force of hell coulde not faſten, our ſoules might for euer be deliuered from comming thither.

This condemnation of the bodie to the graue, and of the ſoule to hell for ſinne, is that [1] law of humane neceſſity, which Hilary ſpeaketh of, (wherto the Lord Ieſus ſubmitted himſelf; not that his fleſh ſhould ſee corruption, or his ſoule taſt of damnatiō, but y by the preſence of his body in the graue, & of his ſoule in hell he might ſhew himſelfe inuincible to both, and ſo deliuer vs from both. [m] The archangels, powers, and principalities (in heauen) doe with vnceaſing and euerlaſting voices glorifie the ſonne of God (ſaith Hilary) *quia homo natus ſit, mortem vicerit, portas Inferni fregerit, cohærede ſibi plebē acquiſiuerit, carnem in æternitatis gloriam ex corruptione tranſtulerit;* becauſe he became man, vanquiſhed death, brake the gates of hel, purchaſed vnto himſelfe a people to inherit with him, and tranſlated his fleſh frō corruptiō to eternal glory. Theſe two places the graue & hel, wherto ſinners were adiudged to haue their bodies in the one to be corrupted, their ſoules in the other to be tormented, Fulgentius doth expreſly purſue; as his wordes before do plainly teſtifie; and reſolutelie concludeth, that Chriſts manhood for the ful effecting of our redemption muſt SO FAR DESCEND, [n] *quouſque homo ſeparatus à deo peccati merito*

[1] *Hilar. in* Pſal, 138.

[m] *Hilar. de trinitat. lib.* 3

[n] *Fulgent. vt ſupra.*

merito cecidiffet ; HOVV FAR MAN SEVERED FROM
GOD, FEL BY THE DESERT OF SINNE; THAT IS,
TO HELL, VVHERE THE SOVLE OF THE SINNER
VSED TO BE TORMENTED, and to the graue where
the FLESH OF THE SINNER vfed to putrifie. Nowe if
anie man thinke the foule of man feuered from God, did
not fo2 the wages of finne deferue the place and paines of
the damned, he had mo2e nœde bee catechifed then confuted.
Fo2 fince without repentance men ° perifh in their finnes; °Luke 13.
and P the foule that finneth, that foule fhall die; the death of PEzech.18
the foule after this life is no where but in hell, where bodie &
foule do perifh euerlaftinglie. With thefe fo meth Saint Au-
ften as touching the place. *Si in illum Abrahæ finum Chri-* ¶Auguft.epi. 99
ftum mortuum veñiffe fanctæ fcriptura dixiffet, non nomina-
to inferno eiufque doloribus; miror fi quifquam ad inferos eum
defcendiffe afferere auderet. Sed quia euidentia teftimonia &
infernum commemorant & dolores, nulla caufa occurrit, cur
illò credatur veniffe faluator, nifi vt ab eius doloribus faluos
faceret. If the holie Scripture had faide, that Chrift after his
death came to Abrahams bofome, and not mentioned hell and
the paynes thereof, I maruaile if anie woulde haue beene fo
bolde, as to haue auouched that Chrift defcended into hel. But
for that euident teftimonies do name hel, and the paines (of hel)
I yet fee no caufe, why our Sauiour fhould bee beleeued to haue
come thither, but to deliuer fró the paines thereof. Wherefo2e
when the fcriptures teach vs, ý Chrifts foule was in hell; wee
muft not by hel mean Abrahams bofome, o2 Paradife, but ý
very place of the damned, where the foules of finners are to2-
mented. Fo2 Chrift to redœme man that was condemned
fo2 finne, defcended as lowe, as man fell by the punifhment
of finne in this life o2 the nexte, and fet vs backe from the
fentence of death p2onounced againft vs, by p2efenting
himfelfe in our ftœde to the verie places, that were p2epared
to reuenge our tranfgreffions : his flefh refifting the pow-
er of the graue, and his foule represfing and b2eaking the
paines

paines of hell, that neither ſhoulde bee able to hinder the ſpæde of his reſurrection, oꝛ weaken the woꝛke of our redemption.

As the place whither Chꝛiſt deſcended, is expꝛeſſly named in the ſcriptures to be hell, and ᾅδης, where the wicked are euerlaſtinglie toꝛmented; ſo the purpoſe of his deſcent is plainelie pꝛofeſſed in the ſame, to bee the ſpoiling of Satan, and deliuering of man from the power of hell. And theſe two are ſo linked together, that the one is alwaies included in the other; Chꝛiſt entring Satans houſe to this ende, that he might diuide the ſpoiles. Firſt then let vs ſee, what the ſcriptures ſay of mans deliuerance from the hande of Satan; and afterward heare what ſome of the ancient wꝛiters haue there to added, oꝛ therein doubted. The pꝛomiſe made in the pꝛophet Eſay, that God [r] will deſtroie death for euer, and likewiſe in the pꝛophet Oſee; [ſ] I will redeeme them from the power of hell; I will deliuer them from death : ô death I will be thy death, ô hell I will bee thy deſtruction : was not peculiar to this oꝛ that age, noꝛ pꝛoper to thoſe that were alreadie dead, oꝛ then boꝛne when this was ſpoken; but generall to all the faithfull from the beginning to the ende; whereby God aſſureth them, that [t] hell ſhall bee deſtroied, and [u] Satan troden vnder feete, and [x] death ſwallowed vp in victorie. Zachary Iohn Baptiſtes father is the beſt expoſitoꝛ of all theſe pꝛomiſes, when he ſaith. [y] Bleſſed be the Lord God of Iſrael, becauſe he hath viſited, and redeemed his people . And hath raiſed vp an horne of ſaluation for vs, in the houſe of his ſeruant *Dauid*, (as he ſpake by the mouth of his holy prophets, which were from the beginning) euen ſaluation from our enemies, and from the hand of all that hate vs. (Which was) the othe, that hee ſware to our father *Abraham*, that he would cauſe vs ; being deliuered out of the hande of our enemies, to ſerue him without feare in holineſſe and righteouſneſſe before him all the daies of our life. The ſaluation which God hath wꝛought for vs in Chꝛiſt, doth not frée vs from afflictions and troubles, ſince [z] all that will
live

liue godly in Christ Iesus shall suffer persecution; but it bring-
eth vs DELIVERANCE FROM OVR (ghostly) ENEMIES;
& saueth vs from the hand of al that hate (our soules); that be-
ing quieted from their power and feare, we should serue God
in holines all the time of our life. And albeit in this life, our
eies [a] are opened, that we may turne from darkenesse to light,
and from the power of Satan, to God; and receaue forgiuenesse
of sinnes, and inheritance amongst them, which are sanctified
by faith in Christ: yet the feare of death is not taken from vs,
till we be assured, that hell is conquered; and no cause lefte
why we should tremble at death, that now is an entrance to
a better life.

DELIVERANCE then, FROM THE HAND OF ALL
that hate vs, (which Christ hath purchased for vs,) hath in it
not onelie remission of sinnes, and resurrection from death, but
also the destruction of Satan: whereby God acquiteth vs from
the power of darkenesse, that is, from the feare of hell in this
life, and from the danger thereof in the next, and fully tran-
slateth vs into the kingdome of his deere sonne; and this deli-
uerance belongeth to all the members of Christ without ex-
ception, as well liuing, as yet vnborne. Christ (saith the A-
postle) through death [b] destroied him, that had power of death,
euen the diuell, and DELIVERED ALL THEM, which for
feare of death were al their life long subiect to bondage. If ALL
BE DELIVERED, that were oppressed with the feare of
death, then sutelie the liuing must needs be discharged from
the bondage of Satan; and redemption from the power of
hell, which God promised vnto his seruantes, was not pro-
per to anie that were in hell at the time of Christes descent,
but it was, and is extended to all the faithfull before and after
Christs comming; that in this life they should be secured, &
in the next saued from him, that had the power of death, and
from the gates of hell. Fulgentius teacheth this doctrine as
Catholike. [f] Sicut mortuus pro nobis, omnes nos sibi commori
fecit, sic solutis doloribus inferni, omnes fideles ab ijsdem doloribus

side notes:
[a] Actes.26

Deliuerance was performed as well to the liuing and vn-borne, as to the deade.

[b] Hebre.2

[f] Fulgent. ad Trasimundum. lib.3.

Bb 1. libe-

liberauit. As (*Christ*) dying for vs, made vs all to die with him; so dissoluing the paines of hell, he DELIVERED ALL THE FAITHFVLL from the same. As all the godlie, that euer were, are, or shall be, died in Christes flesh vnto sinne; so all the faithfull from the beginning of the world to the end therof were deliuered from the paines of hell, by the presence and power of Christs soule breaking the strength, and loosing the sorrowes of death euen in hell. And therefore hee saith,

Ibidem.

Christ called himselfe free among the dead, [d] *vt ostenderet animam suam à peccato liberam, in infernum pro* NOBIS PECCA-TORIBVS DESCENDISSE, to shew that his soule cleere fro sinne descended into hel FOR VS SINNERS. So that Christ descended to hell FOR ALL THE FAITHFVL, and FOR VS SINNERS, to deliuer them and vs from the sorrowes of the second death; and not for certaine whom he found in hel, when he came thither.

De trinitate l.4

Hilarius ioyneth in the same confession, that Christ [e] killing death in hell, confirmed the faith OF OVR HOPE with

Ibidem.lib.3

his resurrection; [f] and breaking the gates of hell, purchased a people that shoulde inherite with him. Athanasius euerie where treadeth the same steppes; teaching vs that Christ

Athanas.de salutari aduentu Christi.
Idem de incarnat.Christi.

[g] perfited his resurrection FOR VS, and out of hell and the graue brought immortalitie and incorruption, releasing OVR DETENTION. And againe, Christ [h] brake the chaines of death as God, that where death raigned ouer mens soules, there he being present as a man might demonstrate immortalitie (in his soule) and so MAKE VS PARTAKERS of his incorruption. And lastlie, where death both of soule and bodie was inflicted on man for sinne, the one in the graue, the

Ibidem.

other in hell; [i] hee that gaue the iudgement, dissolued the sentence in his owne person, vnder the shewe of a man condemned; but in deede vncondemned, and free from sinne, that hee might reconcile MAN to God, and bring THE VVHOLE MAN into libertie. FROM THE GRAVE THEN, AND FROM HEL MAN VVAS FREED CHRIST DELIVE-RING HIM.

And

And least it should seeme strange, that our soules were deliuered from hel by Christs descent thither, where they neuer were; S. Austen expounding Dauids words, ᵏ Thou hast deliuered my soule frō the nethermost hell, sheweth that men may bee deliuered as well from DANGERS CONSEQVENT AS PRESENT; and as well from that which is DESERVED, as from that which is INFLICTED. And first ẏ Christ deliuered OVR SOVLES from hell by his comming thither (though we were not there) his words are plaine. *Est aliud (infernum) inferius, quò eunt mortui: vnde voluit deus eruere* ANIMAS NOSTRAS, *etiam illuc mittendo filium suum. Propterea vox eius est in illo psalmo, non quoquam homine coniiciente, sed Apostolo exponente, vbi ait: quoniā non dereliquisti animam meā in inferno. Ergò aut ipsius vox est hic, et eruisti animā meam ab inferno inferiori, aut nostra vox est per ipsum christū dominū nostrū, quia ideo ille peruenit vsq; ad infernū, ne* NOS REMANEREMVS *in inferno.* There is a lower hel, whither ẏ dead go; whēce it pleased God to deliuer OVR SOVLES, by sending his son thither. Therfore those are Christs words in ẏ psalme, not by mās coniecture, but by the Apostles exposition, where he saith; ẏ hast not left my soule in hel. So ẏ this verse, *Thou hast deliuered my soule frō the nethermost hel,* is either the voice of Christ in this psalm, or it is our voice in the person of Christ our Lord, because he therefore went to hell, LEAST VVE SHOVLD ABIDE (for euer) IN HEL. And to proue this speach to be vsuall ẏ we are deliuered from the dangers & places in which we neuer were, but should haue bin, if wee had not bin saued thence; hee addeth.

ᵐ *Recte dicis medico, liberasti me ab egritudine, non in qua iā eras, sed in qua futurus eras. Mittendus erat (quis) in carcerem: venit aliui defendit eum; gratias agens, quid dicit? eruisti animam meam de carcere. Suspendendus erat debitor; solutum est debitum pro eo; liberatus dicitur de suspendio. In his omnibus non erant, sed quia talibus meritis agebantur, vt, nisi subuentum esset, ibi essent, inde se recte dicunt liberari, quo per liberatores suos non sunt permissi perduci.* Thou sayest rightlie to

Bb 2.   thy

We are deliuered, not from being in hell but from comming thither.
ᵏ Pfal. 85.

ˡ Auguſt. in Pſal. 85.

ᵐ Ibidem.

thy phyſitiã, you haue deliuered me frõ this ſicknes, not in which thou waſt, but into which thou waſt like to fall. A man is about to be caſt into priſon; another commeth and reſcueth him. What ſaith he when he giueth thanks? you deliuered me out of priſon. A debtor was in danger to be hanged; the debt is paid for him, he is ſaid to be deliuered from hanging. In all theſe things, they were not; but becauſe ſuch were their deſertes, that vnleſſe they had beene holpen, they had fallen into them, THEY RIGHT-LY MAY SAY THEY VVERE DELIVERED thence, VVHITHER THEY VVERE NOT SVFFERED TO COME, by thoſe that deliuered them. Tertullian declining to Montaniſme in his booke de anima, and defending the ſoules of al the faithful after Chꝛiſts comming to be kept, apud In-feros, in the region of hell till the date of iudgement, ſaue of martyꝛs, to whome onely he opened Paradiſe, confeſſeth the other ſide, which in deed were true chꝛiſtians; made this

* Tertullian. de anima. cap. 55

obiection againſt him. ⁿ Sed in hoc, inquiunt, Chriſtus in feros adijt, ne nos adiremus. Cæterum quod diſcrimen ethnicorum & chriſtianorum, ſi carcer mortuis idem? But to this end, they ſay, Chriſt went to hell, that we ſhould not come thither. For what difference between the Ethnickes and Chriſtians, if after death they be both in one priſon? So that in all ages this doctrine was pꝛeſerued in the church, which the ſcriptures doe war-rant, that Chꝛiſt by his death deſtroied the deuil, and deliuered all the godlie from the feare, not of the firſt death, which they cannot auoide, and need not to feare; but of the ſecond death in hell, which is ſufflie to be feared, and can no way be pꝛe-uented, but by the power of that redemption, which we haue in Chꝛiſt Ieſus.

Where the ſoules of the righteous were before Chriſts comming, is nothing to this queſtion.

[But all the fathers with one conſent affirme, that Chꝛiſt deliuered the ſoules of the patriarks & pꝛophets out of hel, at his comming thither; and ſo ſpoiled Satan of thoſe, ÿ were in his pꝛeſent poſſeſſion.] The doctrin of Chꝛiſts deſcending into hel to ſaue al his mẽbers from cõming thither, muſt not be confounded with this diſputation, whether ÿ ſoules of the

pꝛophets

prophets and Patriarks were before Chrifts refurrection in hell or no; but whatfoeuer we determine or imagine of this later queſtion, the other poſition ſtandeth vncontrolled, both by Scriptures and fathers : yet for their ſakes, that happilie maie ſtumble at this blocke, I will not refraine to ſpeake what I thinke of this aſſertion; ſo as I bee firſt allowed to ſay with ſaint Auſten. *Quod dicimus fratres, hoc ſi non vobis tanquam certus exipoſuero, ne ſuccenſeatis. Homo enim ſum, & quantum conceditur de ſcripturis ſanctis, tantum audeo dicere, nihil ex me. Infernum nec ego expertus ſum adhuc, nec vos ; & fortaſſis alia via erit, & non per infernum erit. Incerta ſunt enim hæc.* That which (in this queſtion) I ſay brethren, if I can not auouch it as certaine, you muſt not bee offended . I am but a man , and what I am aſſured by the Scriptures, that I dare affirme, and of my ſelfe nothing. Hell neither I haue yet experience of, neither you ; and perchance there ſhall bee another way, and by hell it ſhall not bee. For theſe thinges are altogither vncertaine. The thinges after this life God will not haue particularlie knowne vnto vs, whiles here wee liue; and therefore to make ſodaine reſolutions of them, can haue neither certaintie nor ſafetie ; yet ſo much as the ſcriptures reueale, we muſt neceſſarilie beleeue, and may boldlie profeſſe without anie danger.

Touching the ſtate of the dead in the olde Teſtament, I ſee a number of auncient writers incline to this concluſion, that the ſoules of the righteous before Chriſtes death and deſcent were in hell; but as the foundation of their opinion is verie weake, ſo the conſequents are plainlie contradicted, both by Scriptures and fathers . This aſſertion firſt grewe from the confeſſion of the Patriarkes and Prophets, that they muſt after this life, DESCEND TO SHEOL; which the Septuagint doe allwayes expreſſe by the worde ἅδης, and the Latine interpreter, by Infernus ; whereupon the fathers both Greeke and Latin ſuppoſed the ſaints in the old Teſtament departing hence DESCENDED TO HELL.

° Auguſt. in pſal. 85.

The reaſon why the fathers thought they were in hell.

HELL; But the ſignification of the worde Sheól is ſo manifeſtlie miſtaken, that it is nowe no great maſterie to finde the foile. When Iacob ſaith, [r] I will go downe to SHEOL mourning to my ſonne ; and againe, [q] You will bring my gray haires with ſorrow vnto Sheól; and likewiſe Iob; [r] Sheól is my houſe; oh that thou wouldeſt hide me [ſ] in Sheól till thine anger were paſt; as alſo Dauid, [t] what man liueth, that ſhall deliuer his ſoule from the hand of Sheól? And laſtly [u] Ezechias, I ſhal go to the gates of Sheól : If by Sheól in theſe places wee vnderſtand hell, as ſome Greeke and Latine interpreters and writers haue done; we muſt needes confeſſe the faithfull dying in the former Teſtament deſcended into hell ; but if wee take Sheól for the graue, where life endeth and the bodie lieth; then make they no kind of proofe, that the ſoules of the godly before Chriſts comming, were in hel, but only that their bodies were in the graue; of which there was neuer any queſtion amongſt chriſtians or pagans.

Nowe that Sheól in the Scriptures noteth as well the graue where mens bodies putrifie, as the place where the ſoules of the wicked are after this life detained and puniſhed, to him that conſidereth the circumſtances of theſe and other ſuch places, will ſoone appeare. The words of king Ezechiah at large are theſe. [x] I ſaid in the cutting off of my daies, I ſhall goe to the gates of Sheól, I am depriued of the reſidue of my yeares. I ſaide, I ſhall not ſee the Lord in the land of the liuing; I ſhall ſee man no more amongſt the inhabitants of the worlde. I haue cutte my life in ſunder like a weauer. Here is a full deſcription of death, not of hell ; and leaſt wee ſhoulde dreame, that both are linked togither, in the end hee ſaieth; [y] Sheól can not confeſſe vnto thee, neither can death praiſe thee, nor they that deſcende into the pitte, truſt in thy trueth; but the liuing, the liuing, hee ſhall confeſſe thee , as I doe this day . It is manifeſt impietie to ſaie that the ſoules of the Saints departed did neither CONFESSE, NOR PRAISE GOD, NOR TRVST

IN

[r] Gen. 37.
[q] Gen. 42.

[r] Iob. 17.
[ſ] Iob. 14.
[t] Pſal. 89.
[u] Eſai. 38.

Sheól ſignifieth as well the graue as hell.

[x] Eſay. 38.

[y] Ibid. ver. 18. & 19.

IN HIS TRVTH: but in the graue where the bodie wan-
teth fenfe and life, this is moft true, which Ezechias de-
liuereth, and confirmed by the holie Ghoft in diuerfe
places of the Scriptures. ² In death there is no remem-   ² Pfal. 6.
brance of thee (faieth Dauid to God) and in Sheól who
fhall confeffe (or praife) thee? The foules of iuft and per-
fect men did then moft praife GOD, when they were
loofed from the warfare of this life; therefore they were
not in Sheól; for in Sheól none fhall confeffe vnto God,
nor truft in his truth. ³The deade praife not the Lord, nor   ³ Pfal. 115.
all that goe downe into filence . DEATH, SILENCE,
and SHEOL, are taken for one and the fame thing; and
in none of thefe is God praifed, or confeffed. And what
can bee plainer then that Dauid faieth in the 141. Pfalme?
ᵇ Our bones lie fcattered at the mouth of Sheól, as chippes   ᵇ Pfal 147.
hewed on the earth. Their bones I truft lay not fcattered
at the mouth of hell, but at the mouth of their graues, where   ᶜ Iob. 17.
their bodies were buried. Iob in like maner; ᶜ though I
hope, yet Sheól muft bee mine houfe, I fhall take vp my
bedde in darkeneffe. I fhall fay to corruption, thou art my
father, and to the worme, thou art my mother, and my fifter,
Darkeneffe, corruption, and the worme are the partes of
Sheol; and thefe confume the bodie, they wafte not the
foule. Salomon fhall feale vp this iniquifition, where hee
faieth; ᵈ All that thine hande is able to doe, difpatch it in   ᵈ Ecclef. 9.
thy ftrength; for there is neither VVORKE, NOR THOVGHT,
NOR KNOVVLEDGE, NOR VVISEDOME in SHEOL
whither thou goeft. If the foules of the righteous nei-
ther DOE, NOR THINKE, NOR KNOVVE anie thing, they
bee furelie a fleepe, and neither in ioy nor paine; but
if this bee abfurde and wicked to affirme either of hell, hea-
uen, paradife, or of Abrahams bofome, then certainlie
SHEOL, where none of thefe things are, is THE GRAVE;
and there it is euident, all thefe thinges are wanting.
Since then without queftion Sheol fignifeth as well the
graue,

graue, where the bodie lieth dead and rotten, as the place where the ſoules of vniuſt and ſinfull men are kept and tormented; if in the wordes of the Patriarkes and Prophets, confeſſing they muſt go to Sheól, we vnderſtand the graue, which indæde they ment; there is no ſhew in the ſcriptures, that the faithfull before Chriſtes death went to hell, as ſome fathers haue collected out of theſe and ſuch like ſayings of the godlie before Chriſtes birth; but rather the places that mention their ſtate after death, do euidently import the contrarie.

The Church of
the Iewes
thought the
ſoules of the
righteous to
be in peace.
ᵉ Sápient. ca. 3.

The booke of Wiſedome, though it be not Canonicall; yet doth it ſhewe what opinion the Church of the Iewes had of the ſoules of the righteous departed this life; and how much ſome ancient writers were deceiued in this their perſwaſion, that the ſpirites of the Patriarks and Prophets were in hell at the time of Chriſtes deſcent thither. ᵉ The ſoules of the righteous are in the hand of God, and no torment ſhall touch them. They ſeemed in the eyes of the vnwiſe to die, and their ende was counted miſerie, and their departure hence deſtruction; but they are in peace . For though in the ſight of men they were puniſhed, yet their hope is full of immortalitie. They were nourtured in ſome fewe thinges, but they ſhall bee rewarded in greate thinges, for God tried them, and founde them meete for himſelfe. Hee prooued them as gold in the fornace, and receiued them, as the fruites of a perfect offering. In the time of their viſitation, they ſhall ſhine, and iudge the Nations, and raigne ouer peoples, and he that is Lord ouer them ſhall raigne for euer. They that truſted in him, ſhall vnderſtande the truth, and the faithfull ſhall remaine in his fauour; for grace and mercie is with his Saints, and a due regarde had of his elect . The ſoules of the righteous, before Chriſtes comming were in peace, euen in Gods hande, receiued as a perfect offering. Grace and mercie was with them, and a ſpeciall fauour towardes them, no torments did touch them . If this were hell, what

greater

greater ioy and bliffe coulde they haue in Paradife? And this is in effect the verie fame; that Dauid hoped for, when hee faide, God fhal deliuer my foule from the power of Sheôl; for he wil receiue me, Selah.

Pfal. 19.

And if this bee not plaine enough, our Sauiour in his life time defcribed Abraham to be fo farre aboue the place of torment, and Lazarus in his bofome; and fo huge a diftaunce betwixt, that there was no paffing from the one to the other; yea the thiefe was the fame daie that Chrift died in Paradife; and yet our Sauiour raifed nor reduced none from Hell; by their owne confeffion, till the third daie, that hee rofe from the deade. If Abraham were not in hell, nor Lazarus, that laie in his bofome; if the riche man woulde haue his fiue brethren warned, leaft they came into that place of torment; how can it bee true, that the Prophets, and Patriarkes were in hell, when Chrift defcended, and not thence deliue-red, but by his refurrection? Saint Auftens cogitation vpon Abrahams bofome, is woorth the hearing. *h Ad-*

t Luke 16.
Chrift himfelfe placed ÿ foules of the righte-ous far aboue hell in côfort.

h Auguft. epi. 99

dunt quidam hoc beneficium antiquis etiam Sanctis fuiffe con-ceffum, Abel, Seth, Noe, & domui eius; Abraham, Ifaac, & Iacob, alijfque Patriarchis & Prophetis, vt cum Domi-nus in infernum veniffet, illis doloribus foluerentur. Sed quo-nam modo intelligatur Abraham, in cuius finum pius ille pauper fufceptus eft, in illis doloribus fuiffe; EGO QVIDEM NON VIDEO: explicant fortaffe qui poffunt. Solos autem duos, id eft Abraham & Lazarum in illo memorabilis quie-tis finu fuiffe, antequam Dominum in inferna defcenderet; & de ipfis tantum duobus dictum fuiffe illi diuiti; Inter vos & nos chaos magnum firmatum eft, vt ÿ qui volunt hinc tranfire ad vos non poffint, néque inde huc tranfmeare; nefcio. vtrum QVISQVAM SIT, CVI NON VIDEATVR ABSVRDVM. Porro fi plures quam duo ibi erant, QVIS AVDEAT DICERE non ibi fuiffe Patriarchas & Prophetas, quibus in Scripturis Dei iuftitia pietatifque tam infigne teftimonium perhibetur?

Cc 1   *Quid*

Quid ergo is præſtiterit, qui dolores ſoluit inferni, in quibus illi
non fuerunt, nendum intelligoȝ præsertim quia ne ipſos quidem in-
feros vſpiam Scripturarum locis in bono appellatos potui repe-
rire. Quod ſi nuſquam legitur, non vtique ſious ille Abrahæ,
id eſt ſecretæ cuiuſdam quietis habitatio, aliqua pars inferorum
eſſe credenda eſt ; quanquam in his ipſis tanti magiſtri verbis, vbi
ait dixiſſe Abraham, Inter nos & vos chaos magnum firma-
tum eſt, SATIS VT OPINOR APPARET *, non eſſe quan-*
dam partem & quaſi membrum inferorum tanta felicitatis ſinum.
Some adde that this benefite was yeelded vnto the Saintes of
the olde Teſtament, *Abel, Seth*, *Noe* and his familie, *Abra-*
ham, *Iſaac*, and *Iacob*, and to the reſt of the Patriarkes and
Prophets, that when Chriſt came to hell, they were deliuered
from thoſe paines there. But how *Abraham*, into whoſe bo-
ſome that godlie poore *Lazarus* was receiued, can bee imagi-
ned to haue beene in theſe paines, I for my part doe not ſee,
let them DECLARE IT THAT CAN. But that onely two,
Abraham and *Lazarus*, were in that boſome of memorable
reſt, before the Lorde deſcended to hell ; and that it was ſaid
of theſe two onelie ; *betwixt you and vs is a mightie gulfe ſet-*
led, (ſo that ſuch as would goe from hence to you, can not ; nor
anie that woulde come from you to vs,) I knowe not whether
there be anie man, to whom IT SEEMETH NOT ABSVRD.
And if there were mo then two , WHO DARE SAY, the
Patriarkes and Prophets were not there, to whom the worde
of God giueth ſo great teſtimonie of righteouſneſſe and god-
lineſſe ? What benefite hee did them, by looſing the paines of
hell, in which they were not, I yet vnderſtande not ; ſpeciallie
ſince I cannot finde the name of *Inferi* (oȝ hell) in any place of
ſcripture vſed for any good. The which if it bee no where in the
diuine authoritie to be read, then ſurely the boſome of *Abraham*
which is an habitation of ſecret reſt, is not to be thought any part
of hell; albeit in the verie wordes of ſo great a teacher(as **Chȝiſt**
is)where he maketh A*braham* ſay, betwixt you and vs there is a
mightie diſtance eſtabliſhed, it is euident enough, as **J thinke,**
                                                            that

that the bofome of fo great happines is no part nor méber of hel.

Saint Auften examineth the opinion of fome aunctent
wzlters, that Chzift defcended to hell to deliuer ý patriarks,
pzophets, and the righteous of the old teftament thence, ¶ not
onely refufeth, but after his maner mildly refuteth that fan-
fie, which had poffeffed many of the fathers befoze him. Out
of Chzifts wozds in the 16. of Luke he deriueth two conclu-
fions; one that Abrahams bofom was a place OF REST AND
HAPPINES, oz as the fcripture fpeaketh, OF COMFORT;
and confequently not of paine oz. tozment, as was hell; the
other, that BETVVIXT THEM IS AN HVGE DISTANCE,
fo that by no meanes Abrahams bofome can be taken to bee
ANY PART OR MEMBER OF HELL. Out of the princi-
ples of diuinitie he dzaweth two other pofitions, the firft, that
Abrahams bofome was not made for Lazarus onelie; which is
fo abfurd, that he thinketh no man will be fo foolifh as to em-
bzace it. Abrahams bofome muft be open to the reft of his
childzen, which did the woozkes of their father Abraham, as
well as to Lazarus; with God is no refpect of perfons; and
[i] From the Eaft and Weft fhall come manie, , and fit downe   [i] Mat. 8.
with Abraham, Ifaac and Iacob, in the kingdome of heauen,
faith our Sauiour. The fecond is, that if moze befides A-
braham and Lazarus were in that bofome of reft , the Pzo-
phets and Patriarks, muft néds be there, who foz fidelitie
and pietie are commended by the witneffe of Gods fpirite,
and placed in the foundation of the Church with the Apo-
ftles next the heade cozner ftone, as [k] HOLIE MEN OF   [k] 2. Pet. 1.
GOD, infpired and mooued by the holie ghoft. Thefe deduc-
tions being found and fure, whereof there can bee no doubt,
it is certaine, Chzift went not to hell to fetch the Patriarkes
and Pzophets thence, foz they were not there ; but in Abra-
hams bofome, which was an habitation of REST, COM-
FORT and BLISSE; fo farre diftant from the place of toz-
ment, that by no meanes it coulde bee a PART oz
MEMBER THEREOF.

The fumme of
S. Auftens col-
lections out of
the 16. of faint
Luke.

Cc 2   [But

S. Auſtens cō-iecture that ſome were de-liuered out of hell is verie weake.

[But Auſten himſelfe ſaith, hee doubteth not, but Chriſt deliuered ſome from the paines of hell at his deſcent thi-ther.] Saint Auſten refelleth the receiued opinion of o-thers before him, that Chriſt deſcended to hell, to deliuer thence the Patriarkes and Prophets that were there detai-ned; and addeth, that becauſe he then preſentlie ſawe no cauſe why Chriſt ſhould deſcend, but to ſaue from the paines of hel; he doth not doubt, but Chriſt deliuered ſome frō thence. But when he commeth to make proof for this his opinion, he fain-teth, and ſaith, the words of Peter, that Chriſt looſed the paines of hell, may bee taken in that ſenſe; and that Adam was then looſed, A L M ò s T the whole church conſented. Howbeit both theſe proofs are no more then probable, & ſcant ſo much; and therfore they compell no man to receiue S. Auſtens confec-turall inclination; but leaue vs at libertie, as wel to examine his reaſons, as to ſuſpend our iudgemēts, till we ſee ſtroger & better motiues to induce our conſent. For touching Peters words, himſelfe confeſſeth they may bee referred to Chriſt.

[1]*Quod ſcriptū eſt in morte Chriſti factū, ſolutis doloribus inferni, vel ad ipſum poteſt intelligi pertinere, quod eos hactenus ſolue-rit, hoc eſt irritos fecerit, ut ab eis ipſe teneretur, praſertim quia ſequitur, in quibus impoſſibile erat teneri* E V M*: vel ſi cauſa quæ-ritur cūr venire voluerit in infernum, vbi dolores illi eſſent, qui-bus omnino teneri nōn poterat; hoc quod ſcriptum eſt, ſolutis do-loribus inferni, non in omnibus, ſed* I N Q V I B V S D A M A C C I-P I P O T E S T, *quos ille dignos iſta liberatione iudicabat.* What the Scripture ſaieth was perfourmed in the death of Chriſt, T H E P A I N E S O F H E L L B E E I N G L O O S E D, may either bee vnderſtoode to pertaine to Chriſt himſelfe, that hee looſed, that is, fruſtrated thoſe paines from taking anie holde of him; ſpeciallie whereas it followeth (in the Text) O F W H I C H P A I N E S I T W A S I M P O S S I B L E H E E S H O V L D E B E H E L D E: or if wee aske for the cauſe, why he woulde come to hell, where thoſe paines were which coulde take no hold of him; theſe words (looſing the paines of hel) may
bee

bee taken not of all, but of fome, whome he thought worthy to be deliuered. Either way thefe wordes make nothing to S. Auftens fuppofition, that fome were in the paines of hell, when Chrift did thence deliuer them. For if we applie them to Chrifts perfon, which in deede S. Peter doth, they note that Chrift brake before him the ftrength of hell, when he approched to his refurrection. If wee refer them to mans deliuerance thence, that Chrift in our names and for our fafetie lofed the forrowes of hell; this will proue, wee fhould haue gone to hell, if Chrift had not faued vs thence; but that wee were there, it no way proueth. For hee deliuered all his, as wel liuing, and not then borne, as dead, from all the right and claime that hell had to them; and as we were deliuered, not from being there, but from comming thither; fo the dead might bee acquited and affured from the chalenge that hell had to them, though they were then in reft, and in hope of Chrifts comming to performe their expectation, and perfit their redemption from the power of hell.

As for the confent of the whole church A L M O S T, fince Auften himfelfe leadeth vs to diflike the opinion of all the fathers A L M O S T, that the foules of the righteous were in hel before Chriftes defcent thither; hee openeth the waie for vs to afke how the church came, by that perfwafion; whether by fcripture, or by Tradition: Scripture there is none extant for Adam, more then for all other men. Tradition for things done in hell, where no man liuing was prefent, can none bee pretended. The teftimonie, which Auften alleageth out of the booke of Wifedome, maketh rather againft that pofition, then for it. (Wifedome) [m] kept the firft man that was alone created, euen the father of the world; and B R O V G H T H I M O V T O F H I S S I N N E, and gaue him power to gouerne all thinges. That wifedome brought Adam out of his finne, is here affirmed; but whether by chaftifement and repentance in this life, or by deliuerance out of hell after this life, fince neither is fpecified, the firft is rather to bee receaued. For God both

both

[margin] How y church might beleeue Adams bandes were loofed in hell by Chrifts defcent.

[margin] [m] Sapient. 10

both by puniſhing Adams offence, and by offering him grace
in the promiſed Seede, did make way for repentance; yea
the whole life of Adam was nothing elſe but the meditati-
on of his fall; but that Chriſt ſet him from hell, when hee
deſcended thither, canne by no rules of religion bee war-
ranted. Indeed Chriſt went to hell to looſe the bands of A-
dams ſinne; and ſo the church might well beleeue and profeſſe.
For the guilt of Adams tranſgreſſion, and roote of Adams
corruption, brought vs all to be iuſtlie condemned to hell,
but that the death of Chriſt reconciled vs againe to God by
the remiſſion of our ſinnes; and the perſonall deſcent of
our Sauiour looſed all the bandes, and brake all the chaines
of darkeneſſe that were prouided for vs; and ſo freed Adam
and his offſpring from the power and paines of hell. In this
the whole church might conſent, that Adams ſinne was re-
leaſed, and Adams bandes looſed by Chriſts deſcent to hell;
but other tradition, what ſoules were in hell, and thence
deliuered at Chriſtes comming, as it was altogether vn-
knowne to men on earth, and conſequentlie moſt vncer-
taine, ſo is it rather preſumptuous to define, then religious
to beleeue.

And leaſt I ſhoulde ſeeme to be led with the ſpirit of con-
tradiction, to refuſe both the tradition of the church, and o-
pinion of the fathers, I will plainelie ſhew, what cauſeth me
to conſent to neither. Firſt in theſe ſecret and vnknowne
things, no mans aſſertion is to be truſted without the witnes
of the ſcriptures; and forſomuch as is expreſſed vnto vs in
the word of God, it rather croſſeth, then fauoreth this aſſerti-
on of the fathers. Next the ancient writers heerein doe not
onelie varie, one from another, but euen from themſelues;
to manifeſt that they had no ſettled truth, but ſome coniec-
tures, and thoſe verie ſlender in theſe hidden matters. Tou-
ching the ſoules of the righteous departed this life before
Chriſtes death, to omit the place of the booke of Wiſedome
alreadie recited, which expreſſelie gaineſaieth this ſuppoſall
of

From hel was
no releaſe, by
the doctrine of
our Sauiour.

of the fathers, that the soules of the iuſt were both in hell
and in torments: there is nothing cradlie reuealed vnto vs
in the ſcriptures that are canonicall, till we come to the xbi.
of S. Lukes goſpell, where our Sauiour by the parabolicall
hiſtorie of the wicked rich man and the godlie Lazarus tea-
cheth vs, what became of them both after their deathes; and
conſequentlie what was the ſtate of all the deade before his
time; to wit, that they were either CARIED BY AN-
GELS TO ABRAHAMS BOSOME, OR PVNISHED
IN THE FLAMES OF HELL: Theſe two places,
as they bee farre diſtant the one from the other, both in
SCITVATION and CONDITION, the one beeing full of
comfort, the other of torment; ſo in this they agrée, that
there coulde bee no ALTERATION in either. The rich
man in hell coulde neither obtaine anie meanes to bee re-
freſhed, no not a drop of water to coole his heate; nor expect
anie time to bee releaſed. Our Sauiour maketh Abraham
to ſay to the rich man, which muſt néedes be true, ⁿ between
you and vs there is ſettled a great gulfe, (or mightie diſ-
tance,) ſo that they which would go from hence to you cannot,
NEITHER CAN THEY COME FROM THENCE TO
vs. After this life there was no changing of places, and
namelie from hell there was no releaſe. This our Saui-
our taught for a reſolute trueth in his life time; howe then
coulde the ſoules of the iuſt bee releaſed and reduced from
hell by his deſcent? If Abraham and Lazarus were not in
hell; but in a place of reſt and comforte farre diſtant from
hell, howe then were all the righteous before Chriſtes
time not onlie in hell, but in the ſorrowes and paines of hell?
yea the ſon of God with his owne mouth ſo often in the new
teſtament expreſſing the fire of hel to be ° vnquenchable, and
the worme there neuer to die, how dare we without any war-
rant of the word of God, firſt to bring al the ſoules of the righ-
teous before Chriſt, from Abrahams boſome to hell, and then
to deliuer them thence without anie witneſſe of the holie
scriptures?

ᵃLuke.16

°Mark.9.

ſcriptures? With one breath our Sauiour doth thrice pronounce in the goſpell of Marke that in hell, neither the fire quencheth, nor the worme dieth; and preſume wee to quench the one, and kill the other without any ſcruple?

Mark.9.

[But the ſcripture ſaith, the ſoules of the Patriarkes and Prophets were in hell; and there to leaue them after Chriſts deſcent, were euerlaſtinglie to condemne them.] The tranſlators miſtooke the word Sheòl, calling that hel, which indeed was the graue, where the bodies of all the iuſt both before and after Chriſt were laid; but the teacher of all truth, whoſe doctrine wee by no meanes may diſtruſt, placeth Abraham in reſt, and maketh his boſome a receptacle for the ſoules of the righteous; and therefore we may ſtriue about words if we liſt, but we muſt leaue the ſpirits of iuſt and perfit men before Chriſtes comming, that place, which Chriſt, teaching here on earth, aſſured vs, was aſſigned them of God. And ſince by the doctrine of our ſauiour they were not in hell; it is more then manifeſt, he did not fetch them thence by his deſcending thither.

As for the ſuppoſall of the fathers, that Abraham, Iacob, Samuel, and Dauid, with the reſt of the Patriarks and prophets were in hell; it were eaſie to ſhew their varieties, & contrarieties, if I tooke pleaſure to diſcouer their weakeneſſe. S. Auſten in his 99. Epiſtle to Euodius, and his 12. booke *de geneſi ad literam, cap.33.* exactlie contradicteth the opinion of ᵠTertullian, ʳBaſil, ˢHierom, ᵗᵗAmbroſe, that Abraham & the reſt of the Patriarks and Prophets were in hell; & proueth that Abrahams boſome muſt not be thought to be any part or member of hell. In his 57. Epiſtle to Dardanus hee ſaith, *non facile dixerim,* I cannot readily pronounce. In his 20. booke *de ciuitate dei. cap.15.* he ſaith, *non abſurdè credi videtur, antiquos etiam ſanctos, apud inferos fuiſſe,* it ſeemeth no abſurdity to beleeue, that the Saints of the olde teſtament were in hell, vntill the bloud of Chriſt and his deſcent to thoſe places did deliuer them. And thus he either ſome times ſpared the credites of
thoſe

The fathers varie touching the place of the ſoules departed before Chriſts comming.
ᵠ *De anima. ca. 55.*
ʳ *In Pſal. 48. concio. 13.*
ˢ *In Eccle. cap. 9*
ᵗ *In Epiſtol. ad Rom. cap. 5.*

thoſe that were before him, o2 elſe by wziting hee ſo p2ofiteð,
that where at firſt he ðoubteð o2 yéelðeð to others ; at laſt he
reſolueð the contrarie vpon the newe examining the wozðes
of our Sauiour. Tertullian likewiſe in his booke *de anima*
ſaith. ᵃ *Habes de paradiſo à nobis libellum, quo conſtituimus, om-* ᵃ Cap. 55.
nem animam apud inferos ſequeſtrari in diem iudicij. We haue
written a booke touching paradice, where wee defenðe that all
ſoules are kept in hell vntill the day of iudgement. Anð ſpea
king namelie of Abrahams boſome ; ˣ *Omnes ergo anima pe-* ˣ Idem. cap. 58
nes inferos, inquis ? velis ac nolis ; & ſupplicia iam illic & refri-
geria, habes pauperem, & diuitem. Cur enim non putes animam
& puniri & foueri in inferis? Are al ſoules then in hell, you wil
aske ? will you, nill you ; you ſhall finðe there puniſhmentes,
and refreſhments; as in *Lazarus*, and the rich man. Anð why
ſhoulðe you not thinke that the ſoule may bee both tozmented,
and comfozted in hell ? anð yet in this fourth booke againſt
Marcion, hee contraðicteth that falſe poſition, and cometh
ſounðlie to the truth. *Aliud inferi, vt puto, aliud quoque ſinus* ᶻ Idem contra
Abraha. Nam & magnum ait intercedere regiones iſtas profun- Marcion. lib. 4
dum, & tranſitum vtrinque prohibere. Sed nec alleuaſſet diues
oculos, & quidem de longinquo, niſi in ſuperiora, & de altitudi-
nis longinquo, per immenſam illam diſtantiā ſublimitatis & pro-
funditatis. Eam itaque regionē ſinum dico Abraha, etſi non cœ-
leſtem, ſublimiorem tamen Inferis. Hell is one thing, as I thinke,
and *Abrahams* boſome is another. For (*Abraham*) ſayeth a
great depth is betweene theſe two regions, and ſuffereth none
to paſſe to and fró. Neither coulðe the rich man haue lift vp his
eies, but vnto places aboue him, and far aboue him, by reaſon
of the infinite diſtance betwixt that heigth, and that depth. That
region then, I call *Abrahams* boſome, which though it bee not
heauen, yet is it higher then hell. Ambroſe after the ſame ma-
ner, ſometimes ſaith, that Abraham was, (ᶻ *apud Inferos*) ᶻ In Epiſtol. ad
in hell : ſometimes againe, that *Lazarus* ᵃ *in Abraha ſinu* Rom. cap. 5
recumbens, vitam carpebat eternam: Lazarus lying in *Abra-* ᵃ In Pſal. 118.
hams boſome, enioied euerlaſting life; anð hard it is, that eter- ſerm. 3

nall

nall life ſhould be in hell. In the one and the ſame chapter he alloweth the perſwaſion of the heathen, [b] *quod anima libe-* *rata de corporibus ἀΐδην peterent, id eſt, locum qui non videtur, quē locum Latinè Infernum dicimus :* that ſoules departed from their bodies did go to ἀΐδης, that is, to an inuiſible place, which in latine is called hell; and alſo the aſſertion of true religion, ý the [b] graue was the receptacle of the body only; [b] *animarū autē ſuperiora eſſe habitacula, ſcripturæ teſtimonijs valdeprobatur;* But ý manſions of the ſoules are aboue, as may eaſily be proued by ý teſtimonies of ſcripture. Theſe are the habitatiōs of which Chriſt ſaid, there are [c] many manſions with his father. But I take no delight in reherſing their ouerſights, it will ſuffice that with one conſent, they make Abrahams boſome a receptacle for all the iuſt; and the place of tormente where the rich man was, a priſon for the wicked; calling the one hell, and con-feſſing the other to be the fruition of reſt and happineſſe after this life.

[d] They that depart this world by death are according to their
deeds & deſerts beſtowed (ſaith Origen) *alij in locū, qui dicitur Inferius, alij in ſinū Abrahæ,* ſome to ý place which is called hel, others to *Abrahās* boſom. [e] *Omnes qui patrem habent Abrahā, & virtutū eius ſimiles eſſe meruerunt, requieſcunt in ſinu eius.* Al that haue Abrahā for their father, and obtained to be like him in vertues, reſt in his boſome, ſaith Ierom. [f] *Iuſti in Abrahæ ſinu re-quieſcere leguntur, quod in eius gratia, in eius requie, in eius pla-ciditate requieſcunt, qui conformē ei fidē induerunt, et eandem in bonis operibus fecerunt voluntatem.* The iuſt (ſaith Ambroſe,) are ſaid to reſt in Abrahams boſome, becauſe they reſt in like fauor, in like eaſe, in like contentation, which put on like faith to Abra-hā, and followed his exāple in wel doing. And therfore he ſpea-keth elſe where to Abrahā : [g] *Expande ſinus tuor; vt plures ſuſ-*
cipias, quia plurimi in deū crediderunt. Open wide thy boſom to receaue me, becauſe many haue beleeued in God. [h] *Extendit Dauid ſpes ſuas ad infinitam perennitatis ætatē, nec concluditur mortis occaſu quē ſciat ſibi in Abrahæ ſinibus exemplo pauperis*
Lazari

Lazarieſſe viuendū: Dauid ſtretcheth out his hope to infinite e-
ternity, & endeth it not with ý fal of death, knowing ý he ſhould
liue in Abrahãs boſome, as did that poore *Lazarus,* ſaith Hilary.
Neither Dauid onely, but all the faithfull were, and ſtill are
kept in Abrahams boſome, as Hilarie thinketh, vntill the day
of iudgement. *Exeuntes de corpore ad introitum illū regni ce-* Idem in Pſal. 120.
leſtis, per cuſtōdiā domini fideles omnes reſeruabuntur : in ſinu ſci-
licet interim Abrahæ collocati, quò adire impios interiectum cha-
os inhibet, quouſque introeundi rurſum in regnum calorum tem-
pus adueniat ; All the faithfull departing this life, ſhall bee re-
ſerued in the Lords keeping, for that entrance into the kingdom
of heauen, placed the meane while in *Abrahams* boſome, whi-
ther the gulfe betweene will not ſuffer the wicked to come, till
the time approch that (the godly) ſhal enter into the kingdom
of heauen. This time of entring into the kingdom of heauen,
he maketh to be the day of iudgement. *Excipit* (impios) *ſta-* Idem in Pſalt.
tim vltor infernus : & decedentes de corpore, ſi ita vixerunt, con-
feſtim de via iuſta peribunt. Teſtes nobis ſunt Euangelij diues et
pauper ; quorum vnum angeli IN SEDIBVS BEATORVM,
& in Abrahæ ſinu locauerunt, alium ſtatim regio pænæ ſuſce-
pit. Nihil illic dilationis aut mora eſt. Iudicij enim dies, vel,
beatitudinis retributio eſt æterna, vel pænæ : Tempus vero mortis
habet interim vnūquemq; ſuis legibus, dū ad iudiciū vnūquemq;
aut Abraham reſeruat aut pæna. Hel, as a reuenger, preſently ta-
keth the wicked, and they leauing this body, according to their
liues, do forthwith periſh frō the right way. The rich and poore
man in the goſpel, do ſerue vs for witneſſes, wherof the one was
caried by the Angels, INTO THE SEATES OF THE BLESSED, &.
placed in *Abrahams* boſome ; the other the region of puniſh-
ment did ſtraightway ſeaſe on : No delaie or ſtay may there
be looked for: The day of iudgment bringeth with it the reward
of eternal bliſſe, or paine : but the verie time of death in the mean
ſeaſon ſubiecteth all men to theſe lawes, that either *Abraham*
or hell paines detaineth euerie ſoule vnto iudgement . Theſe
Fathers confeſſe, that all the iuſt, as well before Chriſtes

reſurrection

resurrection as after, were and are still in Abrahams bosome, and there shall continue till the date of iudgement. Howe then could either Abrahams bosome be in hell, or the Saintes of the olde testament be thence deliuered by Christes descent, since they remaine still in Abrahams bosome, as these fathers write; and so shall do, to the end of the world? If Abrahams bosome were in hell, beeing deliuered from hell, they must needes bee deliuered likewise from Abrahams bosome: If they be still in Abrahams bosome, then were they neuer deliuered thence; and that being in hell, as some fathers would haue it, the iust of both testamentes are still in hell; and so none were deliuered thence by Christes descending thither.

[But the calling vp of Samuel by the Witch at Endor, proueth y Samuel & so the rest of the prophets were in hell: For she saw him ascending vp out of the earth, & he saide to Saul,
1 .Samuel.18.
To morrow shalt thou and thy sonnes be with me. Now that
Whether the
soule of Samuel
were in hell,
or no.
Saul being a reprobate, and killing himselfe, should bee in A-brahams bosome, it was not possible. Since then Samuel and Saul after death were both in one place, and that place was beneath in the earth, it is likelier that Samuel was in hell with Saul, till he were deliuered thence, then that Saul was in Abrahams bosome with Samuel.] The raising vp of Samuel after his death by the Witch, hath moued much question in the church of God, whether it were Samuel in deede that rose and spake, or whether it were the diuell transforming himselfe into the likenesse of Samuel, to driue Saul into dispaire. And albeit the matter may be largelie disputed on either side, yet neither opinion will infer that Samuels soule was in hell, which is the point we haue in hand. That it was
Reasons to
proue it was
an illusion of
the Diuel.
not Samuel himselfe which appeared, but the Witches familiar spirit in his likenesse, these reasons preuaile with mee. First, neither by Witches nor Diuels could the soules of the saints bee commanded, or disquieted from their places, where they are in rest and peace. Secondlie, we are assured, by the doctrine of our Sauiour, that God will sende none
*Luke 16.
m from the dead to instruct the liuing: yea all such conference is

is prohibited & pronounced abominable by the law of God; ᵒDeur.18.
not that the dead can arise or aduise the liuing , but because
the diuell vnder that colour should not delude and abuse the
people of God. Thirdlie, that which appeared receiued adora-
tion at Saules h.nds; which the ᵒAngel refused at S. Iohns; ᵒReuel.22.
and the soule of Samuel neither might , nor would haue ac-
cepted. Fourthlie, Saul forsaken & reiected of God, could not
after death rest in the same place with Samuel the elect and
approued seruant of God. Lastlie , the fathers doe for the
most part resolue, it was an illusion of Satan to strike Saul
into desperation.

　　Tertullian disputing against it verie learnedlie, saieth. ᵖTertul. de ani-
ma, cap 57.
ᵖ Ecce hodie (Simonis hæreticos) tanta præsumptio artis extollit, Authorities to
proue the
same.
vt etiam Prophetarum animas ab inferis mouere se spondeant: Et
credo, quia mendacio possuit : nec enim pythonico tunc spiritui mi-
nus licuit animam Samuelis effingere, post deum mortuos consu-
lente Saule. Absit alioquin vt animam cuiuslibet sancti nedum
Prophetæ a dæmonio credamus extractam, edocti, quod ipse Sata-
nas transfiguretur in Angelum lucis, nedum in hominem lucis.
Dubitauit, si forte, tunc Prophetam se Dei asseuerare, & vtique
Sauli, in quo ipse morabatur : ne putes alium fuisse qui phantas-
ma administrabat , alium qui commendabat, sed eundem spiri-
tum & in pseudoprophetide & in Apostata facile metiri, quod fe-
cerat credi : & ideo per quem visurum se credidit, vidit : quia per
quem vidit & credidit. ¶ Nulli autem animæ omnino inferos pa-
tere, satis dominus in argumento illo pauperis requiescentis, & �q Ibid.
diuitis ingemiscentis ex persona Abrahæ sanxit, non posse relegari
renunciatorem dispositionis infernæ, quod vel tunc licere potuisset,
vt Mosi & Prophetis crederetur. Euen at this day the followers
of Simon (Magus) are so puffed vp with the presumption of their
art, that they promise to raise from hell the soules of the Pro-
phets. And I thinke they can easily belie themselues; for so did
the familiar spirit (of the witch at Endor) resemble the soule
of Samuel, when Saul reiected of God, consulted the dead. O-
therwise, GOD FORBID VVE SHOVLD BELEEVE, that the

　　　　　Dd 3　　　　　　　　　　soule

soule of any Saint, much lesse of a Prophet, could bee raised by the Diuell; since wee are taught that Satan is often transfigured into an Angell of light, much more into a man of light. Perchaunce (the Diuell) did doubt to auotich himselfe to bee the Prophet of God, and that to *Saul*, whom hee alreadie possessed; least you should thinke it was anie other which commended the apparition, then hee that procured it; but euen the same spirite both in the false Prophetesse; and to the Apostata (*Saul*)easilie belied that which he had made to be beleeued. And therefore by whome (*Saul*) beleeued hee should see (the ghost of Samuel) by him he saw it; because by whom he saw it, to him he gaue credite. And to teach vs that no soule may rise from the dead, the lord doth sufficiently determine by the person of *Abraham* in that argument of the poore man in rest, & the rich man in torment, that none can returne to report the state of things in hell, which then might haue beene done, to get the more authoritie to *Moses* and the Prophetes. The booke of questions vnder the name of Iustine Martyr being of good antiquitie, if it bee not his; saieth . [*] *Cætera omnia ab ipsa Pythonissa facta sunt, Dæmonis operâ, prastigijs eorum oculos deludentis, qui videbant eum quã Samuel non erat. Veritas autem dictorum à Deo fuit, qui permisit Dæmoni, vt in forma Samuelis Pythonissæ appareret, & res futuras præmonstraret. Et quoniam Samuelem Saul non audierat, dum amissionem regni prædiceret illi, sed post diuinam sententiam ei regnum adimentem, per hariolos imperium retinere satagebat, indignum eum duxit Deus, vt ei ventura significaret per homines sibi adhærentes.* All the rest the witch did by the operation of the *Diuell*, deluding their eies, which sawe one that was not *Samuel*. But the trueth of that which was spoken, was of God, who permitted the Diuell both to appeare to the witch in the shape of *Samuel*, and to foretell the euent of thinges to come. For in that *Saul* would not giue eare to *Samuel*, prophecying vnto him the losse of his kingdome, but sought to retaine it by the helpe

of

of witches, God counted him vnworthie to vnderſtande what
ſhould come to paſſe by anie ſeruants of his. Theodorete in his
queſtions vpon the firſt booke of Kings, doth reiect this opi-
nion, that the witch raiſed vp Samuel, not as falſe only, but as
impious alſo. His words are. ʿ *Quomodo oportet intelligere de*
ventriloqua? Nonnulli dicunt eam verè retuliſſe Samuelem. Nõ-   ʿ *Theodoret. que-*
nulli autem hoc refellerunt. Ego quidem PRIMVM EXISTIMO   *ſtionum, in lib. 1.*
ESSE IMPIVM. *Exiſtimo enim mulieres necromanticas ne quamli-*   *Regum queſt. 62*
bet quidem reducere animam, tantum abeſt, vt prophetæ, & tan-
ti prophetæ. Eſt enim perſpicuum, quod in aliquo alio loco degunt
animæ expectantes reſurrectionem corporum. EST ERGO VALDE
IMPIVM *credere ventriloquam habere vim tantam.* What ſhall
we ſay concerning the witch? Some thinke ſhee truly raiſed vp
Samuel; Some others refell it. I think the firſt to be a W I C K E D
imagination. For I reſolue that witches can raiſe no mans ſoule,
much leſſe the ſoule of a prophet, and of ſo great a prophet. It is
euident that the ſoules (of the dead) are in a place beſides this
world, expecting ẏ reſurrectiõ of their bodies. It is therfore VERY
IMPIOVS to beleeue ẏ a witch hath ſo great power. And where
Theodoret alleageth a place of the Chronicles to proue, ʿ *Quod*   ʿ *Ibidem.*
ipſe deus vniuerſorum efformata vt voluit ſpecie Samuelis, protu-
lit ſententiam, & minime per aduerſarios protulit ſententiã; That
God himſelfe framing the ſhape of *Samuel* as pleaſed him, pro-
nounced the ſentence, and did not giue that iudgement by his
aduerſaries : there are no ſuch wordes in the Text as he que-
teth. For he citeth them thus: ᵘ *Et mortuus eſt Saul in ſuis ini-*   ᵘ *Idem. queſt. 62*
quitatibus, in quibus peccauit domino ſuper eloquium domini, prop-
terea quod ipſum nõ cuſtodiuit, & quod interrogauit Saul in ven-
triloqua, vt exquireret, ET RESPONDIT SAMVEL PROPHETA, &
non exquiſiuit in domino, & occidit eum. Saul died in his ſinnes, in
which he ſinned againſt the Lord, as touching the word of ẏ lord
which he performed not, & alſo in that Saul conſulted the witch,
to know what ſucceſſe he ſhould haue. And *Samuel* the prophet
anſwered him, & *Saul* ſought not the lord, & he ſlue him. Theſe
wordes, AND SAMVEL THE PROPHET ANSVVERED HIM,
                                                                            are.

are not in the booke of ˣ Chronicles; and therefore Theodo-
rets foundation being falſe, his concluſion that God ſpake
theſe wordes, and not the diuell, is no way iuſtifiable. Be-
ſides, if God had ſaide, that Saul and his ſonnes after death
ſhould bee with (God;) as hee that ſpake to Saule ſaide they
ſhould be with him; God had promiſed vnto Saul ETERNAL
LIFE after his departure hence; which is a plaine contra-
rietie to the wordes of the Scripture, that ſaith; ʸ SAVL
DIED IN HIS SINNES. The firſt part then of Theodorets
reſolution, that a witch could not raiſe the ſoule of Samuel, is
ſound and true diuinitie; the ſecond, that God made a ſhape of
Samuel, and thereby anſwered Saul, is not proued by any
ſcripture, though it be ſo ſuppoſed by Theodoret.

S. Auſten diſputing the matter on both ſides, though he no
way yeeld that the witch was able to raiſe vp ſoules; yet hee
ſaith, ᶻ Non eſt abſurdum credere, ex aliqua diſpenſatione diuinæ
voluntatis permiſſum fuiſſe, vt nõ inuitus, nec dominante aut ſub-
iugante magica potentia, ſed volens & obtēperans occultæ diſpen-
ſationi dei, qua & pythoniſſam illam, & Saulem latebat, cõſentiret
ſpiritus Prophetæ ſancti ſe oſtendi aſpectibus regis, diuina eum
ſententia percuſſurus. It is no abſurditie to thinke, that by ſome
diſpenſation of the diuine pleaſure it was permitted, that the
ſoule of the holie Prophet, not againſt his will, nor ouerruled or
forced by anie magicall power, but willing and obeying the ſe-
crete will of God, which was hidde both from the witch, and
from Saul, ſhould ſhewe it ſelfe to the kings ſight, to the end
it might the more aſtoniſh him with the iudgement of God.
And albeit he make this poſſible, yet he inclineth rather to
this opinion as the eaſier, and likelier, that the whole was
but the deceite and worke of Satan ᵃ Quanquam in
hoc facto, poteſt eſſe alius FACILIOR intellectus & EXPE-
DITIOR exitus, vt non verè ſpiritum Samuelis excitatum à ſua
requie credamus, ſed aliquod phantaſma, et imaginariam illuſio-
nem diaboli machinationibus factam, quam propterea ſcriptura
nomine Samuelis appellat, quia ſolent imagines, rerum earum
nominibus

nominibus appellari, quarum imagines funt . Although in this fact, there may bee another more eafier vnderftanding, and freer from (all)difficulties, if wee beleeue that the foule of *Samuel* indeede was not raifed from his reft, but that it was a phantafme, and illufion wrought by the craft of Satan; which the fcripture therefore calleth by the name of *Samuel*, becaufe refemblances are woont to bee called by the names of thofe things which they refemble. The felfe fame word for word hee [b] repeateth in his anfwere to the queftions which Dulcitius propofed vnto him; and albeit in thefe places he fway indiffe-rently betwixt both, or incline faintly to the one; yet in his bookes *De doctrina Chriftiana* he calleth it a Sacrilegious re-prefentation of Samuels image. [c] *Non enim quia imago Samue-lis mortui Sauli regi vera pranunciarit, propterea talia facrile-gia, quibus imago illa prafentata eft, minus execranda funt.* Nei-ther, becaufe the image of dead *Samuel* foretold truth to king *Saul*, are fuch SACRILEGIES, BY WHICH THAT I-MAGE WAS SHEWED, the leffe to be DETESTED.

But if it were the foule of Samuel that appeared, and no illufion of the diuell prefenting himfelf in the habit of Samu-el, the ftorie no way conuinceth that Samuel was in hell. The witch faid, I faw gods afcending out of the earth; but her fight is no good proofe, where the foules of the iuft are, or whence they come, the diuell might eafily delude her; and make her beléeue, hee came out of the earth, that came from another place. Againe if the bodie of Samuel were taken vp for his foule to appeare in; that was raifed out of the earth, though the foule of Samuel came from Abrahams bofome; fo hee ne-ceffarily muft rife out of the earth, if his bodie rofe withall, as we all fhall at the generall refurrection. And where the image of Samuel faide to Saul, [d] To morrow thou and thy fonnes fhall be with vs; he did not meane their foules fhoulde be in the fame receptacles after death, but as Auften faieth: [e] *Mortuus mortem viuo pranunciabat.* He that was dead, fore-fhewed the death of him that liued; *vt non ad aqualitatem feli-citatis*

Marginal notes:
[b] *Ad octo Dul-citij quaeftiones queft.6*
[c] *De doct.Chri-ftiana.li.2,ca.23*

Neither opiniō proueth that Samuels foule was in hell.

[d] 1.Sam.18.

[e] *Ad Simplie. lib.2.queft.3*

citatis, ſed ad parem conditionem mortis referatur: That it ſhould be referred to the like condition of death, & not to the fruition of the ſame felicitie. **For if we ſo take the words,** Thou ſhalt be to morrow with mee, *vtiꝗ, falſum eſt;* it is certainly falſe, ſaith Auſten, [f] *Magno quippe interuallo poſt mortem ſeparari bonos a malis in Euangelio legimus, cum dominus inter ſuperbum illum diuitem, cum iam apud inferos tormenta pateretur, & illum, qui ad eius ianuam vlceroſus iacebat, iam in requie conſtitutum, magnum chaos interiectum teſtetur.* That the good are after death ſeparated from the bad by a mightie diſtance, we read in the Goſpel, where the Lord witneſſeth, that there is a great gulfe interiected, betweene the proude riotſman, where hee was tormented in hell, and the poore Lazare now in reſt, which lay full of ſores at the rich mans gate. **And ſo whether we take it to be the ſoule of Samuel that ſpake to Saul, or a Magicall illuſion of Satan transforming himſelfe into the ſhape of** Samuel, **neither way proueth that** Samuel **was in hell; howbeit I rather imbrace the reaſons that are extant in the ſ. queſtions of the olde teſtament vnder the name of S. Auſten, cited in the Canon law, which though they be not** Auſtens, **are verie ancient.** [h] *Indignum facinus aſtimo, ſi ſecundum verba hiſtoriæ commodetur aſſenſus. Quomodo enim fieri poterat, vt arte magica attraheretur vir & natiuitate ſanctius, & vitæ operibus iuſtus? Aut ſi non attractus eſt, conſenſit: quod vtrumꝗ de viro iuſto credere abſurdum eſt. Porro hac eſt præſtigium Satanæ, qua, vt plurimos fallat, etiam bonos in poteſtate ſe habere confingit: Hiſtoricus mentem Saul, & habitum Samuelis deſcripſit, ea quæ dicta & viſa ſunt exponens, prætermittens ſi vera an falſa ſint. Quid enim ait? Audiens in quo habitu eſſet excitatus, intellexit, hunc eſſe Samuelem. Quid intellexerit retulit, & quia non bene intellexit, contra ſcripturã, alium adorauit quam deum, & putans Samuelem adorauit diabolum, vt fructum fallaciæ ſuæ haberet Satanas. Si enim vere Samuel illi apparuiſſet, non vtiꝗ vir iuſtus permiſiſſet ſe adorari, qui prædicauerat deũ ſolum adorandũ. Et quomodo homo dei, qui cũ Abraham in refrigerio erat dicebat ad virum peſtilentiæ; dignum ardore gehennæ,*

g Queſt. ex ve ſer. teſt mento. queſt. 27.
h Cauſ. 26. queſt. 3. §14. nec mirũ.

gehenna, or as mecum eris? His duobus titulis fubtilitatem fallacie fua prodidit improuidus Satan, quia & adorari fe permifit fub habitu & nomine Samuelis contra legem: & virum peccatis prefa fum, cum magna diftantia peccatorum & iuftorum fit; cum Samuele iuftiffimo futurum mentitus eft. Ad eum enim tranfmigrauit (Saul) quem adorauit, I take it to be a wicked act, if we acknowledge the ftorie according to the words. For how could it be that a man holie in birth, and iuft in life fhould bee drawne (from the place of his reft) by the power of a witch? If he were not drawne (againft his will) hee confented (to come;) both which are abfurd to beleeue of fo iuft a perfon. And this is the fleight of Satan, that to deceiue the more, hee maketh as if the iuft were in his hands. The ftorie doth defcribe the mind of *Saul*, and the fhew of *Samuel*, expreffing what was feene and faid, but pretermitting how true or falfe either was. For what faith it? *Saul* hearing in what habite (the fpirite) was raifed, vnderftoode it to be *Samuel*. It reporteth what (*Saul*) conceiued, and becaufe hee conceiued amiffe, hee adored another then God; againft the fcripture; and thinking it to bee *Samuel*, worfhipped the Diuell, that Satan might reape the fruite of his fallacie. For if *Samuel* had indeede appeared vnto him, the iuft perfon woulde neuer haue fuffered himfelfe to bee worfhipped, which preached God alone to be worfhipped. And how did the man of god, that was with *Abraham* in reft, fay to that peftilent man, worthie of hell fire, to morrowe thou fhalt bee with me? By thefe two wayes Satan afore he was ware betraied his fraudulent fubtilie, becaufe he fuffered himfelfe to be worfhipped vnder the habite and name of *Samuel*, againft (Gods) lawe; and lied, that *Saul* loden with finne fhould after death be with righteous *Samuel*, whereas there is a great diftance betwixt the iuft and vniuft (after this life;) and *Saul* went hence to him, whom he worfhipped.

[If the fathers fo much varie, and diffent from themfelues, and from others, whie do I preffe their teftimonie touching Chrifts defcent to hell?] I preffe them no further then they accord with the words of the scripture, and with the grounds of faith, & wherein they all concurre with one consent. When they swarue aside, or part asunder, I dissemble it not; wishing the reader, as not to regarde their priuate opinions without good proofe, so not to reiect their general confession in matters of faith agreeing with the scriptures, without better demonstration then I yet see made for the contrarie. That the diuell was destroied, and man deliuered by Christs death from the feare of death, is no supposall of mine or theirs, but the manifest conclusion of the holy ghost. That Christ i in his owne person spoiled powers and principalities, and openly triumphed ouer them, that l death and hell might bee swallowed vp in victorie, is not mans imagination, but the Apostles resolution. That Christs m soule was in hell, and there not m forsaken, if Dauids prediction, and Peters application were not plaine inough, S. Lukes interpretation is so pregnant, that without wrong to the word, it can not bee pared. Lay these togither, and see what they lacke of Christs soule descending into hell. His being there must needs inferre his descending thither. And yet least some scrupulous person should stick at the phrase of Christs DESCENDING INTO HEL, I think S.Paul hath words equiualent to them, n Ascending on high he led captiuitie captiue. That he ascended, what is it, but that he FIRST DESCENDED into the lower partes of the earth? He that descended, is euen the same that ascended aboue al the heauens; that he might fil al. If hell be any where, there can be no doubt but it must be in the lower parts of the earth. From the earth vpward is heauen, where hell can not be. Christ then DESCENDED into the lower partes of the earth, and thence ledde captiuitie captiue, that hee might fill all (places) with his presence. Christs sepulchre was in the higher parts of the earth, o hewen out in a rock, and thence he might lead the death of the bodie captiue, but not the diuell, that was ruler ouer death, and had a chalenge to the soules of men that came not neare their graues. Since then ascending from the lower parts of

the

I vrge not the fathers but agreeing with the scriptures and with them selues.

i Heb 2.
k Colof.2.

l 1.Cor.15.

m Acts 2.

o Ephef.4.

o Mat.27.

the earth, he lead captiue, all ẏ powers, that held man in bon-
dage; and thoſe chieſelie were the powers of hell, which had
intereſt into the ſoule of man by reaſon of ſinne; it muſt
needes bee, that Chriſt deſcended to thoſe partes of the earth,
where mans captiuitie was ſtrongeſt, which is in hell: and
thence freed him by his preſence, and led thoſe captiues, that
ruled ouer him, as conquerour of all the power of the deuill
and darkeneſſe, whoſe priſoner man was, before hee was
redeemed. Againe, hee firſt deſcended to the loweſt, and
then aſcended to the higheſt, that he might fill all places with
his preſence. If hee deſcended not to hell, howe filled hee
that place, where hee neuer was, except with the brightneſſe
of his diuine glorie, which is euerie where preſent without
deſcending or aſcending ? But the Apoſtle ſaith he deſcen-
ded to the loweſt, and aſcended to the higheſt, that he might
fill all (places) with the preſence of his manhoode, all knees
in heauen, earth, and hell bowing vnto the exaltation of his
humane nature.

And if the lower partes of the earth, whither Chriſt de- **Chriſts deſcen-**
ſcended to leade captiuitie captiue, bee not lowe enough to **ding into the**
ſhewe the ſettuation of hell: Saint Paul hath plainer wordes **deep, and into**
of Chriſtes deſcending as lowe as might bee; when he wri- **hel are al one.**
teth to the Romanes in this wiſe. P Say not in thine heart, **P Rom.10**
who ſhall aſcende into heauen? (that is, to bring Chriſt downe
from aboue,) or who ſhal DESCEND INTO THE DEEPE?
(that is, to bring Chriſt backe from the deade.) Chriſt dy-
ing DESCENDED INTO THE DEEPE, as riſing
from the deade, hee aſcended into heauen. Nowe the deepe
is ſo lowe, that no place canne be lower; yea hell it ſelfe,
and the priſon of Diuels is knowne by that name in the
newe Teſtament. When the ſpirits, that poſſeſſed the mad
man amongſt the Gadarens, were to bee caſt out by Chriſt, **q Luke.8**
q they beſought him, that hee would not commaund them εἰς **r Reuelat.9.**
τὴν ἄβυσσον ἀπελθεῖν, to departe into the deepe. In the Reue- **verſe 1. & 2.**
lation of Saint Iohn, hell is called, r τὸ φρέαρ τῆς ἀβύσσου,

* Ibidem. ver. 11

the pit of the deepe, and the Diuell is there named ᵗ the An-
gell, τῆς ἀβύσσȣ, of the deepe : yea the verie place, where the
Diuell is ſhut vp, is expreſſed by that word ; ᶠ I ſawe an An-
gell (ſaith Saint Iohn) come downe from heauen, hauing τὴν
κλεῖν τῆς ἀβύσσȣ , the key of the deepe, and a great chaine
in his hand. And he took the dragon that olde ſerpent, which is
called the diuell, and bounde him, and caſt him εἰς τὴν ἄβυσσον,
into the deep, & ſhut him vp. If ἄβυσσος be a bottomles deep,
then which can nothing be deeper ; if in the ſcriptures it pro-
perly ſigniſie the verie dungeon of hel, where the diuels are
kept; the Apoſtle then auouching that Chriſt, when hee died,
DESCENDED εἰς τὴν ἄβυσσον, INTO THE BOTTOMLES
DEEP, doth cleerely confirme that he deſcended into hell. As
therefore, if we aſke who can deſcend into the deep, or aſcend
into heauen, we reuerſe Chriſts being among the dead and
his ſitting at the right hand of God in the heauens, ſo if wee
confeſſe them both to be verified in Chriſt (ᵗ but in Chriſt they
neuer were nor euer ſhalbe verified of any man)we muſt no
more deny ᵖ he deſcended into the bottomles pit, which is hell,
then ᵖ he aſcended into ᵖ heauens, both are neceſſary partes
of our redemption, & euident proofes of his mighty operatiō.
We muſt be freed frō hel, before we can be placed in heauen ;
and if Chriſt haue omitted either, he hath performed neither.

What marnaile then, if the ancient fathers with one con-
ſent, make Chriſts deſcent to hel, a material point of our re-
demption, and preſſe it as an appendix to faith ; ſince it hath
ſo good ground, and iuſt proofe in the ſcriptures, howſoeuer
they or the doubt, where the ſoules of the righteous were, be-
fore Chriſts ſuffering. ᵗ Crux, mors, inferi, ſalus noſtra eſt, ſaith
Hilary; The croſſe, death, and deſcent (of Chriſt)to hell are our
ſaluation. ᵘ Diuinitai neque corpus in monumento, neq, animā in
inferno deſtituit. hic eſt eum, quod dictū eſt per prophetā. non re-
linques animā meā apud inferos, neq, dabis ſanctū tuū videre cor-
ruptionem. Quocirca in ANIMA quidē CHRISTI MORS DEVICTA
EST, reſurrectioq, ab inferis deprompta, & ſpiritibus annunciata
eſt

ᶠ Reuel.20.
κλεῖϑλα.

Chriſt deſcen-
ded into the
bottomleſſe
deepe.

The deſcent
to hell after
death, a part of
our redéption.

ᵗ De Trinitat.
lib.2
ᵘ Athanaſ.de ſa-
lutari aduentu
Chriſti.

*eſt : in corpore vero dei corruptio abolita eſt , et incorruptibilitas e
ſepulchre emicuit.* (Chriſts)deity neither forſooke his body in the
ſepulchre, nor his ſoule in hel. For ỹ is ỹ meaning of the Prophet,
whē he ſaith; Thou wilt not leaue my ſoule in hel, nor ſuffer thine
holy one to ſee corruptiō; Wherfore in THE SOVLE OF CHRIST
DEATH, VVAS CONQVERED, and the reſurrection from hell per-
formed, and ſignified to the ſpirits; (that roſe with him:)In the
body of (him that was) God, corruption was aboliſhed, & in-
corruption ſhined out of the graue. Yea Auſten himſelf putteth
great difference betwixt the certainty of Chriſtes deſcent to
hell, and the vncertainty of deliuering of ſome ſoules thence,
which be found there, as he imagineth. [x] *Teneamus firmiſſime
Quod fides habet fundatiſſima auctoritate firmata ; quia Chri-
ſtus mortuus eſt ſecundum ſcripturas, et cætera quæ de illo reſtante
veritate conſcripta ſunt : in quibus etiam hoc eſt, quod apud Infe-
ros fuit, ſolutis eorū doloribus , quibus eū erat impoſſibile teneri.*
Let vs hold moſt firmly, ỹ which ỹ faith containeth; confirmed
with moſt aſſured authority, that Chriſt died according to the
ſcriptures; & the reſt ỹ is written of him by the teſtimony of the
truth, amongſt ỹ which this is alſo to be nūbred, ỹ he was in hel,
diſſoluing ỹ pains therof. Of which it was impoſſible he ſhuld be
held. Thus far doth Auſten vrge the very articles of our faith
confirmed by the ſcriptures, & that maketh him infer, ỹ who
then but an infidel wil deny that Chriſt was in hell ? But when
he cōmeth to the ſecond point of deliuering ſome from hel,
that were in the paines thereof, he tempereth his ſtile, and
ſaith, [x] *à quibus recte intelligitur ſoluiſſe & liberaſſe, quos voluit,*
from which paines Chriſt may well be conceaued, to haue looſed
and deliuered whom he would; & that which Peter ſaith, looſing
the ſorrowes of hel, [a] *accipi poteſt in quibuſdā,* may be vnderſtood
of ſome, whom he thought worthy to be deliuered. For which
ſince there can bee no ſure proofe, brought out of the worde
of trueth ; we ſhall doe beſt to giue eare to his owne aduiſe
in the like caſe. [b] *Ergo fratres ſive illud ſive iſtud ſit ; hic me
ſcrutatorem verbi dei , non temerarium affirmatorem teneatis.*

[x] Auguſt. epiſt. 99.

[x] Ibidem.

[x] Ibidem.

[a] Ibidem.

[b] Auguſt. in Pſalmum.85.

Therefore brethren whether this or that bee it, heere take me as a ſearcher of the word of God, and not as a raſh affirmer.

All the defence that may be made out of the Scriptures, that Chriſt deliuered ſome of the ſaints out of the preſent poſſeſſion and power of hell, is that which is written in the goſpell of Saint Matthew, touching the bodies of the ſaintes riſing from death. When Ieſus yeelded vp the ghoſt; [c] Behold the vaile of the temple rent in twaine, and the earth did quake, and the ſtones did cleaue, and the graues did open themſelues, and many bodies of the Saints, which ſlept, aroſe; and came out of the graues after his reſurrection, and went into the holy cittie and appeared to many. The death of the bodie, as it is parte of the wages of ſinne; ſo is it the [d] gate of hell; and the Diuell is ſaide in the ſcriptures to haue the [e] power thereof. So that howſoeuer the ſoules of the iuſt were in the handes of God, and at reſt in Abrahams boſom, their bodies lying dead in the graue, & rotten with corruption were within Satans walke; and when Chriſt raiſed them out of their ſepulchers to an happie life, he toke them from the power of darknes; and tranſlated them into the kingdome of light. [f] Death is an enemie, though the laſt that ſhall be deſtroied; and [g] death, as well as hell, ſhall be caſt into the lake of fire; and therefore Chriſt toke the keyes both of [h] death, and of hell; and by his riſing from the dead inſulted againſt both; ô death, where is thy ſting? ô hell, where is thy victory? It is the force of ſinne that killeth the bodie; and likewiſe the force of ſinne that rotteth the bodie; ſinne being the ſtrength of hell againſt bodie and ſoule. As then our ſoules are freed from the power of hell, when our ſinnes are remitted; ſo our bodies are deliuered from the handfaſt of hel, when corruption, the conſequent of ſinne, is aboliſhed. In this ſenſe it may bee ſaide, that Chriſt deliuered ſome from the power of hell, that is, their bodies from the ſepulchers where the plaſe turned into duſt. For by death and corruption the ſinnefull fleſh of man is till the reſurrection ſubiected to the range of Satan, hee beeing the

Chriſt deliuered the bodies of ſome ſaints, from the power of hel, that is, he raiſed them from death.
[c] Matth. 27

[d] Eſay. 38
[e] Hebre. 2

[f] 1. Corinth. 15
[g] Reuelat. 20
[h] Reuel. 1.
[i] 1. Corinth. 15

the ᵏ Prince of the ayre, and ˡ gouernour of darkneſſe, and ᵐ ru-
ler of death.

ᵏEphef.2
ˡEphef.6
ᵐHebre.2

Saint Auſten doubteth, whether thoſe bodies of the faints
were wholie freed from corruption; or late down againe in
death after they had giuen witneſſe to Chriſts reſurrection.
ⁿ *Scio quibuſdam videri, morte domini Chriſti iam talem re-
ſurrectionem præſtitã iuſtis,qualis nobis in fine promittitur;Qui
vtique ſi non iterum repoſitis corporibus dormierunt, videndum
eſt quemadmodum Chriſtus intelligatur primogenitus à mortuis
ſi eum in illa reſurrectione tot præceſſerunt.* I know (faith Au-
ſten) fome thinke, that at the death of the Lord Chriſt the fame
kind of reſurrection was performed to the iuſt, which is promi-
fed to vs in the ende of the worlde : but if they ſlept not againe,
by laying downe their bodies, we muſt looke howe Chriſt can
be vnderſtood to be the firſt borne of the dead, if ſo many went
before him in that reſurrection. But his reaſons are of no ſuch
force, as to perſwade, that the bodies of the faintes, which
rofe with Chriſt, ſlept againe in their graues, and returned
to corruption; yea that would ſomewhat impeach the power
of Chriſts reſurrection, if it were able to raiſe them to life,
but not preſerue them in life; and the whole fact will ſeeme
rather an apparition, then a true reſurrection. His firſt ob-
iection is anſwered in the tert it ſelfe. For the faints did not
riſe before Chriſt, but after Chriſt; and ſo ſtill Chriſt was the
firſtborne from the dead. The wordes of the tert are; ° manie
bodies of the faintes, which ſlept aroſe ; and came out of the
graues AFTER HIS RESVRRECTION. Nowe to thinke
that they rofe preſentlie vpõ his death, ₊ ſtated aliue in their
graues till he was riſen, is a vaine imagination, and a waie
rather to puniſh them with a wearifome life, then to prefer
them to a comfortable reſurrection. His ſecond reaſon hath
ſome more ſhew, but it is not ſufficiẽt to conclude his inten-
tion. ᵖ It ſeemeth hard (faith he) that *Dauid* ſhould not be in
that reſurrection of the iuſt, if it were eternall, of whoſe ſeede
Chriſt is ſo often commended to vs with ſo great honor and eui-

Whether the
bodies of the
faints, that
rofe with chriſt
ſleptagaine
or no.
ⁿ Auguſt.epiſt.
99.

°Matth.27.

ᵖ Augu 7. E-
piſtola. 99.

dence.

a Actes. 3.

dence. And if Dauid rose with them, Peters proofe vnto the Iewes is verie weake, when hee saith, ʤ Dauid is deade and buried; and his sepulchre remaineth with vs vnto this daie. For if Dauids body were risen before the speaking of those words, his sepulchre was emptie; and concluded nothing for Peters purpose. For aunswere hereto, the holie Ghost had

Dauid saw corruptió though he were then risen from corruption, but Christs flesh neuer putrified

no meaning by Peters mouth to proue that Dauid laie then in his graue, when those words were spoken; but onelie that Dauid saw corruption, as his sepulchre remaining to that daie conuinced; wherein his bodie was buried aboue a thousand yeares before Christes comming, and consequentlie must needs be turned into dust many hundreds before Peter spake the words. His prediction therfore, that God would not suffer his holy one to see corruption, could no wais pertaine to himselfe, but must bee verified in some other, which was Christ; and so Peters argument was verie sound and cleere; whether Dauids ashes were then in his sepulchre or no. Peters other allegation, that Dauid is not ascended into heauen, doth

a Acts. 2. ver. 34

not hinder, but Dauid might be translated into Paradise, with the rest of the saints, ꝑ rose from the dead, when Christ did; but it is a iust probation, that Dauids body was not then ascended, when Christ sate in his humane flesh at the right hand of God; which expresseth the power and glorie, whereunto the bodie of Christ was exalted by his ascension into heauen. So that here Austen hath some hold to proue, that Dauid did not ascende in body, when Christ did; or at least not to heauen, whither Christ ascended; because in plaine words Peter saith, Dauid is not ascended into heauen; but either the bodies of ꝑ saints slept againe, when they had giuen testimony to Christs resurrection; or they were placed in Paradise, and there expect the number of their brethren, which shall bee raised out of the dust; or lastlie Dauid was none of those, that were raised to beare witnesse of Christes resurrection; but onelie such were chosen, as were knowne to the persons

. Augast. de ge-

then liuing in Hierusalem. Whatsoeuer it was, ʃ melius est dubitare

Aubit que de occultis, quàm litigare de incertis. It is better (as Au-
sten faith) to doubt of things (vnknown and) hid, then to striue
about things vncertain. The last reason of S. Austen, that God
so prouided for vs, that the fathers of the olde testament without
vs, should not be perfect, proueth not, that al the saints in Pa-
radise lacke their bodies; for then we must deny that Henoch
was translated, not to see death; and that Elias was taken vp
by a whirlewind into heauen, as also that he was seene on the
mount talking with Christ, which are directlie affirmed by the
scriptures; but it wil make some proofe, that they haue not the
same perfection of ioie and blisse, which they shall haue, when
all the members of Christ are receaued into glorie.

10 There remaineth one obiection, which must be eased, before
I ende. And that is, Christ saide to the thiefe which confessed
him on the crosse: This day shalt thou be with me in Paradise;
how they could Christ be three daies in hell, except we
grant it might be in manie places at once. S. Austen laboreth
in his 57. epistle to remoue this stumbling blocke; and af-
ter some turnes and wrenthes, he thus concludeth. *Est au-
tem sensu multo expeditior, & ab his omnibus ambiguitatibus li-
ber, si non secundum id quod homo erat, sed secundum id quod deus
erat, Christum dixisse accipiatur: Hodie mecum eris in paradiso. Ho-
mo quippe Christus, illo die secundum carnem in sepulchro, secun-
dum animam in inferno futurus erat. Deus vero idem ipse Christus
vbique semper est.* The far easier vnderstanding, and free from al
these ambiguities is; if wee take Christ to speake those wordes,
This day shalt thou bee with mee in Paradise, not of his
manhoode, but of his Godhead. For the man Christ was that
day in the graue according to his flesh, and in hell as touching
his soule; but the same Christ as God is alwaies euery where.
And though this answere please that learned Father well,
that Christ shuld speake of the thiefes soule, and his diuine
presence in Paradise, yet wee haue no warrant in the word
of God so to fasten Christs soule vnto hel for the time of his
death, that it might not bee in Paradise before it descended

Margin notes:
nes ad literam li.
8. cap. 5.
Hebre. 11.

Hebre. 11
4. Regum. 2
Matth. 17

Luke. 23

August. epist.
57.

into hell; and he firſt ſhew himſelfe to the ſaints to their vn-
ſpeakeable comfort, before hce went to ſubieet the powers
of darkeneſſe vnder his yoke. That hee [b] deſcended into the
deep, muſt be receaued, becauſe it is auouched by the apoſtle;
but what time he went, or how long he ſtaid, as alſo what ma-
ner of triumph he brought thence, cannot bee limited by a-
nie mortall man; In all theſe caſes I thinke it ſafeſt to par-
ticularize nothing, which is not defined in the worde of God:
there may be likelihoods, but the conſciences of the faithfull
muſt not bee enforced, except to certainties. This is that
I thought fit to be ſaide touching Chriſtes deſcent to hell;
vrging the force and fruite of his going thither, or appea-
ring there, to ſubiect the whole ſtrength and kingdome of
Satan vnto himſelfe, and to acquite all his members from
comming thither; but the time or manner of his deſcen-
ding, I dare not determine, leaſt I ſhould auert you from
truth to fables.

Farre ſurer is the former doctrine, teaching the redemp-
tion of mankinde by the death of Chriſt to bee all-ſufficient
and euerlaſting, wherein the ſcriptures being euident and the
Fathers conſonant, I ſhall neede no moe words; I will there-
fore cloſe them both with the confeſſion of Fulgentius, who
liued 500 yeeres after Chriſt, and ſo commend you to God.

[c] *Deus verus & viuus, imo deus veritas et vita æterna, niſi idem*
verus homo fieret, mortē guſtare non poſſet. Et idē homo qui mor-
tem guſtauit, ſi verus deus & vita æterna non eſſet mortē vincere
non valeret. Excepto illo, qui ſic homo eſt vt idem ſit deus, quis eſt
homo qui deſtruxerit mortem, aut quis eruet animam ſuã de ma-
nu inferi? niori autem filij dei, quam SOLA CARNE *ſuſcepit*
YTRAMQVE IN NOBIS MORTEM, *anima ſcilicet car-*
niſque deſtruxit, & reſurrectio carnis eius gratiam nobis & ſpi-
ritualis & corporalis reſurrectionis attribuit, vt prius iuſtificati
per fidem mortis & reſurrectionis filij dei, reſuſcitemur ab infi-
delitatis morte, & poſt primam reſurrectionem ſcilicet ani-
marum, quæ nobis in fide collocata eſt, etiam iſta carne, in

Marginal notes:

[a] Rom. 10

[c] Fulgent. de in-
carnat, & gra-
tia dom. noſtri
Ieſu chriſti. ca. 8,

qua nunc viuimus, reſurgamus, nunquam denuo morituri. The
true and liuing God. yea the God that is truth it ſelf, and liſe euer-
laſting, if he were not alſo true man, could not haue taſted death.
and that man which taſted death, except he had beene likewiſe
the true God, and eternall life, hee could not haue conquered
death. Sauing he that was both God and man, what man could
haue deſtroied death, or deliuered his own ſoule from the power
of hell? But the death of the ſonne of God VV H I C H H E S V F-
FERED IN HIS FLESH ONELIE, deſtroied both deaths in
vs, as well of ſoule as bodie; and the reſurrection of his fleſh gaue
vs the grace both of a ſpirituall and corporall reſurrection, that
being firſt iuſtified by faith in the death and reſurrection of the
ſonne of God, we might bee raiſed from the death of infideli-
tie; and after the firſt reſurrection which is of the ſoule, (from
ſinne,) giuen vs by faith, we may alſo riſe in this fleſh, in which
we now liue, neuer to die anie more.[d] *Cum* S O L A C A R O M O-* d Fulgent: de
R E R E T V R E T R E S V S C I T A R E T V R I N C H R I S T O. *prop-* paſſione domini
ter vnitatem perſonæ dei & hominis, filius dei dicitur mortuus. ad Traſim. lib. 3.
Totum igitur H O M I N E M *cum ſuis infirmitatibus ſine pec-*
cato dei filius accepit; in tota traditus idem Chriſtus, S E C V N-
D V M S O L A M C A R N E M M O R T V V S, *Totus Chriſtus ſe-*
cundum ſolam animam ad infernum deſcendit. Humanitas ergo
vera filij dei, nec tota fuit in ſepulchro, nec tota in inferno, ſed in
ſepulchro ſecundum carnem Chriſtus mortuus iacuit, & ſecundum
animam ad infernum Chriſtus deſcendit. Secundum diuinitatem
vero ſuam, quæ nec loco tenetur, nec ſine concluditur, totus fuit in
ſepulchro cum carne, totus in inferno cum anima. At per hoc ple-
nus fuit vbiq; Chriſtus, qui non eſt deus ab humanitate, quam
ſuſceperat ſeparatus, qui & in anima fuit, vt ſolutis inferni dolo-
ribus A B I N F E R N O V I C T R I X R E D I R E T, & in carne
ſua fuit, vt celeri reſurrectione corrumpi non poſſet. Whereas
O N E L I E T H E F L E S H died, and was raiſed againe in Chriſt,
yea for the vnitie of the perſon, being God and man; the ſonne of
God is ſaid to haue died. The whole nature of man then with
our infirmities, the ſonne of God tooke vnto him for our ſakes,

but

but without ſinne . in the whole, nature the ſame Chriſt beeing deliuered, DIED ACCORDING TO THE FLESH ONLY, and whole Chriſt deſcended into hell according to the ſoule on-lie. So that the true manhood of the ſonne of God, was neither wholie in the ſepulchre, nor wholie in hell, but in the ſepulchre Chriſt lay dead in his true fleſh; and in his ſoule Chriſt deſcended into hell. But as touching his diuinitie, which is nei-ther comprehended in place, nor meaſured with end, whole Chriſt was in the graue with his fleſh, and whole Chriſt in hell with his ſoule. And thereby whole Chriſt was euery where: be-cauſe his Godhead was not ſeuered from his manhood; but was with his ſoule, that diſſoluing the ſorrowes of hell, it might re-turne conquerour from hell; and with his fleſh, that ſpeedilie ri-ſing, it might not ſee corruption.

The darke places of Peter, that Chriſt by his e ſpirit prea-ched ynto the ſpirites (that are now) in priſon, which in the daies of Noe were diſobedient whiles the Arke was preparing: and likewiſe that f the Goſpell was preached ynto the dead; I omit as nothing pertinent to Chriſts deſcent to hell; the firſt be-ing verified in the time, and by the mouth of Noe; and the ſe-cond performed by the preaching of the Apoſtles, as Saint Auſten long ſince obſerued, who ſaith of the firſt, Conſidera-ne forte totam illud quod de concluſis in carcere ſpiritibus, qui in diebus Noe non crediderant, Petrus Apoſtolus dicit; omnino ad inferos non pertineat, ſed ad illa potius tempora, quorum formam ad hæc tempora tranſtulit. Take heede, leaſt happily all that which Peter ſpeaketh of ſpirits cloſed in priſon, which beleeued not in the daies of Noe, doe not at all pertaine to hell, but rather to thoſe times, which Peter compareth with our age: and of the ſecond, h Quod Petrus dicit, propter hoc & mortuis Euange-lizatum eſt, ut iudicentur ſecundum homines in carne, viuant autem ſecundum deum ſpiritu, non cogit apud inferos intelligi Propterea enim in hac vita & mortuis Euangelizatum eſt, id eſt, infidelibus & iniquis, ut cum crediderint iudicentur ſecundum hominem in carne, hoc eſt, in diuerſis tribulationibus & in ipſa

e 1.Pet.3.

f 1.Pet.4.

g Auguſt. epiſt. 99.

h Ibidem.

morte carnis . That which Peter faieth ; (to this purpofe was the Gofpel preached vnto the deade, that they might bee iudged according to men in the flefh, but liue according to God in the fpirit;) hath no necefficie to be applied to hell . For the Gofpel is preached in this life to the dead, that is to the infidels and finners, that when they beleeue they might be iudged in the flefh after the maner of men, by diuerfe troubles, and euen by the death of the flefh. This I repeate the rather, becaufe fome late writers haue borrowed Saint Auftens expofition, and fuppreffed Saint Auftens name; as if they were the firft that euer looked into the truth of thefe places . Other reafens there are, but they are not worth the ripping vp; I will therfore trouble you no further.

To the father that fpared not his owne fonne , but gaue him for vs all; to the fonne that laide downe his life for vs, and redeemed vs with his precious bloud ; to the holie Ghoft which fealeth the fufferings and comforts of Chrift in our harts; euen to the king euerlafting, immortal, inuifible, and God onelie wife, be honour and glorie, for euer and euer. Amen.

The Conclusion to the Reader, for   225
the cleering of certaine obiections
made against the doctrine
before handled.

I Promised thee (Christian reader) in ye
preface of this booke, to giue thee a tast
in the conclusion how rashly & weak-
ly the doctrine, which thou hast now
read, was confuted, before it was
printed, by one that professeth " *He* " [1] *Pag. 3.*
could not forbeare but imploy his talent "
to cleare the holy cause (as he calleth it) "
" *from all the corrupt fansies and vaine imaginations of men:* "
which, God willing, I meane now to performe. Thou must
not looke that I will wast time and paper to settle a giddie
head, or stoppe a running tongue; but when by some particu-
lars I haue made it appeare how vnfit he is to bee refuted,
or so much as regarded by mee; I will leaue him to the depth
of his follies. For though he point plainlie to my sermons,
in directing his treatise: [b] *contrary to certaine errors publikly* " [b] *pag.1*
preached in London, and sticketh not to [c] *name me*; yet because
he flyeth from the state of the chiefe Question, which I im- ' *Pag: 89:*
pugned, and taketh the paines to ouer skip all my authori-
ties with silence, if not with contempt, and in reporting my
reasons forgetteth and dissembleth what pleaseth himselfe,
as also in the defence of his holie cause he roueth as he li-
steth, neither keeping himself to any order, nor bringing any
matter of moment, but confusedlie powring out the hastie
resolutions of his owne braines, spiced euerie where with
ignorant & absurd positions : neither my leasure nor my li-
king suffer me to seeke him out, that hath so farre lost him-
selfe, nor to vouchsafe him an answere, that so proudlie despi-
seth all authoritie and antiquitie, which sorteth not with his
fansie . I will therefore shew thee (good Reader) some exam-

ples of his insolent retecting the fathers, of his forgetfull
or wilfull altering my reasons, of his impertinent proouing
that which is not questioned, and skipping that which should
bee proued, of his erroneous and dangerous assertions, of
his intolerable ignorance in the tongue, whereof he so much
vaunteth, and then leaue thee to God, if thou loath not the rea-
ding, as I did the writing before thou come to the end.

Galat 6.   Where I tooke for my text, these words of S. Paule,
[a] God forbid that I should reioice but in the crosse of our Lord
Iesus Christ, whereby the world is crucified to me and I to the
world. This cōfuter would beare men in hand, that I mistooke
my text, & forced a false conclusion from it. [b] *This (saith hee)*
is not onely an obiection, but euen a foundation and principall
ground of this errour, but so mistaken and forced as nothing may
be more. My reasō hee maketh to be this; *Christs soule was not*
crucified but only his bodie; therefore Christs bodie onlie suffe-
red, and not his soule. By this (gentle reader) it may plainlie
be perceiued, how well this gainsaier obserued my proofs. I
drewe no reason from these words, but proposing them for
my theine, tooke occasion from them to laie downe; first the
contents of Christs crosse, how far it extended; and then the
effects of Christs crosse, how much it performed, which is the
generall methode of the whole treatise. In the contents of
Christs crosse my words are these. Rightly then maie the
Crosse note all manner of miseries, forsomuch as our Sauiour

Vide pag. 4.   going from the garden to the graue suffered all sorts of afflicti-
ons; which I before specifying amongst others named these,
shame, reproch, and all sorts of deadlie paines, besides heauines
of hart, and agonie of mind, which oppressed him in the garden;
and this I made no different signification, but rather a partici-
pation of the crosse of Christ. When I came to Christs suffe-
rings on the Tree, as Peter speaketh, I vsed these plaine
words: the rest (of his torments) which went before, not being
excluded as superfluous, but continued and increased by that
sharp & extreame martirdome which he suffered on the Crosse.
Did

Did I then make any such conclusion out of these words of Paul as you imagine, Sir confuter? or did rather your wit & memorie so slenderlie serue you, that you could not conceiue or carry away the maine methode of my sermons, diſtinctly laid downe at my firſt entrance into this matter? But as you begin with my Theme, so you continue with the whole discourse, mistaking, forgetting, peruerting and maiming all that I alledged or concluded.

d Neuertheleſſe you take it to bee cleare, that this text was *d* Pag. 32. *mistaken by me, for the Apoſtle here ſpeaketh not of the perſonall ,, ſufferings of Chriſt, but of the godlie, which they ſuffer for Chriſts ,, truth ſake.* To dimme mens eyes twy light is clearer then Sunne ſhine; and to a man of your vnderſtanding falſehood may bee clearer then truth; but knowe you Sir H. I. that I miſtooke not my text. For albeit the CROSSE bee ſome times taken for the afflictions of the godlie; yet THE CROSSE OF CHRIST is no where in the ſcriptures ſo taken. Again though we be ᵉ permitted and ᶠ commanded to reioice in our afflictions, yet to make it a thing deteſtable to reioice in ᵉ 2. Cor. 11. anie thing elſe, as the Apoſtle here doth, by ſaying, God for- verſ. 30. bid that I ſhould reioice but in the Croſſe of Chriſt; hath no ᶠ Jacob. 1. ver. 2. ground in diuinitie. Himſelfe ſaieth elſe where; ᵍ Of ſuch ᵍ 2. Cor. 11. a man (as was taken vp into Paradiſe) will I reioice; of my ſelfe I will not reioyce, except it bee of mine infir- mities. Our Sauiour ſaieth to his Diſciples, ʰ Reioice ʰ Luke. 10. rather becauſe your names are written in heauen. But of Chriſt crucified, it is pietie and dutie to ſaie; God forbid that wee ſhould reioice but in the Croſſe of Chriſt. For as to the Co- rinths the Apoſtle refuſeth ⁱ all knowledge ſaue of Chriſt, and ⁱ 1. Cor. 2. him crucified: ſo here hee renounceth all reioycing ſaue in the Croſſe of Chriſt, that is in Chriſt crucified. This to bee the full and plaine meaning of the Apoſtle in this place is to me as cleare as daie light, and I hope will ſo ſeeme to thee (Chriſtian Reader) if thou marke the words of Saint Paul in the 12. verſe of this verie Chapter, where hee chargeth

Gg 2 the

the false Apostles with vrging Circumcision , because they
Gal.3.6.ve.12 would auoid persecution for the crosse of Christ: They con-
straine you (saith hee) to be circumcised , onely because they
would not suffer persecution for the Crosse of Christ; protesting
the contrarie for himselfe in these wordes , but God forbid
that I should reioice but in the Crosse of Christ, VV H E R B Y
THE VV OR L D IS CRVCIFIED TO ME, AND I TO
THE VV OR L D : Meaning he doth not onely refuse the fa-
uours, but despise the terrors of the worlde for the crosse of
Christ. In the first part of this comparison betwixt himselfe
and those that flattered the Iewes with teaching circumci-
sion for feare of affliction, put your interpretation to y wordes
of the Apostle, and see how absurdly it matcheth with them.
They constraine you to bee circumcised , onely because they
would not suffer persecution for the crosse of Christ , that is as
you expound it, because they would not *suffer persecution for*
" *the afflictions of the godlie.* Hath this exposition either sense or
reason in it ? Or else is it euident that the Apostle here mea-
neth by the crosse of Christ, the slander & shame of Christs suf-
fering on the Crosse, which the Iewes so abhorred, that they
pursued all that preached or beleeued it ? Then consequentlie
Paules reioycing in nothing but in the crosse of Christ contra-
rie to their course must needs import, that he reioiced in no-
thing so much as in that shamefull death which the Sauiour
of the world endured on the crosse; and to that end he saieth
in the former Chapter , where hee more largelie handleth
Gal.5.ver.11. this matter ; If I yet preach circumcision, why doe I yet
suffer persecution ? Then is the slander of the crosse abolished;
meaning there was none other cause why the Iewes hated
and persecuted him, but for preaching Christ crucified, to bee
the true and onlie meane of our saluation, without circum-
cision or whatsoeuer ceremonies of the law.

As the text is cleare with the sense which I followed, so the
Tract.in Io. h.10,43. fathers concurre with the same. Christ (saieth Austen) chose
that kind of death to hang on the crosse, that a Christian might
say,

saie, far be it from me to reioice but in the crosse of Christ. Chrysostome **vpon this place**, [a] what is the reason (saith hee) that *Paul* so reioyceth in Christes crosse? because Christ for my sake tooke the shape of a seruant, and for my sake endured that hee suffered. **Adding farther.** [a] *Annon est gloriandum, quum ille dominus, qui verus est deus, non erubescit pro nobis crucem subire?* Haue we not good cause to reioice when that Lord, which is true God, was not ashamed to endure the crosse for vs? *Paul* **doth** [b] not reioice (saith Ierom) in his owne righteousnesse or knowledge, but in the faith of the crosse, by which all my sinnes are pardoned me. *Christ* [c] bearing his crosse on his shoulders, (saith Bede) commendeth it, that *Paul* might saie, be it far from me to reioice but in the crosse of Christ. He was despised in the eyes of the wicked for that, wherein the heartes of the Saintes should reioice. **I staie somewhat longer (gentle Reader) on this point; for that, as it had bin a childish ouersight in me at the verie first entrance to mistake the meaning of my text; so it is more then a malepart tricke in him vniustlie to chalenge me for it; but I maie the better content my selfe with it, since this Refuter sticketh not to vse all the Fathers with like disdaine, whereof I will giue thee an example or two, that thou maiest see the headinesse of this hasty writer.**

In the contents of Christs crosse, I obserued out of [d] Augustine, [d] Ierom, **and** [d] Bernard **that no violence of death wrested Christes soule from him, as it doth ours; but when he sawe his time, hee euen at an instant laide it downe of himselfe, no paines hastening his death.** [e] *This is a paradoxe in Nature* (saith this **Controller**) *and contrary to scripture which saith, he was like vs in all things sinne only excepted.* **You might giue the learned and auncient Fathers better wordes Sir trifler, whatsoeuer you do me; your wits are too weake to refute their resolution. For where like a Puni, you prate you know not what, they ground themselues on the plaine and expresse wordes of the scriptures.** [f] No man (**saith our Sauiour**) taketh (my soule) from mee, but I laie it

downe

[a] Chrysost. in Galat.6

[b] Ierom.in Galat.6

[c] Beda. in Galat.6

[d] Vide pag.7

[e] Page.53
,,
,,

[f] Iohn.10

downe of my selfe: I haue power to laie it downe, and haue power to take it againe. Howe thinke you Sir; coulde anie violence or paines of death take Christes soule from him; or had hee power to laie it downe when and as he woulde, which no man else euer had or shall haue? you replie, *he was like vs in all things, sinne only excepted.* Such proofes became well your person. Was he like vs in his birth? can we lie in the graue without corruption, as he laie? or raise our selues from death as he did? Reade more for shame and write lesse, till you bee better aduised, or better instructed. Upon these wordes of Christ, I haue power to laie down my soule, and haue power to take it againe, Chrysostom writeth thus; [g] *vtrumq; nouum fuit & præter communem consuetudinem. Potestatem habeo ponendi eam: hoc est, ego solus potestatem habeo, quæ vobis non est.* Both these (powers) were strange and aboue the common course of men. I haue power to laie down my soule, that is, I ALONE haue this power, which you haue not. If you denie this that Chrysostom saith; remember what God himselfe saith: [h] ô foole this night shal they fetch away thy soule frô thee, which Christ saith none could do from him, because he had power by his fathers appointment to laie it down of himselfe.

[g] Homili. 69 In Iohannem.

[h] Luke. 12

In like sort, when I shewed not mine own opinion, but the iudgments of the ancient fathers as well for the causes that might be of Christes [i] agonie in the garden, as for the meaning of his [k] complaint on the crosse, my God, my God, why hast thou forsaken me; obserue (gentle Reader) I praie thee, how absurdly he roleth from the one to the other, & how insolentlie he reiecteth al the fathers, for that they vphold not his humour of hell paines to be the ground of both. I alleaged Ierom and Chrysostom, that Christ on the crosse cited the beginning of the 22. Psalme, My God, my God, why hast thou forsaken me, that the Iewes might knowe they had fulfilled the words of the prophet Dauid in that psalme foreshewing the passiô of Christ. His answere is, [l] *this sence is most absurd.* To Athanasius, Augustine, and Leo, that Christ spake those

[i] Vide pag. 19

[k] Vide pag. 34

[l] Pag. 66

wo;ds in the person of his church, which then suffered in him
and with him, he saith, ^m *This is no lesse absurd then the former,*   ^m *Pag. 67*
there is no reason or likelihood for it. When I b;ought Ierom, „
Ambrose, Austen, and Bede, that in the garden Christ might
so;row fo; the reiection of the Iewes, who would pul the ven-
geance of God on their owne heads, to the vtter destruction
of their whole nation by putting him to death, this Confu-
ter foolishly and fo;getfully maketh this an interp;etation of
Christes complaint on the crosse, and addeth; ⁿ *This is more*   ⁿ *Pag. 63.*
fond and absurd then the other. So when among other causes „
of Christs agony in the garden that might be, (fo; I twke vp-
on me to determine none) being sixe in number, I b;ought
this fo; one out of Ambrose, that Christ sorrowed fo; vs, was
SAD fo; vs, and GRIEVED fo; vs, he LAMENTED OVR
VVOVNDES, not his, OVR VVEAKENES, not his owne
death, ^o *This in effect (saith hee) is nothing but what wee*   ^o *Pag. 68.*
affirme, howbeit this ought not to haue anie place heere;   ^p *Pag. 69.*
P. how could these wordes hang together, when hee meaneth to tell „
his father howe zealous hee is for his glorie, to saie; My God, „
my God, why hast thou forsaken me? There is no fashion in
them thus signifying. What you speake boldlie but errone-
ouslie of the sonne of God; ^q *It cannot bee strange if often*   ^q *Pag. 55.*
times Christ fell amazed, confounded and forgetfull of him- „
selfe for feare and griefe; I maie trulie and iustlie say of you; „
it is not strange to see you amazed, confounded and fo;get-
full in your w;iting. What I spake of Christes agonie
in the garden, you applie to his complaint on the crosse, and
saie, *the words will not hang together.* God Sir awake out „
of your sleepe, and learne at least to vnderstand befo;e you
aunswere.

As this p;esumer euerie where with disdaine casteth away
the iudgements of the fathers which I p;oduce, & p;efer reth
his owne peenish conceite before them all: so when he repo;-
teth my reasons, he either igno;antlie mistaketh them, o; pur-
poselie peruerteth them, ŷ they may the lesse encumber him.

Ii

Vide page. 58

In the effectes of Christes crosse I noted out of the Apostle to the Hebrues three properties of the true propitiatorie sacrifice which tooke awaie the sinne of the world; It was a bodilie, a bloudie, and a deadlie sacrifice; and amongst manie reasons to confirme the same, I brought these two, which the confuter after his forgetfull maner roueth at. The first in effect was this, The true sacrifice for sinne, which the Redeemer should offer, was shadowed and foreshewed by the sacrifices which God commanded and accepted in the old testament: but the sacrifices of the Patriarches and of the faithfull appointed by Moses foreshewed and figured a bodilie, bloudie, and deadlie sacrifice, and no paines of hell; therfore the true sacrifice for sinne was made by the bodie, bloud and death of the Redeemer, and not by the paines of hell suffered in his soule. The second this; As the sacrifices of the law prefigured what the Sauiour of the world should do for the abolishing of sinne; so the sacraments of the newe testament confirme and seale that performed in the person of Christ Iesus, which was the true propitiation for our sinnes, and price of our redemption: but the sacraments of the new testament, and speciallie the Lordes supper, declare and confirme vnto vs the bodie of Christ giuen for vs vnto death, and his bloud shed for the remission of our sinnes; therefore this was the true propitiation for our sinnes, and price of our redemption, and not the paines of hell suffered in the soule of Christ, as some imagine. To the first the Confuter answereth; *The proposition is false taking it generally. The carnall sacrifices of the Iewes signified that which they were apt to signifie, but not anie further. The sacrifices of beastes coulde not prefigure the personall vnion of God and man, nor the reasonable and immortall soule of Christ, nor his resurrection, all which were necessarie pointes in the meritorious sacrifice.* Secondlie he denieth the assumption. *For certaine of the Iewes sacrifices set foorth the sufferinges of the soule of Christ also: As the scape Gote in the 16. of Leuiticus, which was a sin offering*

Page. 11.
Page. 12.

ring, though it were sent awaie free and untouched . To the
reason drawne from the Sacraments, hee saieth), *Wee are to* ᵖPag. 14.
answere as we did before . These are bodilie and earthlie Ele- „
ments, and therefore fitte to set foorth bodilie and apparant ef- „
fects in Christ ; they cannot set out the spirituall and inuisible „
effects in him. And yet the ceremonie of breaking the bread which „
is to shewe that Christes bodie was broken for us, can not belong „
properlie to the bodie, but to the soule . These I trust are pour
woꝛds; now heare my replie. I had no such pꝛopoſition as
pou frame to pour ſelfe, that either the ſacrifices of the lawe,
oꝛ Sacraments of the Goſpel, were figures of our whole
and abſolute redemption, which is (as pou expound it) of all
the fruits and cauſes of our redemption. This is pour crea-
tion, not my pꝛopoſition ; I tolde pou that as God had pꝛo-
miſed, ſo the faithfull beléeued, that his owne ſonne ſhould be
the Seede of the woman, and by his death and bloud ſhould
purge their ſinnes . To continue this pꝛomiſe and con-
firme the faith of all befoꝛe and under the lawe, God ap-
pointed bloodie ſacrifices , as continuall remembꝛances
and figures, not of the perſon, noꝛ of the function of Chꝛiſt;
but of the Sacrifice, by which hee ſhoulde aboliſh ſinne;
to witte, by his bodie ſlaine, and his bloud ſhedde, which
the carnall ſacrifices were fitteſt to reſemble , ſince
God would not haue the bloud of anie man, but of his
owne ſonne ſhedde foꝛ remiſſion of ſinnes . My pꝛopo-
ſition then ſpeaketh of the true ſacrifice foꝛ ſinne , and a-
uoucheth that to bee the true ſacrifice foꝛ ſinne, which was
ſhadowed and figured by the death and bloud of thoſe beaſts,
that God commaunded to bee offered unto him. This pꝛo-
poſition pou doe not denie , foꝛ pou graunt, ᵗ *The Iewes* ᵗPag. 11.
ſacrifices ſignified what they were apt to teach, and ſignifie: „
but they were apt and oꝛdained of GOD to teach the
Iewes, that, by the death and bloud of the Meſſias, they
ſhoulde bee redeemed and ſaued from their ſinnes ; ergo
they were apt and oꝛdained of God to figure and ſhadowe

the

the true propitiatorie ſacrifice. And ſo the patriarkes and Prophetes beleeued and expected, whoſe faith and hope could neither be vaine nor fruſtrate, ſince they were thereto directed by Gods owne appointment.

This propoſition, be you Chriſtian or Iewe, you may not denie; and therefore you doe well to denie the aſſumption, and to affirme that certaine ſacrifices of the Iewes, as namelie the ſcape Goate in the 16. of Leuiticus did ſigni-

Pag: 12:

"fie the immortall ſoule of Chriſt , which was f *a ſacrifice* "for ſinne , and did properlie beare our ſinnes, and ſuffer for our "ſinnes. But Sir, if a man aſke you howe you proue that the ſcape Goate ſignified the ſoule of Chriſt, what haue "you to ſaie? *Becauſe both Goates* (ſaie you) *are a ſacrifice* "*for ſinne, as the Text ſpeaketh.* You abuſe the Text, and de-ceiue your ſelfe. The wordes are . Aaron g ſhall take of

g Leuit.16 verſ.5.

the aſſemblie of the children of Iſrael two hee Goates for a ſinne offering , that is to make a ſinne offering of one of them, on which the Lordes lotte ſhall fall ; So followe the wordes in the 8. verſe of that chapter. Aaron ſhall caſt lottes ouer the two hee Goates, one lotte for the Lorde, and another lotte for the ſcape Goate. And Aaron ſhall offer the Goate on which the Lords lot ſhall fall, and MAKE HIM A SINNE OFFERING. The taking of the Goates from the people doth not make them ſacrifices for ſinne , but the of-fering them vnto the Lord by the Prieſt : ſo that though two were taken, yet lots were caſt which of them ſhould bee the ſinne offering, and which of them the ſcape Goat, which con-ſequentlie was no ſinne offering, becauſe that was made a ſinne offering, on which the Lords lot fell. And ſo if the ſcape Goate did ſignifie the ſoule of Chriſt, as you affirme more boldlie then wiſelie, then was not the ſoule of Chriſt a ſinne offering, neither did it ſuffer for ſinne , if your owne ex-ample maie bee truſted. Howbeit what the ſcape Goate ſignified, I am not ſo forwarde to pronounce as you bee, though I haue better warrant ſo to doe then you haue.

For Cyrill, or as some thinke, Origen writing vpon that place of Leuiticus saieth; [h] If all the people of God were holie , there shoulde not bee two lottes cast vpon the Goates, one to bee offered to the Lorde , the other to bee sent to the desart ; but there should bee one lotte, and one offering to the Lord alone. But nowe where in the number of them that come to the Lord, some belong to the Lord, some deserue to bee cast awaie, and seuered from the Lordes offering; therefore part of the sacrifice which the people bring, to wit one of the Goates, is offered to the Lorde, the other is cast off, and sent into the Desart.   Ambrose in the like sense.   [i] As of two founde in the fielde one is taken , the other forsaken ; so are there two Goates, one fitte for sacrifice , the other to bee sent awaie into the Desart. Hee serued for no vse , neither might hee bee eaten or tasted of by the children of the Priestes.   Beda ioyneth with them .   [k] If all the people were holie, there shoulde not bee two lottes vpon the Goates , but one lotte, and one offering ; nowe when manie are called and fewe chosen, part of the peop'es sacrifice is offered to the Lord, the other parte is cast awaie.   Or else this maie bee vnderstoode of Iesus and *Barrabas* , that one of them, which was the Lordes lotte, euen Iesus was slaine ; the other accursed caitife was sent into the Iewes Desart , bearing the sinnes of the people that cried, Crucifie him. So that the scape Goate by the iudgement of these fathers signified the reprobate among the people; and not the soule of Christ ; as you boldlie auouch. But did it signifie the soule of Christ; what gaine you by that ? The scape Goate was neither done to death, nor made anie sinne offering, as you falslie suppose, but was separated from the Lords offering, and let go free and vntouched . Then by your owne similitude the soule of Christ neither died anie death , as you after falselie and absurdlie conclude, that the soule of Christ died , and was crucified; neither was it anie part of the offering for sinne to G O D, which you so much endeuour to proue . Such is

your

[h] In Leuit.lib.9

[i] Lib.1. epist 4.

[k] In Leuit.ca.16

your vnderstanding,that by your owne examples,you ouer-
throw your owne positions , whiles you labour to establish
them with faint conceits of your owne deuising.

[But in the burnt offering or holocaust prescribed,Leui.6
you find more helpe then in the scape Goate , to proue that
Christ soule suffered for our sins as wel as his body.]If you
meane th it Christs soule suffered the paines of hel, I would
faine see how you proue that out of the holocaust or burnt of-
fering. If you thinke the name of fire doth somewhat relieue
you,remember, Sir,besides the sundrie references that fire
*Leuit.7. ver.2 hath in the scripture,the [1] holocaust was first slaine,and after
burnt;and therefore vnlesse you will fasten the fire of affictió
as you call it,to Christs body or soule after his death,the bur-
ning of the dead sacrifice by fire will little further your pur-
pose.Again, in one and the same fire was the holocaust con-
sumed. If this therefore touch the death and passion of Christ,
his bodie and soule must iointly suffer one and the same kind
of affliction;which is the thing you so much impugne . And
*pag:11 since by your owne position the bodies of beasts [m] could not
"prefigure the immortall and reasonable soule of Christ,how com-
meth it now to passe that y body of the holocaust after death
shall signifie as wel the soule as the bodie of Christ? Can
you thus plant and plucke vp with a touch? It is no waie
denied or doubted by mee, that the soule of Christ was af-
flicted and tormented with sorow and paine all the time of
his passion; which this Crister so much laboureth to proue;
and therefore if the holocaust did signifie the whole manhood
of Christ suffering for our sinnes,it could not preiudice anie
thing, that I did or doe teach, as anon thou shalt (gentle
Reader) more plainlie perceiue; but yet whie the burning
of the holocaust should signifie Christes affliction on the
Crosse, either in bodie or soule , I see no proofe made by
this Confuter;and why it should not resemble Christes af-
flictions before death,these two reasons moue me. First it
was burnt after it was dead; next it was wholie consumed
by

by fire; neither of which can accord with Chzistes sufferings oz the crosse: but by the burning of that sacrifice, I take rather the acceptation of Chzistes death, oz his incorruption after death to be significd. Foz that part of each sacrifice which God reserued foz himselfe, and receiued to himselfe, (was alwayes burnt with fyze; and the Hebzue wozd, HOLAH, which the Scripture vseth foz the holocaust, signifieth [n] that which ascendeth vp to God (by fire;) whence God is often saide in the scriptures, when hee accepteth an holocaust, to smel a sweete sauour. Which wozds saint Paul applieth to the death of Chzist in saying, Christ gaue himselfe for vs to be a sacrifice vnto God of a sweet smelling sauour, that is well pleasing and acceptable vnto God. So likewise because the fire consumed in the holocaust all that was subiect to cozruption, the holocaust may signifie Chzistes incozruption after death. This sense S. Austen appzoueth, when he saith. [o] *Sic leuetur holocaustum vt absorbeatur mors in victoriam*; Let the holocaust so ascend that death bee swallowed vp in victorie. And againe, [p] *Quando totum consumitur igne diuino, holocaustum dicitur. Totum meum consumat ignis tuus, nihil inde remaneat mihi, totum sit tibi. Hoc erit in resurrectione mortuorum, quando mortale hoc induerit immortalitem. Cum absorbet ignis diuinus mortem nostram, holocaustum est.* When the whole sacrifice is consumed with heauenlie fire, it is called an holocaust. Let thy fire (ò Lord) consume me wholie, let nothing therof remaine mine, let the whole be thine: this shall bee in the resurrection of the dead, when this mortalitie putteth on inmortalitie. When Gods fire consumeth our Death, then is it an holocaust. An other kinde of holocaust is mentioned by Saint Austen, which I mislike not. [q] *Holocaustum est totum igne consumptum. Est quidam ignis flagrantissimæ charitatis; totus exardescat igne diuini amoris, qui vult offerre Deo holocaustum.* An holocaust is when the whole is consumed with fire. There is a fire of most feruent charitie, hee must wholie burne with the fire of the loue of God, which will offer to God an holocaust,

[n] Gen. 8.
Exod 29.
Leuit..

[o] August. i.
psal. 50.

[p] August.
psal. 65.

[q] Idem. in psal. 49.

No man euer burned with this fire comparable to Chꝛist
Iesus; whose loue towardes God and man flamed, as vnto
death, so after death, most feruentlie. So that touching the
holocaust the Confuter pꝛesumeth but pꝛoueth nothing; and
yet if his supposall were granted, it weakeneth not the fojce
of my reason, since by the bodily and bloudie sacrifice shado-
wed in the law, I do not exclude the toꝛments on the crosse
imparted to the soule, oꝛ rather holy discerned by the soule
of Chꝛist, but onelie the paines of hell which were neuer fi-
gured by anie sacrifice, noꝛ sealed by anie Sacrament of the
old oꝛ new testament, though now they bee made the pꝛinci-
pall part of our redemption, which indœde was purchased
by the death and bloud of Chꝛist Iesus.

In auoiding the reason which I dꝛewe from the Sacra-
ments of the new testament, and namelie from the Loꝛdes
Supper, in the length of sir lines (Sir refuter) you contradict
the definition and institution of that Sacrament, as also the
plaine resolution of S.Paul, and the pꝛinciples of naturall
   reason. The Sacraments (you saie) *are earthlie elements, they*
   cannot set out spirituall and inuisible effects in Christ. I had
thought Sacraments by their nature had bœne visible
signes of inuisible graces, which definition is so common in the
schooles, that no smatterer in diuinitie besides you is igno-
rant of it. ¶ *Si tu incorporeus esses, nude dona ipsa incorporea tibi*
tradidisset. quoniam vero corpori coniuncta est anima, in sensibili-
bus intelligibilia tibi traduntur. If thou hadst been without a bo-
die, God would haue giuen thee his spirituall gifts vncouered; but
because thy soule is ioined with thy bodie, in sensible thinges are
deliuered thee spirituall (oꝛ inuisible) graces. ͬ Where all the Sa-
craments were common, (saith Augustine) Grace which is the
vertue of the Sacraments, was not common to all. ˢ In the Loꝛds
Supper, that there should be no horror of bloud, & yet the grace
of Redemption might remaine, for a resemblance thou receiuest
the Sacrament, but thou obtainest the grace & vertue of (Chꝛists)
true nature. So that if those earthly elements of water, bꝛead
and

chylost. in
Mt.homil. 83.

ᵖPsal.77.

ͬ Ambros.de
sacramentis.
lib.6. cap. 1.

and wine, did not set out and exhibite the spiritual and inuisi-
ble effects in Christ, they were no Sacraments. [But the Ce- ᵗPag. 14.
remonie of breaking bread (say you) cannot properly belong to the »
body, but to the soule.] In the first institution of his Supper »
did not Christ breake the bread, and deliuer it saying, Take
eate, this is my bodie? If breaking belong to the bread, then
breaking belongeth properlie to the body of Christ; for the
bread was ordained to shew forth the body of Christ, & that S.
Paul noteth in expresse words. ᵗThe bread which we break, is it ᵗ1.Cor.10.
not the Communion of the body of Christ? But Christs body (you
say) was not properly broken; because ŷ scripture saith "not "Iohn.19.
a bone of him shalbe broken. A speculation fit for such a diuine
as you are; had Christs body nothing in it but bones? Had he
not as well flesh as bones? ˣA spirit, saith our sauiour, hath not
flesh & bones, as you see me haue. Then if Christs flesh were ˣLuke.24.
rent & torne with whips, with nailes, with a speare, as it cer-
tainly was, though his bones were whole, his body was pro-
perly & truly broken. For the cutting or tearing of the flesh,
is the breaking of the flesh, and from a part the whole maie
and doth properly take his denomination. And therfore Paul
spake truly and properlie when he thus expresseth the words
of Christs institution, y This is my body, which is broke for you. y1.Cor.11.
Neither doth he in that word varie from Christs institution,
but he rather teacheth vs, that as the bread is broken, and the
wine powred out in the Lords supper; so was the flesh of the
Lords body giuen to be broken & torne on the crosse for vs, &
his bloud likewise shed for the remission of our sinnes. ᶻThe ᶻPag.10.
nailes & spear, (you grant) did pearce him, but in no sort can that »
be called breaking or bruising in peeces, as the worde in Esay doth »
plainlie signifie. Wherefore the meaning is the torments of his »
soule did bruize and breake him in peeces. Your Hebrue,
your Greeke, & your Philosophie, came all out of one forge,
they are so like. You can not finde that Christes flesh was
broken and bruised on the Crosse by grieuous stripes and
wounds, but you haue spied, that his soule was broken in
                                    péeces.

peeces and that properlie . If one of the Prentices before whome you were wont to talke , should aske you into howe manie péces it was broken, your heade would ake to shape him a wise answere. [But the word DACHA which Esay vseth doth plainly (you say) signifie to breake in peeces.] Doth it alwaies and euer signifie properlie to breake into péces? How can it then be applied to the soule, but improperlie and by a figuratiue kinde of speech? A Mole hill with you is a Mountaine. The worde doth signifie to treade vnder foote, to bruise, to oppresse, to humble. When Dauid saith the enemie [a] hath cast my life downe to the ground; Will you saie he hath broken my life in péces? When Iob saith, [b] How long will yee vexe my soule, and afflict mee with your wordes, will you adde, and breake mee in peeces with your wordes? When Ieremie saith of the men of Iudah. [c] They are not humbled vnto this day; Will you phrase it, and say, They are not broken in peeces to this day?

In the power of Christs death to proue the bloud of our sauiour to be the true price of our redemption, and that as wel of our soules as of our bodies; I alledged the words of Peter [d] You were redeemed with the precious bloud of Christ; and of the souls in heauen saying vnto Christ, [e] Thou wast killed, & hast redeemed vs to God by thy bloud; when their bodies were rotten in ÿ earth. Hence I reasoned. if our soules be not redeemed fro death by the bloud of christ, our bodies haue in this life no benefite of redemption, I meane from death; for wee die as doe infidels, and our bodies rot in the graue as theirs doe till the daie of resurrection. But S. Peter saieth, wee are redeemed, not we shall bee; and the saints say to Christ when their bodies lie in the dust, Thou hast redeemed vs by thy bloud; ergo that redemption which we haue in this life, must be referred to our soules; and our bodies must expect the generall daie of redemption in the ende of the world. To this our Confuter replieth , [f] *What a paradox, yea what impietie is this? Haue our bodies no good at all by Christes death,*

Marginal notes:
[a] Psa. 143. ve. 3
[b] Iob. 19. ver. 2
[c] Ier. 41. ver. 10
[d] 1. Pet. 1.
[e] Reuel. 5.
[f] Pag. 23.

no

no more then the bodyes of infidels,becaufe wee die ftil as wel as „
they? God Sir remember, Redemption from death is the „
point which I vrged; ý our bodies in this life haue not, no
moze then the bodies of Infidels haue, but muſt expect it.
And therefoze if our Soules be not redœmed by the blœd of
Chriſt from Sinne & death, we haue prefentlie no redempti-
on by the blœd of Chriſt, but muſt ſtaie foz the time of our
refurreation befoze we ſhall haue it. Which is contrarie to the
wozds both of Peter and of the Soules in heauen, that faie
to Chriſt when their bodies bœ rotten in earth, Thou haſt re-
deemed vs by thy blood. Here ý tell vs of the iuſtification,
moztification, and fanctification of our bodies., as alſo of
the expectation of glozie, which our bodies ſhall haue, and
thinke to make a great conqueſt of the wozds, NO GOOD
AT ALL; but pull in your hoznes. Beſides that my meaning
is verie plaine, whatſœuer the wozdes were, which I might
vſe, which I do not acknowledge to be theſe that you bzing,
but that our bodies haue no benefitte of Redemption from
death; marke well the condition annexed to the pzopoſition,
If our foules bee not redeemed by the death and bloud of
Chriſt; and then all theſe abſurdities which you thought to
faſten on mee, fall full on your owne head. Foz if our foules
be not redœmed by the blœd of Chriſt, our bodies haue vt-
terlie no good, euen no good at all by the death of Chriſt.
[They haue you faie *Iuſtification, mortification, fanctificati-* „
on,& hope of refurrection, beſides the *lawfull poſſeſſion* of earth „
ly things.] Haue our bodies theſe things of themſelues,
oz from our foules firſt iuſtified, moztified, fanctified and af-
fured of life? I truſt you dare not faie that our bodies haue
anie of theſe, but foz and from the Soule. Then if the foule
be not redœmed by the death of Chriſt, the bodie can haue
none of theſe, and confequentlie my wozds are found. and
gœd; & yours, if you ſtand to them againſt the condition an-
nexed to mine, are pzophane and falſe. [But I alter my
wozds, you will faie, to my beſt aduantage, when I ſœ your
obiections to pzeuent that danger.] It had bene fitteſt foz

you to haue ſtated the printing of mine owne woꝛdes, and
then you might haue charged me with them, and not bee
repelled as a foꝛgetter oꝛ miſconſtruer of them, oꝛ to haue
gotten you a copie of that which I deliuerd out that verie
ſummer to men of great honour and learning, a yeere and
moꝛe before I euer heard oꝛ thought of your pamphlet, be-
cauſe I founde ſo manie humoꝛous headed miſconcea-
uing and miſrepoꝛting my woꝛdes. But your haſte
was ſuch, you coulde not; oꝛ your ſkill, you woulde not
ſtaie the ſight of mine owne woꝛdes, leaſt they ſhoulde
trouble you moꝛe then you were ware: and therefoꝛe out
of your owne ill conceaued, and woꝛſe digeſted Rapſo-
dies, you frame obiections as pleaſeth your ſelfe, which
either were not mine, oꝛ not ſo propoſed by me. And that
maketh me purſue no moꝛe of your aunſweres, by reaſon
I ſpende moꝛe time in recalling you to the trueth of my
woꝛdes, then in refelling your exceptions, which haue
neither waight noꝛ witneſſe, moꝛe then the buꝛ̃ing of
your owne bꝛaine. Let vs therefoꝛe view howe well you
behaue your ſelfe in your owne proofes, which you cannot
foꝛget oꝛ miſtake.

　In propoſing the queſtion, and purſuing the proofes, there
is ſome hope (chꝛiſtian Reader) the holines of the confuters
cauſe wil lead him to go plainly & ſoundlie to woꝛk. Thus ther-
foꝛe he beginneth. §*The whole controuerſy hath in it two points.*

§*Pag.*1.
" 　　　*1. That Chriſt ſuffered for vs the wrath of God.*
"
" 　　　*2. That, after his death on the croſſe, he went not into hel*
" 　　　*in his ſoule.*
" *Now then for the former, thus we ſaie and conſtantly auow: Chriſt*
" *Ieſus did ſuffer in his whole manhoode for the redemption and ſa-*
" *tisfaction of our ſinnes: yea he ſuffered properly and immediatelie*
" *in his ſoule and not in his fleſh only. Therefore he ſuffered for vs*
" *the wrath of God. This conſequent is manifeſt and cannot be de-*
" *nied. The antecedent or firſt part of the former generall reaſon is*
" *denied and confidentlie reiected, yet how falſelie by Gods helpe ſhal*

　　　　　　　　　　　　　　　　　　　　　　　eaſily

easily appeare. Touching the first part of this controuersie; were you awaked or a sleepe (Sir refuter) when I preached of these thinges, that you so constantlie auowe this was the question, whether Christ suffered for vs the wrath of God or no? If you were present and not a sleepe, it is too much boldnes to outface the world in print, that this was the position which I impugned. There were to manie witnesses there, for mee to denie, or you to belie the question; you knowe it well enough, but you cannot tell how to proue that which I then reproued, and therefore you shrink from that, and dallie with generall and doubtfull termes, which according as they are expounded, may either make with you, or against you. The question proposed by me, was, whether it could be proued by the scriptures, or by necessary consequent from them, that Christ in his soule suffered the true paines of hell such as the damned doe suffer, and wee shoulde haue suffered, had we not beene redeemed by him? I added, if we tooke the paines of hell metaphoricallie for great and extreame sorrowes and paines, as Dauid and Ionas did, the speach might be tolerated; but if wee tooke them properlie for the verie same which the damned doe and shall suffer in hell, as there is no proofe in it, for there is no truth in it. To this you saie nothing, and so to all wise men make a confession that you cannot iustifie that, which I then disallowed. Ye bee come since to tell vs that certainelie Christ suffered the wrath of God for vs; which if it be granted you, I doe not see what it canne helpe your cause, or hurt mine. For the wrath of God extendeth to all paines and punishmentes as well corporall as spirituall, in this life and the next, be they temporall or eternall. So that no paine or punishment small or great coulde befall the bodie or soule of Christ, but it must needes proceed from the wrath of God. Wherefore your idle discourse of 32. leaues, in which you labor to proue that Christ suffered the wrath of God for sinne, might wel haue bin spared. Three lines directlie to the purpose had bin more worth

I i 2.   then

then so many leaues thus wastfullie spent. But in the ende
you conclude like a Clark, Christ suffered the wrath of God,

ᵇ Pag. 33.   " ʰ *which we affirme is equall to hell it selfe , and all the tormentes*
"*thereof.* What you affirme I little regarde ; what you can
proue is that I intend. And out of this proposition Christ suf-
fered for vs the wrath of God for sinne, you shall neuer con-
clude ; Ergo hee suffered the true paines of hel. Were your
proposition generall that Christ suffered all the wrath of
God for sinne, that is the whole wrath of God and euery part
thereof due to sinne, you might well conclude; Ergo he suffe-
red the true paines of hell; for hell indœde as it is the last, so
is it the greatest effect of Gods wrath against sin ; but from
an indefinite proposition as yours is , which maie signifie
the VVHOLE OR SOME PART OF GODS VVRATH due
to sinne , you shall neuer inferre what part you list, as here
you doe.

Will you, to make your consequent good, amend your an-
tecedent and make it generall; that Christ suffered the whole
wrath of God, & euery part thereof due to sinne? Then heare
good Sir, mine answere . That proposition, besides that it
no waie followeth vpon your first antecedēt; Christ suffered
properlie and immediatlie in his soule, therefore he suffered
the whole wrath of God and euery part thereof due to sinne:
besides I saie that there is no coherence, no consequence be-
twixt these two propositions; the later of them , that Christ
suffered the whole wrath of God due to sinne, and euery part
thereof, is most impious and blasphemous. For so neither vtter
desperation, nor finall reiection, nor eternal damnation are ex-
cepted, but Christ did and must suffer them all; since they are
partes , yea the chiefest partes and effectes of Gods wrath
against sinne. This is far from your meaning, as you often
protest. Trulie I belœne it; charitie leades me to thinke,
though you be somewhat foolish in this cause, that yet you are
not so diuellish as to fasten these things on the sonne of God.
But you must also be so wise as to sœ, that if your antecedent
be

be general, these wil follow, whether you mean them or no: if your antecedent be not general, but indefinite, as, Christ suffered the wrath of God due to sinne, that is some partes and effectes of Gods wrath due to sinne, you shall neuer make choise in your conclusion which parts he suffered, as namelie the true paines of hel & of the damned. Now those which you will, either the inualiditie of your argument, or the impietie of your antecedent; the one will proue you to lack learning, that you sée not the difference; the other that you want christianity, if you should not with mouth disclaim, and with hart detest that horrible blasphemie.

You wil pretend I know, your conclusion is not general: no more indéed is it; your words are , *therfore Christ suffered* ,,
for vs the wrath of God; but this conclusion bceing indefinite, ,,
and verie doubtfull, will do you no good in the fortifieng of your cause. For Christ may suffer the wrath of God in his bodie, yea in his soule hee maie suffer it, and yet not the paines of the damned , or of hell : but because you make this the maine foundation of your whole matter, let vs looke somewhat better into it. You labour to proue by a long processe that Christ suffered the wrath of God for sinne . First then what meane you by the wrath of God? I hope you doe not meane anie inwarde affection or perturbation in God, but as you expounde your selfe [i] *the verie effectes of his iust* ,, [i] *Pag 33:*
wrath; you shoulde saie, of his iustice and power punishing sinne. And this warning (gentle Reader) if thou bce simple I must giue thee, (for the learned knowe it of themselues,) that when thou readest in the scriptures, or hearest me reason of the wrath of God, thou doe not imagine that God is mooued with anie inwarde mutation, but the punishment ordained for sinne by the iustice of God, or inflicted on vs when we haue sinned by the hand of God, (whatsoeuer mean it please him to vse) is called the wrath God. Ambrose saieth well ; [k] *Ira est non ei qui iudicat, sed illi qui iudica-* [k] *In cap.3. ad*
tur; It is no wrath to God that iudgeth , but to him that is Rom.

[1] Greg. moral.
lib.10.cap.14
[m] Auguſt. de
ciuitate dei.
lib 15.c:p.25

[n] Auguſt. in
Pſal.7.

is iudged. [1] *Quia culpas percutit iraſci dicitur*, ſaeth Grego-rie; God is ſaide to be angrie, becauſe he puniſheth our ſinnes. And ſo Auſten. [m] *Ira dei non perturbatio animi eius eſt, ſed iudicium quo irrogatur pæna peccato*. The wrath of God is no affection of mind in him, but his iudgment whereby puniſh-ment is inflicted for ſinne. **The concluſion is;** [n] *nomine iræ intelligitur vindicta iniquitatis*, by the name of (Gods) wrath is vnderſtoode the puniſhment of iniquitie. **It is then eui-dent that by the name of (Gods) wrath, throughout the ſcrip-tures, is vnderſtœde the vengeance oʒ puniſhment pʒepa-red oʒ inflicted foʒ the ſinnes of men. Nowe what particu-lar puniſhmentes God hath pʒonided foʒ ſinne as well in this life, as the next, to chaſtiſe and reuenge both the bo-dies and ſoules of ſinners, woulde aſke long time to re-hearſe. The greateſt and ſoareſt are theſe iudgementes, which are executed on the wicked, in the woʒlde to come; to witte, reiection from the kingdome of God, and condem-nation to hell fire, where not onelie darkeneſſe amaʒeth the eies, and remembʒance of ſinne committed afflicteth the conſcience, but an intolerable flame of fire toʒmenteth both ſoule and bodie foʒ euer. Theſe terrible iudgementes of GOD againſt ſinne the Scriptures publiſh and de-nounce to men in this life, that if the loue of heauen doe not winne them to obedience, the feare of hell ſhoulde hold them from reſiſting and contemning God. The greateſt toʒment that in this life canne befall a ſinner is deſperati-on; when the ſoule of man, conuinced in her ſelfe by the number of her hainous offences, loſeth all hope of life to come, and caſteth her eies wholie on the fearefull toʒmentes of hell pʒepared foʒ her; the continuali thought and fright whereof doe ſo amaʒe and afflict the comfoʒtleſſe ſoule, that ſhee ſinking vnder the burden feeleth in her ſelfe the horrour of hell befoʒe ſhee come to it. So that the loſſe of heauen, and feare of hell maie toʒment wicked and deſperate perſons in this life; but the execution thereof,**
after

after this life, shall breede an other manner of astonishment
and torment, then they canne yet conceaue.. If the thought
of these iudgementes and punishmentes, ordayned by Gods
power and iustice for sinners, so afflict men, what shall
the sight doe? if the feare of hell bee so intolerable, what
shall the flame bee? when therefore you saie (Sir Re-
futer) Christ suffered for vs the wrath of God; wee must
not content our selues with that generall worde, you must
tell vs in particular what partes and effectes of G O D S
wrath Christ endured, before you canne auouch that which
hee suffered, to bee equall to hell and all the tormentes
thereof. Did hee suffer hell fire either in soule, or in bodie?
the damned shall suffer it in both. Did hee finde or feare
himselfe to be excluded from the kingdome of God: the dam-
ned doe see themselues shut out for euer. If hee neither felt
nor feared the MYST, the VVORME, the FIRE of hell, nor
so much as DOVBTED the LOSSE of Gods kingdome,
what tormentes equall to hell canne you name vs? [The
wrath of God you will saie, is equall to hell and all the tor-
ments thereof]. The wrath of God is hell, and so are all the
tormentes of hell; yea they are the sharpest effectes of Gods
wrath against sinne. And therefore neuer plaie with gene-
ralities and ambiguities, but expresse plainly what other ef-
fectes of Gods wrath you meane. For since the losse of hea-
uen, the darkenesse, worme, and fire of hell, and the feare
of both bee the greatest and forest iudgementes of God a-
gainst sinne, that are decreed by his iustice, reuealed by his
word, and executed by his power, in this life or the nexte:
wee plainelie and truelie saie you can name vs none other
effectes of Gods wrath equall to these. If then it be hay-
nous impietie to saie, Christ suffered these, and none other
are equall to these, take backe your lauishing vntruth, that
Christ suffered the effects of Gods wrath, *equal to hel and all*
the tormentes thereof, for my part I see neither sense nor rea-
son in it.

But

" [*But it shalbe soundlie and euidently prooued.*] Will you prooue you know not what? Tell first what effects of gods wrath you meane, and then on with your proofes. Your meaning may be such as you shall neuer prooue. It may be such as we wil easely graunt. For teaching your words which you take for the castel of your cause, *Christ suffered for vs the wrath*
" *of God*; know you good Syr, Christ suffered nothing at his Passion either in bodie or soule, were it little or great, but it was an effect of Gods wrath punishing Sinne, or as you delighte to speake, it was the wrath of God. Well, if you bee so loath to expresse your mind, for feare you bewraie your
" cause, let vs heare your proofes; ° *Thus wee saie and constantlie*
" *auow : Christ Iesus did suffer in his whole manhood for the Re-*
" *demption and satiffaction of our Sinnes; yea he suffered properlie*
" *andimmediatlie in his soule and not in his flesh onlie :* As you haue begonne so you will goe on; talking is your profession, you did your selfe wrong when you came to writing. This Antecedent as you vtter it, (your meaning is secret to your selfe) doth neither good nor hurt to the Question. That christ suffered in his whole manhood for the Redemption of our Sinnes is a thing by mee neuer doubted, nor denied; the doubt is, what he suffered in his whole manhood; and what in ech part of his manhood; for that he suffered all that he suffered in his whole manhood your selfe doe disclaime in the next page, when you saie, P *This greeuous Passion was in his soule*
" *properlie andimmediatlie, seeing then his bodie was not touched*
" *with anie smart.* And when I gaue sixe causes that might bee of Christs agonie in ÿ garden, did I so much as pretend that anie of them then touched his bodie, when he was affeard with this passion of mind? And except this be your meaning, that Christ suffered some things for our Redemption in his whole manhood, and some things properlie andimmediatlie in his Soule, your Antecedent hath a flatte contradiction in it selfe. For if he suffered all, that he suffered, in his whole manhood, how could hee suffer anie thing properlie and immediatlie

° Pag. 4

P Pag. 5.

immediatelie in his soule? which is the second part of your owne Antecedent. And if that bee the drift of your generall reason, about which you spende 32. leaues, you maie sit downe and begin againe a newe pamphlet, that shall haue some more certaintie then this hath. For heere you roue, neither expressing, nor indéede knowing what you woulde haue; onlie you hide your selfe in this generall phrase, that *Christ suffered the wrath of God for sinne*; but vnlesse you speci- fie what he suffered, I do not meane to brabble with you, or with anie other, about generall and vncertaine speaches. What hee suffered more then the scriptures expresse, (for I faithfullie beléue all that is there written) I doe not casilie admit you, or anie other such presumer, to deliuer vpon your credits; when you declare what you meane, and prooue that you saie, you shall soone haue an answere.

[*Christ* (you saie) [i] *assumed not our nature, nor any part of it, but* ONLY *to suffer in it properly and immediately, euen for the very purchasing of our redemption thereby. Otherwise he had no neede to assume both, but either the one part or the other.*] See what it is (good Reader) for a man to loose himselfe in the wildernesse of his owne wit. To proue that Christ suffered both in bodie and soule, which is a thing by no man denied (for the question is, what he suffered, and not whether soule and bodie were ioined in Christes sufferings?) this Refuter lea- peth ouer head and eares into absurdities, not onely against diuinitie, but euen against nature, and the verie law of our first creation. That the sonne of God had no END nor PVR- POSE in taking our nature vnto his in the vnitie of person, but ONLY to suffer for our sinnes, is a bolde and lewd ouer- sight; his ende and purpose in taking our nature was not onlie to suffer for vs, but to doe all that for vs, which in his life time, and after his death, by his resurrection, ascension, and mediation he did, doth, and will do for vs. By his owne mouth he reuealed to vs his fathers will from heauen; by his example of life he taught vs all perfection of holinesse;

[i] Pag. 17?

Pag. 16?

Pag. 17?

by

by his rising he swallowed vp our death; by his intercession wee receaue all the giftes and graces of God, which wee haue oz shall haue; by his sitting in heauen with our flesh, he giueth vs assurance that our mortall bodies shall bee changed, like to his glozious bodie; yea the verie vnion of our nature to his is an effectuall meane to make vs one with him, as he is one with God. Had Christ not béene man, we could haue had no interest in the fulnes of his obedience, in the riches of his graces, in the Communion of his spirit, in the fellowship of his glorie, which are the helpes, suppoztes, and meanes of our saluation, as well as his suffering foz vs: and man hee coulde not bee without a soule and a bodie; neither part ioyned with his diuine nature was sufficient to make him a man. By the lawe of our first creation we are men consisting of bodies and soules; and therefoze Christ as our heade must haue both, NOT ONELIE TO SVFFER FOR SINNE, but also to quicken, sanctifie, and glozifie both our soules and bodyes that hee may perfite our saluation, and bzing vs to GOD, without reiecting oz excluding either parte of our nature. Yea so aduised you are, Sir Refuter, in your reasons, that by your owne assertion you conclude Christes flesh to bee needclesse foz our Redemption: foz thus you saie; " ¶ *This suffering* (of the soule by her bodie which is *na-*"*turall* and *by sympathie onelie*) PROPERLIE DID NOT "MAKE TO OVR REDEMPTION. What is suffe-ring, good Sir, in your learning? The receauing of the blowes, oz the feeling of the paine ? If you beate oz cut a deade carkas, that hath neither life noz sense, will you saie it suffereth? J thinke not. There must then bee life and sense in the bodie, befoze it canne suffer oz feele a-nie paine. Nowe, life and sense, pertaine they to the bo-die oz else to the soule? If you knewe not befoze, as by the vnlearned discourse it seemeth you did not, Saint Au-sten shall teach you; except you will skozne him in this point,

¶ Pag. 18.

point, as you do in others. [t] *Si diligentius consideremus, dolor,* *qui dicitur corporis, magis ad animā pertinet. Animæ enim est do-* *lere, non corporis, etiam quando ei dolendi causa existit a cor-* *pore, cum in eo loco dolet, vbi læditur corpus. Sicut ergo dici-* *mus corpora sentientia & corpora viuentia cum ab anima sit cor-* *poris sensus & vita; ita et corpora dicimus dolentia, cum dolor* *corporis nisi ab anima esse non possit.* If wee well consider, the paine which is called bodilie paine, belongeth rather to the soule. The soule feeleth the paine, not the bodie euen when the cause of paine commeth from the bodie, and the soule greeueth in the place where the bodie is hurte; As then wee saie bodies are liuing and feeling, when the life and sense of the bodie is by the soule; so saie wee bodies full of paine, when the paine of the bodie cannot bee felte but by the soule. And so againe; [f] *Dolores qui dicuntur car-* *nis anima sunt in carne & ex carne; dolor carnis tantummo-* *do offensio est anima ex carne.* The paines which are called bodilie paines, are the paines of the soule in the bodie and by the bodie. For bodilie paine is nothing else but the griefe of the soule by the bodie. Whereof Diuines maie not doubte, since naturall reason and experience teacheth, that as the soule seeth by the eies, and heareth by the eares of the bodie; so the soule feeleth paine and offence by euerie part of the bodie, when it is wounded or wronged. If this suffering of Christes soule, by communion with his bodie, did not properlie *make to our Redemption*, which are your owne words; then neither the stripes, woundes, nor death of Christ did any way make to our redemption; since of all these violences offered to Christes bodie, the flesh it selfe had not the feeling but onlie the soule of Christ by communion with her bodie, or as you terme it, by *Sympathie*. Yea farther, by your owne rule, the flesh of Christ was needelesse in the worke of our Redemption, for so much as his flesh could not properly and immediatlie feele any paine; but of force

must

[m] August. de ciuitate dei. lib. 21. cap. 3

[f] Idem de ciui- tate dei. lib. 14. cap. 15

must leaue the feeling of all that was suffered to the soule; and so whiles you talke so much of the proper and immediate suffering of Christes soule, you haue cleane excluded all the sufferings of Christ, which the scripture expresseth, as not making proper lie to our redemption.

Pag.19.

" [But ᵗ insteede of a false argument of mine, you will returne a
" reason better grounded, and of certaine truth; which is this;
" Whereby Adam first, and we euer since doe most properlie commit
" sinne, by the same hath Christ our second Adam made satisfac-
" tion for our sinne. But Adam first, and we euer since most proper-
" lie commit sinne in our soules, our bodies beeing but the instru-
" ments of our soules, and following the soules direction and will.
" Therefore Christ in his soule chieflie and most properly made satis-
" faction for vs.] Thou shalt perceiue (christian reader) by the answere to this argument, howe ill I spend the time in pursuing this Trifler, which neither can tel what he would haue, nor what he should proue, nor whether his own reasõs make with him or against him. I made no such argument as here he pretendeth; the effect of my reason was this. The flesh of Christ must be as able to redeeme vs as Adams was to condemne vs: but we inherit pollution and condemnation from Adams flesh; wherefore the flesh of Christ must both quicken and clense vs. The Maior is euident, vnlesse we make the diuell more able to destroie vs by an other, then God is able to saue vs by himselfe. The Minor is cleere, without intermedling with the question, whence soules be deriued. I vtterlie refused to ground anie reason vpon that difficultie; I vsed Dauids words, in sinne my mother conceiued me, and as Ambrose saith, " prius incipit in homine macula quam vita; pollution (which is originall) beginneth in man before hee hath life. Now the soule is the life of the bodie. Then if pollution cleaue to the flesh before life come, and consequentlie before the soule come, whence soeuer it commeth; it is euident that Adams flesh defileth and so condemneth vs. As for my conclusion that Christes flesh must quicken and clense vs, if the

Vide pag e.104

ᵃ In Apologia Dauid.ca.11.

                                                                premisses

premisses would not support it, which they fully doe; the
Scriptures will maintaine it.ˣ He that eateth my flesh(saith
our Saniour)and drinketh my bloud, hath eternall life, and I
will raise him vp at the last daie. I am that bread of life. If anie
man eate of this bread, he shall liue for euer, and the bread that
I will giue, is my flesh, which I will giue for the life of the world.
My reason standing good, Sir Refuter, let vs looke a little
to yours, that you saie is so well grounded, and of certaine
truth. How proue you your first proposition, *In which part*
Adam did first sinne, by that part Christ must satiffy for sinne?
Satiffaction for Sinne the Scripture acknowledgeth none
but by death;because ƥ Iudge in prohibiting Adam to trans-
gresse threatned death;ʸ In the day that thou eatest therof thou
shalt die the death;and the Apostle saith plainlie; ᶻChrist is the
mediator of the new testament, that THROVGH DEATH,
which was for the REDEMPTION of the transgressions in the
former Testament, they which were called might receiue the
promise of eternall inheritance. If nothing might satiffie for
sinne but death;then consequently the Soule of Christ which
could not die, could not paie the satiffaction for our Sinnes,
howsoeuer Adam did, and we still doe sinne, most properlie
with our Soules. This is but a straw in your waie; for you
sisse, but absurdly, if not impiously defend, that Christ died
the death of the Soule; yet because the Scriptures and Fa-
thers with one consent auouch the contrarie, yea S. Austen
is so peremptorie therein that he asketh, QVIS AVDEAT
DICERE, WHO DARE AFFIRME IT? you shall giue mee
leaue to tell you that the Apostle denieth your Maior, till you
can make it good, not by your own vnlearned frensie, but by
good testimonie of Scripture, that Christ did die the death of
the Soule. Now by your assumption, that Adam *most proper-*
lie committed sinne in his soule; If you mean that Adams soule
was the agent, his body the Instrument which the soule vsed
as in all sins;so in this;that indeed is most true, but directly
repugnant to your conclusion. Put that for your Minor, that

ˣ Iohn 6.

ʸ Gene.2.
ᶻ Hebrues 9.

Vide pag 79.

Bk. 3.   Adams

Adams soule transgressed the commaundement with hir bodie
and by hir bodie ; the conclusion then followeth in spite of
your hart; ergo in satisfying for sinne the Soule of Christ
must be punished with hir bodie & by hir bodie; which is the
thing you labour to ouerthrowe with all the wits you haue.
Meane you otherwise that Adam brake the Commaunde-
ment of God, not by his bodie properlie, but by his soule ?
Then is your assumption a manifest contradiction to the fact
of Adam. For with his eares he heard the perswasion of the
woman, with his eies he liked the forbidden fruit, with his
hand he tooke it, with his mouth he did eat it, which was the
fact that God preciselie did prohibit. God did not saie to A-
dam thou shalt not like it, or desire it, which the soule of Adam
did, but THOV SHALT NOT EATE THEREOF, which
could not bee performed but by the hand and mouth of A-
dam: and therefore Adam transgressed the commaundement
not by his soule, but by his bodie, euen as in murder, theft, &
adulterie, these facts men commit by their bodies and not
by their soules.

[But in that and all other sinnes brought to effect,
the soule, you will saie, is the principall agent, the bodie
is but the Instrument.] I grant it willinglie; and thence
I conclude, ergo in the satisfaction for sinne, the soule
must be the principall patient and dolent, and the bodie by
Gods iustice must be the instrument of her paine. And here
marke I praie thee (Christian Reader) whether this one ar-
gument doe not vtterlie ouerthrow all that this idle discour-
ser hath doone, and would doe in this whole pamphlet. For
nothing is more proportionable to Gods iustice, then to
ioine them in paine, that were ioyned in sinne; and to re-
taine the same order in punishing, which they kept in offen-
ding. But all prouocations and pleasures of sinnes the soule
taketh from her bodie, all acts of sinne she committeth by
her bodie: therefore the iustice of God both temporallie and
eternallie

eternallie punisheth the soule by the bodie ; that as it hath beene the Instrument of her pleasure , so it shall bee of her paine. And if GOD obserue this course as well in his temporall as eternall vengeance on the sinnes of men, whie then shoulde not the sufferinges of Christes soule by his bodie bee truelie and properlie a satisfaction for sinne, which this great Doctor a little before said, *made not properlie* ,, *to our Redemption?* ,,

Pag. 18.

For thy better instruction, gentle Reader, and my discharge, that the soule taketh her occasions to sinne, vseth her delightes in sinne , and perfeurmeth her attemptes of sinne, with and by the bodie, giue mee leaue in this point to bee somewhat the longer . ᶻ *Caro est officina spiritus, qui in ea et per eam, quæcunque affectauerit, peragit & consummat .* The flesh (saith Cyprian) is the forge of the soule, which in that and by that acteth and performeth, whatsoeuer it affecteth . ᵃ *Per quinque sensus, quasi per quasdam fenestras vitiorum ad animam est introitus .* By the fiue senses of the bodie (saieth Ierome) as it were by certaine windowes, vices (or sinnes) haue their entrance into the soule. ᵇ *Nusquam anima sine carne est quamdiu est in carne;* NIHIL NON CVM ILLA AGIT *, sine qua non est ; siquidem in carne , & cum* carne *, & per* carnem *agitur ab anima , quod agitur in corde .* The soule (saieth Tertullian) is no where without the flesh , as long as it is in the flesh. SHEE DOTH NOTHING VVITHOVT THAT , without which shee is not . Euen that which is done in the heart, the soule doth in her flesh , with her flesh, and by her flesh: Yea hee presseth it farther and saieth; ᶜ *A deo non sola anima transfigit vitam, vt nec cogitatus licet solos, licet non ad effectum per carnem deductos, auferamus a collegio carnis. Et sine opere et sine effectu cogitatus, carnis est actus. Negent factorum societatem, cui negare non possunt cogitatorum. Et si anima est, quæ agit & impellit in omnia, carnis obsequium est .* So farre it is that the

ᶻ Cyprian in prolog de natiuitate Christi

ᵃ Hier. contra Iouin. lib. 2

ᵇ Tertullian. de resurrect. carnis.

ᶜ Ibidem.

the ſoule alone doth perſourme this life , that the VERIE
THOVGHTS IN THEM SELVES, neuer brought to effect,
we take not frō the fellowſhip of the fleſh. Yea the very thought
VVITHOVT ACT, VVITHOVT EFFECT, iS A DEEDE of
the fleſh, Let them now denie that to be the ſoules companion
in works , which they cannot denie to bee her companion in
thoughts. For though it be the ſoule, that mooueth and leadeth
to all things, yet the fleſh addeth her ſeruice. And leaſt it ſhould
ſeeme ſtrange that he affirmeth, he pointeth to the words of
our Sauiour , ᵈ out of the hart come. euill thoughts. How
trew this is that Tertullian here voucheth thou ſhalt ſone
perceiue (gentle Reader) if thou behould men in SLEEPE, in
FRENSIES, in LETHARGIES, in APOPLEXIES; where
the ſubſtance of the ſoule is no waie touched or decaied; but
onelie the Inſtruments of her bodie, which ſhe vſeth in per-
ceiuing, remembring, vnderſtanding anie thing, are diſtem-
pered, or obſtructed. The experience hereof, is ſo caſie and eui-
dent euen to the ſimpleſt among men. that I ſhall nede to
ſpend no more words to the learned. Tertullians concluſion
is this. ᶜ deum non licet aut iniuſtum iudicē credi, aut inertem: in-
iuſtū, ſi ſociam bonorum operum a præmiis arceat; inertem, ſi ſociā
maloru a ſuppliciis ſecernat. Non ſit particeps in ſententia caro. ſi
non fuerit & in cauſa. Non poſſunt ergo ſeparari in mercede, quas
opera coniungit. We maie not thinke God to bee an iniurious, or
a negligent Iudge : iniurious, if he exclude the (ſoules) compa-
nion in good works from (the ſoules) reward; negligent, if he ex-
cuſe the (ſoules) partner in euill, from the (ſoules) puniſhments.
Let the fleſh haue no part in the ſentence, if it had no part in
the cauſe. They cannot be ſeuered in wages, that were ioyned in
worke. If Tertullians aſſumption be true, that in this life the
ſoule can neither work, ſpeake, perceiue, deſire, nor think good
or euill without the Inſtruments of her bodie ; (excepting
alwaies Gods power to inſpire what pleaſeth him; for hee
that framed the ſoule can alter and chaunge it at his liking,
by the immediate working of his ſpirit;) if Tertullians con-
cluſion

ᵈ Matth.15.

Ibidem de re-
ſurrect. carnis,

clusion be true, that God the righteous iudge of the world in his euerlasting reward of obedience, & likewise in his eternall vengeance for sinne will ioine and couple both bodie and soule togither; then apparentlie NO SVFFERINGS ARE SO FIT IN THE PERSON OF THE REDEEMER FOR THE SATISFACTION of sinne, as those VVHICH ARE COMMON TO BOTH PARTS OF MAN, & namely which the soule suffereth from her bodie & by her bodie; which ouerthroweth all the Confuters vnsalted and vnsettled discourse of the soules proper and immediate suffering in the person of Christ Iesus.

Doe I then denie that the soule hath anie sufferings in this life and the next, which come not by the bodie? By no meanes. For though those conioined sufferings be most answerable to sinnes committed; yet the soule hath some proper punishments in this life, as sorrow and feare, when the bodie hath no hurt, from which Christ was not free as appeereth by his Agonie: and so in the next the soules of the wicked haue griefe and remorse besides the paine of fier. The remembrance of sinne shall not a little torment the wicked, but perpetuallie afflict and gnaw their consciences as a worme that neuer dieth. The losse of Gods fauour and kingdome shall not a little grœue them, when they see others receiued into that eternall ioye and blisse, and them-selues excluded. [t] *Gehenna grauius est a dei beneuolentia exci-dere*; to fall from Gods fauour (saith Chrysostome) is more grieuous then hell it selfe; and againe, [s] *Ego illius gloriæ amissionem multo amarius quam ipsius gehennæ supplicium esse dico. Intolerabilis quidem res est gehenna: quis nesciat & suppli-cium illud horribile? tamen si mille quis ponat gehennas, nihil tale dicturus est quale est à beatâ illius gloriæ honore repelli.* The losse of that (euerlasting) glorie I saie is farre bitterer then the totments of hell it selfe. Hell is an intolerable thing, and an horrible punishment: who knoweth it not? Yet if a man

would

an Reader)how scornfully this Confuter reiecteth the iudg-
ments of the auncient fathers by mee alleaged touching
the causes of Christs agonie in the garden, and his com-
plainte on the Crosse; as likewise how forgetfullie hee
changeth, or purposelie maimeth my reasons, that hee
maie the better auoyde them : and thirdlie, how vncer-
tayne his propositions, and how lame his conclusions
are, that hee maketh for his owne side, yea often such
as ouerthrowe his owne assertion; Thou shalt heare now
some of his speciall reasons, as hee calleth them; but
as the trueth is, some of his speciall absurdities, and impie-
ties: wherein I will be no longer then of force I must bee; I
take little pleasure in raking such an vncleane sinke.

_{k Pag. 34.}   " The first is:[k] *Christ suffered the paines and sorrowes for*
    " *sinne which we should.* This proposition (Sir confuter) if
you take it indefinitlie as it lieth; proueth nothing for you:
you maie do well to goe to the Vniuersitie againe, whence
you came afore you were wise, and there learne to put
quantitie to your propositions, that wee maie know when
you speake of any thing, whether you meane A L L or s o m e:
for if you meane here, that Christ suffered A L L that wee
should, this proposition is an horrible blasphemie: then
Christ suffered the L o s s e of G o d s G r a c e, s p i r i t e,
f a v o v r, l i f e, and k i n g d o m e, for so should wee;
then hee was plunged into finall desperation, irreuocable
malediction, and eternall condemnation; for so should wee.
[You are farre from that frensie, you will saie.] I hope
so too; neither doe I charge you with it; but if your propo-
sition bee generall you cannot auoide it; and therefore,
after your loose and trifling manner, you sette downe
a doubtfull assertion, that maie serue for all, or for part of the
which wee should haue suffered. If you meane but part, then
your proposition proueth no such thing, as you intend. For
you would faine from hence inferre, that Christ suffered
the paines of hell, which were due to vs; & if hee suffered but
part

part of that which wee should, a wise Christian will suppose anie part, rather then the paines of hell; howbeit the Apostle teacheth mee to saie that ¹ Christ died for our Sinnes according to the Scriptures, and that death was the death of the Crosse, ᵐ He humbled himself & became obedient vnto death, euen to the death of the crosse. [That is no sufficiēt answere, you wil saie; because on the Crosse ⁿ He sustained our sorrowes, as Esaie said he should.] The wordes of Esaie are not, as you would faine haue them, he bare A LL our sorrowes, for then he must haue sorrowed for the losse of gods grace, fauour & kingdome, as I said before; but the prophet saith, he bare our sorrowes, which maie receiue a double construction, and either of them verie religious and christian. The first, whatsoeuer hee felt or suffered it was ours, not his owne, that is for our sakes, and for our Sinnes. This the Prophet in the words following confirmeth, He was wounded for our transgressions, He was bruized for our iniquities. The next is, he sustained our sorrowes that is such weaknes, faintnes, & wearines, as are incident to our nature; and that the Prophet confesseth in the words before, He is a man full of sorrowes, and hath experience of infirmities, euen of such as naturallie offend & afflict vs. But when the scripture faileth you, you flie to similitudes of your owne making, and where Paule saith, ° Christ gaue himselfe a ransome for all; you saie, ᴾ the Scripture speaking heere after the common vse, and custome of redeeming captiues taken in warre, doth meane that Christ paid for vs THE SAME PRICE which else wee should haue paid. First whoe told you that the Scripture speaketh here after the common vse of Enimies, since in our Saluation the sonne of God interposed himselfe as a mediator with his father, to answere what the iustice of God would require at the hands of his sonne, for the pardoning of a seruant, that had offended? You and your friends cannot abide to heare, that the enimie who had vs in captiuitie should haue any price for our deliuerance; you condemne that as a Manicheisme;

and

¹ 1 Cor.15.

ᵐ Phil.2.

° Esai.53

° 1Timot.2.

ᴾ Pag.34

and doe you no'we for an aduantage vrge that the ene-
mie must haue a price for his captiue? Secondlie· the price
that wee shoulde haue paide was eternall condemnation
of bodie and soule into hell fire. If Christ paide the same,
loke wel least with seeking helpe from an enemie, you light
not on open blasphemie. Lastlie to ioyne with you in your
owne similitude, is it not the common vse in warres to
redeeme captiuitie with monie? The Captiue himselfe is
tyed to perpetuall imprisonment or seruitude; hee that
will ransome a prisoner is not bounde to bee a Prisoner
himselfe, but to yeelde such recompence in money or other-
wise, as the conquerour shall demaunde. So that e-
uen by your owne comparison, it is euident, the sonne
of GOD in redeeming vs was not tied to our captiui-
tie, but might yeelde his Father a greater recompence
for our absolution, then our condemnation woulde haue a-
mounted vnto.

Your seconde speciall follie (Sir Confuter) is groun-
Page. 35. " ded vpon the wordes of Saint Paule. *Christ redeemed vs from*
" *the curse of the Lawe beeing made a curse for vs*. Whence
" you reason; *It is vaine and senselesse to thinke that the A-*
" *postle speaketh here of two seuerall kindes of curses. And if Christ*
" *sustained anie curse for vs, what curse could it be? not the curse*
" *of the lawe? or what was it? not the curse of God?* If you aske
to learne, you may bee soone taught. If you aske to brag,
you maie be soone cooled. The curse of God vpon the sinne
of man proceedeth from the wrath of God against the sinne
of man; howbeit God curseth not onelie sinners, but other
his creatures, with whom he is not angrie, but only because
they shoulde not serue the pride and lustes of the wicked.
When Adam transgressed, God cursed the earth for his
p Genes. 3 sinne in saping, p Cursed is the earth for thy sake, thornes and
thistles shall it bring thee. For not onelie the soules and bo-
dies of the wicked are cursed and consumed with plagues
resting in them, and on them; but all that they take in hand,
and

and all that belongth to them is accursed likewise. ¶ If thou wilt not (saieth Moses) obey the voice of the Lorde thy God to doe all his commaundementes, then all these curses shall come vpon thee and ouertake thee. Cursed shall thy basket bee, and thy store. Cursed shall bee the fruite of thy bodie, and the fruite of thy lande, the increase of thy kine, and the flockes of thy sheepe. The Lorde will sende vpon thee cursing in all that which thou settest thine hande to doe, vntill thou bee destroyed and perish, because of the wickednesse of thy workes. The rest of GODS curses there numbred vnto the ende of that Chapter, and laide vpon bodie and soule, wife and childzen, goods and landes, life and death of such as transgresse; peruse (gentle Reader) at thy leasure, and thou shalt easilie see, how farre the curse of GOD in this life pursueth sinners; besides the horrible tozmentes of the nexte life kept in stoze foz them. So that as I did in the wzath of God, I must in the curse of God aske you (Sir Confuter) whether you meane that Chzist suffered foz vs the whole curse of the lawe, oz parte thereof? if you aunswere the whole; looke in that place which I now cited, how manie kinds of curses there be reckned, which neuer touched our Sauiour; besides the graunde curse which closeth vp all, and continueth foz euer; ʳ Depart from me ye CVRSED into euerlasting fire. If you saie a parte; then pzoue you nothing with pour hot and sharpe spurres as you thinke, when you saie; *what curse could it be? not the curse of the law? or what else? not the curse of God?* Chzist suffered a parte of that curse, which God by his owne mouth laid on Adam and all his posteritie foz sinne. ˢ By one man sinne entred into the worlde (saieth Paul) and by sinne death; hee also suffered other partes of the curse, which GOD by his ᵗ lawe thzeatned vnto sinners, to wit ᵘshame and TROVBLE, ˣ VVRONG and VIOLENCE, ʸ CAPTIVITY and MISERY, ⁷ THIRST and NAKEDNES, ᶻ GRIEFE and PAYNE of bodie and minde. Besides, the verie kinde of death, to which

ᑫDeutero.28

ʳMatth.25

,,
,,

ˢRom.5.

ᵗDeut.28
ᵘverse 20.37.
ˣ 33.
ʸ 48.
ᶻ 65.

'Galat.3

which he submitted himselfe was accursed by speciall words in the law, ᵃ accursed is euery one that hangeth on the Tree. Now to verifie the words of S. Paul, that Christ redeemed vs from the curse of the law due to our sinnes, being made a curse for vs; it sufficeth that the sonne of God, being equall with his Father in glorie and maiestie, vouchsafed to vndergoe not all the partes of our curse, but some partes there of. Gods euerlasting curse which is most due to sinne, I hope you will free him from. Gods spirituall curse, by which he depriueth the wicked of his trueth, of his grace and other giftes of his spirite, you must likewise cleare the sonne of GOD from. Hee cannot be subiected to that parte of Gods curse without apparant impietie. Take from him trueth, you make him a lyar; take from him grace you charge him with a reprobate minde; take from him the Spirit of GOD, you giue place to Satan to worke in him as in the children of vnbeliefe. I trust (Sir Refuter) you bee neither so wicked as to thinke, neither so desperate as to defend, that the sonne of God might suffer any of these curses. Then haue you boldelie, but falsely and lewdly con-

ᵇ Pag.40.

“ cluded out of S. Paul, that he putteth ᵇ *a part of the iust curse*
“ *of the lawe, thereby meaning the whole.* Are you so well acquainted with Saint Paules minde, that of your owne heade, to vphold your humorous fansie, you will vrge his meaning without his wordes, to support a manifest falsitie? The whole curse of the law containeth infatuation of minde, obduration of heart, desperation, damnation; and what not? Did Paul meane, that Christ was made these thinges for vs? or could hee haue redeemed vs, if in these things he had beene poked with vs? But that I thinke (Sir Refuter,) you sinne of ignorance, not meaning to maintaine these blasphemies, and yet including them within the largenesse of your words, through the weaknesse of your wit, I must by the duty which I owe to God, and his truth, haue giuen you other termes, then now I do; but I had rather fatherly warne you to take

heede

hæde of these toles in time, least they bzing the whole curse of God vpon your owne soule, which you would so faine saFen on Chzists.

Notwithstanding your follie thus to pzesume without all pzofe vpon the Apostles meaning besides his wozdes, you haue a good conceit of your self, & like a proper man you say, *I vrge then, let it be noted, Christ is said to be made a curse for vs;* „ 'Pag. 37. *and before I shewed this curse was Gods curse And againe.* d *The* „ *Scripture it selfe affirmeth, hee did all that for vs: therefore who* „ dPag. 36. *dareth denie it? Who either man or Angel shall presume to say* „ *nay?* You haue vzged it, I haue noted it, and so haue manie wise and good men moze; and will you heare what I conceiue? Trulie this; you haue moze néede of Phisicke to cure your bzaines, then of labour to rebate your arguments. So many, and those *speciall reasons;* so proudlie proposed, so weaklie performed, so falselie concluded, did I neuer reade as long as I haue liued. Thou wilt thinke perchance (chzistian Reader) I speake this to disgrace the encounterer, and so to pzeiudice his cause with thee; mine heart God knoweth; but if thou bee not of the same minde with mee befoze I ende with his *speciall reasons,* as hee calleth them, I much deceiue my selfe; specialie if thou thy selfe bee intelligent and indifferent.

I hope, though I vaunt not, as he doth, there can bee no doubt, but the curse of God foz sinne containeth these partes which I propose; to wit, the externall, corporall, spirituall, & eternall plagues and punishments, wherewith God pursueth the wicked that rebell against him. I count it as cleare, that neither the eternall, noz the true spirituall curse of God could take hold on the soule of our Sauiour. Foz as the greatest blessings that God giueth vs in this life, after he hath by mercie pardoned our sinnes, are the faith of his truth, to direct vs, the strength of his grace, to assist vs, the earnest of his spirite to perswade our hearts of his fatherlie clemencie to vs, and to inflame vs againe with the loue of his name, hope

of

of his promises, and desire of his kingdome; so the greatest
curse for sinne, that in this life maie befall men, is to
haue his holie spirite taken from them, with all his gra-
ces and gifts, that anie waie tende to saluation, and to bee
giuen ouer into a reprobate sense, that with blindnesse and
hardnesse of heart, they may runne headlong to their owne
destruction. With these impieties and blasphemies, I trust
no Christian will burthen the soule of our Sauiour; and yet
these are the true spirituall curses of God against sinne. If
Iohn.1. sin in the soule of Christ were alwayes ^e full of grace and truth,
and the abundance of his spirite such, that ^e wee all receiue
of his fulnesse; If in the perfection of his holinesse, innocen-
cie and obedience there coulde bee no defect; nor anie feare
or doubt in that stedfast assurance of faith, hope and loue,
which our Sauiour alwayes retained; howe could hee bee-
ing so fullie and perpetuallie blessed of God, bee also trulie
accursed of him? The curse of God is not in wordes, but
in deedes. Then euidentlie saint Paules meaning is and
must be, that Christ, voluntarilie vndertaking some part of
the curse due to our sinnes, (for the whole hee could not vn-
dertake without reprobation and damnation;) not onlie dis-
charged vs of the whole, but gaue vs the blessing of God pro-
mised to Abraham. And to this ende I brought the testimo-
nies of saint Austen, Chrysostome, and others, fullie confir-
Pag.35. ming that I said: to which you replie, as your custome is; *It
is vaine and senselesse to thinke that the Apostle here speaketh of
two seuerall kinds of curses.* Indeede it is vaine and fruitlesse
to reason with him, that preferreth his ignorant imagina-
tion, before the iudgements of all the learned, and aunctent
fathers in Christs church; but Sir, your follies will sticke fast
by you, when their expositions shall passe with all wise men
for cyrrant and good.

You quarrell as your manner is, with those parts of the
curse, which I say Christ indured. For where I proposed a
SHAMEFVL, WRONGFVL & PAINFVL death to be that
part

part of the curse, which Chꝛiſt ſuffered foꝛ vs; you ſkirre at
euerie one of theſe; And of the firſt you ſay: ᵍ *Will any man of*   ᵍ Pag.38.
common reaſon affirme that (to be openly hanged on a tree) *was* „
all the curſe that Chriſt bore for vs? Nothing but the ſhame of „
the world, becauſe it was an ignominious death? Whether you „
account ſaint Auſten, and ſaint Chryſoſtome, men of com-
mon reaſon J know not; The Church this 1200.yeeres hath
taken them foꝛ reuerend and learned fathers. You adde, *It* „
is more then abſurd ſo to ſay. Judge thou (Chꝛiſtian reader) „
whether this Pꝛater be well in his wits, that in his frenzie
thus repꝛocheth, not onelie the fathers of Chꝛiſtes church,
but euen the Pꝛophets and Apoſtles themſelues, as men
moꝛe then abſurd,and not of common reaſon. Moſes from
Gods mouth thꝛeatneth ſuch as tranſgreſſe the lawe, that
God will ſend them ʰ trouble and ſhame,and will make them   ʰDeut.28.
a ⁱ wonder,a prouerbe,and a common talke among all people.   verſ20.
Eſay foꝛeſhewing Chꝛiſts ſufferings, reckoneth this not foꝛ   ⁱ & ver.37.
one of the leaſt; ᵏ He was deſpiſed,reiected & numbred among   ᵏ Eſay.53.
ſinners; we did iudge him plagued and ſmitten of God,and tur-
ned our faces from him. Dauid in the perſon of Chꝛiſt, com-
plaining of the wꝛongs receiued at the time of his paſſion;
putteth this as the firſt and the chiefeſt,ˡ I am (as) a worme   ˡPſal.22.
and not a man; a ſhame of men, and the contempt of the peo-
ple. All they that ſee mee haue mee in deriſion;they make a
mowe, and nod the heade, ſaying, he truſted in God, let him
deliuer him, let him ſaue him. They gape vpon mee with their
mouthes. Saint Paule himſelfe vꝛgeth as much the ſhame,
as the paine of the croſſe; ᵐ Looke to Ieſus the authour and   ᵐHeb.12.
finiſher of your faith, who for the ioy ſet before him endured
the croſſe and deſpiſed the ſ H A M E. He endured ſuch contra-
diction of ſinners leaſt you ſhould faint in your mindes. How of-
ten doth God thꝛeaten ſhame and confuſion of face to thoſe
that fall from him? Howe earneſtly doth Dauid euery where
pꝛay againſt it? Howe truly doth Daniel make this confeſ-
ſion to god?ⁿO Lord to vs belongeth O P E N ſ H A M E becauſe   ⁿDaniel.9.

we haue finned againſt thee ; the CVRSE is powred vpon vs written in the law of *Moſes*; becauſe of our ſinnes, Ieruſalem and thy people are a REPROCH to all about vs. If the ſcriptures were not cleare, that ſhame and reproch is a chiefe part of Gods curſe againſt ſinne, howe manie wiſe men and good men chooſe death before ſhame? What generous nature doth not more decline ſlandering then wounding? In common reaſon to which you appeale, howe can it bee leſſe wrong or griefe, to whippe the ſoule with reproches, then the bodie with ſcourges? Verſly our Sauiour who beſt knoweth the waight of both, giueth like rewarð to both :   ° Bleſſed are you when men reuile you, and ſpeake all maner of euill againſt you for my ſake, falſelie ; reioice and be glad, for great is your reward in heauen.

Matt. 5. (margin)

As you ſhuffle with the ſhame, which our Sauiour ſuffe-red on the Croſſe, ſo you doe with his death; affirming that " *Death may* P *in no ſort heere be called a curſe, becauſe death* " *to the godlie is no* q *curſe properlie, nor puniſhment of ſinne,* " *but a beneſite and aduantage.* You are too yoong a Doc-tor to controll Saint Auſten, whoſe wordes I haue alledged in the Treatiſe at large. His reſolution is, that when Paule ſaieth, Chriſt was made a curſe for vs, he meant Chriſt died for vs. *Idem eſt mortuus quod maledictus, quoniam mors ipſa ex maledicto eſt.* It is all one to ſaie, Chriſt died for vs, and hee was accurſed for vs ; becauſe death came from the curſe. This you denie ; for that the godlie after death goe to heauen, which is rather a beneſite then a curſe to them. Good Sir, it is no beneſite of death it ſelfe, but Chriſtes bleſſing after death, that departing this life, wee goe to heauen. Did you incourage men to die, ſince of force for ſinne dwelling in their bodies they muſt die; it were well ſaid, that death is reſt from their labours, and an en-trance into bliſſe, for ſo Chriſt hath prouided for his, when they goe hence : but if you will reaſon what death is in it ſelfe, you muſt reſolue it to be a part of Gods curſe inflicted on
Adam-

P Pag. 45. (margin)
q Pag 44.
Vide pag. 92 (margin)

Adam for sinne, and from him naturallie deriued to all his posteritp;from which though our soules be exempted,and our bodies shall be restored,yet it remaineth to this day a part of Adams punishment, which can not bee auoided, though it must not bee feared, because Christ hath ouerthrowne the force and feare therof with his death. By one man(saith Paul meaning Adam)sinne entred into the world, and by sin death. I hope it entred not as a blessing;God doth not vse to blesse sinne:but it entered as a part of the wages of sinne, or curse for sinne, and so it doth and shall continue,to the ende. The last enemie that shall be destroied(saith Paul)is death;when this mortall hath put on immortalitie,then is death swallowed vp in victorie; till then the sting of death is sinne. If the death of the bodie be an enemie and must be destroied by Christs second comming,then is it no blessing;for those shall increase,when he appeareth in glorie. If Christ be in you(saith Paul)the spirit is life for righteousnes sake, the bodie is deade because of sinne. If sinne bee the cause of death yet seazing on our bodies,it can bee no blessing,that riseth from so badde a cause; neither could the resurrection of our bodies,which Christ hath promised,and we expect at the last day, bee so great a ioy as it is; if the corruption of our bodies in the meane time were a blessing. Gods blessings be not contrarie one to the other.S.Austen learnedlie resolueth this question in this sort. Boni bene moriuntur,quamuis mors sit malum. The godlie die well, though death be euill. Mori hominis ex pœna peccati est, quia ex peccato factum est vt moriatur.The death of mans body commeth from the punishment of sinne, becouse sinne brought it to passe, that man dieth. This conclusion in exact wordes Prosper collecteth out of saint Austen. Mors etiam piorum pœna peccati est.The corporall death euen of the godlie is the punishment of sinne. This collection to bee true,S.Austen himselfe confirmeth. Si vero quem mouet,cur vel ipsam patiantur, si & ipsa pœna peccati est, quorum per gratiam reatus aboletur tam ista quæstio in alio nostro opere, quod inscripsimus de Baptismo

Rom 5.

1.Cor.15.

Rom.8.

August.de ciuitate dei. lib.13.cap.5. August.contra Faustum.lib. 14.cap.3. Prosper in sentent.ex August.148. August.de ciuitate dei lib.13.cap.4.

*tiʃmo paruulorum tractata ac ʃoluta eʃt.*If it moue any man, why they, whoʃe ʃinne is aboliʃhed by grace, doe yet ʃuffer the death of the bodie, if that death bee a puniʃhment of ʃinne, that Queʃtion I haue handled and reʃolued in another worke of mine, intituled of the baptiʃme of infants. **The effect of his reʃolution here is this.** * *Per ineffabilem dei miʃericordiam & ipʃa pæna vitiorum tranʃit in arma virtutis, & fit meritū iuʃti, etiam ʃuppliciū peccatoris, NON QVIA MORS BONVM ALIQVOD FACTA EST, QVAE ANTEA MALVM RVIT, ʃed tantam deus fidei præʃtitit gratiam, vt mors inʃtrumentum fieret, per quod tranʃiretur in vitam.* By the vnʃpeakeable mercie of God, the verie wages of vice becommeth an inʃtrument of vertue, and the puniʃhment of a ʃinner is made the merite of the righteous: not that death, VVHICH BEFORE VVAS EVILL, IS NOVV BECOME ANIE GOOD THING, but God hath ʃhewed ʃo great fauour to our faith, that death is the waie or meane by which wee ʃhall paʃʃe to life. **And ʃo concludeth, that** y *Pie fideliterque tolerando auget meritum patientiæ, non aufert vocabulum pænæ;* By induring (**the death of the bodie**) religiouʃlie and faithfullie the merite of patience is increaʃed, but the name of the puniʃhment is not altered. **And if death were nowe no part of the puniʃhment of our ʃinnes, but a gaine to the godlie as you woulde haue it, by what meanes I praie you came it ʃo to bee? Not by the reʃurrection of Chriʃt conquering death, and changing the nature of it? When till Chriʃt was riʃen, death was a puniʃhment to the faithfull themʃelues; and conʃequentlie when Chriʃt died for our ʃinnes, hee tooke vpon him a part of our curʃe, which after he turned, as you ʃaie, into a bleʃʃing.** z *Primus parens propter tranʃgreʃʃionem mortis pænam intulit, verum ʃuperueniens Chriʃtus hæc omnia abʃtulit. Neque enim mors, vltra mors eʃt, ʃed nomen tantum habet mortis.* Our firʃt parent by his tranʃgreʃʃion brought in the puniʃhment of death: But Chriʃt comming after tooke all away. For death is no longer death, but hath onelie the name of death, a *Ipʃam mortem*

Marginal notes:
*Ibidem.

? Ibidem cap. 5

ᶻ Chryʃoʃt. in gen. Homil. 29.

ᵃ Auguʃt. de ciuitate dei. lib. 10. cap. 24.

tem,quamuis esset pæna peccati,pro nobis tamen sine peccato Christus persoluit. Death it selfe, (saieth Austen)though it were the punishment of sinne, yet Christ that was without sinne vndertooke it for our sakes. And so for anie thing you haue yet said, or shall euer be able to say, Saint Austens assertion, which I cited before,standeth good ; that because the death of the bodie was a part of the curse inflicted vpon Adams sinne, Christ vndertaking that part of the curse for vs , that is, dying in his bodie, loosed vs from the whole curse of the lawe.

Againt Chrysostomes iudgement, that not onelie death, but the very kind of death which Christ died,was accursed by the very words of the lawe, saying, accursed is hee that hangeth on a tree;you replie: [b] *Not euery one that is hanged is cursed: for manie innocents and martyrs are hanged, who are most blessed ; but euerie one that is iustlie hanged is accursed; and so, was Christ here* [c] *condemned by the iust sentence of the lawe to paie his debts , for whome hee had willinglie and aduisedlie vndertaken. And so indeede he bare the true curse of the lawe.* Chrysostoms iudgement is as I reported it. [d] *Crux signum erat mortis maledicta,mortis omnium diffamatissima. Hoc enim solū mortis genus maledictioni erat obnoxium.* The crosse was a signe of a cursed death,of a death most infamous . This onelie kinde of death was subiected to the curse.And againe. [e] *Non quēuis mors isti similis est,ista namq; omnium videbatur esse probrosissima,ista plena dedecore, ista maledicta.Propterea Iudæi satagebant eum ista morte interimere, vt si nemo abstineret ab eo quod esset occisus, abstineret tamen vel ideo,quod hoc pacto esset occisus.* Not euerie death was like to this. This seemed most reprochfull,most shamefull and accursed.Therefore the Iewes laboured to put him to this kind of death,that if no man would refuse him because he was killed, at least yet they should forsake him, for that he died this vild kinde of death. The kinde of death which Christ submitted himself vnto was a shameful, + a cursed kind of death,as for the cause of christs death,Chrysostom was far

from

Marginal notes:
[b] *Pag.38.*
[c] *Pag.39.*
[d] Chrysost.in demonstrat. quod Christus sit deus.tom.5.
[e] Idem in epist. ad philip.ser.7.

from thinking Chriſt was iuſtlie hanged; he ſaith Chriſt thus honoured his father, *Non coactus, nec inuitus, ſed & hoc ex ſua ipſius virtute;* not conſtrained, nor vnwilling, but of his own virtue or humilitie. And the Apoſtle warranteth Chryſoſtoms ſpeech, for he ſaith; g Chriſt humbled himſelfe, and was obedient to the death, euen to the death of the croſſe. But what warranteth

" your ſpeech that h *Chriſt was hanged on the tree by the iuſt ſen-*
" *tence of the lawe?* I had thought he had ſuffered the i iuſt for the vniuſt; and hauing no ſinne had beene willinglie, and by no ſentence of the law, hanged on a tree. k *Is it wrong (you*

" *aſke) for the law to lay the penaltie on the ſuretie, when the debtor*
" *cannot diſcharge it? But if it be meere and true iuſtice, and no*
" *wrong, then was Chriſt by the iuſt ſentence of the lawe hanged on*
" *the tree, and ſo he bare indeed the true curſe of the law.* l *For though*
" *God alwayes loued and imbraced Chriſt in regard of his owne in-*
" *nocent perſon, yet in another regard of our perſon, which he ſuſtai-*
" *ned, we may ſay God* HATED *him, God* CVRSED *him.* m *Yea he tooke*
" *our perſon on him, and ſo became by our ſins,* SINFVLL, DEFI-
" LED, HATEFVL, & ACCVRSED. Is this the holines of your cauſe you haue in hand, Sir refuter, with a ſimple ſimilitude againſt the ſcriptures, againſt the faith, againſt the fathers, againſt the conſciences of gods people, openly to pronounce the eternall and euerlaſting ſonne of God SINFVL, DEFI-LED, HATEFVL, & accurſed of his father; for that he took vpon him the puniſhment of our ſinnes? Your ſimilitude had need be ſound, that ſhall beare the waight of theſe wordes; if you faile, can you tell howe deeply you come within the iuſt ſentence of gods law, for opening your irreligicus mouth against God, and his ſonne? but thereof anon.

In the meane while, becauſe with ſcorning Chryſoſtom, you make way to your vnholy conceit, that Chriſt being truly ac-curſed in ſoule for the guilt of mans ſinne n *was iuſtlie hanged*
" *by the ſentence of the lawe, and ſay it is* VAINE *and* SENCE-
" LESSE *to thinke the Apoſtle ſpeaketh there, of two kinds of cur-*
" *ſes (as Chryſoſtom affirmeth) but rather that* o *hanging on a tree*

is

f Ibidem.

g Phil.2.

h Pag.39.

i 1.Pet.3.
k Pag:39

l Pag.42.

m Ibidem.

n Pag.35

o Pag.40

is set downe as a part for the whole execution of Gods iust curse, „
and argueth the whole to be on Christ, let vs see whether you, „
oz Chrysostom, bee deceiued. ᵖ As many as are of the workes
of Gods lawe, are vnder the curse, (saith Paul;) for it is written, ᵖGalat. 3
Cursed is euery man that continueth not in all things which are
written in the booke of the lawe, to do them. We shall agree
I hope that this is Gods curse, both temporall and eternall,
laid on the bodies and soules of sinners, foz transgressing a-
nie part of Gods commandementes, pzoposed in his lawe;
and to this all that haue sinned are subiected, because it is the
GENERALL curse, EXECVTED by God himselfe vpon ALL
sinne committed, either in deede, word, oz thought. ᑫ From
this curse (saith Paul) Christ hath redeemed vs, beeing made a ᑫGalat. 3
curse for vs, as it is written, Cursed is euerie one, that hangeth
on a tree. If this be all one with the other, then euerie man
that transgressed Gods law in thought, wozd, oz deede, was
by the sentence of the lawe to bee hanged on a tree. Shewe
that sentence in the lawe, and Chrysostom shall yeelde vnto
you; if you cannot, then haging on a tree is no necessarie part
of the generall curse of God vpon all sinners, and conse-
quentlie being no part of it, it is not all one with it, neither
can it argue the whole to haue been in Christ. [*How standeth* „
the Apostles reason then that Christ was made a curse?] where in „
sinne there are two thinges, the committing of it, and the
reuenging of it by God oz man in this life oz the next; and
magistrates had vnder Moses, as they haue vnder Christ,
power giuen them from aboue ʳ as Gods ministers to take ʳRom. 13.
vengeance (in this life) on him that doth euill; the Apostle
knowing that Christ, though he committed no sinne, was yet
content to beare the punishment due to sinne in his bodie on
the tree; and by his smart to abolish our fault: citeth a place
out of Moses, where the Iudiciall and corporall punishment
of a man by death is not onelie called a curse, but counted a
satisfaction foz sinne, which being suffered the law had ended
his forme vpon the sufferer. And so concludeth that Christ
ℕ n i.   receauing

receauing a Iudiciall, and corporall punishment of death for our sinne, not onlie therein suffered the curse, but satisfied the force of the law, & by that curse of his suffering redeemed vs from the curse of our transgressing. The place cited out of Moses is this; ʃ if a man haue committed an offence worthy of death, and is (by the lawe) to die, and thou hang him on a tree: his body shall not remaine all night on the tree, but thou shalt bury him the same day; for the curse of God is (alreadie laid or executed) on him that is hanged. This most apparantly was a publike punishment executed by the magistrate vpon the body of the offender; and because by his open and shamefull death, which Moses rightlie calleth the curse of God, hee had satisfied the sentence of the Iudiciall lawe, God commandeth no farther reproch to be offered his bodie, in suffering it to hang in all mens eies any longer, but to bee buried the same date; For that by his death the curse of God ceased. The difference betweene these two curses is soone perceiued. Euerie sinne receaued the first curse, whereof Paul spake before; fewe crimes receaued the iudgement of this seconde kinde of curse which was to bee hanged. The first was inflicted by God himselfe: the second was executed by the magistrate. The first touched bodie and soule, in this life and the next; the second ended with the death of the bodie. The first was committing of sinne, the seconde was suffering for sinne. And therefore Chrysostomes exposition is verie true, when hee saieth; ᵗ The peoplewere obnoxious to another curse, which was this; Cursed is euerie one, that continueth not in that which is written in the booke of the lawe, for there was not one of them that had fulfilled the whole Lawe; but Christ insteede of that, tooke vpon him another curse, which said, cursed is euery one that hangeth on the tree. He that should take away the first curse, must not bee subiect to the same, but vndertake an other in place thereof, and by that dissolue the first. As if one being adiudged to die (for some crime) an other, no way guilty of the same, but willing to die for him, should deliuer him from the

punishment.

ʃ Deuter.21

ᵗ Chrysost. in ca.3. ad Galat.

punishment: So did Christ; not being subiect to the curse of trãs-gression, insteede thereof he tooke an other curse, and dissolued the curse that laie on them.

[Before a man can be accursed by his death, hee must, you saie, be iustlie hanged; for manie *Innocents and martyrs are hanged who are most blessed.*] Innocentes and martyrs, bee their soules neuer so blessed, maie beare in their bodies a shamefull death, as Christ did in his; and that is a kinde of corporall curse, though by men bniustlie inflicted, euen as death in the godlie is a remnant of Gods curse bpon sinne, though their soules bee blessed before and after death. Pea the worde KALAL whence the Hebrewes deriue that which with them signifieth a curse, noteth also to make vilde and contemptible, as if shame, reproch, and contempt were the greatest outwarde curse, that coulde befall anie man in this life. The cause why ince suffer it, shall make it iust or bniust; but wee must call thinges by those names, which GOD first allotted them. Nowe death, shame, wrong, reproch, and such like, God ordayned at first to bee punishmentes of sinne, and so partes of the curse due to sinne. If wee suffer at mens handes for pietp, that which God appointed to be the wages of iniquity, so wee bee patient and willing to abide the triall, which is righteous with God, though iniurious from men, the name is not altered, but the rewarde increased. Pea God it is, that causeth iudgement to beginne at his own house oftentimes, by the handes of persecutors; hee doth bs right, when men doe bs wrong; and dealeth not with bs according to our sinnes in the greatest wrongs that can be done bs. Therfore martyrs and innocents may do well to remember, that God hath cause enough, though man haue none; and so submit themselues as worthie of worse from Gods handes. But none of these thinges may be saide of our Sauiour, who alone among all the children of men wanted sinne, and suffered wrong; and therefore his punishments with God were

iust,

iuſt, not by his deſeruing, but by his deſiring to ſuffer foʒ man. How then commeth it to paſſe, that martyʒs, which are ſinners befoʒe God, are vniuſtlie hanged, becauſe they deſerue no ſuch thing at mens handes ; and Chʒiſt who was moſt innocent befoʒe men, and moſt righteous befoʒe God, you wil needs haue to be iuſtly hanged?

[*The ſuerty* (you ſay) *by his ſuertiſhip is a debtor to the creditor and to the law; and ſo* Chʒiſt, *though moſt innocent in himſelf, yet was hee iuſtlie hanged, as our ſuretie, by the iuſt ſentence of the law.*] You miſtake, Sir Confuter, as wel the ſentence of the lawe, as the ſuertiſhip of Chʒiſt. Foʒ though mans lawe permit, which is the rule of charitie, that men ſhould beare each others burdens, and vndertake one foʒ another in money matters, and ſuch like things which God leaueth in each mans will and power; yet tell me I pʒaie, what lawe, Gods oʒ mans, permitteth a murderer oʒ like offender to be ſpared, and an other, that is willing, to bee hanged in his ſteede? I thinke mans law will allow you no ſuch ſuertiſhip, I am ſure Gods lawe will not. [u] As I liue, ſaith the Lord, the ſoule that ſinneth, that ſoule ſhall die. The wickednes of the wicked ſhall bee vpon himſelfe. Hee ſhall haue then no ſuerties to die foʒ him, much leſſe ſhall his ſuertie be compelled to die by the ſentence of the law. Their monie men may giue awaie; but their liues they may not, till God call foʒ them; and if not their liues, much leſſe their ſoules by anie ſentence of the law. The ſonne of God did not by LAVV, but by LOVE interpoſe himſelfe to beare our ſinnes; [x] So God loued the worlde, that hee gaue his onely begotten ſonne, that whoſoeuer beleeueth in him ſhould not periſh, but haue euerlaſting life. Yea [y] the ſonne of God loued vs, and gaue himſelfe for vs, not by anie obligation to the lawe, foʒ hee was aboue the lawe, and could not be bound by the lawe; and we were condemned by the ſentence of the law, and not put to finde ſuerties. The eternall wiſedome and counſell of God then out of his ineſtimable loue towardes vs, without the lawe, and

Marginal notes:
[u] Ezech. 18
[x] Iohn 3.
[y] Galat. 2

and before the law decreed, as to create vs, so to redeeme vs, by Christ his sonne. And the sonne not as debtour to anie, nor for anie, but of his good will and fauour toward vs, offered himselfe to suffer for vs whatsoeuer the iustice of his father would impose. Wherein he became not a Suertie bound to the law; but a Mediatour to God, and a Redeemer of man. Suerties that stand bounde and must paie the debt, may not looke to be Mediators; and he that redeemeth a prisoner from the enemie is not bound, but content so to doe. And that the death of Christ should be paide as a debt to the lawe whereto Christ was bounde, is to mee a strange position. I tooke Christes sufferings all this while for a voluntarie oblation to God, and not for a due obligation to the lawe, and himselfe to be a mediatour, not a debtour; his death I reckned to bee a richer offer, then man coulde owe, and a greater price then the lawe could exact. And therefore the newe testament of mercie, grace, and glorie was made by his bloud, which are other manner of purchases, then the due paiment of mans debt. Howe coulde that bee due vnto the lawe, which ouerthrew the lawe? Sinners, such as we are, were to die by the lawe; but that the sonne of God should die for vs, what lawe did or coulde require that at his handes? you shall doe well therefore to leaue these dangerous discourses, and learne to saie with the scripture and fathers, that loue, not lawe; desire, not debt; mercy, not necessity brought the sonne of God from his throne in heauen, to his crosse on earth.

[Such was the sentence of the lawe, you will saie, that without death he could not redeeme vs.] Naie such was his loue, you should saie, that euen with his death hee would redeeme vs. *Cum posset nobis etiam non moriendo succurrere,* [1]Greg. moral. *subuenire tamen moriendo hominibus voluit: quia nos videlicet* lib.20.cap.16. *minus amasset nisi & vulnera nostra susciperet, nec vim suæ dilectionis nobis ostenderet, nisi hoc quod a nobis tolleret, ad tempus ipse sustineret. Passibiles quippe mortalesque nos reperit, & qui nos existere fecit ex nihilo, reuocare etiam sine sua morte potuit à passione. Sed vt quanta esset virtus Compassionis ostenderet, fieri pro nobis dignatus est, quod esse nos voluit, vt in semetipso temporaliter mortem susciperet, quam à nobis in perpetuum fugaret.* Christ when he might haue succoured vs without dying, woulde rather helpe man by dying (saieth Gregorie:) because he had loued vs lesse, if he had not taken to himselfe our woundes, neither had hee shewed vs the strength of his loue, vnlesse hee had for a tyme sustayned that, from which he deliuered vs. Hee founde vs miserable and mortall; yet hee that made vs of nothing might haue recalled vs from our miserie without his owne death. But that hee might declare howe greate the vertue of Compassion is, hee vouchsafed to bee that, which hee appointed vs to bee, that receauing a temporall death in himselfe, hee might chase it from vs for euer. [a] Those (saieth Austen) that aske, did GOD so want meanes to deliuer men from the miserie of this mortalitie, that hee woulde haue his onelie begotten sonne to bee made a mortall man, and to suffer death; It is not enough so to refute that wee shewe this waie to be good and agreeable to the diuine excellencie, whereby God vouchsafed to deliuer vs by the Mediatour of God and man Christ Iesus, *verum etiam vt ostendamus* NON ALIVM MODVM POSSIBILEM DEO DEFVISSE, *cuius potestati cuncta aqualiter subiacent, sed sananda nostra miseria conuenientiorem alium modum non fuisse, nec esse oportuisse;* but also that wee shewe God VVANTED NOT OTHER MEANES, to whose power all thinges are subiect, but that neither there was, nor coulde bee a more conuenient way to heale our misery. For what was so needefull to raise vp our hope, and to free mens mindes from despairing immortalitie, being alreadie deiected by the condition of their mortalitie; as to make euident shewe ynto vs, how much God esteemed vs, and how much hee loued vs? whereof what plainer or perfiter proofe could be made, then that the sonne of God, remaining that he was, would take from vs & for vs that which he was not, and vouchsafe to be amongst

[a] August. de Trinitate lib. 13.cap.10

vs : and firſt without anie deſerte of his to beare our miſeries, and vpon vs, then beleeuing how greatly God loued vs, and hoping where afore wee deſpaired, to beſtowe without all merit of ours, yea when wee deſerued euill at his handes, the giftes of his grace, with bounty no way prouoked by vs. And ſo Ambroſe.

[b] By one mans death the world was redeemed, Chriſt might, if hee woulde, haue refrained from death ; but hee neither refuſed death as vnprofitable, neither could he haue ſaued vs any better waie then by dying. So that no legall neceſſitie, much leſſe Judiciall ſeueritie, brought Chriſt to his Croſſe, but to teach vs obedience to God by his example, to demonſtrate his loue to vs by refuſing nothing for our ſakes, and to declare his owne power, whoſe weakeneſſe was ſtronger then all his and our enemies, and to ſtrengthen our patience, and giue vs comfort in all the troubles of this life, he choſe the paynefull and ſhamefull death of the Croſſe, and there ſhewed ſo perfitte a patterne of obedience, innocence, patience, that the Angels themſelues did admire it.

[b] Ambroſ. de fide reſurrect.

So farre you make Chriſt ſuertie for vs that in taking [c] our perſon on him, hee became by our ſinne ſinnefull, defiled, hatefull and accurſed. Similitudes, if you ſucke nothing from them but that which is agreeable to þ truth, in teaching may be tolerated; in concluding they will halt. That Chriſt is [d] a ſuerty, we find it once mentioned in the ſcriptures; but not to þ law to pay our debtes, but [d] of a better teſtament, euen of the new couenant of grace eſtabliſhed in his bloud, wherof he is alſo the mediator & prieſt. Now he died for vs, not as a ſuertie bound to þ law, but as a mediator to God for vs, he interpoſed himſelf of his own accord, to yæld ſuch recompence vnto his father, as hee ſhould be pleaſed to accept for vs. If you will næds vſe ſimilitudes, vſe rather the ſimilitude of a mediator, and Redæmer, which the ſcriptures often call him, then of a ſuerty; therby to bind him not onely to ſuffer the paines of hell in our ſtæde, but alſo to defile him with our ſinnes

[c] Pag. 42

[d] Hebre. 7

and

and make him hatefull to God by our curse. No similitudes "can proue Christ in *taking our person on him to be* S I N N E-"F V L L, D E F I L E D, H A T E F V L, *and* A C C V R S E D; and therefore your vncleane mouth, and vncleaner heart, that thus speake, and thinke of the sonne of God, are worthier of castigation, then of refutation. I know you will pretend the Apostles wordes, ᶜ God made him sinne for vs that knewe no sinne; but howsoeuer some late writers turne sinne into sinner, and thence giue cause of these and the like speaches, the church of God from the beginning hath warilie declined such irreuerent wordes, and yet plainelie confesse the truth. That God M A D E H I M S I N N E, hath two good and approued senses; one that he made him a sacrifice for sinne, and so the clenser of sinne, and no waie defiled by our sinne: the other, that he punished our sinnes in him, and vsed him as hee doth sinners. ᶠ They that know(saith Austen) the scriptures of the olde testament, acknowledge this that I saie. Not once, but often and verie often it is found; Sacrifices for sinnes, are called sinnes. Then him that knewe no sinne God made sinne for vs, that is a sacrifice for sinne. Christ was made sinne in that he was offered to abolish sinne. And againe, ᵍ *peccatum vocabatur in lege sacrificium pro peccato, assidue lex hoc commemorat, non semel, non iterum, sed sapissime. Tale peccatum erat Christus. Peccatum non habebat, & peccatum erat; peccatum erat, quia sacrificium pro peccato.* The sacrifice for sinne is in the law called sinne. The lawe still so vseth the word, not once, nor twice, but verie often. Such a sinne was Christ, he had no sinne, and yet he was sinne. He was sinne, because he was the sacrifice for sinne. So Ambrose. ʰ Because Christ was offered for sinne, worthilie is he said to be made sinne, because in the lawe the sacrifice that is offered for sinne is called sinne. This waie if you conster S. Paules wordes, they conclude directlie against your irreligious supposition. For if Christ when hee tooke vs into his bodie, did clense our sinnes by the offering of himselfe; hee became not defiled by our sinnes. Hee did not clense vs

that

ᵉ 2.Cor.5

ᶠ Aug.de verbis do. secund. Iohan.serm.48

ᵍ Idem de verbis Apostoli. serm.7.

ʰ Ambros in 2. Corinth.ca.5

that was defiled by vs. Howsoeuer you take those wordes; ¹ Such an high priest it became vs to haue (saieth the Apostle)as was holy,harmlesse, VNDEFILED, SEPARATE from sinners. If the Priest were defiled, the sacrifice could not be accepted. If Christ were separate from sinners, then was hee not polluted by sinners. He tooke our sinnes vnto him, not to drawe anie pollution from them, but to make þ purgation of them. He that coulde clense vs from our sinnes, howe much more coulde hee keepe himselfe from breeing defiled with our sinnes? If we follow the other sense of S.Pauls wordes, that Christ was made sinne for vs, that is the punishment of our sinne, wee must take heede that wee bring him not within the guiltinesse of our sinnes, as we doe within the punishment of our sinnes. ᵏ *Suscepit Christus sine reatu supplicium nostrum, vt inde solueret reatum nostrum, & finiret etiam supplicium nostrum.* Christ vndertooke (saith Austen) our punishment without our guilt, that so hee might remit our guilt, and ende our paine. ¹ Christ (saieth Cyprian) endured by *Moses* and his owne Apostle to bee called a curse, and sinne, *pro similitudine pœna, non culpa*, for the likenesse of the paine, not of the fault. ᵐ *Dilexit*(nos Christus)*dulciter, sapienter, fortiter. Dulce nempe dixerim,quod carnem induit; cautum,quod culpam cauit;forte,quod mortem sustinuit.* Christ (saith Bernard) loued vs sweetelie, wiselie, stronglie. Sweetelie in that he tooke our flesh; wiselie, in that hee shunned our guiltinesse; strong'ie, in that he suffered death for vs. If Christ tooke the paine, but not the guilt of our sinnes, howe came hee to bee defiled by our sinnes? It must needes be either in ioining and vniting himselfe vnto vs, or in answering and suffering for vs . Our vnion with Christ doth sanctifie vs, it defileth not him. We are as neere ioyned to Christ nowe raigning in heauen, as wee were to Christ suffering on the Crosse. As wee died with him then in the bodie of his flesh , ⁿ so wee sitte togither with him in heauenlie thinges . But our vnion and communion nowe , though wee bee sinfull and

mortall

Marginal notes:
ⁱ Heb.7.

ᵏ August.cont. Faustum.lib.14 cap.4

ˡCyprian de passione Christi.

ᵐBernard in cantic.serm.30

ˣEphes.21

mortall , doth no waie defile him , no moze did it then, when hee suffered foz vs . If you sate our sinnes wera imputed vnto him , when he was crucisied foz them; that increaseth the perfection of his loue , it argueth not anie pollution of his soule. To die foz wicked men , did not touche him with anie taint of our sinnes , but °GOD (saieth the Apostle) setteth out his loue towardes vs in this, that whiles wee were yet sinners Christ died for vs . The iust therefoze did die foz the vniust, and was no partner of our iniustice ; hee that saued vs from our sinnes , did not defile himselfe with them . And where all this is grounded vppon a simple similitude , that a suertie by vndertaking foz a debtour , maketh the debt his owne, though hee neuer bozrowed the money; it is easilie and trulie aunswered , that Christ did not vndertake wee shoulde not sinne, noz that wee shoulo paie the debt which wee did owe; but when wee had sinned, and were able no waie to aunswere the iustice of GOD, but by our euer-lasting destruction of bodie and soule; it pleased the sonne of God to interpose himselfe, and no waie bound to vs, oz foz vs; to intreate his father ᶠ that in his owne per-son hee might make recompence foz our sinnes ; and so as a Mediatour allowed of God, hee tooke our nature: and freelie, not indebted; willinglie, not constrained; P. Hee gaue himselfe for vs a sacrifice of a sweete sauour vn-to God. As if the whole people of anie lande rebelling against their King, and beeing subdued and readie to be destroied, the Kinges sonne (loath to see his fathers king-dome dispeopled, and so manie wretched men , women, and childzen put to fire and swozde) shoulde impoztune his father at his request to bee gratious vnto them, and to late on him , though hee bre his onelie sonne , what chastisement the father in his wisedome and iustice shall thinke fitte foz the repzessing of the like outrage hereaf-ter : maie anie of those subiectes without extreame ingra-titude

°Rom.5.

P Ephes.5.

titude, and intolerable contumelie reproch the Kings sonne, when hee suffereth for their sakes , that hee is guiltie of their treason, and both DEFILED with it, and HATEFVLL for it ? I will not applie , becaufe it will preffe you too farre; but as mine owne perfwafion is , that no fuch finfull and hatefull wordes haue, or fhould be vfed in the Church of God to the difhonour of his fonne;fo my counfell to the fober and wife reader, is, to ftop his eares, and fhut his eies againft fuch defiled and accurfed fpeeches.

Yon proceede to another proofe, and where the Apoftle faith, Chrift fpoiled Principalities & powers, and made a fhew of them openlie, triumphing ouer them ; vpon thefe wordes you inferre. ¶ Thefe principalities are the diuels ; therefore it is cer- „ ¶Pag 45. taine Chrift FELT THEM to bee the verie inftruments that „ VVROVGHT THE VERIE EFFECTS of Gods wrath VPON „ HIM. This is the firft place where you fpecifie anie effect of „ Gods wrath againft Chrifts foule(for you will haue the foule of Chrift properlie and immediatelie to fuffer the effectes of Gods wrath;) and that you prooue learnedlie and wifelie like your felfe. The diuels haue nothing to do with the foules of men, but either to tempt them to worke in them, or to torment them. To tempt is to trie how faft the faints ftand in the feare and loue of God. And for that caufe the wifdome of god hath from the beginning fuffered all his faints, his owne fonne not excepted to be tempted of fatan. For Chrift coulde not be tempted by the corruption of his heart as we are, but by Satans voice, or by Satans members. Of vs Iames faith ʳEuerie man is tempted, when he is entifed and drawne away by his owne concupifcence. Concupifcence there was none in Chrift. He had no law in his flefh rebelling againft the lawe of his minde, as wee haue; It is in vs the rage of originall finne from which he was free, and therefore he coulde not bee tempted but by the eare, as he was in the defart by fatan himfelf, & by Satans members al the time of his abode on earth. In the harts of men when the diuel preuaileth with temptation

ʳ.Iames.ʃ

there he worketh,leading ſuch as conſent and yęld vnto him
ᶠEpheſ.2. into all wickedneſſe, euen with grœdineſſe:Soᶠhe worketh
in the children of diſobedience, as the Apoſtle teſtifieth. This
ᵗ1.Pet.2.
ᵃ1.Iohn 3. can haue no place in Chriſt, becauſe ᵗ he did no ſinne,neither
was there anie guile found in his mouth. ᵃ He that committeth
ſinne(ſaith ſaint Iohn)is of the diuel,and for this purpoſe appea-
red the ſonne of God, that hee might diſſolue the workes of the
diuell. Then ſince inward temptation by the hart Chriſt could
haue none, and outward temptation by the mouthes ϟ handes
of the wicked is no effect of Gods wrath, but rather a triall
of Gods gifts and graces beſtowed on vs ; It remaineth
" that if *Chriſt felt the diuels as the very inſtruments that wrought*
" *the verie effects of Gods wrath vpon him*,that is vpon his ſoule,
" (for that part of Chriſt you ſay muſt *properly* and *immediatelie*
" *feele the wrath of God*) it reſteth I ſaie by your owne wordes
ϟ Chriſt FELT THE DIVELS TORMENTING HIS SOVLE.
And indeede for ſo much as in executing the true paines of
hell, and of the damned, God hath none other inſtruments
but diuels,you cannot defend that Chriſt ſuffered the paines
of hell, but you muſt graunt that Chriſt felt the diuels, as
inſtruments executing thoſe paines on his ſoule . Nowe
the bodie of man they may torment with touching , as they
did Iobs ; the ſoule they can not, but by poſſeſſing it. For
they can not woorke but where they are , and therefore
they muſt poſſeſſe the ſoule which they torment. Is not here
(Chriſtian Reader)an wholeſome clearke,and an holie cauſe,
that concludeh Chriſtes ſoule was poſſeſſed and tormented of
diuels on the Croſſe? And the proofe is as ridiculous , as
the poſition is impious. Chriſt ˣ ſpoiled principalities and
powers,and openlie triumphed ouer them, ergo (ſay you) hee
ˣPhilip.2. " felt them the inſtruments *of Gods wrath* , by tormenting his
ſoule. If your learning and Logicke ſerue you ſo well, you
may procęde Doctor in dotage when you will. For my part
(Chriſtian Reader) I will giue none other anſwere to theſe
lewd and wicked abſurdities, but that which Iacob ſaid to Si-
meon

meon and Leui; y Into their secret my soule shall not come. To ⟨y Gen.49.⟩
strengthen thee, thou maieſt remember, that Peter saide of
Chꝛiſt. z God anointed Iesus of Nazareth with the holy ghoſt, & ⟨z Acts.10.⟩
with power to heale all that were oppreſſed of the diuell; foꝛ God
was with him; oꝛ elſe that Chꝛiſt ſaid of himſelfe, a The prince ⟨a Iohn.14⟩
of this world commeth, and hath naught in me; oꝛ at leaſt that
the diuels themſelues ſaid to Chꝛiſt; b Iesus the sonne of God ⟨b Matt.8.⟩
WHAT HAVE WE TO DO WITH THEE? Art thou come
to torment vs before the time? And ſo in the Goſpell of ſaint
Luke, the c foule ſpirit when he ſaw Iesus cried out, what haue I ⟨c Luke 8⟩
to doe with thee, Iesus the sonne of God moſt high? I beseech
thee torment me not.

[But perchance I miſtake him.] would God there were
ſo much grace in him, as to reuoke it, oꝛ refuſe it; I woulde
gladlie confeſſe mine errour in miſtaking his woꝛdes: but
what if he go on from bad to woꝛſe? What if he heapeth vp
reaſons as he thinketh, but indæde trifles void of ſenſe and
reaſon to confirme the ſame? c *This reaſon will proue the* ⟨c Pag.45⟩
ſame (ſaith hee) taken from the leſſe to the more. d *Thus do the* ⟨d Pag.46.⟩
members of Chriſt ſuffer. Therefore of neceſſitie Chriſt our head
ſuffered the like. *Yea to the Hebrues hee ſheweth a reaſon which*
can neuer be refuted by the witte of man. e *Chriſt ſuccoured vs* ⟨e Pag.47⟩
not, but wherein hee had experience of our temptations and infir-
mities: but he ſuccoureth vs euen in theſe our temptations of feel-
ling the terrours of God and the ſorrowes of hell. Therefore hee
himſelfe had experience of the ſame. f *Adde hereunto that of* ⟨f Pſa.48.& 49⟩
all abſurdities, this is the greateſt, that meere men ſhould ſuffer
more deeply and bitterly then Chriſt did. You haue moꝛe woꝛds
then witte (Sir Confuter) that pꝛopoſe theſe childiſh argu-
ments foꝛ inuincible reaſons. Your ſelfe ſhall ſæ the weake-
nes of them. g *Whatſoeuer the members of Chriſt, ſay you, did or* ⟨g Pag.46.⟩
ſhall ſuffer, of neceſſitie Chriſt our head ſuffered the like. Meane
you in bodie? oꝛ in ſoule? oꝛ in both? If in bodie, then Chꝛiſt
had his eies put out, foꝛ ſo had Sampſon; he was ſwalowed vp
by a whale, foꝛ ſo was Ionas; hee was caſt into a burning

Dd 3 ⟨furnace,⟩

furnace, for so were Sidrac, Mishac, and Abednego; he was stoned to death, for so were Naboth, Steuen, and others. You meane not in bodie; meane you then in soule? Inwarde assaults of error, lust and sinne Christ neuer had. He was free from all conflicts of heart., that rise in vs from the roote or remorse of sinne; that increase with weakenesse of faith, want of grace, and quenching of Gods spirite. The terrors of minde which wee feele through conscience of our vnworthinesse, ignorance of Gods counsell, and distrust of Gods fauour hee neuer felt : his faith admitted no doubting, his loue excluded all fearing, his hope reiected all despairing. So that howe you shoulde make a falser proposition, and more repugnant to the Apostles wordes which you alledge then this which you haue made, I by no meanes can conceiue. Hee was tempted in all thinges a like except sinne. Then neither the rootes, partes, nor fruites of sinne must bee in him. But the Apostle that excepteth sinne, excepteth all sinnefull adherentes. The punishment of sinns which proceedeth from the iustice of GOD, and is no sinne, that Christ might and did beare; but in no wise those terrours and feares of conscience which proceede from sinne, and augment sinne, as doubting, distrusting, despairing, in which GOD reuengeth sinne with sinne; these muste bee farre from Christ, vnlesse wee will wrappe him within the snares of our sinnes. The feare of Gods Maiestie armed with mightie power to reuenge sinne, is profitable to keepe vs from sinne; therein Christ may communicate with vs, though not to that ende, for he could not sinne; but fearing, doubting, or distrusting that God will for our manifold sinnes cast vs from his presence, and condemne vs to hell, commeth in vs from the guiltinesse of conscience and weakenesse of faith and hope, which in Christ neither had, nor coulde haue anie place.

[But

[But *the Apostle* (you saie) *sheweth a reason, which can neuer bee refuted by the witte of man. Christ succoured vs not, but wherein he had experience of our temptations.*] Are those woordes in the Apostle? No(you will saie)but collected from the Apostles woordes, where hee saith k In that Christ suffered being tempted he can helpe those that are tempted. Hence you conclude vpon your owne warrant,that Christ can succour vs in no temptation but whereof himselfe had first experience; and this you proclaime to be irrefutable. Such lips such lettice; such doctors such diuinitie. Your collcaion, Sir Refuter, is not onelie farre different from the Apostles woordes, but euidentlie repugnant to the christian faith and truth. The Apostle giueth not here the cause why Christ is able to helpe vs in our miseries and necessities, for he is able in that he is God to do what he will; but hee sheweth that our high Priest is l faithfull and mercifull, that is willing and readie to heare vs, and helpe vs in all our afflicions and troubles, for so much as in his owne person hee woulde feele our temptations and infirmities,that he might be the better able to helpe vs in hauing more compassion on vs. And this is that the Apostle saith in the fourth chapter of this Epistle: m Wee haue not an high Priest , which can not bee touched with the feeling of our infirmities, but was in all things (or through-lie) tempted alike except sinne . So that his sufferinges made him the more mercifull and faithfull ; because he knoweth best as well our naturall infirmities, as our manifolde miseries.

This for the sense of the Apostle, nowe to the truth of your collection. C H R I S T S V C C O V R E T H V S N O T, *but wherein he hath felt the same.* Meane you Christ is not able or not willing? For you saie, hee succoureth vs not. To saie hee is not able, is blasphemie ; because he is God,and God I hope can succour vs in all our miseries, without suffering those things which we doe. To say he will not(though the Apostles word bee Δύναται, hee is able) is as false in

Pag.47.
Heb.2.
Heb.2.ver.17
Heb.4.

it.

it selfe, and as iniurious to Christ.   For then Christ will
neuer helpe anie man that is sicke, because hee neuer felt
anie disease of bodie, nor anie whose bones are broken, be-
cause his were whole: nor anie Martyr that burneth in fire,
because hee died on the crosse; the blinde, deafe, dumbe,
lanie, and a thousand such like Christ will neuer heare, nor
helpe, because he suffered not the same . [You speake of
ghostlie temptations, you will saie, not of bodily afflictions.]
Saint Paule speaketh of both, and Christ had experience of
both; and therefore if your collection be false and absurde in
the one, it will neuer bee sound and assured in the other.
But come to your owne pitch . Will Christ deliuer no
man from blindnesse and hardnesse of heart, because hee
neuer endured either? Will he not aide vs to represse the
lusts of our flesh, because he neuer was tempted with them?
Will he not helpe our vnbeliefe, because his faith was al-
waies strong? Will he not saue anie from desperation, be-
cause he neuer despaired? Will hee not cure frenzie, and
furie, because hee was neuer out of his wittes? Nei-
ther did hee, nor will hee cast out Diuels, because him-
selfe was not possessed? Is this the reason that cannot
bee refuted by mans witte which euerie childe maie pre-
sentlie controlle ? In deede you speake truer then you
are ware of, if your deuise maie bee receiued . For
you doe not sticke to defile Christ with our sinnes, to asto-
nish and amaze all the partes and powers of his minde, to
torment him with Diuels, and in the ende to adiudge him
to the death of the soule, which hath in it blindnesse and
hardnesse of heart, infidelitie, and what not? Yea it is with

" you: ⁿ of all absurdities the greatest, that meere men, although
    " they bee reprobates, shoulde suffer more deepely then Christ did,
" ᵒ For Gods iustice, saie you, shoulde bee as seuere on Christ, as
    " on anie reprobate, and yet they suffer reprobation, despera-
tion, damnation.

From hence you go to another of your holie mysteries;
and

and as if you had not done the Lord of glorie wrong enough with these irreuerent and irreligious speaches, you take from him in his passion at your pleasure, not only his vertues & graces, but euen his sense, memorie & vnderstanding, & leaue him often times when you list your selues, *amazed, astonished, and forgetfull of himselfe for feare, yea so distempered, disturbed, distracted, & ouerwhelmed &* ALL CONFOVNDED *in his whole humanity, both in all the powers of his soule and senses of his body, that he knew not what he said or did.* God grant, (Sir Refuter) you be wel in your wits, that depriue the Sauiour of the world when you will, of all sense, memorie, & vnderstanding. [The euangelists, you wil say, in expresse words affirme that Christ in the garden was *astonished* & grieuously perplexed.] Haue you the skill, when the scriptures saie, that Christ beganne to bee astonished and perplexed, to stretch ye beginning to the highest degree of all astonishment that maie light on the Reprobate in this life, or the damned in the next? when the holie ghost toucheth a naturall infirmity common to Christ with all the godlie in the like cases, doth your conscience serue you to make of that not onlie a general and total distemper, but an Infernall confusion of all the powers of his soule, and senses of his bodie? had you consulted S. Ierom, hee would haue taught you an other lesson. *Dominus vt veritatem probaret assumpti hominis, vere quidem contristatus est; sed ne passio in animo eius dominaretur per propassionem capit contristari. Aliud est enim contristari, aliud incipere contristari, &c.* The Lorde to shew himselfe a true man, was sorrowfull in verie deede, not that any passion ouerswaied his minde, but he began to be touched with the affection of sorrow. It is one thing to be sorrowfull, and an other to begin to be sorrowfull; his sorrow was not for any feare to suffer, since he came of purpose to suffer, and reproued *Peter* as too feareful, but for that most wretched *Iudas,* and the weakenes of all his Apostles, and the reiection of the whole nation of the Iewes, and the miserable destruction of Ierusalem, And if heretickes doe interpret

Pag. 55.
Pag. 53.

*Mark. 14.
*Math. 26.

*Ierom. in Matth. ca. 26

this

this sorrowe of heart, not for our Saviours affection towardes them that shoulde perish., but for a perturbation of minde, let them answere me, howe they expounde that which *Ezechiel* speaketh in the person of God, and in all these thinges thou didst make me sorrowfull. Saint Ierome saieth, the wordes enforce no more, then that Christ began to bee sorrowfull and perplexed, and if anie man stretch them farther hee giueth him the note of an hereticke; and though I refraine that worde because I hope you doe it of ignorance and not of malice, yet I cannot excuse you from a dangerous errour, and that in foure speciall pointes. First you mistake the cause whence this feare arose; secondlie you extende it farther then in trueth you shoulde; thirdlie you continue it longer then with anie warrant you may; and fourthlie by pretence thereof you chalenge Christes prayers in the garden not onelie with want of good memorie, but with flat repugnancie to the knowne will of God; which is euident sinne,

Concerning the first I am resolued, as in the treatise before I haue specified, that the cause of Christes agonie, could not procede, but from his submission to the maiestie of God sitting in iudgement, or from his compassion on mans miserie, or from both. You will haue it procede from " *the intolerable horrors of Gods fiery wrath equall to hell*; And where Cain saide, The horror of my sinne is heauier then I can beare, you doubt not but ˣ *Christ as touching the vehemencie of the paine, was as sharpelie touched euen as the Reprobates themselues, yea if it may be, more extraordinarilie.* You that are so well acquainted with the horrors of the Reprobate for their sinnes, that you dare attribute them to Christ, can you tell what they are? is it speculation that you speake of, or experience; that you dare thus subiect the sonne of God to the same terrors and horrors of conscience; which namelie Cain as you saie, and other reprobates haue felt? I praie you, Sir, in so waightie matters as maie amounte to

heresie.

Vide pag. 17

ᵃ Pag. 80

ˣ Pag. 81,

heresie and open blasphemy, plaie not with generall termes, so as neither you vnderstande pour selfe, noz anie man else can conceiue pour meaning . The terrozs of the wicked in this life wee can coniecture , you canne perhaps liuelie describe them, but foz ought that wee learne by the scrip, tures they are such , as without hozrible impietie you cannot ascribe vnto the Sauiour of the wozlde. Remozse of sinne committed, vexing and gnawing the conscience, is the first of their paines , which suffereth them night noz daie to take anie rest . Secondlie , the feare that God, whome they haue despised, hath likewise reiected them and is become their enemie, and therefoze from him they looke foz nothing, but the iust vengeance of their sinnes both in this life and the nexte , so pursueth them , that they tremble and flie when no man followeth them . Thirdlie the griefe to foz see themselues excluded from the fellowship of that ioie and blisse, which is pzouided foz the saintes of GOD, which Chrysostom saieth is far more bitter then the paine of hel , doth make them sinke foz sozrowe . Lastlie the continuall terrour of that dzeadfull iudgement which shall be pzonounced , of that hozrible confusion which then shall o- uerwhelme them ; and of those eternall and intollerable flames of fire in which they shall burne; the verie terrour I saie and hozrour thereof doeth so afflict and tozment them, as if they pzesentlie felt it . Moze wozdes may bee vsed, and perhaps moze vehement to amplifie their paine ; but these are the partes and causes of that feare and hozrour, which pursueth the wicked foz their haynous offences . Can anie of these, (Sir Refuter,) bee applied to Chzist? Dare you but offer so much as the mention of the least of them to bee founde in the sonne of GOD ? I thinke you dare not; I hope you will not. What meaneth then this matching of Chzist with Cain ? yea this touching of Chzist deeper then anie of the Repzobate? In hozrour and paine you saie, *y Christ was like them who be separated in deede* ;: y Pag.79.

from

" *from the grace and loue of God , yet himselfe neuer separated, but*
" *alwaies most intirely beloued.* The horrour and paine, which the
Reprobate heere feele, riseth from the remorse of their owne
conscience, and from the distrust and feare of their owne
hearts; which pursueth them euen in this life before iudge-
ment. The execution of his terrible vengeance indœde God
hath reserued to the next life. The greatest terror that the A-
postle noteth in the wicked here in this worlds is, [z] a fearefull
expectation of iudgment and of burning fire which shall deuour
the aduersaries. What horror then like the reprobate coulde
the conscience of Christ fœle, that had no remorse, distrust,
or feare of anie such thing as they haue, but was assured and
secured of Gods euerlasting fauour, and loue in the highest
degree was there paine without horrour and feare in the
soule of Christ? If you meane the paine that is consequent
to our naturall affections, as to sorrowe and feare, you saie
nothing to the purpose. Saint Iohn saith [a] *timor habet pœnam;*
Feare hath in it paine, and so hath sorrowe, euen as hope hath
ioye; [b] Reioice in hope; but this is not the paine which the
Reprobate fœle, much lesse which the damned suffer; I
trust their paine is more then a naturall oppressing and af-
flicting of the heart with humane feare and sorrowe. And
therefore if I conceaue anie thing, you misse the truth verie
much, Sir Confuter, when you saie that Christ was touched
in horrour and paine as dœpelie as the Reprobates are; and
yet your conceite reacheth farther. For you defende that he
suffered as much as the damned in hell, which is more then
the reprobates doe in earth, howsoeuer to shewe your lear-
ning you make hell and heauen heere on earth. For my
selfe (Christian Reader) whence I thinke, the astonishment
of Christ in the garden might rise, thou hast it in the treatise
before, I shall not nœd to repeat it againe.

In like maner you extend Christes agonie too farre; for
where it was an agonie of minde, which did not bereaue him
neither of sense, memorie, nor vnderstanding, you haue
wrought

[z] Hebre.10

[a] 1.Iohn.4

[b] Rom.12.

brought vs a far dell of phrases, to expresse that *all the senses* ,,
of his bodie, and al the powers of his soule were amazed, astonished, ,,
distempered, disturbed, distracted, forgetfull, ouerwhelmed, and ,,
all confounded; and you thinke you neuer haue words enough
to expresse your follie, in dreaming of the greatest astonish-
ment that maie be, because the scripture saieth, he began to
be astonished. But Sir, how proue you this you saie? as in
feares and sorrowes there bee diuers degrees; so are there
likewise in astonishmets. To be astonished is to ioine feare
with admiration, which draweth the minde so wholie to think
on some speciall thing aboue our reach, that during the time
we turne not our selues to anie other cogitation. Euen as
the eie, if it be bent intentiuelie to behold anie thing, for that
present it discerneth nothing else: So fareth it with ye soule, if
she wholie addict her selfe to thinke on anie matter, she is a-
mused; if it bee more then she conceaueth, or more fearefull
then she well indureth, she is amazed, or astonished; but not
of necessitie so, that she loseth either sense or memorie; one-
lie for that time she conuerteth neither to anie other obiect.
The present beholding of the diuine maiestie sitting in
iudgement; and of his iustice armed with infinite power
to reuenge the sinnes of men, might iustlie astonish the hu-
mane soule of Christ; seeing therewithal how mightilie God
was prouoked by the manifold and wilfull transgressions of
men; but this religious astonishment, though it might for a
season suspend all other thoughtes in our Sauiour, yet is
there no neede it shoulde depriue him of vnderstanding,
sense or memorie. When Paul saieth [c] worke your saluation   [c] Philip.2
with feare and trembling, doth hee meane they should want
memorie or vnderstanding? When Moses receaued the law
from God, [d] so terrible was the sight that hee saide, I tremble   [d] Hebre.12
and quake. Was Moses therefore voide of sense or reason
at that present? [e] An horrible terror (saith Dauid) hath taken   [e] Psal.119.
mee for the vngodlie that forsake thy lawe. Was Dauid for
their sakes besides himselfe, and all confounded in bodie and

soule,

soule, as you speake here of Christ? Our whole conuersation
shoulde bee as Paule professeth of himselfe, when hee saieth,
I f was among you with much trembling and feare. Should
therefore Christians bee alwayes besides themselues?
"[g *Christ often praied vnto his Father,* you saie, *and then pre-*
"*sented himselfe before the Maiestie of God; and yet wee do not*
"*reade that euer hee was vexed, terrified, and amazed in so do-*
"*ing.*] Sir Refuter, if your vnderstanding and memorie be
not lost, I tolde you that the humane nature of Christ pre-
sented it selfe before the maiestie of God in iudgement,
there to suffer man euerlastinglie to perish, whome hee
deerelie loued, or to vndertake in his owne person that
burthen, which the iustice of God, displeased with our sinnes,
should laie vpon him. And if you doe not thinke this a cause
sufficient for the manhoode of Christ to feare and tremble,
yea for the time to bee astonished at the number of our
sinnes, and terrour of Gods vengeance, prouided for our
eternall destruction both of bodie and soule, you bee so deepe
in your hellish paines, that your wits and senses are con-
founded. Absurdities and contrarieties are so rife with
you, that you thinke other men can hardlie auoide them;
but first vnderstand your owne, and then you shall the bet-
ter charge others.

After you haue spent the whole strength of your small elo-
quence and lesse intelligence, to infer and amplifie the most
"h *wonderfull and piteous agonies, feares, sorrowes, miseries, out-*
"*cries, teares, astonishment, forgetfulnesse, and confusion of the*
"*powers of nature with which the sense of Gods wrath afflicted, dis-*
"*tracted, amazed, ouerwhelmed, and all confounded* our Sauiour
"*in his whole humanity;* You suddainlie, euen in the twinkling
of an eie free him from all, and set him cleare, as if all this
had beene but a dreame. For vpon Christes speaking of
these wordes, i Father, if it bee possible let this cuppe passe
"from mee; you inferre, k *if Christ had thus praied aduisedly*
"*and with good memorie, against the knowne will of God hee had*
　　　　　　　　　　　　　　　　　　　　　　　　　　sinned

f 1 Cor. 1
g Pag. 61.
b Pag. 73.
i Matth. 26.
k Page 57

sinned. And in the words presentlie following without state
or pause betweene , yet not my will, but thine bee doone,
you imagine that Christ , [1] *as it were comming suddainly to*   „   [1] Pag.71.
himselfe quickly controled his former words . And thus when it   „
pleaseth you, you put the sonne of God into [m] *a wonderfull*   „   [m] Pag.73
and piteous confusion and forgetfulnesse of all the powers and   „
partes of his bodie and soule ; and least you shoulde be convin-   „
ced of a manifest, and irreligious vntrueth, in the verie
nicke of the nexte worde, which Christ spake with the same
breath , you restore him to his perfect senses , and dis-
charge him from your hellish confusion and paynes. But
good Sir, if it were so *vnsupportable and intolerable a bur-*   „
den , and confusion as you dreame of , howe came our   „
Saviour to bee so lightlie and quicklie ridde of it , as if
there had béene no such thing? was that heauie and fierie
wrath of GOD against our sinnes equall to hell so soone
quenched? or was the sonne of God no longer able to en-
dure it? [n] *Of all absurdities (* your selfe beeing iudge , for   „   [n] Pag.48.
it is your position) *this is the greatest , that meere men should*   „
suffer more deepelie then Christ . Then if Cain endured this   „
all his life long , if Saul and Iudas had no intermission
of their payne , if the damned in hell , (from whome
you fetch your patterne) doe euerlastinglie suffer it , howe
commeth it to passe , that after you haue so hotlie stirred
for it , you are so soone wearie of it ? will you make vs
beleeue, that Christes obedience and patience was tried
with a touch of this hellish paine, and so an ende ? or will
you returne it as often as please you? and if this cuppe
did so quicklie passe from our Saviour , howe did hee
then praie against the knowne will of God; which is an o-
ther of your foundations, when as , in the vttering of these
words, the cup did passe from him, by your owne confession?
In like sorte to excuse Christ from sinne , [o] *in praying a-*   „   [o] Pag.55
gainst the will of his Father, you cast him into a wonderfull   „
confusion

" confusion and forgetfulnesse of all the powers of his soule , and sen-
" ses of his body : and in the same page, for an other aduantage,

ᵖ Pag.59. " you auouch that in that praier , Chꝛist ᵖ PERFECTLIE
" KNEVV the dominion of death shoulde not holde him. Were all
the powers of his souls ouerwhelmed and all confounded,
and yet did he euen in that whole confusion of sense , memo-
rie, and vnderstanding PERFECTLY KNOVV the domini-
on of death should not holde him? can a man haue his know-
ledge and memorie all confounded and ouerwhelmed , and
yet retaine PERFECT KNOVVLEDGE? coulde Chꝛist foꝛ-
get his fathers will in that praier through astonishment, and
in the speaking of the woꝛds remember he praied amisse, and
in the nexte woꝛde quicklie coꝛꝛect himselfe? Surelie these
be conceittes answerable to your cause ; and deuices fit foꝛ
your diuinitie ; But (Sir Refuter,) let passe your dꝛeames,
and shewe vs your pꝛoofes , that Chꝛist praird against the
knowne will of his father, which you make the groundwoꝛk
of this confusion : and when you haue so done , then pꝛooue
that your hellish paine was the cause of this astonishment.
Manie thinges might astonish our Sauiour foꝛ the time,
besides the paines of hell; and in that astonishment, if Chꝛist
ᑫ Luc. 9. had spoke he knew not what (which I beléeue not) as ᑫ Peter did
when he sawe his gloꝛie in the mountaine, it had béene a de-
fect in nature, and no contempt of Gods counsell, much lesse
such an infernall confusion as you describe.

ᵣ Pag.59. " [It is manifest (you saie) that Chꝛist ᵣ in plaine words praied.
" contrarie to Gods known will :] It is moꝛe manifest that you
knowe not what you saie. Howe coulde he pꝛate against his
ˢLuc.22. Fathers will that praied expꝛeslie with this condition, ˢ O
Father IF THOV VVILT take awaie this cup from me.[That
is a coꝛꝛection after the pꝛaier (you will saie) and no conditi-
on in the pꝛaier.] Are you so captious against Chꝛist, that
ᵗMat.26. you will not supplie one Euangelist with an other ? ˢ Luke
and ᵗ Matthew put a plaine condition vnto the pꝛaier of
Chꝛist; the one saying, father if thou wilt; the other, father if

x

it be poſsible, that is to ſtand with thy will, and mans ſal-
uation. And though Marke omit the condition in the tenor
of the praier, yet doth he fullie expreſſe his meaning to bee al
one with the reſt. For thus he ſaieth of our Sauiour, " hee   *Mark. 14.
fell downe on the grounde, and praied that IF IT VVERE
POSSIBLE, that houre might paſſe from him. So that all
three Euangeliſtes concurre, that Chriſt praied not onelie
with a reſeruation of his fathers will, but annexed that con-
dition vnto his praier; and therefore in all mens eies ſaue
yours, hee praied not in plaine wordes contrarie to Gods
knowne will. And this erroneous and contumelious poſiti-
on you ſet downe to the worlde, as the chiefeſt fortreſſe of
your helliſh paines, wherein you plainly wreſt the ſcriptures
from their expreſſe wordes.[But S. Iohn, you will ſaie, repor-
teth Chriſtes praier to bee ſimplie made, ˣ Father, ſaue mee   ˣIohn. 12
from this houre.] Saint Iohn ſpeaketh of an other time and
place; and his wordes import a deliberation of two partes
propoſed by our Sauiour, with his reſolution in the ende;
what ſhall I ſaie? Father deliuer me from this hower; that is,
ſhall I ſaie deliuer me from this hower? but therefore came
I into this hower. Father glorifie thy name. Chryſoſtom thus
expoundeth Chriſtes wordes : Y NON DICO libera me ex   ʸChryſoſt.in
hac hora, ſed pater glorifica nomen tuum. I SAIE NOT, de-   Ioan. Homil.66
liuer me from this hower, but father glorifie thy name. And ſo
doth Epiphanius. Quid dicam pater ? ſerua me ex hac hora, hoc   Epiphan. lib. 2
inquit dicam? at propterea veni in hanc horam. What ſhall I   Hæreſ 69.
ſaie ? Father ſaue mee from this hower ? ſhall I ſaie ſo ? but
therefore came I into this hower . But what better expoſi-
tor canne wee haue then Saint Paul , who plainely ſaith that
Chriſt in making this praier was heard, & ᶻ deliuered from   ᶻHebre. 5
that he feared. Hee praied not againſt the knowne will of
God, whoſe praiers God heard and performed. And where
you flie to this helliſh confuſion to ſaue Chriſt from ſinne;
by pretending to cleere him from ſinne , you charge him ra-
ther with ſinne. For the praier which is not made in faith

is sinne. Nowe can the heart be assured it shall receaue that
it asketh at Gods hands, if it bee neither directed to aske ac,
cording to the will of God, nor prepared to aske with that de,
uotion which is fit for God? So that when you make Chrsit
to triple his praiers with vehement teares and cries, & still
repugnant to the will of God, you chalenge the sonne of
God with open sinne, from which you would seeme to excuse
him. And as for your double relapse into the same astonish-
ment still, when Christ was twice cleere from it, it is a foolish
deuice of your idle braines, as if the Lorde no sooner retur,
ned to his praiers, but your hellish confusion did waite at
his heeles, to interrupt and ouerwhelm him; and within
sixe wordes againe to leaue him. If your cause be holie,
iest not thus prophanelie with the sonne of God, nor bereaue
him of his wits, when you thinke good. If it were a ne-
cessarie effect of Gods wrath, then after it lighted on our
Sauiour in the garden, it must continue till man was re-
deemed, and Gods wrath appeased, which was not done but
by the death of Christ? And therefore make your choise: ei-
ther let the wrath of God cease in the garden, when Christ
ended his praiers; or if that still continued to the death, let
also this astonishment still continue, or at least bee no ne-
cessarie effect of Gods wrath. One of these you must take,
take which you will; the rest will serue to subuert your tower
of Babell.

[I doe you wrong, you will saie, to call your opinion the
tower of Confusion;] you do your selfe wrong (Sir Re-
futer) in the chiefest point of Christian religion to leaue the
faith confessed by the whole Church of Christ for these
1500. yeares, and to walke in such ambiguities, and ab-
surdities as your selfe doe not vnderstande. For I praie
" you, Sir, this *wonderfull confusion and astonishment in*
" *all powers of the soule, and senses of the bodie*, is it a ne-
" cessarie consequent to the wrath of G O D, or no? If
" it bee, (for you saie, *Christ coulde not but sinke, and bee*
" *confounded vnder that burden*) howe commeth it to passe,
that

Pag. 54.

that the reprobate and desperate, feeling the sense of
GODS wrath vpon them, doe not loose their wits, and
senses as Christ by your assertion did? will you affirme
they are astonished and all confounded as Christ was? then
if you excuse Christ from sinne, in disliking and declining
his Fathers knowne will, because hee was astonished;
you must likewise excuse all the wicked and Reprobate
from their sinnes, after they once feele the sense of Gods
wrath, because they cannot but bee astonished and con-
founded vnder that burden? Againe, coulde Christ not
sinne, whiles hee felte the wrath of God vppon him, be-
cause he was astonished? Ergo neither coulde bee merite
all that while, and so neither his obedience, patience, hu-
militie, nor charitie coulde haue anie place, or vse, so
long as the sense of GODS wrath dured. Haue you not
deuised vs a goodlie sense of Gods wrath, that shall exclude
Christ Iesus from the exercise of all his graces, vertues,
and merites? This palpable absurditie you thinke to
skippe, (Sir Refuter,) but your wit is too weake, or your
cause not good; it will not bee. [a *If a man in distresse fall*
a sleepe, saie you, *or be astonished with some violent blowe*
on the heade, in such an one there is no decaie of faith, nor of
obed·ence, nor of patience, nor of loue ; euen so in Christ there
was no defect of grace, but an infirmitie of nature .] Was
Christ a sleepe or in a swoune? astonished you thinke, he was.
Was hee so astonished that his senses were taken from
him? did hee not walke? did he not speake? did hee not pray?
whie then compare you this to a sleep or a swoune, wheras in
Christ was neither? and though you plainelie faile in your
comparison; yet, were it so, as you would haue it, for your life
you cannot auoide my conclusion. For a man in a sleepe
or a swoune, though he loose not the habite of faith and pati-
ence, obedience and loue , yet hath hee no vse of them for
that time; much lesse doth hee serue God with them. But
Christ Iesus by all his sufferinges must merite, which a

a Page. 57.

Q q 2·   man

man a sleepe oʒ amazed cannot doe. And therefoʒe remem-
ber, (Sir Refuter) this reason amongst the rest is yet vn-
answerd; and I thinke wil somwhat trouble pour bʒaines
befoʒe it bee answered. All that Christ suffered for our Re-
demption was, and must bee, meritorious with God. But the
suffering of hell paynes, which astonish and confounde all
the powers of the soule, and senses of the bodie, neither was,
nor coulde bee meritorious with God; Christ therefore did not
suffer such hellish paynes as did confounde and astonish all the
powers of his soule and senses of his bodie. And thus, by
pour amazed position, you haue wholie confounded pour
owne opinion.

Thou hast heard (good Reader) a number of the Refu-
ters speciall follies; I haue some fewe moʒe to trouble thee
with, and so I will leaue him to his holie cause, and thee to
the mercies of God. To shewe himselfe learned as well in
the Gréeke tongue, as in philosophie, hee vndertaketh an o-
ther reason that I made, and spoʒteth himselfe somewhat
handsomlie with it. Out of the fift to the Hebʒewes where
the Apostle saieth, [b] Christ in the daies of his flesh did offer
vp prayers and supplications with strong cryes and teares vnto
him that was able to saue him from death, and was heard in that
he feared, oʒ deliuered from his feare: I collected two things.
Firit that Chʒist in his pʒaiers made in ϸ garden(foʒ to those
the Apostle pointeth) did but feare, and not as then suffer
that he feared. The nexte, he was deliuered from his feare;
and consequentlie neuer came to suffer that from which hee
was deliuered. This Confuter replieth, as hee thinketh,
verie soundlie, and verie sufficientlie. Thou shalt heare the
whole. My reason hee maketh to bee this. [c] *That wherein*
" *Christ was hearde and deliuered from by praier, he feared but felt*
" *not. But Christ was heard and deliuered by prayer from the wrath*
" *which he feared, therefore he felt it not.* His answere is. [d] *Nay*
" *euen therefore he felt it. Wee deny therefore the first proposition.*
" *For hee was in some sense of it, when hee praied against it, and was*
　　　　　　　　　　　　　　　　　　　　　　　　　heard

[Hebre.5]

[Pag.24.]

[Ibidem.]

heard. He had then some foretaft but the extremity came after,
which hee before feared. And finallie hee being in all this
was heard (as the verie word (εἰσακουσθεὶς) *) seemeth to im-*
port) and delyuered from it, that is at leaft, not before hee
had felt it. Againe very the fearing of Gods wrath is a true
feeling, I saie not a ful feeling, but a true feeling:but it is gran-
ted that now in this Agonie hee feared the wrath of God:
Therefore hee truelie felt it. Therefore the Queftion is gran-
ted. You wrote this in the morning, Sir Refuter, when you
were fresh and fasting, it is so short and sharpe; but belike
it was darke, or your eies were dull you could not see
neither what I said, nor what your selfe saie. The force of
my reason consisted in this, that where feare goeth before
suffering, and is no longer called feare when suffering com-
meth; If Christ at the time of his praiers in the garden
were deliuered from his feare, much more from anie suffe-
ring of that hee feared. And since by your owne positions
you affirme hee feared in his agonie the paines of hell; I
concluded hee suffered them not. Let vs now see howe you
impugne this reason. You first change suffering into fee-
ling; and because the soule in all hir affections hath a kind
of feeling, you inferre, *naie therefore Chrift felt it.* Your
manner is too shrowde your selfe with generall and am-
biguous words that maie signifie anie thing, and then you
shew your learning in speaking you knowe not what. But
vse the word suffering which I did, or take feeling for suffe-
ring, in which sence it maie stand; and then see how absurd-
lie and falslie you take my reason at this rebound. For
then you must saie. Fearing is a kind of feeling, Christ fea-
red the paines of hell, ergo Christ suffered them; and so by
your logicke whosoeuer feareth captiuitie or death, is a
captiue, and dead; and hee that feareth to loose his purse,
hath lost it; yea hee that feareth to offend God, doth offend
him; and hee that feareth to bee an hereticke, is an here-
ticke. I thought though your diuinitie had not, yet your

Vide Pag. 29.

Qq.3.   Philophie

Philosophie coulde haue serued you to vnderstand; that ^e *metus est mali impendentis, ægritudo præsentis*; feare is of an euill approching; griefe or paine, of an euill present. If you scorne philosophers, whom for the propzietie of words, you pzeferre before all the diuines in the world, as anon shall appeare; Lactantius telleth you, that of ^f Desire, ioy, feare and sorrow, the two first (desire and ioy) are for good things approching or present: the two last (feare and sorrow) for euill likewise approching or present. S. Ambrose will teach you that, ^g *ante dolorem est timor, post dolorem tristitia*: feare is before griefe or paine; after paine followeth heauines. And likewise Gregorie, ^h *In his vita tormentis, timor dolorem habet, dolor timorem non habet, quia æquaquam mentem metus cruciat, cum pati iam cæperit, quod metuebat.* In the torments in this life feare hath some griefe, but griefe hath no feare; because feare doth not afflict the mind, when a man once suffereth that, which he feared. This were enough to make my argument good, but it hath yet moze strength from the Apostles words: Christ pzaying in the garden was heard from his feare; that is was deliuered from his feare. Now is a man deliuered from his feare by suffering that he feared? So wee lest with men, when we will giue them their deserts, and let them stand no longer in suspence; but God so tested not with his sonne, as to rid him from his feare, by pzesent punishment. God therefore heard Chzists pzayer and deliuered him from his feare, when as yet he did not suffer it; and being deliuered from it in the garden, how came he to suffer it moze extremely on the Crosse? For you sate, ⁱ *Christ was in some sense of it, when hee praied against it, he had then some fortaste of it, but the extremitie came after, which he before feared.* Syr confuter, if you can test & gybe thus with the Apostles words, I must leaue you as lacking both conscience & commō sense; & so will all ỹ be godly. Christ pzaying in the garden was deliuered from his feare, saith Paul; that is say you, after he *had suffered on the Crosse, the extremitie of that which he before feared.* So the for

Christ

Cicero. Tuscul.quæst.lib.4

Lactant:de vero cultu.li. 6.ca.14

Ambros.de Iacob et beata vira li 1.ca 3.

Gregor.moral.li.9.cap.39.

Pag.74.

Chzist to be deliuered, from that he feared, was (by your conſtruction) to ſuffer the extremitie of that he feared. Will you that God ſend you ſuch deliuerance in the time of need, that ſo prophanely play with the deliuerance of his ſonne? [He was deliuered you will ſay, from the continuance of it.] No (good Syr) Chziſt neuer feared the paines of hell ſhould continue on him after death; it is hozrible blaſphemy ſo to think; & vnto death you ſay they continued. How was he then deliuered from his feare? oz haue you ſo ſoone fozgotten your owne wozds, if you regard not myne? [k] *It is abſurd to ſaie he praied in feare againſt that which he perfectly know ſhould neuer come vnto him, namely that the Dominion of Death ſhould hold him.* If the dominion of death ſhould not hold his bodie, much leſſe ſhould hell hold his ſoule.

[But the Græke word, εἰσακουσθείς, you ſaie, ſeemeth to impozt a deliuerance after Chziſt was in that he feared: εἰσακουσθείς, [l] *Hee was heard being in it*.] As is your diuinitie, Syr confuter, ſo is your Græke. Foz if Chziſt were heard; then God did heare him; & ſo if εἰς ioyned to the paſſiue of ἀκούω ſignifie that Chziſt was heard being in the paines of hell; then εἰς, ioyned to the Actiue, and referred to God, muſt likewiſe impozt that God being in ye ſame paines did heare him. Haue you not bzought vs a learned obſeruation out of your Græke ſtoze, that God which heard, and Chziſt that was heard, were both in the paines of hell? But indeed εἰσακούειν is to hearken vnto, as wee do when we bend our eare to anothers ſpæch; and εἰσακουσθείς is harkned vnto oz heard. The word is fiue times vſed in the new teſtament, but in the Septuagint nothing moze frequent to ſignifie that we harken to Gods voice when we obey him, and God harkneth to our voice, when hee graunteth our pzaiers. Feare not ſaith the Angell to Zacharie, εἰσηκούσθη ἡ δέησίς σου, thy praier is heard, thy wiſe Elizabeth [m] *Luc*☧*:1* ſhall bring thee a ſonne, Soe the Angell to Cornelius, εἰσηκούσθη σου ἡ πϱοσευχὴ thy praier is hearde. [o] with [n] *Act*:10 ſtrange

[k] Pag.59.
[l] Pag.63.
[m] Luc☧:1.
[n] Act:10.

* 1 Cor: 14

† Eccles· 3:

¶: Iob: 22:

ʳ Pſal. 55
ˢ Eſa.59.

ᵗ Pag.74.

ſtraige toonges will I ſpeake to this people, ſaith the Lord, ϰαὶ ουδ᾽ ούτως ἐισακύσονταί μυ, and neither ſo will they harken vnto mee. The wiſe man in like manner, P ὁ ἐισακύων κυρίυ, hee that harkeneth vnto the Lord, giueth reſt to his mother. And the Septuagint, Whē thou praieſt, ſaith Eliphas in the booke of Iob, ¶ ἐισακύσεταί σε, God will heare thee.ʳ Earlie, ſaith Dauid to God, ἐισακύση τῆς φωνῆς μυ, ſhalt thou heare my voice. So in Eſaie,ˢ the eare of the Lord is not ſhutte, μὴ ἐισακῦσαι not to heare . Infinite eramples might bee bꝛought to the ſame end, but theſe are ſufficient to conuince your ignoꝛant miſtaking of the Græke tongue ; yet the Queſtion you ſaie is granted.ᵗ For fearing "is a true feeling, and if Chriſt feared the wrath of God, ergo he "felt it. You recken a pace when you recken alone, but when you come foꝛ allowance you will lacke a faire deale of your reckning . If fearing were ſuffering , which is moſt abſurd; if there were no kind of feare, but your amaʒed and all confounded feare , as there be moꝛe other kinds of feares ; if there were noe moꝛe parts of the wꝛath of God, but hell paines, as there be ſundꝛie moꝛe ; if no man might feare but foꝛ himſelfe, as in charitie wee may, and in duty we ought to feare foꝛ others, and Chꝛiſt in loue might and did foꝛ vs ; then had you ſome hope, that he which granteth the one, would admit the other: but if this be all you can ſaie, that feare is a kind of feeling, I am as farre from granting the Queſtion, as I was in the firſt beginning. Foꝛ though you dallie with doubtfull woꝛds, and thinke it enough to catch here and there at a likeliehood, my courſe is not ſo. Indæde out of theſe woꝛds I reaſoned vppon your owne pꝛinciples: and ſuppoſing it foꝛ the time to be true which on this place ſome auouch, that Chꝛiſt feared the paines of hell, I concluded if Chꝛiſt were deliuered from fearing, he was certainlie deliuered from ſuffering the paines of hell . And befoꝛe you anſwere the argument, you triumph as if the Queſtion were granted. But Syꝛ remember it is is the suffering of hell paines that we talke of, and not of a Metaphoꝛicall kinde of féeling ; which you substitute in stéd thereof. Againe all the effects of Gods wꝛath Chꝛist did not feele, noꝛ feare, as namelie, neither repꝛobation , noꝛ desperation, noꝛ eternall damnation , which is the chiefest and sharpest effect of Gods iust wꝛath against sinne. Some partes thereof if hee did feare, and so in affectien feele, howe doth it followe hee felt oꝛ feared hell paines ? Thirdlie, hee did sustaine as well our person, as our cause ; hee had not onelie compassion on vs, but conionction with vs ; and in that respect as our head hee might woꝛthilie feare the euerlasting destruction of his bodie, if he did not interpose himselfe, and auert Gods wꝛath from them , by healing them with his owne stripes, and bearing their sinnes in his owne bodie. Fourthlie he might feare the power of Gods wꝛath , able to punish euen the bodie of Chꝛist with farre moꝛe smart, then his humane flesh was able to endure. Last-lie, hee might carefullie shunne and decline both our sinne and the wages of our sinne, which is eternall death with a re-ligious feare, as content to redeeme vs, but not to destroie both himselfe and vs.

And this commeth néerest the signification of the Gréek woꝛde there vsed, which is no confused oꝛ amazed feare, such as you woulde cunninglie conuey vnder the name of a [n] *perplexed feare* , but a carefull and diligent regarde to be-ware and decline that, which wee mislike oꝛ doubt. And therefoꝛe εὐλαβὴς is not onelie one that feareth God by taking good care not to displease him, but a circumspect and warie man in other thinges ; and εὐλάβεια is circum-spection and warinesse in pꝛiuate oꝛ publique affaires, as well as Religion to GOD . Nowe because the bol-der men are, the sooner they aduenture on anie thing, and the moꝛe fearefull, the moꝛe héede they take what they do; εὐλάβεια by consequent signifieth an inclination rather to feare, then pꝛesumption; but it is lesse then φόβος , which

„ ·Pag 74.

Kr 1　　　　　is

is the vsuall worde in Greeke for feare, as maie plainelie be proued by Plutarch in his Treatise of Morall vertue; where, noting howe men couer vitious affections vnder the names of vertues, he saieth, ⁎ τὸ αἰσχύνεσθαι αἰδεῖσθαι καλῦσι, καὶ τὸ ἥδεσθαι χαίρειν, καὶ τὸς φόβὸς εὐλαβείας; They call blushing reuerence; mirth gladnesse, and feare warinesse. Euripides in the person of Eteocles king of Thebes, saieth, ἥδ᾽ εὐλάβεια χρησιμωτάτη θεῶν, Circumspect care is the most profitable Goddesse. And where you quote the 2 3. of the Acts for proofe of your conceit, the place is rather against you then with you. For when the Councell dissented about Paule, and some tumult began to arise, the ᶻ Tribune doubting least some hurt might happen vnto Paule then his prisoner, preuented it, and sent his souldiers to take him away from the midst of the throng. This feare of the tribune was for another man, not for himselfe, neither was a perplexed or amazed feare, but a doubt forecasting the worst, and preuenting it. So is it written of Noah, that being admonished by God of the flood which should come vpon the world, by faith ᵃ εὐλαβηθεὶς, fearing, declining and preuenting (what God had threatned to others) he made ready the Arke, for the sauing of his housholde. This could be no distrustfull feare, what should befall him and his house ; for his faith is commended by the Apostle in preparing the Arke , for the safetie of himselfe and his children; but he shunned that which he saw would light on others; and that the scripture there calleth εὐλαβηθεὶς. The rest that maie concerne Christs praier in the garden, or might occasion that agonie which there hee sheweth, thou hast (gentle Reader) in the ᵃ treatise before; which I will not here resume, least I wearie thee with ouer much tediousnesse.

 For a farewell to his speciall reasons, the Confuter hath reserued matters of most speciall moment to the last : and because they are weightie and neede good proofe, hee hath searched the bottome of his studie , and sheweth vs here

the

⁎ Plutarch. de virtute moral.

7 Euripid. in Phœniss.

ᶻ Acts. 23.

ᵃ Heb. 11.

ᵃ Vide pag. 17.

the depth as well of his reading, as vnderstanding. Out of
the Epistle to the Hebrues he citeth these wordes ; [b] *Chrift
through death abolished him that had the power of death , that
is the Diuell.* From hence hee reasoneth thus. [c] *Surelie
the worde* DEATH *hath the same meaning in both places : ve-
rie fonde it were to take it here otherwise. Nowe it is quefti-
onleffe , in this latter place , death fignifieth the death of the
foule, the tormentes and forrowes of the damned, which are fepa-
rated from the life of God : of which death the Diuell is fayde
to haue the power and execution. Therefore in the former place
death fignifieth fo to, euen the death of the foule, that is the tor-
ments and forrowes due to the damned, and* [d] *confequently Chrift
fuffered the death of the foule. And becaufe this reafon will
feeme altogether vnreafonable and harfh in the eares of fome,
to faie the leaft of it , let them foberlie confider it, and it is moft
true and euident:* Or if this will not perfwade men to be-
leeue that Chrift died the death of the foule, [e] *men liuing be-
ing furprifed with grieuous forrowes and paines, will faie* (as
Terence witneffeth, *occidi, perij, interij) they die, they perifh.
So likewife the death of the foule fometimes maie bee vnderftoode
and that moft fitlie for the paines and fufferinges of Gods
wrath , which alwayes accompanie them that are feparated
from the grace and loue of God.* And if Terence bee not au-
thoritie fufficient, Saint Peter againft whome lieth no ex-
ception, [g] *faith, that Chrift in his fuffering for vs was done to
death in the flefh , but made aliue by the fpirite. And in the
Scripture whenfoeuer the flefhe and the fpirite are oppofed to
gither,* [h] *the flefh is always Chriftes whole humanitie , I faie,
not his bodie onelie, but his foule alfo. From hence nowe it fol-
loweth, that Chriftes foule alfo died , and was crucified accor-
ding to the death and crucifying, which foules are fubiect vnto,
and capable of.* I haue (Chriftian Reader) neither per-
uerted the reafons, nor pared the authorities, on which
this Confuter groundeth his conclufion , that Chrift died

[b] Heb. 2.

[c] Pag. 7 ¶

[d] Pag. 7 5.

[e] Pag. 76

[f] Pag. 77.

[g] Pag. 7 8.

[h] Pag. 7 9.

the death of the soule, and that Christs soule was also cruci-
fied as well as his bodie; I haue onelie sette them togither,
that thou maiest with one biew behold both the deepnes and
soundnesse of this bpstart writer; and in thy secrete and bp-
right iudgement, is it not patience enough to heare and en-
dure a two legged creature to talke in this sort without all
learning, religion or discretion, controlling all the fathers
as foles, for thinking otherwise then hee doth, commaun-
ding the Scriptures pretor-like, to serue his ignorant and
lewd assertions, and esteeming none to be sober or conside-
rate, except they confesse his shamefull absurdities to bee
most true and euident? But I haue not learned nor bsed
to giue reuiling speeches, the Lorde reprooue his follie.
Though it bee not worth the answering, yet for their sakes
that bee simple, I will not refuse to speake to it, and to
let them see what difference there is betwixt truth and
errour.

    Your maine reason (Sir Refuter) is this, in these wordes
“ of the Apostle, *Christ through death abolished the diuell that*
“ *had power of death.* This worde DEATH (say you) *hath the*
“ *same meaning in both places,* the proofe you make for it is this,
“ *verie fond it were to take it here otherwise.* Your assumption is,
“ *but death in the latter place questionlesse signifieth the death of*
“ *the soule; Therefore Christ died the death of the soule.* It were
as easie for nice to saie, it is not so; as for you to saie,
it is so; but that course which you holde is but prating of
euerie thing, it is no proouing of anie thing. Howe ma-
nie kinds of death there are, wee shall better learne by the
graue father Saint Austen, then by the young louers in

[3 August. serm. 129.] Terence: [1] *Dicitur mors prima, dicitur & secunda. Prima*
mortis duæ sunt partes, vna qua peccatrix anima per culpam
discessit a creatore suo : altera qua iudicante Deo exclusa est
per pœnam à corpore suo. Mors autem secunda ipsa est cor-
poris & animæ punitio sempiterna. There is a first death and
a second Death. Of the first death there be two parts: one, when
                                 the

the sinfull soule by offending departed from her Creator; the o-
ther whereby the soule for her punishment was excluded from
her bodie by Gods iustice. The second death is the euerlasting
torment of bodie and soule. The same partes and kindes of
death are often repeated by him in his 13. booke *de ciuitate
Dei*; as namelie, [k] *Mors animæ fit cum eam deserit Deus, sicut* [k Augustде
corporis cum id deserit anima. Ergo vtriusq́; rei, id est totius ho- ciuitate dei.
minis mors est, cum anima à Deo deserta deserit corpus. Ita enim lib. 13. cap. 2.
nec ipsa viuit ex deo, nec corpus ex ipsa. Huiusmodi autem totius
hominis mortem illa sequitur quam secundam mortem diuino-
rum eloquiorum appellat authoritas. Nam illa pœna vltima &
sempiterna recte mors animæ dicitur. The death of the soule is,
when God forsaketh her, as the death of the bodie is, when the
soule forsaketh the bodie. So ẏ death of both, that is of the whole
man is when the soule forsaken of God forsaketh her bodie. For
so neither she liueth by God, nor the bodie by her. This death of
the whole man, that other death followeth ; which the diuine
scriptures call the second death, for that last and euerlasting pu-
nishment is rightlie called the death of the soule. Here are three
kindes of death; sinne, which separateth vs from God, bodilie
death, which separateth the soule from the body, and eternall
damnation which tormenteth body and soule for euer. In the
Apostles words to the Hebrues, that Christ through death abo-
lished ẏ diuell that had power of death; you will by no meanes
haue the death of the bodie intended ; that is a benefite and
gaine to the godlie. When of sinne and eternall damnation
the diuell must be said to haue power, and indeede so he hath.
• For hee is the perswader and leader to sinne, and the ex-
ecutioner and tormentor in damnation. And so by your di-
uinitie Christ must sinne, and be euerlastinglie condemned
to hell fire, before he can abolish the Diuell that hath power
of both these. For he must abolish him, by the same kind
of death, whereof hee hath power. Looke, Sir Resu-
ter, what an wholsome exposition of the Apostles words you
haue made vs, which the diuell himselfe durst not aduenture,

it

it is so blasphemous. God forbid you will say, this should be
anie part of your meaning. But if such bee your ignorant
rashnesse, that you will so expound scriptures, as these con-
sequents shall necessarie followe, you must leaue writing,
and fall to learning an other while, till you be able to foresee
what may iustly be inferred vpon your positions. Deaths
of the soule there are none mentioned in anie Scripture, or
father, but sinne and eternall damnation. Leaue the pa-
theticall, hyperbolicall & metaphoricall phrases of Terence,
to boies in the Grammer schoole, speake at least like a di-
uine, though you bee none. If your cause bee so holie a
truth as you talke of, it hath both foundation and approba-
tion in the Scriptures. You shall not neede to runne to
heathen Poets to prooue that the Sauiour of the worlde
died the death of the soule. What the death of the soule is,
what consequentes it hath, and what maine and moste
sufficient reasons there are, why Christ neither did, nor
might die the death of the soule, thou hast (good Rea-
der) before in the Treatise it selfe : if this fumbler either
will skippe them, or can not answere them, I must not
repeate them as often as hee will neglect them. Yet to
ease thee of going backe, I will here giue thee the effect
thereof.

Vide pag. 73.

The life and death of the soule is in manie hundred
1 August. in Io-
han. tract. 47. places learnedlie and trulie touched and prooued by Saint
Austen.[1] *Mori carni tuæ est amittere vitam suam ; mori anima
tuæ est amittere vitam suam . Vita carnis tuæ anima tua, vita
anima tuæ Deus tuus. Quomodo moritur caro amissa anima, quæ
vita eius est ; sic moritur anima amisso Deo, qui vita est eius.*
For thy bodie to die, is to loose his life ; and for thy soule to
die, is to loose her life. The life of thy bodie is thy soule. The
life of thy soule is thy God . As the bodie dieth when the
soule is departed , which is his life ; so the soule dieth when
m August. de
verbis Apost.
serm 30. God is departed which is her life. And againe. [m] *Quomodo
ergo mortua est anima de qua viuit corpus ? Audi ergo &
disce*

disce; corpus hominis creatura Dei est, & anima hominis creatura dei est. De anima deus viuificat carnem, ipsam autem animam viuificat de seipso, non de seipsa. Uita ergo corporis anima est, vita anima Deus est: moritur corpus cum recedit anima, moritur ergo anima si recedit Deus. Carnem iacentem sine anima vides; animam miseram sine Deo videre non potes? Crede ergo, adhibe oculos fidei. How dieth the soule then by which the bodie liueth? Hearken and learne. The bodie of man is the creature of God, & so is the soule. By the soule God giueth life to the flesh, but the soule her selfe God quickeneth by himselfe, and not by herselfe. The life of the bodie then is the soule, the life of the soule is God. The bodie dieth when the soule departeth, ergo the soule dieth if God depart from her. Thou seest the flesh lying dead without a soule, and canst thou not see the soule wretched without God? Beleeue then, and open the eies of faith. And speaking of the particular consequents to the life and death of the soule, the same father saith: [n] *Quomodo cum anima est in corpore, præstat illi vigorem, decorem, mobilitatem; Sic cum vita eius Deus est in ipsa, præstat illi sapientiam, pietatem, iustitiam, charitatem; veniente itaq; verbo & audientibus infuso resurgit anima à morte sua ad vitam suam, hoc est ab iniquitate, ab insipientia, ab impietate, ad Deum suum qui est illi sapientia, iustitia, charitas.* As when the soule is in the bodie, shee giueth vigour, comelinesse and motion to the bodie; so when God her life is in the soule, he giueth her wisedome, pietie, righteousnesse and charitie, The worde (of God) then sounding and infused to the hearers, the soule riseth from her death to her life, that is from iniquitie, follie, and impietie, to her God, who is to her wisedome, righteousnesse, and charitie. If this were not plaine inough; the Scriptures themselues are so euident, that no man can mistake the life of the soule, except hee will purposelie blinde himselfe, least hee shoulde come to the knowledge of the truth. For the sonne of God is [o] life, and comming down from heauen, [p] gaue life to the world, [q] quickning whom hee would [r] with the waters of life, that is

by

[margin notes:]
a August. in Iohan. tract. 19.

o Iohn. 1.
p Iohn. 6.
q Iohn. 5.
r Iohn. 7.

f Rom. 8.
t Iohn. 6.
u Iohn 15
x Galat. 3.
y 1. Iohn 4.
z 1. Iohn. 5.
a Colos. 3.
b Reuel. 22.

by the f spirite of life, yea t whosoeuer beleeueth, and u abideth in him , hath life and beareth fruite in him. For the iust shall x liue by faith, and he that dwelleth in y loue, dwelleth in God, and God in him, for God is loue. So that not onely Christ is our life, z and he that hath the sonne hath life, but a with him, and in him, alwaies was, and alwaies will bee , the b fountaine of life, which neuer did nor can drie vp: how then could Christ die the death of the soule , whose soule was personallie vni- ted , vnto the worde that was life in it selfe ?   And if the grace and spirite of God in vs, make vs liue by God, and in God; if faith and loue knitte men to the life of God; howe coulde the soule of Christ alwaies full of grace and truth, alwaies full of faith and loue, and of the holie Ghost, bee deade?

[But this Refuter meaneth another death of the soule.] What his meaning is , is not materiall, but whether hee meane truth or no. If he wil frame vs a monster in christian religion, what haue I to do with that, but to detest it ? There is another death after this life, mentioned both in scriptures and fathers, which is the second death. But I hope this Con- futer will eate and sleepe vpon the cause before hee wrappe our Sauiour within euerlasting damnation. That is, a death in deed from which God blesse and saue vs all . They must needes bee good Christians that labour to bring Christes soule within the compasse of the second death. c *Hac mortali-*

c August in psa. 43.
d Idem in Io- han. tract. 43

tas est vmbra mortis; vera mors est damnatio cum Diabolo. Our death is here but a shadow of death; the true death indeede is damnation with the diuell, saith Austen. And againe d *Quid est ista mors ? Est relictio corporis , depositio sarcinæ grauis : mors secunda, mors æterna , mors gehennarum , mors damnatio- nis cum Diabolo, ipsa est vera mors :* What is this death ? It is the leauing of the bodie, and the laying downe of an heauier burthen; for the second death, the death that is eternall , the death of hell, the death of condemnation with the Diuell, that is the true death . Which of these two deathes of the soules,

ſoules, you will haue the ſoule of Chriſt ſubiected vnto, you
muſt tell vs, (Sir Refuter,) if you will néedes haue him die
the death of the ſoule; and the choiſe is ſo good, that take
which you will, you incur hainous and horrible blaſphemie.
I wiſh you to bee better aduiſed, then to proceede to the de-
fence of ſo wilfull a frenſie. As for new deaths of the ſoule,
you haue no commiſſion to inuent anie; ſhewe what ſcrip-
ture or Father ſpake it before you, or you muſt giue the
godlie leaue to thinke you no fit founder of a newe faith. S.
Auſten was of opinion that no Chriſtian durſt auouch that
Chriſt died the death of the ſoule, [c] *Nam quod Ieſus anima*   [c] Idé epiſt. 99
mortificatus fuerat, quis audeat dicere, cum mors animæ non ſit
niſi peccatum, a quo ille omnino immunis fuit? That Chriſt was
dead in ſoule VVHO DARES AFFIRME IT, whereas the
death of the ſoule (in this life) is nothing but ſinne, from which
hee was altogether free? you not onelie auouch it, but you
thinke no man ſober that will not conſent to it. But you did
well to propheſie of this conceite of yours, that it woulde
ſeeme harſh and altogether vnreaſonable in the eares of ſome, to
ſaie the leaſt of it; In the eares of all that bee wiſe and lear-
ned it will ſound worſe, for it is a flat repugnancie not only
to all the Fathers, but euen to the chriſtian faith, that Chriſt
died as well in ſoule as in bodie; and as meane a man as
I am, I thinke I ſhall bee able to make that good which I
ſaie. For if the ſoule of Chriſt were alwaies perfectlie vni-
ted vnto life, fullie poſſeſſed of life, and aboundantly able to
giue life, tell me I praie you howe it maie ſtande with the
trueth of the ſcriptures, that the ſame ſoule was for anie
time deade? you may euen as well defende that Chriſt ſin-
ned, as that his ſoule died, for the death of the ſoule is ſinne
in this life, and damnation in the next. [f] *Certe anima Chriſti*   [f] Aug. epiſt. 99
nulla mortificata peccato vel damnatione punita eſt, quibus dua-
bus cauſis mors animæ intelligi poteſt : Surelie the ſoule of Chriſt
was deade with no ſinne, nor puniſhed with any damnation,
which are the two waies that the death of the ſoule may bee

Sſ 1.   poſsibly

possibly conceaued.

g Pag.77. " [The death of the soule, say you, g *may be vnderstood, & that*
" *most fitly, for the paines and sufferings of Gods wrath, which al-*
" *waies accompany them that are separated from the grace and loue*
" *of God. This death of the soule* yee affirme *(Christ suffered;*
" *yet hee himselfe neuer separated, but most intirely beloued, yea*

h Pag.42 " *most* h *holie, most innocent, and most blessed,*] You contradict,
(Sir Refuter,) not onlie the scriptures and fathers, but euen
your selfe in one and the same sentence, and reele like a
man whose braines are not steadie. i *Secundum scripturas*

i Ambros.de fide resurrect. *triplicem esse mortem accepimus. Vna est cum morimur peccato,*
deo viuimus. Beata mors quæ a mortali nos separat, immortali
conseruat. Alia mors est vitæ excessus cum anima nexu corporis
liberatur. Tertia mors.est de qua dictum est, anima quæ pecca-
uerit, ipsa morietur. Ea morte non solum caro sed etiam anima
moritur; hæc mors non est perfunctio huius vitæ, sed lapsus erro-
ris. By the scriptures (saith Ambrose) we learne there is a tri-
ple death. One when we die to sinne and liue to God. This is
a blessed death, which seuereth vs from that which is mortall,
and ioineth vs to that which is immortall. The second is the de-
parture out of this life, when the soule is deliuered from the
bandes of her bodie. The thirde death is that of which it is
written; the soule that sinneth, shall die; this death dieth not
onelie the flesh, but the soule also; for it is not the ending of
this life, but the running into errour. k The first is the life

k Ibidem. of the soule, and the death of sinne, which is spiritv-
all; The second is the ceasing of this life which is na-
tvrall; the thirde is not onelie sinne but destruction,
which is penall. Which of these agreeth to Christ,

l Ibidem. Ambrose himselfe will tell you. l *Quid est Christus nisi*
mors corporis, spiritus vitæ? What is Christ but the death of
the bodie, and the Spirit of life? Then Christ died not the
death of the soule, for the spirit of life cannot die, vnlesse
you will make life it selfe to bee death. Yea, they which in
this worlde die the death of the soule are separated from
Christ.

Chzist, for did they abide in him, they shoulde abide in life; he is ᵐ the waie, the truth, and (not onelie liuing, but) life it selfe; This testimonie our Sauiour giueth of himselfe, ⁿ Verilie, verilie I saie vnto you, hee that beleeueth in mee hath eternall life. If they cannot die the death of the soule, which beleeue in Chzist, howe much lesse can Chzist himselfe die that death? And heere, (Sir Refuter) you bzoch so grosse and palpable an errour, that women and childzen will deride you. Foz if the tozmentes of hell and paines of the damned *do always accompany them that are separated from the grace and loue of God*, howe manie hundzed thousand thousandes of all sortes, sexes, and ages in all kingdomes and countries shoulde bee disturbed, distracted, and confounded in all the powers of their soules and senses of their bodie? where are the ᵒ riches of Gods bounteousnesse, patience and long suffering which the Apostle so highlie commendeth, as leading vnto repentance? Howe could Abraham with anie truth saie to the rich man in hell; ᵖ Sonne remember thou in thy life time receauedst thy good thinges and *Lazarus* paines; where if your position be true, the paines of Lazarus coulde not bee comparable to the tozmentes and paines that ALVVAIES ACCOMPANIE the wicked? I assure thee (christian Reader) a man could not with fewer and foolisher wozdes then these, moze crosse the whole tenoz of the scriptures. Foz the wicked here in this life abound with all wealth, ease, and pzosperitie, insomuch that manie of the godlie haue baene and still are offended with it. Reade the 72. Psalme, and see whether these intolerable and hozrible feares, sozrowes, paines, and tozmentes of hell and the damned, do alwaies accompanie them heere in this life. ᵠ My feete were almost gone (saith Dauid) when I sawe the peace of the wicked. There are no bands in their death, they are lustie and strong, they are not in trouble, nor plagued with other men, their eies stand out for fatnesse, they haue more then their heart can wish. Lo these are the wicked, yet PROSPER

ᵐIohn.14

ⁿIohn.6.

ᵒRom.2

ᵖLuc.16.

ᵠPsal. 72

THEY

THEY ALVVAIE, and increase in riches. This was too hard for me till I went into the sanctuarie of God, then I vnderstood their ende. So that God ʳ with much patience suffereth the veſſels of wrath prepared vnto deſtruction, who according to their harde and impenitent hearts, ſ heape vp wrath vpon themſelues againſt the daie of the declaration of the iuſt iudgement of God, whoſe ſuddaine deſtruction is then neareſt, when they ſhal ſay ᵗ peace and ſafety.

And what maruell you croſſe the ſcriptures in confounding the wrath of God to come with the wrath of God preſent in this life; when you doe not ſee your owne wordes to be contrarie one to the other? For if Chriſt died the death of the ſoule, which is ᵘ an alienation from the life of God, howe was he neuer ſeparated, but alwaies intirely beloued and moſt bleſſed? If hee were neuer ſeparated from the life of God, howe came he to die the death of the ſoule, which muſt nœds be a ſeparatiõ for the time from God, vnleſſe you can match light and darkeneſſe, death and life together, and make the one to be the other, and both to cleaue to God himſelfe? But that cannot you do, that can make the paines of the damned, and torments of hell the onlie true and perfectlie accep- " ted ſacrifice to God? Theſe are your words. ˣ *Such a ſorrow* " *indeed of a broken and contrite heart is the only true and perfectly* " *accepted ſacrifice to God, and is in effect nothing but what we af-* " *firme.* You affirme that Chriſt died the death of the ſoule, " which you interpret to bee ſuch ʸ *paines and ſufferings of Gods* " *wrath, as alwaies accompany them that are ſeparated from the* " *grace and loue of God:* You affirme that Chriſt ſuffered ᶻ *won-* " *derfull and piteous aſtoniſhment, forgetfulneſſe and confuſion of* " *the powers of nature, euen of* ᵃ *all the powers of his ſoule and ſen-* " *ſes of his bodie*, yea he ᵇ *felt the verie diuels as the inſtruments,* " *that wrought the verie effectes of Gods wrath vppon him; and* " *though the* ᶜ *wicked oftentimes find farre more intolerable hor-* " *ror of their ſinnes then any other, yet you doubt not, but* " ᵈ *Chriſt as touching the vehemencie of paine, was as ſharply tou-*
cbed

ʳRom. 9

ſRom. 2

ᵗ 1. Theſſa. 5

ᵘEpheſ. 2

ˣPage. 68.

ʸ Pag. 77.

ᶻ Pag: 73.

ᵃPag. 53.

ᵇPag. 45.

ᶜPag. 80.

ᵈPag. 81.

ched euen as the Reprobate themselues, yea, *if it may be,more ex-*
traordinarily. All this you affirme, and by your owne words, "
all this is the ONLY TRVE, *and perfectly accepted sacrifice to* "
God. So then whosoeuer feeleth not all this, hath no broken "
nor contrite heart, nor anie longer then hee feeleth these hel-
lish torments in his soule. And if this be the ONLY TRVE
sacrifice to God, I will not aske what shall become of the
sacrifice of praise and thanksgiuing , but howe vnhappie
are the goodlie that at anie time are free from the paines of
the damned, and from the tormentes of hell, since the suf-
fering thereof is the ONLY TRVE and perfectlie accepted
sacrifice to God? ^c*Godly sorrow, saieth the* Apostle,*causeth* ᵉ 2.Corin.7
repentance vnto saluation; those wordes please you not ; such
^f *hellish sorrowes* , and *intolerable horrors* as the *Reprobate* „ ᶠPag.45 in
themselues feele, yea as *the damned doe suffer,* this saie you is margine.
the ONLY TRVE *and accepted sacrifice to God.* You must „
haue other sacrifices, and those accepted, before you come to
heauen; or else the Reprobate and damned will bee there as
soone as you : God send you his grace,and grant your wits
and senses bee not distempered and distracted; you talke so
much of hellish paines, and torments executed by diuels, as
the *only true sacrifice of a broken and contrite hart.* „

The Apostles wordes, whereon you first grounded this o-
dious assertion, haue no such intention, as you imagine. By
death Christ conquered him that had power of death that is the
Diuel. Aske the simplest childe ŷ is catechised in your charge,
if you haue anie , what death Christ died for vs, and hee will
answere you out of his Creede, Christ was crucified, deade,
and buried ; and that is the death which the Scriptures de-
scribe and deliuer. ^g I deliuered vnto you (saieth Paul)that ᵍ1Corin.15.
which I receiued,how that Christ died for our *sinnes,*according
to the scriptures; what death if wee aske the Apostle, he will
answere the death of the Crosse . For ^h ye preach (saieth he) ʰ1.Cor.1
Christ crucified ; and I esteemed not to know any thing among ᶦ1.Cor.2.
you but Christ Iesus and him crucified. Christ crucified then,

that is by his death on the crosse, destroied him that had powor of death . [Of what death, you aske , hath the diuell powor?] as well of the seconde death which Christ coulde not suffer ; as of the first which hee did suffer. [Christ, you will saie , coulde deliuer vs from no death , but from the verie same which he suffered himselfe.] If so you saie, or so would saie, it is no lesse then heresie, or blasphemie. Hee deliuered vs from euerlasting death, which hee neither did, nor coulde suffer . If you saie hee deliuered vs not from euerlasting death, it is open heresie; if you saie Christ suffered euerlasting death, it is blasphemie . Yet hath the diuell power of both deaths, as well temporal as eternall. What power, you

*Sapient. 1,
:Sapi, 2,

aske, hath the diuel of this death which our bodies die? [k] God made not that death, but by the [l] enuy of the Diuell it came into the world . He was the first procurer of it by perswading sinne, and still reioiceth in it as the verie gate to hel.

[m] Esa. 38

[m] I shal goe, (said Ezechiah) to the gate of hell, which was the death of his bodie; that waie the wicked passe to hell. Yea the Apostle

[n] 1.Corin. 15.

calleth the corruption of our bodies the sting of sinne , wherewith the diuell pearced vs; [n] when this corruption hath put on incorruption, ô death where is thy sting?

For the exposition of the Apostles words, I may either say

[o] Auguft. de pecc.merit.& femiss.li 2,c.32

with [o] S, Austen, *Ipse Dominus mori voluit, vt, quemadmodũ de illo scriptum est, per mortem euacuaret eum qui potestatẽ habebat mortis, id est Diabolum, & liberaret eos qui timore mortis per totam vitam rei erant seruitutis . Hoc Testimonio satis illud monstratur, & mortem istam corporis principe atque authore Diabolo, hoc est ex peccato accidisse, quod ille persuasit. Neq, enim ob aliud potestatem habere mortis verissimè diceretur.* The Lord himselfe would die, that is it is written of him, by death he might destroie him that had power of death, euen the diuell, and deliuer them which for feare of death were all their life long subiect to seruitude . By this testimonie it is sufficientlie prooued that this verie death of our bodies came from the Diuell as the Authour and chiefe dooer thereof; that is from the sinne which hee perswaded,

swaded. He cannot for any other cause be said to haue power of death, which here is most truly spoken. Ambrose, Chrysostom, and Cyril referre death throughout that sentence to the death of the bodie: In these wordes (saie they) the Apostle ᴾ noteth an admirable thing, that whereby the diuel had power, thereby was he ouerthrown. The weapons which were his strength against the world, that is death, by ŷ Christ strooke him. Why treble ye? why feare ye death? now death is not terrible, but acceptable as the end of labor and the beginning of rest. ꝗChrysostom hath almost the same wordes. Cyrill verie often expoundeth death in that place for the death of Christs bodie. ʳ The sonne of God was partaker of flesh and bloud, that yeelding his ʙᴏᴅʏ to death, he by nature as God being life it selfe, might quicken it againe: otherwise how had hee abolished the imperie of death, vnlesse he had raised againe his dead ʙᴏᴅʏ. And againe; ˢBecause it was aboue mans nature to abolish death, yea rather it was subdued of death, the son of God, that is life, took vnto him mans nature subiect to death, ŷ death as a cruell beast inuading his flesh should cease frō his tyranny ouer vs, that should thereby be abolished. If by death in the second place we vnderstand the death of body and soule with Fulgentius, I am not against it, this being alwaies remembred, that Christ died no death but the death of the bodie.ᵗ Mors filij Dei, quam ꜱᴏʟᴀ ᴄᴀʀɴᴇ suscepit vtramẽ, in nobis mortẽ, animæ scilicet carnisẽ destruxit. The death which the sonne of God suffered ᴏɴʟʏ in his flesh, destroied ʙᴏᴛʜ ᴅᴇᴀᴛʜꜱ in vs, as well that of the soule, as that of the body.

The Confuter hauing bestirred himselfe in his special and choise arguments, as thou hast heard (christiā reader) & now drawing to an ende, purposeth like a politicke captaine so to entrench himself, that no force shal fetch him out of his hold. And because wordes are the weapons that can endanger him; he taketh the readie waie with them, to turne & wind them at his will, and so maketh anie thing to be euerie thing, that nothing should hurt him. The scriptures affirme, that

Chris

ᴾ Ambros. in, Hebre. ca. 2

ꝗChrysost. in Hebre. ca. 2
ʳCyril de recta fide. lib. 1. ex Hebr. ca. 2

ˢIdem de recta fide lib. 2.

ᵗFulgent de incarnat. & grat. christi. c. 8

Chꝛiſt crucified is the wiſedome and power of God to all that be called, and that we are "reconciled to God by the death of his ſonne, and our ſinnes redeemed, and the ʸ diuel deſtroied by the death of Chꝛiſt Jeſus; as alſo that hee ʸ ſuffered for vs in the fleſh, yea he ᶻ ſuffered for our ſinnes being put to death in the fleſh. And leaſt it ſhould hence bee collected, that Chꝛiſt died not ꝗ death of the ſoule; but rather the death of his bodie was a ſufficient pꝛice foꝛ the life of the woꝛlde; the Refuter vndertaketh this place of Saint Peter, that Chꝛiſt was ᵃ done to death in the fleſh, and thence will pꝛoue, that the fleſh com-"pꝛehendeth bodie and ſoule, and that the ſoule of Chꝛiſt ᵇ DI-ED *and was crucified* as well as the bodie. Reaſon oꝛ authoꝛi-tie beſides his owne he bꝛingeth none, but out of the hinder part of his head he giueth an obſeruation, which, if he ſate the woꝛde, muſt needes pꝛoue ſounde and good; and this it is. "ᶜ *Whenſoeuer in ſcripture the fleſh and the ſpirit are oppoſed to-*"*gether, the* ᵈ *fleſh is alwaies Chriſtes whole humanitie, as well* "*his ſoule as his bodie. From whence it followeth that Chriſts ſoule* "*alſo died and was crucified.* How pꝛoue you this note, (Sir Refuter?) had you ſaide that whereſoeuer the fleſh of Chꝛiſt liuing is ſpoken of, there the fleſh of a man endued with a humane ſoule is intended; you had ſaide well: foꝛ Chꝛiſt was perfect man and perfect God, in one and the ſame perſon: but when you will ſtretch all the attributes of the bodie, and make them common to the ſoule, becauſe Chꝛiſt had a ſoule as well as a bodie, it is no true obſeruation de-riued from the ſcripture, but a partiall ſuppoſition intended to further your helliſh ſoꝛrowes. In the 26. of Matthew, when Chꝛiſt telleth his diſciples ᶜ that the ſpirit is readie, but the fleſh weake, doth hee take ſpirit there foꝛ the godheade, as if that were readie to ſuffer anie thing; oꝛ foꝛ the ſoule which was willing, but that the fleſh was weake? In the 24. of Luke when Chꝛiſt ſaieth, ᶠ a ſpirit hath not fleſh and bones as you ſee me haue, had his ſoule fleſh and bones, and thoſe to be ſeene as his bodie had? To the Romanes when Paul ſaith,
                                                ᵍChriſt

Marginal notes:

ᵘRom.5.
ˣHebre.2.
ʸ1.Peter.4.
ᶻ1.Peter.3.

ᵃ1.Peter.3.

ᵇPag.79

ᶜPag.78
ᵈPag.79

ᵉMatth.26.

ᶠLucæ.24

g Christ our Lord was made of the seede of *Dauid* according to the flesh, and declared to be the sonne of God, touching the spirit of sanctification, by the resurrection from the deade; will you conclude that Christes soule was made of the seede of Dauid and came from Dauids loines as Christes flesh did? The like he repeateth in the same Epistle: h of the Israelites came Christ according to the flesh, which is God ouer all to be blessed for euer; where if your obseruation faile not, Christes soule must be kinne to the Iewes as well as his flesh. Whie then, when Peter saith, i Christ was put to death according to the flesh, but quickned by the spirit, doe you make it so cleere a case that the worde flesh there compriseth both bodie and soule; and therefore by Peters confession, Christ died in soule as well as in bodie? so when Paul saith; k Christ was crucified through infirmitie, yet liueth through the power of God, what leadeth you to imagine, that his soule was crucified as well as his bodie? who did crucifie him I praie you, God or the Iewes? Peter saieth to the Iewes, l Iesus of Nazareth, a man approoued of God, after you had taken with wicked hands, you haue CRVCIFIED and slaine. So againe, m the holy and iust one ye denied, and killed the Lord of life. And likewise. n By the name of Iesus, whom ye haue crucified, whom God raised againe from the deade, doth this man heere stande whole, who before was a creeple. If the Iewes then crucified and killed the Lorde Iesus, coulde they crucifie and kill his soule? Are you so simple that you remember not the wordes of our Sauiour, o Feare not them which kill the bodie, but are not able to kill the soule? And you make it not an ouersight; but a positiue point of your holie truth, as you call it, that Christes soule was crucified and died; and consequentlie that the Iewes directlie against the wordes of Christ were able to kill and crucifie the soule of Christ. Will you saie that God crucified the soule of Christ, for what will you not saie, that say Christs soule was crucified & died? in what scripture shall wee reade that God crucified

g Rom. 1.

h Rom. 9

i 1. Pet. 3

k 2. Corin, 13

l Actes. 2.

m Acts, 3.

n Acts 4

o Matt. 10

Tt 1. the

the soule, as the Iewes did the bodie of Christ? you woulde seeme to conclude it out of the scripturs, which whensoeuer they speake of Christ crucified, they note the shamefull and cruel death which the Iewes executed on him, not anie thing that God did vnto him. And out of that word, euerie where in the scriptures referred to the Iewes, to inferre that God also crucified his soule, is as much madnesse as the former. If you feare not the paines of hell, because you are so well acquainted with them, feare at least the shame of the worlde, least they deride you to skorne, as lacking that common vnderstanding which boies in the streetes, and prentices in the shoppes haue. But what if your selfe, being be like amazed, and (as you saie of Christ) all confounded in all the powers of your soule, and senses of your bodie, when you wrate in defence of your holie cause, do contradict your selfe, and call your owne assertion ABSVRD and MOST FALSE, and that not ten or twelue leaues off, but in the verie same place where you labour to iustifie this position, and prouing and pronouncing it to be absurd and most false, you presently conclude it as a principle of your newe faith? well, if it bee not so, then I must confesse I was asleepe when I thought you did so. But if it fall out to be true which I saie, I hope (christian Reader) thou wilt thinke my time anie waie better imploied then longer to reason with such a braine-sicke babler.

° 1. Pet. 3. ver. 18.

The words of Peter are; ° Christ hath once suffered for sinnes, the iust for the vniust, and was put to death in the flesh, but quickned by the spirit. Saint Austen writing vpon this place obserueth this for a sure rule to expounde the whole.

? Aug. epist. 99

P *In ea re quippe viuificatus est, in qua fuerat mortificatus.* Christ was quickned in that verie part, wherein hee suffered death, or was put to death. This rule hath in it a mightie truth that maie not be resisted. For if any part of Christ died, which was not againe quickned, but still left dead, then that parte suffered perpetuall death; which is not onelie

plainelie

plainelie false but openlie blasphemous. Then must this
stande for an vndoubted grounde; that whatsoeuer part of
Christ was dead, the same must be quickned againe, to auoid
the eternall death of anie part. And if anie part of Christ nee-
ded not quickning or restoring to life, it neuer died; for
quickning is heere the restoring of life to that which was
dead, and not the giuing of life to that which had none be-
fore. Then if Christs soule died, of force it must either be quick-
ned againe, or kept vnder eternal death; but to saie that Christs
soule was quickned or made aliue IS ABSVRD AND MOST
FALSE: *Ergo* to saie that Christes soule died IS ABSVRD
AND MOST FALSE. You will aske me howe I proue the
Minor or second parte of this Argument? If Saint Austen
did not helpe me to proue it, the Confuter will. Loe (Sir
Refuter,) your own words in the very same place, take care
I praie you, that I misrepeat them not, for if I hit the right,
you wil proue your selfe as verie a baby as euer suckt a bot-
tle. ¶ BOTH THESE, saie you, ARE ABSVRD AND MOST FALSE, „
that Christ was made aliue either in his HVMANE SOVLE, „
OR BY THE SAME. See and shame, if there be anie grace, „
or sense in you, that going about purposelie to proue that
Christs soule died and was crucified, you set this for a pre-
face vnto it, *it is* ABSVRD *and most* FALSE *that Christ* „
was made aliue in his humane soule; which without any shift or „
colour, you do saie & must saie, before your conclusion can be
true; except you wil flie to this, that Christes soule died
in deede, but was neuer restored to life, or made aliue a-
gaine; which if wee come to, I must proclaime you no longer
foolish but blasphemous. Howbeit I hope you will rather
see your follie, then fall to this frensie; for my part, I wish
you better counsell and more reading; and althongh you
tell me of ʳ *errors*, ˡ *corrup: fansies and vayne imaginations*, „
ᵗ *shameful questiōs*, ᵘ *toyish fables*, ˣ *fond, absurd, without sense* „
or reason, when I doe but repeat the iudgementes of the „
ancient and learned Fathers; yet I will beare them at „

ᵗPage.78
linea.28.

ᶠPag.1.
ᵗPag.3
ᵗPag.54.
ˣPag 81.
ˣPag.48

Lt 2,   your

your hand, and from my heart doe pittie your ignorance, for
I hope it bee but ignorance; howsoeuer you take vpon you
to controle all as fond and absurde, that yeelde not to your
humour.

For the cleering of this place of Peter, wherein the Con-
futer hath so much ouer-seene himselfe, I stand not vpon the
aduantage of his wordes, but vpon the sounde and learned
expofition of Saint Austen, whose antiquitie and authoritie
concurring with the truth of the scriptures doth please me, &
I truft (chriftian reader) wul content thee. *Chriftus spiritu vi-
uificatus est, cū in passione esset carne mortificatus. Quid est enim,
quod viuificatus est spiritu, nisi quod eadem Caro, qua sola fuerat
mortificatus viuificante spiritu resurrexit ? Nam quod anima
fuerat mortificatus Iesus, hoc est eo spiritu qui hominis est, quis
audeat dicere, cum mors anima non sit nisi peccatum, a quo ille om-
nino immunis fuit ? Certe anima Christi non solum immortalis,
secundum naturam cæterarum, sed etiam nullo mortificata pec-
cato, vel damnatione punita est, quibus duabus causis mors ani-
ma intelligi potest; & ideo non secundum ipsam dici potuit Chri-
stus viuificatus spiritu. In ea re quippe viuificatus est, in qua
fuerat mortificatus; ergo de carne dictum est. Ipsa enim reuixit
anima redeunte, quia ipsa erat mortua anima recedente. Mor-
tificatus ergo carne dictus est, quia secundū solam carnē mortuus
est, viuificatus autem spiritu quia spiritu operante, etiā ipsa caro
viuificata surrexit. Christ was quickned by the spirit, when in
his Passion he was put to death in his flesh. What meaneth it,
that he was quickned by the spirit, but that the same flesh, in
VVHICH ONLY HE DIED, rose againe by the quickning
of the spirit ? For that Iesus DIED IN SOVLE, I meane in
his humane spirit, VVHO DARE AFFIRME IT, where as
the death of the soule is nothing (in this life) but sinne, from
which he was wholie free ? Surelie the soule of Christ was not
onlie immortal by nature, as others are, but neither died by sinne
nor was punished by any damnation, which are the two waies
how

*Aug.epift.99

how the foule maie poffiblie die. And therefore Chrift could not bee faid to bee quickned in foule by the fpirite: for in that part was hee quickned, in which hee died . Therefore it was fpoken (by Peter) of Chrifts flefh . That reuiued when the foule returned, becaufe that died , when the foule departed. Chrift then is fayd to bee done to death in his flefh, for that hee died ONLY IN HIS FLESH , and to be quickned by the fpirite , becaufe that verie flefh rofe againe being quickned by the working of the fpirite. Thefe learned and found conclufions of S. Auften, are deredlie repugnant to your weake and falfe obferuations, Syr Refuter. Chrift died in the flefh (faith Peter) that is faith Auften, in THE FLESH ONLY ; for the foule of Chrift died not, fince the death of the foule is either finne in this life, or damnation in the next, both which were farre from Chrift. You tell vs that Chrifts foule not onlie died, but was alfo crucified ; and all the proofe you bring for it, befides Terence, is that Peter faith Chrift died in the flefh. Now the flefh faie you, fignifieth as well the foule as the bodie, and fo Chrift died in both: but fuch proofes, if you vfe them often, will proue you to haue a great deale leffe religion and learning, then you would feeme to haue.

What death the Scriptures affirme Chrift died for vs, if you bee now to feeke at thefe yeares, it is pittie your fhoulders haue beene fo long troubled with your head. Can there bee fuller, or plainer words then thofe which the foure Euangelifts vfe in defcribing the death, buriall, and refurrection of the bodie of our Sauiour ? Shew but one fuch word in Scripture or father , that Chrifts foule died at the time of his Paffion, and take the caufe.[He layd downe his soule vnto death, you will faie;] You fhould haue done well in your pamphlette at leaft to haue laid that downe for a fhewe , and not vpon your fingle word to haue vouched fo weightie a matter as the death of Chrifts foule is; but you muft be borne with, your wits are often not at home. What is ment by this that Chrift laid downe or yeelded his Soule.

Lt.3. vnto

Efai.53.

vnto death, S. Austen largelie disputeth in his 47 treatise
vppon S. Iohns Gospell. The effect is, when Christ laid
downe his soule vnto death, his bodie died, and not his
soule. [a] *Quid fecit Passio, quid fecit mors, nisi corpus ab anima
separauit? Si enim mortuus est dominus, immo quia mortuus est
Dominus (mortuus est enim pro nobis in cruce) sine dubio caro
ipsius expirauit animam. Hoc est ergo ponere animam, quod est
mori. Cum ergo exit anima a carne, et remanet caro sine ani-
ma, tunc homo ponere animam dicitur. Carni hoc tribue, caro
ponit animam suam, & caro iterum sumit eam. Caro ponit a-
nimam suam expirando. Ipse Dominus Christus dictus est sola
caro. Audeo dicere, et sola caro Christi dictus est Christus. Con-
fiteris illud quod habet fides, in eum Christum te credere, qui cru-
cifixus est & sepultus. Ergo sepultum Christum esse non negas,
& tamen sola caro sepulta est. Ergo Christus erat etiam caro
sine anima, quia non est sepulta nisi caro. Disce hoc etiam in
Apostolicis verbis, Humiliauit semetipsum factus obediens
vsque ad mortem. Iam in morte* SOLA CARO *a Iudæis est
occisa,& tamen carne occisa Christus occisus est. Ita cum caro
animam posuit, Christus animam posuit, & cum caro vt resur-
geret animam sumpsit, Christus animam sumpsit.* What did the
Passion, what did the death of Christ, but separate his bodie
from his soule? If the Lord died for vs, yea rather because in-
deede the Lord did die for vs: (for hee died for vs on the crosse,)
doubtlesse his flesh did breath out his soule. Soe that to laie
downe his soule and to die is all one. When the soule departeth
from the flesh,& the flesh remaineth without any soule, then a
man is said to lay downe his soule. Vnderstād this of the flesh,
for the flesh laieth down her soule,& taketh it againe, the flesh
laieth down her soule by breathing it forth. The Lord Iesus is
called his flesh alone. I dare be bold to auouch it, THE ON-
LY FLESH of Christ is called Christ. Thou confesse st, as it is in
thy Creede, that thou beleeuest in that Christ, which was cru-
cified & buried. Then thou acknowledgest Christ to be buried,
& yet only his flesh was buried. Therefore flesh without a soule
was

was Chrift, becaufe nothing of him but his flefh was buried. Learne the felfe fame in the Apoftles words, Chrift humbled himfelfe & was obedient vnto Death, Now in his death ONLY HIS flefh was killed of the Iewes, and yet the flefh being flaine, Chrift was flaine. So when the flefh laid downe her foule, Chrift laid downe his foule, and when the flefh tooke her foule againe to rife, Chrift tooke his foule againe. To men that do not wilfullie blind themfelues thefe words are cleare e-nough, and they haue for their warrant the full confent of Scriptures, Councels, & Fathers, for 1400 yeares, without diffenting from it. bChrift fuffered for you, (faith Peter) lea-uing you an enfample that you fhould follow his fteppes, who himfelfe bare our finnes in his bodie on the Tree, that we being dead to finne, fhould liue in righteoufnes. Then when Chrift died to fin, his body died on the tree, his foul liued in righteouf-nes: So muft we do, for fo did he, when he left vs an example how to follow his fteppes. Our foules muft not die before we can refemble his death; they muft liue in righteoufnes as he did. cEuery where (faith Paul) we beare about in our bo-die the dying of the Lord Iefus, that the life of Iefus might alfo be made manifeft in our bodies; which he thus expoundeth af-terward. Therefore we faint not, but though our outward man perifh, yet the inward man is daily renewed. Then in our bodies we carrie about the death of Chrift, who for our ex-ample died in his bodie vnto finne, that we fhould follow his fteppes. And why doubt we hereof, fince the fame apoftle doth in as plaine & expreffe words, as might be fpoken, tefti-fie, that Chrift, when cwe were enimies, reconciled vs IN THE BODY OF HIS FLESH THROVGH DEATH; to make vs holy, and without fault in his fight, grounded and ftablifhed in faith, and not mooued awaie from the hope of the Gofpell? What could the hart of Paul inuent, or his tong vtter more effectuall then this, that Chrift THROVGH DEATH IN THE BODIE OF HIS FLESH reconcileth vs to God and maketh vs holie;.

b 1Pet.2

c 2.Cor.4

d Ibid.vers.16

e Colof.1.

holie, and without fault in his fight? If you can quarrell with thefe words (Sir Refuter) you maie do what you will with the Scriptures. No words will bind you, that take bodie for foule, life for death, faith for amazed feare, hope for intolerable horror, defcending for afcending, and hell for heauen. What is this els but to make a confufion of all Religion, and giue open defiance to the trueth by taking one contrarie for the other? You do not fo, you will faie. Leaue fo doing and thefe Queftions will foone be determined. I prooue there was alwaies in Chrift euidence of faith, affurance of hope, Ioy of loue euen in the midft of his paines on the

^f *Pag.7.* "croffe: and you graunt there was ^f *not anie the leaft dimi-*
"*nution in Chrift of his faith, patience or obedience to God,*
"neither was Chrift fo much *as touched with anie wauering,*
"much leffe fearing in his *truft and confidence of Gods loue and*

^g *Pag.77* "*protection towards him.* How then can the ^g horrour of Gods
"*feuere iuftice and wrath,* like them that indeed be feparated from the grace and loue of God, bee in Chrift? Or how can the forrowes of the damned which are feparated from the life of God bee found in Chrift? how could Chrift fuffer ^h *the fame*

^h *pag.46.* "*terrours of Gods wrath and affaults of the Deuill, yea far grea-*
"*ter then the godlie féele in their confciences, for want of faith,* and feare of Gods difpleafure? What are thefe but plaine

ⁱ *pag 57* "contrarieties? Againe in Chrift, you faie, ⁱ *was no defect of*
"*grace;* how then could the foule of Chrift replenifhed with the fpirite of life, and liuing in all fulnes of grace and trueth, bee dead? can you make one and the fame part of Chrift both aliue and dead? Soe likewife if Chrift had but ^k *feared*

^k *pag.64.* "*to bee vtterly forfaken with the hatred of his Father,* that indéed
^l *Pag.49.* "you faie *were defperation, which God forbid.* And yet you doe
^m *Pag.70.* "not doubt but *Chrift was as* ^l *deepelie touched with the* ^m *vn-*
ⁿ *Pag 80.* "*fpeakeable horror of Gods* ⁿ *feuere wrath due to finne as the* ^o
^o *Pag.81* *Reprobates themfelues.* A number of thefe hogepots you haue made vs; fpeaking of things which your felfe cannot, or dare not expreffe. Sometimes you would faine affirme
it

it in generall words, and when you come to particulars, you renounce it againe. In the verie case that gaue vs occasion of this rehearsall, when the Apostle saith, we are Preconci- ᵣRom.5. led to God by the death of his sonne, and explaining him- selfe, saith the death that reconciled vs to God, was the death which Christ suffered ⁹ in the bodie of his flesh; Is it ˢCol.5. not as cleare as daie light, that the bodilie death of Christ, which he suffered on the crosse, is by the scriptures resolued to bee the sufficient price of our redemption, and meane of our reconciliation to God, except you take the bodie of Christ for the soule of Christ, and the stripes and woundes of his flesh for the paines of hell? ᵗYee were redeemed ᵗ1.Pet 1. with the precious bloud of Christ, saith Peter.   Can there bee plainer wordes, that Christes ˢbloud shedde for the re- ʳMat.26. mission of our sinnes is the perfect price of our redemption, without the death of the soule, or paines of hell, which you interpose? So likewise, when Peter saieth ᵗ Christ bare ᵗ1.Pet 2. our sinnes in his bodie on the Tree, in that hee ᵘ suffered ᵘ1.Pet.3. once for sinners when hee was put to death in his flesh; are you not forced to peruert these wordes for defence of your fancie, and to take the flesh for bodie and soule, that you maie make the death of Christe to bee common to both? [It is one thing, you will saie, to take the fleshe for the whole man, and another to take the bodie for the soule.] I knowe it right well, but the one will not serue your turne without the other. By a part to name or note the whole man, is no newes in the Scriptures; but to ascribe the attributes of one part to the other, because the name of either part is sometimes ta- ken for the whole, that is a generall subuerting of all the trueth of the Scriptures. Saint Austen tolde you euen nowe, that Christes dead flesh is called Christ; will you therefore referre the properties of Christes dead flesh vnto his soule, and not thinke you take the waie to dissolue as well the vnion as communion of two natures in Christ,

Bb 1   and

and of the distinction of two parts in his manhood? The body indæde is more distinguished from the soule, then the name of flesh is, because the vnregenerate part of the soule is in the Scriptures euerie where called flesh; but this hath no place in Christ, by reason no corruption of sinne cleaued vnto his soule, and therefore the name of fleshe doeth no where signifie the soule in Christ, as it doeth often in vs; onelie by naming flesh in Christ, the scripture sometimes intendeth, that he disdained not the weakest and basest part of our nature, when he came to redéeme vs. And

* Iohn. 1.

so Saint Iohn saith, * The worde was made flesh, meaning the true and eternall sonne of God, vouchsafed to take not onelie our reasonable and humane soule vnto him, but euen our vilde and mortall flesh into the vnitie of his person, and so became man, that hee might restore man nowe fallen from God, and perished in his sinnes, to the fauour and life of God againe. But when the Scriptures saie, that Christ died for our sinnes, the auncient fathers and Councels with one consent applie that to the death of Christes bodie on the Crosse, and not to the death of the soule, or to anie paines of hell. And though in the Treatise before I haue cited such as sufficientlie witnesse that doctrine to be sounde and Catholike, yet will I not bee greeued to let thee see (Christian Reader) that there was nothing more commonlie, nor constantlie professed in the Primitiue Church, then the doctrine which I am now forced to defende against the rage and reproch of this slaunderous impugner.

7 Athanasius de incarnat. verbi dei.

7 Post edita per facta diuinitatis suæ monumenta, reliquum iam erat, vt pro omnibus sacrificium offerret, pro omnibus templum suum morti tradens, quo omnes innoxios & liberos à veteri præuaricatione efficeret, seque declararet mortis victorem. Corpus igitur quod communem cum omnibus habebat naturam (corpus enim humanum & mortale erat) ad similitudinem sui generis mortem excepit; verbum enim quoniam mori non potuit, vtpote immortale

immortale, corpus sibi sumpsit, quod mori poterat; illudque vt suu pro omnibus obtulit, vt ita pro omnibus, omnibus ipse corpore coniunctus, mortem patiens, compesceret eum, qui mortis habebat imperium, hoc est Diabolum, & liberaret eos quotquot formidine mortis per omnem vitam obnoxy erant seruituti. After Christ by his deedes had declared his diuinitie, it remained that hee shoulde OFFER A SACRIFICE FOR ALL, yeelding vnto death the temple (**of his bodie**) for all, thereby to deliuer and discharge all from the olde transgression, and to declare himselfe the conquerour of death. His bodie therefore, which in nature was like all ours (for it was an humane and mortall bodie) died in like maner as bodies doe. For the sonne of God, because he could not die being immortall, tooke a bodie vnto him that might die, and offered that as his owne for all men, that so being ioined in bodie to all, and suffering death for all, he might represse him that had power of death, euen the Diuell, and free those, that for feare of death were all their life long subiected to seruitude. Epiphanius **treadeth in the same steppes.**[z] When the sonne of God (**saith he**) would suffer of his owne good will for mankinde, because his diuinitie coulde not suffer, beeing of it selfe impassible, hee tooke τ̀ ἡμέτερον παθητὸν σῶμα, OUR BODIE THAT MIGHT SVFFER, that therein hee might yeelde to suffer, and admitted our sufferings, his Godhead being present in his flesh, the godhead suffreth not. For he that saith I am life, how can he die? But God remaining impassible συμπάσχει τῇ σαρκὶ, suffereth by his flesh, that his passion may be accounted to his deitie, though it suffered not to the ende our saluation shoulde bee from God. In his flesh was the suffering, least wee should haue a passible God. Which indeede is impassible, imputing that suffering vnto himselfe, according to his free choise, and not of anie necessitie. Ambrose **in like sort.**[a] *Laqueus contritus est, & nos liberati sumus. Non potuit melius conteri laqueus nisi prædam aliquam diabolo demōstrasset, vt dum ille festinaret ad prædam, suis laqueis ligaretur. Qua potuit esse præda nisi corpus? Oportuit igi-*

[z] *Epipha. hær. res. 69.*

[a] *Ambros. in Lucam. lib. 4 de duct. Christi in desertum*

tur

tur hoc fraudem Diabolo fieri, vt si sciperet corpus dominus Iesu & corpus hoc corruptibile corpus infirmum, vt crusigeretur ex infirmitate Si enim fuisset corpus spirituale, non dixisset, spiritus promptus est; caro autem infirma. The snare is broken, and we are deliuered. The snare could not bee better broken, then by shewing the diuel some pray, that whiles he hastned to the pray, he might be wrapped in his owne snares What pray could there be beside the bodie (of man?) It was therefore requisite the diuell should bee thus deceiued, that the Lord Iesus should take a body vnto him, euen this corruptible & weake body of ours, that he might be crucified through infirmitie. Had it beene a spiritual bodie that he tooke, he would neuer haue said, the spirite is rea-
• Idē. de incarn. Sacrament. ca. 5
die, but the flesh is weake. [a] The same Christ suffered, and suffe-red not; died and died not, rose againe and did not rise; because hee raised vp his owne bodie. For that which fell, that rose a-gaine; that which fell not, needed not rise. Hee rose then accor-ding to the flesh, which being dead did rise againe. Ergo also he died in our nature which he tooke vnto him, and suffered in the body which he tooke, that we might beleeue he tooke a true bo-die. To the vnbeleeuer asking, Shall I beleeue God in flesh, God borne of a woman, God crucified, whipped, dead, woun-
ᵇ August. de verbis domini secundum Io-han. serm. 42.
ded, buried? [b] Austen answereth, thy God remaineth vnchange able; feare not, he perisheth not. Christ was borne of a woman, but in his flesh. Hee was an infant, but in his flesh. Hee suc-ked, increased, was nourished, and grewe in age, but in his flesh. Wearied he slept, but in his flesh. Hee hungred and thirsted, but in his flesh. He was taken, bound, whipped & mocked: yea he was CRVCIFIED AND KILLED, BVT IN HIS FLESH. Why art thou afraid? The word which was God remaineth for euer. He that despiseth this humblenes of God wil neuer be cured from the deadly swelling of pride. The Lord Ie-sus therefore by his flesh gaue hope to our flesh. To be borne, and to die were here on earth common, to liue for euer was not here. Christ found here our earthlie wares, which were vilde, and brought with him his heauenlie, which were strange. If

thou

thou feare (his) death, loue (his) refurrection. c He came to the
place of our pilgrimage to take that which aboundeth here, euē
mocks, whippes, blowes, spittings in his face, reproches, hanging,
the croſſe and death. Theſe things abound in our region, to this
entertainment hee came. What hath he giuen thee here? Inſtruc-
tion exhortation, and remiſſion of ſinnes. What hath he promi-
ſed thee O mortall man ? that thou ſhalt liue for euer. Doeſt
thou not beleeue it ? Beleeue it, I ſay, beleeue it, It is more that
he hath alreadie done, then that hee hath promiſed. It is more
incredible, that the eternall died, then that the mortall ſhall liue
for euer. If God died for man, ſhall not man liue with God ?
But can God die ? Hee tooke from thee wherein to die for
thee. THERE COVLD NOT DIE BVT FLESH, THERE
COVLD NOT DIE BVT A MORTALL BODIE. Hee
clothed himſelfe with that wherein hee might die for thee; hee
will clothe thee, wherin thou ſhalt liue with him. d In that (part)
Chriſt died, in which thou ſhalt die: in that (part) Chriſt roſe
in which thou ſhalt die. Thou wilt pardon mee (Chriſtian
Reader) if among ſo much lothſome ſtuffe of reprobate hor-
rors, damned paines, and helliſh torments, as this Confu-
ter hath heaped together , I ſolace my ſelfe ſometimes
with the longer comfort of ſounde and ſweete doctrine,
ſo ſincerelie and ſenſiblie deliuered by the learned and
auncient Fathers . I will alledge one place more where-
in thou ſhalt ſee the full conſent of prouinciall and ge-
nerall Councels, not to bee gaineſaide by anie man that
will beare the name of a Chriſtian, and ſo ſhutte vp this
point.

Cyrill writing to Neſtorius, to ſtay and ſuppreſſe that
falſe doctrine which hee beganne then to ſpreade; teacheth
vs verie plainelie howe the ſonne of God is ſaide in the
Scriptures to SVFFER, DIE, AND RISE AGAINE for
vs, and our ſaluation. e So wee ſaie (the ſonne of God) ſuf-
fered and roſe againe ; not that the ſonne of GOD ſuffe-
red in his owne nature, either the ſtripes , or the boaring of

the

c Auguſt. in
pſal 148.

d Idem in pſ. 70

e Cyril epiſt. 8
ad Neſtorium.

the nailes, or the reſt of the woundes , ἀπαθὲς γὰρ τὸ θεῖον, ὅτι
καὶ ἀσώματον, the Deitie coulde not ſuffer by reaſon it is no
bodilie ſubſtance; but becauſe THAT BODIE, which hee
made his owne,ſuffered theſe things, himſelfe is ſaide to ſuffer
theſe things for vs. ἦν γὰρ ὁ ἀπαθὴς ἐν τῷ πάσχοντι σώματι,
He that coulde not ſuffer was then in his bodie which ſuffe-
red. After the ſame manner wee thinke of his dying . The
ſonne of God is by nature immortall, incorruptible, life and the
giuer of life ; but becauſe the bodie , which was his owne, ta-
ſted death for all by the fauour of God , as *Paule* ſpeaketh,
hee himſelfe is ſaide to haue ſuffered death for vs, not that hee
had experience of death as touching his owne nature, (it
were a madneſſe ſo to thinke, or ſay) but for that as I ſaide e-
uen nowe, his fleſh taſted death : So his fleſh riſing againe,
it is called his Reſurrection , not that hee fell to corruption,
God forbidde; but that his bodie roſe againe . When this
ſtayed not the frenzie of Neſtorius the heretike , but that
hee replied in ſwelling woordes , Cyrill called a Coun-
cell at Alexandria, and there with one conſent , they ap-
prooued the trueth, and ſent it vnto Neſtorius to bee con-
feſſed in theſe woordes amongſt others ; [f] If anie man doe
not confeſſe that the Sonne of GOD ſuffered in his fleſhe,
was crucified in his fleſh , and taſted death in his fleſh, let
him bee accurſed . Dilating this and the reſt of their Ar-
ticles in their Synodall Epiſtle ſent to Neſtorius , they
ſaie , [g] Wee confeſſe that the onelie begotten God, euen the
ſonne borne of God his father, though hee were impaſſible in
his owne nature , yet ſuffered hee in his fleſh for vs accor-
ding to the Scriptures ; καὶ ἦν ἐν τῷ σαυρωθέντι σώματι, τὰ
τῆς ἰδίας σαρκὸς ἀπαθὰς οἰκειούμενος πάθη; and was in his
bodie that was crucified, accounting the ſufferings of his owne
fleſh as proper vnto him,though he were without ſuffering;and
by the grace of God taſted death for all, διδοὺς αὐτῷ τὸ ἴδιον
σῶμα, when he gaue his owne bodie vnto death. This doctrine
came to bee ſcanned in the third generall Councell helde at
                                                Epheſus,

[f] Syn. Alex-
and anathe-
matiſmus. 12.

[g] Epiſtola Sy-
nodi Alex-
andrinæ ad
Neſtorium in-
ter Cyril.epiſt.
10.

ʰEphesus, and being there deliberatelie read, was woorde for
woorde allowed of the whole Councell, as agreeable to the
Scriptures and the Nicene fathers. The like approbation it
had, not onelie in the Councell of Constantinople vnder Flu-
uianus, but in the great councell of ⁱChalcedon, where the pro-
ceedings of both these Councels were afresh examined,
and the former woordes of Cyrill repeated and confirmed,
with the ful consent of that general Councel, as most sound
and catholike.

So that he shall ill deserue the name of a christian, that
after so manie fathers, and Councels, both Prouinciall and
Generall, will begin to teach vs a new faith, and tell vs that
the Scriptures meane Christ was crucified and died, as wel
in his soule, as in his bodie; since the whole Church with one
assent hath euer so conceiued and expounded the Scrip-
tures, that Christes crucifying and dying must bee refer-
red to his bodie; and consequentlie that the ioynt sufferings
of Christ (the soule feeling what the bodie suffered) were
most auailable for our redemption . For when they a-
scribe the crucifying and death of Christ to his bodie ;
they doe not exclude the soule from the sense and feeling
of the paine , which is a naturall consequent to the con-
iunction with her bodie, but they shew what part of Christs
manhoode suffered the crosse and death , that the Scrip-
tures so much speake of , and whereby wee are redee-
med and reconciled vnto GOD . One place repeated
in the Councell of Ephesus, maie serue in steede of manie,
to declare their meaning . ᵏHowe can the Creator of all
thnges, who is neither visible, palpable, nor mutable, sustaine
the Crosse and death ? Wee saie the sonne of God sustained
the Crosse and death in his owne flesh, that hee might deli-
uer vs from death and corruption. Hée laide downe his soule
for vs, not as an alien and straunger to the sonne of God, but
vnspeakeablie vnited vnto him, as himselfe saith ; I haue power
to lay downe my soule, and I haue power to take it againe.
ΤΆΥΤΗϹ

ʰ Ephesin. con-
cil ii. Sess. I.

ⁱ.Concil.Chal-
cedon. act. I

ᵏ Interrogatio
& respō. in cō-
cil. Ephesino
propositæ,

τάυτης ἰδιον τὸ ἀδημονεῖν, τὲ λύπην ὑπομένειν, ᾗ ἐκδημεῖν ἀπὸ τᾶ σώματῷ· ὡς ἡμὶ σαρκὸς τ κοπιᾷν, τ ςαυρᾶϛαι, τὸ ἀνίϛαϛαι. It is proper to the soule to bee pensiue, to feele paine and griefe, to depart from the bodie; as it is proper to the flesh to be wearied, to be crucified, to be raised againe. So the violence was offered to the bodie, the sense whereof reached vnto the soule; and these are the sufferings of the crosse, and of death, which the Scriptures attribute to the sonne of God for our saluation; Insomuch that your long discourse of the proper and immediate suffering of Christes soule for sinne without and besides the bodie, maie be hanged on the hedge, as discoursing both from the scriptures, and all the Catholike fathers, that either haue priuatelie testified the truth by their writings, or publiklie confirmed it by their assemblies. And as for your hellish paines, when your selfe can tell what they are, and make some better proofe, then yet you haue done, that they were, or might be in the soule of Christ, you shal receiue further answere.

These are the Refuters exquisite arguments, which he calleth his speciall reasons, being indeede rather so manie monsters in Christian Religion, then matters to perswade anie man were he neuer so simple, and but that a straunge faith muste needes haue such straunge groundes as these bee, I should thinke hee did rather expose this conceipte of Hell paines, to bee derided of the worlde, then to bee beleeued, hee euerie where so secondeth his badde cause with woorse proofes; but where better foode wanteth, Akornes are good meate, and blacke Moores maie bee beautifull, when others bee swate. I woulde heere make an ende of his first parte, but that as his manner is, when hee hath stumbled absurdlie a long while at hell hee steppeth on the suddaine as vnhandsomelie to heauen. [1] *Knowe therefore* (saieth hee) *hell, as we take it is euen in this life founde sometime, as heauen is likewise; for as* [m] *touching materiall fire in hell, what a toyish fable*

[1] Pag. 80.

Pag. 81

fable is that? elſe I praie you how may the ſoules of the damned ſuf- ,,
fer by materiall fier, ſeeing they are ſpirits, and therefore with ,,
them and fier materiall there can be no communion. But let it bee ,,
as it may be; the locall hell of the damned we ſpeake not of . You ,,
ſlacke your hell paines (Sir Refuter) towardes the ende,
as if all this while you had beene too hot in them; and heere
you giue three qualifications to them; or rather contradicti-
ons to your former ſpeeches . *Hell as you take it is* SOME- ,,
TIMES *found in this life.* But two leaues before you tolde ,,
vs the ⁿ *paines and ſufferings of Gods wrath, which are the hell* ,,   ⁿ*Pag. 77.*
that you ſaie Chriſt ſuffered, ALVVAIES *accompanie them* ,,
that are ſeparated from the grace & loue of God; how commeth ,,
ALVVAIES to bee ſo quicklie changed into SOMTIMES?
were there fewer wicked when you ſpake the laſt wordes,
then when you ſpake the firſt? or are you better aduiſed; re-
membring what a groſſe abſurditie it woulde bee to caſt all
infidels and hypocrite, wicked and diſobedient perſons into
hel torments all the time of this life before the iudgment of
God taketh hold of them? Secondlie, ᵒ *as there is heauen* ,,   ᵒ*Pag. 80.*
euen in this life in ſome meaſure, euen ſo, ſaie you, *there may* ,,
be hell. You doe not meane that here on earth are the verie
ſame ioies and bliſſe that are in heauen, nor anie way equall
to them; if you did, it were a lewder abſurditie then the for-
mer. For here ᵖ we reioice, that our names are written in hea-   ᵖLuke.10
uen ; (as the Apoſtle teacheth vs to doe) �q wee reioice vnder   qRom.5
the hope of the glorie of God . ʳ Now hope that is ſeene, is not   ʳRom 8.
hope. For howe can a man hope for that which hee ſeeth (or
poſſeſſeth?) but when we hope for that we ſee not, we doe with
patience abide for it. In this life ſ wee walke by faith, not by
ſight; and whiles we dwell in the bodie, we are abſent from the ſ2.Cor.5
Lord. For though t we be now the ſonnes of God, it appeareth ᵗ1.Iohn.3
not as yet what we ſhal be ; ᵘ our life is hid with Chriſt in God;   ᵘColoſ.3
when Chriſt, who is our life ſhall appeare, then ſhall wee alſo
appeare with him in glorie. If you therefore affirme of hea-
uen as you do of hell, that the VERIE SAME ioies which are

in heauen, o2 EQV'ALL with them are here sometime found on earth, it is a wicked errour flatlie repugning to the trueth of Gods p2omises, and to the verie nature of our Ch2istian faith and hope. (Fo2 ˣ faith is the 'grounde of thinges hoped for, and the euidence of thinges not yet appea-ring,) but if you meane that as wee conceaue HOPE of heauenlie blisse, so wee must nædes REIOYCE in it; this position is verie true, but plainelie opposite to your imagi-nation of hell paines. Fo2 then must there in this life bee no mo2e felte of hell, but the FEARE thereof, and the griefe arising from that feare; euen as the HOPE of hea-uen maintaineth our ioye. Nowe in Ch2ist coulde nei-ther the feare of hell possiblie bee founde, no2 anie griefe, o2 so2rowe arising from anie such feare, since there was "in his soule no wante of faith no2 hope, *no ʸ not anie the* "*least diminution* of either, as your felfe confesse; but as the Apostle faieth, ᶻ FOR THE IOY THAT VVAS SET BEFORE HIM he endured the (paine of the) crosse, and de-spised the shame. And here you may fæ by your owne com-parison the follie of your owne assertion. Fo2 if your hellish "so2row? *be the only true and perfectly accepted sacrifice to God,* (as you faie) and ᵇ without faith it is impossible to pleafe God; which alwaies hath hope, and consequentlie, ᶜ the ioie of fal-uation annered vnto it, which you call heauen; then can no man pleafe God, o2 offer anie facrifice to God, till hee bee both in hell and heauen at one and the fame time; and the ioyes of heauen are fo coupled with the paines of hell, that none of the faithfull can be in the one without the other, but in both togither. And thus haue you b2ought heauen and hell not onelie to bee euerie where, but by your co2rupt con-ceites to bee alwaies linked together. Laftlie, the fire of hell doeth fomewhat trouble you, and therefo2e you labour vtterly to quench it; and aske, ᵈ *what a toyish fable is that?* but good Sir, if you would b2ing no mo2e fables then I doe, you might haue spared not euerie leafe, but euerie line in
                                                                this

ˣ Hebre.11.

ʸ Pag.71.

ᶻ Hebre.12.

ᵃ Pag:68.
ᵇ Hebre.11.
ᶜ Pfal. 51.

ᵈ Pag.31.

this poure vnaduised pamphlet. I spake not in my sermon one word either of materiall, or corporall fire in hell, but I vrged the fire of hel to be a true created fire, and not any metaphoricall flame, as you here dreame: from which since the bodie and soule of Christ were both free, he did not suffer the true paines of hell, nor the same torments which the damned do in hell; and which wee should haue suffered, had wee not béene redéemed.

^c *This (you saie) is great iniquity, yea plaine sophistry to amplifie against you, and to make your most holie truth odious with the people onely by the ambiguitie of the worde hell.* Begin you nowe to finde the sensible absurditie of your mishapen fancie? if you woulde haue taken the name of hell metaphorcallie for great and excéeding paines, this question had béene sooner calmed, and our Créede fréed from your neine found exposition. But to father your opinion vpon the créed with more likelihood, where the word hell is properlie taken, (though you now hatch vs a new signification of hell out of Socrates,) you then vrged as your selfe in this present confutation do still vrge, that Christ must haue the ^f FVL VVAIGHT AND BVRDEN *of our finnes laid vpon him, and* ^g *suffer those forrowes and paines for finne,* VVHICH ELSE VVE SHOVLDE; *that his price* VV AS THE SAME *which elfe wee shoulde haue payde; that feeing it* ^h *was possible for him to feele* THE FVLL SMART *of our finnes, yea* ALL OVR SMART, *and Gods strict iustice so required,* IT VV AS SO, AND MVST BE SO; *as also, that* ⁱ *it is not proportionable with iustice, that an easier nishment should satisfie for a greater finne, and* ^k *of all absurdities the greatest, that meere men shoulde fuffer more deepelie then Christ did; and therefore,* ^l *Christ sustained euen the sense of Gods wrath* DVE *to our finnes, and had the* ^m VVHOLE CVRSE *of God for finne executed on him, that is the* ⁿ DEATH OF THE SOVLE *and the* ⁿ TORMENTES *and forrowes* DVE TO THE DAMNED. Without anie

X x 2 sophistrie

^e Pag. 80.

^f Pag. 28.
^g Pag. 34

^h pag. 37.

ⁱ pag. 2
^k pag 48

^l Pag. 73.
^m Pag. 40.

ⁿ Pag 77.

Sophistrie Sir, what is the FVLL BVRDEN of our sinnes, and THE SAME PRICE which we should haue paide, what is OVR FVLL SMART yea ALL OVR SMART, and the VVHOLE CVRSE OF GOD; what is the DEATH of the soule, and the TORMENTS DVE TO THE DAMNED, but those verie things which I by the warrant of Gods word told the people were prepared and threatned to the wicked, and shall bee executed on them in hell, as they shoulde haue bin on vs, if we had not bin redeemed by the blond of Christ? you must recall all your reasons, and vnsaie all these positions before you can auoid that which I obiect. If Christ did, and must by Gods iustice suffer the VVHOLE, the SAME, and ALL that was due to vs for our sinnes; shewe me, good Sir, I praie you (for I confesse it passeth my reach) how you can free him from the darknes, destruction, reprobation, malediction, worme or fire of hel? yea those words, if you looke not well to them, and rebate them in time with some fresh write, they will carrie with them both the PLACE and PERPETVITY of hell; for both these were DVE to our sinnes, and are parts of Gods CVRSE, and should haue béene executed on vs, as they shall bee on the damned; and out of ALL, the VVHOLE, and the SAME, how can you except anie, but by an

ᵒ Pag. 81. " open *Vray dire* of dotage? [ᵒ *The local hel of the damned you* " *speake not of.*] Speake of what you will; so long as your assertions, in full and plaine termes inferre and conclude so much; well your words may runne without your wits; but I tell you trulie what is the consequent of them, and leaue those words, and then your most holie trueth is left naked without shew or shadow of proofe. For these generals, the VVHOLE, the SAME, and ALL giue life, such as it is, to your childish reasons. Without them you cannot open your mouthe to make one conclusion.

But because hell fire so much crosseth your cause, that you would faine be rid of it, and burneth your fingers so fast, (Sir Refuter,) that you striue to cast water on it; giue mee

leaue

leaue a little to let you vnderſtand, it flameth more fiercelie, then that you can quench it with the licour of your mouth. And the rather for that in the eares of all men it is a moſt ſenſible reproofe of your vnſauorie poſition. For if Chriſt ſuffered not the fire of hell in bodie nor ſoule, then moſt apparantlie he ſuffered not the F V L L burden of our ſinnes, nor paid the S A M E price which wee ſhould haue paide, nor endured A L L our ſmart, nor felt the VV H O L E curſe of God, nor ſuſtained the tormentes D V E to the D A M N E D; and therefore the true kindeling of this fire, is the vtter quenching of your new deuiſed hell paines. Knowe you therefore (Sir Refuter) that your metaphoricall fire in hell is a phantaſticall errour of yours; and you ſhall doe well to tremble at the terrible iudgement of God threatned in his worde with more religion, then to caſt off that fire as a _toyiſh fable_. I ſhall not nœde to rehearſe, how often it is denounced in the Scriptures, and in what behement and conſtant manner; let vs learne rather carefullie to ſhunne the place, then cunninglie to ſhift the word, which they ſhall finde to bee no figure, that feele it. P A fire (ſaith God himſelfe) is kindled in my wrath, and ſhall burne to the bottome of hell, it ſhall eate through the earth, and the depth thereof, and ſhal inflame the foundations of the hils. q Behold, (ſaith Eſay) the Lord wil come with fire, that he may recompence his anger with wrath, and his indignation with the flame of fire, for the Lorde ſhall iudge with fire. The ſlaine of the Lorde ſhall bee manie, their Worme ſhall not die, neither ſhal their fire be quenched. Which wordes our Sauiour directlie referreth to hell. r It is better to enter into life haulting, then hauing two legs to bee caſt into hell, into the fire that neuer ſhall bee quenched, where their Worme dieth not, and the fire neuer goeth out. ſ If wee ſinne willinglie (ſaieth the Apoſtle to the Hebrues,) there remaineth no more ſacrifice for ſinnes, but a fearefull expectation of iudgement, and raging fire, which ſhal deuoure the aduerſaries. As Sodome and Gomorra and the cities about

them

p Deutero.32

q Eſa.66

r Mark.9.

ſ Hebre.10

t Iud.r.epiſt.

them are set forth for an ensample, and suffer the vengeance of eternall fire. [u] The fearefull and vnbeleeuing, the abhominable and murtherers, and whoremongers, and sorcerers, and Idolaters and all lyars shal haue their part in the lake which burneth with fire and brimstone, which is the second death; **To whome the Iudge shall saie, when they shall see the truth thereof before their eies** , [x] Depart from mee ye cursed into euerlasting fire, prepared for the Diuell and his angels. [y] For the Lord Iesus shall shewe himselfe from heauen with the Angels of his power in flaming fire rendering vengeance to them which know not God, and obey not the Gospell. **That the fire with which Christ shall appeare to iudge, shall bee corporall and visible to all mens sights can bee no question, it** [z] shall dissolue the heauens, melt the elements, and burne vp the earth with the workes that are therein, as Peter affirmeth: **and that the wicked shall euerlastinglie burne therein, all the Fathers with one consent acknowledge.** [a] Ignorance (saith Austen) of such as are not willfully, but simplie ignorant, shall excuse no man from burning in euerlasting fire. For it is not saide without cause: Christ shall come in flaming fire to render vengeance to those ȳ know not God. [b] In flaming fire rendering vengeance; this (saieth Ierome) *Paul* speaketh against them because they dreampt of the paine of conscience, and thought this impossible. If the flame by Gods commandement did not so much as touch the three men (**that were cast into it,**) [c] why by the same power shoulde not fire be beleeued to bee sharper to some, and easier to others? [c] Christ shal come (saith Ambrose) with his heauenlie armie, and with fire as his minister to giue vengeance on the Pagans which knewe not God, and the Iewes which beleeued not the gospell of Christ, all which the fire shall burne, that they may bee punished with euerlasting destruction, alwaies feeling it, and neuer failing in it, that the verie paine which consumeth them, may euer renewe them. **And so** Chrysostome. [d] Thinke on this fire, and thou wilt count the pleasure of sinne to bee no pleasure. If
the

Marginal notes:
- [a] Apoc. 21.
- [x] Matt. 25
- [y] 2. Thessa. 1
- [z] 2. Pet. 3
- [a] August. de grat. & lib. arbitr. cap. 3
- [b] Hierony. in 2. Thessa. ca. 1
- [c] Ambros. in. 2. Thessa. ca. 1
- [d] Chrysost. in 2. Thessa. ca. 1

the onely fight of a deade man fo quaile our hearts, howe much
more hell, and the fire which cannot be quenched? becaufe the
very remembrance of it is able to drawe vs to do well, therefore
God hath appointed the very threatning of it, as an wholefome
medicine for our foules.

Your fœuelefle obiections againft thefe and the like pla-
ces, that if there be *true fire* in hell, why not a true *worme* as
well, and *much wood*? And if this fire were prepared for Di-
uels that are fpirits, what communion hath fire with fpirits?
thefe trifles of yours I faie, S. Auften hath long fince fullie
confidered, and learnedlie refuted, and plainlie refolued, that
all thefe toyes notwithftanding, the fire of hell is not onelie
a TRVE fire, which were my wordes, but a CORPORAL fire
that fhall punifh both men and diuels; at which you fo much
wonder. *Mitti in gehennam ignis, vbi vermis eorum non
moritur, & ignis non extinguitur, non piguit vno loco eadem
verba ter dicere. Quem non terreat ifta repetitio, & illius pœnæ
comminatio tam vehemens ore diuino?* To be caft into hell fire,
where their worme dieth not, and the fire quencheth not, Chrift
did not loath in one place, to repeate the fame wordes thrice.
Whome woulde not this repetition terrifie, and the threat-
ning of that paine fo earneft by Chriftes owne mouth? Both
thefe, the fire and the worme, fuch as woulde haue them to be-
long to the paines of the foule, and not of the body, faie; that fire
may be here fitlie taken for burning griefe; as the Apoftle fpea-
keth, *who is offended, and I burne not?* the fame kinde of
griefe they thinke, may be vnderftood by the worme; for fo it is
written, *As the worme wafteth woode, fo doeth griefe
the heart of man.* On the other fide thofe that doubt not, but
in hell the bodie and foule fhall be both punifhed, they affirme
the body fhall bee afflicted with fire, the foule with a kinde of
forrowe, as it were with a worme. The which though it bee
MORE LIKELIE, becaufe it is ABSVRD, that in hel fhould
want either paine of bodie or of foule; I rather beleeue that both
PERTAINE TO THE BODY, then that neither; and that the
fcripture

* Auguft. de
ciuitate dei.
lib. 21. cap. 9

f 2. Corin. 11.

s Prouerb. 25

scripture in these wordes suppresseth the griefe of the soule, because it followeth as a consequent, though it be not expressed, that the bodie beeing so tormented, the soule must likewise bee afflicted with an vnfruitfull repentance. For it is writte n in the bookes of the olde Testament, [h] the vengeance on the flesh of the wicked is fire and worme. Let euerie man choose what best pleaseth him, to attribute fire to the bodie, the worme to the soule, the one properly the other figuratiuely ; or both to the bodie properly. For I haue afore sufficientlie shewed, that certaine creatures liue euen in the fire in burning without consuming, in payne without death, by the maruelous power of the Almightie Creator; which to be possible whosoeuer denieth, knoweth not by whome all wonders are wrought. Let therefore euerie man choose of the twaine, which he liketh best, whether he will referre the worme properlie to the bodie, or to the soule, by a kinde of translation of thinges corporall to spirituall, so that BY NO MEANES HEE THINKE the bodies in hell shall bee such, that they shall not be touched with the paine of fire. [i] Heere riseth another question, if the fire that shall afflict (in hell) bee not incorporall, as the griefe of the soule is, but CORPORALL AND HVRTING WHERE IT TOVCHETH, that bodies may therein bee tormented, howe the wicked spirits shall bee punished by the same ? For the same fire is prouided to punish both men and Diuels as Christ saieth, [k] *Depart from me yee cursed into euerlasting fire prepared for the Diuel and his Angels.* Why should we not say that incorporall spirits may be afflicted by the paine of corporall fire, after a true but a maruailous manner, when as the spirits of men beeing also incorporall, may nowe bee inclosed in the members of their bodies, and shall then bee tied to the bandes of their bodies without dissolution ? therefore the spirits of Diuels, or rather the spirits that are Diuels, though they bee incorporall, shall be FASTENED TO CORPORALL FIRE, thereby to be tormented after a strange and vnspeakeable maner: Fastened I saie, to receiue torment from the fire, not to
giue

[h] Ecclesiast.7

[i] Idem de ciuitate dei lib. 21.cap.10

[k] Matth.25.

giue life to the fier. And hell it selfe which is called the lake burning with fire and brimstone, SHALL BE A CORPORAL FIER, and shall torment the bodies of men with their soules, and the diuels that are spirits without bodies feeling paine, but not giuing life to those CORPORALL FIERS. The steps of Austen doth Gregorie followe : [1] Corporall fier to continue needeth corporal nourishment: but contrariwise the fier of hell (which is incorporal) and SHAL CORPORALLY BVRNE the wicked cast into it, is neither kindled with mans industrie, nor fed with wood, but once created remaineth vnquenchable, and needeth no kindling, and wanteth no burning. Therefore the Scriptures, to shew that the reprobate burne within & without, say, they are deuoured with fier, and made as an ouen, that by fier they may bee tormented in their bodies, and by griefe burne in their mindes. And though the word *incorporeus* bee crept here into Gregories text in stead of *Corporeus*, as appeareth by the comparison and words adioyning, (for it were no straunge thing that a metaphoricall fier should neede no kindling of man, nor nourishing of wood; & how can an incorporall fier CORPORALLY burne the reprobate, which are the words presently following?) yet to put that out of doubt, his opinion is cleere to the contrarie in his Dialogues, where hee saith: [m] That the FIER OF HELL IS CORPORALL, I haue no doubt, in which it is certain bodies shall be tormented. And if the diuell and his angels being incorporall shal be tormented with CORPORALL FIER, what maruell if the soules before they receiue their bodies feele corporall torments?

Neither were they the first that made this resolutiō; that an actuall and sensible fier shal torment the bodies & soules of the damned; the Church of Christ from the beginning beleeued the same. [n] The prophane Philosophers (saith Tertullian) know the difference of this common and that hid fier; so far distant is this which serueth mans vse, from that which in Gods iudgement appeareth, whether it flash with thunder from heauen, or break through the earth by the tops of hils. For that consumeth not, what it burneth; but rather repayreth what it eateth, as the

mountaines

[l] Greg. moral. li. 15. cap. 17.

[m] Idem. dialog. lib. 4.

[n] Tertul. in apologetico versus finem.

mountaines euer burning doe still continue, and he that is blasted from heauen liueth and turneth not to ashes. This is a testimonie of that eternall fier, this is an example of that perpetuall iudgement, which maintaineth punishmēt. The hils burne and dure; how then shall the wicked and the enemies of God?

o Lactant. de diuino prae-mio li.7.ca.21.

Lactantius in like fort: ° The holy Scriptures teach vs how the wicked shall be punished. Because they sinned in their bodies, they shall take their flesh again, that they may be punished in their bodies; yet that flesh which God will clothe man with, shall not bee like this earthly flesh, but indissoluble and remaining for euer, that it may suffice for torment, and for euerlasting fier. The nature of which fier is diuerse from this which wee vse about the necessaries of this life. For that fier alwaies liueth and burneth of it selfe without any nourishment. The same diuine fier therefore with one and the same strength and power shall burne and continue the wicked, and shall yeeld it selfe euerlasting maintenance, so as it shall only burne and torment without any decay to the bodie. Cyprian is often and earnest in this cause:

p Cyprian. ad Demetrianū.

P *Cremabit addictos ardens semper gehenna, & viuacibus flammis vorax poena, nec erit vnde habere tormenta vel requiem possint aliquando, vel finem:* Hell alwaies burning shall broyle them that are adiudged to it, and paine shall deuoure them, with continuall flames; neither shall their torments haue ease or end. And againe,

q Idem de laude martyrij.

q *Saeuiens locus cui gehenna nomen est, eructantibus flammis per horrendam spissae caliginis noctem, saeua semper incendia camini fumantis expirat; globus ignium atratus obstruitur, & in varios poena exitus relaxatur:* The cruell place, which is called hell, casteth vp fearfull fiers, like a burning chimney, the flames breaking through the horrible darknes of ÿ thick mist; a whole globe of blackish fier standing and resoluing into diuers sorts of torments.

r Idem de ascensione chri-sti.

r *Stridorem illum Dentiū flammae inextinguibiles agitabunt, immortales miseri viuēt inter incendia, & inconsumptibiles flamma nudū corpus allambent:* Vnquenchable flames shall force that gnashing of teeth, immortall wretches shall liue in the midst of fier, and flames neuer consuming shall wrap their naked bodies. Hell as Chrysostome writeth, hath fier and darknes, but far worse then these which we are acquainted.

quainted with. ʃFor if there be fier(saith he)how is there dark- ʃ Chryʃoʃt. in
neʃʃe? thou ʃeeʃt that fier is more grieuous then this our fier,for it hebre ca. t.
hath no light: if it bee fier,how doth it burne for euer?thou ʃeeʃt homilia.1.
it is worʃe then ours,for that is not to be quenched,and therfore
is called vnquenchable. Let vs then thinke with our ʃelues how
great a miʃerie it is,to burne for euer, to be in darknes, to make
continuall lamentation,and to gnaʃh the teeth and not to be re-
garded? if darknes alone doe ʃo terrifie, and trouble our hearts,
what ʃhall it do when ʃuch grieʃes & flames of fier come with it?

Minutius Felix in his dialogue betwixt an Ethnicke and a
Chriʃtian, cited by Lactantius in his firʃt booke De falʃa reli-
gione cap.11. ʃaith: ᵗAs the lightnings touch mens bodies,but t Minutius
conʃume them not;and the flames of the hils Ætna & Veʃuuius, Felix in Octa-
and of other parts of the earth do burne & not waʃte;ʃo that pu- uio.
niʃhing fier(inhell)feedeth not vpon the decayes of their bodies
that burne, but continueth without eating or waʃting their bo-
dies.The ʃame compariʃon doth Pacianus,ẏ died vnder Theo-
doʃius,make in his exhortation vnto repentance againʃt the
Nouatians:ᵘPoʃt animarum tēpeʃtiua ʃupplicia rediuiuis quoque u Pacianus in
perpetua corporibus pœna ʃeruatur: After the due puniʃhment paræneʃi ad
of the ʃoules,(of the wicked) a perpetuall torment is prepared pœnitentiam.
for their bodies that ʃhall be reʃtored to life. The force whereof
you may coniecture by the things which are in this world.Ætna,
Liʃaniculus, and Veʃuuius in Campania doe caʃt out vnceaʃing
flames of fier, and to manifeʃt to vs the perpetuitie of that (ter-
rible) iudgement, they ʃtill breake & waʃte,and yet neuer end.

Sibylla whom ˣ Lactantius, ˣ Euʃebius,and ˣ Auʃten alledge x Lactantius
and allow as inʃpired by God,deʃcribeth the laʃt iudgemēt lib.7.ca.20.
with theʃe words : The earth cleauing ʃhall lay open the dun- x Euʃebius de
geon of hell ; all kings ʃhall come before the Tribunall of God, vita Conʃtant.
and a flood of fire and brimʃtone ʃhall fall from heauen (vpon x Auguʃt. de
the wicked.) ᵞ Chriʃtus in ʃuo tunc terrore videbitur, eíque ciuitate Dei
ignis iudicij in reproborum vindicta famulabitur, quia videli- li.18.ca.23.
cet Ignis iƚƚe Iudicij, qui cœlum, aerem, & terram concremat, y Greg. in E-
peccatores inuoluit; quos proculdubio in pœna ʃua damnationis zechiel ho-
confringit : Chriʃt then ʃhall be ʃeene in his terror,and the fier mil.2.
of iudgement ʃhall ʃerue him to reuenge the Reprobate,by rea-

son the very fier of iudgement, which melteth the heauens, the ayre and the earth, wrappeth in sinners, whom doubtlesse it crusheth in the torment of their damnation. ᶻ Yea, the flame of hell shineth not to the Reprobate for their comfort, and yet giueth light for their punishment; that to the eyes of the damned though the fier of their torment shine with no brightnes, yet it sheweth for their further griefe in what sort they are punished. How thinke you Sir Refuter, is it a TOYISH FABLE worthy of such contempt as you make it, or a point of Christian doctrine deliuered by the Prophets and Apostles, and receiued by the Fathers in all ages in Christs Church, that the FIRE of hell shalbe VISIBLE and SENSIBLE to the bodies of the wicked, and shall ETERNALLY and CORPORALLY punish the damned according to their deserts without quenching it selfe, or consuming thē? And your foolish Philosophie that things corporall cannot worke vpon things spiritual, must giue place to the power and will of the Almightie; by whose appointment wee see in this life nothing more common, thē that the soule which is spirituall, suffereth from her bodie all kindes of paines; and therefore it is as easie for God to make the soule feele fier in the next life without the bodie, as with the bodie; whose power if it please you to impugne, you must leaue the name of a Christian, and get you some other profession. So then the paines which the damned feele, besides the griefe of heauen lost, is FLAMING FIER intolerably tormenting both bodie and soule; and as ª Cyprian obserueth; *Omni tormento atrocius desperatio condemnatos affliget* : Desperation, which shall afflict the condemned worse then al their torments. To these if you subiect the Sonne of God, you know what will follow; from these if you free him, as you needes must, then is the Question at an end: for in euery mans sight, Christ did not suffer the paines of hell, nor the torments of the damned, which the scripture maketh to be these, ɛ not those which you can neither expresse nor proue.

Frō slender reasons you come (Sir Refuter) to slenderer authorities; and though you quote but few, and not one of them

---

ᶻ Idem moral. li.9.ca.39.

ª De ascensione Christi.

them speaking one word to your purpose, yet before you
produce them, you chalenge them as vnsufficient to testifie
in this, or any cause against your liking. For where they
may not be iudges, nor with you so much as witnesses of
the Scriptures sense, (you so reiect their expositions euerie
where with pride & disdaine) yet you in your wisedome take
vpon you to build vpon the words of the holy Ghost, what
absurdities and follies you list; and your best reason is, *it* „
were fond to thinke otherwise: but be more sober, if you will be „
ruled by me; it is the way to hazard your own wits, & not
their credits, to entertaine thē in this maner. [They speake
not plainly, nor fully you say, because it was neuer in que-
stion in their time.] Touching the redemption of man by
the death & blood of Christ Iesus, they speake as plainly and
fully as it is possible for men to speake; and kǣpe exactly the
forme of wholesome doctrine deliuered in the Scriptures;
touching your hell paines they say nothing in dǣd, because
it was neuer heard of in ȳ Church of Christ in their times;
but that Christ died NOT THE DEATH OF THE SOVLE;
and by the ONLY DEATH OF HIS BODY, and shedding of
his blood sufficiently ransomed & redǣmed vs, this cannot
be spoken in plainer and exacter termes, then they haue pro-
posed it and proued it. And therfore you and others shal doe
well not to make al the ancient & learned lights of Christs
Church so ignorant in their Crǣd & Catechisme, as not to
know, how they were saued by ȳ Crosse & death of Christ,
before your hellish paines of the damned were of late deui-
sed. Your better sifting of this matter, is the open wresting
and forcing of the scriptures against their true, proper and
perpetual sense, to serue your strange conceits. And as you
do with the scriptures, you must be suffered to do with the
Fathers which you produce, that is; to put thē quite from
their own meaning, & frame their words to your fancies,
before any man can tell to what end you cite them.

The first word you quote out of Ierom, you falsifie by
putting *maledictum* to it, where Ierom doth not so, but sim-
ply saith, VVH AT VVE should haue suffered for our sinnes,

that

that he suffered for vs. The very next words that are his owne, (for he interposeth a place of Scripture, that in his flesh Christ dissolued our enmitie with God, and healed vs with his stripes) are these. [a] *Ex quo perspicuum est, sicut corpus flagellatum & laceratum, ita animam verè doluisse pro nobis.* Whereby it is euident, that as his bodie was whipped and torne, so his soule truely sorrowed for vs. Here you must be permitted to adde of your owne, besides Ieroms meaning, that this sorrow was your hellish sorrow, or else I cannot see why you cited Ierom, except it were to falsifie him. But how, and why Christ sorrowed for vs, when Ieroms own words were alleaged by me, your answer was; this [b] *is more fond and absurd than the other.* Cyprians words you neither vnderstand, nor like; he saith that Christ [c] taking our person and cause vpon him sayd in our names, that he was forsaken: *Quod pro eis voluisti intelligi qui deseri à Deo propter peccata meruerant, quorum reconciliationis causam agebas,* which he would haue to be vnderstoode of vs (or for vs) who deserued by our sinnes to be forsaken of God, whose reconciliation he then vndertooke. So S. Austen expounded those words of Christ, My God, my God why hast thou forsaken me? [d] *Illa vox membrorum ipsius vox erat, non capitis,* that voyce was the voice of his members, and not of the head; but you could not endure either Austen or any other father so to say, without controlement. [But Cyprian saith Christ endured like punishment to those that be sinners & accursed.] In part, not in all; otherwise he must haue suffered eternall death of bodie and soule: and therefore expounding himselfe in the next sentence, he saith, [e] *In tantum infirmis compateris, vt nec crucifigi, nec mori, dum illi viuant & non pereant, nec erubescas nec formides.* So far didst thou suffer with the weake, that thou didst neither shame to be crucified, nor feare to dye, so they might liue and not perish. Ambrose saith; With the sorrow of his soule Christ abolished the sorrow of our soules; Here you must haue leaue to bring in your hellish sorrowes against Ambroses minde, or else this is but lost labour: the causes of Christs heauines and sorrow when I repeated out of this

very

Marginal notes:

[a] Hierony. in Esa. ca. 53.

[b] Pag 68.
[c] Cyprian. de passione christi.

[d] August. in Psal. 21.

[e] Cyprian. Ibidem.

berp place of Ambrose, you reiected them as f*fond and false,* f *Pag.*67.
and now with the bare name of sorrow you think Ambrose
dreamt of your hell paines. For shame reade out the chap-
ter, and leaue these mistakings.

[But * Ambrose saith, the man (in Christ) now readie to *In J uce.ca. 23. de commendatione spiritus.
die, by the separation of the Diuinitie, cried, my God, my God,
why hast thou forsaken me.] A man dieth when his soule lea-
ueth his body. Christ therefore readp to die the death of the
body, which was left of y deitie vnto death, by withdraw-
ing it selfe for a time, vttered these words. Death of the
soule, or dereliction vnto hell paines, there are none to be
found in Ambrose, nor any words sounding that way, vn-
lesse you peruert them at your pleasure. The words next
going before are these : g *Gloriosa Dei professio, vsque ad mor-* g Ambros. ibidem.
tem se pro nostris descendisse peccatis, vel euidens manifestatio
contestantis Dei secessionem Diuinitatis & CORPORIS. It was
a glorious profession of God, that he descended euen vnto death
for our sins; or an euident manifestation of God witnessing the
departure of his Diuinitie from HIS BODIE, (when it dyed.)
The next words of Ambrose why you alleage I doe not set,
but to make vp the number, which is very smale, and lesse
forcible. Who doubteth but Christ offered that, which he put
on? He put on his body, & his body he offered. S. Paul will
tell what Christ offered, h We are sanctified by the offering of h Hebre.10.
the bodie of Iesus Christ once made. Your own author Saint
Ambrose writing vpon these words alleaged by Paul, i thou i Ambros. in Hebre.ca.10.
hast fitted me a bodie, saith ; *Hoc ex persona dicitur eius, qui*
CORPVS SVSCEPIT *nostræ mortalitatis, vt pro nobis habe-*
ret quod offerret. This is spoken in his person, who put on our
MORTALL BODIE, that he might haue what to offer for vs.
k *Vna quippe oblatio corporis Christi perfectos facit sanctificatos* k Ibidem.
quæ remissionem integram facit peccatorum. The one OBLATI-
ON OF THE BODIE OF CHRIST maketh perfect, such as
be sanctified, and giueth full remission of sinnes. If you thinke
Ambrose mistake the matter; heare Athanasius. l *A nobis si-* l Athanas. de incarnatione verbi Dei.
mili corpore mutuato, eo quod omnes mortis corruptioni obnoxij
essemus, pro omnibus ID IPSVM *in mortem deditum patri suo*
SACRI-

SACRIFICAVIT, *vt homines à morte ad vitam* CORPORE *suo, quod proprium sibi fecit, renocaret.* IMMOLATIONE *enim* SVI CORPORIS *& legi nobis infesta finem posuit, & primordium vitæ nobis renonauit spe resurrectionis nobis data.* The son of God BORROVVING FROM VS A BODIE LIKE OVRS, becaufe we all were fubiect to the corruption of Death did SACRIFICE THE SAME to his father by yeelding it vp vnto Death, that BY THE BODY which he made his own, he might recall men from Death to life. For by the OFFERING OF HIS BODIE, he ended the lawe that oppreffed vs, and renewed the beginning of life vnto vs, giuing vs hope of Refurrection. Cyrill with the whole Synode of Alexandria, which I mentioned before, wrote thus to Neftorius. m Chrift is made the mediator of God and man, and a reconciler of peace, offering himfelfe to God, & to his father as a fweet fmelling facrifice, for he OFFERED HIS OVVN BODIE FOR VS, to bee a fweete fauour. But of the true facrifice for finne, which Chrift offered, I haue fpoken enough before, as well in this conclufion, as in the Treatife. It muft haue the BODIE, the BLOOD, and the DEATH of the offerer: none of which agree to the foule of Chrift, though the bodie without a foule could be no reafonable facrifice; I therefore I exclude not the foule whofe obedience, innocence, & patience concurred to fanctifie this facrifice; but I note the parts of the facrifice for fin by the Apoftles doctrine were thofe, which I named, the blood and death of the Sacrificer; both which muft needs be found in his body and not in his foule.

m Epiftola Synodi Alexandrinæ ad Neftorium.

From Ambrofe you roue to Tertullia, & there you find that which I neuer doubted of. n The Son fuffered, forfake of his father. *Hæc vox eft animæ & corporis, id eft hominis.* This was the voice of foule & bodie, that is of man. Did you think the body could fpeak without the foule, before you read in Tertullian that this was the voice of both? If you did, you were deeply learned; if you did not, why doe you bring it as a matter worth the hearing, that bodie and foule ioyned in fpeaking? But you help it ouer y̆ ftile with a falfe tranflatió, & where Tertullian faith, this was the voice of foule & flefh, you englifh

n Tertullian contra Praxeam.

it

it, [o] *this is meant of the flesh and of the soule*, to wit, as you ex- „
pounde it, that both soule and bodie died forsaken of God.
Take back, Sir Refuter, your false and unsauerie glozes
that corrupt the text, Tertullian neuer heard, nor thought of
the death of Christs soule, nor of anie such forsaking, as you
imagine; hee expoundeth himselfe without your additions,
in the verie same place, plaine enough. [p] *Denique posuit* [p] Tertullian aduersus Praxeam in eodem loco.
spiritum, & statim obijt. Spiritu enim manente in carne, caro omnino mori non potest. Ita relinqui a patre fuit mori filio; filius igitur & moritur, & resuscitatur. Dicendo denique Christus mortuus est, id quod unctum est mortuum ostendit, id est, carnem,
Christ laid aside his spirit, and PRESENTLY DIED. For his
spirit remaining in his flesh, the FLESH by no meanes coulde
DIE. So to be forsaken of the father, was for the sonne TO DIE.
The sonne therefore died and was raised againe. Then in saying
Christ died, (*Paul*) shewed that died which was annointed, euen
the flesh of Christ. Of the death of Christes flesh Tertullian
speaketh, which hee saith, could not possiblie bee, so long as
Christes soule remained in his bodie. Christ then died no
death of the soule whiles he liued, and breathed on the crosse;
but the death which hee died was the laying aside of his
soule, and leauing his bodie unto death. You ende with
Cyril that [q] Christ made his flesh a Redemption for our flesh,
and his soule a Redemption for our soules. Cyril meaneth no- [q] Cyril de recta fide ad Theodosium.
thing lesse then that, which you would implie, that with the
death of either part in himselfe, Christ redeemed each part
in us; But Cyril knowing that Christ in his sufferings on
the crosse ioyned both partes together, the one to receaue
the violence and rage of the wicked, which was his bodie; the
other to feele & endure the smart thereof with all obedience
patiẽce, which was his soule; saith truly that Christ ioyning
both soule and bodie in suffering for us, redeemed both soule
and bodie in sauing us; which wee acknowledge to bee true
without exception. For had not the soule of Christ beene
partner, yea chiefe patient in those bodilie sufferinges of

Chriſt , they could not haue profited vs; neither doe we at
anie time otherwiſe ſpeake or thinke of Chriſts ſufferings,
but that the bodie was the inſtrument whereby the ſoule of
Chriſt did admit and feele all thoſe paines, wrongs, ſhames,
wounds and whatſoeuer he endured on the croſſe , or before
at their hands, which put him to death. But theſe paines and
ſorrowes of Chriſts ſoule, you ſaie, MAKE NOT TO OVR
REDEMPTION, and vnleſſe the ſoule properlie and imme-
diatlie (not from , or by her bodie) feele helliſh paines and
ſorrowes, ſuch as the damned doe , you make no reckning
of all that Chriſt otherwiſe ſuffered . And this is your error
which you ſhrowde vnder the name of a moſt holie trueth,
where indeede, if it be vrged & followed, as you beginne, it
will fall out to be a moſt hainous contemning of all that
Chriſt ſuffered for vs; and a dangerous ſubſtituting of other
deuiſes, which Chriſt neither did nor could ſuffer, as you
propoſe them.

    You end, Sir Refuter , as you beganne with egregi-
ous lyes, that *not the moſt or the beſt*, BVT ALL AND EVE-
RY ONE, *both churches and writers in the world, that are pro-
teſtants, teach as you doe, and that your doctrine is publiklie au-
thorized by the lawes of this Realme,* as appeareth by the booke
of Homilies, where it is ſaid, that *Chriſt put himſelfe betweene
Gods deſerued wrath and our ſinne.* But (Sir confuter) if you
haue this propertie of Mydas ÿ you can turne all Fathers,
Churches, writers, and lawes with touching them, to be of
your opinion, you muſt haue Mydas eares too; vnleſſe you
looke better about you. Such an inſolent and impudent ſpeech
would well become an ale-houſe, where no man ſhould be are
you; but in the face of the world to bray after this ſort is to-
lerable in no man, but in you, that neither know what you
ſay, nor ſee what you ſhould prooue, nor vnderſtãd what ma-
keth with you or againſt you. You no ſooner reade in any mã
new or olde mention of Gods wrath, or of death, but you
ſtraight fanſy that he meaneth your hel paines, & the death of

the

Pag. 37.
Pag. 9.

the soule; and so you play with the homilies allowed by the lawes of this Realme. Where because you find that Christ interposed himselfe betweene the wrath of God & vs, to auert it from vs, you forthwith resolue, the Homilies teach your doctrine. But awake, Sir Refuter, and you shall see great difference betwixt the doctrine taught in the booke of Homilies, and publikely approued by the lawes of this Realme, & your frenzies; that Christ DIED THE DEATH OF THE SOVLE; that the VVHOLE CVRSE of God was executed on Christ; that he was by our sins *defiled, sinful, hateful, & accursed; that al the* ,, *powers of his soule & senses of his body were ouerwhelmed, distrac-* ,, *ted, and all confounded, that he felt the verie Diuels to be instru-* ,, *ments, executing the wrath of God vpon him, that the sufferings* ,, *of Christs soule,* by *Sympathie* as you call it, (that is from and ,, by the body) *make not to our redemption; that Christs soule died* ,, *and was crucified, where it is absurd and most false to say Christ* ,, *was made aliue ether in his humane soule, or by the same;* these and an hundred such absurdities and impieties haue no allowance in the bookes of Homilies, nor any thing sounding towards your hellish paines of the damned. The doctrine there taught is sound, true and plaine, that we are redeemed by the death and bloud of Christ Iesus; that such was the iust displeasure of God against our sinnes, that though he were his owne son, that vndertooke the cause for vs, the iustice of God pursued him with most painfull smart and anguish euen vnto death; and forced the weaknesse of his humane flesh to crie, my God, my God why hast thou forsaken mee. But you content not your selfe with this; you must haue him suffer the verie paines of the damned in Hell, or nothing. His bodilie death were it neuer soe paynefull and sharpe, you make light ac- ,, [Pag.51] count of; [the theeues crucified with Christ, suffered, you say, *as* ,, *great bodily violence as he did; yea wicked & vngodly men indure* ,, *with boldnes & great ioy far more exquisite & barbarous tor-* ,, *mēts & sharper tortures, as touching the body, then Christ could* ,,

*Pag 51

*Ambrof.in
Lucæ ca. 22
de Triftitia
Chrifti.

x Aug.tractat.
in Iohan.36.

y Bernard.de
paſsione Chri-
ſti.cap.5

" endure, and therefore in plaine words you saie, ' ſuch follie in
" the ſonne of God, bee it farre from y u once to imagine, as that he
" ſhould ſtagger, ſhrink or faile for any corporal tormentes whatſoe-
uer, forgetting that Ambroſe writeth; " Neque enim habent
fortitu.inis laidem, qui ſtuporem magis vulnerum tulerunt, quã
dolorem: it can haue no praiſe of fortitude to be deſperately con-
firmed, rather then patientlie ſubiected vnto paine of torments.
And what Auſtē confeſſeth, x Nihil erat tunc IN CARNE IN-
TOLERABILIVS, there was nothing more intolerable in the
fl.ſh then the croſſe of Chriſt; as likewiſe that Bernarde re-
ſolueth y Nec aliquo modo dubitandum, quin infirmitatem &
exterminationem corporis incomparabilem ſuſtinuerit; it muſt
not be doubted,but Chriſt ſuffered incomparable weakenes and
torment of body. For this if you did ſtriue, it were to be to-
lerated; for that which no father euer teſtified, nor ſcripture e-
uer affirmed, when you ſhew your ſelfe ſo eager;you betray
your humor, you benefit not your cauſe.

  Thou haſt heard chriſtian Reader,what things I haue miſ-
liked in the firſt part of this opponents pamphlet; but no-
thing more then this, that he waſteth ſo manie wordes, and
neither expreſſeth what hee meaneth, nor proueth what hee
pretendeth. All that he hath ſaide is this in effect;Chriſt ſuf-
fered in ſoule the wrath and curſe of God for our ſinne, or
due to ſinne; but theſe are ſo generall termes that in parte
they bee true, in parte they bee falſe, and therefore hee that
walketh in theſe cloudes,and deſcendeth not to particulars,
meaneth to hide his heade vnder the Couert of theſe ge-
neralities when neede is; and out of theſe to faſhion to
himſelfe ſuch aſſertions as pleaſe beſt his humour. The
waie to come by a trueth, is to ſpecifie the partes of
Gods wrath and curſe, which they ſuppoſe Chriſt ſuffered,
and then ſhall wee in fewe wordes trie whether thoſe ſuffe-
rings accord with the rules and groundes of the ſcriptures,
or no. And this I foretell, becauſe if hee or anie other
for him bee diſpoſed to reuiue his cauſe, hee muſt not
bring

bring a sacke full of woꝛds foꝛ so waightie matters;but plainlie and particularlie declaring what he holdeth, and pꝛouing what he affirmeth,go directly to the point,and then by Gods grace we ſhall ſoone trie where trueth ſtandeth. But if anie man will dꝛaw the grounde of our redemption to generall and ambiguous termes , which ſhall ſtill increaſe contention to noe purpoſe; J meane not to repell woꝛds with woꝛds ; till they anſwere theſe pꝛoofes , J will not trouble my ſelfe with their emptie phꝛaſes.

In the ſecond Queſtion of Chꝛiſts deſcent to hell,J ſhall not hold thee long (gentle reader) becauſe this babler foꝛgetting what J ſayd,concerning the pꝛoofe and purpoſe of Chꝛiſts deſcent to hell,runneth a new courſe to Pagans and Poets foꝛ help , to expound that article of our Creede; and there pꝛeſumeth himſelfe to be ſo ſtrong, that of the reſt he doth pꝛats without reaſon oꝛ remembꝛance. The end of Chꝛiſts deſcent to hell, J noted out of Athanaſius , Fulgenſius and others , and pꝛoued their ſpeach confoꝛmable to the Scriptures;the places thou haſt in the latter part of the treatiſe, J meane not to increaſe this cloſe with needleſſe repetitions. The Cöfuter , belike diſtracted and diſtempered with the cogitation and confuſion of his hell paines, vtterly miſtaketh oꝛ foꝛgetteth the whole. He ſuppoſeth Chꝛiſts deſcent to hell had none other purpoſe,but *to triumph and inſult vp- „ *Pag. 64. on the thrice miſerable and wofull wretches in their preſent vn- „ ſpeakeable damnation,infinitely confounded alreadie,& inferreth; „ Sure a verie ſcrie triumph this were for the ſonne of God which e- „ uen among men were nothing but diſhonorable;but if his bꝛaines „ be ſo bꝛickle,that he can neither conceaue, noꝛ carrie a- waie what J ſayd;J muſt not beate it into his head: that J then pꝛeached , is here now pꝛinted , let him refell it if hee can. Soe when J made the ſubduing of hell and treading on Satan with all the power of darkneſſe , a chiefe part of the gloꝛie of Chꝛiſts reſurrection,this ſcoꝛner in his fooliſh conceite mocketh at it,and ſaith *a worthie *Pag. 54. priuiledge

"" *priuiledge surelie, and verie honorable. All men would thinke it*
"" *a greater honour neuer to haue come in hell at all. For his actuall*
"" *triumphing in hell all the world knoweth, is the most inglorious*
"" *and vilest debasing.* In sadnes (Syr refuter) if these be your
best exceptions against Chꝛists triumphing ouer hell, all the
world will know, that you are a woꝛthie man, to weare a
wodden dagger. The Apostle made it a part of Chꝛists high
exaltation,[b] that euerie knee, as well of things vnder the earth,
as of things in heauen, should bow vnto him, and euerie toong,
confesse that Iesus Christ is the Lord; and do you thinke it a
méete matter to be mocked and deried? Paul saith; Christ
spoyled principalities and powers (of hell & darknes) and made
a shew of them openlie, and triumphed ouer them in his owne
person, (foꝛ so I must reade till you shew me better authoꝛitie
against it, then I haue bꝛought foꝛ it;) & your selfe both sée and
say, that [c] *whyles Christ suffered and whyles he died, it was a mi-*
"" *serable triumph, yea* [d] *a piteous triumph it was indeede, where*
"" *himselfe remayned in such woful torméts, where appeared no shew*
"" *of conquest, but rather of being conquered; & [e] still he suffered til he*
gaue vp the ghost. What letteth them I pꝛaie you, since these
woꝛds were not verified on the Crosse, but they did take
place in his resurrection, as I teach; and therein as by the
effects it was most euident and apparant to the eies of all
men, he did spoyle powers and pꝛincipalities, & made a shew
of them openly, and triumphed ouer them in his owne per-
son? Doth the holy ghost attribute this as a great honour to
the humane nature of Chꝛist, that [f] ascending on high he led
captiuitie captiue; and doe you make a merriment of it,
appealing to the whole woꝛld foꝛ their censure on your
side?

"" Pour stronge st foꝛt is this; [g] *There can bee no commoditie*
"" *nor benefit to the godlie by it. For what good is there so much*
"" *as pretended? The generall redemption of all Gods elect and*
"" *chosen people was wrought and fullie finished on the Crosse.* [h]
"" *what could his going downe to hell adde more?* Is the subduing of
hell

Pag.156.

[b] Philip.2.

Coloss.2.

[c] Pag.156.
[d] Pag.159.

[e] pag.156.

[f] Ephes.4.

[g] pag.163

[h] Pag.164.

hell powers, and the treading on all their force, and the re-
straining of all their furie, so small a matter with you, that
it doth no good to the godlie? Hee hath triumphed and spoy-
led them to free vs from feare; and hath taken the [i] keyes   [i] Reuel. 1.
of death and of hell, into his owne hands; to shew that all
power is giuen him in heauen, earth, & hell, and that he can re-
straine and [k] bind Satan at his will and pleasure. Is the per-   [k] Reuel. 20.
formance and assurance of these things no comodity nor be-
nefit to the godlie? [*The redemption of Gods elect, was (you*   "
say) fully finished on the Crosse.] Deserued and obtained it   "
was on the Crosse, and by the crosse, but not there executed.
There were our sinnes pardoned, and our selues reconciled
to God; but as Christ died for our sinnes, so he rose for our
iustification. His resurrection in that glorious manner, which
I haue mentioned in the treatise, & his ascension are necessa-
ry parts of our Saluation; and therefore vse not the force of
Christs crosse to exclude, but to induce the rest. For so doth
the Apostle when he saith. [l] Christ humbled himselfe, & became   [l] Philip. 2.
obedient vnto y̆ death of the crosse. Wherfore (that is euen for
that his humility & obedience) God hath highly exalted him
& giuen him a name aboue euerie name; that at the name of Ie-
sus should euery knee bow of things in heauen, in earth, & vnder
the earth. So that his descending, rising, and ascending added
nothing to the force of his death, but shewed the fruite there-
of; and tend all to our good, since wee are presentlie secured
from the power of hell and Satan, and shall be certainelie
raysed and receaued to glorie. Christes death without
his resurrection and ascension had beene our confusion,
and no redemption; for if sinne had slaine him with-
out rising, it must needes haue damned vs without
hoping: now in his Resurrection as euery Enemie was
most mighty, so was there most need he should be subdued.
But hereof I haue spoken so largelie before that I
shall not neede to rehearse it againe; with turning the
page

page it maie soone bee sene.

ᵐ Pag. 148. " [But ᵐ *The Scriptures (you tell vs,) are cleare-*
" *ly againſt Chriſts going to Hell. For this daie (ſayd Chriſt*
ⁿ Page. 150. " *to the theefe) thou ſh lt bee with mee in Paradiſe.* ⁿ *All*
" *this muſt needes be of his humane ſoule verelie without all queſti-*
" *on. There is none can conſider herein his Deitie. If anie thinke*
" *his ſoule might goe to hell firſt, and preſentlie goe thence to hea-*
" *uen yer night alſo, that is ridiculous and toyiſh.*] You haue ſo
manie topes in your head, Sir Refuter, that a coloured cap
would well become it: when you come to a non plus in your
proofes, then you crie, this is ridiculous and topiſh. Go like
your ſelfe, and looke to the ridiculous topes that you bring
vs in euery page almoſt. You would proue, forſooth, that the
SCRIPTVRES ARE CLEARE againſt Chriſts being in
hell at anie time betweene his death, and his Reſurrection;
& for your warrant you bring his words to the theefe on the
croſſe; this daie thou ſhalt bee with mee in Paradiſe; and at his
death when he ſayd; Father into thy hands *I* commend my ſpi-
rite; And when the places conclude no ſuch thing as you
would haue them, nor anie thing neere it; then you helpe it
° Pag. 152. " with outcries, and ſaie; ° *There is no man of ſenſe conſidering*
" *theſe circumſtances that can iudge otherwiſe.* But will your
wiſdome remember that S. Auſten in his 57. Epiſtle diſ-
cuſſing this place of purpoſe, to day thou ſhalt bee with mee
in Paradiſe; ſaith the word MEE maie verie readily and
eaſily bee referred to Chriſts Godhead, promiſing the thiefe
Paradiſe that preſent daie; and all the childiſh amplificati-
ons that you haue brought vs to the contrarie, are not
worth a nut-ſhell to conteruaile S. Auſtens iudgement.
But graunt it were ment of Chriſts ſoule; are you ſo per-
fect in the length of the waie from hell to Paradiſe, and the
wearines of Chriſts ſoule in going to both, that you be ſure
he could not do both that daie? You thinke belike Chriſt
would not goe thither, but to view the deuils one by one,
and call their names to ſee who were abſent. You haue for-
gotten

gotten that P with his presence, or with his word whiles hee r Luke 8
liued here on earth, hee could torment the diuels, and therefore if it pleased him but to chewe himselfe, who hee was, whom they had so despitefullie pursued by the handes and tongues of the wicked on the Crosse; all hell must not onelie bende and bowe vnto him, but feare and fall before him. Againe, what coulde hinder though he did not descende that date which hee died, but hee might so doe the date that hee rose ; and euen when hee was to rise to loose all the strength of hell before him, and to let Satan see that his kingdome was ouerthrowne by that death, at which hee so much insulted and reioyced? The time I doe not determine, though I thinke it pertained rather to the glorie of his resurrection, then otherwise ; as I haue in the treatise more at large expressed.

[Was not his soule, you will aske IN HIS Fathers handes, till the time of his Resurrection?] Who doubteth that? As if to subdue hell with the glorie of his presence did not prooue the hande of G O D to bee rather mightilie with him, then anie waie to leaue him, and that to bee true, which was forespoken by Dauid in his person, q Thou wilt not leaue my soule in hell ? [The q Psal.16. handes of God, you thinke, signifie heere his ioyfull presence, and the possession of heauen.] Who tolde you so? Was Dauid dying when hee saide ; r Into thine handes r Psal.31. I commende my spirite, thou hast redeemed mee Lord God of truth? Was Sion not on earth but in heauen, when the Prophet saith of her ; ſ Thou shalt bee a crowne of glorie in the hand of the Lord, and a royall Diademe in the hande f Esai.62. of thy God, it shall no more bee saide to thy land, Desolate, for thy land shall haue an husbande ? Was the king of Iudah then in heauen, when God saide of him, t Though t Iere.22. Coniah the sonne of Iehoiakim king of Iudah were the Signet of my right hand, yet would I plucke thee thence? Gods hand signifieth his power, and protection ; and could there

greater fauour, power, o? pretention bee ſhewed to the ſoule
of Chriſt, then fo? God in raiſing him from the dead, not
onelie to treade death, but euen hell and Satan vnder his
feete? Call you this a moſt inglorious and vile debaſing, fo?
the humane nature of Chriſt, to haue all power in hea-
uen, and earth, (in which Hell alſo muſt bee compriſed,)
to bee deliuered vnto him; and to bee made Lorde o-
uer all, not onelie men, and Angels, but euen enemies
and diuels? From this honour and power, whereof it is
ſaid; ᵃThou haſt ſubiected all things vnder his feete; maie no
creature in heauen, no? in hell be excepted? And therefo?e
if this bee a vile debaſement, I knowe not what glo?ie mea-
neth. The purpoſe then of Chriſtes deſcent to hell, giueth
honour to him ouer all his enemies, and comfo?t to vs
againſt the power and terrour of hell, which wee ſee
diſſolued and ſpoyled by our heade in our names, and fo?
our ſakes; fo? ſo much as beeing ioyned to him as ˣmem-
bers of his bodie, of his fleſh, and of his bones, hell hath
nowe no mo?e right to vs then to him; ſince it is not
poſſible but the heade muſte bee where the members are:
And Chriſt himſelfe ʸhungreth, and thirſteth, and is naked,
and ſicke, impriſoned, and perſecuted, in euerie one of
his members, euen in the baſeſt and loweſt of them; and
this no mo?e impeacheth the all ſufficient merite of Chriſtes
Croſſe, then his reſurrection from the dead doeth the third
daie after his death, and all things finiſhed on the Croſſe,
needefull to bee ſuffered fo? our redemption; which in
your franticke humour you ſeeme to deteſt as ᶻBLAS-
PHEMOVS.

[The p?oofe that hee went thither, you will ſaie, is
all; if that were once cleered, the reſt woulde ſoone bee
acco?ded.] I maie not fo? your pleaſure (Sir Refuter)
ſtande to rippe vppe and repeate the thinges which were
then deliuered, and are now publiſhed; there you may looke;
If you like them not, giue mee ſome reaſon beſides your
owne

ᵃ 1.Cor.15.

ᵇEpheſ.5.

ʸMat.25.
Acts 9.

ᶻPag 156.

owne rouing conceit , and it ſhall bee ſoone anſwered.
[It is no where written in the Scriptures you will ſaie.]
Saint ꝩ Auſten iudiciallie and reſolutelie telleth you, it is
written in the Prophet Dauid, and ſo expounded by Saint
Peter ; and of that iudgement were all the Fathers of
Chriſtes Church without exception. ᶻ Athanaſius ſaith it is
a parte of the Catholike faith , without beleeuing the
which we can not be ſaued. And ſure the words be plaine e-
nough, if you leaue wreſting them from their right and true
ſignification to ſerue your affections. What can be plainer,
ᵃ Thou wilt not leaue my ſoule in hell ; beſides the Article of
our Creede, He deſcended into hell ? Your anſwer is: ᵇ *This*
is euident that the worde hell in our vulgar Creede is vn-
fit , corrupt and ſtarke naught. For this I affirme , it is onelie
the Fathers abuſiue ſpeaking, and altering the vſuall and auncient
ſenſe of Hades, that hath bredde this errour of Chriſtes deſcen-
ding into hell. Their vnapt and perilous tranſlating into La-
tine, Inferi , and our naughtie and corrupt tranſlation in Eng-
liſh, hell, hath confirmed the ſame. ᵈ *And note here firſt it is*
a thing too rifewith the Fathers , yea with ſome of the aunci-
enteſt of them to alter and chaunge the authenticke vſe of words,
whereby conſequentlie it is eaſie for errours and groſſe miſ-
takings to creepe in . As Chirotonia *to ſignifie ordination of*
Miniſters , when it ſignifyeth authenticallie the peoples giuing
of voices in election : Kleros, *to ſignifie onelie the Cleargie, when it*
ſignifieth all the flocke. Euen ſotrulie the Greeke fathers vſe Ha-
des, *and the Latine* Inferi , *to ſignifie hell properlie and particu-*
larlie, that is , the place of the damned ᵉ *But this is a meere and*
plaine abuſion of theſe wordes, and ſpeciallie of our worde moſt in
queſtion, that is Hades, They haue much altered and changed the *
authenticke and true vſe thereof. You begin nowe to ſhewe
your ſelfe in your right hue . All the Greeke and Latin fa-
thers that euer were in the Church of Chriſt; all the Engliſh
teachers that haue béene ſince this nation receiued the faith,
neuer vnderſtood the ſignification of the word Hades, til you
Aaa 2　　　　came

ꞋEpiſt. 99.

ᶻAthanaſ. in
Symbolo.

ᵃPſal. 16.
ᵃAct. 2.

„ᵇ Pag. 124
„ᶜPag. 95

„ᵈPag. 96.

„ᵉPag. 97.

came of late to bring vs newes of Socrates fansie , and
Ciceros diuinitie to correct the Creede ; Ignatius, Clemens,
Origen, Athanasius, Eusebius , Basil , Nazianzene , Epi-
phanius, Chrysostome, Cyril, Eustathius, Theodorete, with
a thousand more naturallie borne Greekes ; and manie of
them nothing inferiour to Plato, or whom you can name,
euen for their eloquence in the Greeke tongue , were they
all ignorant of the worde Hades , which boies in Gram-
mar schoole doe well vnderstande ?   Or did they all
conspire one after another to falsifie the faith ? Irenæus,
Tertuillian , Cyprian, Lactantius, Ierome , Ambrose, Au-
sten , Hillarie, Prudentius, Prosper, Fulgentius , with in-
finite others great Schollers and pillars in the Church
of GOD, had none of them the skill to knowe what
Infernum or *Inferi* meant , till you sprang vp to restore
the Latine tongue to his originall integritie ?   Or did
they all concurre purposelie to corrupt the Creede?
Which will you take from all these fathers religion , or
learning ?   If you leaue them so much vnderstanding as
the boies haue nowe in Paules Schoole , they coulde not
mistake either Hades, or Inferi. And therefore you may talke
thus long enough before you shall gette vnto sober Rea-
der to beleeue you. Ye must bee as farre infected with this
frenzie as you your selfe are, before this will anie way sinke
into his head, that none of these vnderstode their owne na-
turall language. [But they haue mistaken other wordes,
you saie, as well as these ; namelie, χειροτονία and
κλῆρος] In deede you, or they haue grosselie mistaken the
one ; the other is not, that I knowe in question , vn-
lesse you take vppon you so greate a commaunde in the
Church of GOD, that no worde maie bee vsed by anie
man without your consent. Doeth anie father in ex-
pounding the Scriptures, put the Cleargie for the peo-
ple ; as if the rest had no part in the kingdome of
Christ?

Chrift? but if they wanted a word to note them, that were
called to the publike feruice of Chriftes church; and thought
beft to name them clerici, clerkes; what haue you to do with
it? or what reafon to fpeake againft it; fo long as the reft
of Gods people are not thereby depriued of their parte in
Gods heauenlie inheritance? And what if they tooke this
tearme from the fcripture and deriued the verie word from
the Apoftles mouthes? are you not well occupied to quarrel
with them? Peter doth twice vfe that worde for a parte, or
place in the publike miniiterie and feruice of the church, with
which the people did not medole. [a] Iudas (faieth) Peter) was [a] Acts, 1.
numbred with vs, καὶ ἔλαχε τὸν κλῆρον τῆς διακονίας ταύτης,
and had his place in this minifterie. So againe to Simon Ma-
gus; [b] οὐκ ἔσι σοι μερὶς, οὐδὲ κλῆρος ἐν τῷ λόγῳ τότῳ. Thou [b] Acts, 8
haft no part nor lot in this bufineffe or function. Where Peter
in both places calleth the charge of an Apoftle κλῆρος, not
that Iudas, or the reft of the twelue were chofen by lots, but
that he had a part with them in that function.

As for χειροτονία, I thinke there bee more faide, then you
will be able to anfwere; you know where to finde it. Could
you proue that the Apoftles did make elders with the peo-
ples voices, which you fhall neuer bee able to doe, you had
fome reafon to thinke the worde might imporie fome fuch
thing; but where the worde in his owne nature is but to
ftretch out the hande, and it is certaine by the fcriptures the
Apoftles in ordaining elders did vfe impofition of handes,
which is plainelie χειροτονία; (electing by voices they did not
vfe for ought that can bee prooued;) what a malepart gueff
are you to faie, _It was a rife thing with the fathers, yea with the_ ,,
ancienteft of them to alter & change the authentick vfe of words; ,,
becaufe the Athenians in Demofthenes time had a courfe in
their publike affemblies to giue their confentes to make
lawes and decrées with holding vp their hades, which he cal-
leth χειροτονία? But you bite on the bridle I perceiue, and fo
you muft, till you learne to be more fober then to condemne

so manie learned and religions fathers of ignorance and corruption; which in such a companion as you are, might well be beleeued; in men of their religion and iudgement can by no reason be mistrusted. This by the way, because you glance at χειροτονία, though therein you accuse not me that alleage them, but the fathers themselues as corrupters of church discipline, and peruerters of their own language; howbeit hades is now in question and not κλῆρος, or χειροτονία; and therefore saie for hades what you can, or rather for your selfe; since all wise men will hold you more then rash and presumptuous, if you condemne so many without great cause:

Pag.97.

«[*The classical writers, you say, the maisters of the Greek tongue*
«*do vse* HADES *in proper sense only in generall for the* STATE
«*OF THE DEADE, the* WORLD OF THE DEADE, *the*
«*WORLD OF SOVLES DEPARTED, indifferently, and in-*
«*definitely, meaning as wel those in eternal ioies, as those in paines.*]

Labour you (Sir Refuter,) to bring into the creede the marybones of a greeke phrase, or an article of the christian faith? if you be so idle headed, that you striue to haue a new phrase into the Creede, remember the kingdome of God is not in

1.Corinth.4

speach but in power. If you intende an article of the faith, pagans and Poets are no such classicall maisters, to be cited or followed in the mysteries of christian religion. What if it were true, which here as your maner is, you auouch with a brazen face, ß Homer, Plato, & Plutarch did so vse the word; is it therefore a consequent the scripture must so speak: how many hundred Greeke words haue with Pagans their general significations, which the holie ghost restraineth to expresse Gods truth, and serue Gods will? The greeke wordes for Apostle, elder, Bishop, Deacon, Gospell, Scripture, faith, hope, repentance, sinne, the law, conscience, concupiscence, and infinite such like, doe they not with Pagans import one thing, with Christians an other thing, and that by the warrant of Gods worde? touching hell it selfe; with your classicall wri-

ters

ters, and maisters of the Greeke tongue, (I meane euen
Homer, Plato, and Plutarch) are not δαιμόνια, taken for good
and blessed spirits, yea for Gods, which the scriptures vse on-
lie for diuels? Plutarchs booke περὶ τȣ̃ σωκρᾱτȣς δαιμονίȣ; of
Socrates spirit; which thing also Plato mentioneth in his Apo-
logie and dialogue *De sapientia*, meaneth not Socrates Di-
uell; neither doth Isocrates prescribe vnto Demonicus by this
rule, ἅμα τὸ δαιμόνιον, that hee shoulde worship the diuell,
but rather God; and yet by that word the new testamēt and
the Septuagint in the olde intend onelie diuels. Διάϐολος
with the maisters of the Greeke tongue is but a carper or re-
prehender, insomuch that most of Platoes schollers were cal-
led Διάϐολοι, and yet in the newe testament this is the pro-
per name for the diuell. Τάρταρος Plutarch doth take for the
ayre, and deriueth that word from colde; τάρταρος ὑπὸ ψυ-
χρότητος κέκλη· δηλοῖ δὲ καὶ ἡσίοδος εἰπὼν Τάρταρον ἠεροεν-
τα. καὶ τὸ ῥιγȣ̃ντα πάλλεσθαι καὶ τρέμειν, ταρταρίζειν. *Tartarus*
is so termed from colde, whence *Hesiode* calleth it the ayrie tar-
tare; and he that shaketh and trembleth for cold, is sayd *tarta-*
rizein. Yet your instructor maketh τάρταρος the saple and
prison in hell, and saith, S. Peter when hee telleth howe God
condemned the Angels, taketh all the words from *Homer* and
HIS PROSE COMMENTARIE. If he meane Eustathius
the Christian Bishop, it is a foule ouersight; if hee meane a-
nie other, he shall do well to proue, and not to presume that
Peter read Homer and his prose commentarie to expresse
the punishment of Diuels. Nowe if δαιμόνιον, διάϐολος,
and τάρταρος haue other significations and acceptions with
the maisters (as you make them) of the greeke tongue, & yet
in the new testament are wholy & onlie referred to note hell
and the diuels thither adiudged; whie may not the word HA-
DES in like sort be taken from his prophane vse among the
heathen writers, and bee applied by the Euangelistes and
Apostles to signifie hell? yea if the opinion which the pagan
Poets

Apud Athen.

Plutarch. de
primo frigido.

Poets, and prophane Philosophers holde of HADES were false and repugnant to the christian faith, howe could the canonicall writers of the new testament vse the word, and not change the sense? dare you so much as dreame, that the holy Ghost woulde canonize the Poets fables and the Philosophers fansies of the world to come? or if you be so foolish, as to forget the difference betwéene light and darknes, truth & falshood, wil any wise man entertaine your poeticall furies? " [The Gentiles, (you will saie,) tooke HADES for the worlde " of the deade, the worlde of soules departed; generallie and inde-" finitelie, were they in hell or in heauen, and this is no error, (you " think,) against the faith.] But this is an open falshood committed against your owne classicall writers; and if your cunning in the græke Poets bee no profounder, the boies in Grammer schooles will deride it. I praie you sir by your Greeke Poets, Homer, Hesiode, and others what is HADES originallie, the name of a person, or of a place? I aske you none other question, but that which euerie childe acquainted with your Poets canne readilie tell, which your maisters of the Græke tongue, Plutarch, and Plato confesse; which euerie speech that you, or your Instructor bringeth out of his Poets doth confirme. And here (christian Reader) I must praie thy patience and pardon, if I turne from the scriptures and fathers to the Poets and their fables; I haue no desire to it, nor delight in it; but such is the insolence of these men grounded vpon ignorāce, that it may not bee endured, and without some entering into these matters, it will not bee displaied. I will saie no more then I must néedes, and omit what is not materiall.

Homer the first and eloest of your classicall writers imagineth that the thrée sonnes of Saturnus, whom hee supposeth to bee Gods, deuided the gouernement of the whole worlde betwéene them; Iupiter taking the skie and the aire; Neptune the water, with her déepes and riuers : and Pluto the heart of the earth with all the dead of what sort soeuer. This thirde

sonne

fonne of Saturne, and owner of the deade, is hee that Homer and all the Poets call ἀΐδης HADES; his name being diuerslie declined and inflected to serue their verse, but still the same person. Homer in the 15. of his Iliades maketh Neptune thus to speake. We are three brethren, the sonnes of *Saturne* by *Rhea*; *Iupiter* and I, τρίτατ⊙ δ' ἀΐδης ἑνέροισιν ἀνάσσων; the third is HADES the ruler of those ŷ lie (dead) in the earth. The whole was deuided into three parts ; my lot was to dwell alwaies in the sea, ἀΐδης δ' ἔλαχεν ζόφον ἠερόεντα, and HADES lot was to haue the darke mist ; and to *Iupiter* fell by lot the large heauen with the skie and clowdes. This HADES or God of the deade Homer calleth [b] ζεὺς καταχθόνιος, the god vnder the earth, and giueth him in the same booke these properties, ἀΐδης τοι ἀμείλιχος, ἠδ' ἀδάμασος,

Homer Iliad. 15.

[b] Iliad. 9.

τόνεκα καὶ τέ βροτοῖσι θεῶν ἔχθιςος ἁπάντων ; HADES implacable & fierce;& for that cause of all ŷ gods the most odious to men. Hesiode agreeth with Homer, that *Rhea* companying with *Saturne* brought him notable children.

[c] ἰφθιμόν τ' ἀΐδην ὅς ὑπὸ χθονὶ δώματα ναίει,

[c] Hesiod. in Theogonia.

ΝΗΛΕὲς ἦτορ ἔχων, euen mightie HADES that dwelleth in housen vnder the earth and hath a cruell and mercilesse heart. The same Hades he maketh the gouernour of the deade, as Homer doth.

Τρέας ἀΐδης δ' ἑνέροισι καταφθιμένοισιν ἀνάσσων :

Ibidem.

HADES was afraid that is ruler of the deade vnder the earth. This is that hades which you so much talke of, to whose house your Poets make all the dead iust & vniust, good and bad to come; and therefore the most of your authorities out of the Greeke Poets and others haue εἰς ἅδε, vnderstanding δόμον or οἶκον, to shewe that the deade go or come to HADES HOVSE or dwelling.

The rest of your classicall writers and masters of the Græke tongue, both Plato and Plutarch alleadge and approue this fable of Homer. Plato in his dialogue of rhetorick called Gorgias, maketh Socrates thus to sate ; [d] Heare then a

[d] Plato in Gorgia.

Bbb 1. very

very excellent tale which you will thinke a fable, but I a good leſſon. That which I will ſaie, I will ſpeake to you for a trueth. As *Homer* reporteth, *Iupiter*, *Neptune*, and *Pluto* deuided the gouernement, after they receaued it of their father. There was a lawe touching men vnder *Saturnus*, and euer was and ſtill is with the gods, that ſuch men as led a iuſt and holie life, when they departed hence ſhoulde goe to the Iles of the bleſſed, and there liue in all happineſſe without any euill; and they that had beene wicked and vngodlie ſhould goe to the priſon of puniſhment and vengeance which is called *Tartarus*. The iudges of theſe matters, in *Saturnes* time, and in the beginning of *Iupiters* raigne were the liuing of ſuch as yet liued, and gaue iudgement the ſame daie that each man ſhould die, wherefore their iudgement was corrupt. P L V T O thē and the Gardians of the bleſſed Ilands going to *Iupiter* tolde him, that there came vnto them men to either place vnmeete for that condition. To whome *Iupiter* aunſwered, I will ſee it redreſſed. The iudgementes are therefore now amiſſe, becauſe they that are iudged are couered round, for they are iudged aliue, and ſo many that haue wicked ſoules are compaſſed with beauty, nobility, & riches, and manie come to the place of iudgement, & depoſe they liued honeſtlie, and ſo the iudges are aſtoniſhed; as alſo the iudges thēſelues are clogged, hauing their ſoules wrapped with their eies, and eares, and the reſt of their bodie. Firſt therfore men muſt be kept from foreſeeing the time of their death. Thē they muſt be iudged whē they are naked from all theſe thinges, that is after death, and the Iudge likewiſe muſt be deade alſo, that he may be free frō theſe lets, and with his ſoule he muſt view the ſoule of euery man newly dead, forſaken of all his kind, & ſtripped of al worldly pompe, that the iudgement may be ſincere. And I foreſeeing this before you, haue appointed Iudges, two of my ſons *Minos* & *Rhadamanthus* out of Aſia, and a third which is *Aeacus* out of Europe. Theſe when they are dead ſhall iudgē in an open meade in the meeting of three waies, whereof two ſhall leade, one to the Iles of the bleſſed, another to Tartarus. The ſoules of *Aſia* ſhall be

iudged

iudged by *Rhadamāthus*, & thoſe of Europe by *Aeacus*, to *Minos* will I giue the prerogatiue to decide ỹ doubts that ſhall ariſe in either place : ỹ the iudgmēt may be very euē which ſhal ſend ſoules to their places. This is that wich I haue heard, & beleeue to be true, & by their ſpeeches am perſwaded there is ſome ſuch thing. Thus far Plutarch citeth out of Plato ỹ iudges ᵹ places for the dead, ᵹ al this within Plutoes kingdom vnder ỹ earth, which they cal HADES: where as well the places, ᵹ pleaſures for the good, as the priſons ᵹ puniſhmentes for the bad are in their conceit prepared ᵹ ſetled. And this if you doubt, read either Vliſſes deſcent to HADES deſcribed by Homer in the I I. book of his Odiſſeas, or Aeneas iourney to hel, ſet forth by Virgil in the firſt booke of his Aeneidos, or Dyoniſius voiage to ſee Euripides, expreſſed by Ariſtophanes, as alſo the like aduentures of Hercules ᵹ Theſeus mentioned by Euripides, ᵹ others, ᵹ you ſhall ſee THE VVORLD OF THE DEAD, OR THE VVORLD OF SOVLES, be they good or bad, to be in Plutoes kingdom, which the greek Poets cal HADES: ᵹ therfore vnleſſe the diſtemper of your braines make you weary of Chriſtian religion, and incline you to Paganiſme, I doe not ſee what reaſon moueth you to bring Homers HABES to expounde the Creede. And were you permitted ſo to doe, what gaine you by it? For Homers HADES is ỹ region vnder the earth, where the good are kept in pleaſant fields, and the wicked in places of puniſhment, and this is euidentlie the hell of the Poets and Pagans, to which by your own claſſicall ᵹ authentical expoſition Chriſt did deſcend, if their HADES be receaued into the creede.

[But Plato the wiſe *Maiſter taketh it ſometime for hea-* "
uen; as namelie in his Phædone, where ſpeaking in the perſon "
of Socrates a little before his death he ſaith. The ſoule beeing an "
inuiſible thing goeth hence to another place like to it ſelfe, that "
is, to a noble, pure, and inuiſible, in HADES; *in truth to a* "
good and wiſe God; whither if God will my ſoule ſhall preſent- "
lie goe.] Did you not propoſe Plato to bee an expounder "
of the Creede] and preferre him as a wiſe maiſter be-
fore

ᵉPlutarch.de conſolatione ad Appollonium ad finem.

ᶠAriſtophanes in ranis ᵍ Euripides in Hercule furente.

[Tertul. de anima.

fore all the fathers, because you thinke hee fitteth your humour right, I coulde suffer him to haue his praise; but in this case I must saie of him as Tertullian doeth, *Doleo bona fide Platonem omnium hæreticorum condimentorium factum; Illius est enim & in Phædone, quod anima hinc euntes sint illinc, & inde hinc;* I am sorie in good sadnesse that *Plato* is becom the Apothecary of al heresies. For it is his opinion euen in his *Phædone*, that soules go hence thither, and thence hither. Your wise Masters report of HADES AND PLYTO, was the priuate opinion of Socrates against the common consent of Homer and all the poets, and against the receiued perswasion of the people. The conceite it selfe is full of pride, errour, and paganish infidelitie, absurditie, and blasphemie. And yet all this being verie true, Platoes wordes importe no such thing, as you imagine, that HADES is that heauen where God and his sauntes remaine. And therefore, Sir Confuter, if you be wearie as well of the Apostles, as of the fathers, and insteed of Christ will haue Plato to teach men the mysteries of the kingdome of heauen; Englande (where God be thanked there is a religions, vertuous and wise prince, ruling with christian lawes, and a number of learned and graue both Counsellors, Bishops, Iudges, and others that will endure no such prophanenes) is no fit place for you to bring in Platoes heauen. If I proue not these exceptions which I take to your wise maisters imagination, let me beare the shame; if I do, look you & your fellowes how well you deserue of Christian religion to make the sauntes to rest, and Christ to raigne either in Platoes heauen, or in Homers hades.

For the first it is euident; the Poets all with one consent placed HADES BELOVVE VNDER THE EARTH, and not aboue in the skies, nor in heauen. Homer and Hesiod you haue hearde. ᵇ Aristophanes maketh Dionysius desirous to see Euripides nowe deade, and therefore sendeth him to Hercules to learne the waie, to whome professing that no man shall perswade him not to goe.

ᵇ Aristopha in Ranis.

to

to Euripides, Hercules replieth, πότερον ἐις ἅδϰ κάτω; wilt thou goe TO HADES BELOVVE, to see him? where Plutoes kingdome is described aunswerable to the rest of the Poets. In Euripides the ghost of Polydor beginneth the first tragedie thus. [h] Here am I come leauing the dennes of the dead, and the gates of darkenesse· ἵν' ἅδϰς χω-ρὶς ᾤκισαι θεᾶν, where HADES hath his seate seuered from the gods. Pindarus speaking περὶ τᾶν εὐσεβέων ἐν ἅδϰ, of the godlie that are in HADES, saith, [i] τοῖσι λάμπει μὲν μένος ἀελίϰ τὰν ἐνθάδε νύκτα κάτω; to them the strength of the sonne doth lighten the NIGHT that is there BELOVV. [k] Euripides maketh Hercules after the murther of his wife, and children to saie, θανὼν ὑπερπερ ἦλθον, ἔιμι γῆς ὑπο. Dying I will go vnder the earth whence I came; Nowe whence Hercules came is expressed before [l] ἀνελθὼν ἐξ ἀνελίων μυχᾶν ἅδϰ κόρϰς ἔνερθεν returning from the darke chambers of the queene of HADES BELOVV. In like sort Sophocles maketh Aiax to saie. [m] τὰ δ' ἄλλ' ἐν ἅδϰ τοῖς κάτω μυθήσομαι, the rest I will speake to the spirites BELOVV IN HADES. So Hercules remembring his workes, saith, with these armes I drew by force, that inexpugnable Monster [n] τόνθ' ὑπὸ χθονὸς ἅδϰ τρίκρανον σκύλακα, the three headed whelpe of HADES VNDER EARTH. Simonides shewing how manie waies men end their liues, some by sickenesse, some by warre, some by sea, saith; such as are tamed or conquered in warre [o] πέμπει μελάινϰς ἄιδϰς ὑπὸ χθονός, HADES sendeth vnder the blacke earth. [p] Orpheus one of the eldest Maisters of the Greeke tongue without comparison, that liued in the time of the Iudges of Israel, as Suidas testifieth, and not so farre infected with fables, as those Philosophers and Poets that came after him, describing the true God, that, as he saith, Moses wrote of, calleth him, ἀιθέρος ἠδ' ἄιδϰ, πόντϰ, γάιϰς τε τύραννε, δάιμονες ὃν φρίασσι θεᾶν δὲ δέδοικεν ὅμιλες; the king of the heaues, of the earth, of the sea, AND OF HADES, before whom Diuels do tremble, and the whole companie of

gods

Margin notes:
[h] Euripin Hecuba.
[i] Apud Plutarch de consolatione ad Apollonium.
[k] Euripid: in Hercule furete
[l] Ibidem.
[m] Sophocles in Aiace flagellifero.
[n] Sophocles in Trachiniis.
[o] Simonides in vitâ humanam
[p] Orpheus de deo.

gods (or Angels) doe feare. Where in olde Greeke and good diuinitie HADES is ſeuered from heauen, ſea, and earth, and conſequentlie muſt be properlie HELL. And ſo if you runne ouer all the Poets, you ſhall finde that with one generall conſent they placed Hades not onelie κάτω below, but ὑπὸ χθονὸς, vnder the earth. This was the opinion of the people.

k The common people (ſaith Lucian) perſwaded by Homer, Heſiodus, and the reſt of the poets, and taking their poems for a law τόπον τινὰ ὑπὸ τῇ γῇ βαθὺν ᾅδην ὑπειλήφασι, beleeue: HADES to bé a deepe place vnder the earth ; and that Pluto Iupiters brother raigneth ouer that gulph, the kingdome of the deade falling to him by lotte , and hee ordering howe they ſhall liue there belowe . The place was ſo called from the name of the perſon whome they ſuppoſed to bee gouernour of it ; otherwiſe HADES was the proper name of Pluto, as Plato himſelfe confeſſeth in Cratylo , l ὁ δὲ ᾅδης οἱ πολλοὶ μέν μοι δοκοῦσιν ὑπολαμβάνειν. τὸ ἀειδὲς προσειρῆθαι τῷ ὀνόματι τούτῳ, καὶ φοβούμενοι τὸ ὄνομα, Πλούτωνα καὶ λεσιν αὐτόν. As for HADES the moſt part of men ſeeme to me to conceiue by the name that, which is darke , or which can not bee ſeene , and fearing the name they call him PLVTO.

And howſoeuer Socrates in that place, with a very falſe and fond reaſon goeth about to proue, that the name of HADES, as hee thinketh was not thence deriued but rather ἀπὸ τὸ πάντα τὰ καλὰ ἀειδέναι, from knowing al good things; which in deede is but a teſt, and by no poſſibilitie can come within the compaſſe of that word; yet both Plutarch, and the proſe commentator vpon Homer, neglect this vtterly, and vphold that which Socrates refuſed. m τὸ ἀειδὲς αὐτὸ καὶ ἄχρασον, ἄδικος καὶ ἀχέραν ἐπίκλησιν ἔσχον. Hades and Acheron (ſaith Plutarch) haue their names from (the aire) that is not ſeene, nor hath any colour. And in his diſcourſe, whether a ſecrete and ſilent life be beſt, or no, Plutarch propoſeth this etymologie as truer a elder then Socrates ſaints. τὸν ἥλιον Ἀπέλλανα κατὰ τὰς παλαιὰς καὶ παλαιοὺς θεσμοὺς νομίζοντες Δήλιον καὶ Πύθιον προσα-
γο-

k Lucianus de luctu

l Plato in Cratylo.

m Plutarch de primo frigido.

n Plutarch de occulte viuédo

γορεύωσι: τὸν δὲ τῆς ἐναντίας κύριον μοῖξας,εἴτε θεὸς εἴτε δαίμων, ἐςὶν,ᾅδην ὀνομάζωσι,ᾅς,ἐὰν εἰς ἀειδὲς καὶ ἀόρατον ἡμῶν, ὅταν διαλυθῶμεν,βαδίζοντων,νυκτὸς ἀιδῶς ἀεργηλοῖο θ᾽ ὕπνω κοίρα-νον. Men ACCORDING TO THE AVNCIENT TRADI-TIONS OF THEIR FATHERS,thinking the sunne to be A-póllo, named him Delius, and Pythius. And the RVLER of the contrarie deſtinie (to life and light) whether he bee a God, or a DIVEL,they termed HADES,being the MASTER of dark night,and dead ſleepe; for that when wee depart hence,wee go into an vnknowne and vnſeene place. So that Socrates deri-uation of Hades was both falſe and newe, euen as his opini-on of HADES to be an eloquent and bountifull God; and his reaſon is woꝛſt of all, that becauſe men returne not backe againe after death, therefoꝛe °HADES doeth detaine them with eloquent perſwaſions, and great rewards, which maketh him to be called *Pluto*.   Foꝛ the ſcripture aſſureth vs, that men dead can not returne againe, though they were neuer ſo willing; and though God of his goodnes beſtoweth euer-laſting bliſſe on his Saints; yet the reſt would faine bee rid of their eternall miſerie,and can not; neither are they held in their ſtate with faire pꝛomiſes, oꝛ large benefites, but by the vnalterable rigoꝛ of Gods iuſtice. Euſtathius vpon Ho-mers woꝛdes, that Achilles ſent many a woꝛthie ſoule to HA-DES, ſaith; ἔςι γὰρ ᾅς τόπος σκοτεινὸς ὑπὸ γᾱν, ἀφανὴς,ἀφαι-ρισμένος ψυχαῖς.ᾅς, is a darke place vnder the earth, not to be ſeene, appointed for ſoules, and is deriued from ἀ the pꝛiua-tiue,and εἴδω to ſee, and is called alſo ἀιδῆς , and by con-traction HADES. So when Homer bꝛingeth in Hectors wife complaining of her miſerie and ſaying,

° Plato in Cratylo.

P σὺ μὲν ἀϊδλω δόμως ὑπὸ κεύθεσι γαίης

ᵖ Iliad.22

ἔρχεαι,Thou huſband art gone to HADES houſe vnder the dennes of the earth. Euſtathius addeth; τόπος ἐςὶν ὑπόγαιος, καὶ ὅτω κε-κρυμμένος ; διὸ καὶ ἀΐδης λέγεται ῾ήγαν ἀὴρ ἀφανὴς,ὃν οὐκ ἔςιν ἰδεῖν. This is a place vnder the earth, and ſo hidde from vs. Therefore it is called Hades, that is an inuiſible aire; which wee

can

can not fee . And howfoeuer Socrates pleafed himfelfe in framing this heauen, as you call it, for himfelfe , and a fewe others (for hee admitteth none but Philofophers into it) Lucian in his Dialogues of the dead, bitterlie mocketh him, as being in Hell with all the ref ; howfoeuer he dreamed of an heauen for himfelfe after his departure hence.

In dialog.
Aeaci & Me-
nippi.

How Paganifh, and not onelie ridiculous but blafphemous Platoes heauen is , appeareth by this, that Socrates maketh s v v a n n e s his fellow feruants to Phœbus, & imagineth they fing that day they die, προειδότες τὰ ἐν ἅδε ἀγαθά, FORESEEING THE GOOD THINGS THEY SHALL HAVE IN HADES. And further faith that whē they perceiue they muſt die, then chiefly and moſt of al they fing γεγηθότες ότι μέλλυσι παρὰ τὸν θεὸν ἀπιέναι ὕπερ εἰσὶ θεράποντες; reioycing that they SHALL GO TO GOD whofe feruants they are. And thofe wordes which Socrates fpake of Swannes, forefǣing THE GOOD THINGS IN HADES, you, Sir Confuter, in the abundance of your wit, note to proue HADES to be heauen. And to this heauen though Socrates admitte Swannes, yet he accepteth no men, but fuch as haue bǣne Philofophers, & thofe of the pureſt fort. As for fuch as vfe popular and ciuil vertues, as iuſtice and temperance, gotten by care and continuance without Philofophie , his words are expreſſely thefe; ¶ τούτυς εἰκός ἐςινεἰς τοιᾶτον πάλιν ἀφικνᾶθαι πολιτικὸν καὶ ἥμερον γένος, ἤπς μελιττῶν, ἤ σφηκῶν ἤ μυρμήκων ἤ καὶ εἰς ταυτόν γε πάλιν τὸ ἀνθρώπινον γένος· εἰς δὲ γε θεῶν γένος μὴ φιλοσοφήσαντι καὶ παντελᾶς καθαρῷ ἀπιόντι ὺ θέμις ἀφικνεῖθαι ἄλλῳ, ἤ τῷ φιλομαθεῖ. It is fit that fuch (foules) fhould returne againe into fome fuch politicall and tame kinde either of B E E S, V V A S P E S, or E M M E T S, & after that into men again. But into the kinred of the Gods it is not lawful for anie to come that hath not beene a Philofopher , and verie pure at his departing hence. Others that were flouthfull and filled their bellies, hee faith muſt be turned into Affes, and fuch other beaftes

pPlato in Phedone.

Pag. 91.

qPlato in Phædone.

beaſts; and oppꝛeſſours and wꝛong doers into Wolues, Kites and Hawkes. Of theſe his plaine reſolution is ʳ that ᵣIbidem. ſuch ſoules wander, vntill by the earneſt loue of their bodilie na-ture, which followeth them, they PVT ON BODIES againe. And ſuch bodies (of birds and beaſts) they put on as reſemble the manners of their former life. Here is a godly world of ſoules to be bꝛought out of Plato into the Creede; and Socra-tes heauen, whp you ſhould fanſie, I cannot geſſe, except it be, that none but very pure and preciſe perſons ſhall come thither, to whom you would faine be the ringleader. But this is not all. In making HADES AND PLVTO, bp which the Poets meane the diuell, to bee a wiſe and bountifull God, hath not your wiſe Maſter fitted his new heauen with an excellent head? Plutarch moueth the doubt whe-ther HADES be a God oꝛ a DIVELL, that hath power ouer darknes and death: Homer & Heſiode affirme, he dwelleth vnder the earth, and is implacable, cruell, and hated of men. Porphyrie, no meane follower of Plato, concludeth PLVTO (which is all one with HADES as * Plato confeſſeth) to *In Cratylo. be the chiefe of all wicked ſpirites. Porphyries woꝛds are, ſτὰς δὲ πονηρὰς δαίμονας ἐκ εἰκῇ ὑπὸ τὴν σϕαίραν ὑποτίθεμεν. εἰ᾿ ἐκ τῶν συμ- ſ Citatur ab βόλων μόνον ἀνατειθέντες, ἀλλ᾿ ὅτι τὰ μειλίγματα, ἡ τὰ τέτων Ἀποτρόπαια περὶ Euſebio de τὸν πλύτωνα γίγνεται, ὡς ἐν τῷ πρώτῳ ἐδείκνυμεν: ὁ ἀυτὸς δὲ τῷ πλύτωνι ὁ θεὸς, preparat. e- ἡ διὰ τἀτο μάλιςτα δαιμόνων ἄρχων, ἡ σύμβολα διδὸς περὶ τὴν τέτων ἴλασιν. uangelica lib. We doe not without cauſe coniecture that all wicked ſpirites 4. cap. 12. are vnder Serapis; being led ſo to thinke not onely by his cere-monies, but becauſe offerings to pacifie, and ſacrifices auer-ting rage are done to PLVTO, as we haue ſhewed in our firſt booke. Now Serapis is all one god with Pluto, and therefore he is the greateſt prince of Diuels, and one that giueth charmes to driue away ſpirits. Loe, here is Socrates wiſe and bounti-full god, HADES AND PLVTO, concluded by a great Platonicke, to be the chiefe diuell; whoſe iudgement Euſe-bius followeth. And in deede conſidering his place where he dwelleth, his rage that he vſeth againſt men, foꝛ which

he

hee is so feared and hated of them, and his sacrifices in which hee delighteth, as also his power ouer death and darkenesse, it is a cleare case that Platoes HADES OR PLVTO is the great diuell in hell; whose craftes and sleights, because hee knew not as a Pagan, he hath promoted him to bee a wise and liberall god; and you haue learnedly cited this wise deuise to make him ruler of your heauen, whither you send Christ and his Saints to liue there for euer.

Now were it graunted vnto you, that Pluto and HADES (which by the description of all your classicall Poets is in deede the diuell) were one of Platoes gods; are you so little acquainted either with Plato or with Paganisme, that you presently conclude hee is the true God of Heauen? Or that this inuisible place must needes bee the kingdome of God? Looke but in the latter end of this booke, which you alleage for this very purpose: and there you shall see what pretie fansies Socrates hath of another inuisible earth farre aboue this, and waters likewise, and trees, and flowers, and fruites, and beastes, and men that liue longer than we doe here below, and without sicknes; where also there are temples & woods, in which the gods dwell familiarly; ᵗ ἄςη αὐτῶν ἰδεῖν, ἢ ϑέαμα ἰλαμίνων ϑεατῶν, That to see that

r Plato in Phædone circa finem.

earth is the sight of the blessed. But what be these wicked fancies either to the Creede or to Christian Religion? Seeing therefore your Greeke Poets with one consent make HADES to be a god below vnder the earth; and put vnder his power as well the Elisian fields and seates for the iust soules, as the prisons and dungeons for the vniust; and this fantasticall conceite of Socrates touching a speciall place for himselfe and such Philosophers as hee was, together with Swannes, beasts, trees, flowers, fruites, as it was singular and secret to himselfe, so it was most absurd and wicked; you may by no meanes bring your Classicall writers that were Pagans to expounde the

Creede;

Crǣde; much lesse must you binde the holy Ghost in the new Testament, to vse the word HADES, as the infidels did; since the holy Ghost onely knoweth and speaketh trueth; and their imaginations of the dead, or as you speake of the world of soules, was not onely false and foolish, but impious and blasphemous. And yet if you doe admit them to bee interpreters of the Crǣde; which I vtterlie refuse for the causes I haue tolde you; they make directly againſt you. For HADES with them was the Ruler or place of soules that were beneath vnder the earth, were they in rest or in paine; and that Christian Religion will assure you must nǣdes be hell, howsoeuer to breake out your broken matter you beginne halfe to doubt where hell is.

[*The authenticke authors of the Greeke tongue vsed hades* ,,
for the place of the blessed soules (you say) *and not properlie* ,,
for hell. So Leonidas cheered vp his men not to feare such ,,
a blessed death; to suppe in hell had beene a colde comfort ,,
vnto them.] You reade nothing your selfe belike, that you ,,
hit nothing right. In Plutarch whome you alleage, this
is no comfort giuen by Leonidas; but hǣ sǣing the Persians now in sight, as his men were dining; and in number so infinite aboue his, who were but an handfull, willeth them to make short, and saith; So dine, as men that must suppe in HADES; that is, care not for meate since death is so neere; but prepare to fight for your Countrey. It sheweth a resolution to dye, but no consolation after death more than they knew before; which was, that in HADES were places as well for the good to rest, as for the bad to bǣ punished; but both were below vnder earth, and in Plutoes kingdome, as the Gentiles supposed. Neither did Homer meane to make a new heauen, for such as Achilles slue, but to send them to the place where hǣ thought all soules did abide; and therefore hǣ put Achilles soule in Plutoes region vnder the earth, as

well

well as the rest of the Grecians and Troians, that died in that Battaile. And because your Proctor will needes haue the words that Achilles spirite spake to Vlisses at his descent to hell, to bee a dictionarie for hades, what place it is, against which if the Creede had gone, it had been a skoffe to all Hellas, and had hindered all the proceeding of the Gospell: Let vs see whether his owne dictionarie will not returne all his allegations vppon his owne head. If HADES in the Creede must bee the same place, where Achilles spirite was, whither Vlisses descended, and where he saw and spake with so many Ghostes, then apparantly HADES must bee the Poets HELL. At Vlisses entrance Homer telling how the soules came about him saith,

a Odiss. 11.
　　a αἰδ᾽ ἀγέροντο ψυχαὶ ὑπὲ ἰξ ἐρέβευς :
The soules flocked together out of Erebus; now ἐρέβῷ is the very place where the Poets place Cerberus, and whence the same Poet saith, Hercules

b Iliad. 8.
　　b Ἐξ ἐρέβευς ἄξοντα κύνα ςυγερᾶ ἀΐδαο :
Was sent to fetch from Erebus the dogge of HATEFVLL HADES. Againe Vlisses mother asking him how hee came to that place, saith

c Odiss. 11.
　　c τέκνον ἰμὸν πῶς ἤλθες ὑπὸ ζόφον ἠερόεντα,
My sonne how camest thou vnder this darke mist? Of Aiax Ghost, who would not for anger speake to Vlisses, Homer saith,

d Ibid.
　　d βῆ δὲ μετ᾽ ἄλλας ψυχὰς εἰς ἐρέβῷ :
Hee went away to other soules in Erebus. There Vlisses saith hee saw Sisyphus

e Ibid.
　　e κρατέρ᾽ ἄλγι ἔχοντα,
Suffering grieuous torments, as also Titius and Tantalus to endure the like. There he saw 　f βίην ἠρακλῆίην

f Ibid.
　　εἴδωλον αὐτὸς δὲ μετ᾽ ἀθανάτοισι θέοισι :
τέρπεται. Hercules strength a Ghost: for hee himselfe was in ioye with the immortall Gods. There Achilles spirite

g Odiss. 11.
toke so small comfort, that when Vlisses said, g There is none

none happier then thou Achilles; before , whiles thou li-
uedſt , wee honoured thee as a God , and now art thou a
great commaunder among the Dead ; bee not therefore ſo
ſadde ; hǽ replied , Praiſe not death to mee Vliſſes, I had
rather ſerue any poore man (on earth) as his drudge, though
hee were ſcant able to liue, then to raigue here ouer all the
dead. If the place bee darke and dǽpe ᵻᵻᵻᵻᴑ : if Cerberus
bǽ there which the * Poets make the very kǽper of
hell; if there bǽ grieuous and cruell puniſhmentes for
ſuch as deſerue them, if the beſt haue there ſo little ioye
of the place, as Homer maketh Achilles ghoſt here to
confeſſe, what place can this bǽ but that hell, which
all the Poets acknowledge; though in ſome part there-
of there bǽ worſe puniſhmentes then in other ?

*Heſiod. in
theogonia.
* Virgil.li.6.

[This is not that Tartarus, you will ſaye , which the
Poets make the Iaple and Priſon for the wicked .]
What is that to the purpoſe, if ſome puniſhmentes in
hell bǽ worſe than other ? Looke to thoſe whome the
Poets place without the dungeon, and ſǽ whether they
bǽ in heauen or no? And becauſe you and your friends
talke ſo much of the worlde of Soules, and of heauen
to bǽ found in HADES , and INFERI; and your ſelfe
bring Virgill as one of your Claſſicall authors to proue
this matter, ʰ *Who though hee were a Poet, and fayned* „
many things, yet hee ſpake (you ſay) *familiarlie, and after* „
the vulgar vſe , and for the ſubſtance of the matter vttered „
touching heauen and hell , the opinion of the worlde then : „
I muſt pray the Readers leaue and patience, whiles I
follow you in your owne fantaſticall deuiſe, though a-
gainſt mine owne liking, to let the ſimple ſǽ what your
worlde of ſoules, and your heauen is, euen in thoſe very
writers, which you produce for this purpoſe; and whe-
ther they bǽ fitte things to bǽ Preſidents for the Crǽde
or no. In Plutoes kingdome vnder earth, whether Æne-

ʰ *Pag.67.*

as went to ſée his Father Anchiſes, ¹Virgil your authen-
ticke author maketh beſides *Tartarus*,ᵏ *and your goodly Eliſi-*
an fields the eternall habitation (as you call it) *of the bleſſed,*
many lodgings. As firſt for ¹ſicknes, care, weeping, pouertie,
labour, warres, diſcord, dreames, and death, beſides for Cen-
taures, Briareus, Hidra, Chimera, Gorgon, Harpies, and Gerion,
and ſundrie other monſters. There wander the Ghoſts, whoſe
bodies are not buried a hundred yeare before they can get ouer
the foule and filthie riuer of Styx. The other ſide of Styx, is
kept by Cerberus the Dogge with three heads; where firſt
are placed the ſoules of infants weeping and crying ; then
ſuch as were vniuſtly condemned to death, next, ſuch as being
wearie of their liues killed themſelues, now willing to ſuffer
pouertie, or any paine on earth, ſo they might returne to life
againe. In the fourth place are *Lugentes Campi*, the wo-
full fields of ſuch as died for loue ; in the fift, Warriers and
ſuch as purſued each other with the ſword, where Æneas ſaw
all the Grecians and Trojans that dyed at the ſiege of
Troy. Of all theſe places, where yet are no puniſhments,
the Poet maketh Deiphobus to ſay to Æneas, what cauſe
driueth thée,

   Vt triſtes ſine ſole domos, loca turbida adires,

To come to the wofull houſen without ſunne, and lothſome
places? Then leadeth the left hand to Tartarus, which
theſe men ſo much harpe at, compaſſed with fierie Phlege-
ton, and there are the puniſhments of the wicked ; then
Plutoes palace, and on the right hand, *Amæna vireta*
fortunatorum nemorum ſedéſque beatæ, The ſweete ſprings of
the fortunate woods, and the bleſſed ſeats. Here is the hea-
uen which this confuter alleageth out of Virgil, and here
Æneas found his father Anchiſes, in a greene vale, viewing
the ſoules that dranke of the water of obliuion, and were
to take new bodies on earth againe. His words are,

   * *Anima quibus altera fato,*

i Æneidos 6.
k Pag.101.
l Æneidos 6.
*Æneidos 6.

Corpora

Corpora debentur, Lethei ad fluminis vndam
Securos latices & longa obliuia potant.

The foules who by deſtinie are to take bodies the ſecond time, doe here at the Riuer of Lethe drinke the waters of vtter forgetfulnes, no way remembring whatſoeuer they ſaw or knew, either whiles they firſt liued, or during the time of their abode vnder earth. And becauſe it ſeemed ſtrange to Æneas, that ſoules ſhould come to take other bodies, though this be right Platoes fanſie in his Phædone, Anchiſes telleth his ſonne the ſecrets of Platoes Purgatorie, heauen, and reſurrection, as Virgil conceiued them, who was a great Platoniſt. When men die (ſaith he) all the infections of their bodies cannot preſently be taken from their ſoules.

Æneidos 6.

❧ *Ergo exercentur pœnis, veterúmq; maloru͂ ſupplicia expendunt,*
Therefore the ſoules (of ſuch as are curable, for the deſperate and inſanable, are caſt into Tartarus, and neuer come thence by Platoes owne words) are purged with paines, and abide the puniſhment of their former infection, ſome are hanged vp to the winde, ſome are plunged vnder water, ſome are clenſed by fier:

Quiſque ſuos patimur manes, exinde per amplum
Mittimur Elyſium, & pauci lata arua tenemus,
Donec longa dies perfecto temporis orbe
Concretam exemit labem, purúmque reliquit,
Æthereum ſenſum, atque auraï ſimplicis ignem.
Has omnes vbi mille rotam voluêre per annos,
Letheum ad ſluuium Deus euocat agmine longo,
Scilicet immemores ſupera vt connexa reuiſant,
Rurſus & incipiant in corpora velle reuerti.

m Æneidos e.

Wee euery one of vs ſuffer our clenſing, and after that wee are ſent out into the large Elyſian fieldes, where but a fewe of vs inhabite theſe pleaſant places, vntill long time hath taken awaye the bodilie infection, and leaueth the æthereall ſenſe pure, and the vigour of the fierie and

ſimple:

simple ayre. Then after a thousand yeares God calleth all these soules (thus purged and placed in the fortunate seates) to the flood of Lethe, that they may goe to the earth againe, with vtter forgetfulnesse of all things, and beginne to desire to returne to new bodies. To these Elysian fields when Æneas should come, the Poet maketh Sybilla say,

Æneidos 6.　　*Ad genitorem imas Erebi descendit ad vmbras*;

Æneas descendeth to his father, euen to the soules below in Erebus : And that Erebus is one of the infernall Gods, as the Poets call them, can bee no question. For when Dido minding to kill her selfe prepared *Sacra Ioui stygio*, Sacrifices to the infernall Iupiter, the Poet maketh her Priest

Æneidos 4.　　to inuocate, *Tercentum tonat ore deos Erebúmque Chaósque*, Three hundred gods, and Erebus and Chaos.

This is the worlde of Soules that Virgil deliuered in his time; which hée collected out of Plato; this is the heauen, that is contayned in HADES and INFERI. Iudge thou Christian Reader, whether this be not the high way to Paganisme, to tell vs that this is the heauen, where the Saints of God are in rest, and whether Christ ascended. For my part, but that I thinke this confuter talketh of that hée knoweth not, I must haue proclaymed him for a Pagan; and therefore after hée séeth it, if hée persist to say that heauen is either Homers HADES, or Virgils INFERI, I may not spare to discharge the dutie of a Christian man, to let the whole realme vnderstand, that this is open infidelitie, cloaked vnder the name of Puritie. Platoes world of Soules where it altereth from this, is rather worse than better. For hée saith, the soules of euill men are clogged with their bodilie vncleanenes,

n Plato in　　and wander, [n] ὥσπερ λέγεται ἀεὶ τὰ μνήματα τε ᾗ τάφες, about tombes
Phædone.　　and graues, as it is said, and then put on the bodies of beastes, birds, or wormes. And you, Sir Confuter, lighting on the first part of these wordes, openly falsifie them, and
　　　　　　　　　　　　　　　　　　　　　　　　lewdly

lewdly misapply them. For in steede of (as it is said) you translate, (*as it is commonly said*) and by that worde „ *Pag. 98.*
COMMONLY of your owne adding, and referred to the former words, where there is a manifest distinction or pause betwixt them, you bid the reader note that HADES *is commonly called heauen.* For thus you write : Againe, *Plato saith of heauen, that it is an vnseene estate, euen* HADES, „ o *Pag. 98.*
as it is commonly called, which you will by the side to be *noted;* „ where Plato in that place speaketh not one word of hea= uen. But such is the miserie of your cause, you must belie your authors, or else you will lacke proofes for your hu= mours. And touching the soules of all men that are borne, Plato holdeth their soules had bodies before, and staye in HADES, vntill the time come that they must haue bodies againe, and therefore all our knowledge heere is but the remembring of that wee knew before, when our soules were in other bodies ; which is the opinion that Tertullian chargeth him with : His owne words are, p πάλαι μὲν ἄν ἐςι τίς ὁ λόγος ἄτε ὃ μεμνήμεθα οἷς εἰσὶν (αἱ ψυχαὶ) ἐν= p Plato in θένε ἀφικόμεναι ἐκεῖ : ἢ πάλιν γε δεῦρο ἀφικνῦνται ἢ γίγνονται ἐκ τῶν τεθνεώτων. Phædone.
There is an auncient assertion which wee remember, that soules departing hence are there, and come hither againe, and are new borne from the dead . And least you should thinke hee did not consent to it; hee saith somewhat after, q ἢ ἡμεῖς τὰ αὐτὰ ταῦτα ἐκ ἐξαπατώμενοι ὁμολογῦμεν : ἀλλ᾽ ὅτι ἢ τῷ ὄντι, q Ibid. ἢ τὸ ἀναβιώσκεθαι, ἢ ἐκ τῶν τεθνεώτων τὰς ζῶντας γίγνεθαι. Wee are not deceiued confessing all this; but there is in very trueth a re= turning of soules to liue againe on earth; and of the dead spring the liuing. Consult you and your Instructor whether you will bring this HADES or world of soules into the Creede; or whether the thiefe from the Crosse ascended to this hea= uen, together with the soule of our Sauiour. But if these bee intolerable and abominable heresies to haue soules passe from bodie to bodie; and Platoes HADES be nothing

else but a continuall chopping and changing of soules from
life to death, and from death to life againe, hale backe your
HADES from the Creede, howsoeuer your Hellas will take
pepper in the nose to see her follies refused.

    Cicero is your last authenticke writer that you bring
to proue *Inferi* to bee heauen, out of whom you note three

g Pag. 107.   " things. *r First, that he vtterlie misliked the opinion of the olde*
    " *Latines, that thought the world of the dead was vnder the earth,*
    " *and therefore gaue this terme* INFERI, *to signifie the same:*
    " *this hee openly misliketh, that the damned soules were beneath*
    " *in the earth, or at least in such kinde of torments as many did*
    " *imagine. How much more did he condemne them, that thought*
    " *all the deceased soules were beneath, vnder, or in the earth?*
    " *The blessed hee thought rather, as Plato did, to ascend vp to*

ſ Pag. 108.   " *heauen.* ſ Secondly, you note, *That although hee reiected*
    " *the opinion of the former Latines, yet hee retayned the La-*
    " *tine phrase, as being now common and familiar euery where;*
    " *which rose of olde from that opinion, thinking all the dead af-*
    " *ter this life to be* infra, *beneath. He had learned to thinke wise-*
    " *lier, but yet he spake so, as the vulgar phrase had preuailed, ac-*
    " *cording to Aristotles rule; we must thinke as the wise doe, but*
    " *speake as the people doe.* Thirdly, *Tullie saith of this opinion*
    " *followed great errors.* If a man would hire you to speake
against your selfe, you cannot doe it in plainer manner
than here you doe. You confesse that Cicero was the first
(for before him you bring none) that misliked the opi-
nion of the olde Latines (whose seate and tongue in Ita-
lie was then 1200. yeares olde) that the world of the dead
was vnder the earth, and to signifie so much, they vsed
the worde Inferi; which had continued in the mouthes of
all men learned and vnlearned, till Ciceroes time, to
expresse the state of the dead. Secondly, you say the phrase

t t " *was so common and familiar euery where for the worlde*
    " *of the dead,* that Cicero himselfe, though hee thought

                                        otherwise

otherwise durſt not depart from *the vulgare phraſe which had ſo generally preuayled.* Then by your owne confeſſion wee haue thus much, that *Inferi* for twelue hundred yeares in the mouthes of all men ignorant, and learned among the Latines and Romanes did ſignifie the ſtate of ſuch ſoules as were vnder the earth. Now let Cicero ſay what he can to the contrarie; his authoritie is no waie ſo great that it ſhould ouerwaigh ſo long and ſetled a conſent. Great errors followed hereof Tullie ſaith. And you affirme the like, but not ſo great as Tullie himſelfe mayntayned in reiecting that opinion. For he in ſome pride of his tongue and conceite of his wit brought heauen and hell to be vtterly nothing.

That the old Latines thought all men after death to go vnder the earth I ſee no proofe; I find rather the contrarie confeſſed by your owne author. He alleageth out of Ennius, *Romulus in cælo cum dijs agit æuum, vt fama aſſentiens dixit Ennius.* Romulus leadeth his life in heauen with the Gods, as Ennius approuing the ſame writeth. And againe; *Abijt ad Deos Hercules. Vetera iam iſta, & religione omnium conſecrata.* Hercules is gone to the Gods. Theſe things are ancient and ſealed with the religious conſent of all men. So that Ciceroes words which you alleage, cannot import that they thought ſo of all men, for then they muſt ſo haue thought of Romulus and Hercules, which Cicero confeſſeth all men acknowledge to be in heauen; but they ſuppoſed ſo of moſt men; which amongſt Pagans, as they were, was no ſuch great error, as you would make it, nor any way ſo great as that which Cicero laboured to eſtabliſh in place thereof. For he through the inſolencie of his opinion of himſelfe, or inconſtancie of his diſpoſition, or both, would ſomtimes haue an *Inferi,* or hell below; and ſometimes he would haue none. Examples whereof are euident in his writings. In his ſpleene againſt Antonie, he ſaith; *Illi igitur impij, quos occidiſtis*

t Tuſcul2. quæſt.li.1.

uPhilippic.2.14

diſtis, etiam ad Inferos pœnas parricidij luent: vos autem qui ex-
tremum ſpiritum in victoria effudiſtis, piorum eſtis locum et ſe-
dem conſequuti. Thoſe wicked, whom ye ſlew, ſhall IN HELL
ſuffer the puniſhment of their parricide: you that loſt your liues
in obtayning the victorie haue obtayned the place and ſeate of
the bleſſed. In his brauerie defending Cluentius, he caſt it

x Pro Clu-
entio.

all off as a fooliſh fable. × Quid tandem illi mali mors attulit?
niſi forte ineptijs ac fabulis ducimur, vt exiſtimemus illum a-
pud Inferos impiorum ſupplicia perferre, et actum eſſe præcipitem
in ſceleratorum ſedem atq̃ regionem: qua ſi falſa ſunt, id quod
omnes intelligunt, quid ei tandem aliud mors eripuit præter do-
loris ſenſum? What harme could (Cluentius) do vnto (Oppi-
anicus condemned and baniſhed for his lewdnes) by killing
him? vnleſſe wee belecue toyes and fables to thinke he endured
the puniſhment of the wicked in hell, and that he was caſt head-
long into the region and priſon of the vngodly? which (con-
ceits) if they bee falſe, as all men may eaſily vnderſtand, what
hurt could death doe him, but take from him all ſenſe of griefe?
To make a reaſon for his Client, that by killing his ad-
uerſarie, afflicted with penurie and miſerie, he ſhould rather
doe him a good turne, then a ſpite, he vtterly reiecteth, as a
fable, that the wicked haue any puniſhments after this
life; which in the former place againſt Antonius ſouldiers
he vrged as vehemently for a truth.

And though in this place he tare, as you ſay, the ignorance
of the olde Latines, yet in another place, hee commendeth

y Oratio in
Catilin. 4.

their wiſedome, for the ſelf ſame poſition. y Itaq; vt aliqua in
vita formido improbis eſſet poſita; apud Inferos eiuſmodi quædam
illi Antiqui ſupplicia impijs cõſtituta eſſe voluerũt, quod videlicet
intelligebant his remotis non eſſe mortem ipſam pertimeſcendam.
Therfore to terrifie the wicked in this life, THOSE AVNCIENT
Fathers held there were ſome ſuch puniſhments appointed IN
HELL for the wicked, becauſe they ſaw without the death was
no way to be feared. And, Sir Refuter, are you a Chriſtian,
that thinke it worth the noting out of a prophane Orator,

that

that it is a foolish fable to thinke, the wicked are punished
after this life in hell? Vphold you the proude and lewd con-
ceite of a Pagã against the setled and reueled iudgements
of God by his word? dare you adde of your owne head (for
your author hath no such word)ᶻ *that the ignorance* OF THE „ z *Pag.* 106.
TRVTH *beganne this opinion, that Inferi were vnder the earth,* „
and the terrors of hell also? I see your deuise; you would haue „
hell euerie where; and TORMENTS OF HELL you would
haue none, but such as Christ by your assertion suffered in
his soule here on earth; and because you want good autho-
ritie to countenance this matter, you reade vs a Lecture
out of Cicero, that he thought so before you, and that he is a
verie authenticke and Classicall writer. But keepe this
lesson till you get none but Atheists and Infidels to bee
your hearers; they will thanke you for it; Christian eares
doe abhorre it; and will detest your prophanes as much as
they doe Ciceroes. For if there bee no punishment in hell,
sure there is no hell, and he that decreaseth the terror, de-
creaseth the truth of it: therefore the olde Latines did not
erre. But your New Orator thinketh hee may buyld and
ouerturne hell and heauen at his pleasure.

As he dealeth with hell, so doth he with heauen; som-
tymes he will haue one, and somtimes he cannot tell whe-
ther there bee any such habitation for soules or no. And the
heauen which he would haue, is a Mansion of his owne
making. Such authors you bring vs to expound the
Creede, and to outface all the Fathers, that they them-
selues cannot tell what they say. Where he purposely dis-
puteth of the seate and sanctuarie for the soule after death,
he concludeth the whole discourse, as doubtfully as he be-
ganne. ᵃ *Si supremus ille dies non extinctionem, sed commutati-* a Tuscula.
onem affert loci, quid optabilius? sin autem perimit ac delet omni- quæst. lib. 1.
nò; quid melius quàm in medijs vitæ laboribus obdormiscere, et ad finem.
ita conniuentê somno sepeliri sempiterno? If the daie of our death
bring not a perishing but changing of places, what can be more

Ddd 3 to

to be wiſhed for? But if it vtterly quench and extinguiſh (bodie and ſoule) what can be more acceptable amidſt the troubles of this life, then as it were wincking to ſlumber, and ſhutting our eies to fall into an euerlaſting ſleepe? *Habes ſomnum imaginem mortis, eamḡ, quotidie induis, & dubitas quin ſenſus in morte nullus ſit, quum in eius ſimulachro videas eſſe nullum ſenſum?* Thou haſt ſleepe which thou daylie trieſt, for an image of death; and doubteſt thou but there is no ſenſe in death, when thou findeſt no ſenſe in ſleepe, which is the patterne of death? Now on the other ſide for Ciceroes heauen, which you will needs bring into the Creede vnder the name of *Inferi*, hee maketh it no reward of vertue, nor gift of grace to be beſtowed where it pleaſeth God; but he affirmeth there is a fierie aire aboue, of which ſoules are made; and therefore as ſoone as the ſoule is looſed from the bodie, it flieth vpward as fier doth, by a naturall motion, vnto the place, which is like to it ſelfe, and there ſtayeth, and is nouriſhed with the ſelfe ſame things, with which the ſtarres are nouriſhed.

Qua quum conſtet, perſpicuum debet eſſe, animos quum é corpore exceſſerint, ſiue illi ſint ſpirabiles, ſiue ignei, ſublime ferri: accedit vt eo facilius animus euadat ex hoc aere, quem ſæpe iam craſſum appello, eumḡ, perrumpat, quod nihil eſt animo velocius. Qui ſi permanet incorruptus, ſuiḡ, ſimilis, neceſſe eſt ita feratur, vt penetret & diuidat omne cœlum hoc, in quo nubes, imbres, ventiḡ, coguntur. Quam regionem quum ſuperauit animus, naturamḡ, ſui ſimilem contigit, & agnouit, vinctus ex anima tenui, & ex ardore ſolis temperato ignibus inſiſtit, et finem altius ſe efferendi facit. Quum enim ſui ſimilem & leuitatem & calorem adeptus eſt, tanquam paribus examinatis ponderibus, nullā in partem mouetur. Eaḡ, ei demum naturalis eſt ſedes, quum ad ſui ſimilem penetrauit, in quo, nulla re egens, alitur & ſuſtentatur, yſdem rebus quibus aſtra ſuſtentantur & aluntur. It is long and tedious (good reader) to be troubled with theſe prophane follies; but becauſe the confuter laboureth ſo much to haue

Ciceroes

Ibidem.

Ibidem.

Ciceroes wozld of foules and his heauen into the Creede, and in refpect of him difgraceth all other wziters as igno=rant of the latine tongue, thefe woz9s will playnly fhew thæ, what an audacious, irreligious, and heathenifh at=tempt that is; and how abfurdly and lewdly he faith, Cicero had learned to thinke wifelyer then they, that faid hell was below in the earth. Foz they deliuered a trueth, and this of Ciceroes is a falfe, foolifh and wicked fanfie. The Englifh of his woz9s is in effect this. Thefe things being certain, it ought to be a cleare cafe, that our foules when they leaue the bodie, whether they be of an aerie or fierie nature, do mooue vpward. A good helpe for the foule with more eafe to paffe and breake through this groffe ayre heere below is this, ẙ nothing is fwifter than the foule. Which remayning vncorrupt, and alwaies like it felfe, OF NECESSITIE MVST ASCEND, and pearce, and deuide all THIS HEAVEN (oz ayze) in which the cloudes, windes, and rayne engender. Which region when the foule hath once paffed, and touched, and perceiued a nature like to it felfe, mixed of a fubtile ayre, and the temperate heate of the funne; in that fierie region, IT STAYETH, and maketh an ende OF AS-CENDING ANY HIGHER. For when it hath gotten like both heate and purenes (of the ayze) balanced as it were with equall waights, it moueth no way. AND THIS IS THE NATVRAL SEATE OF THE SOVLE, when it commeth to a like ayre to it felfe; in which needing nothing, IT IS NOVRISHED and fed with THE SELFESAME THINGS, VVITH VVHICH THE STARRES ARE NOVRISHED and fuftayned. Ciceroes heauẽ is nothing but an heap of heathenifh impieties. The firft, that the fubftance of the foule confifteth of fier oz ayre; the fecond, that of neceffitie it afcendeth vpward as fier doth. The third, that when it commeth to a pure ayze and tem=perate heate of the funne, it ftayeth there, and afcendeth no higher. The fourth, that this is the naturall feat foz the foule, and thence it moueth no way. The fift, that it is there nourifhed and fuftayned with the felfe fame things,

with:

with which the ſtarres are. The conſequents to this hea-
uen are moſt horrible. Firſt that all ſoules by neceſſitie of
their nature being in this place, there are conſequently
none in HELL, nor none in heauen, and ſo both thoſe places
are vtterly emptied by your eloquent Maſter. Next that,
when the ſtarres & ſkies ſhall be melted and diſſolued with
fier, then muſt the ſoules of all men be likewiſe diſſolued,
conſiſting of the ſame matter, which they doe, and ſo vtter-
ly extinguiſh. Laſtly, Gods promiſes, and threats are all
fruſtrate, if he can doe his enemies no more hurt, nor his
ſeruants more good, then this heauen affoordeth. And ther-
fore if you bring the world of ſoules, or this heauen into the
Crede, I muſt refuſe the Article for open and euident
points of Infidelitie, which I ſuppoſe, the Apoſtles, nor A-
poſtolicke men neuer meant, when they made the Crede.

Yet this place ſuch as it is, Cicero, you ſay, called it *In-*
feri. Syr if you leaue lying, you muſt leaue writing. For
you can ſhant write a true word. Cicero doth no where
call this place *Inferi*; but howſoeuer he had his priuate
conceits as a Philoſopher, yet when he ſpake before the
ſenate, or the people, he was forced to yeld to ſuch opiniós,
and to vſe ſuch words as were commonly receiued with
all men, and that is the direction which Ariſtotle giueth by
the rule which you alleage, that though we muſt learne to
think as wiſe men do; yet we muſt be content to ſpeake as
the people doe, not that by ſo ſpeaking we muſt alter the
nature and proprietie of the words, which wee vſe; but
mynding to aduiſe or perſwade the multitude, we muſt con-
diſcend as well to their vulgar phraſes, as to their generall
and receiued opinions. And therefore as the people thought
all men dying to deſcend vnder the earth to *Inferi*, ſo Ci-
cero ſpeaking in open place vſeth this ſame phraſe, whatſoe-
uer he priuately thought of the place where the dead were.

From Pagans (Syr Refuter) you returne to Chriſtiás, &
whom before you accuſed for altering & changing the auth-é-
ticke

vſe of words, you now alleadge as obſeruing the true pro-
prietie of the ſame word, for which you did chalenge them
before. *b Hereunto let vs adde (ſaie you)that the latter learned* ,, *b Pag.101.*
writers euen Chriſtians haue alſo eſpied and graunted this pro- ,, •
prietie of the latin word Infernum or Inferi, as alſo of the Greeke ,,
H A D E S. Ierom *ſaith, Infernus is a place where the ſoules are in-* ,, in Oſe:ca:13.
-cluded either in reſt or in paines. The farder you go, the more
you ſhew, you vnderſtand neither Pagans nor Chriſtians.
The fault you found with the latin Fathers was, that they
c vſe the word Inferi to ſignifie hell properlie and particularlie, ,, *c Pag.96.*
that is the place of the Damned: or elſe an other particular place ,,
vnder the earth apart of hell and not farre from hell it ſelf where ,,
ſoules remayned if not in paines, yet in priſon, & far from the place ,,
of eternall bleſſednes & ioy, but this you affirme *is a meere and* ,,
plaine abuſion of the word. And within two leaues, when Ierom
ſaith the veric ſame thing, which you miſliked before, and cal-
led a meere and plaine abuſion of the word; you confeſſe hee
eſpied the true proprietie of the word Infernus. This is banding ,,
of Balles in a tennis Court, and not anie ſearching after a
truth in the church of God. But when your learning reacheth
no furder, you muſt needes breath out your ignorance, or bri-
dle your toong, which hath runne ſo long on a voluntarie,
that you cannot tell when you bee out, nor when you bee in.
Ierom indeede was of opinion that before Chriſts death
the ſoules of all, as well good as bad, were ſhut vp in a place
within the earth; the good in reſt and expectance of Chriſts
comming thither, by him to bee deliuered; the badde in
paines and torments. This place common to both ſorts,
but with different effects, Ierom calleth Infernus, which in our
Engliſh toong is hell. Of this place he ſaith. *d Infernus locus* *d in Oſe:ca:13*
eſt in quo animæ recluduntur ſiue in refrigerio. ſiue in pœnis. Hell
is a place in which ſoules are included, either in reſt or in
paine. Here you ſaie Ierom eſpied the proprietie of the
latine word Infernum *or* Inferi. Bee it ſo ſince you will
needes haue it ſo. But Infernum in this place doth

no waie ſigniſie the kingdome of heauen ; Ergo the true pro-
prietie of the worde *Infernum* doeth not ſigniſie the king-
dome of heauen. The Maior is your owne. The Minor by
Gods grace I will prooue euen out of Ierom. Marke well
his wordes.

Hiero.in epi-
taph Nepot ad
Heliodorum.

Quid ſimile Infernus & regna cælorum ? What likenes haue
Infernus and the kingdome of heauen ? you ſaie Infernus is
taken by Ierome for the kingdome of heauen; Ierome him-
ſelfe telleth you the one hath no likeneſſe to the other. Are
you not caught like a long bealied thing in your owne grin?
and becauſe you ſhall perceiue it is not a tricke, but a truth
that I preſſe you with out of Ierom, that INFERNVS by no
meanes is the kingdome of God, and conſequentlie muſt be
properlie hell ,(except you will builde newe receptacles for
ſoules after Chriſts aſcenſion where they may bee, neither in
hel nor in heauen,)you ſhal haue more out of Ierom touching

In Amos.ca.9

the true proprieties of theſe wordes. CERNE PROPRIE-
TATES; AD INFERNVM DESCENDITVR, AD COE-
LVM CONSCENDITVR. MARKE THE PROPRIE-
TIES(of theſe two wordes:)TO HELL MEN DESCEND,
TO HEAVEN MEN ASCENDE. And againe, *No-*

In Eccleſiaſt.
cap.9.

ta ante aduentum Chriſti , quamuis ſanctos , omnes Inferni
lege detentos. Porro quod ſancti poſt reſurrectionē domini nequa-
quam teneantur inferno teſtatur Apoſtolus dicens;melius eſt diſ-
ſolui & eſſe cum Chriſto;Qui autem cum chriſto eſt , vtique non
tenetur in Inferno . Note that before Chriſts comming all,euen
the ſaints thēſelues, were detained vnder the lawe of hel:but that
after the reſurrection of our Sauior they are not helde in hel, the
Apoſtle witneſſeth when he ſaith;It is better to be diſſolued and
to bee with Chriſt. And he that is with Chriſt certainely is not
detained in hell. There is no ſhifting from the force of theſe
wordes.Afore Chriſts comming the ſaints were in *Inferno*,af-
ter his aſcenſion they were not. For hee that is with Chriſt
is not in *Inferno .* Saie if you dare that *Infernus* here is the
kingdom of God. For then theſe abſurdities will purſue
you.

you: That after Christes ascension the saintes are not in the kingdome of heauen, and he that is with Christ is not in the kingdome of Christ: therefore maugre your bearde, if you haue anie, *Infernus* with Ierom is trulie and properlie hell, and in no wise the kingdome of heauen, as you imagine. Thus thriue you by your own authors, whom you produce to make the world beleeue that formerlie HADES & INFERI did signifie heauen: such heauens if you be wise, keepe your selfe from, neither professe to expound the Creed by the Classicall maisters of the greeke tongue, being Poets & Pagans. What is to be thought of that opinion of the Fathers that the saints before Christs comming were in *Inferno*, in hel, but free from feare or torment, though in some darknes, as also whence they tooke the ground of that assertion, I haue shewed in the end of the ª treatise before as much as needed to this question, there with ease it may be perused.

ªVide pag. 189. et sequent.

[They mistooke, you will saie, the word *Infernum* in the old testament, and thence grew their opinió, that the Patriarks and prophets before Christes comming went to hell; but the scriptures had no such meaning; for neither the worde Sheol with the Hebrues, nor the worde Hades with the Septuagint had any such sense, to signifie hell. And this a notable argument, ý Hades signifieth the world of soules, or generall state of the dead, were they in hel or in heauen.] Wee are all this while out of our proper element to sift heathen philosophers & Poets for the meaning of the creede, & a little smattering in the Greeke tongue made the Refuter so arrogant, that hee bid defiance to all the fathers both greeke and Latin, as vnable to vnderstande one poore word in the Creede, which the church of Christ proposed to euerie childe to learne, and to euerie catechist to knowe. But now wee are returned to the scriptures againe, (for Fathers they leaue as corrupters of the olde both faith and phrase) wee shall goe through with more ease, and ende with more speede. That Sheol or Hades doe signifie heauen, either in the Scriptures of the

olde

olde o2 newe Testament, o2 with the Septuagint which are
the tranſlators of the Hebrue into Grœk , J vtterlie denie;
and no man liuing ſhall euer bee able to make anie p2oofe
thereof; on which iſſue I am content to ioyne with any man
that is learned and ſober , fo2 the hazard of either of our cre-
dits. If Sheol, and Hades in the ſcriptures neuer ſignifie hea-
uen, then can they not ſignifie THE VVORLD OF SOVLES;
fo2 ſo much as there is no one place common to all ſoules de-
parted this life , but ſome are in hell , and ſome in heauen;
and fo2 one wo2d to ſignifie both hell and heauen ſo farre diſ-
tant one from the other, and ſo much repugnant one to the o-
ther,is ſomwhat ſtrange, except it could be ſtrongly p2oued.
Chaos did impo2t the whole maſſe of heauen and earth be-
fo2e they were diſtinguiſhed, but ſince they were ſeuered,
and ſetled by the wonderful wiſedome and mighty power of
God ſo far apart one from the other, and ſo much vnlike one
to the other , there are wo2des in the ſcripture which note all
that God made , but none that comp2iſe heauen and hell,ex-
cluding the reſt . S. Paul vſeth ᵃ κτίσις fo2 the creature', and
ᵇ καΐαβολη κόσμʊ fo2 the making of the world, and our ſaui-
our vſeth ⁱ αἰὼν fo2 this world and the next , where nothing is
excepted; but that heauen and hel ſhould come to be included
in one wo2d & the reſt excluded, I ſee neither whie, no2 howe
it ſhould be . Fo2 where wo2des are common, ſome thinges
muſt alſo be common, as nœdefull to bee exp2eſſed by thoſe
wo2des;but to ſoules in heauen and hell no poſitiue thing is
common;all things are rather contrarie. Their bodies they
want in both places,becauſe they are ſoules;otherwiſe their
ſtates be as repugnant in all points,as light and darkneſſe,
Ch2iſt and Belial,yea as heauen and hell in which they are ;
wherefo2e as light and darknes,faith and infidelitie,truth and
errour haue no common wo2de to comp2iſe them being
contraries each to other ; no mo2e haue heauen and hell
as they are the rewardes of the iuſt and vniuſt ; fo2 ſo much
as all things in either are directlie repugnant each to other.
                                                              Againe

ᵃ Rom.8.
ᵇ Epheſ. 1
ⁱ Matth.12.

Again that s h e o l o2 h a d e s may poſſiblie ſignifie heauen
I vtterlp denp, becauſe in heauen beſites the ſoules of men,
there are the elect angels of God, to whom if anie man dare
applie sheol o2 hades, he muſt giue me leaue to thinke his
iudgement to be weake, and his faith vnſound.

[Sheol and Hades, you will ſaie ſignifie all that are deade
in either place.] But pou muſt remember, that both theſe
wordes in the Scriptures doe p2operlie ſignifie places and
not perſons. Fo2 though the ancient Græbes vſed the word
h a d e s , firſt fo2 a perſon, and then fo2 the place which that
perſon gouerned; yet the holie ghoſt (knowing that the per-
ſon which the Pagans meant was in deede the Diuell) v-
ſeth the worde fo2 the place, and not fo2 the perſon, except
the terte bee figuratiue. In Sheol it was neuer doubted
but that it alwaies ſignified a place, and neuer anie per-
ſon. Nowe if neither Sheol no2 Hades canne ſignifie both
places, I meane heauen and hell, then canne they not ſig-
nifie the worlde of ſoules; fo2 they bee diſperſed in both
thoſe places.

[It cannot be denied, pou wil ſaie, but the olde teſtament
referreth Sheol, as the Septuagint doe Hades, both to the
godlie and to the wicked after death.] It is moſt true that
Sheol in Hebzew, and Hades in Greeke are applied in the
olde Teſtament both to the good and bad; The Queſtion
is not to what men, but to which parts of men, good o2 bad,
Sheol and Hades are referred. To the bodies of men,
good and bad, lping deade in the graue they are ſometimes
applied; to the ſoules of the godlie, as detained in either,
they are neuer applied. Sheol and conſequentlie h a d e s
with the Septuagint, impo2teth the whole death that is
due to ſinne, and euerie part thereof; but by no meanes
heauen, where the ſoules of the ſaintes are, no2 anie part of
that bliſſe, which they poſſeſſe. Since then as well the death
of the bodie in this worlde, as the death of the ſoule in
the nert worlde were the wages of ſinne; Sheol and Hades·

doe sometimes signifie the generall state of deade bodies, as when the Scripture describeth rottennesse, silence, forgetfulnesse, senselessenesse, contempt, dishonour, and such like to bee in Sheol. And the same worde when it is referred to the soules of the wicked as there detained, or of the godlie as thence deliuered; for so much as the soule cannot be inclosed in the graue; of necessitie the pit prepared for the soules of sinners must bee, by all such textes of Scriptures, intended. But that Sheol or Hades shoulde signifie the worlde of Soules, as well in heauen as in Hell, neither hath this Refuter brought anie Texte or reason for it, neither will hee euer bee able to prooue it. And howsoeuer one of late hath taken vppon him to talke of those thinges, like one of the Titanes with bigge and bombasted tearmes; I, seeing nothing in that fardell of his but Riddles and raylinges, meane not to alter my course.

Then touching the sense of Sheol in the olde Testament, I take it to bee cleare, that it sometimes signifieth the graue or the state of deade bodies; but neuer the worlde of soules, which phrase the Refuter hath caught by the ende, hoping at length to conueie it into the Creede. But hee must first shewe vs where hee findeth anie such thing in the Scriptures, before wee maie suffer him to make it an Article of our faith. Against it euerie place is a proofe; but for it none that I reade, or they haue yet alleaged. They shifte handes, and in steede of the worlde of soules they bring in the graue, or the state of deade bodies; which is but a vaine flourish, to propose one thing, and to prooue another. And though you (Sir Refuter) goe to harping of "phrases which I thinke is your best skill; as, [k] *The state of* " *the deade, the worlde of the deade, the worlde of soules departed;* yet I must let you vnderstande there is great difference betwixt these speeches. Sheol may extend to their bodies whose soules doe liue in heauen: to their soules it cannot; and therefore

[k] *Pag.* 97

therefore you must not chop in the one for the other, as your instructor doth, who when he would proue the world of soules, falleth vp about head and eares into the graue. The one you shall euerie where light on, of the other there is no mention. As when Iacob said to his sonnes, [l] you will make my hoare haires descend to *Sheol* with sorrow; and likewise when Dauid said to Salomon, [m] thou shalt make (*Shemeis*) hoare haires descende to *Sheol* with bloud: are there white haires or bloud in the worlde of soules, as there are in the graue? this is the state of deade bodies, but not of soules departed. In the destruction of Core, Dathan and Abiran, the Scripture saieth; [n] the earth opened her mouth & swallowed them vp, and their howsen, and they descended, and all that were with them aliue to *Sheol*. Aliue is both bodie and soule in euerie mans eie. For had those two bene seuered, they had bene dead. Doe the bodies of men descende to your world of soules? or is it plaine that in this place must be meant by Sheol either hell which receiued both their bodies and soules that were in that rebellion against God; or at least the heart of the earth, which receaued them liuing, whereas other men die before they are committed to the earth? [o] like sheepe (saieth Dauid) shall they bee laide in Sheol. Are there sheepe, or anie resemblance of sheepe in your worlde of soules; or doth Dauid rather meane, that, as sheepe are bounde, and then slaine, and cast on heapes, so shall the wicked bee handled? nowe as manie places in the scriptures as note Sheol to be below, cannot be referred to your worlde of soules; for they are as well on high in heauen, as below in hell. And therefore of force Sheol must in all those places either importe hell which is belowe, or the graue which is lower then the earth wheron men doe liue. [p] Thou hast deliuered my soule (saith) Dauid) from the lower *Sheol*. And Esaie of the King of Babell: [q] *Sheol* belowe was afraide at thy comming, and raised vp her mightie men to meete thee, and to saie vnto thee, art thou also weakened, as well as wee? is thy pride depressed to *Sheol*? This cannot

be

[l] Genes.42.

[m] 3.Reg.2

[n] Numb.16

[o] Psal.49.

[p] Psal.86.

[q] Esa.14.

bee meant of the generall and indefinite state of the deade nor of the worlde of soules, for manie of them were on high in strength and ioie; not in feare and weakenesse, as here they are described in Sheol. And therefore ruffle you and your a-bettour as long as you list with tauntes and tearmes; fell crakes fray not such as bee priuie to your lame legs. Againe, heauen is namelie expressed, and opposed to Sheol; how can heauen be included in Sheol? e To the high heauens what wilt thou do? it is lower then *Sheol*, how wilt thou know it? Will your learning serue you to make the high heauens a part of the lowe Sheol? f If I ascend to heauen, thou art there, (saieth Dauid to God.) if I lie downe in *Sheol*, there art thou also. So God himselfe by Amos: t If they dig to *Sheol* there shall my hande fetch them; if they ascend to heauen thence will I bring them downe. And to the king of Babilon. u Thou saiedst in thine heart I will ascende to heauen, and climbe aboue the highth of the cloudes: but thou shalt be pluckt down to *Sheol*, euen to the sides of the pit.

To men of anie meane capacitie I thinke it be manifest, that ascending here cannot be descending; & consequentlie that heauen is no part of Sheol, but a place rather opposed a-gainst it; albeit your impudencie be such p in the Creed you expound, he descended into hell, by the cleane contrarie, that is, he ascended into heauen. But that will not men of your face and fansie doe? I hope all good men will beware of such expositions. We deride the Glosse of the Canon lawe for saying *Statuimus, id est, abrogamus*, we establish, that is, we abrogate. How ridiculous and audacious then is this pre-sumption, to sate Christ descended into hel, that is he ascended vp to heauen; but hereof in the close when we haue first clea-red your fonde conceites of SHEOL AND HADES. x The dead praise thee not (saith Dauid to God) nor all that descende into silence. If the scriptures affirme as much of Sheol, how can Sheol be the worlde of soules? yea how can Sheol bee hea-uen, where the soules night and daie, that is euerlastinglie,

Dd

e Iob. 11.

f Psal 139

t Amos. 9

u Esa. 14.

x Psal. 115.

do nothing but praise God, and confesse vnto him the honor
of his name? ʒ Sheol (saieth Esay) cannot confesse vnto thee,   ʒ Esa.38.
neither can such as descende vnto the pit trust in thy truth. Yea
(saieth Salomon,) ᶻ There is no worke, thought, knowledge,   ᶻ Ecclesiast. 9
nor wisedome in *Sheol*, whither thou goest. If Sheol bee the
world of soules, they be all a sleepe, that neither doe speake,
nor thinke anie thing. Small are their ioyes, and lesse are
their paines, which they neuer so much as thinke of. So that
neither hell, nor heauen, nor any part of your world of soules
can bee heere vnderstoode by Sheol in Salomons wordes;
but of meere force it must be the Graue where the bodie ly-
eth voide of sense, speach, action, or cogitation. The rest of
the places of the olde Testament where Sheol is named, con-
curre with these; and import either the graue, which is
common to the godlie with the wicked; or else that pit which
is prepared for the soules of the wicked, which can bee none
other place, but preciselie and properlie HELL. What
textes they are of the lawe and the prophets, where Sheol   Vide pag. 147.
is named, that cannot bee referred to the graue, I haue
in the treatise before specified and handled such of them, as
I thought sufficient, especiallie receauing no answere to
my reasons, but the Sphingicall perplexities of an high
minded Maister; whose wordes with mee, though they
bee of the largest size, are but winde. And therefore I rest
vpon the same groundes and proofes, which I make before,
and stande to iustifie, that in no place of the olde or newe te-
stament, where SHEOL OR HADES are named, their
world of soules is, or canne bee vnderstoode; let them name
mee the places, I will presentlie send them by Gods grace
an answere.

As for HADES (good Reader) by which worde the Sep-
tuagint expresse the Hebrue SHEOL; in all these textes,
where thou seest the worde SHEOL, thou maiest assure thy
selfe the Septuagint vse HADES in steede thereof, and the
verie same reasons that serue for Sheol, serue for HADES in

Fff 1.   euerie

euerie point without exception: And that maketh me who-
lie to skippe the handling of HADES in the Septuagint;
and to referre the discussing thereof till I come to the pla-
ces of the newe Testament. Now the consequent of that
I haue alleaged either heere or before, is this; that by
SHEOL and HADES in the olde Testament must needes be
meante either HELL, the GRAVE, or their WORLDE
OF SOVLES, which they so much talke of; if no place in
the olde Testament doe necessarilie enforce their worlde
of soules to bee vnderstoooe by either of these wordes,
then it remaineth, that in what textes the graue maie not
bee endured to bee the meaning of either of these wordes,
there wee conceaue the place of the damned must bee in-
tended in either of them. Peruse both the obseruations and
Vide pag. 147 allegations before, and thou shalt see both the textes and
the proofes, whie the place of the damned must often bee vn-
derstoode by Sheól in the bookes of the law and the prophets.
I hope thou wilt thinke it superfluous for mee to defende it,
or enlarge it, before anie man doe particularlie impugne it.
So that whatsoeuer you prate (Sir Refuter) without
waight or warrant touching Sheol, I count it lip labor; when
you or your helpers bring anie thing worth the regarding,
you shal find me readie to receaue it, or refute it; as the mat-
ter deserueth.

Sheol then in the olde Testament, and Hades in the Sep-
tuagint signifiyng somtimes the state of deade bodies which
is the graue; sometimes the place of deade soules, which is
hell; but neuer the world of soules, whereof some are in hea-
uen; let vs see what force HADES hath in the new testament;
or whether it can thence be proued, that Hades importeth the
world of soules. As ý mysteries of God ware more fully de-
clared by the gospel, then by the law; so the kingdom of hea-
uen was more precislie seuered from the kingdome of Sa-
tan by Christ, then by Moses. What Moses darkelie sha-
dowed vnder figures, that Christ reuealed in plaine wordes;
and

and therefore hell fire, which is obscurelie mentioned in the law and prophets, is often and openlie named by the mouth of our Sauiour; and HADES, which before extended to good and bad, is nowe by the writers of the newe testament restrained to the place of the damned. So that Hades with the signifieth hell, and the powers thereof, and not the death of the bodie, much lesse the world of soules. Examples hereof I haue giuen thee (gentle Reader) in the ᵘ Treatise before; saue that I then reasoned the death of the bodie was not signified by HADES, which note these deuisers haue changed into the VVORLD OF SOVLES. I must therefore nowe ouerrun all those places againe, and shewe that the VVORLD OF SOVLES cannot bee expressed by anie of those places. Which I will with as much breuitie as I canne, considering the wise Reader will soone bee able to discerne this newe Camisadoe latelie offered with the VVORLD OF SOVLES. The first place is, ˣ Woe to thee *Chorazin*, and woe to thee *Bethsaida*, saith our Sauiour: ʸ And thou *Capernaum* exalted to heauen, shalt bee brought downe euen to hell; it shall bee easier for Sodome in the day of iudgement then for thee. What is Gods curse and threates to impenitent sinners? HELL, or the VVORLD OF SOVLES? and in the daie of iudgement, when their punishment shall bee greater then the Sodomites, shall they go to hell fire, or to the VVORLD OF SOVLES? I praie you (Sir Refuter,) where are the Sodomites at this houre? in hell or in your VVORLD OF SOVLES? In hell I thinke. Saint Iude saith, ᶻ They do sustaine the punishments of euerlasting fire. Is that your VVORLDE OF SOVLES? If it be not, they shal certainlie be where the Sodomites are, yea in worse case shall they bee, and that I suppose must bee in hell, and not in heauen. The second place is in the wordes of Christ to Peter, ᵃ Vpon this rocke will I builde my church, and the gates of hell shall not preuaile against it, and I wil giue thee the keyes of the kingdom of heauen. The VVORLD OF SOVLES doth not impugne the church, therfore it is no signe

ᵘ Vide pag. 171

ˣ Matt 11
ʸ Luc 1.10

ᶻ Iud. epist.

ᵃ Matth. 16

of Gods fauour, for that not to preuaile against the church. Againe, whatsoeuer preuaile not, yet if hell preuaile, what safetie hath the church? Heresie and iniquitie are the gates of hell fighting against the church, as well as crueltie. [b] *Ego portas Inferni reor vitia atque peccata, vel certé hæreticorū doc-trinas, per quas illecti homines ducuntur ad Tartarum. Nemo itaque putet de morte dici, quòd apostolici conditioni mortis sub-iecti non fuerint, quorum martyria vides coruscare.* I thinke (saith Ierom,) the gates of hell to be vices and sinnes, or else he-resies, by which men being enticed are led to hell. Let no man therefore imagine it is spoken of death, as if the Apostles were not subiect thereto, whose martyrdoms thou findest so famous.

[c] *Digna ædificatione illius Petra, quæ infernas leges, & Tartari portas, & omnia mortis claustra dissolueret.* It was a Rocke (saith Hilarie) worthy of Chrifts building, which should dissolue the lawes of hell, the gates of *Tartare*, and all the Cloisters of death. So Origen, [d] *Porta inferorum dicentur etiam principa-tus ac potestates, aduersus quas nobis est colluctatio.* The gates of hell may the powers and principalities bee called, against the which we haue to striue. [e] *Portas inferni hæreticam prauitatem nominat, siue vitia & peccata, vndé mors ad animam venit.* The gates of hel Christ calleth *Hæresies*, (saith Bede) or else vices and sinnes, by which the soule dieth. So Ambrose, [f] *Quæ autē sunt portæ Inferni, nisi singula quæque peccata?* What are the gates of hell, but all kind of sinnes? And Gregorie; [g] *Portæ Inferni hære-ses sunt, quæ quasi inferorum aditum pandunt.* The gates of hell are heresies, which open as it were the passage to hell. The fifte generall councell of Constantinople with one full consent alloweth the same. [h] *Porta inferni non preualebunt aduersus e-am, id est hæreticorum lingua mortifera.* The gates of hell that is the deadlie tongues of heretickes, shal not preuaile against the church. You might haue more, but these are enough. Here (Sir Refuter) you tell a long and a foolish tale of death out of your owne heade, as if Christ did promise his Apostles protection against the violence of Tyrants, but not against

[b] Hiero. in Matth. 16

[c] Hilarius. in Mat. cano 16

[d] Origenes in Matth. ca. 16.

[e] Beda in Mat. 16.

[f] Ambros. lib 6. in Lucæ ca 8.

[g] Greg. in. Psal. 5. pænitentiale

[h] Synod. 5. con-stantinop. Sessione. 8.

the rage of Satan; *To vnderstande sinnes and errours as some* „ ¹*Pag.111.*
of the ancient writers doe, the circumstances of the texte, you „
saie, doe seeme not to beare it. Your ignorant humour is „
loth to haue it so; otherwise the wordes of Christ, respect
the trueth of Peters confession, that himselfe was Christ
the sonne of the liuing God; against the which faith no policie,
nor tyrannie of Satan shoulde preuaile, and so by your leaue
the Fathers goe direalic to the meaning of the texte; and
you woulde wrest it to your priuate fansie, least HADES
shoulde signifie HELL; and yet at length vpon aduisement
you ᵏ *confesse it may bee heere the* GATES OF HELL, „ ᵏ*Pag.113.*
and that HADES *is thus vsed sometimes, and namelie in the* „
last example out of the 16. of Luke. It is well then that in „
the 16. of Luke you yeelde HADES doeth signifie HELL,
where the wicked are tormented, and did you denie it, the
Scripture auoucheth it; the wordes are plaine, ¹ I am tor- ¹*Luc.z.16.*
mented in this flame: & again, least they come into this place
of torment. Then HADES without anie other addition no-
teth HELL, and when Christ faith, the rich man IN HADES
LIFT vp his eyes; he addeth this as a necessarie consequent
being in tormēts, to shew that HADES is the place of torment,
and not the vvorld of sovles.

From thence you leape to the Reuelation; and there, when
Saint Iohn sawe ᵐ one sitting on a pale horse whose name was ᵐReuelat.6
death, and HADES followed after him, that is, saie you, *the*
world of the dead. ⁿ *It cannot be hell certainely, becaufe hel slai-* „ ⁿ*Pag.116.*
eth none in that sort. Again, to saie preciselie that the fourth „
part of the world should go to hell, I take it to bee a strange phrase „
in scripture. Here first is a plaine profe, that death and HADES „
are two seuerall things, the one following after the other. For
nothing doth follow it selfe. The doubt is now what HADES
importeth. *The world of the dead,* saie you. The worlde of the „
dead, if thereby you mean dead bodies, is al one with death;
if you vnderstand the world of foules, that hath two partes
heauen and hell, which of these two did follow after death to

help destroy the fourth part of the earth? the kingdom of hea
 uen is neuer proposed in the scriptures as a destroyer, but
the diuell hath his proper name in this booke, ⁿ ὁ ἀπολ-
λύων the destroyer. Againe, this vision S. Iohn saw at the
opening of the fourth Seale, but the world of soules in hea-
uen was shewed him in the opening of the fift Seale, which
presentlie followeth in the next verse in these words. And
when (the lambe) had opened the fift Seale, I saw (saith Iohn)
vnder the altar the soules of men slayne for the word of God,
and for the testimonie of the Lambe. The world of soules in
heauen was seene in the opening of the fift seale; therefore
that world of soules was not seene in the opening of the
fourth Seale; but of force, if by HADES you will vnder-
stand anie world of soules, it must be of those that were in
HELL. Howbeit because hee did accompanie death that
was sent to destroy, I take it rather to bee the power of
the deuill, that is there described; then anie world of soules,
as you dreame. And that the diuell destroyeth as well the
bodie as the soule; if it be strange to you, you are a greater
stranger in the Scriptures then you would seeme to bee.
Who threw the house vpon the heads of ⁿIobs Children can
you tell? or who smote Iob himselfe with that loathsome
disease? [But the fourth part of the earth, you saie,
could not go to hell;] God graunt no more then the
fourth part go thither. Neuer reade you, ^o many called
and few chosen? and ^p though the number of the children
of Israel be as the sand of the Sea, yet but a remnant
shall be saued. And why might not the dragon as well de-
uoure the fourth part of þ earth, as ^q draw downe from heauē
with his tayle the third part of the starres? Or if there you take
a certayne nomber for an vncertain, which is S. Iohns man-
ner of writing in this booke, why not as well here as else
where? these therefore are a couple of idle quarrels; if these
be your best, you are more willing, then able to do harme.
But by þ same words in the same booke, we shall better vn-
derstand

ⁿ Apoca.9.

Apoca.6.vers9.

ⁿ Iob.1
Iob.2

^o'Math.22.
^p Rom:9.

^qApoca.12

derſtand what is ment by HADES, then by your wandring and weake gloze. Death and HADES, ſaith S. Iohn were caſt into the lake of fier. ʳ It were abſurd (you adde) to ſaie death and hell were caſt into hell. True; but moze abſurd, and moze blaſphemous to ſaie, that death and the wozld of ſoules ſhall bee caſt into the lake of fier. For then not onlie the Saints of God, but heauen it ſelfe ſhould bee caſt into hell fier. Yet if we take the containing foz the contained, which is the moſt vſuall phzaſe of the Scripture, as ˡ wo be to thee Chorazin, wo to thee Bethſaida, & thou Capernaum; as like-wiſe ˢ Ieruſalem, Ieruſalem which killeſt the prophets; & it ſhal be eaſier for Tyrus & Sydon, with a thouſand ſuch euery uher occurrent; then is it an eaſie & true ſpeach, that hel, to witte the powers of hell; euen the diuels themſelues ſhall be caſt into the lake of fier. And ſo doth Andreas Biſhop of Ceſaria expound it, ᵘ πονηράς δυνάμεις, τάς τόν ἅδην ἐχύσας, the wicked ſpirits the poſſeſſours of HADES, ſhall be caſt into hel fier. And ſo Bede ˣ Mors & Infernus miſſi ſunt in ſtagnum ignis. Diabolum dicit et ſuos, quem ſupra in equo pallido ſedentem Infernus ſequebatur. Death & hel ſhall be caſt into the lake of fier. He meaneth the diuel & his, who before ſitting on a pale horſe hell followed. As yet then HADES in the new Teſtament is not onlie a thing different from death, but euen hell it ſelfe; and your wozld of ſoules in none of theſe texts can find any hold oz help. Let vs ſee the reſt.

That Chziſt triumphed ouer hell and Satan, & not ouer death onely; the Apoſtle fully affirmeth when he ſaith; Chriſt ʸ ſpoyled principalities & powers, made an open ſhew of them, and triumphed ouer them in his owne perſon; that likewiſe hee hath the keyes of hell and not of death onlie, S. Iohn plainlie ſheweth when ᶻ he ſaw an angell come down from heauen, hauing the key of the bottomeles pit, and there binding & ſhutting vp the diuell. The ſame key of the bottomeles pit was, in the 9 Chapter of the Reuelation, giuen to the Star that ſlode from heauen. This keye muſt Chziſt haue, foz hee ſaith:

„Apoca.20.
„1 Pag.116.

ˢ Math.11.
ᵗ Math.23.

ᵛ Andreas c.xL. in Apoca.ca..

ˣ Beda in apoca.ca.29.

ʸ Coloſ.2.

ᶻ Reuelat.3.

saith of himselfe that he ^a hath the key of Dauid, which ope-
neth and no man shutteth, which shutteth and no man ope-
neth. Since then there are ^b keyes not of heauen onlie which
Christ committed to Peter and his fellow labourers; but of
the ^c bottomles pitte, where Satan lyeth bound; which of force
must bee HELL; when Christ professeth in the first of the
Reuelation that he ^d hath the keyes τȣ θανάτȣ καὶ τȣ ἅδȣ
of death and of HADES; who seeth not that HADES there must
signifie hell it selfe, the key whereof is so expreslie mentio-
ned in that booke? And so when the Apostle maketh two
parts of Christs conquest against death and hell, ^e ô death
where is thy sting? ô HADES where is thy victorie? what reason
is there to exclude out of these words, Christs victorie ouer
HELL, since the same Apostle witnesseth, that Christ had a
glorious triumph against hell, and the word HADES in all
the places of the new Testament, which we haue yet viewe-
ed, inferreth hell? [The Apostle (you saie) ^f speaketh not of
"the Damnation of the wicked; but of the resurrectiõ of the dead.]
And so do I; and therefore inferre, that when the bodies of
the saints shall be raised from death, whose soules be alreadie
saued from hell; then shall these words be openlie verified, ô
death where is thy sting? ô hell where is thy victorie? For since
by sinne hell gate possession of both parts of man as well
of his bodie as of his soule; the full deliuerance of man must
free both parts, and the full conquest ouer hell is the losse of
both parts, which in the resurrection of the dead shall be per-
formed and not afore; and therefore then is the time for all
the faithfull to thanke God, for their full victorie ouer DEATH
AND HELL, and to saie with the Apostle ô death where is
thy sting? ô HELL where is thy victorie? But what hath your
world of soules to do with these words, or with anie other;
where HADES is named in the new testament? All these
places serue fitlie for hell, and the most of them necessa-
rilie; since either is expressed as a diuerse thing from
HADES, or not to bee comprised in the name of HADES.

But

Marginal notes:
^a Reuelat: 3.
^b Math. 16
^c Reuelat: 20.
^d Reuelat: 1
^e 1 Corinth 15
^f Pag. 117.

But your world of soules is most absurd and false in euery one of these, and can not stand with the circumstance of the text, the first of the Reuelation onelie excepted, where though there be no woordes to impugne it, yet are there none to approue it. For is it anie curse for Capernaum, to bee brought to the world of soules, except you meane hell? Doth your world of soules impugne the Church of Christ? or destroy the fourth part of the earth? or shall it be cast into the lake of fire? And what victorie shal the soul haue against the world of soules in the last day; since their owne soules reioice to receiue their bodies; and against the soules of the wicked they neither may nor will insult? It therefore remaineth that though HADES with the Septuagint signifie either BODILIE DEATH or HELL; yet in the new Testament where HADES is described as a different thing from DEATH, and following AFTER DEATH, HADES of necessitie, being NOT DEATH, must needes import HELL. Of the place in question, Thou wilt not leaue my soule in HADES, I will yet saie nothing, but will come to the words of the Creede, Christ descended to HADES, and search what must be the meaning of HADES in that article.

What I take to be the meaning of Hades in the Creede, where it is said, Christ descended to HADES, as also what reasons lead me thereunto, thou hast, Christian Reader, in the former [a] treatise, thou shalt with more safe finde it there, then I repeat it here; howe much this Confuter confesse thor resisteth, that must I now examine. When I obiect that in a short sum of the Christian faith made for the simple and common people, to repeate one thing twice were needlesse, and against the nature of the Creede: and to vse a darke and . . . . . . after a plaine and easie, is vnreasonable . . . . he answereth, §It is true. I hold it vnreasonable altogither i . . . . short and vulgar Creed, appointed euen for the common Chri . . . to vse words darke and difficult. An In len the same thing . . . by diuers words expressed, the later ought to be the lighter and . . . rer. Therefore I fullie grant, in the Creede, . . . the phrase . . . must be familiar, triuiall, easie and plaine. I vrged three things to be obserued in the ex-

[a] Vide Pa. 171.

Ggg　　　　　　pounding

pounding the Creede, the words to be proper and euident with-
out figuratiue obscuritie, the things to be different without idle
repetition, and the order to be consequent without anie confu-
sion. The Confuter agreeth with me in all these; and he doub-
teth not but his exposition is such.   Since then there be three
expositions of that article, Christ descended to HADES; that is
either to the GRAVE, or to HELL, or to the WORLDE OF
SOVLES, which in Christes case (you saie) was HEAVEN;
which of these three, Sir Refuter, commeth neerest to the na-
ture of a short, easie, and orderlie summe of a Creede? The first
you like not, because it expresseth that in darke and hard cir-
cumloquution, which was familiarly and plainely said before,
he was dead and buried. The question then resteth betweene
the two last, which of the twaine best expresseth the proper

b Pag. 125. " sense, and vulgar vse of the worde HADES. *For the Apostles*
   " *and Apostolike men* (you confesse) *did so write and speake, as the*
   " *people then might best vnderstand.* If it bee so, then your expo-
sition, (Sir Refuter) is cleane thrust out of doores. For nei-
ther with the auncient Maisters of the Græke tongue, which
were the Poets, nor with the Septuagint, nor with the
writers of the newe Testament, nor with the people of that
time, in their vnderstanding, did HADES euer signifie the
worlde of soules without anie limitation of state, or place.
Againe that generall and indefinite worlde of soules, without
respect of hell or heauen, is no point nor part of the Christian
faith. For faith touching Christ must not be generall or am-
biguous, but particular and certaine. It is no faith, much
lesse an article of the faith, to saie, Christes soule after death
went some whither; the Creede musse specifie the place
whither it went before it can bee a matter of faith, that must
bee beleeued. And therefore HADES doeth point out the
particular place, as hell or heauen whither Christes soule
went after death, before any man may chalenge it to be the
true meaning of that article.

i Pag. 128. "   If anie doe aske particularlie whither is this? You aun-
   " swer, *namely into heauen: for whither should the Saints go else?*
                                          This

This in déede is a familiar, triuiall, easie, and plaine expofition, Chriſts ſoule DESCENDED DOVVNE TO HADES; that is, it ASCENDED VP TO HEAVEN. And ſo by taking heauen for hell, and aſcending vppe for deſcending downe, you haue quickelie made an ende of this matter. Whie then goe on with your wife Maiſter, and make HADES, which is the chiefe Diuell, to bee God, and you haue made a perfect expofition of the Creede, fitte for ſuch as attribute to Diuels, what they ſhoulde attribute vnto GOD. Was this the plaineſt and eaſieſt waie for the Apoſtelihe men to teach the people, Chriſtes ſoule aſcended vppe to heauen, by ſaying hee DESCENDED TO HADES? And did the people ſo beſt vnderſtande them? You that expounde this by the cleane contrarie, and ſaie they be beſt ſo vnderſtœde, no maruaile if you arrogate ſo much vnto your ſelfe in framing the Scriptures to your fanſies; you maie with little ſtudie prooue a ſpeedie expoſitour of the Scriptures. But, Sir, wiſe men that regarde their faith more then your follyes will aſke; where you finde deſcending for aſcending, and Hades for heauen? If you pretende Plato, they will tell you, that to embrace a priuate conceite of Socrates againſt all the former Greekes, againſt the Septuagint, againſt the Euangeliſts, and Apoſtles, and euidentlie againſt all the fathers is not to expounde an Article of the faith, but the next waie to bring Paganiſme into the Creede; and that by ſo licentious and lewde a trade of open peruerting the wordes of the Creede, and taking ſowre for ſweete, colde for heate, euill for good, that nothing ſhall ſtande ſounde if this bee admitted. [¹ It is, you ſaie, an Hebrewe phraſe. k So *Iacob ſpake, I will goe downe mourning to my Sonne vnto Sheol, yet Iacob thought not to goe to hell to his ſonne, but among the ſoules of the godlie deade, that is to ſaie, into heauen.*] It hath benne meetelie well tolde you, that Sheol neuer ſignifyeth Heauen in all the Scriptures, but that Iacob meant hee woulde goe mourning vnto Sheol, that is to his Graue, refuſing to take anie comfort whiles he liued, ſince his ſonne

k Pag: 186

was dead. You like a tyrant ouer the Scriptures , will haue
what sense pleaseth you in euerie place; and then you saie it is
plaine and common. In deede your ignorance and insolencie is
verie plaine and common; but the interpretations which you
make of Scripture, be absurde and more then foolish. A man
liuing maie well be said to descend into his graue; liuing hee
standeth, dying he lieth downe; and the face of the earth on
which we are, is higher then the bowels of the earth where wee
lie buried; but of a soule ascending vp to heauen, to say it de-
scendeth to hell, is a phrase of your making, and fit for your
faith, which is guided more by will then by truth. When you
proue these two points, that HADES IS HEAVEN in the Scrip-
tures, and that DESCENDING IS ASCENDING, we will
hearken to your exposition; till then wee will leaue it as a dis-
temper of your vntetled braine.

For the last exposition of the three which remaineth, I haue
shewed thee (Christian reader) by the particular circumstances
of the Scriptures, that in the continuall vse of the new Testa-
ment HADES signifieth HELL, which is the place where the
wicked after this life are in torments. I haue also in the ser-
mons before examined the words of Dauid, alledged and ap-
plied by [m] Peter to Christ, Thou wilt not leaue my soule in hell,
whence Peter concludeth Christs soule was not left in hel; as like-
wise the words of Paul importing that Christ descended εἰς τὴν
ἄβυσσον to the bottomlesse deepe, which worde throughout the
new testament doth signifie nothing but HEL; I haue noted
how anciently Christs local descent to hel was preached in the
church, euen by one of the [n] seuentie disciples (that were conuer-
sant with Christ) & continued to this daie with the full consent
of the fathers, both Greeke & Latin without exception, and by
the whole church of Christ receiued; I must not iterate that
which there is so latelie written. The words are faire and plain,
there is no danger nor difficultie in them, the end of Christs
descending thither being both honourable to him, and comfor-
table to vs, as I haue before deliuered it. Lastly, I see no cause
either in this Confuters ridiculous pamphlet , or in his abet-
tors

Vide pag. 170
& sequent.

[m] Psal. 16.
[m] Act. 2.

[n] Luke. 10.

tors tempestuous and furious libell, why anie man should dislike or distrust this exposition, as vnfit for the wordes, or vnsound for the faith of the Creede. To load thee with authorities were to make an other volume; thou shalt onelie see I haue not deuised it of mine owne heade, but that it hath both antiquitie for it, and authoritie with it, and so I will make an ende. Cyprian in his Sermon of Christs passion; [o] *Ipse dicit ad patre, non derelinques animam meam in inferno, nec sines corrumpi carnem meam in sepulchro, quia vbi in præsentia illius, effractis inferis est captiuata captiuitas, præsentata victrice anima in præsentia patris ad corpus suum sine dilatione reuersus est,* Christ saieth to his Father, Thou wilt not leaue my soule in hell, nor suffer my flesh to rotte in the graue, becaufe as soone as captiuitie was subdued, hell being broken vppe in his presence, and his triumphing soule presented to the sight of his Father, hee without delay returned to his bodie. Arnobius writing vppon the hundreth thirtie and seuenth Psalme; [p] *Postea vidit inferos, & longè factus est non solum à cælis, sed & ab ipsa terra: Abyssi profunda descendens scidit, & quia inde reuerteretur ad superos, & quia a superis remearet ad cælos.* Afterward Christ went to hell, and was farre not onelie from heauen, but from the earth: descending hee brake the bottomlesse deepe, that hee might thence returne to life; and from thence to heauen. Lactantius in his verses of the resurrection, saith;

> [q] *Tristia cessarunt inferna vincula legis,*
> *Expauitq́, Chaos luminis ore premi.*
> *Depereunt tenebræ, Christi fulgore fugatæ,*
> *Æterna noctis pallia crassa cadunt.*

The fearefull bands of the infernall power ceased, and Chaos was afraid to be oppressed with the light of his presence. The darknesse of hell was chased away with the brightnes of Christ, and the grosse couerings of eternall night vanished. Athanasius, [r] *Ipse est dei virtus, qui infernum expugnauit, & imperium Diaboli demolitus est, qui Deus in descendendo, deus in ascendendo, corpus suum à morte excitatum patri repræsentauit, ac vindicauit à morte sub cuius imperio tenebatur.* Christ is the power of God, which surprised hell,

[o] Cyprian de passion Christ.

[p] Arnobius in psal.137.

[q] Lactan.phœnix de resurrect.

[r] Athanas.ad Liberium.

and

and outthrewe the kingdome of the diuell , who beeing God in descending, and God in ascending, presented his body raised from death to his father, and tooke it from death, vnder whose power it was helde. Hilarius. [f] *Hic ergo vnus est mortem in inferno perimens, spei nostræ fidem resurrectione confirmans, corruptionem carnis humanæ gloria sui corporis perimens.* Christ alone is hee that in hell killed death, confirmed our hope with his resurrection, and destroied the corruption of mans flesh , with the glorie of his owne bodie. Basil: *Habes ergo myrrham ob sepulturam, guttam ob descensionem ad infernum, quod non inefficax in sepulchro permanserit, sed ad infernum descenderit, gratia dispensationis circa resurrectionem absoluenda, vt quæ de seipso erant oracula Prophetarum, vniuersa expleret:* Thou hast (in this Psalme) myrrhe for his buriall, dropping for his descent to hell, because hee lay not in his graue without force, but descended into hell to dispatch thinges needfull for his resurrection, that hee might fulfill all that the Prophets forespake of him. Nazianzene maketh Christes mother to say of him, [u] *At vbi veneris in atram nocte Plutonis domum, Infernum acerbo iaculo defixeris.* But when thou wentest to the house of Pluto , where darke night is ; thou diddest thrust thorow hell with a wounding speare. Fulgentius : [x] Dauid spake of Christes resurrection, that his soule was not left in hell, nor his flesh saw corruption. In this then the Godheade of Christ shewed the power of his impassibilitie, that being euery where, alwaies, and vnspeakeablie present, it wanted not to his flesh , when it suffered not his soule to feele any paine in hell, neither forsooke his soule in hell, whiles it kept his flesh from rotting in the graue . Beda our countriman shall be the last, [y] My flesh (saith Dauid of Christ) shal rest in hope, expounding in what hope; to wit in this hope, that though my soule descend to hell, yet thou wilt not leaue it to bepossessed of hel. The rest go all cleare that way, applying ẏ wordes of Dauid cited by Peter, Thou wilt not leaue my soule in hell, to Christs descent thither after death. And howsoeuer the fathers incline to thinke, as Ierom did, that the saints before Christes comming were inclosed in a place vnder the earth , expecting Christs comming to bee carried vp to heauen (of which I haue

spoken

Marginal notes:

[f] Hilarius de trinitat. lib. 4.

[t] Basil. in psa. 44.

[u] Nazianzen. in christo patiente.

[x] Fulgentius ad Thrasimundum. lib. 3.

[y] Beda in Psal. 15.

spoken as much as is needfull in the z treatise before;)yet they *Vide pag.189. absolutelie acknowledge that Christ descending destroyed & sequent. the kingdome of Satan, and freed all the faithfull from euer comming thither.

The rest of the Confuters talke is like ye froth of the sea, which wind & waues roll to and fro;sometimes he runneth this way, and then backe againe another way;saying and vnsaying hee knoweth not how,nor what. Sometimes he saith the Creede, and *namely this article Christ descended to Hades could not bee made long after the Apostles time;whereof Ignatius and others most* ” Pag.93. *ancient do speake.* In another place he saith; *We find almost all the* ” Pag.166. *Creedes,certainlie the most ancientest, and the best of them to want* ” *these wordes of Chrifts descending into hell.* In one place he saith, ” *The Creedes which we find in Ignatius, Irenæus, Iuftinus Martyr,* ” b Pag.167. *Tertulliã, Origen, Athanafius, Auguftinus, the Nicene, Cõftantino-* ” *politan, Toletan, Ephefine, al these neuer thought that Chrifts going* ” *downe to hell,was anie diftinct or certaine Article of the Christian* ” *faith.* And yet before he confessed ye *Ignatius and others most aun-* ” Pag.93. *cient doe speake namelie of this Article.* But, Sir, haue these ” Creedes which here you cite, all the rest of the Articles that are in the Apostles Creede ? I hope there want in some of them a good manie . For these rehearsals in the eldest Fathers doe but touche some of the Articles of the Creede, and shewe that there was such a compendious briefe of the Faith receiued amongst Christians from the beginning. The Councels of Nice, Conftantinople, Ephefus, and others, want euerie one of them sundrie Articles that are in the Apostles Creede, and adde other that are not there; so as in deede they are rather expofitions then recitals of the Apostles Creede. And yet I hope Athanafius creede hath this Article in precise a Igna ad Trall. wordes,and rehearseth it as a part of the Catholike faith,that b Iren.li 5.c.3 1 Chrift descended into Hell . Neither is there anie one of lo. cum tryph. these Fathers whome heere you haue named, as a Ignatius, d Tertul. de. b Irenæus, c Iuftinus Martyr, d Tertullian, e Origene, f Au- anima. guftine, but they expreffelie touche and teache Chrifts lo- e Orig.in cap. call descent to Hell , as all the rest doe without exception. f Aug.epi.99. And

And if Councels will content you, you shall not goe farre for both Prouinciall and Generall. The Councell of Alexandria that wrote to represse the heresie of Nestorius, maketh the spoiling of hell a part of Christes resurrection, and saieth; [d] *Tertia Die reuixit, expolians infernum,* Christ rose againe the thirde daie, hauing spoyled hell. This confession was read and allowed as Catholike in the first generall Councell of [e] Ephesus, in the great Councell of Chalcedon, and in the fifth generall Councell of Constantinople. So that fathers and Councels both oecumenicall and prouinciall, haue receiued and approoued this article euen from the foundation of Christs church; as a part of Christes resurrection, howsoeuer they did not alwayes annexe it to their Creedes.

With like follie and inconstancie, he saith it is [f] *the naturall and necessarie deuision of the articles of the Creede, that these, Christ suffered, was crucified, dead, buried, descended into hell, should concerne Christs humiliation,* and hee supposeth euerie sensible man will confesse so much whereas he himselfe expoundeth the last of them to haue this meaning, that Christes soule ascended to heauen. Now to ascend to heauen euery boy knoweth is a part of Christes exaltation, and not of his humiliation. Howe his note booke deuideth the Creede, I know not, but Saint Paule whence this diuision hath his ground, saieth this is [g] Christs exaltation, that at the name of Iesus euerie knee should bow of things in heauen, earth, and vnder the earth, which is hell. His humiliation stretcheth no farther then the death of the Crosse, then beginneth his exaltation. With like discretion when I alledged the Parable from Christes owne mouth, that his triumph ouer Satan must haue three parts, the [h] ouerrunning, the binding, the spoyling of Satan, and his kingdome; and further from that Parable I deriued nothing; This wisdome to shew himselfe learned, crieth out, [i] *a fine toy or rather a shamefull gloze by vnsauorie allegorizing to corrupt the Text. Is this a good waie to prooue Articles of the fayth, videlicet by Allegories?* As if the moste parte of Christes doctrine were not deliuered by Parables and Allegories?

She

[d] Epist Cyril. & Synod. Alexan. ad Nestor:
[e] Vide acta cōcilii Ephesini & 5. Synod. Constan. Sess. 7.

[f] Pag. 166.

[g] Philip. 2.

[h] Mat. 12. Luke. 11.

[i] Pag. 161.

The parables of the Sower, of the labourers in the vineyard, & the husbandmen killing the heire, of good trees & straight gates, of the lost sheepe, vniust Steward, and vnrighteous Iudge; of Tares sowed by the enemie, and haruest at the end of the world, of the great Supper, and wedding garment, of the wounded Samaritane, and wise virgins, of the prodigall sonne, and euill seruants, one y neglected his maisters talent, the other that imprisoned his fellow, of the rich man & Lazarus; to be short the allegories of light, of salt, of leauen, of chaffe, of the vyne and branches, of the good shepheard, and a thousand such in the prophets, Euangelists and Apostles, do they teach no matters of faith? What Buzzard was euer so blind as so to saie, no points of faith maie be proued by allegories? Had I extended the Parable farder then Christ himselfe did, or applied it to anie other purpose then he did; there might haue brene some cause of quarrell, but keeping my selfe preciselie both to the Scope and words of our Sauiour, I could not tread awrie. But in a brauerie to chalenge all the Parables and allegories in the Scriptures, as vnsitte to teach points of faith, neuer came in anie sober mans head.

As you vse the Scriptures, so you vse the Synode of this Realme, that is you arrogantlie and absurdlie falsifie it. *The manifest meaning of the whole Synode (of this Realme,) which is our publik doctrine and established by law in England .* APPARENTLY RENOVNCETH, (saie you) *this doctrine of Christs going downe to the hell of the damned. If you proue that you saie, I must confesse it is verie material; & by Gods grace I my selfe will reuoke all that I haue said in this point; but if you brag not onlie without cause, but against the verie trueth and tenor of their proceedings, are you not worthie in steede of* H. I. *to be named* W. F ? *but let vs heare how this appeareth? Euen thus; the Synode before holden in king Edwards time affirmed this doctrine directly and expresly (in their article of Christs descent to hell.) This Synode comming after repeateth andratifieth a part (*of that article*)in expresse words; but part of it euen all and euerie whit that containeth this doctrine expreslie of Christs going downe to the hell of the damned, all this I saie our Synode,* (anno 1562) *cutteth off, it putteth out, it casteth awais .* The words are these of the former Synode, *Quemadmodum Christus*

k *Pag.* 172

Pag. 173

Hhh i.

Articlu.3

Chriſtus pro nobis mortuus eſt & ſepultus, ita eſt etiam credendus ad Inferos deſcendiſſe. Nam corpus vſque ad reſurrectionem in ſepulchro iacuit, ſpiritus ab illo emiſſus cũ ſpiritibus qui in carcere ſiue in inferno detinebantur fuit, illiſq; prædicauit, quemadmodum teſtatur Petri locus. As Chriſt died for vs and was buried; ſo alſo it is to be beleeued, that he went down to hel. For his body lay in the graue vntil the reſurrection; his ſpirit which he breathed out was with the ſpirits that were in priſon or in hel, and preached vnto them, as the place of *Peter* vvitneſſeth. ᵇ But our Sy-

Pag.172.

" node ſince correcteth it herein & ſaith but thus only, Quemadmo
" dũ Chriſtus pro nobis mortuus eſt & ſepultus, ita eſt etiã credẽ
" dus ad inferos deſcendiſſe. *As Chriſt died for vs and was buried,*
" *ſo we are to beleeue alſo, that he went vnto the dead. This therfore*
" *in thẽ is ſeene manifeſtly (as I ſaid) to renounce and abrogate this*
" *particular ſenſe of Chriſts deſcẽding,* ỹ ʜᴇ ᴠᴠᴇɴᴛ ᴀꜰᴛᴇʀ ᴅᴇᴀᴛʜ ᴛᴏ
ʜᴇʟʟ. Is this all you haue to ſaie (Sir Refuter,) then when pro-
uender is deuided you ſhall haue a part for your good collectiõ.
You collect that ỹ later Synode by leauing out certain words
of the former renounceth that ᴄʜʀɪꜱᴛ ᴀꜰᴛᴇʀ ᴅᴇᴀᴛʜ
ᴠᴠᴇɴᴛ ᴛᴏ ʜᴇʟʟ; and that which it retaineth of the former
Synode in expreſſe words is this; ɪᴛ ɪꜱ ᴛᴏ ʙᴇ ʙᴇʟᴇᴇ-
ᴠᴇᴅ ᴛʜᴀᴛ ᴄʜʀɪꜱᴛ ᴠᴠᴇɴᴛ ᴅᴏᴠᴠɴ ɪɴᴛᴏ ʜᴇʟʟ, So in
your iudgement by beleeuing that Chriſt wente downe into
Hell, they renounce, that Chriſt went to hell. If it were
a matter of ſight I ſhoulde aſke whether you had anie eies or
no; nowe it is a matter of reaſon I muſt more doubte whe-
ther you haue your fiue wittes or no. Set your inference to
the biewe of all men. The Synode in her Maieſties time a-
greeth, It is to be beleeued that Chriſt vvent downe into hell.
Ergo they apparãtly renounce that Chriſt went to hel. This is
your concluſion; ſhew it to any tapſter or tinker in England
and ſee whether he will reward you with a mocke or no.

⸢But they leaue out the latter part of the Article which the
former Synode concluded.⸣ So they leaue out that Chriſts
bodie vvas in his graue vntill his reſurrection, which are the
words of the former Synode. Is the omitting of this a ma-
nifeſt renouncing and abrogating of it? God forbid ⸢But the
firſt Synode in king Edwardes time added farther, you ſaie,
that Chriſts ſpirit vvas vvith the ſpirits detained in Priſon or in
hel,

hel, and preached vnto them,] First then tell your abettor, that al the Realme wil take him not only for a Railor against al honesty, but for a lier against al duty, that voucheth so confidently king *Edward* the sixt and his subiects held that Christ his soule neuer vvent to Gehenna; & the realme knoweth the Q. othe; as also the Q. aduentureth her eternal state. These be no states to come within the compasse of his vncleane mouth: He may doe well to remember who they be, of whom it is written; They despise gouernment, & speak euil of those that are in authoricie, as raging vvaues of the Sea, foming out their owne shame; And to take heed, that he proue not too true a prophet against himselfe in paying the price of misusing his liege and Soueraigne Ladie, and her whole Realme. But I wish him repentance and so I leaue him. Secondlie, (Sir Refuter) you maie see three thinges in the latter wordes of that Article in king Edwardes Synode, which are verie wiselie with silence ouerskipped by the Synode in her Maiesties time; and wherein for my part I thinke they did verie well not to adde to this Article, anie time, purpose,. or prisoners, when, why, or to whome Christ descended. But therein to imitate the wisedome of the best ages, who kept this Article as they founde it without enterlacing it with anie newe additions. For in the later wordes of that former Synode nowe left out are three thinges that cannot bee iustified by the Scriptures. 1. that the Spirits of the iust vvere in hell. 2. that Christ there preached vnto them. 3. that he staied there till his resurrection. These three pointes contained in the Article of that Synode; were aduisedlie and profitablie suppressed by the Synode kept in her maiesties time; and these are the pointes which I my selfe impugne in this Treatise, as hauing no iust nor tolerable grounde in the Scriptures. But these thinges being drowned by omission, what is that to the rest of the article, which the later Synode imbraceth as a matter necessarie to be beleeued? for thus they resolue; As Christ died for vs & vvas buried; so also it is to be beleeued y̆ HE VVENT DOVVN INTO HELL. And though you woulde weaken their resolution with a false translation, as your maner is, by making them saie, vve are to beleeue that Christ vvent vnto the dead, yet may you gain no thing by that, for we haue publike assurance & allowance that

Iudæ epistola.

Articul 3.

their words were and are IT IS TO BE BELEEVED THAT CHRIST VVENT DOVVNE INTO HELL. Their words in Latin were, you will say, *Credendus est ad inferos descendisse?* But the same Bishops & the same Clergie that were at the first Synode in the 5 of her Maiest[y], assembling again in the 13 yeare of her highnes raign, did themselues english it as I report it, and offered it to the Prince & Parliament in those words to be cōfirmed, which accordingly that high Court did. So ŷ now not these words, Christ descended into HADES, though they be true as being the originall words, much lesse yours Christ went to the dead, but prcciselie these, Christ went downe into hell, are the faith & doctrine which the Church & Realme of England professeth, or which the lawe establisheth; and what they meane, were it not for your addle quirckes, is soone perceaued euen of the simplest.

Page.173

" You conclude that the *publike sentence of our Church*, yea
" *the publike law of our land is against this opiniō of Christs descen-*
" *ding into hell.* And I conclude likewise that which is in the bone will neuer out of the flesh; with arrogance and ignorance you began, and so you will end. If HELL in english be HELL, & GOING DOVVNE be DESCENDING, thē both the Church & the law of England directly, expressely, precisely mayntayneth CHRISTS DESCENDING INTO HELL. If HELL in english be HEAVEN, & GOING DOVVN be GOING VP, then the Church and lawe of England fauoureth your fansie. And hereof I am wel content thou shalt be Iudge (Christian Reader) that vnderstandest best thine owne toung. For the latine INFERNVM and the Greeke HADES I am content to be tried by all the Fathers, Greeke & Latine that euer wrate in the Church of Christ. If these men cānot keepe their quarter cleere nor vpholde their conceite, but they must exclude all Greeke, Latine, and English diuines since Christs time from vnderstanding euerie man his owne naturall toong; I will see their braines better settled, and their mouthes better tempred, before their philosophicall follies and Rabbinicall fansies the one sorte being strangers, the other enimies to the faith of Christ, shall draw mee from my Creede. And so I wish thee (Christian Reader) as my selfe, mercie and grace from the Lord Iesus, and commit thee to God.

FINIS.